the Beatles

The Dream Is Over

Off The Record 2
By Keith Badman

OMNIBUS PRESS
London/New York/Paris/Sydney/Copenhagen/Madrid/Tokyo

Cover designed by Chloë Alexander
Picture research by Nikki Lloyd & Keith Badman

ISBN: 0.7119.8802.1
Order No: OP 48378

Exclusive Distributors:
Music Sales Limited,
8/9 Frith Street,
London W1D 3JB, UK.

Music Sales Corporation,
257 Park Avenue South,
New York, NY 10010, USA.

Macmillan Distribution Services,
53 Park West Drive,
Derrimut, Vic 3030,
Australia.

To the Music Trade only:
Music Sales Limited,
8/9 Frith Street,
London W1D 3JB, UK.

Typeset by Galleon Typesetting, Ipswich
Printed in Great Britain by Creative Print & Design (Ebbw Vale) Wales

A catalogue record for this book is available from the British Library.

www.omnibuspress.com

Author's Notes

Two years ago now, I completed work on my first Omnibus publication, *The Beatles After The Break-Up 1970-2000* and never in my wildest dreams could I wish for the acknowledgements that the book would receive. It was voted 1999's 'Rock Book Of The Year' in *Record Collector* magazine and considered as one of the ten most essential Beatles books ever published in *Q*. To quote The Rutles, "I was shocked and stunned." Naturally, I am extremely proud of that book as well as *The Beatles: Off The Record*, the follow up, which featured original, largely unpublished quotes to tell The Beatles' story. That book concluded in April 1970 and left you all wondering what happened next.

Well, the answer is sitting in your hands now. May I present *The Beatles: Off The Record Volume Two - The Dream Is Over*, another weighty tome which, just like in the first volume, uses original interviews and newspaper cuttings to tell the story of The Fab Four's lives. But this time, the book focuses on the period when they were no longer being Beatles. Covering the same time span as *After The Break-Up*, this book varies from the original in the way that it deals more comprehensively with their solo albums, songs, inspirations, concerts, feelings, pains, betrayals by past colleagues, the re-packaging and ripping off of The Beatles' music and the incessant, largely irritating, 'Beatles To Reform' rumours. It focuses more the story than simply lists what occurred. To compliment these quotes and stories, I have added (chronologically) recollections by various dedicated Beatles followers who, for instance, attempt to explain what it is like to endure modern day *Beatlemania*.

Unlike *After The Break-Up*, this book doesn't list the dates when Wings played in America unless there is a story to accompany a certain concert. I have made a point in this book of collating interviews with John, Paul, George, Ringo and assorted colleagues that, for one reason or another, have not seen the light of day (if at all) since their first airing or printing. I've tried to offer an almost totally fresh reflection of The Beatles' lives from April 1970, covering 31 years right up to an eye witness account of Paul's brief *Adopt-A-Landmine* concert appearance in June 2001, including along the way, for the first time ever, the true behind-the-scenes stories about Paul's historic return to the Cavern Club in Liverpool in December 1999.

This is not a replica of *After The Break-Up*, but a loving companion. The Beatles story will never end so expect an updated version of this book sometime in 2030...

Acknowledgements

For their help on this book very special thanks, in no particular order, go to my quite remarkable reliable regulars, Pete Nash, Pete & Fenella Walkling, Stephen Rouse, Mike Dalton, Bob Boyer (USA), Dirk Van Damme (Belgium), Richard Porter, Laurence Moore, Gary Crowley, Terry Rawlings and Jean Herbaut. A very special 'thank you' goes to Billy Heckle, Dave Jones, Ray Johnston and Colin Jones of Cavern City Tours, Mathew Street, Liverpool, the proud organisers of Paul's historic Cavern concert in December 1999.
In addition, I must also thank Beatles related celebrities such as Denny Laine, Neil Innes, Steve Holly and Laurence Juber with whom I was able to spend some time with at various Beatles conventions through the years. Pieces of these interviews appear in this book.
Also, special thanks must go to the following: Andy Davis & Daryl Easlea (*Record Collector* magazine), Mike Websell & Neil Somerville (BBC), Paul Wayne (Tracks), Steve Vallis, Andy Neill, Bill King (USA), Matt Hurwitz (USA), Rene Van Haarlem (Holland), Tony Rouse, Steve Holmes (Beatles For Sale), Greg Schmidt (USA), Spencer Peet, James Fielding, Lesley Benson, Dave Carter, Dave Withers, Mark Saunders, Brian Durrant, Robert Batchelor, Alan Smith, Anne-Marie Trace, Allison Devine, Diane Machin, Michael Randolph, Dr. Bob Heronimus (USA), Jim Keays, Danny Wall, Betina Drake, The Rutles fan pages and Steve Marinucci of the marvellous *Abbey Road* Beatles website. Please check it out at http://www.best.com/~abbeyrd/fabnews.htm

A note of thanks must go to the following Beatles-related books and magazines . . .

The Beatles Book Monthly, John's *Playboy* interviews, George's *I Me Mine, Lennon Remembers, Beatlefan* (USA), *Harrison Alliance* (USA), *Every Little Thing* (USA) and *Beatles Unlimited* (Holland)

Beatles-related television and radio programmes . . .

Parkinson (BBC), *Today Show* (NBC), *Rockline* (USA), *Aspel & Co.* (LWT/ITV), *Robert Klein Radio Show* (USA), *The Old Grey Whistle Test* (BBC), *Paul McCartney Now* (CBS), *Up Close* (USA), *Insight On Wings* (Radio One)

Film and video archives of . . .

BBC Worldwide, Much Music (Canada), BVL Enterprises, MPL, Radio Luxembourg, LBC, BBC Radio One, Radio Monte Carlo, VH-1,

Radio stations . . .

WPLJ (New York), WNEW-FM (New York), KCSN, KLOS-FM (Los Angeles), VARA (Holland), Capital Radio, Radio Clyde, RKO Radio (USA), BBC World Service, GLR, 92.3WXRK-FM (CBS USA), CNN (USA), KHJ Radio (USA)

Websites/ Chat sites

AOL, Century 21, Yahoo!

The following libraries and their respective staffs who so excellently assisted me with my research . . .

The BBC Written Archives Centre, Slough public library, Westminster Reference library and the Colindale Newspaper library, plus the hundreds of other sources for information, but sadly, too many to list . . .

Newspapers, magazines and news agencies . . .

Melody Maker, Disc & Music Echo, Daily Mirror, Rolling Stone, Life, Musician, New Musical Express, Evening News, Daily Sketch, Sunday Times, The People, The Sun, Daily Mail, New York Herald Tribune, The Guardian, New York times, The Tenessean, Redbook, Modern Hi-Fi & Music, Record Mirror, Hit Parader, Rock Around The World, United Press International, Woman, News Of The World, Newsweek, Playboy, Liverpool Echo, New Standard, Modern Drummer, Daily Record, LA Times, Detroit News, The Register, The Globe, Titbits, Daily Star, Kansas City Star, Tucson Weekly, Time Out, Woman's Own, USA Today, The Hartford Courant, Michigan Daily, The Times, The Times Of India

A personal note of gratitude must also go to the following people who have contributed to this book, by either interviewing or reporting on the individual Beatles from April 1970. In order of appearance, they are: Derek Taylor, Howard Smith, Christine Stevens, Michelle Bernel, Tess Basta, David Spinoza, Carolyne Mitchell, Roy Shipston, Mike Ledgerwood, Richard Green, Jann Wenner, Mike Hennessey, John Reader, Frankie McGowan, Stella Shamoon, Les Perrin, Kenny Everett, Richard Perryman, Peter Bennett, David Hughes, Celia Heddon, David Walley, Kip Cohen, Lisa Mehlman, Robert Bury, Al Aronowitz, Patrick Doncaster, Freda Kelly, Michael Cable, Peter McCabe & Robert Schonfield, Gavin Petrie, Martin Marriott, Geoff Liptrot, James Johnson, Paul Dacre, John Blake, Elga Eliaser, Robert Ellis, Robin Denselow, Joe Hall, Robert Brinton, Sandra Shevey, David Blundy, Roy Carr, Tony Tyler, Murray Davies, Charles Shaar Murray, Linda Solomon, Beverley Legge, Julie Webb, Adam Wall, Graham Saunders, Ian MacDonald, Neil Splinter, Dave Cash, Tony Prince, Frank Goldsworthy, Chris Van Ness, Lisa Robinson, Jerry Bailey, Eve Zilbart, Denis Elsas, Jim Ladd, Ben Fong-Torres, Lenny Kaye, Lynn Thirkettle, Colin Irwin, Scott Muni, Nicky Horne, Rosemary Horide, Piers Akerman, Jack Anderson, Robert V. Weinstein, Ray Fox-Cummings, Wendy Hughes, Derek Jewel, Dave Gelly, Alan Freeman, Mark Dowdney, Laura Gross, Ray Coleman, James Johnston, Mr. Cut, John Rockwell, Jeanette Smith, Maureen Orth, Alastair Buchan, Robert Palmer, Dan Bennett, John Collins, Angie Errigo, Chris Hutchins, Steve Wright, Joe Pumphrey, Nelson Segal, Voyle Gilmore, George Martin, Aunt Mimi Smith, Judith Simons, Stuart White, Stuart Robertson, Lachie MacKinnon, Keith Dalton, James Erlichman, Bill Goldsmith, Cliff Wayne, Paul Gambaccinni, Fred Weiner, Philip Finn, John King, Michael Nally, Patrick Walker, Glenn Gale, Simon Kinnersley, Barbara Graustark, Ian Pye, Andy Peebles, Paul Williams, Laurie Kaye, David Sholin, Paul Goresh, Michael Leapman, John Hilpern, David & Victoria Sheff, John Chartres, Anne Nightingale, Stephen Pile, Tracy Harris, Tony Luscombe, Kathy Turner, Garth Pearce, Alan Dunn, Jonathan Kirby, Andrew Golden, Alwyn Thomas, Len Adams, Hunter Davies, Christina Appleyard, Bob Coburn, Peter Kent, Ted Hynds, Ellie Buchanan, Clement Burton, David Wigg, Steve Turner, Kevin Connal, David Sinclair, Simon Bates, Linda Duff, Max Bell, Geoff Baker, Philip Norman, Mark Wheinberg, Tony Parsons, Allan Kozinn, Samuel Roberts, Louise Gannon, Rebecca Fowler, Pete Clark, Chrissie

Hynde, Howard Stern, Viva, Dominic Mohan, Roger McGough, Greg Nowak and Dave Herman

Inspirational thanks must (as usual) go to Arsene Wenger who, despite the betrayal of a couple of his (so called) star players, is still the finest football manager in the world and has continued to make Arsenal FC the greatest club in the land . . .

Lastly, and by no means least, a very special thanks go to Kathleen, Sheila, Pauline, Michael and everyone else close to me (they know who I mean) who assisted me in my latest Beatles book madness. And to Bob Wise, Nikki Lloyd (picture researcher extrordinaire) and Chris Charlesworth of Omnibus Press, who commissioned this book, and Peter Dogget who helped Chris edit it. Of course, a very special thanks goes to Chris who, three years down the line, has continued to be a gem to work with and a tower of strength as we pieced this book together. Anyway, I hope you all enjoy it as much as I enjoyed researching and compiling it, a story that just will never end . . .

Keith Badman,
Berkshire, England
June 2001

Ringo "If I had any regrets, I think it would be that I was never in the audience at a Beatles concert. I would have liked to have seen it from another angle. It must have been amazing! It was amazing on stage but to sit in the audience, it must have been fantastic . . . There were too many super parts about being in The Beatles. Being big in England was great. Then we were big in Europe and suddenly we got to America and we did *The Ed Sullivan Show*. We did the Palladium show and I was sick with fear. Then we did Shea Stadium. If you look at our career, which one are you going to pick? Sailing Loch Ness in a rowing boat with John? That was a big time!"
(1976)

Paul "When The Beatles split, it was a terrible blow. It was like finding out that you're unemployed. It was depressing and I really felt useless. I knew how the unemployed felt. That's the reason I said one day, 'Let's go. We'll be a group. We'll do something.' So I asked some musicians, bought a bus and we were on the road again giving concerts. That's the way I am. I'm a musician. If I don't play or sing, then I'm unhappy. And then, everybody wanted to talk about The Beatles. It was awful! I didn't even want to talk about that time. I wanted to be treated like Paul, a musician with his band, Wings. But to the rest of the world, I was still a Beatle. It's like the fellow who finished in the army. I was a civilian again and I didn't want to be called Sergeant . . . The Beatles split up because of The Beatles. We had reached the limit of what was possible for us. We wanted to become famous and we were the most famous band in the world. We needed five years to gain that success and we spent five years at the top. The cake was left in the oven too long and it was going to burn . . . Our egos collided. We had spent night after night roaring with laughter, only the four of us in cars or vans on the roads of the world. We were four guys completely united and happy together, but suddenly we couldn't communicate anymore. The break-up was like the atom bomb. We all got grey hair . . . It was our wives who helped us bring it out and you can't condemn men for falling in love, can you? It happened to John first. We can't begrudge John for falling in love with Yoko. If I could live my life over again, I don't think I'd change one thing except the break-up. I'd want to be able to come back and say, 'Listen, guys, we're going to split, but we're going to do it peacefully because whether you like it or not, this business is going to keep going until the end of our days.' "
(1984)

George "We consciously stopped being The Beatles because it was just too much. Everyone was growing too much and The Beatles were too small to hold four people. I think there was not much of a reason for it to end like it did. It's sad because it made it look as though nothing good has come from it. Everybody was angry with everybody else but there was so much good. We had many good times but we had bad times, too. If you counted them up, we had more good times than bad. But unfortunately, we all had so many different opinions about the business and it was the business that broke us up. John, Ringo and myself are still very close and Paul I'd like to be friends with . . ."
(1971)

John "Talking about The Beatles getting back together is an illusion . . . The Beatles only exist on film and on record and in people's minds. You cannot get back together what no longer exists. We are not those four people anymore . . . Why should The Beatles give more? Didn't they give everything on God's earth for ten years? Didn't they give themselves? Didn't they give all?"
(*Playboy*, September 1980)

Thursday, April 9

John "I received a phone call from Paul on Thursday afternoon. He said, 'I'm going to leave The Beatles as well.' I was happy to hear from Paul. It was nice to find that he was still alive! Anyway, Paul hasn't left . . . I sacked him."

Paul "When people say I let it out, it was actually months after we had broken up. No one was saying anything and I was putting out this crazy press release with the *McCartney* album because Peter Brown said to me, 'We need some press on this. You'd better do something,' and I didn't want to be interviewed. I didn't feel secure enough to do that. So I said, 'Okay, we'll do a question and answer thing.' So I said to Peter, 'Write me out a questionnaire of what you think they'd ask me.' He wrote it all out and I just filled it all in, like a questionnaire, and it all came out weird."

Friday, April 10
Paul's announcement that he has left The Beatles appears on the front-page of the *Daily Mirror* . . .

Paul "The press got it and it looked like I was doing a real number. John then thought, 'Aha, he's done the announcement of The Beatles' split.' But it was months after. Someone's got to do it. In actual fact, we signed contracts that were saying that The Beatles were still going and that was one of the terrible things when The Beatles broke up. But I became known as the one who broke The Beatles up."

Derek Taylor, The Beatles' press officer "This is the truth about Paul McCartney. He cannot make that Beatle scene any more because what we know as The Beatles and love as The Beatles and prized and valued and changed our lives by, is not what it was. It is a hang-up, it's a drag and it is a prison for four souls screaming for freedom. It was once a garden with tangerine trees and marmalade skies and girls with kaleidoscope eyes and cellophane flowers of yellow and green. Nothing can take that away. As long as all of us are alive we should all be on our knees with our stereo phones on our ears thanking God it happened . . . It was the only dream I ever had that came true. I love them for it. The Beatles. They have done enough for you and you have done enough for them. For every dollar you spend on them, they give you a dollar's worth of themselves. I am sick at heart, press, public, Beatles, we seek too much of each other."

Disc & Music Echo reports "Apple was fraught with the usual scenes, which come when The Beatles hit the headlines. The road outside No. 3 Saville Row, W1, was jam-packed with pressmen, excited fans and onlookers. But inside, everyone went about their business in the normal way. Only the press office, with Derek Taylor and Mavis Smith at the helm, seemed in any way to have anticipated the avalanche of calls and callers. One floor down, Allen Klein, The Beatles' business boss, was undisturbed. The first thing he said when confronted by reporters was that he hadn't even seen Paul's statement, and as far as he was concerned, the whole situation was the same as it had been for the last six months."

Paul "Klein was not the exclusive reason why The Beatles broke up. We were starting to do our own things before he arrived, but it certainly helped. There were various reasons why we split. I don't think even the four of us know all the reasons, but Klein was one of the major ones . . ."

Linda McCartney "I knew I hadn't broken up The Beatles. I'd pleaded with them to stay together. It really broke my heart to see Paul so upset that he didn't have a band anymore, that he felt completely washed up and redundant."

Derek Taylor "Paul McCartney has not left The Beatles, nor has Richard Starkey, George Harrison or John Lennon. The Beatles left *them* at an unrecorded moment in time. Neither has it anything to do with Linda McCartney or Yoko Ono."

Yoko Ono "I hated being blamed for the break-up of The Beatles. I wasn't responsible. It was John's decision after Ringo and then George told him they wanted to leave. He persuaded them to change their minds and then he changed his mind. He wanted to say, 'I started the group and I broke it up.' In the end, though, it was Paul who announced the break. John was angry about that because Paul had a new album out at the time and John thought he did it to attract publicity."

George "When we broke up, I thought, 'Thank God that's over!' The idea of The Beatles was like having a job and you are either fired or the factory burns down. For me, I was glad that we burned it down. It was too stifling. It's not gloomy, it's just that it wasn't as much fun for us in the end as it was for all of you."

Paul "The inevitable thing after The Beatles, really, was that you were actually facing up to growing up. The thing of finally being on your own. The biggest trouble for me was the break-up of The Beatles. The Beatles' break-up was shocking. It totally screwed my head. It was not easy being in a top job one day and the next day you haven't got a job. I asked myself, 'Am I any use to anyone? I was very useful yesterday playing bass and singing, but now we've broken up.' That was very hard."

Ringo "I went back to my luxury home in Weybridge and just sat in the garden for months, wondering what on earth I was going to do with myself. Playing with The Beatles had been my whole life for ten years and now it was over and I didn't feel qualified to do anything else. The initial break-up was so emotional, mainly for me, but not so much for the others. We had been together for so long and then suddenly I had nothing to do. I sat in my garden thinking, 'My God, where do I go from here?' I felt so absolutely lost. I was not interested in being in a new band right away. I was bigger than any band I could have joined. I went into hiding to escape the pressures. You just sit around the house like everyone else does. You go into London or you go shopping or see a film or you watch telly. I was sick really, and then, one day, I jumped up and I thought, 'Hell, I'm going to get myself together. I can't sit here for the rest of my life,' so I went off and did an album, which was a limp way to get in again, but it was a start."

The break-up of The Beatles produces an opinion from Mick Jagger, of The Rolling Stones "Obviously The Beatles could have got somebody else," he insists. "It's not impossible. It's never going to be the same band without Paul McCartney, but it would be another band, probably as good or a bit different. John's got a good voice and George has quite a good voice and they could have easily got another bass player who doubled on organ or something. The only thing to me was that they can't have wanted to play together that much because they would have got another bass player."

Paul "After all we'd been through, I thought that they knew me. I think we were all pretty weird at the time. I'd ring John and he'd say, 'Don't bother me.' I rang George and he came out with some effing and blinding, not at all Hare Krishna. We weren't normal to each other at the time."

Paul's *Daily Mirror* announcement that he has left the group reaches John and Yoko who are at 20 Devonshire Place, London, where they are undergoing primal scream therapy with Arthur Janov at his clinic . . .

John "Janov's book came to me in the mail and the name *Primal Scream* intrigued me. I mean, Yoko's been screaming a long time. Just the words, the title, made my heart flutter. Then I read the testimonials, 'I am Charlie so-and-so, I went in and this is what happened to me.' I thought, 'That's me. That's me.' We were living in Ascot and there was a lot of shit coming down on us. And these people say they get to this thing and they scream and they feel better, so, I thought, let's try it. They do this thing where they mess around with you until you reach a point where you hit this scream thing. You go with it, they encourage you to go with it, and you kind of make a psychical, mental, cosmic breakthrough with the scream itself."

Amidst all the commotion, Paul, Linda and the family leave their St John's Wood home and head off to their farm in Scotland to escape the prying eyes of the media. He will stay there, almost undisturbed, for months . . .

Paul "I went off to Scotland for a while, because I just couldn't handle being in London, with the music business and people saying, 'When are you going to get together with the lads, Paul?' That was the big question. It's like asking a divorced couple when are you going to get back together. You just can't stand the thought of going back to your divorcee . . . I was a city boy, but lived far enough out of town to see a bit of the country. The farm is 600 acres and just right for the family and me. I can breathe the air. It never ceases to amaze me that I put seeds in the ground, the sun shines at the right time, the rain comes on at the right time, then something grows and you can eat it. That's something to give thanks for . . . We don't eat meat because we've got lambs on the farm and we just ate a piece of lamb one day and suddenly realised we were eating a bit of one of those things that were playing outside the window, gambolling peacefully. But we're not strict, I don't want to put a big sign on me, 'Thou Shalt Be Vegetarian'. I like to allow myself. I like to give myself a lucky break . . . I just love to find that, even in this day of concrete, there are still horses alive and places where grass grows in unlimited quantities and sky has clear in it. Scotland has that. It's just there without anyone touching it . . .

"We were in Scotland and we decided to take a trip to the Shetland Islands, so we piled in the Land Rover with the two kids, our English sheepdog, Martha, and a whole pile of stuff in the back with Mary's potty on the top. On the second day, we get up to a little port called Scrabster at the top of Scotland. But when we tried to get on the big car ferry, we got in the queue but we were two cars too late, we missed it. We thought, 'Don't despair. We really didn't want to go on that big liner, a mass-produced thing. Let's beat the liner,' but we gave that up and instead we decided to try and get a ride in one of those little fishing boats. So I went to a bunch of boats but they weren't going to the Orkney Islands, so I went on another one, this trapdoor thing, and they were sleeping down below. The smell of sleep is coming up through the door. At first, the skipper said, 'No,' and then I said there was thirty quid in it for him and then they say they'll take us. It was a fantastic little boat called the Enterprise and the captain was named George. We brought all our stuff aboard and it was low tide, so we had to lower Martha in a big fishing net and a little crowd gathers and we wave our farewells. As we steam out, the skipper gives us some beer and Linda, trying to be one of the boys, takes a swig and passes it to me. Well, you shouldn't drink before a rough crossing to the Orkneys. The little one, Mary, throws up all over Linda, as usual and that was it. I was already feeling sick and I gallantly walked to the front of the boat, hanging onto the mast. The skipper comes up and we're having some light talk but I don't want it. He gets the idea and points to the fishing baskets and says, 'Do it in there.' So we were all sick, but we ended up in the Orkney Islands and we took a plane to Shetland, it was great . . .

"When The Beatles broke up, there we were, left with the wreckage. It was very difficult to suddenly not be in The Beatles, after your whole life, except for your childhood, had been involved with being in this very successful group. I always say I can really identify with unemployed people, because once it was clear that we weren't doing The Beatles anymore, I had real withdrawals and had serious problems. I started drinking and not shaving. I just didn't care. I just thought, 'That's the end of me as a singer, songwriter, composer,' because I hadn't got anyone to do it with, unless I work out another way to do it. Gradually Linda got me out of that. She'd say, 'Come on, this can't go on, you know. You're good. You're either going to stop doing music or you'd better get on with it.' "

Saturday, April 11

In light of the fact that 18 to 20-year-olds can now vote, the music paper *Disc & Music Echo* publishes the results of its pop opinion poll where they asked its readers: "If you could choose a pop personality as your local MP, who would you like it to be?" John tops the poll with 22% of the votes. T. L. Graham, of Glasgow, Scotland, writes "John is the only pop star interested in politics and the only one with guts to say what he thinks."

Friday, April 17
In the UK, Paul releases the album *McCartney* . . .

Paul "After John said he was leaving, I hung on for months, wondering whether The Beatles would ever come back together again and hoping that John might come around and say, 'All right, lads, I'm ready to go back to work.' None of us knew what to do, but we decided to wait until about March or April until our film, *Let It Be*, came out. But I was bored. I like to work. I'm an active person. Sit me down with a guitar and let me go. So, naturally enough, in the meantime, I began to look for something to do. I decided I was not going to sit there, sucking my thumbs, waiting for everyone to come back, so the album *McCartney* turned out to be the answer in my case. I had just got a new recording machine in my house and I found that I liked working on my own. At first it wasn't going to be anything serious but it turned out to be a great time. When we had to go to the (Morgan) studios, Linda would make the booking and we'd take some sandwiches and a bottle of grape juice and put the baby on the floor and it was all like a holiday. So, as a natural turn of events, from looking for something to do, I found that I was enjoying working alone as much as I had enjoyed the early days. So, anyway, *McCartney* came out and Linda and I did it totally, the record, the cover, the ads, everything presented to the record company. Then there started to appear these little advertisements. On the bottom was 'On Apple Records', which was okay. But somebody had also come along and slapped on 'An ABKCO managed company'. Now that is Klein's company and has nothing to do with my record. It's like Klein taking part of the credit for my record. All those little things kept happening, such trivia compared to what happened. Maybe that sounds petty, but I can go into other examples of this kind of thing. All these things that are continuously happening makes me feel like I'm a junior with the record company, like Klein is the boss and I'm nothing. Well, I'm a senior . . . The income from the *McCartney* album is still being held by Apple and Linda and I are the only ones on the record."

Derek Taylor, The Beatles' press officer on *McCartney* "I didn't enjoy it as much as *Sgt. Pepper*, but that's my hang-up, and neither as much as *Revolver*. But *McCartney* is a very, very personal art form and it makes me sick this morning, lovely morning though it is, to have to cry out in pain on behalf of this brilliant man who is trying to discover who he is in music."

'The Lovely Linda'

Paul "When the Studer 4-track was installed at home, this was the first song I recorded, to test the machine. On the first track was vocal and guitar, second, another acoustic guitar, then overdubbed hand slaps on a book and then finally, bass. I wrote this in Scotland, and the song is a trailer to the full song, which will be recorded in the future."

'That Would Be Something'

Paul "This was written in Scotland in 1969 and recorded at the mike, as the mixer and VU meters hadn't arrived."

'Valentine Day'

Paul "Recorded at home and made up as I went along, acoustic guitar first, then drums. Maybe drums were first . . . Electric guitar and bass were added and the track is all instrumental. Mixed at EMI."

'Every Night'

Paul "This came from the first two lines, which I've had for a few years. They were added to in 1969 in Greece (Benitses) on holiday. This was recorded at EMI with vocal, acoustic guitar, drums, bass, lead guitar, harmony to the lead guitar, double tracked vocal in parts and electric guitar (not used)."

'Hot As Sun'

Paul "A song written in about 1958 or 9 or maybe earlier, when it was one of those songs that you play now and then. The middle was added in Morgan Studios, where the track was recorded recently."

'Glasses'

Paul "Wine glasses played at random and overdubbed on top of each other. The end is a section of a song called 'Suicide', which is not yet completed."

'Junk'

Paul "Originally written in India (in 1968) at Maharishi's camp and completed bit by bit in London. Recorded vocal, two acoustic guitars and bass at home and later added to at Morgan."

'Man We Was Lonely'

Paul "The chorus, 'Man we was lonely', was written in bed at home shortly before we finished recording the album. The middle, 'I used to ride', was done one lunchtime in a great hurry, as we were due to record the song that afternoon. Linda sings harmony on this song, which is our first duet together . . . The steel guitar sound is my Telecaster played with a drum peg."

'Oo You'

Paul "The first three tracks were recorded at home as an instrumental that might someday become a song. This, like 'Man We Was Lonely', was given lyrics one day after lunch, just before we left for Morgan Studios, where it was finished that afternoon."

'Momma Miss America'

Paul "An instrumental recorded completely at home. Made up as I went along, first a sequence of chords, then a melody on top. Piano, drums, acoustic guitar, electric guitar. Originally, it was two pieces but they ran into each other by accident and became one."

'Teddy Boy'

Paul "Another song started in India and completed in Scotland and London, gradually. This one was recorded for the *Get Back (Let It Be)* film but later not used. Re-recorded partly at home and finished at Morgan. Linda and I sing the backing harmonies on the chorus and occasional 'oohs'."

'Singalong Junk'

Paul "This was Take 1 for the vocal version, which was Take 2 and a shorter version. Guitars and piano and bass were put on at home and the rest added at Morgan Studios. The strings are Mellotron and they were done at the same time as the electric guitar, bass guitar and sizzle cymbal."

'Maybe I'm Amazed'

Paul "Written in London at the piano, shortly after I had first gotten together with Linda. It was one of those songs that just came out. It was very special. I added the second verse slightly later . . . Recorded at EMI. Linda and I are the vocal backing group. Mixed at EMI. I enjoyed doing it, I enjoyed singing it."

'Kreen Akrore'

Paul "There was a film on TV about the Kreen Akrore Indians living in the Brazilian jungle and how the white man is trying to change their way of life to his, so the next day, after lunch, I did some strumming. The idea behind it was to get the feeling of their hunt. So later, piano, guitar and organ were added to the first section. The second had a few tracks of voices (Linda and I) and the end had overdubbed breathing, going into organ and two lead guitars in harmony. Done at Morgan, the engineer is Robin Black. The end of the first section has Linda and I doing animal noises (speeded up) and an arrow sound (done live with bow and arrow – the bow broke) then animals stampeding across the piano case . . . We built a fire in the studio but didn't use it, but used the sound of the twigs breaking."

George on the *McCartney* album " 'That Would Be Something' and 'Maybe I'm Amazed' I think are great and everything else I think is fair, you know, quite good, but um, a little disappointing. Maybe I shouldn't be disappointed maybe. It's best not to expect anything then everything is a bonus, you know. I just think those two tracks in particular are really very good. And the others, I mean, just don't do much for me . . . The arrangements of some of those songs, like 'Teddy Boy' and 'Junk', with a little more arrangement they could have sounded better. I suppose it was the only thing he felt he could do at the time, you know, and he started off just testing his machine. Eddie Cochran did something like that, didn't he? On 'Summertime Blues' and 'C'mon Everybody' he played bass, guitar and drums."

Saturday, April 18

The music journalist Penny Valentine reviews Paul's album *McCartney* in *Disc & Music Echo.* She writes, "I don't know what he was thinking when he planned this album. Perhaps he is laughing at us all. That's fine, but it's a pretty cruel way of doing it . . . almost a betrayal of all the things we've come to expect."

Saturday, April 25

Disc & Music Echo publishes a Public Post Office Telegram from **Paul** and Linda, replying to Penny Valentine's review of the *McCartney* album. It reads, "Dear Penny hold your hand out you silly girl I am not being cruel or laughing at you I am merely enjoying myself you are wrong about the McCartney albumn (*sic*) it is an attempt at something slightly different it is simple it is good and even at this moment it is growing on you love – Paul and Linda McCartney."

Tuesday, April 28
In New York, during a visit to see the new Apple office at 1700 Broadway, **George** finds himself in a lengthy conversation with the WPLJ DJ, Howard Smith . . .

"We just cut a track in London of Ringo's song called 'It Don't Come Easy', and so maybe he'll put that out as a single . . . Paul and John and myself have just got so many songs. If we do our own albums, that way we don't have to compromise . . . Paul wants to do his songs his way, he doesn't want to do his songs my way, and I don't wanna do my songs their way, really. And I'm sure that after we've all completed an album or even two albums each, then that novelty will have worn off."

Smith "You think The Beatles will get together again then?"

George "Uh, well, I don't know. I couldn't tell, you know, if they do or not. I'll certainly try my best to do something with them again, you know. I mean, it's only a matter of accepting that the situation is a compromise. And it's a sacrifice, you know, because we all have to sacrifice a little in order to gain something really big, and there is a big gain by recording together, I think, musically and financially and spiritually and for the rest of the world, you know. I think that Beatle music is such a big sort of scene that I think it's the least we could do is to sacrifice three months of the year at least, you know, just to do an album or two. I think it's very selfish if The Beatles don't record together."

Smith "But everything looks so gloomy right now."

George "It's not really, you know. It's no more gloomy than it's been for the last ten years. It really isn't any worse. It's just that now over the last year, what with John and lately with Paul, everything that they've thought or said has come out, you know, to the public. It's been printed, it's been there for everybody to read, or to comment about, or to join in on . . ."

Smith "But the things. The feelings had been there all along?"

George "No, I wouldn't say that. We're just like anybody else. Familiarity breeds contempt, they do say, and we've had slight problems. But it's only been recently, you know, because we didn't work together for such a long time in the John and Yoko situation, and then Paul and Linda. But really, it's not as bad as it seems, you know . . . We're all having a good time individually."

Smith "There seems like there's so much animosity between Paul and John. It seems like Paul is saying it's all over."

George "It's more of a personal thing, you know. That's down to the management situation with Apple, because Paul, really, it was his idea to do Apple and once it started going, Paul was very active in there and then it got really chaotic and we had to do something about it. And when we started doing something about it, obviously Paul didn't have as much say in the matter and then he decided he wanted Lee Eastman, his in-law, to run it and we didn't. That's the only reason, you know. But that's only a personal problem and he'll have to get over it because the reality is that he's out-voted and we're a partnership. We've got these companies, which we all own 25 per cent of each, and if there's a decision to be made then, like in any other business or group, you have a vote, you know. And he was outvoted 3 to 1 and he doesn't like it, it's a real pity.

We're trying to do what's best for The Beatles as a group or best for Apple as a company. We're not trying to do what's best for Paul and his in-laws, you know . . . It is because it is on such a personal level that it is a big problem, you know. When I go home at night I'm not living there with Allen Klein, whereas, in a way, Paul's living with the Eastmans, you see . . . It's not really between Paul and us, you know, it's between Paul's advisors who are the Eastmans and our business advisors, which is Allen Klein. But it's all right."

Smith "I somewhat detected some kind of animosity between Yoko and Linda. Is that part of what it's all about?"

George "Ah, I don't know. I don't think about it, you know. I refuse to be part of any hassles like that, you know. Hare Krishna, Hare Krishna, Krishna, Krishna, Hare, Hare. And it'll be okay, you know. Just give 'em time because they really do love each other. I mean, we all do. We've been so close and through so much together . . . The main thing is, like in anybody's life, they have slight problems and it's just that our problems are always blown up and shown to everybody. But it's not really a problem; it's only a problem if you think about it . . . I get on well with Ringo and John and I try my best to get on well with Paul. Whatever happens, it's gonna be okay. In fact, it's never looked better from my point of view. It's really in good shape; the companies are in great shape. Apple Films, Apple Records, my song company is in good shape because I've been productive over the last year or so. It's really good that we got back a lot of money that a lot of people had that was ours, a lot of per cents that different people had."

Smith "Did Klein do all that for you? Were you really that broke or were all of you just crying poor?"

George "We weren't broke. We had earned a lot of money but we didn't actually have the money that we had earned, you know. It was floating around because of the structure of things. Since 1962, the way everything was structured was just freaky. None of us knew anything about it. We just spent money when we wanted to spend money, but we didn't know where we were spending it from, or if we paid taxes on it, you know. We were really in bad shape as far as that was concerned, because none of us really could be bothered. We just felt as though we were rich, because really we were rich by what we sold and what we did. But really it wasn't the case because it was so untogether, the business side of it. But now it's very together and we know exactly where everything is and there's daily reports on where it is and what it is and how much it is, and it's really good."

George goes on to explain his conflict with Paul . . .

"He'd written all these songs for years and stuff, and Paul and I went to school together. I got the feeling that everybody changes and sometimes people don't want other people to change, or even if you do change, they won't accept that you've changed, and they keep in their mind some other image of you. Gandhi said, 'Create and preserve the image of your choice.' And so different people have different images of their friends or people they see."

Smith "So what was his image of you?"

George "Well, I got the impression it was like, he still acted as if he was the groovy

Lennon/McCartney. There was a point in my life where I realised anybody can be Lennon/McCartney, you know, 'cos being part of Lennon/McCartney really I could see, you know, I could appreciate them, how good they actually are. And at the same time, I could see the infatuation that the public had, or the praise that was put on them. And I could see everybody's a Lennon/McCartney if that's what you wanna be. But the point is nobody's special, there's not many special people around . . . If Lennon/McCartney are special then Harrison and Starkey are special, too. What I'm saying is that I can be Lennon/McCartney too, but I'd rather be Harrison, you know."

Thursday, April 30
John and Yoko meanwhile continue with primal scream therapy by visiting Arthur Janov's clinic in Los Angeles, California . . .

John "We were there six months. We had a nice house in LA. We'd go down to the session, have a good cry, and come back and swim in the pool. You'd always feel like that after acid or a good joint, you know, sort of in the pool tingling and everything was fine. But then your defences would all come up again, like the acid would wear off, the joint would wear off, and you'd go back for another fix. Now I can cry, that's what I learnt from Primal Therapy."

Friday, May 8
In the UK, the *Let It Be* album is finally released by EMI . . .

John "There was twenty-nine hours of tape, just so much tape, twenty takes of everything because we were rehearsing and taping everything. Nobody could face looking at it, so we let Glyn Johns remix it, because we didn't want to know. We just left it to him and said, 'Here, do it.' It's the first time since the first album that we didn't have anything to do with it. None of us could be bothered going in, Paul, nobody could be bothered about it and the tapes were left there. We got an acetate each and we called each other and said, 'What do you think? Oh, just let it out.' "

Paul "We walked away from that LP. We didn't really want to know. The best version of the album was before anyone got hold of it. Glyn Johns's early mixes were great but they were very bare, very Spartan. It would be one of the hippest records going if they brought it out. That was one of the best Beatles albums because it was a bit avant garde. I loved it. It was purely as we recorded it, down there in Apple or up on the roof. It had a good sound on it, from Glyn Johns, just a couple of mikes over the drums, it was very basic and I loved it."

Ringo "It was a strange time for us then, because we weren't doing anything and that album needed fixing, but he (Phil Spector) couldn't fix it unless we said so. So we said, 'Yes.' "

John "He worked like a pig on it. I mean, he always wanted to work with The Beatles, and he was given the shittiest load of badly recorded shit with a lousy feeling to it ever, and he made something out of it. He did a great job."

Ringo "Even at the beginning, Paul said, 'Yes,' and then he heard it. I spoke to him on the phone and said, 'Do you like it?' And he said, 'Yeah, it's okay.' He didn't put it down, and then, suddenly, he didn't want it to go out. It was two weeks after that that he wanted to cancel it."

John "When I heard it, I didn't puke. I was so relieved after hearing six months of this like black cloud hanging over, that this was going to go out. I thought it would be good to go out, the shitty version, because it would break The Beatles, you know, it would break the myth. 'That's us, with no trousers on.' We were going to let it out in a really shitty condition, and I didn't care. I thought it was good to let it out and show people what had happened to us, 'This is where we're at now. We can't get it together. We don't play together anymore, you know, leave us alone.' "

Paul "When the *Let It Be* album came out, there was a little bit of hype on the back of the sleeve for the first time ever on a Beatles album. It said it was a new phase Beatles album and there was nothing further from the truth. That was the last Beatles album and everybody knew it. There was no new phase about it all. Klein had it re-produced because he said it didn't sound commercial enough."

'For You Blue'

George " 'For You Blue' is a simple twelve-bar song following all the normal twelve-bar principles, except that it's happy-go-lucky."

'I Me Mine'

George, in his book *I Me Mine* " 'I Me Mine' is the ego problem. There are two 'i's, the little 'i' when people say 'I am this' and the big 'I', i.e. OM, the complete whole, universal consciousness that is void of duality and ego. There is nothing that isn't part of the complete whole. When the little 'i' merges into the big 'I' then you are really smiling! I suppose having LSD was like somebody catapulting me out into space. The LSD experience was the biggest experience that I'd had up until that time . . . suddenly I looked around and everything I could see was relative to my ego, like 'that's my piece of paper' and 'that's my flannel' or 'give it to me' or 'I am'. It drove me crackers, I hated everything about my ego, it was a flash of everything false and impermanent, which I disliked. But later, I learned from it, to realise that there is somebody else in here apart from old blabbermouth. Who am 'I' became the order of the day. Anyway, that's what came out of it, 'I Me Mine'. The truth within has to be realised. When you realise that, everything else that you see and do and touch and smell isn't real, then you may know what reality *is* and answer the question 'Who am I?' "

'Two Of Us'

Linda McCartney "As a kid, I loved getting lost. I would say to my father, 'Let's get lost.' But you could never seem to be able to get really lost. All signs would eventually lead back to New York or wherever we were staying. When I moved to England to be with Paul, we would put Martha, Paul's sheepdog, in the back of the car and drive out of London. And as soon as we were on the open road, I'd say, 'Let's get lost,' and we'd keep driving without looking at any signs. Hence the line in the song, 'Two of us going nowhere'. Paul wrote that on one of those days out."

'The Long And Winding Road'

Paul "We were never asked if it was okay to put all that stuff (orchestra/backing vocals) on 'The Long And Winding Road'. If I had been asked, and someone had said, 'Is it okay to do it, I'd like to do it like this,' then I might have said, 'Yeah, it's okay to do it.' But I was moaning about it because I was just presented with this finished record. Allen Klein said, 'Phil (Spector) had mixed the record.' In fact it says on the record, 'Reproduced for disc, a new phase'. It wasn't so much that I hate screaming violins and women singing, which is how it came out like. I love that. In fact, I really love Phil for that. He's the master of that. But the point is, I hadn't been asked. If I had put it on it, I wouldn't have minded. But the thing is, it just appeared and they say it's your new record and I'm saying, 'What? Who did all that?' That was the problem."

Beatles producer, George Martin "I thought the orchestral work on it was totally uncharacteristic. We had established a particular style of music over the years, generally overlaid music on most Beatles tracks, and I felt that what Phil Spector had done was not only uncharacteristic, but wrong. I was totally disappointed with what happened to *Let It Be.*"

Apple Records promoter, Pete Bennett "Having spent numerous hours and days during the editing process, the song made a long and winding impression on me. During the editing process, everybody was eating banana sandwiches and celery."

'Across The Universe'

John "I was lying next to me first wife in bed and I was irritated. She must have been going on and on about something and she'd gone to sleep and I'd kept hearing these words over and over, flowing like an endless stream. So I went downstairs and it turned into a sort of cosmic song rather than an irritated song."

'Get Back'

Paul "When we were doing *Let It Be*, there were a couple of verses to 'Get Back' that were actually not racist at all. They were anti-racist. At the time there were a lot of stories in the newspapers about Pakistanis crowding out flats, living sixteen to a room, or whatever. So in one verse of 'Get Back', which we were making up on the set of *Let It Be*, one of the outtakes has something about 'Too many Pakistanis living in a council flat', which, to me, was actually talking out against overcrowding for Pakistanis. If there was any group that was not racist, it was The Beatles. I mean, all of our favourite people were always black. We were the first people to open international eyes, in a way, to Motown."

Wednesday, May 20
The Beatles' *Let It Be* film is premiered in London at the London Pavilion and in Liverpool at the Gaumont in Camden Street . . .

George "This film is just pure documentary of us slogging and working on the album. The whole of the album was filmed because we want this film to go out simultaneously. Originally, we were rehearsing the songs we were planning to do for some big TV spectacular. We had an idea of doing it as a TV show, but we didn't really know the formula of how to do it. We didn't want to do another *Magical Mystery Tour*, as we had already been on that trip, and we didn't want to do the *Tom Jones Spectacular*, and we were always trying to do something different. So, we were down in Apple rehearsing and we decided to film it on 16mm, maybe to use it on a documentary and the record happened to be the rehearsal of that record."

John "The film was just a film of us making the LP. It's in documentary form, but it's a very interesting film. You see what you go through to make a record. It's not that simple, it's a long process, and a lot of it is captured on film. Obviously, we played a lot of music that we were interested in at the time. We don't have any set style. We're not always going to record in one style or another."

George "The film, rather than a TV show, happened to be the film of us making the record. So, it's very rough in a way, but it's nice, you know, because you can see our warts, you can hear us talking, you can hear us playing, tuning, and you can even hear us laughing, and all of those things. It's the complete opposite to the clinical approach that we normally had."

Ringo "It was supposed to be 25 per cent each, and I've got about two shots, you know. I did a lot of my comedy for them. I ran around, hiding and peeping and looning about, but they never used any."

John "There was a couple of jam sessions in *Let It Be*, with Yoko and The Beatles playing, but they never got in the movie, of course. I understand it all now . . . That film was set up by Paul for Paul. That's one of the main reasons The Beatles ended. I can't speak for George, but I pretty damn well know, we got fed up of being sidemen for Paul. After Brian died, that's what happened . . . The camerawork was set up to show Paul and not to show anybody else, and that's how I felt about it. And, on top of that, the people that cut it, cut it as 'Paul is God' and we're just lying around there. That's what I felt . . . There were some shots of Yoko and me that had been just chopped out of the film for no other reason than that the people were orientated towards Engelbert Humperdinck . . . I felt sick."

Paul reflects on the January 1969 *Let It Be* sessions, "It simply became very difficult to write with Yoko sitting there. If I had to think of a line, I got very nervous. I might want to say something like 'I love you, girl', but with Yoko watching, I always felt that I had to come out with something clever and avant garde. She would probably have loved the simple stuff, but I was scared. I'm not blaming her; I'm blaming me. You can't blame John for falling in love with Yoko any more than you can blame me for falling in love with Linda. I told him on the phone the other day that, at the beginning of last year, I was annoyed with him. I was jealous because of Yoko and afraid about the break-up of a great musical partnership. It's taken me a year to realise that they were in love, just like Linda and me."

The English journalist Roy Shipston reviews the film "*Let It Be*, the latest, and possibly the last Beatles film, is hardly a feature film in the usual sense – it is a documentary, an explanation of why the group is in the state it is in; almost an apology. It reveals three more or less disinterested Beatles, and one with frustrated enthusiasm, trying to keep it all together . . . Paul. There is no plot, no script, only what they happen to say at the time, and not much of that quality, which abounded in their early films . . . humour."

Saturday, May 23
The current success of a fragmented Beatles, forces the release of a syndicated UK news report entitled "Beatles Album Hits American Jackpot" . . .

The report reads "Beatles have hit the jackpot again! In America, the *Let It Be* album looks like becoming the biggest seller of all time, and 'The Long And Winding Road', the track released as a single there, has already outsold 'Yesterday'! Figures released by Beatles boss Allen Klein this week, show that, despite recent publicity about personal and professional rifts, John, Paul, George and Ringo are still the darlings of America. Said Apple's Mavis Smith, 'It's quite incredible! They're certainly selling more records now than they've ever done. Even at the height of the "scream era".'"

Saturday, May 30

The underground release of the bootleg album *Get Back To Toronto – High Quality Stereo Recordings With Love From John And Yoko*, forces an Apple spokesman to remark "We are aware of the existence of a bootleg Beatles album, which we understand is a very poor recording of *Let It Be*, but we're not at all worried by it."

JULY

From his Scottish farmhouse, **Paul** is quoted as saying, "John Lennon, George Harrison and Ringo Starr are the most honest and sincere men I have ever met. I don't mind being bound to them as friends, I like that idea and I don't mind being bound to them musically. I liked them as partners and I liked being in their band. But most of all, we must change the business arrangements we have for our own sanity. Only by being completely free of each other, financially, will we ever have any chance of coming back."

Friday, July 31
Cynthia Lennon rushes around London in the sun, preparing for her marriage tomorrow to the 28-year-old Italian, Robert Bassanini . . .

Cynthia "Of course I'm nervous this time, of course I'm afraid. I so want it to go right. I'm not any tougher but I'm wiser. I don't feel as though I could be hurt any more but if I were hurt again, I'd face it in a different way. I'd fight. I'll work very hard at my marriage this time. I want a complete partnership, because last time, I retired too much. I was a little bit too complacent. I didn't know things were going wrong. The end for me was very sudden. I had no doubts, I was very happy and I'm easily contented. All I ever wanted was to be a housewife. I was happy to be in the sun. It's difficult getting married again when you've already got one failure behind you, but this time I'm very sure. I've thought a lot about losing confidence in myself. I've fought it and got over it. There were moments when I was very low down. Moments when I thought nobody would ever love me again. In the beginning, it was very hard . . . Robert and I wanted it to be a very private, very quiet affair but the whole thing seems to have got out of hand. I'm just wearing a simple floral dress that I've worn before and I always do my own hair. I want to be just as I am for my own wedding."

Saturday, August 15

Meanwhile, a headline in today's Disc & Music Echo reads, "*The Long And Winding Road* Is Beatles New Film." The report by Mike Ledgerwood continues "The Beatles are to make another film. A special documentary of their spectacular career, made up mainly from cinema and TV sequences, is currently being compiled at their Apple HQ. I understand that a tentative title is *The Long And Winding Road.* The movie, which has been in production for about a year, features every foot of film ever shot and screened of the group . . . The Beatle weddings, their MBE awards, their TV shows, the group's concerts around the world, their meetings with the Maharishi, stretching right back to the beginning in Liverpool's Cavern Club. The mammoth task of collecting the film from movie, TV and newsreel companies, both in Britain and abroad, has been organised by Apple's Neil Aspinall, who is at the moment editing the epic down from 100 hours of material. I was told at Apple, 'It will be a full documentary on the rise of The Beatles. We've had a huge task getting everything together. Also included is everything we at Apple have ever filmed. We don't know when it will be ready for release.' "

Also inside this week's edition of *Disc & Music Echo*, Mike Ledgerwood reports on the eerie silence now surrounding The Beatles' Apple headquarters at 3 Saville Row . . .

"The big black flag with the embroidered green apple is suspended motionless above No. 3 Saville Row, W1, dipped as in mourning. The street is strangely still. You realise suddenly the reason. The fans, whose determined doorstep rituals had become a familiar sight, have gone. Inside too, the atmosphere of Apple has changed. There's an air of uncertainty. Things aren't what they used to be at Apple. Even the employees of the multi-million pound Beatle-bossed Empire have to own up. 'People don't come to see us anymore,' they say. 'Where have all our friends gone?' they ask. Once the Apple offices fairly buzzed with activity. It was rush hour all the time . . . Apple was once a place where you learned to expect the unexpected – and usually accepted it without question. 'Did you see a donkey on the way up in the lift?' Derek Taylor, The Beatles' highly respected PR man inquired once. And he wasn't joking either. Today, however, it's sadly different, and suspiciously silent. The gloss is gone. And lately there have been rumours that the whole Apple idea has turned sour, and the company is to close down . . . The Beatles themselves are conspicuous by their absence these days. Paul was never an ardent Apple man, but you could expect to stumble over Ringo Starr on the stairs, or exchange a few words of greeting with George. And the Lennons, too, were often in and out. John and Yoko have been in America for ages now and George is engaged in marathon recording sessions. Only Ringo has been around, and word has it that even the friendliest Beatle has been unsociable of late . . . Lately, there has been more tightening up. Derek Taylor has departed to write a book. Peter Brown, part of the Apple hierarchy, has assumed the role of pressman. And entertaining expenses – the welcome whiskey-and-Coke extended to visitors – have been curbed considerably. An integral and important part of the unique Apple atmosphere was always the friendly freedom which abounded. Producers, journalists, disc jockeys, a wide cross-section of showbiz, could come and go. The building was 'open house' to all and sundry. A meeting place for all pop people. And it paid dividends. Apple was held in high esteem. You'd drop in for a drink with Uncle Derek, do your thing and split. Now, this is no more. Now, Apple is a shadow of its former self. The shine has gone. There's an air of despondency and uncertainty among the staff. They're aware of the rumours that the axe is poised yet again . . . and they're worried. And outside, the faithful fans – often the first to know – seem to have deserted the shrine. Is the writing on the wall?"

Friday, September 25 (UK)
Ringo releases his second solo album; the Nashville-influenced *Beaucoups Of Blues* . . .

Ringo "That came about after I had met Pete Drake in the studio with George Harrison (*All Things Must Pass* sessions). Drake noticed that I had a lot of country tapes in my car. I told him I liked country and he said, 'Well, why don't you do a country album?' And I said, 'Oh no. I'm not going to sit around in Nashville for six months,' because that was how long it used to take us to do an album. He said, 'It doesn't take that long. I did *Nashville Skyline* (Bob Dylan) in two days.' I said, 'Are you kidding?' I mean, I am sure it didn't take only two days for *Nashville Skyline*. It probably took four! Anyway, I said, 'Okay, I'd love to do one. Can you get it together?' We went into the studio on a Thursday and I had ten tracks done by the Friday, the next night! We did ten tracks in the morning and ten tracks at night. I think some of my finest vocals are on that album, because I was relaxed. At first, I was really nervous and Pete would say, through the glass, 'Hoss, if you don't get loose, I'm going to come up in there and stomp on your toes!' "

Saturday, September 26
John begins recording his *John Lennon/Plastic Ono Band* album at Abbey Road Studios in London. In adjoining studios are George, concluding work on his album, *All Things Must Pass*, and the Australian rock band, The Masters Apprentices, recording their first UK EMI album. Their lead singer is Jim Keays . . .

"Meeting John Lennon was amazing," Jim recalls. "Actually, I met him in the toilet. I was having a 'wee' and he came in and stood beside me and I looked around and it was John Lennon! I'm not usually stuck for words. I would have spoken to the Queen of England if she had come in there, but I just couldn't utter a syllable. I didn't know what to say to him. He left and I still didn't say a word to him and I was kicking myself that I didn't have a conversation with him. One other day, I looked in John's studio and I thought that there was nobody in there. So I thought I'd take a look to see what was happening, if anything, and there was no one in there, except for John. He didn't know I was in there. I looked through the glass and there he was, sitting, writing a song. Then, all of a sudden, the song came out. He sang, 'A working class hero is something to be.' He wrote that song, right there and then as I was watching. That was a great thrill to see that happen."

George "I was in one room singing 'My Sweet Lord' and John was in another room, in Abbey Road, singing 'I don't believe in Jesus, I don't believe in nothing.' He went through that situation with Primal Scream, which was really not the best thing I recommend for anything. Maybe he needed to do it, but it was the point in time where we were totally the extreme to each other and that song, 'Working Class Hero', reminds me of that."

Saturday, October 17
Today's *New Musical Express* features an interview with George Martin, carried out by Richard Green. The conversation headlined "Beatles Record Again? The Odds Are Much Against It", takes place in Martin's recently opened, £400,000 complex, AIR Studios, situated in London's busy Oxford Circus . . .

Green "What is the possibility of further Beatles recording sessions?"

Martin "It all depends on Paul and John and if they want to work together again . . . I think The Beatles would have liked these studios. They would have liked a place of their own, but it never came about for various reasons. That is a pity. The formation of Apple was an example of putting the wrong people in the wrong jobs. Even if The Beatles did decide to record together again, they may find it hard to do so when they choose to. They're the sort of people who decide in the morning that they want to make a record that night. With all the demand for studio time at the moment, they would probably find it difficult to be able to record in that way. They never really made set plans for recording. It was all done on the spur of the moment. They'd ring me and say, 'We want to go into the studio today.'"

The costs to hire Martin's new studios, planned as far back as 1965, are not cheap. Studio 1, with its 16-track facilities, is £35 an hour . . .

Martin "The swing in recording costs began at about the time of *Sgt. Pepper*. That cost £15,000 in studio costs alone, but with an album like that, that sells millions and millions, it is well worth all the expense and effort involved."

Saturday, October 31
Stuart Sutcliffe's mother, Millie, breaks years of silence to talk about her departed Beatle son . . .

"Stuart persuaded me to go down to the Cavern to hear these boys called The Beatles . . . As long as I live, I'll never forget that sound. It lifted the soul out of my body. I couldn't believe it came from those little boys. John and Stuart formed a friendship so deep that few could appreciate it. They were very loyal to each other and even after Stuart split from The Beatles to continue his painting in Hamburg, the pair corresponded constantly. Today, I believe that John still has two bundles of letters to each other. In 1961, John broke his arm defending Stuart in a fight. Later, he modestly shrugged off the injury, to his Aunt Mimi, as a sprain, sustained in a fall. Stuart was playing with The Beatles in Litherland, a suburb of Liverpool, and the popularity of the group was growing daily. The girls were growing crazy for them. I always waited up for Stuart to come home. It was 3am, when he finally came in, without his glasses. He told me, 'You've no reason to wait up this morning. We've been attacked. I got knocked out . . . unconscious. I was hit from the back. My glasses are nonexistent. I couldn't even pick up the pieces, but John got the thug, and he broke his wrist giving him what he'd given me.' Stuart refused to see a doctor after the fight. He had no time to be ill. He was too fond of life. He said if I called a doctor, he'd be gone before he arrived. Stuart died a little less than a year later. The death certificate said, 'Cerebral haemorrhage with mass bleeding. Cause unknown.' Yet, to this day, I am convinced that whatever happened in that brawl might have been a factor in Stuart's death. Stuart died loving The Beatles, having hope and faith in everything they did. And I dare say he believed that his friend, John, would get together with me to see things were worked out okay. I'm just hoping that one day, John will do."

Tuesday, November 17

The *Evening News* reports, "A caravan bought by Beatle John Lennon and his wife, Yoko Ono, to provide gypsy children with a school, has been wrecked – by gypsies! No lessons have been held since Easter at the blue-painted 32-foot caravan, named Romano Dron, and bearing a plaque with John and Yoko's names. Since, gypsies have smashed every window, ripped out all cupboards and fittings, destroyed books and furnishings and fire has burned a hole in the roof. The caravan has been left on the outskirts of Luton on the Caddington Road. Nearby, on the verge site area, are seven gypsy caravan lorries, scrap and bonfires. In December, John Lennon and Yoko Ono donated £100 so that the 32-foot caravan could be bought. Mrs Mary Marriott, of Caddington, who with her husband George helped to organise the school, said, 'It is a frightful mess and very disappointing.' "

Monday, November 23

The Liverpool publicist, Bill Harry spends time reminiscing, recalling the times a decade ago, "I signed The Beatles' manager Brian Epstein as a contributor after my pop paper, *Mersey Beat*, became a runaway success, selling over the counter in record shops. Eppy (Epstein) agreed to try a dozen. Eventually, he sold twelve dozen! Later, he expressed a desire to write the record reviews, and it was because we were always writing about this group called The Beatles, that he became interested. That business about someone (Raymond Jones) walking into the record shop and asking about a record called 'My Bonnie' is a load of nonsense. Brian knew about The Beatles before that!"

Friday, November 27 (USA)
George releases the three-album set *All Things Must Pass,* which features production from Phil Spector . . .

George "Towards the last years (of The Beatles), when I was writing a lot of songs, John and Paul continued writing, and Ringo also started writing a lot of songs, it was hard to get songs on an album. That's why *All Things Must Pass* had so many on it, because it was like being constipated for years and suddenly being able to let loose. I did *All Things Must Pass*, the basic tracks, seventeen of them, just one after another. I suddenly thought, 'I had better check out and see what I have got here,' and I found out that I had seventeen tracks, some dating back to '66 and '67. Then I had to decide which ones to use. In the end, I thought, 'Use them all,' because a lot of them were a backlog and, in order to clear the way for what I was writing, at that time and in the future, I used all of them. Even before I started I knew I was gonna make a good album because I had so many songs and I had so much energy. I had a lot of songs from The Beatles time and I was writing all the time, and I wrote a few while making the album as well. Some songs I used on this album were written about four years ago . . .

"Ringo played on almost the whole album and Phil Spector never considers a session a session unless the entire floor is covered with a multitude of mess, with musical instruments everywhere . . .. I felt it was good music. I liked the first song that was on the album, 'I'd Have You Anytime' and particularly the recording of it, because Derek & The Dominoes played on most of the tracks and it was a really nice experience making that album, because I was really a bit paranoid, musically. Having this whole thing with The Beatles had left me paranoid. I remember having those people in the studio and thinking, 'God, these songs are so fruity! I can't think of which song to do.' Slowly I realised, 'We can do this one,' and I'd play it to them and they'd say, 'Wow, yeah! Great song!' And I'd say, 'Really? Do you really like it?' I realised that it was okay. They were sick of playing all that other stuff."

Pete Drake, who plays steel lead guitar on the record "George is a fantastic person! He's a lot like (Bob) Dylan; their personalities are an awful lot alike . . . It cost them $10,000 just to fly me to London to play on it and about $80,000 or so for the whole album. I saw a lot of things in England in the short time I was there. John Lennon's chauffeur zipped me from my hotel to the studio in the Rolls Royce. But the thing I learned a lot about was their studios and how they make records."

Alan Smith of the *New Musical Express* "George Harrison's three-album set *All Things Must Pass*, which finds its way into the shops this week, will prove that it's a long time since so much love and care and work have been wrapped into one package by one specific artist. Like the *McCartney* album, all I can say is that *All Things Must Pass* stands head and shoulders above just about any other solo album released this year."

'I'd Have You Anytime'

George "I liked 'I'd Have You Anytime' because of Bob Dylan. I was with Bob and he had gone through his broken neck period and was being very quiet, and he didn't have much confidence. That's the feeling I got with him in Woodstock. He hardly said a word for a couple of days. Anyway, we finally got the guitars out and it loosened things up a bit. It was really a nice time with all his kids around, and we were just playing. It was near Thanksgiving. He sang me that song and he was very nervous and shy and he said, 'What do you think about this song?' And I had felt strongly about Bob when I had been in India years before, the only record I took with me along with all my Indian records was *Blonde On Blonde*. I somehow got very close to him, you know, because he was so great, so heavy and so observant about everything. And yet, to find him later very nervous and with no confidence. But the thing he said on *Blonde On Blonde* about what price you have to pay to get out of going through all these things twice, 'Oh mama, can this really be the end.' And I thought, 'Isn't it great?' because I know people are going to think, 'Shit, what's Dylan doing?' But as far as I was concerned, it was great for him to realise his own peace and it meant something. You know, he had always been so hard and I thought, 'A lot of people are not going to like this,' but I think it's fantastic because Bob has obviously had the experience. I was saying to him, 'You write incredible lyrics,' and he was saying, 'How do you write those tunes?' So I was just showing him chords like crazy, and I was saying, 'Come on, write me some words,' and he was scribbling words down and it just killed me because he had been doing all these sensational lyrics. And he wrote, 'All I have is yours, All you see is mine, And I'm glad to hold you in my arms, I'd have you anytime.' The idea of Dylan writing something, like, so very simple, was amazing to me."

'What Is Life?'

George " 'What Is Life?' was written for Billy Preston in 1969. I wrote it very quickly, maybe in fifteen or thirty minutes, on the way to the Olympic Studios in London when I was producing one of his albums. Although Billy was such a great artist, I didn't think his songs were potential hits. Before the session, I just suddenly thought, 'Let's see if I can write a sort of uptempo song for Billy,' and I wrote 'What Is Life?' in about half an hour. And as it happened, we got to the session and Billy and the musicians had arrived and had already started rehearsing for some of the songs and that's the reason why we never got round to recording it. So I did it myself and recorded it. It was one of those tracks that Phil wasn't there for, because Phil was coming and going during the sessions. In fact, we did most of the basic tracks with Phil and then he disappeared and I finished the recording. I recorded 'What Is Life?' one way and didn't like it. I decided it wasn't right. Then we worked on it a second time and then I came up with the bass line, which I play on my bass guitar, and then I got the feel to it, then it was okay and we re-recorded it and it came out much better."

'Wah-Wah'

George " 'Wah-Wah' was written during the *Let It Be* sessions (January 1969). We had been away from each other after having a very difficult time recording the *White Album* (1968), which went on so long. It went on forever. When we came back from holiday, we went straight back into the old routine. I remember Paul and I were trying to have an argument and the crew carried on filming and recording us. I couldn't stand it and I decided, 'This is it! Thank you, I'm leaving!' 'Wah-Wah' was a headache as well as a foot pedal. It was written during the time in the film where John and Yoko were freaking out and screaming. I wrote this tune at home."

'Awaiting On You All'

George "Some songs I've written when I wasn't even writing a song. There's a song called 'Awaiting On You All'. I was just going to bed and I was cleaning my teeth, strumming my teeth and suddenly, in my head, came this, 'You don't want a . . .' And all I had to do was pick up a guitar, find what key I was in and fill in the missing words."

Apple Records promoter, Pete Bennett "George felt very apprehensive about coming out as a solo artist and not as a member of The Beatles. He was very nervous. While in New York City, George, Phil Spector and I were mixing the *All Things Must Pass* album at Media Recording Studio. After the mixing was completed, I requested fifty acetates, which would be sent to all the key radio stations across the country on an exclusive basis. Even after all this, George was still concerned about being out as a solo artist. He asked me whether he would have a No. 1 album and single like John Lennon did. I told him, 'No. 1 all the way.' "

(Note: The *All Things Must Pass* album will become a collectors item shortly following its release, after copies of the sleeve are impounded by airport customs. Consequently, buyers cannot get the album in the shops. A spokesman for Apple will later remark: "The triple LPs are pressed here, along with the presentation package; but all the sleeves and colour posters of George are printed in the States. We sold out of initial supplies and couldn't get any more through because around 250,000 altogether were stuck in freight at London's Heathrow Airport. Apparently, there were hang-ups over import papers or something. As a result, nearly 100,000 *All Things Must Pass* albums could not be sent to retailers around the country between December 18 and January 15, 1971." He adds: "George will not be doing radio and TV promotion for his hit. He's not interested in publicity. He says he's just a musician, that's all.")

Regardless of the lack of promotion for the album, *All Things Must Pass* becomes a massive hit around the world. But his three former Beatles colleagues are not forthcoming to heap congratulations about the album upon George . . .

Paul "I remember John saying to me about George's record *All Things Must Pass*. 'He's a hip boy,' he said. 'Still, he's got to follow it up, hee hee.' "

George "I remember John was really negative at the time. I was away and he came round to my house and there was a friend of mine living there who was a friend of John's. He saw the (*All Things Must Pass*) album cover and said, 'He must be fucking mad, putting three records out. And look at the picture on the front . . . he looks like an asthmatic Leon Russell.' There was a lot of negativity going down . . . I felt that whatever happened, whether it was a flop or a success, I was gonna go on my own just to have a bit of peace of mind."

Saturday, November 28

Christine Stevens and **Michelle Bernel**, two long-time Beatles worshippers, announce why they have stopped standing every day, in all weathers, at the gates of Paul's home in St John's Wood, London . . .

"Paul changed when he got married," Michelle laments. "He's not the old Beatle Paul we used to love. Well, he isn't even a Beatle anymore, is he? He was always so friendly. He often used to chat with us . . . I think it might even be true about him dying, because he's not the same person. In the early days, when Paul went out, he would always tell fans what time he was coming back so that they didn't have to hang around pointlessly. And he even used to pose for them to take photos. Before he was married, he didn't mind us taking photographs. It must be something to do with Linda, that's what most people think. She must have got something across him. You could tell he was changing. It was when she came along that he started dressing differently, wearing Levi's and bovver boots."

Christine "Just before he announced that he didn't want to be a Beatle anymore, he told us that he was sick of it, and he didn't think he would ever be able to live it down . . . None of the other Beatles have visited Paul for years. Ringo was the last one to go round there and that was ages ago. John hasn't been since he got married to Yoko and George told us once at Apple that, 'Paul thinks he's it! He always has.' Even his own brother won't go round now."

December

Carlo Mendez/Jotta Herre release the single 'Penina', a track written by Paul back in December 1968 when he and Linda had gone to Portugal to visit The Beatles' authorised biographer, Hunter Davies . . .

Paul "I gave this song to a group when I turned up in Portugal, 'cos I turned up pissed out of my skull one night and wanted to drink in this hotel, you know, about 12 (midnight). I sat in on drums, and they said, 'Give us a song,' so I said, 'Yeah . . . I've been to Alberferra, I had a great time there,' you know. It was called 'La Penina', which was the name of the hotel, and I ended up in La Penina and they were all digging and singing along. It was good, you know. It was one of those that was right, you know. So,

William Hickey said that I had given away this £20,000 song. But then, Derek Taylor said, 'It's not that he gave away a song, he gave away more of a riff for them to build around.' "

Tuesday, December 8

In his rented New York Greenwich Village apartment, John holds an in-depth controversial conversation with Jann Wenner of *Rolling Stone* magazine, later published in the book *Lennon Remembers* . . .

"I'm not The Beatles. I'm me," **John** announces. "Paul isn't The Beatles. Brian Epstein wasn't The Beatles, neither is Dick James. The Beatles are The Beatles. Separately, they are separate. Nobody is The Beatles, how could they be? We all had our roles to play . . . One has to completely humiliate oneself to be what The Beatles were, and that's what I resent. I didn't foresee it; it just happened bit by bit, gradually, until this complete craziness is surrounding you and you're doing exactly what you don't want to do with people you can't stand. The people you hated when you were ten . . . like sitting with the Governor of the Bahamas when we were making *Help!* and being insulted by these junked-up middle class bitches and bastards who would be commenting on our working-classness and our manners. I couldn't take it . . . I would go insane, swearing at them . . . I'd always do something. I couldn't take it. It was awful . . . It was a fuckin' humiliation."

Paul, in *Life* magazine "I ignored John's interview in *Rolling Stone*. I looked at it and dug him for saying what he thought, but to me, short of getting it off his chest, I think he blows it with that kind of thing. I think he makes people wonder why John needs to do that. I did think there were an awful lot of inconsistencies, because on one page you find John talking about how Dylan changed his name from Zimmerman and how that's hypocritical. But John changed his name to John Ono Lennon and people looking at that just begin to think, 'Come on, what is this?' But the interview didn't bug me. It was so far out that I enjoyed it, actually. I know there are elements of truth in what he said and this open hostility, that didn't hurt me. That's cool. That's John."

Friday, December 11

Simultaneously in both the UK and USA, John releases the album, *John Lennon/Plastic Ono Band* and Yoko releases *Yoko Ono/Plastic Ono Band* . . .

Ringo on John's album "It was fantastic! It was such a heavy album for me. I was on it so maybe I was just getting off on it because of that, but the songs were so great and there were three guys and the cuts are really terrific."

John, in conversation with Jann Wenner of *Rolling Stone* magazine "I learned a lot on this album. I didn't have to learn so much before, because usually there'd be George, Paul and I all listening to it and I wouldn't have to think so much about each individual sound . . . Most takes are right off and most times I sang it and played it at the same time. I can't stand putting the backing on first then singing, which is what we used to do a lot in the old days . . . I wrote 'Mother' in England and 'Isolation' in England, and a few more. I finished them in California . . . At the beginning of 'Mother', the beginning of the album has this bell going 'Dong . . . dong . . . dong.' It's a church bell, which I slowed down to thirty-three, so it's really like a horror movie, and that was like the death knell of the Mother-Father Freudian trip. 'Look At Me' was written around The Beatles' double-album time (1968). I just never got it done. There are a few like that lying around . . ."

'God'

John "I don't believe in The Beatles, that's all. I don't believe in The Beatles myth. I don't believe in them whatever they were supposed to be in everybody's head, including our heads for a period. It was a dream. I don't believe in the dream anymore."

Yoko Ono/Plastic Ono Band . . .

John "The first track is called 'Why' and it was the first real rock'n'roll take we ever did together. It's Ringo, Klaus, me on guitar and Yoko on voice. And the fascinating thing is even we didn't know where Yoko's voice started and where my guitar ended on the intro. But you can tell."

Disc & Music Echo review: "John and Yoko Lennon's latest LPs are alike in many respects. Both sleeves, for instance, bear similar colour covers, each with a childhood photo on the reverse. And both use basically the same backing group, The Plastic Ono Band. But that's where the similarity ceases. John's material is predictably mysterious and way-out, with him singing in the persuasive suggestive style, and appearing to enjoy every moment . . . But, it's senseless to try and define Yoko's efforts. They are simply a wicked waste of wax! Lennon – four stars. Yoko – no rating."

Saturday, December 12

The *New Musical Express* asks, "Could Beatles Re-Unite In '71 With New LP?" The report continues "Could 1971 see a grand Beatles reunion, if only in the recording studios? There is wideworld speculation in music circles that the famous foursome will get together again in the new year to record a new album despite the fact that 1970 has seen John Lennon, Paul McCartney, George Harrison and Ringo Starr emerge as highly successful solo artists. The Beatles are said to be closer than at any time for the last eighteen months, and a meeting of the three of them in New York would appear to have strengthened the likelihood of a professional reunion. Indeed, all four might have met up had Ringo's new baby not kept him at home. An Apple spokesman remarked on the possibility of a reunion, 'We would probably be the last to know, as The Beatles are not obligated to tell us their plans in advance.' But, when he was tackled on the subject by our correspondent in New York, George Harrison confined himself to the cryptic comment, 'Stranger things have happened!' "

While Mike Ledgerwood writes in today's *Disc & Music Echo* "Come Together! The Beatles May Play Again Live!" The report goes on to say: " 'Beatles on stage in concert in Britain for the first time in five years' . . . That's the hint for the new year following reports that Paul McCartney's rift from John, George and Ringo is about to be patched up. I understand that the paths of John, Paul, George and Ringo crossed in New York recently, when there was rumoured talk of a reunion, including a surprise concert appearance. In fact, a friend of The Beatles confided, 'I can't see them doing anything official again, but they certainly seem serious about working together. There have been definitive discussions in that direction.' He added that Paul, in particular, wants to work again, 'Although it was he, originally, who has always been hesitant in the past.' Apple spokesman Peter Brown was evasive. He said, 'No comment!' "

Thursday, December 31
The year ends on a bad note when it is revealed that the break-up of The Beatles' partnership will be settled in the High Court of London . . .

Paul "I really felt that Klein had to be got rid of because I could see that he wasn't doing us any good. He got $5 million off us in the first year he managed us and he wanted more and I was just trying to fight for us. I was saying, 'Don't give him 20 per cent, give him 15. We're a massive group,' and they were saying, 'Oh come on, you've got to give him twenty.' And I was saying, 'What do you mean?' It all got so crazy that I decided that I had to sue Allen Klein. So I got all my lawyers and I said, 'I've got to get out. We've got to do this or else he's going to have everything that I've worked for, and the others.' That's the way I saw it. The lawyers then got on the case and they said, 'Oh, oh, we can't sue Allen Klein.' And I said, 'Why not?' And they said, 'He's not a party to any of the agreements. You'll have to sue The Beatles.' So I said, 'Well, I can't do that. There's no way that I can do that.' So about two months later, while I was on the hill up in Scotland, with the mists, I was thinking, 'I've got to do something. But I can't do what I've got to do.' It took me two months to decide that I had to do it, sue The Beatles! It was murderous. I had a knot in my stomach all summer. It didn't matter, they were parties to Klein and I had to actually go and sue them. You can imagine what I had to go through suing my best mates and *seen* to sue my best mates. That was the worst and knowing that no one would understand it. No one would understand why I had to do it, not even if I put out 50 million press releases . . . My lawyer, John Eastman, he's a nice guy and he saw the position we were in, and he sympathised. We would have these meetings on top of hills in Scotland; we'd go for long walks. I remember when we actually decided we had to go and file suit. We were standing on this big hill, which overlooked a loch; it was quite a nice day, a bit chilly and we had been searching our souls. The only alternative was seven years with the partnership, going through those same channels for seven years . . .

"There was a partnership contract put together years ago (January 1967) to hold us together as a group for ten years. Anything anybody wanted to do, put out a record, anything, he had to get the others' permission. Because of what we were then, none of us ever looked at it when we signed it. We signed in '67 and discovered it last year. We discovered this contract that bound us for ten years. So it was, 'Oh gosh, oh golly, oh heck,' you know. (I said) 'Now, boys, can we tear it up, please?' But the trouble is, the other three have been advised not to tear it up. They've been advised that if they tear it up, there will be serious, bad consequences for them."

Paul discusses the problem further in a conversation with the BBC reporter Mike Hennessey . . .

"It all comes down to one basic fact, which is, in my opinion, The Beatles haven't finished as a group and me being in a new group, with a new line-up. I believe that, no matter what the consequences are, the tax consequences, or, 'Sorry boys, you can't do that, we've got a contract.' The relationship in which we started the group was that if any one of us was in trouble and wanted to get out and was in a sticky situation, our view was that we'd sit down and see what we could do about it. Well, in fact, it's just the opposite that has happened. It all boils down to one fact, they have my contract."

Friday, January 1

Following yesterday's announcement, Paul talks at his Scottish farmhouse about his apparent rift with John and the other Beatles. Sporting a large beard, **Paul** remarks, "I dig John. There is a rift, but it's not a bad one. I just want to get out of this trap. I want to dissolve The Beatles' partnership. I suppose it ceased to be a working partnership eight months ago. I left in June. Songwriting between John and I came to a halt a year ago, but The Beatles' partnership goes on for seven more years (*sic*) and this is why I want out now. The other three of them could sit down now and write me out of the group and I would be quite happy. I could pick up my cash and get out. I don't know how much is involved but I don't want Allen Klein as my manager. For my future, I am just going to write songs and they will be better than ever. I have got an album ready for release now."

Monday, January 10

Recording sessions for *Ram* start at the A & R Studios in New York . . .

Paul "We went to New York to try and find the best recording studio in the world. But I tried them all, and I still think No. 2 at Abbey Road is the best. It's the one that suits me best, anyway. It's also got so many facilities there. In America, if you suddenly decide that you want a harmonium, you have to ring up a firm, 'Yes, we want a harmonium. Yes, we will pay for it. Yes, we'll pay for delivery costs,' all this business. Here in England, I just say to Tony (Clark, engineer), 'Can we have a harmonium,' he phones the man downstairs and he wheels one up. Anyway, in New York we got to Harlem on the subway, we had a great evening at the Apollo Theater and we had a walk through Central Park after hours. You may find us murdered one day . . . It was snowy like moonlight in Vermont, just fantastic and I figure anyone who scares me, I scare him."

Linda "While we were in New York making *Ram*, twenty kids would follow us everywhere we went, everywhere, hotels, rehearsals, the studio. After a while I asked them to lay off and one of them turned and said, 'Well, what the hell did you expect?' I wasn't expecting that."

American Beatles fan, Tess Basta "The first time I ever saw Paul was when he was in New York recording his *Ram* album at the former CBS Studios. I know I went there a couple of days. One day, the first time I saw him, I saw him about three times. When I arrived, he was already there. There were a lot of people there every day and I was told, which I found out myself, that he is usually in a vicious mood. This was his bad period. I saw him come out for lunch with Linda and I was in heaven! To finally see him in the flesh was too much. Believe it or not, he decided to stop right outside the doorway and let people take pictures of him but he wasn't too thrilled about it. And, believe it or not, my camera decided not to work. My trusty Instamatic suddenly became my untrustworthy Instamatic. When he left to go to lunch, he and Linda simply walked up the block and people were following him up to the corner, but didn't dare follow him any further. He came back about an hour and a half later and, all of a sudden, people looked and noticed him bopping down the block from the same direction that he left in. He simply walked in and that was that. Afterwards, I saw him leave for the day around 6pm. As a joke, everyone decided that when he came out to leave, we would all be quiet and not even say goodbye or anything for that matter. But you should have seen the look on his face as he walked to the cab! And when he got into the cab, he turned around to look at all of us and we still weren't doing anything. He had such a perplexed look on his face.

"My next encounter with him was a couple of days later. We got there at 9am and no one was there. We couldn't figure it out. We found out later that he absolutely, positively does not want to see anyone there in the morning and he scared them enough that no one went. We were standing there saying how great it was that we were the only ones there when, finally, he pulls up in a cab with Linda, Mary and Heather. My friend and I were standing in front of the doorway entrance while he is paying the driver and scowling at us from inside the cab. Everyone gets out and he stops directly in front of us, only three feet away. We say good morning to him and not only does he not say good morning to us, he says absolutely nothing but continues to stare at us, and I mean really looking at us. We were a little uneasy and my friend Linda finally asks him if we can take a picture and he says, 'Not in the morning', and leaves it at that and walks in. Linda and I found out afterwards that we were very lucky, as there were a few bad incidents with girls there in the morning. Then we knew why he was staring at us the way he did. He was looking to see if he recognised us, if he had previously warned us not to be there at that time of day. Obviously realising we did not know, he didn't go into a tirade. In spite of the fact that most of the time he was in a miserable mood, Linda and I were glad that he didn't decide to randomly abuse us that morning, considering we were innocent. It showed us that his good nature was still intact under all the hostility apparent at the time."

Paul "When we were in New York to do *Ram,* I held auditions for a drummer. It was embarrassing. I've never auditioned anyone before. I hired a depressing basement with a tatty drum kit in it. I'd auditioned quite a few drummers and then Denny (Seiwell) walked in. Apart from anything else, he was a lot younger than the others. Some drummers just couldn't play in there. Denny went straight for the tom-toms and within seconds, the room began to throb. I was sold! He's also a technically good drummer, and has a bass voice."

A session musician on the recordings is the top-rated 21-year-old guitarist David Spinoza. He had previously played the guitar part on Freda Payne's monster hit 'Band Of Gold' . . .

"All I remember is getting a phone call from Linda McCartney," David says, "who addressed herself as, 'Mrs McCartney', and I said, 'Who?' She said, 'My husband would like to meet you.' And I said, 'Did I ever work for your husband before?' She said, 'This is Linda McCartney and my husband is Paul McCartney', like I was supposed to know Paul McCartney was calling my house. She didn't make it clear what they wanted me for. I thought it was for a meeting or a recording session, but it turned out to be an audition. I took down the address and I went to this place on 45th Street, which was a dirty loft. They must have been there for three days auditioning people. It seemed weird for him to come to town and audition the heaviest musicians in the business. Cats who had been in music for fifteen years and played with just everyone and who, as musicians, The Beatles just couldn't stand next to as instrumentalists. You don't have to audition these cats; they can play everything under the sun. I had heard that some of the studio guys had given them a hard time, which I really didn't want to do because I wanted to work with them. When I get there, there are three guitar players, but you had to be called. You couldn't walk in off the streets with your guitar. Paul, with a three-day-old beard, introduced himself to me and we are alone in this gigantic room. There is nothing but amplifiers, piano and drums and, of course, Linda. He wanted me to play something. He played a blues, and a solo and some folk and said he wanted me to do that. I played it and then he just said, 'Sorry I couldn't spend more time with you but I have a lot of people to see,' and so I said, 'Fine.' As soon as I got home, the phone rang and Linda said Paul wanted me to do the sessions the following week.

"The date started out going really smoothly, but then what was happening was that although originally they had told me they wanted me for four whole weeks, days were getting cancelled out and they weren't booking definitive dates. So I had to keep asking, not to be a drag, but to keep my book straight and to know what other work I could take. I kept asking but I wasn't getting a straight answer. Finally, after I had heard from them, Linda rang me up on a Sunday night, and told me that they wanted me to do all the following week, just like that. But I couldn't, because I had asked if we would be working and they had said probably not, so I had taken other dates. I had told them that I couldn't keep every week open because when Paul goes back to England, there are other people that call me all year and they are going to keep me eating, not him, although I would love to do his sessions. So she calls me and I said I could make two of the days, not all five and she got very indignant. That's the vibration I got. I got vibrations like, 'It's Paul McCartney's session, you're supposed to keep life open indefinitely.' Finally I just did those two days and the next week I still couldn't get a straight answer and it seemed like I was dealing with Linda and not Paul . . . Working in the studio with them was fine. Paul knew what he wanted. I think the whole album was done in the same form as the *McCartney* album, only we played the parts for him. We were told exactly what to play. He knew exactly what he wanted and he just used us to do it. He just sang us the parts he wanted and the tune developed as we went along. We added things and we made suggestions. But I would say that two out of ten times he took one of our suggestions, or at least if he did, he modified it and made it into a Paul McCartney thing. It always comes out Paul McCartney regardless of the suggestion.

"Linda didn't have much to do in the studio, she just took care of the kids. The kids were there all the time, every day. They brought the whole family every day to the studio and they stayed no matter how long Paul stayed. If he was there at four o'clock in the morning, everybody stayed. I thought to a certain degree, it was distracting. It was a nice, loose atmosphere, but distracting. I really don't know what Linda did in the studio aside from just sit there and make her comments on what she thought was good and what she thought was bad. She sang all right. I heard some of the things she sang on the album and she sings fine, like any girl that worked in a High School glee club. She can hold a note and sing background. Paul gives her a note and says, 'Here Linda, you sing this and I'm going to sing this,' and she does . . . There's one track, which is a cute thing, a blues tune, which I think has a pretty unique sound and I had fun doing '3 Legs'. Paul likes to double track a lot of things. We both played acoustic on some tracks and then tripled. Sometimes Paul played piano but he never played bass while we were there. He overdubbed the bass. It was a little weird, because bass, drums and guitar would have been more comfortable, but that's the way he works . . . Working with Paul was fun, in as much as it was good to see how he works and where he's coming from. But as a musician, it wasn't fun, because it wasn't challenging or anything like that. But it was very good. Paul is definitely a songwriter, not a musician, but he writes beautiful songs. In the studio he's incredibly prompt and businesslike. No smoking pot, no drinks, or carrying on, nothing. Just straight-ahead. He came in at nine in the morning. We were all there and we would listen to what we had done before so that it would get us psyched ready to do the day's work, then we went into the studio and it was eight hours of just playing. He's not a very loose cat, not eccentric in any way at all. Very much of a family man. He just wants to make good music."

Friday, January 15
Following extensive radio airplay, George releases the single 'My Sweet Lord' . . .

George "I went to see Delaney & Bonnie & Friends, which was with Eric Clapton, he was one of the friends, playing at the Albert Hall in London (December 1, 1969), and sometimes you go to a show and I go, 'Wow, I'd love to be up there playing. It looks so nice.' And other times, I think, 'Oh no, I'm glad I'm not in that band.' But with Delaney & Bonnie & Friends with Eric, it looked so good. They played so well and I just sat there in the box with Ringo. The next day, they pulled up in a car outside my house and said, 'C'mon.' So I slung on my guitar and went with them. We did a tour of England and then we went round Europe. I remember Eric and Delaney & Bonnie were doing interviews with somebody in either Copenhagen or Gothenburg, somewhere in Sweden and I was so thrilled with 'Oh Happy Day', by The Edwin Hawkins Singers. It really just knocked me out, the idea of that song and I just felt a great feeling of the Lord. So I thought, 'I'll write another "Oh Happy Day",' which became 'My Sweet Lord' . . . As far as I'm concerned, 'My Sweet Lord' was a hit because of the sound and its simplicity. The sound of that record, it sounds like one huge guitar. The way Phil Spector and I put that down was we had two drummers, a bass player, two pianos and about five acoustic guitars, a tambourine player and we sequenced it in order. Everybody plays live in the studio. I spent a lot of time with the other rhythm guitar players to get them all to play exactly the same rhythm so it just sounded perfectly in synch. The way we spread the stereo in the recording, the spread of five guitars across the stereo, made it sound like one big record. The other things, I overdubbed, like I overdubbed the voices, which I sang all the back-up parts as well and overdubbed the slide guitars, but everything else on it was live. There's Ringo and a drummer called Jim Gordon . . . They then sued me over a song written by a guy who died a while back that I had never even heard of anyway, although I'd heard the song ('He's So Fine') . . . 'My Sweet Lord' was written in a dressing room while Delaney & Bonnie were being interviewed. It turned out not to be 'Oh Happy Day', but more like The Chiffons' 'He's So Fine' . . .

"I was brought up almost a Catholic, where they told me, 'Just believe in what we're telling you. Don't expect to see Jesus because he's not there. We nailed him up 2,000 years ago. He's dead.' But Jesus never went away. This is the joke. The thing that really impressed me in India or from India was Swami Bifficonada and he contradicted exactly what I had been taught in Catholicism, which was, 'If there's a God, let's see him. If there's a soul, let's perceive it, otherwise it's best not to believe. It's better to believe an outspoken atheist than a hypocrite.' Whereas, he's saying, 'If there's a God, let's see him,' and I'm right with him there. Okay, if there's a God, come on, let's see him. Now there is a way to see him. You have to really struggle to see him but he can be seen. You have to practise . . . Musically, anything any good that comes out of me, it's a blessing through that and all the crap that comes out is me. If anything any good comes out of my life or out of my music or out of my mouth, then let the glories be to the Lord, for blessing me with whatever talent or with whatever I have that is honest and that all the deceitfulness or lies, which I am also pretty good at, that's me."

Tuesday, January 19
Meanwhile, back in London, the break-up of The Beatles' partnership begins in the High Court . . .

Paul "When we were starting to break up, we found a contract which bound us together for ten years and it had another five years to run. We had signed this and then forgotten about it. Klein insisted that we kept to it and that's why I had to sue the others, because I could not sue Klein . . . It's not the boys; it's not the other three. The four of us, I think, still quite like each other. I don't think there is bad blood, well not from my side anyway. I spoke to the others quite recently and there didn't sound like any from theirs. It's a business thing. It's Allen Klein . . . Klein is incredible. He's New York. He'll say, 'Waddaya want? I'll buy it for you.' I guess there's a lot I really don't want to say about this, but it will come out because we had to document the stuff for this case . . . We began to talk about the suit, over and over. I just saw that I was not going to get out of it. From my last phone conversation with John, I think he sees it like that. He said, 'Well, how do you get out?'

"In England, if a partnership isn't rolling along and working, like a marriage, then you have reasonable grounds to break it off. Good old British justice! But before I went into this, I had to check out in my mind, is there such a thing as justice? Like, I throw myself into the courts and I could easily get caught, tell the story, put it all in there and then justice turns around . . . I mean, these days people don't believe in justice. I really think the truth does win, but it's not a popular thought. But then, all my life, I've been in love with goodies as against the baddies . . . People said, 'It's a pity that such a nice thing had to come to such a sticky end.' I think that too. It's a pity. I like fairy tales. I'd love it to have The Beatles go up in a little cloud of smoke and the four of us just find ourselves in magic robes, each holding an envelope with our stuff in it. But you realise that you're in real life and you don't split up a beautiful thing with a beautiful thing."

The highly publicised London High Court case will run until Friday, March 12 . . .

Paul "Yes, I did take The Beatles to the High Court, which was a highly traumatic time for me. Imagine fronting that one out. It was crazy. It was just insane. I felt so insecure, which is the reason why I grew that beard. It was a cover-up. I went to the High Court and the judge said Klein had 'The prattle of a second-class salesman.' My whole life was on the line. This was the fire, this was the furnace and we all had the shakes in our voices. It was something that we had never ever had before. I remember Neil Aspinall quite clearly, nervously trying to speak."

During which time each of The Beatles will present, via their solicitor, Mr Morris Finer, QC, written statements in their defence against Paul . . .

John "The Beatles' company, Apple, became full of spongers and hustlers after the death of Brian Epstein. The staff came and went as they pleased and were lavish with money and hospitality. We have since discovered that, at around that time, two of Apple's cars had completely disappeared, and we also owned a house, which no one can remember buying. Within a few weeks of Mr Allen Klein's being appointed as manager of The Beatles, the hustling and lavishness was stopped. Incompetent or unnecessary staff were dismissed and discipline and order were restored to the company. Each of The Beatles started to receive regular statements of his financial affairs, including copies of bills with explanations. Mr Klein repeatedly told George, Ringo and I what he was doing almost to the point of boring us . . . There had been a lot of arguing, mainly about musical matters. I suppose Paul and George were the main offenders but from time to time, we all gave displays of temperament and threatened to walk out. According to Klein, the muddle he found was enormous and went back for years, and Paul and the Eastmans were continually obstructing him and refusing information and documents he needed from them. I have not the slightest doubt that Klein was being truthful to me about both these matters."

George "To get a peaceful life, I always had to let Paul have his own way, even when it meant that songs of mine weren't being recorded. At the same time, I was helping record Paul's own songs and into the bargain I had to put up with him telling me how to play my own instrument. Matters came to a head in a dismal and cold studio at Twickenham, when we were filming *Let It Be*. In front of the cameras, Paul started getting at me about the way I was playing. I decided I'd had enough and I told the others I was leaving the group. After a few days, the others asked me to return and, since Paul agreed he wouldn't try to interfere or teach me how to play, I went back. Since the row, Paul has treated me more as a musical equal, and I think this whole episode shows how a disagreement can be worked out so we all benefit."

Ringo "Paul is the greatest bass guitarist in the world, but he has behaved like a spoilt child . . . I was shocked and dismayed after Paul's promises about a meeting in January that a writ should have been issued on December 31. I trust Paul and I know he would not lightly disregard his promise. My own view is that all four of us together could even yet work out everything satisfactorily."

Aside from the case, **Paul** remarks in *Life* magazine "You can read the other boys' side to find out that I'm a stinker. I think I'm right but don't we all . . . Because I've had to take this action against the others, it looks like we can't stand each other. I can really only speak for myself but I still like the other three. And maybe it's deeper than 'like', but at the moment, I'm not stuck on them. I'm not pleased. We are not amused at the moment. I am not loving them but I know that when it's over, I will really like them."

Wednesday, January 20
With The Beatles' High Court trial brewing, John and Yoko head off to Japan, where John meets Yoko's parents for the first time. The informal meeting takes place at the family's seaside home, 50 miles from Tokyo . . .

Mrs Isako Ono "It was delightful to meet him. He seemed a very pleasant man. I think all those articles in the papers about his odd behaviour are silly nonsense. He appeared to be a quiet, thoughtful and very gentle person to me. It was I who took the phone call announcing their arrival. I was absolutely astonished when Yoko telephoned and told me she was in Japan. What they are doing here is not entirely clear. When they were here at our unworthy home, John made his own concession to our custom by taking off his white tennis shoes and leaving them at the door. We offered them tea at a table with chairs but John said it would be more appropriate to behave in the Japanese style. I thought that was very charming. So they knelt on tatami (straw matting), drank o-cha (tea) and talked. Most of the time it was about Yoko's brother and two sisters, but we also talked about their home in England. It sounds beautiful. We would love to go there, but I am afraid we are too old."

John Reader, *Daily Sketch* "Yoko has confided to friends that she and John went to Japan because of the unpleasantness of living in London during Paul McCartney's court action to try and dissolve The Beatles' Apple company."

Thursday, January 21

The *New Musical Express* reports, "Beatles Rock'n'Roll Oldies To Be Issued Before Long?" The article continues, "Now that The Beatles have ceased to function as a group, notwithstanding continued reports that they may reunite to record a new album, it seems likely that some of their previously unissued material may soon see the light of day. There are known to be nearly 50 tracks by The Beatles, which have never been released, and these include a large number of rock'n'roll titles, which the foursome recorded on the *Let It Be* film set. Among other items in the vaults are The Beatles' live concert at the Hollywood Bowl and a little known Beatles album, which they cut in Italy when they were undertaking their famous European tour. This was issued briefly in Holland three years ago, but was subsequently withdrawn."

Saturday, January 23

As The Beatles' High Court action continues to besmirch the worldwide media, The Beatles' former 'nurse' Peter Brown quits his job at Apple and heads off to America for his new employment as the president of The Empressarios, the newly formed US branch of the Robert Stigwood Organisation. Before his departure, a party, arranged by the singer Cilla Black, is held in his honour in London . . .

"It was a roaring success," he announces to the reporter Frankie McGowan. "Ringo was there to bid me bon voyage but the other Beatles did not attend. George is not a partygoer. Paul I will see in New York and John is still in Tokyo. He is a sensitive subject at the moment. I think I am in his bad books. John thinks I cut Yoko the last time we met, but it is terribly unfair. When I walked into that room, I was anxious because I was aware that I wasn't just meeting two old friends who had been away for six months. John had gone through a total transformation. I think I greeted him in much the same way as I always would, with a hug, and then I turned to Yoko and said hello. John said I cut her because, for some reason, I didn't kiss her. But that is John."

Brown admits to McGowan, "My relationship with the four Beatles is one of the few genuinely close ones they have in common. It has survived because I have been a discreet, loyal and devoted man. But I never felt that I could replace Brian Epstein in their lives. No one could ever have done that. He was the only person they would listen to. I was accepted and invited to family parties because I was a friend. They turned to me when he died because there were some things, private things, that someone had to attend to. During the past eighteen months, my job has spread and I became more involved with Apple on the administration side. I don't think they will need to replace me. Since they have started developing separately, they have naturally found other people to help them."

This turbulent year also sees Paul moving into the sometimes lucrative world of music publishing . . .

"I owe it all to Linda's dad, Lee Eastman and her brother, John," **Paul** announces. "Linda's dad is a great business brain. He said originally, 'If you are going to invest, do it in something you know. If you invest in building companies or something, you can lose a fortune. Wouldn't you rather be in music? Stay in music.' I said, 'Yeah, I'd much rather do that.' So he asked me what kind of music I liked and the first name I said was Buddy Holly. Lee got on to the man who owned Buddy Holly's stuff and bought that for me because the Buddy Holly stuff was up for sale. Norman Petty just happened to be selling it. EMI was interested in it, Chappels was interested in it, Allen Klein was interested in it and I think, secretly, that's what got me interested. I had always said I liked Buddy, he was one of my big influences when I first started writing. When it came up for sale, I had to spend my money somehow and I thought, 'Well, I'd rather have that than anything else.' Not so much to be greedy, but to just, kind of, be able to look after those songs and do stuff for them, because it's stuff that I'm really interested in. I like the publishing thing because it's clean. It just takes care of itself. So I was into publishing now. The strange thing is that we, The Beatles, never owned our own publishing. It was always getting bought and sold. Someone else owns 'Yesterday' not me. So it was a kind of compensation, really, for that."

Monday, February 1
At Pinewood Studios in Iver, Buckinghamshire, Ringo begins shooting *200 Motels*, his next solo film, a bizarre and surreal musical movie starring the rock star Frank Zappa and his backing group, The Mothers Of Invention . . .

Zappa "I thought that it would be the ultimate absurdity to have Ringo Starr play Frank Zappa, and especially having him say the dialogue, which he had to deliver in the front part of the film. Ringo accepted it because he was getting a bit browned off with his good-guy image."

Ringo "I played Frank Zappa because he couldn't play himself. He would only play his guitar. *200 Motels* was great and very fast because we did it on videotape. We did all the editing on tape and then transferred it onto film. It has some weird effects. I've never seen the whole movie."

Monday, February 8

Meanwhile, **Paul** features today in a syndicated press report, revealing that "Beatle Paul McCartney has twice been turned away from New York's most fashionable restaurant, Twenty-One. He went to lunch at the restaurant, which is frequented by Aristotle and Jackie Onassis, with his 18-month-old daughter, Alice (*sic*). But the manager, Monte Seldman, turned Paul away because he was wearing sneakers – and no tie. The same evening, Paul returned to Twenty-One for dinner with his wife, Linda. He was wearing a long overcoat and he rushed upstairs to the restaurant, keeping the coat on. He said he was cold. But when the management asked him to take his coat to the cloakroom, they discovered he was wearing neither a tie nor a jacket. Once again he was asked to leave. Paul and his family are in New York visiting his in-laws and 'getting away from it all'."

On **Saturday, February 13**, in the annual *Disc & Music Echo* poll, The Beatles are placed in the top spot in the 'Top Group – Britain' section, and beaten into the second spot by Led Zeppelin in the 'Top Group – World' category.

Friday, March 12

In the UK, John releases the single 'Power To The People'.

John "I wouldn't take weeks to make a record like that. I just sort of throw it out quick . . . They're sort of throwaway records . . . That was the expression going round those days . . . Tariq Ali had kept coming round wanting money for the *Red Mole* or some magazine or other and I used to give anybody money, kind of out of guilt, because I was thinking, 'Well, I'm working class and I am not one of them. But I am rich, so therefore I have to.' So, any time anybody said something like that, I would fork out, you know . . . He was hustling for whatever he was hustling for and I kind of wrote 'Power To The People' in a way kind of as a guilt song . . ."

Paul "John has a new record out with a song called 'Power To The People' and there's a line in it, a sort of shouting to the Government, 'Give us what we own', and to me, Apple's the Government thing. Give me what I own."

Appearing on the B-side is Yoko's controversial recording, 'Open Your Box' . . .

John "I don't know what the hell 'box' means in America, apparently it means crotch, or whatever."

Yoko "This song has been banned and I believe it is because I am a woman. One of the reasons is because the word 'box' has many different meanings, especially in America, where it refers to a certain part of a woman's body. If a man makes a statement like that, he can easily get away with it. I think the fact that it was a woman, supposedly making an obscene statement, that really shocked people. Men sing about legs a lot . . . The song is not really that crude, and then it's banned, just like that. 'Box' is a very philosophical song, about opening everything up, minds, windows, your country, it's sort of like 'We're All Water'."

Monday, March 15

Stella Shamoon, London City Writer reports "Linda McCartney, American wife of Beatle Paul, is the centre of a financial row between her husband and the song publishers, Northern Songs, over whether she helped Paul write his new hit single, 'Another Day'. Paul McCartney insists she did and is claiming her entitlement to half the copyright earnings. But Northern Songs rejects the claim and means to take the McCartneys to court if necessary. Mr Jack Gill, chairman of Northern Songs, said, 'We will require McCartney to prove that she is capable of composing such music if she persists i claim. We find it extremely strange that a person who never wrote music bef marriage, should have helped write "Another Day". Mrs McCartney's clai copyright earnings of "Another Day" would cut The Beatles' share of th song.' Lennon remarked, 'It's not very nice, is it?' "

Paul "Linda and I have been writing songs together and my p they don't believe she wrote them with me. You know, sud suddenly she's writing songs. 'Oh sure, wink, wink, oh s actually, one day I said to her, 'I'm going to teach you ho strap you to the piano bench. I'm going to teach you the wa music anyway. I just write by ear and I like to collaborate on s

36

in another room and write, it's too much like work, like doing your homework. If I can have Linda working with me, then it becomes like a game. It's fun, so we wrote about ten songs . . ."

John "What Paul's mistake here was that he tried to take it all for 'Another Day'. Now, I wrote 'God Save Us' with Yoko, and 'Do The Oz' and there's one track on the album she wrote. She had even written other things like 'Julia' back in The Beatles' days, although I never put it on. What we did was we just called Lew Grade and they know she writes music and we said, 'Look, we've done it. So what do you want to do about it?' And he said, 'Well, let's split it,' and so we just split it, Ono Music and Northern Songs. The thing with Paul is, he wants all the action. He wants it all. It's not just the money, it's the principle. For instance, Paul's cost us probably over a million (pounds) since he started this (High Court) thing and his tax counsel's just come up and given us exactly the tax advice we gave him two years ago, to tell him exactly not to do all what's he done. So it's cost us quite a bit trying to see it his way. It's like Monopoly, only with real money, and it's costing us a fortune. The sooner it's over the better."

Paul "The first time I actually saw cheques was when I left Apple and it wasn't even me who saw them, it was Linda, because we had co-written a few of our early things. She had written a few words, so I put her down as co-writer, which ATV and Sir Lew Grade didn't like. In fact, they sued me for a million in England, a million in New York. 'Very charming,' I thought, after all I had done for them. Lee Eastman stepped in and settled. He's a top man. The royalty cheques I saw came to Linda. I thought, 'Wow, I bet I've got a few of them somewhere.' But mine never came to me. They went to an 'aforementioned party'. They always went into a big well, and we never saw any."

Linda "We were getting sued by a publisher, saying that I was incapable of writing. So Paul said, 'Get out and write a song.' So I wrote 'Seaside Woman', which is a reggae number. So then I thought, 'We need a B-side for it,' so we went in and recorded a number called 'Oriental Nightfish', which turned out so good that we thought, 'Now we've got two A-sides,' so now we needed to do two B-sides . . ." (1973)

Saturday, March 20

Les Perrin, the official spokesman for John, George and Ringo, issues the following statement: "Following a newspaper report which states 'The Beatles Are Back' and adding that the new Beatle was Klaus Voorman, I am instructed as press and public relations representative for John Lennon, George Harrison and Ringo Starr, Apple Corps Ltd, Mr Allen Klein and ABKCO Industries Inc., to state that this story is completely incorrect. I am advised that a) The Beatles are not re-forming – and that, consequently, Klaus Voorman does not replace Paul McCartney: b) Messrs. Lennon, Harrison and Starr did not meet last Friday night (March 19) at the Apple HQ to discuss future recordings: John Lennon, George Harrison and Ringo Starr did not send Paul McCartney a cable announcing that the group was recording, detailing times to attend the recording . . . I wish to reiterate my earlier statement that an appeal was launched last Friday (19) by solicitors acting on behalf of John Lennon, George Harrison and Ringo against a High Court decision in Paul McCartney's favour, appointing a Receiver . . . to look after The Beatles' affairs."

John "There aren't any Beatles anymore. They've been disbanded. But if you'd said that George, Ringo and John had an idea they might do a live show or two, then Klaus would be our man to play with us. It's just an idea. We can't say whether it will happen or not. Sometimes we get the urge to have another go and then we think we've done it all before and what do we want to suffer it again for? So, for the moment, Klaus backs us on our individual sessions."

Saturday, March 27

John is a guest on Kenny Everett's live Monte Carlo radio show. The 1am show, a somewhat late promotional vehicle for John's *Plastic Ono Band* album, comes direct from Tittenhurst Park in Ascot . . .

Everett "Now, over to Ascot. Well listeners, here we are in John's luxurious 72-acre studio, built into his home here at Ascot."

John "We are."

Everett "Seeing as this isn't television . . ."

John "Yes, we're in the studio, five by eight."

Everett "Now, why did you buy a studio in your own house, when you've got one in your office as well? In fact, how many have you got?"

John "Well, the one in the office hasn't been finished, you see, and that's going to be 16-track, and this is 8-track. And it just means you can record when you want and you can go to bed."

Everett "Or have a cup of tea."

John "Right."

Everett "If ever you feel during this interview like coming out with an original song, recorded just for Radio Monte Carlo, please feel free."

John (singing) "The man that broke the bank of Monte Carlo."

Everett "Oh my god. Well tell us about your LP, John. It seems not to be as jolly as your last ones."

John "Jolly as what?"

Everett "Well, as the rest of them."

John "Well, such as?"

Everett "*Revolver, Sgt. Pepper . . .*"

John "Ah, well that was a group effort, you see."

Everett "Do you reckon yourself the sad member of the group?"

John "Well, I wouldn't say they're all particularly much happier than me. But, they might emphasise the happier side, that's all."

Everett "Are you thinking of doing a jolly album?"

John "If I feel jolly, you see. I mean, I was sort of going into the things that I wrote about on the album. So, they weren't particularly jolly, they were more like life, you know. Life isn't jolly; it's a bit of both. The album is a bit of both."

Everett "It seems to be mostly centred around your childhood."

John "Well, yes, it is. That's true. Kenny, very good."

Everett "Oh, he sources his facts this interviewer."

John "Anyway, it's not unusual for me to write about childhood, because there were a few old tracks of The Beatles I did about childhood."

Everett "Like?"

John "Well, the middle-eight to 'She Said She Said', 'When I was a boy, everything was right.' All that bit and 'Help!' 'When I was younger so much younger than today.' So it's not surprising. And sad songs I wrote then, you know, 'I'm A Loser' and I can't think of half of them, but it's not extraordinary, you know."

Everett "Track by track, let's go through the LP. What's the first track? 'Mother'."

John "Yeah, well what about it?"

Everett "Was that about your mother?"

John "Yeah, but it's really about most people's mothers I reckon, you know."

Everett "But they can't be all as bad as that."

John "But I think you don't need to take it literally. The mother I had, you never had me, meaning, my mother left me or my mother died. The fact that lots of people, say Yoko for instance, had their mother all their life, and had them with them, but they didn't have literally enough love from them. Well, lots of us suffer that because parents have got their own hang-ups."

Everett "It's good to have parents that aren't too much, because then they kick you out of the nest and you've got to forage."

John "Yeah, I know, but maybe it's just that the last generation, you know, somebody would say, 'Oh, don't feed them by the breast, it's fashionable not to touch the child,' you know, which I don't think is very good for them. Well, things like that you know."

Everett "Didn't have enough of mummy. But you should be the happiest man of the century."

John "Why?"

Everett "I mean, you've been through all that hell and damnation of being dragged up by the heels to the heights of stardom. And now, you've sort of, secured yourself in your own little studio, in your own huge house, in 70 acres of delightful scenery . . . So let's have a jolly LP, John!"

John "All right then, (singing) Ha, ha . . ."

Everett "Thank you."

John "Something like that you mean?"

Everett "Yeah that'll do."

John "Yes, well on the next track, we roll right on towards . . . 'Hold On John'."

Everett "What was that all about?"

John "It was about (plays guitar). Like that you see."

Everett "Well, there must be something spectacular happening to you at the moment."

John "Well, I am being sued, that's pretty spectacular."

Everett "Oh."

John "But we're not allowed to talk about that. 'Hold On John', so that was just about holding on, you see. Even though it's not all that hot, let's hold on."

Everett "Which is your favourite track?"

John "I don't really know, you see. I like 'Working Class Hero', but I like it as a song or a poem or whatever it is. I like 'Isolation' just to listen to."

Everett "Yeah, that's pretty, isn't it?"

John "And . . . I can't quite remember, maybe parts of 'God', you know. I never just have one I like."

Everett " 'Love' seems to stand out, like it was written ages ago, on that album."

John "It wasn't. It was written at the same time, you see. It's not a miserable song at all, is it?"

Everett "No, it's lovely."

John "Right."

Everett "Now, what about this latest record of yours. I mean you can't really mean 'Power To The People', like my mum and dad."

John "Yeah."

Everett "But my dad wouldn't know what to do with it."

John "No, but it's like saying, you know, imagine there wasn't any government, and somebody says, 'We'll vote a government in,' and you're saying, 'You don't expect my mum and dad to vote, do you?' "

Everett "But that's the ones they've got in anyway. I mean, they've been at it for hundreds of years, they must have it right by now."

John "You think they've got it right?"

Everett "Well, as right as you can get it on earth."

John "Well, that's the only chance you get. If you don't get it right on earth, where are you expecting to get it right?"

Everett "Yeah, but you've got to have bad bits to make the good bits stand out."

John "Well . . . sure, you get that with your respective government, you get that just as a person. Everybody has ups and downs. But I just think people should have more say in what goes on, that's all."

Everett "Can you see a better world emerging because it doesn't seem to have gotten better or worse since it started."

John "I can't see it, but there's no harm in striving for it."

Everett "So you're blindly striving for a better world."

John "Well, I wouldn't say blindly striving. Not blindly."

Everett "That was 'Not Blindly' by John Lennon . . . Do you come in here at all times of night, like if you feel an inspiration coming on, do you pop into the studio and do it?"

John "No, I prefer to stay in bed! No, the point is, still at the moment I need engineers, so I have to book to get people down. But, at one stage, it should be possible to put engineers to set it, one night, and then we just press a button it does it automatic. Then I could pop down in the night."

Everett "Do you think you're better with a lot of 'no people' around?"

John "A lot of 'no people'?"

Everett "You know, in EMI, wherever you record there are a million people staring."

John "Well, not always, but the less people the better, I prefer."

Everett "So, if you came down here on your own you'd write some orgasmic material?"

John "Well, I wouldn't probably write it. I mean, I write just anywhere."

Everett "Give us a startling fact."

John "I'm thirty!"

Everett "Are you?"

John "That's startling, isn't it?"

Everett "I'm only 26. Can you remember when you were 26? What was happening?"

John "No, probably on tour."

Everett "You seemed to be enjoying it while it was happening though."

John "Some of it was good, some of it was bad like anything . . . (changing subject) . . . And then the next track was 'I Found Out'."

Everett "Do you think you'll ever become a complete and utter hermit?"

John "No, I couldn't do that, you know."

Everett "What would you miss?"

John "People."

Everett "Oh, you still like people?"

John "Oh, I like them very much!"

Everett "Do you think you're less popular, nowadays?"

John "Than when I was a Beatle?"

Everett "Yes."

John "I might be."

Everett "Does it matter to you?"

John "Well, it's not nice to be disliked."

Everett "But I meant to be not thought about."

John "Well, not thought about, that would be dreadful wouldn't it?"

Everett "I'm asking you."

John "Well, you know, who was the one who picked up the musical papers, ladies and gentlemen. He said it's not worth reading about when I'm not in."

Everett "And you agreed, you rat!"

John "I agreed, you rat. So that answers your question. It's fun to be talked about in a way."

Everett "Yeah. Is most of what you read about yourself true?"

John "If it's a personal interview with me, it'll be, you know, pretty well true. Typing errors can change the meaning of things but it's pretty well true. If it's written about me, it's usually just rubbish."

Everett "Why don't you write a book about yourself?"

John "Well, I'm trying to make records and that. I mean, I'm not that old. I'll do it when I'm old."

Everett "How can you see your life developing in front of you?"

John "I can't. If you'd asked me two years ago, I couldn't have imagined what was going to happen. So I wouldn't even attempt to guess . . . 'Isolation'."

Everett "That would have been a single I think, you know."

John "Well, I think George said that, or he liked it best."

Everett "You seem to have a load of people around that are collecting . . . Like when we were having a cup of tea, there were two people listening to the radio to see if they were playing your record."

John "Oh, no. That's Val who has the radio on night and day whether we've got stuff out or not."

Everett "You don't listen to when you're on the radio?"

John "Oh, I do. But I have a radio somewhere else. But that music you heard, Val listens to that day and night . . . Val's the housekeeper."

Everett "It's a pretty big house, isn't it?"

John "It's not as big as it seems when you first get here. When you first walk in, you think, 'Jesus,' you know. But, it's like a large version of a small house. Meaning that there are not that many more rooms except for this office section. In the living section, it's just like big rooms, instead of small."

Everett "Who did it belong to before you?"

John "I don't know. I think somebody, Cadbury, or other, had it. But a few people have had it."

Everett (referring to the other Beatles) "You're still friendly with the rest of them?"

John "Well, yeah. I played billiards with Ringo, and discuss records with George. But, of course, we see more of each other now with the court case going on, so in a way, that court case brought Ringo, George and I closely together again, because we had to spend hours on different things. So we're pretty damn friendly now."

Everett "Good, because I'm sure there's a million people out there that would love to see you all jangling together again."

John "Well, it's like 90 per cent that George, Ringo and I would record together again, maybe not as Beatles, you know, under that title. But, like if I wanted a guitarist to play with me, I would ask him. Same as I asked Ringo to play drums."

Everett "Is there any one of the old artists that you would like to play with?"

John "I'm too, sort of, shy in a way to play with people I admire, like B.B. King. I might do it if I was there, but I don't do much going around to other people's sessions."

Everett "What do you think of all the violence that's flaring up all over the place?"

John "I mean, London's violent, compared to Dublin, or someplace."

Everett "Not at the moment."

John "Silly things to say."

Everett "I was talking to Harry Nilsson about two years ago, and he said he wouldn't be you for one thousand pounds, or whatever it was."

John "He wouldn't be me for one thousand pounds?"

Everett "No, because of all the pain and agony."

John "I think his agony and pain is just the same as mine. It looks massive. Just because it's being a public figure and all that crap, it gets talked about. I think Charlie Drake was saying something like that, but the problems I have, it's the same as everybody else."

Everett "But you get a lot more of them, than the average bloke."

John "I don't know whether he has it that easy. I think, because of the type of person I am, I might get meself into trouble, in a way, more than another guy, but not because I'm famous, you know. I might be the oddball of the factory."

Everett "A lot of people probably think you're a mad eccentric."

John "Well, what about it?"

Everett "Tell me John, why are you still plugging this album, because it's been out for an awful long time, hasn't it?"

John "Because in the early days of it, they wouldn't play it on the BBC or anything."

Everett "Why not?"

John "I don't know, probably they thought every line and every lyric must have had something in it. So, I didn't get many plays."

Everett "That's because I wasn't there."

John "Right, they've shifted all the oddballs on me. So that's a reason to keep playing it."

Everett "When the shows are segmented into one hour slots, most of the DJs usually want to just play the jolly, bouncy, popular stuff."

John "But it was literally not played, as a policy at one time. And that didn't do it any good. That was when it was first out. And people do have to hear something before they . . ."

Everett (interrupting) "What do you think the answer is, radio as it is in the States?"

John "Yeah, that would be great."

Everett "Lots of stations?"

John "Yeah, bring back the pirates, for god's sake!"

Everett "It's too lonely out there."

John "Is it?"

Everett "Twelve people playing records to each other for two weeks on end."

John "Well, it was good for the listeners, anyway."

Everett "Yes . . . You're surrounded by an entourage, aren't you?"

John "It depends what you mean. Actually I have four people that work for Yoko and I. We have a driver, a housekeeper, an assistant, a secretary, and another guy that comes from Apple. So I suppose that's an entourage. We have a lot of business going on."

Everett "Yes, you seem to be rushing ahead with things, don't you? It's a hive of industry, this place."

John "Well, I like working, you know. So that's about all there is to do, really, unless you just lie on your head all the time."

Everett "You're very fortunate, really, in a way, in that you can now do exactly what you want, can't you?"

John "Well that's what I was working for, almost."

Everett "But you had the studio in mind from the start?"

John "No, the only reason to try and get money or financial security or whatever it is, it's so you can do whatever you want. We're pretty tied up in a way."

Everett "How?"

John "Well, with contracts and things."

Everett "What's the next track?"

John " 'Love'."

Everett "Oh yes, that's pretty."

John "With the fade-in intro, we did it so low you can't hear it on the radio. That's this one. So that was pretty happy, wasn't it?"

Everett "Yes . . . no it wasn't, it was sad."

John "It wasn't miserable."

Everett "When Paul does a single, do you rush out and buy it and then think, right, 'I'll get him'?"

John "I don't have to buy it, he's on Apple."

Everett "But do you listen to it and think, 'The rat, I'll get him with my next single'?"

John "No, I don't. I just listen to it."

Everett "And what do you think of the sort of stuff he's doing lately?"

John "He's done better."

Everett "Since what?"

John "No, no. He's done better stuff than the stuff he's doing now. It might be because of the situation, or something."

Everett "If you had *Sgt. Pepper* in one hand, and your LP in the other, which would you listen to first, and more eagerly?"

John "Obviously, the one I made."

Everett "But you were chiefly responsible for *Sgt. Pepper*, weren't you?"

John "No, no more than the others."

Everett "So you'd rather have something that you've done by yourself, than . . ."

John (interrupting) "When we were Beatles, we'd always prefer our own tracks unless there was something specific."

Everett "So you never completely wrote together?"

John "Well, yes. But each individual Beatle preferred different tracks."

Everett "Haven't you ever heard something he's done that you thought, 'Wow, I must do something like that'?"

John "I don't know about 'I must do something like that,' but I've enjoyed stuff that Paul's done. Obviously, we all had respect and enjoyed each other's music."

Everett "Do you think you'll ever have tea with him again?"

John "Sure."

Everett "So when the fuss has died down, you'll rush at each other."

John "I don't know about that. But there's no doubt we'll see each other."

Everett "So will the world reverberate to another Lennon/McCartney composition?"

John "I doubt it, because we weren't writing all that much together for the last couple of years, anyway."

Everett "Have you ever considered suicide?"

John "Oh, yes. As a teenager, even, I think everybody sort of thinks about it. I don't remember standing on the edge of a cliff; I've never been that near. But I've considered it. Most of us have been through that. Most have been through things with mothers and fathers; most of us have been through something with religion, or not with religion, whatever; most of us have been isolated or been in love; most of us remembered things and most of us have wondered what love is, you know."

Everett "What is it?"

John (singing) "Love is real, real is love . . ."

Everett "Lovely."

John "There are lots of things, your mind blocks off memories from the childhood, because when you're a child, you can only take so much pain or whatever it is. So, when something happens you tend to block it off and not feel it. And it almost, literally, blocks off part of your pain."

Everett "But that's the bit it doesn't want to know about."

John "Yeah, but it's like not wanting to know about going to the toilet, or having a bath. If you don't do it for a long time it accumulates and emotions are the same and you accumulate them over the years. And they come out in other forms."

Everett "Like violence, or something."

John "Well, violence or baldness, or short-sightedness, something like that. That's part of his theory. It's pretty revolutionary I think, the idea, but from the experience I had there it seemed pretty valid; there's a good basis for that theory. And so what you do is go back or find a way of going back to these emotions that you've blocked off. And you remember things you didn't remember, and experience that emotion, because it's still there. It's like taking a diarrhoea pill, and it all comes out, baby!"

Everett "Are you afraid of death?"

John "No, I'm not afraid of it. I don't want to die. Die nicely would be all right, you know, like quietly is no bother at all."

Everett "In your own studio."

John "Taping it and filming at the same time, something like that."

Everett "Right. What's the next one, there must be one left."

John " 'Well Well Well'."

Everett "Do you like Yoko's singing?"

John "I'm pretty influenced by her singing. If you hear 'Cold Turkey', at the end of it, ladies and gentlemen, if you hear 'Cold Turkey' towards the end of it, I'm getting towards singing, or letting the voice go as much as Yoko does, but not quite. But on 'Well Well Well' I let it go."

Everett "Well, what is it? Are you shouting the way you feel, is that what it is? I don't get it."

John "Almost. It's the same as shouting 'Twist And Shout' or 'Tutti Frutti' only just missing the words. Don't say anything, because 'Tutti frutti a-wop-bop-a-lula' never said anything, in literal terms. And Yoko does the same. She just takes a word or an expression or an idea and works around it. It's like a sax playing it. It's like an instrumental. Anyway, I was telling you, Yoko's doing with her voice what instrumentalists have done over the past 50 years with their instruments but she's doing it with her voice. Why, here's Yoko herself who would do some explaining of the problem."

Yoko "I think we're saying a lot of things in our minds that's too heavy to come out as clean sentences, you know. Like I always feel like I'm stuttering my mind, before I say something. But because of our sort of cultured and refined background, we do manage to say something in very smooth sentences, like, 'How are you, Kenny?' But maybe in my mind I'm saying, 'How-how-how-how-a-a-a-re-you?', you know."

Everett "People listening to your side, will never say, 'Oh, she's trying to say so-and-so,' they'll just hear the sound of it."

Yoko "Well, what you're trying to say in your mind is not that specific, it's more like emotional and it's all abstract."

Everett "But people are clamouring to think, what is she saying, what does she mean?"

John "But it's the same thing about when they brought in abstract art, and that. And any middle-class director's home they have their abstract art. It's just the same."

Yoko "Cafés, you know, or restaurants."

John "It used to be all that, 'I don't know what I like, but I don't like that.' It's just abstract. Anyway, another point is that instead of when you're drowning, which we all are, half the time, you don't say, 'Will you consider possibly helping me to a degree that would save my life?' You just go, 'Aaaagggghhhh!' So that's what she's doing."

Following the lengthy interview, Everett concludes, "Basically a sad chap John, I thought. They're very happy together and a very courteous couple. She was knitting in the control room while we were doing that interview, and he was strumming away on his guitar."

APRIL
An interview with Paul, conducted by Richard Merryman in Los Angeles during the recording sessions for *Ram*, is published in *Life* magazine . . .

"The whole Beatles thing, it's like it was all years ago, like going back a distance more than anything," **Paul** declares. "And that's the whole point. The Beatles are really finished, over with, and it's just each of us alone now, living our lives the way we choose . . . The Beatle way of life was like a young kid entering the big world, entering it with friends and conquering it totally. And that was fantastic! An incredible experience! So when that idea came that we should break up, I don't think any of us wanted to accept it. It was the end of the legend, even in our own minds . . . I think it was great what John said, he told us, 'Look, everything sort of comes together right,' and now I agree. We'd just made this album and it was to be called *Get Back* and on the cover was a photograph showing us in exactly the same position as on the first album we'd made, the whole lettering and the background was exactly reproduced. So John said, 'It's a perfect circle, you know.' . . . Even though The Beatles have really stopped, The Beatles thing goes on, repackaging the albums, putting tracks together in different forms and the video coming in. So that's why I've had to sue in the courts to dissolve The Beatles, to do on a business level what we should have done on a four fellows level. I feel it just has to come. We used to get asked at press conferences, 'What are you going to do when the bubble bursts?' when I talked to John just the other day, he said something about, 'Well, the bubble's going to burst.' And I said, 'It has burst. That's the point. That's why I've had to do this, why I had to apply to the court. You don't think I really enjoy doing that kind of stuff. I had to do it because the bubble has burst, everywhere but on paper.' That's the only place we're tied now . . . The Beatles thing was fantastic. I loved every minute of it. It was beautiful, but it was a very sheltered life. Somebody would ring me in the morning and say, 'You've got to be at Apple in an hour,' it got very nursemaidy. If you are a real human, you've got to wake yourself up. You've got to take on these tedious little things because out of the tedium comes the joy of life. I got fed up with Apple this year over Christmas trees. Did I want one, because the office was buying Christmas trees for everyone? I hated that. Actually we pinched one from a field in Scotland."

Tuesday, March 16

In Los Angeles, Paul and Linda attend the annual prestigious *Grammy Awards* ceremony to collect the award of 'Best original score written for a motion picture or television special in 1970' for The Beatles' song 'Let It Be'. They receive the award from the legendary Hollywood cowboy actor, John Wayne.

Paul "We were really leaping with nerves. Me and Linda do everything ourselves, no chauffeurs or anything. We first drove around the place where the awards was taking place four times, saying all the time, 'Let's go in. No we can't, well we must, but I don't want to, but it'll be okay,' and finally we went in, and we got a little table at the back of the hall, with a chequered tablecloth and a bottle of scotch. We watched the show and when they announced us, we just leapt up there in our sneakers."

John "Paul did this to get back at us and Phil Spector and embarrass us."

Friday, April 9

Ringo releases the single 'It Don't Come Easy' in the UK . . .

Apple Records promoter, Pete Bennett "Ringo was the last of The Beatles to come out as a solo artist. When Ringo sent me the record on tape for a reaction, I told him I loved it. He was very concerned whether I thought it was a hit record or not. I replied, 'Yes, we will make it a hit.' So I started on my heavy promotion again. I received a phone call from Ringo two weeks after the release wanting to know what was happening with it. I told him that the record had gone on fifty top radio stations. Ringo couldn't believe it. Two days later, I received another call from Ringo and I told him the record had a bullet. He started to get convinced that he had a hit record on his hands. Ringo continued calling from London every two days to find out about the record's progress. Even John started calling. We did not miss and I promoted 'It Don't Come Easy' to the top of the charts."

A review by the UK music reporter, David Hughes, "Produced by George, far from being just another jolly Starkey country ditty, this is amazingly good, commercial pop music . . . Ringo wrote the song, though, let's not forget, and sings it well. Unlike John and Paul, he's not trying to say anything, in fact the rustic mood of 'Yellow Submarine', 'Octopus's Garden' and others is still in there somewhere. But, it's by far the most ambitious thing he's ever attempted, and it comes off 100 per cent. An awful lot of people will be very surprised by this record, and it's going to do very well."

Sunday, April 25

The *Sunday Times* reports: "Beatles Drop Case". The report reads "Beatle Paul McCartney has won the first part of his action against John, George and Ringo, to break up the partnership. Yesterday, Allen Klein, manager of the three, advised them to drop their appeal against the High Court order putting Paul's Receiver into The Beatles' own company until the partnership is dissolved . . . Klein has spent much of the time in the Apple headquarters at Saville Row, masterminding the three Beatles' attempt to keep the Receiver from moving in."

John "There's this hysterical idea that Paul put this Receiver in and that it's all over. The fact is that the Receiver came in and he was something to do with the partnership. The partnership is a moot question, but basically it's 20 per cent of The Beatles – that's five per cent each, which looked after lawn mowers, seeing that the house is paid for, that the food is paid for. Eighty per cent is Apple, and Apple the Receiver has nothing to do with. We're still fully in charge of it. We sign all the cheques; we do everything with it. I don't know how the problem will be solved. The Receiver is just as much a problem for Paul as it is for us. It's just a thorn in the side of all of us."

The *Sunday Times* report continues "What finally decided Klein was a long message from the three Beatles' solicitors on Friday evening, saying that the chances of the appeal succeeding were poor. The move means that it is almost certain that a full hearing of Paul's action to dissolve the partnership will never take place. More likely, when Paul's accountants have assessed his share of the assets, he will then be bought out by the other three."

John "If Paul wants out of Apple, we'll buy his bit, simple as that, if he wants to sell. But what they want to do is sell it to some third party who just happens to be a friend of Paul's. We don't want to do that, we want to keep our bit."

While in another report . . .

The *People* newspaper writes "The drumsticks of the Beatle who never made it are hidden under dust sheets in the loft, but he says he is glad now that fame passed him by. Pete Best, 28, was the drummer with The Beatles in their 1962 Hamburg days . . . Pete is now a nine-till-five, £1,100-a-year civil servant in the Department of Employment and Productivity in West Derby, Liverpool. He has a wife, Kitty, and two daughters, Beba, seven, and Bonita, three. They live in a three-bedroomed house in Crosby Green, West Derby." "When the group really hit the big time," Pete recalls, "I used to wonder what it would be like if I had still been one of them. I used to lie in bed at night and dream of the fame and fortune, the adulation of the fans, the whole exciting scene . . . I used to be a real dreamer. But I realise now I am probably far happier and settled in life than I would ever have been if I had gone on to share the glory the group received later. The pressures today when John, Paul, George and Ringo have split up and gone their own separate ways must be terrific . . . I am happily married, with two lovely daughters and my life is well orientated. I have no wish to go back . . . I have not played my drums professionally for six years. I look at them in the loft once a year. My children are too young to know who The Beatles are, and my wife and I rarely talk about the old days . . . I have to watch the pennies these days. It's a 30p lunch for the family now if we all go out together. But I am happy in my work, finding suitable jobs for building workers. It is very satisfying and rewarding, helping others."

Monday, April 26

In an interview conducted on a hillside outside his Scottish farmhouse, **Paul** tells waiting reporters: "The Beatles have stopped playing together. The Beatles will not get together again for financial or any other reasons . . . The reason should be perfectly plain to everyone . . . This life and place could do us for the rest of our lives, but there is nothing settled and I am free to choose . . . I will continue to write music."

Also on this day, figures reveal that The Beatles' income in the past year is estimated at £7,500,000.

Tuesday, April 27

The *Sun* newspaper reports "Farewell To The Amazing Beatles – That's Official". The piece, written by Robert Hart, sadly reads: "The Beatles are finished. After all the bitter squabbles and high-priced legal arguments, the end of the golden pop partnership was formerly agreed yesterday, in the quiet of a courtroom. And it was done with the blessing of three High Court judges. Now, middle-aged men are faced with the job of taking apart the pop-music empire which made Britain a seat of world power again, back in the Sixties. All through those Sixties, most of us loved The Beatles if we were young and liked them if we were not so young. Hated them if we could not bear youths with long hair and a lack of respect, especially if they were making a fortune. All sorts of people seized upon The Beatles' music. Few pop singers have not, at some stage, presented a Beatles song. Symphony orchestras have played Beatles music. And when the Guards do their thing in the grounds of Buckingham Palace, it is often to the music of John Lennon and Paul McCartney. As people got used to The Beatles, and The Beatles got used to fame, the eye-opening quirks began to show. John made taking off his clothes a rather public business . . . George Harrison seemed altogether too keen on strange religions for the taste of some of his bewildered public and Paul McCartney seemed to be always going off somewhere, instead of settling down to work on some more tunes with Beatle John. Nobody complained much about the fourth Beatle, Ringo Starr. He never seemed to get up to anything very peculiar. Anyway, it's all over, now. All bar the clearing up. At the insistence of Beatle Paul, the multi-million pound partnership is to be legally dissolved. Beatles John, George and Ringo have dropped their opposition to a caretaker being put in charge of the group's assets. That caretaker is a Beatles fan, 39-year-old chartered accountant, James Spooner . . ."

Friday, April 30

The *Daily Mirror* reports "Beatles Are Refused Tickets For Cup Final". The article, by Frank Corless, reveals that "Beatles George Harrison and Ringo Starr have been refused tickets to see their home team play in the Cup Final. They had written to Liverpool FC asking for fourteen stand seats at Wembley for themselves and their families for next Saturday's match against Arsenal. But the club turned them down. Secretary Peter Robinson said yesterday, 'We appreciate what The Beatles have done for the city, but they cannot be classed as supporters of the team. There are thousands of fans that turn up every week but have not been able to get tickets. If there were any available, our regular supporters would have to be first in line.' Beatles press agent, Leslie Perrin, said, 'The boys were not expecting any special privileges. They would love to go but they accept the position and appreciate that there are thousands of others in the same boat.' "

(Note: For the record, Liverpool is beaten 2–1 by Arsenal.)

Saturday, May 1

In today's *Daily Mirror*, **John** is asked about a reconciliation between him and Paul . . .

"You never know," he replies. "If he walked through into this room now, we would still be good friends, although I doubt if I could forgive him on one or two things . . . There is little likelihood that Lennon and McCartney will ever write together again. I can't get back to writing fairy tales anymore. I've got to live with the realities of life as it is today and reflect them in my music. Besides, we are all happy doing what we are. Look at good old Ringo; he's hooped one in the charts and George is happy doing an Elvis and The Plastic Ono Band isn't wanting . . . I can't help being the blabbermouth, the one who's done the frontal starkers bit and is sometimes known to sit it out in a plastic bag. That's John being John Lennon . . . Yoko and me still hope for children of our own. Yoko keeps dropping 'em."

Yoko chips in "We are going to keep on trying and in the next two to three years, we just hope we will be lucky."

John "If not, we'll adopt. We'll cop all sorts of children – Jews and Arabs, blacks and whites and polka dot kids, too, if they're any around and going."

Monday, May 10

Celia Haddon, *Daily Mail* "For millions of pop fans, The Beatles have brought pleasure. For vast numbers a new form of human expression. But for a few, the pop age brings a personal commitment beyond that pop idol worship. One such person is Carolyne Mitchell . . .

"The house is empty. The gates are locked. Paul McCartney is in Scotland. But to Carolyne Mitchell, Beatles fan extraordinary, this is the closest she can get to her idol. So she waits outside his home in St John's Wood. For more than two years, she has spent nearly every free moment here, or outside the Apple offices or one of the other Beatles' houses. She is no teenybopper. She is 24 years old from Salt Lake City in America. Not a groupie either, she doesn't smoke or drink as she is a Mormon. Her life is The Beatles, particularly Paul. And it's not an easy one . . ."

Carolyne Mitchell "I came from America to be with Paul and, just my luck, I arrived the week before he got married. The very week! My feelings towards Paul are different from those towards a pop idol, really they are. They're as real as they can get. I don't often go out with boys. I just don't like them. Nobody could replace Paul for me. Maybe I will have to be an old spinster, like some people have told me. I can't help it. I just want a relationship with him that would mean I don't have to stand by the gate. I'd like him to be a friend."

Wednesday, May 12

Paul and Ringo are among the guests attending Rolling Stone Mick Jagger's wedding to the 21-year-old Nicaraguan model, Bianca Perez de Macias. Covering the guests' departure from Gatwick airport is the reporter, Sydney Curtis . . .

" 'This is not a reunion, it's a wedding,' said Beatle, **Paul McCartney**, making the point quite clear as, with wife Linda, their child Mary, and her daughter Heather, he joined a Comet-load of guests at Gatwick airport, bound for the wedding reception of Mick Jagger and Bianca. McCartney, who kept the airline waiting half an hour, joined former colleague Ringo Starr at his table in the departure lounge. Neither said a word to the other. I asked him, 'Why have George Harrison and John Lennon not turned up?' Said Paul, wearing well-worn corduroy trousers with a four-inch square tartan patch on the rear, 'I cannot speak for the others.' I asked him, 'Is there any chance of the rift being healed because of this wedding?' He replied, 'Look, I don't want to talk about that, if you don't mind.' Earlier, Ringo had told me, 'I don't know if all The Beatles are coming. We've made our own arrangements.' The Jagger juggernaut, as the airport staff was calling it, a Dan Air Comet, later flew off loaded with champagne and dolly birds. Friends of Jagger's, musicians and their girl friends were aboard."

Ringo "That wedding was a bit strange because Paul and I hadn't seen each other for a year but we both knew that everything was okay. None of us are going to punch each other or anything like that. It was just like, 'Hello', you know, and we had to get warm together."

Monday, May 17
While in the States, Paul and Linda release the album *Ram* . . .

Paul "When we decided to do the new album, we wanted to make it fun, because it isn't worth doing anything if you can't have fun doing it . . . *Ram* is real sweaty rock'n'roll . . . It strikes me as being a hundred times better than the *McCartney* LP . . . The *McCartney* thing was a whole different trip that I needed to go through. This one, though, is really my music, this is really where I am."

John "I thought it was awful! *McCartney* was better because at least there was some tunes on it, like 'Junk'. I liked the beginning of 'Ram On', the beginning of 'Uncle Albert' and I liked some of 'My Dog's Got Three Legs'. I liked the little bit about 'Hands across the water', but it just tripped off all the time. I didn't like that a bit! That's what he was getting into on the back of *Abbey Road*. I never went into that opera bit. I like three-minute records like adverts. And there were all the bits at the beginning of *Ram* like 'Too many people going underground'. Well, that was us, Yoko and me. And 'You took your lucky break', that was considering we had a lucky break to be with him."

Paul "*Ram* is one of those albums that takes a bit of time to get used to. I can imagine the plight of a lonely little reviewer somewhere, sitting in an office, the heating has been turned off and he's got this record, which he has got to say these wondrous things about. And he's got to keep his reputation, so a whole load of things come into his mind when he puts it on and I think if it isn't totally immediate, you do tend to get these not too hot reviews."

Mike Ledgerwood of *Disc & Music Echo* "My first impression of *Ram*, Paul's latest offering, was one of confusion. It seems too busy, complicated, clumsy even. I struggled desperately to find direction in his writing, a method in his apparent musical madness. Lines like 'ludicrous lyrics', 'unintelligible vocals' and 'over produced', leapt horribly from my notebook after I'd listened to it 'cold' on simple stereo in Paul's publicist, Tony Barrow's, office. Try as I could, I was unable to accept that this was the work of Paul, the beautiful Beatle, behind such songs as 'Yesterday', 'Hey Jude' or ''The Long And Winding Road'. Sadly it seemed that the magic had disappeared . . . As a last resort, I switched over to stereo headphones, turned the tone down a fraction – the result was startling! Paul produced a perfectly splendid LP."

But Alan Smith of the *New Musical Express* does not share his enthusiasm. "Paul, what a mess you've made of it. What in the name of all that has gone before is happening to Paul McCartney?" he asks in his review of the disc. "His newly released second solo album *Ram* is an excursion into almost unrelieved tedium. The melodies are weak, the ideas are stale and the arrangements are messy. Much of it is like listening to the sound of Bobbisox Middle Class America set to music. I first heard the album at a 'listen-in'. Some of those around me were so gripped while it played that for most of the time they called across the room to each other about old times and friends. I thought this slightly ungracious, so in the past few days, I've played *Ram* over and over again in a desperate bid to find its redeeming features. But they were right, you know. It's awful!"

Paul "I suppose musically I'm competing with the other three, whether I like it or not. It's only human to compete, but I think it's good for us. I think George has shown recently that he was no dummy. I think we're really good, each one of us, individually. There's three periods in my life. There's the time when I was at school and just after leaving it. That was when I used to read a lot, Dylan Thomas, paperbacks, a lot of plays, Tennessee Williams, things my literature master had turned me onto. I used to sit on the top level of buses, reading and smoking a pipe. Then there was the whole sort of Beatles thing, and just now again I feel I can do what I want. So it's like there was me, then The Beatles phase and now I'm me again."

Summing up, **Paul** announces in October, "Five months after it was released, *Ram* was still selling. It took about five months for it to sell. Whereas a few records do it in a few weeks."

JUNE

In the UK, Macdonald publish *The Beatles Illustrated Lyrics 2*, which features **John** announcing that "Autographs on signed photographs of The Beatles sent to Prince Charles were written by one of the group's road managers. It was Neil Aspinall who signed the pictures that were sent to Prince Charles." In the book, John adds, "We would never have got it (the MBE) if the Palace had read what I thought about Royalty."

On autograph matters, Neil Aspinall, in charge of Apple business in London, remarks "Every road manager does it. It's an open secret. I don't recall signing photographs for Prince Charles but I suppose it's quite possible."

While a spokesman at Buckingham Palace is quoted as saying, "I don't recall Prince Charles asking for or receiving signed pictures of The Beatles, but that is not to say it is not true. He would have been at Cheam School at that time and it may be that boys there got together and asked for the pictures."

Saturday, June 5

Disc & Music Echo reports "Beatle Bootleg – A bootleg Beatles single, two tracks recorded during the group's *Rubber Soul* era, will be on the market within the next few weeks. Both are Lennon & McCartney numbers, put out as a double A-side. But, in order to avoid legal problems, the single may be released under a pseudonym, similar to a bootleg Bob Dylan album . . . Disc was told, 'Each (Beatles) track lasts about three minutes and they're studio recordings made around the time of *Rubber Soul*. It's genuine, original Beatles material, and good quality recordings. The record may be distributed by mail order, and word of mouth will sell it OK.' One of the tracks is understood to be an uptempo 'Get Back' type song with Paul McCartney vocals. The other is a harmony number, which may be titled 'Baby Jane'."

Sunday, June 6
John and Yoko perform at the Fillmore East in New York with Frank Zappa & The Mothers Of Invention . . .

John "We bumped into him and he said, 'Will you come down and jam with us?' So we thought, 'Great! We'll just go down.' We'd just come from London a week before, or something. We went down there and I did an old Olympics number, the B-side of 'Young Blood' . . . It was a 12-bar kind of thing I used to do at The Cavern . . . It was pretty good with Zappa because he's pretty far out, as they say, so we blended quite well . . . We did a three or four-hour gig and it was beautiful. There was no rehearsal. It's much better like that. I'm sick of going on stage and being judged, you know . . ."

Zappa author, David Walley, "I was there in Zappa's suite up at One Fifth Avenue when the whole caper was planned. It was easy, considering the fact that there has always been some antipathy between The Mothers and The Beatles over the cover design of Zappa's album *We're Only In It For The Money*. Zappa's cover design was a parody of The Beatles' famous *Sgt. Pepper* cover and legal hassles prevented Zappa from releasing the album for months. He was very annoyed. But when John and Yoko arrived with the DJ Howard Smith, WPLJ's redoubtable rock'n'roll yenta, Zappa was the most relaxed I had ever seen in New York. He was sitting on the couch, smiling and smoking. And John was like an enthusiastic child looking extremely fit and tanned. When Howard finished his interview with Zappa, John and Yoko stayed and John asked Zappa about that notorious poster showing Zappa sitting on a toilet and he told John how somebody with a camera happened to catch him in the act in London. Frank likes to tell the story but hates the picture. The subject of playing together came up old-folks style. John seemed anxious and needed encouragement. He hadn't worked out much since his last album and didn't know any rock'n'roll tunes. Much less the Mothers' music. John said, 'I'll be nervous as shit! I hope I'm not nervous.' Frank said, 'Oh, come on. It's just a gig. Don't get up tight. We'll have some fun.' Before the second show at the Fillmore, Zappa, Lennon and Yoko jammed in the second-level dressing room to an overflow crowd of Fillmore cognoscenti and hangers-on."

Kip Cohen, Fillmore manager, "The security arrangements for John and Yoko were incredibly complex. They cleaned out the backstage area within ten minutes."

David Walley "They played old R&B, with Zappa playing lead, John chording rhythm and Yoko playing her Ornette Coleman voice. Zappa also showed John the hand signals he uses to conduct The Mothers, mostly with his middle finger. 'When I do this,' Zappa said, sticking his middle finger into the air, 'everybody's going to scream.' John dug it."

Kip Cohen "There was no warning to the crowd of what was going to happen. Zappa and The Mothers finished their set and when they returned for their encore, John and Yoko were with them. Some of the crowd had already started to leave through the exits. Through the audience you could hear, 'John Lennon's on stage! John Lennon's on stage!' The people walking out came running back. Zappa started telling the audience, 'Just cool it.' Yoko walked directly to the centre stage microphone and John and Zappa took mikes at the side. Lennon was dressed in an off-white suit and Yoko looked petite with her black hair glowing. John announced that he was going to sing a song he used to sing in the pubs. It was called 'Joy'."

David Walley "John's amp wasn't working properly and he kept fumbling with it. His fingers kept getting caught in the guitar strings. When John didn't know the chords, he would motion to Zappa, who would step up next to him and show him the right ones. John was fascinated with Zappa's use of his middle finger as a baton. Frank motioned to John, 'You want to do it? Go ahead and do it.' John turned to the audience and stuck his middle finger up. While Zappa was conducting the audience, Lennon was working with the band, wreaking havoc with the tempos. But no one cared. Yoko, meanwhile, was belting it out with her electronic voice. When they finally got to a number called 'Scumbag', Zappa told the audience, 'We want you, boys and girls, to join along. It's a simple lyric.' One of the singers from The Turtles put a canvas bag over Yoko and her microphone during the song but she kept on wailing. She was still wailing when Zappa left the stage and started walking up the dressing room steps. John was still on stage with Yoko, playing with feedback. It was nearly dawn when the show was over. As the crowd left the Fillmore, you could hear them talking about it in disbelief. 'I can't tell him, I can't tell him,' a voice said. 'He was going to come. He'll kill himself if he found out that he had missed John Lennon.' "

Saturday, June 12
One week later, and the bootleg Beatles single, exclusively revealed in *Disc & Music Echo* in the issue dated Saturday June 5, again features in the paper . . .

"The bootleg Beatles single is now expected to be released under the pseudonym The Quarry Men . . . A major record company is interested in issuing the bootleg single within the next few weeks as a 'white label' release, with the credits rubber-stamped on. The publishing credits will probably be something like Lenin & McCarthy."

Reports will soon emerge that the title track is the song 'Maisy Jones' . . .

John, when asked about the track, says, "It's not really a Beatles track at all . . . 'Maisy Jones'? I've never heard of it."

(His recollections are correct, as the song 'Maisy Jones' turns out to be a recording by the unknown group Nimbo.)

Thursday, June 17
At the Cinecitta Studios in Rome, Ringo begins filming his part in the spaghetti western, *Blindman* . . .

Ringo "I took the part because it was so far apart from anything I had ever done before. I start every scene fairly straight, and end up as an out and out madman, and the energy you have to use for that! It was the first time that I ever saw what actors could get off on. It was the first time, as an actor, that I felt, 'Well, that's why they keep on doing it.' It was one of those things that you can't really describe. The whole thing takes over your body, and you just get elated with it. In that film I was another Mexican. I raped the girl, stabbed her father and beat up everybody, because I was a paranoiac brother of the bandit chief. That was funny, but the only drag was that they kept putting me on horses. I don't particularly like horses, but they found Mount Olympus for me to ride so they had to keep cutting because I couldn't get on this horse. The stirrup was eye level. Every time

I went to get up on the horse, they had to cut and lift me up onto the horse because it was so big."

Saturday, June 26

The columnist, Lisa Mehlman, writes from New York "Go home John and Yoko. No one has come right out and said it, but people are beginning to think that John and Yoko Ono are being a bit touristy in their canvassing of New York. There has been so much news of their activities here for the past few weeks, that I wish they would attempt a bit more privacy. It would almost be a relief when they go home. From their plush accommodation in New York, John and Yoko have been making forays into all areas of New York's underground. They have met famed artists and pop historian, Brigid Polk, at Max's Kansas City, where Brigid made an incredible tape of the conversation; they hung out on the Lower East Side and visited some funny clothing stores. They went to see Warhol superstar Jackie Curtis' play *Vain Victory* at off Off-Broadway. They went to Washington Square Park and heard street singer David Peel perform with his group. They saw radical Abie Hoffman and Jerry Rubin . . . and they were fussed over and jammed with Frank Zappa at the Fillmore East . . ."

Thursday, July 1

Paul tells reporters how he chased a girl fan down a hill on his 700-acre hideaway farm in Scotland but denies the girl's claims that he hit her. "All I did was chase her away," he explains. "I never touched her. If she's injured, she must have fallen on the way down the hill. I moved here for peace and quiet, not to have cranks and sightseers around. If I didn't try to stop girls invading the privacy of my home here, I'd never get rid of them." The girl is the 24-year-old American, Carolyne Mitchell, who had left her home in Salt Lake City two years ago to go 'Beatles chasing' around Britain. She claims that, "I was bruised when Paul chased me away from his High Park Farm at Campbeltown, Argyll," adding, "I've seen Paul at his London flat a few times when I've waited around there. Then I thought he was nice. I came up to Scotland last year after he bought this farm and saw him again. Last weekend, I booked into a Campbeltown boarding house, hoping to catch a glimpse of Paul and his family in the town. I made friends with his neighbour on the next farm on my last trip here, and went to visit them. Paul came driving up in his jeep and hit me and shouted at me to keep away. I complained to the local police after the incident." She concludes, "I won't be back. I think he's nasty."

Thursday, July 15

At the Selfridges store in London, John and Yoko hold a signing session for her recently re-released book, *Grapefruit* . . .

Evening News "John Lennon and Yoko Ono held court today in the middle of a sweltering, screaming, scrimmage of hundreds of fans. Yoko wore purple-and-black hot pants with green sandals and a black beret over her right ear. John was in a yellow T-shirt. Immediately, they were surrounded by a crush of fans and photographers. A film crew clambered over counters to get near them. The near-riot broke out when they arrived 15 minutes late at Selfridges to autograph copies of Yoko's new paperback, *Grapefruit*. Two teenage girls, wearing Lennon-type spectacles, fought and clawed to get a bridgehead in the crush, while others staggered back, near fainting. A pile of the books, they cost 40p, collapsed and were trodden underfoot. An elderly woman with a Liverpool accent said, 'Just to see a couple of twerps! No wonder they're big-headed.' From the back of the struggling mass, someone shouted, 'What are they like?' From the front came the reply, 'Horrible.' An Italian, caught in the crowd, asked, 'Who is this John Lennon?' The book, with a cover showing a human behind emerging from a grapefruit, is a random collection of Yoko's thoughts. Lennon describes it as 'profound and beautiful'."

The *Grapefruit* book . . .

Yoko "I think it's very important that *Grapefruit* comes out now and also that it would reach as many people as possible. I believe in it like the guy who invented penicillin because this is a book for some people to do, you see. Some books are like an adjective or a noun; this book is a verb; something you have to do, that's why children like it because they love to do things and that's why they understand it. The adults can't understand it very well because they're too intellectual, they forget the simple things in life. This book teaches you to be creative, that 'artist' is only a frame of mind, anybody is an artist. Once you read this book, you just become an artist because you don't have to have any skill."

John "We've really been pushing it. We've done appearances in Selfridges, the Claude Gill Bookshop, interviews all day. We're really trying to sell it. Last year we couldn't plug it because we were in therapy. We couldn't plug the hardback and so we only sold 2,000. We had the publisher, Peter Owen, bad mouthing us in the press, saying what bastards we were because we didn't turn up to plug it. But we were in therapy. We couldn't! And then I couldn't get to America to plug the book, of course, because they wouldn't let me in when it came out. I reckon if we push *Grapefruit* then it might sell 5,000 copies here and 200,000 in America, and that's what I am doing it for, because the book is important . . . The book of Yoko's has changed some people's lives. It's on the curriculum of at least ten to fifteen universities in America. It was even at Liverpool University. There's a girl called Charlotte Mormon who used to be a very straight New York School of Music cellist. Then she dropped it all and went out after reading *Grapefruit* in its original form ten years ago, and since then she's gone around the world performing Yoko's pieces. You might have heard of this girl, she's the one who goes around playing the cello with her tits out."

Tuesday, July 20
John and Yoko hold an open house for reporters at their Tittenhurst Park mansion in Ascot, Berkshire . . .

Reporter "What happens when you've finished the promotion of *Grapefruit?*"

John "When that's over, Yoko's having an off-Broadway play in New York. It's based on a book and called *Of A Grapefruit In A World Apart*. She did it ten years ago at Carnegie (Hall) and now she's sort of pepping it up. There might be an off-Broadway play of my book but I've got to read the script and I find it very hard to say yes or no to the people who are going to do it. I've been carrying it around for months. Yoko's directing her play and from September to January we reckon we'll be in the States. We're doing a few things here, so don't worry."

"I'm writing better songs than I have ever done," John announces. "But our main concern at the moment is getting Yoko's daughter, Kyoko, back. Everything else is secondary. That's why we aren't involved with the charity concert for the Bangla Desh refugee children at Madison Square Garden. George has always been more involved with India, and this gig is a direct result of his involvement with Ravi Shankar. He's been working with him in California . . ."

Reporter "When will you perform again?"

John "If we get the problem sorted out with Kyoko, I might feel like singing. I don't know where we'd appear; I would never make a plan. If there's something going, I might just join in, but I don't really want to have the *John & Yoko Festival Of Peace* in Hyde Park . . ."

Reporter "What about your new album?"

John "I've just finished it. I did eighty per cent in the studio here. It took seven days, then I spent the days putting the violins on in New York. We'd already mixed everything and we just did it again over there, down to another stereo or whatever you call it, like they used to do in the old days."

Reporter "When was the last time that you and Paul wrote together?"

John "We haven't written for so long, maybe three or four years. I'm better off on my own. I can't think of the last thing we wrote together. 'A Day In The Life' perhaps, which we didn't write together, we just stuck two bits together as we often did."

Reporter "Are you aware of how much the world still mourns the split of The Beatles?"

John "I know a lot of people would be happier if they got together again and to many, the magic of our songs now has gone, but that's an illusion. I'm writing better songs now than I ever wrote in my life and there's nobody who can tell me no. I don't care who they are. I'm writing better, I don't know about him (Paul). We've got less in common than we had, we were kids then with a goal of making it and all that, and we don't anymore, we're on different ends of the spectrum."

Yoko (interrupting) "It's sad."

John "It's not even sad, it's like the world goes, apples grow, they drop and they have seeds and they grow other things. There's no mystery in it. It's just called life."

Saturday, July 24

A New York Press report "Ten hours after the box office opened for two shows at Madison Square Garden, New York, featuring two of The Beatles, George Harrison and Ringo Starr, more than 36,000 tickets were sold yesterday. Proceeds of the performances, tomorrow week, will go to East Pakistan refugees."

Friday, July 30 (UK)
Shortly after its release, George's new single, 'Bangla Desh' is briefly banned by BBC Radio One on political grounds . . .

Tony Bramwell, of Apple "Plays were erased from six shows, including the Stuart Henry, Rosko and John Peel slots last Saturday. It was something about the song persuading people to recognise Bangladesh, but the record's only trying to persuade people to think about children . . . Now it's to be played without mentioning the title or the charity concerned. It's funny, it takes five minutes to ban a single, and four days to get it on again."

George "I really wanted to tell people about Bangladesh and I wrote this song in ten minutes. I sat at the piano and that was the idea I had. That came out and I made a record of it. I didn't expect it to be a big hit, but I hoped it would be because all the money was going to the refugees."

Sunday, August 1
At New York's Madison Square Garden, George presents *The Concert For Bangla Desh . . .*

John "Years ago, in the Sixties, when we did the live broadcast on the satellite of 'All You Need Is Love', the Stones were there, all of London was there and we often talked about imagining that if we got Elvis and all the people we loved and all the people that were current. You know, Dylan, the Stones, get them altogether, it would be the biggest mother show on earth, for peace or love or whatever. We all talked about it, but we could never get it together. But the nearest thing to it was George's Bangla Desh. But, for The Beatles, it was not the right time. We were not exactly in each other's pockets and were still trying to unstick the glue of togetherness."

The reason for the concert . . .

George "A lot of people were killed by the West Pakistani Government who wouldn't allow them to be as they wanted to be. A lot of people were massacred to death. It was terrible, bigger than the Second World War and so many millions of people ran out of the Bangladesh area into India to get away from the killing and, because one thing and another thing, there was a spread of disease and death. Altogether, it was something like eight million people. I don't understand the political thing, but I know that killing is not a good thing. The main reason I was involved was purely to try and raise some money in order to try and relieve the situation."

But George's journey to the show almost ends in disaster . . .

George "I almost didn't make it. My plane got caught in a violent thunderstorm and was struck three times by lightning. We started bouncing around; dropping hundreds of feet all the time and the lights went out. There were explosions and everybody was terrified. A Boeing 707 went over the top of us, missing us by inches. I thought that the back end of the plane had been blown off. I ended up with my feet pressed against the seat in front, my seat belt as tight as could be, yelling, 'Hare Krishna, Hare Krishna, Krishna Krishna, Hare Hare,' at the top of my voice. Miraculously, the pilot managed to land safely two hours later and I am adamant that my chanting, calling out the Hindu names for God, made all the difference."

Thankfully, the massive charity concert goes ahead as planned . . .

George "First of all, I didn't know anything about it until Ravi Shankar told me about it and he said he was intending to do something, which would have made a bit more money than what he could normally make. He was talking about making something like $25,000 and then he started giving me all these articles showing what was going on there, until I got sucked right into it. He asked me whether I could think of ideas to help make a concert. We started thinking about the concert in July. Then I thought, 'Well, maybe I should go on. That'll add a bit more weight,' and then the idea snowballed. Every time I thought about it, my heart started pounding and I started to think, 'Well maybe I can con a few superstar people into coming on and doing it.' "

John, in conversation with the American writers Peter McCabe and Robert D. Schonfield "I told George about a week before it that I wouldn't be doing it. I just didn't feel like it. I just didn't want to be rehearsing and doing a big show-biz trip."

But the American reporter, Robert Bury, recalls the time somewhat differently. "I was invited to New York to see the George Harrison Bangladesh concert, in which it was planned that John, along with Ringo, Eric Clapton and Bob Dylan, would be playing. But unfortunately I arrived in New York without my bags. After I checked into my humble little room at the Park Lane Hotel, I telephoned upstairs to where the Lennons had taken three connecting suites. 'Come up immediately,' said Yoko. 'We have a problem.' Dutifully, I went up to the 22nd floor. The problem was that George didn't want Yoko to perform on stage and then John and Yoko had quarrelled over the matter with the result that John had gone back to London and Yoko was about to follow. There was, however, a complication. Yoko's sister, Setsuko, had flown to New York especially for the occasion and there was no one to look after her. 'Would you?' Yoko asked and enquired whether I would like to move into the suite and be a companion for the weekend. Yoko offered us free use of her limousine and chauffeur and cash would be provided by the Allen Klein organisation for anything we wanted to buy, and since I had lost all my clothes, I could even wear John's clothes which, characteristically, he had left behind. 'Do whatever you want,' Yoko said. 'You can have anything in the hotel. Just sign it all, "Lennon, plus 15 per cent." ' I thanked her, moved into the suite, and put on John's clothes, a French black leather jacket and a blue gingham shirt. It was a bizarre weekend. Setsuko was shy and reserved but psychically very similar to Yoko and for three days we drove around New York playing at being Beatles. Since the whole city was buzzing with the excitement of the Bangladesh concert, Setsuko was mistaken for Yoko everywhere we went in our limousine and we had to fight our way through the fans in Bloomingdales and Saks. But the biggest buzz came after the concert in Madison Square Garden. We had been advised that the best way out of the building would be to follow the artists through the rear entrance to where a line of limousines would be waiting to take us back to our hotel. As the concert ended, chaos erupted and we tore through the crowds and threw ourselves into one of the limousines and locked the doors. Slowly, the line of limos edged up the ramp under Madison Square Garden. Then, as the police cleared the streets, all nine limos roared out into the night at 50 miles per hour, with police motorcycle riders flanking the procession as we raced the wrong way down one-way streets through red lights and back to our hotel. It was an extraordinary scene. When I got back to London, I telephoned the Lennons to thank them for their kindness and John wanted to know every detail of what had happened. He was very amused by my excitement. 'So what do you think of being a Beatle then?' he asked. I replied, 'I had enjoyed it so much that I am now considering taking it up professionally.' John replied, 'I wouldn't think about that if I were you. It takes talent to be a Beatle, you know.' "

Paul "I didn't play on George's Bangla Desh concert because if I'd turned up and John had turned up, then the headlines round the world would have screamed 'The Beatles Are Together Again!' Quite frankly, I didn't fancy playing there anyway."

John "The thing I didn't like about the Bangla Desh concert was that it was The Beatles playing. It wasn't The Beatles . . . I'm glad I didn't do it in a way because I didn't want to go on as The Beatles. And with George and Ringo there, it would have been that connotation of Beatles. 'Now, let's hear Ringo sing "It Don't Come Easy",' and that's why I left it all . . . I don't want to play 'My Sweet Lord', I'd as soon go out and do exactly what I want."

George "First of all, we said we would do one concert and the person who is my business manager, he anticipated a sellout but I wasn't so sure. I knew The Beatles could always have a sellout but on my own, it was different. We advertised for one concert, and they had to sell the tickets from midnight. The police came because it was such a big queue and the police said they had to open the box office and sell the tickets from midnight and they sold out by 5am. So, because it was such a big demand, we decided to do two concerts. We put in an extra concert in the evening and that was sold out too. And then we sold the seats at the back of the stage where you couldn't see anything. We had requests to sell these tickets, and we sold these, too."

Ringo "I do the odd gig like Bangla Desh, where you just fly over for the show and there are a lot of great guys around, but I never want to do the fab four gig again. I mean we could play with each other. I can play drums with any band you like. Paul can play bass with anyone he likes and John and George can play guitar with any band, but it was more than just playing, that was The Beatles."

George "I organised Madison Square Garden with all these people, like Bob Dylan, Leon Russell, Eric Clapton and Ringo, who were kind enough to do that concert. It enabled the concert to be a special concert. It was nerve-racking. I had never done a concert since 1966 and secondly I had never done a concert in my life where I was by myself. I had always been one of the backroom boys and then, on top of that, we had had very little rehearsal. In fact, we had no rehearsal at all with everybody. I rehearsed with the drummer, the drummer's bass player and Badfinger on guitars and a couple of other musicians. We ran through the songs once and right up until Bob stepped up on stage, I didn't even know if he was coming . . . The newspaper adverts couldn't say 'Bob Will Be On' because he never comes on. He never comes up. He sits at home and reads it in the paper and then he doesn't want to come. So I had to say, 'We'll put an advert in the paper, which will say "George Harrison And Friends" ', and we sold two concerts just on that, so everybody else was a bonus for the audience. They didn't really know who was coming. Bob came because, first of all, he knew it had sold out anyway and he decided he'd like to do this to help a good thing. It was only the night before the concert that we knew he was going to be on the show, but even then it was touch and go. He could have gone home again . . .'

"The concert started with Ravi Shankar, who played with his other musicians for forty minutes. I did 'Wah Wah', 'Awaiting On You All', 'My Sweet Lord', 'Here Comes The Sun', 'Something' and 'Bangla Desh'. Then there was a short intermission where we used seven minutes of a film we had from Dutch television because the BBC, in London, wouldn't let us have it because it was politics. They had a good film showing exactly what was happening and they wouldn't let us have it for some political reasons so we had to try and find a film because I didn't want the audience to be a crazy, rock'n'roll audience. I wanted them to realise what it was all about. So I showed them this film and it really brought the audience down. Then we came on and did the rock'n'roll . . . It was obviously a very successful show. At the time when I was putting it together I had no idea about how it was going to turn out. We were fortunate that it turned out well, but, at the same time, I had no idea about what I was letting myself in for. I had a vague idea but it was all so much bigger than I thought."

Ringo "I enjoyed it immensely. It was a bit weird because it was the first time I had been on stage for about three years. I was crazy with nerves beforehand. But if you have done your job, it's okay. You soon relax. It was nice, anyway, because we had a lot of good pals around. Bob was as nervous as anybody that night. We weren't out just to entertain each other. We wanted to entertain the twenty-five thousand people who had paid to come in. It is no good just standing there with our guitar and freaking yourself out."

The reports on the hugely successful show soon appear in the following papers . . .

Al Aronowitz, of the *New York Post* "The overwhelming spectacle of George Harrison, Ringo Starr, Bob Dylan and Leon Russell performing together on the same stage may not be something you expect to read about in college text books some day. But that's what happened at Madison Square Garden last Sunday and is as much of an event in the history of our times as anything music has to offer."

Daily Express "Half of The Beatles plus Bob Dylan sent 20,000 rock fans wild tonight. It was not far from the hysteria and frenzy that surrounded the four Beatles in the Sixties. Ringo Starr and George Harrison had youngsters queued up for four days sleeping rough for the privilege of paying up to £40 for seats. Dylan ambled on to stage at mid concert, unannounced, wearing a shabby pair of light brown trousers and blue denim shirt and jacket. It was several seconds before the audience realised it was the star who constantly shuns the spotlight. Then they roared . . ."

Daily Mirror "Beatlemania came back last night as George Harrison and Ringo Starr gave a show in front of 40,000 youngsters. The crowd in New York's vast Madison Square Garden jumped up and down and clapped and screamed for ten minutes for the two Beatles at the end of their two performances. The fans paid about £190,000 to see the two Beatles, and all of it will be used to help the victims of the fighting in East Pakistan . . . It was a strange evening. It started with sitar music from Indian, Ravi Shankar, as sticks of incense burned on both sides of the stage. Some of the audience also burned incense and in front of me, four teenage girls smoked marijuana. It was George Harrison's night. He introduced the stars, which included such pop giants as Bob Dylan, Eric Clapton and Leon Russell . . . But the songs were not those that the four Beatles used to sing. George gave us his own hits, such as 'Something' and 'My Sweet Lord'. And Ringo sang his hit, 'It Don't Come Easy'."

Evening Standard "Before a single note was played last night at the Bangla Desh children's charity concert held in New York's Madison Square Garden, George Harrison, the prime organiser of the affair, received what I can only describe as a tumultuous ovation for simply existing. A frenzied roar of 'Welcome back' filled the mammoth hall from the lucky 18,000 plus New Yorkers who had managed to get tickets for the show. And at the end of the day's two performances, by what must rank as the most star-packed rock show ever assembled, approximately a quarter of a million dollars was expected to be taken directly from the Garden to UNICEF with special instructions that it be spent on aid for the children of Bangladesh . . . It was perhaps the most exciting night in rock music I can remember, mainly because pop music was rising above the trivia and greed with which it has, for so long, been associated. The amount of good feeling in the hall last night was warming in its spontaneity, and the fans, some of whom had paid £41 for £4 tickets, were not disappointed. All weekend, New York City has been literally jumping with excitement over the concert. The fact that no one knew until the show started exactly who was to be on the bill helped sharpen the anticipation. If I say that Bob Dylan virtually stole the show, it is intended as no slight upon Harrison and his friends, rather a compliment to one of the most aloof charismatic popular heroes of our age . . . After a short interval in which newsreel films of the tragedy of Bangladesh was shown on two enormous screens, the biggest rock affair I have ever seen was suddenly upon us. Dressed in a white suit, Harrison led a band of six horns, four guitars, two basses, a piano, an organ, two drums and a group of singers . . ."

The British show business correspondent, Patrick Doncaster "I stood backstage in the Madison Square Garden as George triumphantly led world pop names in one big, exciting group sound. 'My Sweet Lord' he sang and the vast arena thrilled to this great hit that preaches Krishna. 'Hare Krishna,' he chanted into the mike before going into the vocal. And you know, he had found something close to happiness."

George "I thought of an idea to go on tour and we do two concerts in every city. One concert we give the money to the charity and the second concert, we'd give it to the musicians. The musicians have still got to live and there are a lot of people on the Bangla Desh concert who gave their services for nothing who don't have a lot of money. There are people like me and Ringo, Bob and Leon and Eric, who can afford to do that, but there is other people who need the money but they still gave their services for free."

John "George came up with a good idea after the concert, which was to take a big tour out and do one show for free and one show for money, in each city. I thought that was good then I thought, 'Well, fuck it. I don't want to earn any more money. I get enough off records. I don't want to do a big Apple/Beatles tour.'"

George "From the gates at Madison Square Garden, we made $250,000, which went through UNICEF to Bangladesh. But it took almost two years after the show to get it all straight with the record and the film. We had money held up for years in the States and in the UK. They'd had it in dribs and drabs but most of it was held up in Revenue. I think it still needs John to sign a bit of paper, though. Soon after the concert, we were told that Ravi Shankar and I would have to pay tax on the money we gave away. But the main thing was that the concert was a success and that we attracted attention to it. That was more important than making the money, because, although the money was required, it was at a point in time when nobody was taking any notice. It was just another disaster."

Before the Bangla Desh concert takes place, the British show business correspondent, Patrick Doncaster, meets George, His Divine Grace A.C. Bhaktivedanta Swami Praphupada and the Hare Krishna movement in a back room in a workaday house in Brooklyn, New York . . .

"George Harrison's Indian spiritual advisor is squatted bare to the waist on some cushions and oozed love and peace," Doncaster writes. "He is His Divine A.C. Bhaktivedanta Swami Praphupada, 77, a yogi from India. People looking like monks, in pink and white robes, bowed and touched their foreheads to the floor in front of him, and he gave me a slice of juicy mango flown in from some devotees in Hawaii and we drank water out of little cardboard cups . . . Here I was in the Brooklyn temple of the Hare Krishna movement and after the Swami, George Harrison is about the biggest noise in it. They talk about him in reverence and the devotees bow their shaved heads at the mention of his name. They tell me George has a temple of his own in his rambling home near Henley-on-Thames. They tell me George has paid for the movement's new book to be printed in Japan and has written the preface to it as well . . ."

George writes, "Everybody is looking for Krishna. Some don't realise that they are, but they are. Krishna is God, the source of all that exists. The cause of all that is, was or ever will be. As God is unlimited, he has many names, Allah – Buddha – Jehovah – Rama; all are Krishna, all are one. If there's a God, I want to see him. It's pointless to believe in something without proof and Krishna Consciousness and meditation are methods where you can actually obtain God perception. You can actually see God and hear Him. It might sound crazy, but He is actually there, actually with you."

Doncaster's report continues, "Now you might wonder why George isn't going around in monkish robes with a Yul Brynner hairdo like the others. 'The shaving of the head is not obligatory,' explains a tranquil American assistant to the Swami. 'George did ask about it and was willing to shave his head, but he is a Beatle, we reminded him and he did not have to do it.' "

Monday, August 2

On the day after George's historic Bangla Desh concert, Paul's spokesman, Shelley Turner, announces in London: "He doesn't want the name McCartney linked with the names of the other Beatles. It's pursuing an illusion, something that no longer exists. He wants The Beatles to become on paper what they are in fact. He wants to be allowed to pursue his career and he's trying his utmost to be simply Paul McCartney."

Tuesday, August 3

Paul contacts Freda Kelly, President of the Official Beatles Fan Club in Liverpool, asking her to tell fans, "Thanks for writing, but I'm not a Beatle anymore."

Freda Kelly "It's true that Paul's trying to break The Beatles' name. He just doesn't want to be associated anymore. For instance, in The Beatles' book, we list the birthdays of all The Beatles' children. Paul claims that his family isn't Beatle children. I suppose that's fair enough. I've been waiting for someone to say something like this."

Thursday, August 5

The *Daily Mail* reports "The Beatles Together? It's Possible". The short piece, by Michael Cable, reads "A London charity concert starring at least three of The Beatles is planned for next month. John, George and Ringo are understood to have agreed to take part in the concert, in aid of Shelter, and Paul has been invited to join them. Paul may sink his differences with the others, at least temporarily, because the concert is for charity. Secret negotiations for the concert have been going on for six weeks between John, George and Ringo, their business manager Allen Klein, Tory MP Jeffrey Archer and Lord Harlech, the former British Ambassador in Washington and head of Harlech Television . . ."

Friday, August 6

Syndicated news report "Apple, The Beatles' company, has received a number of offers for possible purchase of the company. Among the bidders is the Robert Stigwood Organisation, which controls The Bee Gees pop group and other pop names, Frankie Howerd, the *Steptoe & Son* writers, Galton & Simpson and the Alf Garnett creator, Johnny Speight. The directors and majority shareholders of Apple, John Lennon and George Harrison, have referred these approaches to Mr Allen Klein, business boss of the Apple group and chief of ABKCO Industries in New York City. Mr Klein announces, 'The offer would be rejected in its present form. I would estimate that a reasonable offer would be in the region of £3,500,000.'"

On **Tuesday, August 31**, John and Yoko leave London Airport for New York, not knowing that he will never again return to England . . .

John "Yoko and I were forever coming and going to New York, so finally we decided it would be cheaper and more functional to actually live there. We began in the West Village, the quiet part. It was Yoko who sold me on New York. She had been poor there and she knew every inch. She made me walk around the streets and parks and squares and examine every nook and cranny. In fact, you could say that I fell in love with New York on a street corner. Jerry Rubin and Abbie Hoffman (leaders of the Yippee party) were almost the first people to contact me when I came to New York. I must admit that some of my early political activities with Yoko were pretty naive. But Yoko was always political in an avant garde kind of way. She had this idea that you must always make use of the newspaper publicity to get across the idea of peace. Any excuse, such as our wedding, was enough. She believed that you should make people laugh, too. The trouble with Rubin and Hoffman was that they never wanted laughter. They wanted violence but I've never been into violence myself . . .

"My fascination with America began as a kid with people like Doris Day and Rock Hudson and also with the realisation that many of the familiar things around me that seemed so British were, in fact, American. My love with New York is something to do with Liverpool. There's the same quality of energy, of vitality, in both cities. New York is at my speed. It is a 24-hours-a-day city, it's going on around you all the time, so much that you almost stop noticing it. But it's all there if you want it. The telephone can bring you anything and everything. I know there are rough areas in New York but I don't visit them often. The district can change abruptly within one block, but I find I can walk the streets quite freely. People recognise me, but they don't trouble me too much. Sometimes they want to audition right there on the street, which can be a bit embarrassing. The cab drivers are something else. They treat me almost as one of the locals. The younger, hippie types still regard me as a rock superstar. They're always turning right round to ask questions and terrifying me. I like New Yorkers because they have no time for the niceties of life. They're like me in this. They're naturally aggressive, they don't believe in wasting time."

SEPTEMBER
George talks about his current relationship with Paul on the Dutch VARA radio station . . .

"It's got to the point where it's silly," he announces. "He's got my telephone number but I don't have his telephone number and I haven't seen him since last December. It's silly. I've got a lot of good friends, a lot of musicians, so in a way I don't miss Paul. It's easier to live without somebody, but I don't think there is any need *not* to be friends. I think his music now is commercial. It doesn't have very much depth at all. I couldn't go in the studio and make an album like Paul's, because, to me, that's wasting time and energy. I think everything should be maximised, you know, to the limit. Paul's is just like The Monkees. At least John, whether you like John or dislike John, at least he's saying something and doing something. But Paul's, it just seems so lifeless."

George also reveals how he sees himself . . .

"I don't see myself as a rock'n'roll person," he announces. "I can play rock'n'roll. I like rock'n'roll but when I come to write something, I don't often write that style, because I, somehow, seem to write melodies. It's hard to see yourself as anything, really. I suppose, basically, I'm just a human, just another human who can play a little bit of guitar. I can write a little bit. I don't think I can do anything particularly well but somewhere down the line, I feel there is a need for me to be what I am. But it's all very confusing. But I shall just continue to do what I am doing, to try and do it better and stronger."

Thursday, September 2

An underground press release, entitled "Paul McCartney Really Is Dead!" is tacked up on walls around Paul and Linda's New York Lower East Side apartment, situated at 895 Park Avenue. The release reads, "Paul's two solo LPs seemed to be the work of someone whose brain just ain't functioning. McCartney has never given any money to progressive organisations, hasn't done a benefit in years, and wrote lyrics with a complete lack of social commitment." A.J. Weberman of the Rock Liberation Front, an organisation concerned with cultural rip-offs of successful pop stars, heads the demonstration.

Sunday, September 5
From their St Regis Hotel room in New York, John and Yoko give a lengthy interview to the journalists Peter McCabe and Robert Schonfield . . . They ask John his thoughts about touring . . .

John "Allen Klein has made me secure enough, it's his fault that I'll go out for free."

McCabe and Schonfield "You mean tour for free?"

John "Well, I thought I can't really go on the road and take a lot of money. A, what am I going to do with it? And B, how could I look somebody in the eye? Why should they pay? I've got everything I need. I've got all the fucking bread I need. If I go broke, well, I'd go on the road for money then."

Friday, October 8

John releases his *Imagine* album in the UK . . .

Ringo "*Imagine* was a fantastic album!"

Apple Record promoter, Pete Bennett " 'Imagine' was a song I first heard at Phil Spector's house in California. My instant reaction to both Phil and John was that if it was properly recorded, 'Imagine', and the rest of the album, would skyrocket to the top of the charts. My prediction turned out to be quite accurate as a result of my commitment to John, Yoko and Phil to make this a top record."

John "There are ten tracks on it. I had more, but Phil Spector suddenly said that I had no more room, so we stopped. Compared to the last one (*John Lennon/ Plastic Ono Band*), it's less introspective in a way and it's a bit light. There's some heavy stuff, but I call it commercial with no compromise. The last one was so personal . . . I didn't set out to make a super simple album with just piano, bass and drums and anything else would have interfered with it. This time, it's a lot looser; people are playing all over it. George is on a good five or six tracks. He plays some great solos and Nicky Hopkins was a fantastic guy. It's just amazing how he lifts a whole track."

Nicky Hopkins "I get along very well with Lennon. John is egotistical to some extent, but he tells you that. He's a very honest cat. His album was such a gas to do. It was all put together in about a week at the studio in his house because John is very quick. Some strings were added in New York but all the rest was done in his own studio at his home in Ascot. John is very definite about what he wants and there is no uncertainty about working with him. He doesn't want to spend much time recording. I played electric piano on the 'Imagine' track and the main piano track on 'Jealous Guy'. My name was missed off the credits for that one through a mistake. I was on 'Crippled Inside', 'Oh Yoko' and 'Soldier', too. George was there doing it with us, as well as Jim Keltner, two guys from Badfinger and Klaus Voorman."

John "I forgot to mention Klaus Voorman, because he's on everything. I think Mike Pender even plays tambourine on one track. Ringo's missing on the album. I kept asking for him, but he was busy. That's a shame, but I've got George this time, that's good."

The drummer on some tracks on the album is Jim Keltner "I was invited to meet John and Yoko by a mutual friend, the saxophonist Bobby Keys. He asked me to come out to John's studio to watch them do an overdub for Yoko's album. So I went along to watch and they said, 'Why don't you pick up something and start playing.' So I played drums covered with towels while Bobby played a duck call. At one point, Yoko told us she wanted the sound of the wind rushing across the back of a frog, and we managed to get exactly the sound she wanted. They asked me to play on John's *Imagine* album, so I came in and we did 'Jealous Guy' and 'I Don't Want To Be A Soldier'. The whole thing was a ball. I really loved working with John. He knows exactly how to work things out. He's unbelievable. His songs are written in such a way that they virtually arrange themselves. I can't say enough about the guy. He's so musically broad-minded."

John "On the artistic level we controlled it . . . We even made the covers ourselves, you know with Instamatic Cameras and Polaroids. The cover of *Imagine* Yoko took with a Polaroid."

Paul "I liked the 'Imagine' track very much. I listened to it (the album) just to see if there's anything I can pinch. The album was John doing what he does best."

'Imagine'

John "Actually that should be credited as a Lennon/Ono song . . . The song was originally inspired by Yoko's book *Grapefruit*. In it are a lot of pieces saying, 'Imagine this, imagine that.' Yoko actually helped a lot with the lyrics, but I wasn't man enough to let her have credit for it. I was still selfish enough and unaware enough to sort of take her contributions without acknowledging it. I was still full of wanting my own space after being in a room with the guys all the time, having to share everything."

'Jealous Guy'

John "The lyrics explain themselves clearly. I was a very jealous, possessive guy. A very insecure male, a guy who wants to put his woman in a little box, lock her up and just bring her out when he feels like playing with her . . . Melody written in India (1968)."

'How Do You Sleep?'

Paul "John did this big thing about me, saying 'Muzak', 'Rubbish' and 'You couldn't rock if you tried', which was all rubbish. But it did put me off for a while. I must say I'm a bit gullible like that and I sort of listened to him for a couple of years. I kind of listen to people like that. I thought, 'I can't write another of those soppy love songs,' and 'I keep writing those, I've got to get hard.' But, in the end, I thought, 'I've got to be myself. I like all that.' It's the worst to be ashamed of it. It's bolder to say, 'What the hell!' I may be soppy . . . If he was going to do me, he should have done me properly. I mean in 'How Do You Sleep?' he says, 'You live with straights who tell you you were king.' Of course I live with straights, half the world is straight. I don't want my kids to be surrounded by hobnailed boots."

John "It was like Dylan doing 'Like A Rolling Stone', one of his nasty songs. It's using somebody as an object to create something. I wasn't really feeling that vicious at the time, but I was using my resentment towards Paul to create a song. Paul took it the way he did because it, obviously, pointedly refers to him, and people just hounded him about it, asking, 'How do you feel about it?' But there were a few little digs on his album, which he kept so obscure that other people didn't notice 'em, you know, but I heard them. So, I thought, 'Well, hang up being obscure! I'll just get right down to the nitty-gritty.' "

Paul "I never came back at him, not at all, but I can't hide my anger about all the things he said at the time about 'Muzak' and Engelbert Humperdinck. I was in Scotland when I read this in *Melody Maker*. I was depressed for days. When you think about it, I've done nothing really to him, compared to what he said about me . . . John is the nice guy and I'm the bastard! It's repeated all the time. But what did I do to John? Okay, let's try to analyse this. Now, John was hurt. So, what was he hurt by? What was the single biggest thing we could find in all our research that hurt John? Well, the biggest thing I could find was that I told the world that The Beatles were finished. But I don't think that's so hurtful."

On the same day, Yoko releases the album *Fly* . . .

John "Yoko's album isn't as commercial as her last because there's no rock on it, but there's some sort of nice, sweet ballad stuff."

Yoko "I've expressed pain and human emotions in my works. Even in *Fly* it was expressed pretty realistically. But it was expressed in an abstract form. The screaming, people didn't think of it as anything but music, well, some people didn't even think it was music."

The review in *Disc & Music Echo* reads "It's time somebody said it. Yoko Ono offering herself as a singer is the height of impudence. Her appearance on albums the ultimate in self-indulgence. It's the biggest confidence trick since the Trojan Horse! *Fly* is a diabolical liberty as a double-album; merely a recreation on record of her rubbish writing in *Grapefruit*. There's absolutely no artistic appeal whatsoever . . . Frequently, Yoko sounds a cross between Tiny Tim at his most outrageous and a bagpipe band tuning up. It's all a terrible dirge!"

Saturday, November 6

Paul "I phoned John the other day to ask him if I could leave The Beatles. I told him about the set-up as I see it. I tried to tell him that I thought I was right about this thing. He said, 'You always think you're right.' I just want the four of us to get together, write on a piece of paper that we want to dissolve the partnership, then hand it to (Allen) Klein. That's all there is to it. They could then wind up the business and divide the money four ways. No one else need be there, not Linda, Yoko or Klein. The Apple situation is like the Common Market. The Government has decided that the people should go into the market, but they don't give a damn what the people say. I'm being kept in Apple for my 'own good', and they're giving me lollipops. But I don't want lollipops, just my quarter of what we've earned over the past ten years. I haven't received any money for the *McCartney* album, nor *Ram*, and I don't expect any money for *Wild Life*."

Monday, November 8

Paul "I sheared the sheep yesterday before coming. We love it up there in Scotland. Have you heard the Wings album? We're pretty pleased with it . . . Really, this is a very glorified press conference to make sure that everybody came."

At the Empire Ballroom in London's Leicester Square, Paul and Linda hold a party to unveil their album *Wild Life* and their new group, Wings . . .

Paul "We were thinking of all sorts of names. We had a new group and we had to think of a name. We had a letter from an old gentleman in Scotland, which said, 'Dear Paul, I see you are looking for a name for your group. I'd like to suggest The Dazzlers.' So we were nearly The Dazzlers, with the big sequinned jackets. But we thought, 'No,' we need something a little more earthy, so we thought of Turpentine. But I wrote to the guy in Scotland and told him that and he wrote back, 'I don't think you'll be calling yourselves Turpentine because that's something used to clean paint off,' so we thought of Wings . . . I thought of the name Wings when Linda was in hospital having Mary and had persuaded the hospital to let me have a camp bed in her room to be with her. I wanted something that would become a catch phrase like The Beatles. You know, people would say things like, 'We've got beetles in the kitchen,' and there would be some crack about it being us. Anyway, I was thinking for some reason of wings of a dove, wings of angels, wings of birds, wings of a plane. So I said to Linda, 'How about Wings?' It was at a time when most people would be thinking about a name for a child, and there we were talking about a pop group."

UK reporter, Gavin Petrie "Will Wings be going on the road?"

Paul "Yes, we'll go on the road, it may be next year, it may be two years time, but it could be next week. But we'll just do it if and when we feel like it. There would be no tour, no announcement that Wings would be starting a tour at Slough Civic Hall on such and such a date. I'd just like to turn up and play unannounced. I'd even like to bill ourselves as something like Ricky & The Red Streaks. We don't want to be a media group; we don't want our faces turning up on posters, papers or knickers. Like if we were billed as Wings, we'd have to play to million-seater halls . . . Paul McCartney is quite a popular name. I don't want to hire something like the Albert Hall and have all the businessmen sitting like rows of penguins judging me. I don't want to be like John who swallowed his nerves and was sick before appearing at the Toronto festival. I want the band to be loose."

DECEMBER
Surprise visitors to John and Yoko in New York are Paul and Linda . . .

Paul "Linda and I went to see John and Yoko in New York and at first it was a little embarrassing, but once we got talking, it was great. It was the first time we had seen each other for more than two years. The only contact we'd had was reading one another's interviews and speaking through lawyers. But we got talking, and it was really good. The vibes were right. The odd thing was that they were just like me and Linda. They felt the same about music and politics and we had the same sort of thoughts about Ireland. Like how wrong the Government is to go in and crush the people like they're doing. John is a nice guy, and so are George and Ringo. But there is still this resentment about Klein. I make no secret of the fact that I hate everything about him. We were never really the four inseparable mop tops the papers used to write about. We were just musicians who worked well together. But now I feel about them rather like the kids I went to school with. I will keep meaning to go and see them, but somehow I know I will never get around to it. The bad feelings have all gone, but now we are all too busy living our own lives."

Wednesday, December 1

In the States, John and Yoko release the single 'Happy Christmas (War Is Over)', a full year before the UK issue . . .

John in conversation with the BBC Radio One DJ, Andy Peebles "What we wanted to do was have something besides 'White Christmas' being played every Christmas, you know, and there's always war, right? There's always somebody getting shot, so every year you can play it and there's always somebody being tortured or shot somewhere, so the lyrics stand in that respect . . . I've always wanted to write something that would be a Christmas record that would last forever, you know. Maybe that's not the one, maybe."
(December 1980)

Tuesday, December 7, in both America and in the UK, Wings release their album *Wild Life* . . .

Paul "Dylan inspired *Wild Life*, because we heard he had been in the studio and done an album in just a week. So we thought of doing it like that, putting down the spontaneous stuff and not being too careful. So it came out a bit like that. We wrote the tracks in the summer, Linda and I, we wrote them in Scotland in the summer while the lambs were gambolling. We spent two weeks on the *Wild Life* album all together. At that time, it was just when I had rung Denny Laine up a few days before and he came up to where we were to rehearse for one or two days. I was thinking of getting another guitarist and I knew Denny and thought he was a good singer. I thought 'Go Now' was fabulous. He was an old school friend of mine. When we evacuated during the war, we went to Birmingham and then he was Brian Hines, which is his original name, and we went around a bit. I met him later when he was in The Moody Blues. We toured with them and this cemented our friendship."

The guitarist Denny Laine, the former lead singer with the Sixties chart-toppers, The Moody Blues "I was making my own solo album. I had just finished doing the rough mixing when Paul called me up. It was like fate. I somehow always believed that one day I'd be working with someone I knew and really respected. That's the way the circle goes."

Paul "He came round to see me and brought a guitar and we played some things together. We showed him the chords and we went straight into the studios, worked on the backing tracks and, within two days, it was finished. A couple of the tracks were from The Beatles days. I'm writing with Linda now and we're writing a lot . . . I've drawn on my influences. I could never stop drawing on my rock'n'roll influences. I'm drawing from all my influences since my ears started functioning . . .. We recorded that album very quickly, it was almost like a bootleg, which may be a shame and perhaps some of the songs aren't as good as they might be. I wanted the whole album to be loose and free, so that everyone could get into it. Things like 'Mumbo', which scream a bit and have only 'Mumbo' as lyrics may offend a few old ladies, but generally it's got something for everyone."

Tony Clark, balance engineer on the sessions, who first worked with Paul on Badfinger's 1969 track 'Come And Get It', "Paul asked for me to be present on the sessions for the album and the feeling had been very relaxed, marvellous and very enjoyable. The whole essence of the feeling was that whatever was going on, we had to get it as live as we possibly could in the studio. The whole idea was to get a live feel. The album was done over two weeks with most of the songs being done on first and second takes."

Paul "On the album, it wasn't even the first take."

Linda "The first side of the album is taken up with rock numbers. We did that on purpose. It's so it can be played at parties. One side for when you want to get up and dance and the second side for the girls, when they want to smooch around."

Paul "I don't like it if you have a wild rocker and it stops and the next thing is some violins coming in."

'Mumbo'

Linda "We were playing it through for about five minutes and Paul shouted to the others, 'It's in F' and in fact, on the beginning, you can hear him shout 'Take it, Tony,' to the engineer. We were playing it for the first time."

Paul "At the beginning of the cut, you can hear me say, 'Take it, Tony.' We had been going for five minutes and then I suddenly realised that he wasn't recording. So I shouted, 'Take it, Tony,' and he just got it in then."

Paul "After the criticism of *McCartney*, I put so much into *Ram* to try and please myself and the critics. With Wings' *Wild Life*, I don't care if people don't like it . . . I like it . . . I didn't write anything consciously. Sometimes when I'm pissed off with John over the Apple business, a line might creep in. I suppose when I wrote 'Too many people preaching practices/Don't let them tell you what you want to be,' that was at him. If there's anything on this album, 'Dear Friend' is the nearest thing to that."

'Dear Friend'

Paul "It's just about a dear friend, whatever it means to you. It's really 'Dear friend, quit messing around. Let's just throw the wine, have a good time and stop messing.' Like George says, 'Isn't it a pity that we break each other's hearts.' Well, that's me saying, 'Let's not . . .' "

'Wild Life'

Paul "We didn't stand up for millions of causes and stuff, like conservation, but the first song we did saying something was 'Wild Life' and that just said that nature was all right. The wild state is a good state so why are we getting rid of it? Let's not. The animals are in zoos, instead of just running, like they are supposed to. Once I was in a game park in Africa, just doing the tour through and there was a big sign at the entrance and it said, 'All you people in motor cars, remember the animals have the right of way.' I liked that. I like that somewhere the animals have a right of way over you."

'Bip Bop'

Paul "I had a very simple thing going on with my guitar, my bass string, just plonking on it, a simple blues thing. We are very interested in playing chunky music, music that doesn't particularly say anything. We're not too serious; we like to have a bit of a bop.

'Bip Bop' is just a song I wrote. It's the one our baby likes. She knows it and it's easy for her to sing. It might be 'Flip Flop', you know. It could be anything, but it's 'Bip Bop'."

'Love Is Strange'

Paul "We were in Scotland one summer, I was painting the roof and Linda's got this reggae record, one of the *Tighten Up* records. We were just playing it and it was great music. We just loved it, so we started with a backing track."

Linda "It didn't start out to be 'Love Is Strange'. It started out as an instrumental and when we listened to it, that song came to mind."

Paul "We got the band together and just started to play the reggae thing. We did the backing track and decided that 'Love Is Strange' would fit over it so we started singing over it and that's how it ended up. Reggae is the newest and best beat around. There are more possibilities with reggae than anything at the moment."

On reflection, **Paul** remarks, "Critics didn't like *Wild Life* when it came out so I started thinking like them, that it was rubbish. Then, when I heard it a couple of years later, I really liked it and found it interesting. Okay, it didn't make me the biggest blockbuster around but I don't think you need them all the time. I like to have a couple of albums like that because it adds to the whole thing, really. But what made *Wild Life* okay for me was when I saw this fella heading for the hills in California holding a copy of *Wild Life*. So someone liked it."

Wings . . .

Paul "I had the idea for forming a band maybe after John left The Beatles and formed The Plastic Ono Band. So I looked at someone like Johnny Cash and I thought, 'Well, Johnny Cash just takes a couple of guys and goes around Folsom Prison and has a sing. It doesn't particularly matter who's in his backing group.' And I thought, 'Well, I'll just do a similar thing. I'll just get a band and it'll really just be for the playing and singing, just so I don't forget how to do it.' Even if it was a country & western band, I just wanted a band so I could get out there and sing. It was difficult when The Beatles broke up, there's no denying that and I do feel a lot better now, now that Wings has started, because we're getting into our new thing. And it's nice when something's broken up to get into your new thing, rather than just hang around worrying about the old thing. We're just now into a new band, we can see all the new possibilities of working different ways, it's all open, it's like a blank canvas, there's still plenty of things we want to get into that we haven't yet."

Friday, December 10
John and Yoko are found giving an acoustic performance in front of 20,000 spectators at the Chrysler Arena Sports Stadium in the University of Michigan campus. Their appearance is part of a benefit show for the jailed John Sinclair, who was imprisoned for up to ten years on July 28, 1969 for possessing less than a quarter of an ounce of marijuana . . .

The New York columnist, Lisa Mehlman "About two weeks prior to the event, rumours were floating around that the Lennons would be involved, but that they wouldn't allow their names to be used in the advertisements for the concert. Then, about three days before it was due to happen, they let their names be used. The Lennons were filming and documenting everything. They had a professional videotape crew complete with three colour video cameras, 16-track tape recorders and a film crew! Some felt that the performance was hardly worth all that, for it was a bit of a letdown as far as the music was concerned . . . they were on for about 20 minutes tops, and did not receive an encore. John and Yoko then returned to their presidential hotel suite and put the 'do not disturb' sign on the door. They went home the following morning."

John "The concert was marked by the peaceful response to its cause, for which the artists donated their services for free. Strangely, only a couple of days after the concert, Sinclair was released from jail."

Ringo "The guy was released and it doesn't matter if it was John's doing or what. John joined the situation so I would credit it to him and if he never does anything else in his political career, that's enough. But he'll keep on trying, I'm sure."

1972

JANUARY

John replies, "What I miss most is just sitting down with a group and just playing. As you know, we've been playing with The Elephants lately, you know Elephant's Memory. When we were gigging with them, and just rehearsing, it reminded me of the early days of The Cavern. It was really nice just to have a solid group. The fact that we're a solid group was nice and it was really good working with them, and that's the thing I miss most, working with a group."

Ringo remarks "I just don't like Elephant's Memory. I don't like them because they're brash and horrible and they substitute volume and craziness for licks."

John continues, "With The Beatles, it became less group-like when we stopped touring and then we would only get together for recordings. So, therefore, the recording sessions were almost the thing we rehearsed in as well. So, all the playing was in a recording session and sometimes it would be a drag. It's like an athlete, you have to keep playing all the time to keep your hand in and we'd be off for months and we'd suddenly come to the studio and be expected to be spot on again. It would take us a few days to get loosened up and playing again. So therefore, The Beatles musically weren't asked together in the last few years, although we had learnt a lot of techniques. We could produce good records, but musically we weren't as together as in the early years. That's what we'd all miss.

"If you sit down with any of the others, and you talk about the past, it was always pre-making it. We always talk about Hamburg, The Cavern and the dance halls in Liverpool, because that was when we were pretty hot musically. We never talk about after that because, to us, that was when the live music stopped existing. Once we left the dance halls and went into theatres, we had to do a show that would only last 20 minutes. Up to then, we had been doing shows that would last an hour or two. Suddenly, everything had to be done in 20 minutes, and in that 20 minutes, we had to do our hits and we'd do two shows a night, because the theatre only held a few thousand people. That's what started to kill our live music."

Howard Smith "Did they ever attempt to get The Beatles to do commercials?"

John "There were many times that we were offered to do some things, like from Coke and all things like that, but we never wanted to associate ourselves with one product. We always thought it was a bit demeaning."

Howard informs John that the promoter Sid Bernstein claimed that he made next to nothing from The Beatles' August 1965 concert at Shea Stadium . . .

John "Believe me, The Beatles got the least of it all, whatever it was. They got more of it than we ever did. We most probably still haven't got paid for it yet. I wouldn't be surprised. Most of it never got to us. We were all ripped off, really. We ain't got millions in the bank, I'll tell you that. My album *Imagine* and the other album are not owned by me. I don't own the songs or nothing, they just go straight into Northern Songs, you know, Lew Grade's fat pocket. And between Capitol, EMI, Lew Grade and all those people, we get sod all out of it, even now. We were just like all the other musicians, we were ripped off from start to finish."

John is asked about Arthur Janov and Primal Scream . . .

"I think we're past those sort of trips," he replies. "Janov was a lot of Freud too. I saw him on TV saying, 'If people had understood Freud, his idea of Primal Scream would have been developed a long time ago.' There's a lot of truth in that. Primal Scream was worth it for me because it did help me a lot to go through my past childhood and delve into it and try to find out what made me tick. England is very suspicious of psychiatrists. If it hadn't been for his book, I would never have touched a psychiatrist. The fact was, in his book, he came across that his psychiatry wasn't like anybody else's. I always thought most psychiatrists need a psychiatrist. I don't believe that anybody can tell you how you are and one thing about their therapy is that they never told you how you were. You had to tell them. That was the difference. With most psychiatrists you just lie there, telling them how you are. What's the point of that?"

Public Performances?

John "If people knew what it was like to go on stage, it would make you wonder why we did it. One period, during therapy, I asked myself, 'Why am I up there? What am I doing up there, performing like an animal?' You put yourself up in front of the public and it's like the Roman theatre. You put your life in their hands, whether you live or die and it's a very masochistic scene to stand up there, day after day, offering yourself as a target, you know, for their love or their hate, depending on how they feel and how good you feel that night. At one point, I was thinking, 'I'd never do that again,' when I began to see what it meant. I thought, 'Why should I be put up there like a performing flea? Get somebody else to do it.' Now I only do it because I want to do it."

Tuesday, January 25
The guitarist Henry McCullough becomes the latest addition to Wings. He recalls the audition to join the band . . .

Henry "I received a phone call from Ian Horne, my roadie, who asked me to go to a rehearsal the next day. I had a couple of pints of Guinness before I went along the first time. That helped . . . It was a wee room. The equipment was set up and Paul asked me to play and said the rest of them would fit in. We got into some rock'n'roll, things like 'Blue Moon Of Kentucky', 'Lucille', some things off the *Wild Life* album and some reggae. Also there were a couple of new ones he'd written. On one song he was kind of playing away on a tune I hadn't heard before so I asked him what to do. He said, 'We're all just trying it out,' and just continued playing. We all joined in, it went on a bit further and in no time at all, a song was written. It was written on the spot and we all contributed. I've only met Paul twice, but he seems full of energy and enthusiasm. He comes in and throws off his coat and gets right into it. I can't help having respect for Paul and all the songs he's written and what he's achieved. But, it's just another band as far as I'm concerned, and that's the way Paul wants it. Originally Denny Laine was going to be the lead guitarist and vocalist as well, but I felt Denny felt a bit restricted playing guitar and singing at the same time. He probably felt he couldn't do both. Paul's talking about just arriving somewhere, it could be up North somewhere or even Broadway, throwing open the van doors and playing wherever it happens to be."

Paul "We're trying things out in Wings at the moment, but there's nothing too set with Henry McCullough. He might come in. All we really want to do is to get a good band to go round and play with. I don't care if we're three, four or five. So long as it sounds like a good band. What we're doing is working up to going out . . . It's been a long time since I played live, that's why I want to get back. I've really decided that I miss just playing to people."

Denny Laine "The first people Paul took on seemed to think that they ought to be millionaires overnight, because they were working with Paul McCartney and that he should give them each a mansion in the country or something. But Paul wasn't even earning anything then because all the money was tied up in The Beatles' litigation."

The first session with Henry is the recording of 'Give Ireland Back To The Irish' . . .

Monday, January 31
Meanwhile, in New York, John and Yoko begin a week of recording as the co-hosts of *The Mike Douglas Show*. On Wednesday's show, their special guest is the rock'n'roll legend, Chuck Berry, one of John's all-time musical heroes . . .

Berry "I had a call from *The Mike Douglas Show* and they mentioned that John would be there. They asked me what we were going to do, so I said, 'Let's do "Memphis" and "Johnny B Goode".' I know he sings it and I invited him to the microphone as we did 'Memphis' in two-part harmony. It was almost like a gig!"

Saturday, February 5

Disc & Music Echo reports "Lennon Plans Football And Four Hour Show". The report reads "John seems set to jump on the Bangla Desh bandwagon by staging a British benefit on the lines of last summer's Madison Square Garden concerts. Disc understands that the ambitious arrangements involve a unique international soccer match, starring World Cup players like Pele at a London ground (either Chelsea or Fulham), followed by a four-hour all-star concert at which Lennon and friends will perform. The venture may even extend to shops and restaurants in the vicinity, staging a special Bangladesh day, including a Bangladesh menu. Les Perrin, of Apple, told *Disc*, 'John may well do something like this, but at the moment, it's pie in the sky. I know nothing and I know it doesn't figure in Allen Klein's plans.' Meanwhile, *Disc* discovered that the Action Bangladesh organisation has been in touch with Lennon's Ascot home, and John's private secretary there said, 'Nothing has been planned for the next few months, but we can not discount the possibility of such an event taking place.' "

(Note: In the same issue of Disc & Music Echo, the paper prints the results of its 1972 Music Poll Awards. John is voted the 'Best Singer/Songwriter', George the 'Best Musician' and *Imagine* as the 'Best Album of 1971', with Paul's *Ram* coming in at No. 9.)

Wednesday, February 9
Paul, Linda and Wings start an 11-date unannounced tour of UK colleges and universities . . .

Paul "It was the only thing I could think of to do, and it was the craziest thing to do, to bring in your wife who's had no previous musical experience. I said to Lin', 'So how do you fancy it? C'mon, hit a synthesiser for us . . . we'll go and have a laugh. I need ya onstage for my confidence.' "

Linda "It was Paul's idea. We were up in Scotland and Paul wanted to play but he couldn't think of who to play with. He said, 'Why don't you learn? We could do it together.' I told him, 'I can't play a note.' So he took me to the piano and said, 'There's a middle C, now you can learn.' We had a few rows as he tried to teach me. He really put me through it. When anything went wrong, I used to say, 'I thought you knew how to make a group?' So I had to teach myself. I had never realised how hard it all was. I was just telling Paul again and again that I don't quite know if I had the nerve to join him. I mean, how do you go out with Beethoven and say, 'Sure, I'll sing harmony with you' when you've never sung a note? Or 'Sure I'll play piano with you' when you've never played? It was mad."

Paul "I just thought I was doing what I knew, and the only way I knew how to do it was to get back on the boards again, with anything and anyone. I wanted to perform again because, I think, the longer I waited with another day of no work and another day with nothing to go to, the more I was becoming stagnant. It's like after an operation, where you want to rest, but you've got to push it. Your body is going downhill. But I just had to push something, and I thought, 'Well, the man who sings everyday is going to have a better voice because he's practising every day. It's got to be good for you.' So, I hit upon the idea of having a bunch of people around me who would play and we'd go out and it didn't matter if it was big time or small time or anything. I'd still be playing. So, we went out with a couple of line-ups and Linda was there on keyboards, terrified out of her mind, poor kid. She was getting picked on something silly."

Linda "I'm the original 'sticks and stones' person, words haven't hurt me. I knew that the people who said these things didn't know me. They said that I was filthy rich, which was not true at all. My family are New York lawyers."

John "I kind of admire the way Paul started back from scratch, because that's what he wanted to do with The Beatles. He wanted us to go back to the dance halls and experience that again. But I didn't! That was one of the problems . . . he wanted to relive it all or something. I don't know what it was. But, I kind of admire the way he got off his pedestal, now he's back on it again . . . He did what he wanted to do. That's fine, but it's just not what I wanted to do."

Paul "People couldn't accept that we wanted to go back to square one and be a little skiffle group again . . . Linda was absolute rubbish but you don't always form groups with absolute technical musicians. In fact, I was thinking if I formed a super group, like Blind Faith, with Eric Clapton, Ginger (Baker), Stevie Winwood, a lot of kind of stars, that that would have its own kind of failings. It would be so intense that that would have to break up. So, we thought, 'What the hell.' We'd take this van up the motorway and we'll do what I always used to do. At least I'd get to sing and we'd be with people . . ."

Linda "When I first went on stage, I was crying with fright. They said that I couldn't play my keyboard with Wings, but what they didn't know was that I really didn't want to play . . . All I wanted was to be with Paul and have a family."

Paul "Linda broke down one night because she couldn't face the whole thing of everyone being down on her. She felt totally out of place. But she had to start somewhere. We stuck by the idea in the group but two of the guys, Henry and Denny Seiwell, would say, 'What are we doing with her?' And I would say, 'I don't quite know. I can't put it into words, but I know there's a good reason for her being here.' I know it is right, whether it is for the general confidence or to give it some innocence for the group. I like innocence myself . . . With Wings, I was the band leader, the business manager, the this, the that. We didn't have an Apple, we didn't have Brian Epstein, we didn't have anything. It was me doing it all. That was the biggest mistake. In The Beatles, I had been free of all that; we had a manager and we had three other guys, but now I was the only one in control."

The opening concert takes place in Nottingham at the university . . .

Paul "We took off from London with the idea of going on tour, but instead of fixing up dates and gigs ahead of ourselves, we wanted to keep it very loose. So we just took off in the van. We left the motorway at Hatherton, just after Leicester, for no other reason other than I liked the name. Unable to find a hotel in Hatherton, we headed for Nottingham, twelve miles away. Then Henry McCullough remembered that he had played at Nottingham last year with The Grease Band and had liked the place. So, at five o'clock, we casually walked into the Union building, grabbed the nearest executive and suggested that Wings play their debut concert there the next day."

Present in the audience is the UK music reporter, Martin Marriott "Out for a drive, he (Paul) looks at a road map and the superstar's finger falls on a spot marked Nottingham. 'That looks like a good place to start, we'll play there,' he says. Whatever you call a wayward decision like that, it brought Paul McCartney to Nottingham University for his first British live appearance in over five years. Paul and his newly formed group, Wings, took the performing plunge and made an unexpected debut at the University Portland building and the blast of cheers, stamping feet and whistles from over 1,000 students seemed to say, 'Welcome back,' to the nervous but elated star. Wings and the McCartney family were in the concert hall and had their equipment set up before most students realised they had arrived. Press cameras, what few there were, had to stay outside. As the group started up, there were hardly 30 upturned faces around the stage to see the Second Coming of Paul McCartney. After the first few bars of 'Lucille', there was never any doubt of success and the concert took on the air of an historical rock event. Between every number there was a break. 'We don't have too many numbers yet, we're just checking it out,' explained a smiling McCartney. 'That's okay,' roared the crowd in response. To say Wings have few rehearsed numbers is an understatement. After no more than half a dozen recent album tracks, Paul explained, 'We may have to throw a few Blues in here.' 'That's fine,' the crowd screamed back. The Nottingham audience was the first to hear the new Wings single 'Give Ireland Back To The Irish'. It is hardly a musical masterpiece, but it is quite a departure for Paul who seemed least likely of all the former Beatles to pontificate. The McCartney children sat on the edge of the stage and watched puzzled as 'dad' had the audience eating from his hands. Uproar at the suggestion it was time to end the concert brought Wings back for two more rockers, before they made a dash for their van and a quick escape. Without a doubt, the McCartney myth will carry Wings through a number of these concerts, but the group has a long way to travel musically. Paul McCartney has arrived – for the second time."

Geoff Liptrot, *New Musical Express* "As the audience left, people were already dissecting the performance, analysing it unnecessarily, but the fact is Paul McCartney is back. Disregard the critics, it was a concert none of us here will ever forget."

Melody Maker "Paul was reluctant to say much about the group's performance but he was obviously relieved by the tremendous response. 'It was very good for us. We will go on touring the country for a while, playing more of these concerts when we feel like it,' he said. And that they did. The next day saw them at York University. Paul had driven out of Leeds, where he had been due to play, because of too much publicity, and booked himself into the Dining Room at York's Goodricke College only hours before his concert started. Despite the publicity ban, students crowded into the room and another three hundred were locked out as Wings went through a two-hour routine, which built up from a subdued start to wild bop in the final 'Long Tall Sally'. It was vintage McCartney, who on occasions looked as though he had gone straight back to the early Beatles days as he sailed through straight rock numbers like 'Lucille'. Judging from the way the audience appreciated the performance, the group looks like a winner live."

Paul's spokesman, Shelley Turner "I only get to hear from them via the answering service, but they've said that everything's going great, and plan to continue. They are travelling in two trucks, the equipment in one and the group, children, wives and dogs in the other. They'll probably stick to the universities since the audience is ready-made and responsive. With concerts, they're in the hands of promoters and that's something they want to avoid."

Linda "I can understand people saying, 'What's he doing getting his wife in the band,' but the point is that the audiences didn't mind. People who came to see us because of what they'd read were obviously a bit dubious, but afterwards, they went home seeing that's the way it had to be and they loved it. Lots of people came up to me and said how good I was. People weren't hostile, just the British press. I was criticised for not being up to the standards of the rest of the group, but probably rightly so. I'm not the same standard, nowhere near. I never said, 'Hell, I'm great. I'm Carole King, man.' I never did. Paul just asked me and I said, Yes.' I think the only thing that really upsets me is that people have got me wrong. I went into Selfridges and a woman said, 'Aren't you Linda McCartney? Oh, you're so much nicer than I thought you'd be.' "

Paul "I remember one terrible night on the tour of the universities we were doing, just to get some practice, we were going to start the tune 'Wild Life' and Linda was to start with the chords on the electric piano. I looked around and said, 'One, two, three,' nothing! I looked to see a glassy stare in her eyes and she's looking at me, mouthing, 'I have forgotten the chords.' The audience thought it was part of a comedy routine we were working into the act. So I walked to the keyboards, showed Linda the chords and got a great laugh. Christ, if all we ever had in the world was perfection, it would be pretty boring."

Friday, February 25 (UK)
Wings release the controversial, politically inspired track 'Give Ireland Back To The Irish' as their next single . . .

Paul "It's something I woke up with this morning. It'll be our next single if it works out that people want it. It's all about the mess in Ireland."

It is immediately banned by a number of important radio stations including Radio Luxembourg. A spokesman for the station comments, "We will not be playing the single because we feel it is political and we keep away from politics. Also, we have a large audience in Ireland and to present the record at this time would, we feel, be unwise."

Paul "I'm a taxpayer, so that entitles me to an opinion. I'm living in the West, so we're allowed to talk over here, right? So when the English paratroopers, my army who I'm paying rates for, go into Ireland and shoot down innocent bystanders, for the first time in my life I go, 'Hey, wait a minute. We're the goodies, aren't we?' That wasn't very goody and I'm moved to make some kind of a protest, so I did 'Give Ireland Back To The Irish', which was promptly banned in England. But it was No. 1 in Spain of all places! That was rather odd, Franco was in power. Maybe they couldn't understand the words and they just liked the tune."

Denny Laine "We went into the Apple Studios to mix 'Give Ireland Back To The Irish' and he (Paul) looked around those studios and he must have been thinking, 'Blimey, I helped build all this.' He must feel bad that he can't go on being involved."

Friday, March 17 (UK)
Ringo releases his new single, 'Back Off Boogaloo', which features production by George . . .

Ringo "I sat down with Marc Bolan one night and he's using this 'Back off, boogaloo' kind of language. I went to bed and I woke up with this song in my head, 'Back Off Boogaloo, what d'ya think you're gonna do,' and I was saying, 'Where's my tape? Where's my tape?' Because I was frightened I wouldn't remember it. I knew I wouldn't remember it. I ran every tape machine in my house and there were ones that the batteries had run down, ones that wouldn't plug in, and there were ones that the fuses had blown. I was hopping round the whole house trying to keep this tune in my head, which was now turning into 'Mack The Knife' and I started to get panicky. And finally I find a tape and I put it down and that's how it came about. In ten minutes I had the whole song. So I said to George, 'Come on, let's go in and do a single. I've got a single I want to do.' He's a great producer."

Friday, May 5
John and Yoko appear as guests, for the second time, on the ABC TV television programme *The Dick Cavett Show*. They perform 'Woman Is The Nigger Of The World' . . .

John "Dick Cavett had this national TV show and he was willing to let us sing because he was a liberal . . . and the company had a big hullabaloo backstage and we did manage to do it live on his show once, but the hullabaloo was amazing. I mean, it was like I'd trodden on the flag or something. It's just absolutely ridiculous but when you think it's such a beautiful statement, you know, what she was saying is true, woman is still the nigger, and there's only one. You can talk about blacks, you can talk about Jews, you can talk about the Third World, you can talk about everything but underlying that whole thing, under the whole crust of it is the women and beneath them children . . ."

John courts controversy on the show when he announces that he has been the subject of FBI harassment since arriving in New York . . .

"My phones were tapped and they were following us around New York in a car for about three days," **John** recalls. "And when I started saying it, even my own lawyer was saying, 'No, no, it's just paranoia.' Everybody was saying, 'Lennon is a big mouth. He's an egomaniac, so why would they bother with someone like him?' The whole thing started when it got into *Rolling Stone* or something that Yoko and I were going to the Republican convention, which was going to be in San Diego. There was big talk among the Peace movement about having an anti-war thing and these people were calling me out and I was seeing all these people and I was just discussing it. The next thing, it's in the papers that 'John and Yoko are going to lead this vast rally in San Diego with Jerry Rubin and Allen Ginsberg'. Then things started happening. My lawyer, who was as square as the next lawyer, started to agree because he found that his phones were being tapped and he doesn't know how to prove it. He said, 'There's something going on with my phone. It's happening to me.' But he's just a straight lawyer. I lost the case about my phone being tapped because I can't prove it. I just know that there were a lot of repairs going on in that cellar. I know the difference between a phone being normal when I pick it up and when I pick it up and there are a lot of noises. When I told my lawyer I think they're tapping my phone, somebody gave me a number that when you call, if you dial it, and you get this feedback sound, it's supposed to say your phone is tapped. I was paranoid at the time, who wouldn't be? Suddenly I realised this was serious. 'They're coming for me!' They were harassing me and I'd open the door and there would be guys standing on the other side of the street and I'd get in the car and they'd be following me and not hiding from me. They wanted me to see that I was being followed. So I went on a show called *The Dick Cavett Show*, a talk show, and I said it that night. I was very nervous about saying it but I had learnt from Dick Gregory. They've been doing him for years, following him and tapping him, he said, 'The best way is to say it out, say it out and then everybody knows if anything happens to you, what happened to you.' I'm not saying they had other plans other than keeping tabs on me, you know, to see what I was up to, to see who I was seeing, and I said it on the air, on the TV and they went away the next day. There was nobody there."

Friday, May 12 (UK)
Wings release their new single, a surprising choice, the traditional nursery rhyme, 'Mary Had A Little Lamb' . . .

Paul "I got a few knocks with people saying, 'Oh, blimey, "Mary Had A Little Lamb", what are you doing?' as if everything that came from my pen had to be earth-shattering. Beatles records, any records, there's always something daft there. The great thing about 'Mary Had A Little Lamb', for me, I was never wild about it, personally. When we took it on tour, it was the song that got the audience singing along on the 'La las'. That was fantastic because it saved the number for me and kids love it. I'd never realised there was a four-year-old audience. Whilst toymakers have got it sussed around Christmas, no one outside the business, short of The Osmonds and The Jacksons, cater for it."

Wednesday, May 17

New York Herald Tribune "The United States government's deportation proceedings against John Lennon and his wife recessed today for at least two months with a prediction from special-inquiry officer Ira Fieldsteel that 'This thing could go on for years.' Fieldsteel closed the Immigration Department hearing in New York following testimony from the former Beatle and his wife, Yoko Ono, on why they should be granted American residency. They ended their testimony with pleas for mercy. 'I don't know if there is any mercy to plead for here,' Lennon said, 'but if there is, I'd like to plea for it on behalf of her child.' The Lennons have been in the US since last August searching for Yoko's 8-year-old daughter, Kyoko. They were awarded custody of the child by a Texas court with the stipulation that she is raised in America, but they have still not seen Kyoko and contend her father, film producer Anthony Cox, is hiding her. When Government attorney, Vincent Schiano asked Mrs Lennon if she would accept permanent residence even if her husband were deported, she wrung a handkerchief, choked back tears and answered, 'That's a hard decision to make. You are asking me to choose between my husband and my child. I only hope you will understand our situation and consider our child and not consider the technicalities as important in this case.' At the press conference after the hearing, both Lennons were optimistic. John said he believed the government was treating him fairly and Yoko said, 'I still have faith in American justice.' "

Sunday, May 28

From her home in London, which she shares with her Italian husband, Roberto, Cynthia Bassanini announces that "John hasn't seen Julian since he went to America. It is rather a long time. He seems to be occupied with Yoko's daughter now. He does write to Julian, just normal letters, asking how he is getting on at school and things like that. And he sends him presents. He sent him a toy truck at Christmas. I don't keep in touch with John anymore. It's purely through Julian that we keep in contact. Julian loves his father. He follows his career in the newspapers. He goes to a private boys' school where people don't bother who he is. He went to a State school, but he had problems there."

Monday, June 12 (USA)
John and Yoko release their double-album *Sometime In New York City* . . .

John "When we made that album, we weren't setting out to make the *Brandenburg Concerto* or the masterpiece everyone tries to make, paint, draw, film. There was no intention of that. It was just a question of getting it done, putting it out and the next one's coming soon. We needn't have done it. We could have sat on *Imagine* for a year and a half. But the thing is, on *New York City*, we were coming outta minds and we just wanted to share our thoughts with anybody who wanted to listen. It was a quicker decision to make *Sometime In New York City* than any other album. And for that reason, it only took nine days to complete . . . The single from the album is 'Woman Is The Nigger Of The World'. Its title comes from a quote from Yoko, published in *Nova* magazine in March 1969. We both wrote the song and are using the *Nova* cover for the single's sleeve. On the other side is 'Sisters Oh Sisters' . . . The album's cover is designed like the front page of a newspaper, the stories being the lyrics; the headlines being the titles of the songs and the photographs being relevant to the subject matter of the song. For instance, an Irish song would have an Irish scene . . . They banned the picture here (USA). Yoko made this beautiful poster, Chairman Mao and Richard Nixon dancing together, and the stupid retailers stuck a gold sticker over it that you can't steam off."

Saturday, July 8
Melody Maker reports that "Paul McCartney has snubbed Britain", in a piece written by Chris Charlesworth . . .

Paul "It's crazy! That's crazy! You know how they are in the papers. The reason why we never played in Britain at this time was because we were playing in France and that's the only reason. We happened to be doing a tour of Europe and we wanted to break the band in. We're a very new band, you know. And if you go and play Britain, or America, with a new band, you're really on the spot. You've got to be red hot. It's a question of living together a while and bouncing off each other, and that's what we're learning to do on this tour. Hopefully we'll tour Britain next year."

Sunday, July 9
As planned, Wings begin a 26-date, nine-continental-country European Tour . . .

Paul "We did most of the organising ourselves and we certainly aren't doing it for the money. I am making sure I avoid the pitfalls this time around. I am going out of my way to avoid all the thieves and parasites who hang around the music business. The whole scene stinks. I estimate that, when I was with The Beatles, we each got about five per cent of what we earned. All your money is handled for you and you get an allowance. If you want a car, or a house, it will be bought for you but you never get any real money. Linda was talking to Jimi Hendrix shortly before he died and he was over the moon because he had been allowed to have an E-Type Jaguar. The car cost about £2,000 and Jimi couldn't realise that this was only a tenth of what others were getting out of it. Even when The Beatles were earning well over £1,000,000 a year, the four of us only used to get about £50,000 a year each in the way of cars and houses and expenses."

The tour begins with a 95-minute performance at the open-air Greek style Chateau Vallon Amphitheatre in Toulon, France . . .

Paul "We wanted to start at a smallish place and this is quite a small, out of the way place. But we could still get a reasonably sized crowd. Originally, we wanted to end in France and start in Finland. I think the British and American audiences are a bit more critical, unlike tonight's audience, who are just coming out for a good evening. I just want to be ready, that's all. We've hired a London double-decker bus, with an open rooftop to take us through the Continent. I always wanted to do something like this. When I was in The Beatles, we never had time, but now I can sit up there and enjoy the good weather."

Henry McCullough, Wings "On the European Tour, some people were saying to Paul, 'It isn't as good as The Beatles.' But it's not the same sort of band. It's a completely different thing. Mind you, I'd like to do some old Beatles stuff. It would be nice to do."

Linda "I can remember crying my eyes out in a dressing room in Europe because I was so scared! And I was nervous in the first half of the show but by the second half I was having a great time. But we had no soundcheck, no rehearsal, no nothing. We had to go on cold. But we were very hot in the second half."

James Johnson, *New Musical Express* "Toulon, South of France, Sunday. This opening date for Paul McCartney's first tour since The Beatles days of 1966 hardly came over as an all-important, high-energy, event. But then everybody it seemed, especially McCartney, wanted to keep the open-air concert at the Chateau Vallon at low key. He wanted a relatively quiet start. Certainly, McCartney could hardly have chosen a more obscure spot to start. Even local taxi drivers had difficulty in finding the Chateau, which could only be reached after a mysterious drive through the suburbs of Toulon, a half-built housing estate and up a two-mile track through pinewoods. Since local advertising was virtually nil, the thousand or so beach freaks, interested locals and occasional middle-aged sophisticates, were gathered there almost by word of mouth. Unfortunately too, the Press Party, flown out from England for the gig, was still struggling through the woods as the first half of the concert came to an end . . . McCartney later admitted that the show hadn't been that good anyway, and, from what could be heard wafting down through the trees, one was inclined to agree. Certain numbers like 'Blue Moon Of Kentucky' sounded more like something from a local church hall group than a band led by a former Beatle. To me, Linda McCartney is still the weakest link in the group, with most of her contributions fairly ineffectual. And certainly, everyone didn't appreciate her talents. When McCartney said, 'One of these microphones isn't working,' a voice calls back out of the audience, 'Give it to yer missus, then.' After the concert, a small party was thrown in the backstage enclosure, all very civilised, with drinks laid out on trestle tables and lit by discreet floodlights in the trees. With Linda constantly by his side, McCartney seemed in cheerful spirits and full of confidence, although he had little time to relax. As soon as he appeared out of the dressing room door, he was surrounded by photographers, autograph hunters and reporters . . ."

A reporter asks Paul about 'Seaside Woman', a song they have just performed . . .

Paul replies "I'm glad she (Linda) wrote that, just for Sir Lew Grade's sake. You see I don't believe he thought she could write. I think he thought I was doing it in her name."

Reporter "What do you feel is the best Wings number so far?"

Paul "I don't know yet. Maybe 'Maybe I'm Amazed', since it went down well. Also, we've got a new one, 'Hi Hi Hi', which is a nice one we wrote on holiday in about five minutes. We're thinking about it for a single."

Reporter "What did you think of John's last album?"

Paul "It's good, if that's what he wants to do, that's fine."

Reporter "But you don't share his social/political beliefs?"

Paul "Actually, I do. I don't think there's much wrong with a lot of what he says. Often he's quite right, and it's certainly not ineffective."

Linda "We haven't even started to say what we really think yet. I think the trouble with John Lennon is that he preaches one thing but he doesn't go and do it. That's very easy. In fact, we saw him recently, and it was all, 'Yeah, yeah,' all open hearts and Yoko's saying, 'To hell with it, let's break up.' But nothing has happened. Nothing! I don't blame him or the others, particularly. They're only puppets for Klein. They're nice people, but they're being manipulated."

Paul then faces questioning from the BBC Radio reporter Michael Wale . . .

Wale "I was in America recently and everybody asked about Paul McCartney."

Paul "Wonderful! What did they ask?"

Wale "Well, are you dead?"

Paul "Well, I can definitely deny that rumour."

Thursday, July 27
Meanwhile, the film *The Concert For Bangla Desh* opens in the UK at the Rialto Cinema in Coventry Street, London . . .

John "*Bangla Desh* is the most fantastic thing. They're blowing the film up to 70mm and it's going to earn millions for those people. It's fantastic and George is virtually an Ambassador in the World. He's going to go to India and Bangladesh and see where the money's going to go, you know, following it through. He's taken on a great responsibility and he's doing it because he's on his own and he's found something he wants to do. I think it's fantastic."

Tuesday, August 1
Wings' European concert tour reaches Copenhagen and, following a show at the KB Hallen, Per Helge Hansen, a distraught fan of Paul's, is impelled to write a letter, published in several European music papers, which gives his opinions of Wings' performance . . .

"Dear Paul, I hope you will be able to take this letter as well meant criticism," Per Helge writes, "and I'm writing this because the other night in Copenhagen, your act was so sad. I did not go to the Wings concert hoping I would hear music up to The Beatles standards, your records with Wings had told me that would be unfair . . . As The Beatles, Paul, together with John, George and Ringo, you made some incredible music that was important to millions of people all over the world. But now, it seems the muzak you make with Wings isn't important even to yourself. The first thing that struck me when leaving KB Hallen in Copenhagen was that it had been a boring concert. I felt that Wings was no more than a second class Norwegian dance group. If you want to take Wings over to England and survive as a respected composer, singer and musician, a radical change is needed. First of all, is finding better songs. Your musicians are good, except Linda. I wouldn't have the heart to travel to Europe if I played the organ that bad."

Denny Laine "On the European tour, I walked into a club where I had arranged to meet Paul and Linda and found them sheet-white and shaking with fear. Paul shouted out, 'There's a guy over there in the corner. He says he's got a gun and he's going to shoot me.' I'm not the bravest guy in the world but there was only one way to handle it. With our guitarist, Henry McCullough, I walked up to the guy. Henry grabbed one arm and I grabbed the other and one of our roadies searched him. He didn't have a gun and that time Paul and Linda were lucky. But how is he ever to know? Paul is no coward, but he was very relieved and thankful for what we did."

Thursday, August 10
There is a further problem for Paul, Linda and Wings in Gothenburg when Swedish police questions them after a drugs raid. Forty policemen with dogs burst into the Scandinavian Hall where Wings were playing, resulting in Paul, Linda and Denny being driven away in a police car. Friends remark that "Paul was play acting on the way to the station . . ."

Gothenburg Police "Paul McCartney and his wife and another member of the group (Denny Seiwell) were questioned in connection with narcotics enquiries and later released."

Reporter, Paul Dacre "Wings had just finished an encore of the old Beatles number 'Long Tall Sally' for the packed audience of 8,000 when police rushed backstage and grabbed the group's secretary, 20-year-old Rebecca Hinds . . ."

Denny Laine "Then they went for Denny Seiwell in a very stroppy way. By this time, Paul and Linda were talking to the police and trying to explain things. They searched us and our clothes. Then they searched the group's bus. We kept asking them, 'Have you got a warrant?' They refused to answer. Finally Paul and Linda agreed to go to the station to try and sort things out. The police took away a few things, including a pipe that belonged to me. I can assure you that none of us had any drugs."

Reporter, John Blake "Paul, Linda and Denny (Seiwell) were taken to police headquarters ordered to pay nearly £1,000 after being accused of smuggling drugs into Sweden. The police said that customs men had opened a parcel addressed to Paul at Gothenburg and found seven ounces of marijuana. A police chief said that the trio had arranged to have marijuana posted to them each day so that they would not have to carry it through customs."

Mr Lennart Angelin, the Public Prosecutor in Gothenburg "Formal charges will be brought against them later. The trio had been released after having deposited 9,000 Swedish Kronor as preliminary fines. They were not arrested since it was obvious that they were going to use the cannabis themselves and not pass it on. They are now free to carry on their Scandinavian tour or leave the country."

Upon leaving the police station, **Paul** remarks to reporters, "The Swedish police behaved correctly, but they take hash and marijuana far too seriously."

Mr John May, British Consul General in Gothenburg "The group got in touch with our legal advisor when they were interviewed by the police in their hotel. The money they paid is more a surety for future good behaviour than a fine. Everything was quickly settled and the police were apparently very nice to the McCartneys. They have now set off for their next concert."

John Morris, the tour producer "Paul, Linda and Denny did admit to the Swedish police that they used hash. At first they denied it but the police gave them a rough time and started threatening all sorts of things."

Within days of the trouble, Paul Dacre paints an alternate version of the story, "Before arriving in Gothenburg, they had appeared in Helsinki. I understand that during their Finnish appearance, the McCartneys had left a bulky parcel filled with shirts and underwear for laundering at their hotel. Soon after their arrival at their hotel in Gothenburg, McCartney's wife and his secretary, 19-year-old Rebecca Hind, made frequent visits to the front desk asking if a packet had arrived. The packet contained nothing more sinister than a bundle of McCartney's exotic shirts and unexotic underwear . . ."

Rebecca Hind "I went down every hour to see if it had arrived, but it never turned up."

Paul Dacre "This all, apparently, alerted the suspicious minds of the hotel's authorities and then, when a parcel arrived at the hotel, addressed to another member of the group, which turned out to contain a quantity of hashish, the police were duly informed. It was automatically assumed that the McCartney package was the one containing, not laundered clothing, but sinister pot. The result was that the hapless Miss Hind was one of the first to be closely questioned by the Gothenburg police."

The Swedish reporter Elga Eliaser recalls an event from earlier in the day, "Paul McCartney, his hair cropped and dishevelled, didn't hesitate when two burly Scandinavians deliberately bumped into us as we walked through Oslo in the early hours. While I looked the other way and tried to remember the Norwegian for 'Sorry,' he turned towards them, his fists clenched and eyes blazing. In a moment they had gone. But the tough, new McCartney is here to stay. It was no surprise to me when he clashed with the Swedish drug squad later in the day. For the truth is that at the ripe old age of 30, Paul has turned from the chirpy, cheerful Beatle into a very angry young man. He is angry with fans who pester for autographs at an inconvenient moment. He told one to go to hell in an art gallery the other day. He is furious with hotel managers who make life difficult. And most of all, he is bubbling over with rage at all the 'Mr Ninety per cents of the pop business . . .' "

Paul explains to Elga "I have been conned so many times and lost so much money that I am determined never to let anyone off with anything again. I was always very well mannered and polite. My dad brought me up to always tip my cap at my elders and I used to do it until I was about 14 and I didn't wear a cap anymore. Now I force myself not to tolerate people I don't like. If people do something that irritates me, I let them know about it. You can so easily lose your identity in this sort of business. You confuse the myth with the person you really are. Like Marilyn Monroe must have got to the point where she didn't know who she was any more. She was a walking legend, not a person. I make sure that being well known doesn't stop me being an ordinary bloke who won't tolerate people he doesn't like."

Tour producer, John Morris "Paul is paranoid about people trying to make money out of him. There is no agent on the tour, no tour manager, no publicity officer and, at present, his auditor is on the tour, checking the books. It was his wife, Linda, who made him see he was surrounded by con men and leeches."

Saturday, August 19
Wings perform in Groningen, Holland . . .

The music journalist, Robert Ellis "The Martini Hall in Groningen, turned out to be a square box of steel and concrete with a king-sized echo problem. At 8.30pm, the audience began to assemble and they sat on the floor and waited. Someone was playing records over the PA, then, 'Ladies and gentlemen . . . from England . . . Wings.' All of the audience strained forward to get their first view of Paul as the curtains parted. The band were playing 'Eat At Home' straight into 'Smile Away' without a pause . . . The piano and keyboard department is still the weakest link, improved though Linda is, and the harmony singing needs attention."

Following the show, an optimistic Paul and Linda are interviewed by Ellis whilst listening to a playback of the concert in The Rolling Stones' mobile recording studio, parked outside the venue . . .

Paul "Rotterdam was better. We had some of the audience dancing on the stage . . . We're recording more of the gigs, and filming them, too. I have some ideas for the film and maybe we will use it for TV."

Linda "I feel better about my playing now. It's a nice feeling. It's all sort of coming together. I got really carried away on the music tonight, although all the gigs have been good for a long time now, except Copenhagen, which was a bit flat."

Sunday, August 20
During a break from their European jaunt, Paul, Linda and Wings gather in the Dutch VPRO radio station to record an interview for the show *Popsmuk* . . .

Host "Have you ever regretted The Beatles breaking up?"

Paul "You regret it at the time, you know. But since then, I'm really happy that it happened, 'cos it's allowed me to do things I don't think I would have got into if we had still been in The Beatles because it's a little limiting, you know, The Beatles thing. You had to do things in a certain way. If you wanted to spit, it wasn't as easy as it is in this group."

Host "Do you see the other Beatles sometimes?"

Paul "I see them a little bit, on and off. For me and for them, it's a band that has finished, you know. While for everyone in the newspapers, it's a kind of legend that's finished. But, you've got to remember, that for us, it was just a band, you know. As for us, we're just musicians, so the main thing is just to make music still. That's the main thing."

Host "How have the audiences been so far (on this tour)?"

Paul "It's been good, thanks. It's been very good everywhere we've played. Some of them just sit around a bit, you know. They don't realise they've gone for an evening out, which is the main thing. They should loosen up a bit."

Host "Which countries have you played so far?"

Paul "France, all of Scandinavia, Finland, Norway, Sweden, Germany, Switzerland, I think that's about all . . . And Holland, of course."

Host "Could you say in which countries the audiences have been very nice to you?"

Paul "Well, the best audience, just as an audience, you know, nicest to us, was Paris Olympia, I thought."

Host "I see so few interviews with the group, why is that?"

Paul "Well, normally we do millions, actually. But the thing where you might not see 'em so much is if we don't want to do one, we don't do one. It's the normal kind of thing

John and Yoko, pictured at Selfridges store in London's Oxford Street during a signing session for Yoko's *Grapefruit* book on July 15, 1971. *(Rex Features)*

George with his friends from the Hare Krishna Temple, photographed on March 5, 1970 to promote their second single. *(Hulton-Deutsch Collection/Corbis)*

Ringo on the set of *200 Motels* at Pinewood Studios, Iver, February 1971. *(Pictorial Press)*

John in his studio at Tittenhurst Park, Ascot, during the *Imagine* sessions, June 23, 1971. *(S.I.N.)*

John and George working on 'Oh My Love' during the June 1971 *Imagine* sessions at Ascot. *(S.I.N.)*

George on stage with Eric Clapton during his Concert For Bangla Desh at New York's Madison Square Garden, August 1, 1971. *(Bettman/Corbis)*

The last photograph ever taken of John Lennon in the UK, on August 31, 1971, at London's Heathrow Airport. John and Yoko left for New York that day – and he never returned. *(Rex)*

Paul with Wings during the UK university tour in February, 1972; Denny Laine on top and, left to right below, Denny Sewell, Linda, Paul and Henry McCullough. *(Corbis)*

John and Yoko performing 'Memphis Tennessee' on the *Mike Douglas Show* in New York with guests Chuck Berry and Elephants Memory, recorded February 2, 1972. *(Jeff Albertson/Corbis)*

Paul and his father James, pictured at the Chelsea Reach pub in London during the filming for the *James Paul McCartney* TV special, transmitted in the US on April 16, 1973. *(Rex)*

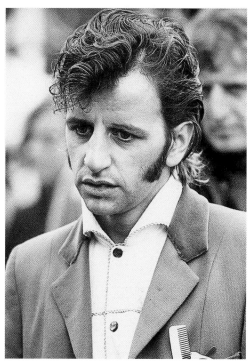

Paul on stage with Henry McCullough and Denny Laine during Wings' European tour in August, 1972. *(Pictorial Press)*

Ringo filming *That'll Be The Day* on the Isle of Wight, October 1972. *(Rex)*

John, newly cropped, and Yoko at the Watergate hearings in Washington DC on June 29, 1973. *(Bettman/Corbis)*

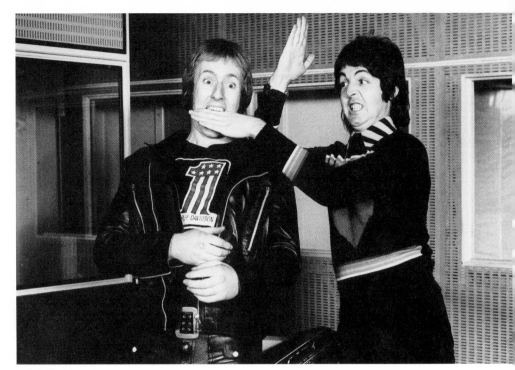

Paul with Wings' second drummer Geoff Britton at Abbey Road Studios in August, 1974. *(LFI)*

George with Billy Preston and US President Gerald Ford at the White House on December 13, 1974. *(Bettmann/Corbis)*

where you have a press agent and he just brings you out in front of everyone, because some of the people we've done interviews with, they're just stupid, you know. So we're trying to avoid those people . . . But it's nice when people want to know what you're doing now rather than what you did ten years ago. The newspapers ask the same questions. It's going over and over and over and over and over all old news that I don't like."

On **Thursday, August 24**, Wings' European Tour closes in Berlin, Germany. Watching the show is Robin Denselow of *The Guardian* newspaper . . .

"Seven weeks on the road and Paul McCartney's new band, Wings, is dramatically improved since the first performance I reported on from the South of France," Denselow pleasantly reports. "Trailing across Europe and playing every night has transformed the band from weak apology to an excellent vehicle for McCartney's, at last, revived talent. At the Deutschlandhalle, a massive concrete barn that is Berlin's answer to the Wembley Pool, Wings faced a large suspicious audience for the first time and defeated them by two encores after a painful uphill fight. At their best, they are now a straightforward rock, dance band with a good line in harmonies, reminiscent at times of The Beatles of *Rubber Soul*. McCartney is rightfully relying more and more on his guitarists Henry McCullough and Denny Laine and the interplay between the three of them is now far tighter and more enthusiastic. His songs are at least giving them some leeway. 'The Mess' for instance, had echoes of The Who in parts, with changes in pace and harmony, a welcome contrast to the nursery rhymes he has been writing of late. Another new song, '1882', was a slow tuneful narrative ballad, a bleak horror story about Victorian England, a thousand times more impressive than his ghastly 'Give Ireland Back To The Irish'. There was a change in McCartney's stage act as well. Faced with hostility, he lost his temper and worked harder than ever. The good material and hopeful finds were all there, but so were some of the early problems. He still includes four or five simplistic songs, presumably so that his wife Linda can play them. These destroy his act and obviously bore the band. Linda's singing was still sub-standard with a tendency to go flat as soon as she moved away from the piano. If McCartney could overcome problems like that, he will be ready for a successful British comeback."

Wednesday, August 30
John and Yoko hold their One To One charity concert at Madison Square Garden in New York . . .

Paul (speaking in November) ". . . John asked me to do a charity concert with him in New York, but I said no, because I knew Klein would have been in the background pulling the strings. It's a pity now that we didn't do it but we *will* do things, I'm sure. I don't see any reason why all four Beatles shouldn't be on stage at some time, all playing together and having a good time. I don't think you'll ever get The Beatles reforming, because that's all gone. The Beatles were a special thing in a special era and I really couldn't see it all coming together again. But I think it's daft to assume that just because we had a couple of business upsets, we won't ever see each other again or that if John has a concert some time, we won't go and play on it. John's great, really. He tells the truth all the time. That's why people think he's a bit crazy. He doesn't seem to hide anything. Really, he and Yoko are very reasonable."

John "That Madison Square Garden gig was the best music I've enjoyed playing since the Cavern or even Hamburg. I really enjoyed that gig. You could see I was on the trip all right. It was just the same kinda feeling when The Beatles used to really get into it . . . I got up from the piano in one number and, Jesus, it was like flowing an act or something. Phew, it was just the same as competing in the Olympics, when you've really got to box your best. It was really weird."

Yoko "When I did 'Open Your Box', I really went to the top and thought, 'That's a climax!' But then, John came on stage and started 'Cold Turkey' and he just surpassed it again and did another climax. We had to top each other. I have never seen John do 'Cold Turkey' in that way, it was a beautiful performance."

But in 1974, **John** will admit that the One To One Concert "was fine because it helped a lot of people but it was really hell for me. I ended up putting the whole thing together. Nobody ever seems to know what they're doing. I really got put off after that. I ended up organising the whole show. I'm supposed to ring everybody and I just thought, 'I've had enough of this.' I really got tired of it and then I get badmouthed for doing it. After it, I got attacked for not being as good as The Beatles. So I thought, 'Sod this for a laugh! I'll just make records.' "

Tuesday, September 19
Paul and Linda's home in Scotland receives unwelcome guests . . .

The *Sun* reports, "Police chemists were last night analysing plants taken from two farms owned by ex-Beatle, Paul McCartney. Paul and his wife frequently use the farm in Kintyre, Argyll, as their West of Scotland retreat. But the McCartneys were in London when Argyll county police made a sudden search earlier this week. Paul knew nothing of the visit until it was over. Once police have a laboratory report, they will prepare a second report for the procurator fiscal. No one has been charged in connection with the search."

Paul "I've been doing horticulture for a couple of years at the farm. My dad's a keen gardener. I think it's rubbed off. We got a lot of seeds in the post and we didn't know what they were. We just planted them all and five of them came up . . . illegal."

Thursday, September 28
Instead of Paul featuring in a news story, it is his old English sheepdog, Martha, the inspiration behind The Beatles' 1968 track 'Martha My Dear', that makes the news when she gives birth to puppies, upsetting Paul's neighbours in St John's Wood due to the litter's constant barking . . .

Joe Hall, *Evening Standard* "But Paul's reply was, 'They're a load of old colonels!' Police had been called into the dispute and neighbours are rather upset by a four-letter word note pushed through one of their letterboxes. The neighbours in the quiet avenue at the back of Lords cricket ground began getting hot under the collar a couple of months ago when Paul's pet Martha gave birth to puppies. They complained that the eight pups were barking all day and keeping them awake at night as well. 'They woke us up at 3:30 one morning and I went round to see him the next day to ask him to keep them quiet,' said one neighbour. 'Unfortunately he was away at the time and I spoke to the McCartneys' nine-year-old daughter, Heather. She said there were ten dogs in the house altogether.' When the noise continued, the neighbour wrote the McCartneys a note asking them to try and keep the dogs quiet. But the barking went on, and on, according to neighbours. So three of the neighbours signed a complaint form, which was delivered by police from their local station. 'It was an order for them to stop the nuisance within 14 days or face a £20 fine,' said one of the neighbours. 'But when the police came back to see us, 14 days later, we decided not to press it any further. The dogs had been much better and we hadn't heard them nearly so much.' But then, a couple of days later, the note sent earlier to the McCartneys was pushed through the neighbour's letterbox. Scrawled across it in red ink was a four-letter word reply. 'It was inexcusable,' said the neighbour. 'There was no need at all to send that to us. We were furious! It just shows a dreadful lack of manners. Our three children used to adore him, but now they have nothing but contempt for him.' "

Paul "The dogs were a little exuberant, but they are much quieter now. They are a load of colonels around here. They're all mad. I don't care what they say."

A neighbour in St John's Wood "There is no question of the dogs being ill-treated. The RSPCA have been to the house in the past and say that the dogs are not being neglected. Apparently, the McCartneys treat them as vegetarians and don't give them meat. But they get fish and other food every day. The real question is whether so many dogs should be kept in the house all the time. The only time they seem to go out is when they are in the garden. There are between 10 and 13 in the house at present. They have been much quieter for the past weeks."

Monday, October 23

At the Butlins holiday camp in the Isle of Wight, Ringo begins filming *That'll Be The Day*, starring the *Godspell* singer, David Essex . . .

Ringo "It's just about a guy, David Essex, growing up and I'm one of the influences. After Butlins, I work in a fairground so I take the guy to work in the fairgrounds and introduce him to his first lady and from then on, he'll have anything . . . camels, donkeys, he doesn't care. I introduce him to the naughtier side of life."

DECEMBER

John and Yoko's 70-minute self-produced film *Imagine* receives a preview screening in Soho, London . . .

John "It's for TV. It's surreal and it goes over the top of probably every track of the *Imagine* album and three or four tracks of Yoko's *Fly* album. We were shooting as we were recording. We're not making it as a documentary. We're making it like TV footage and then we'll send it round the world and hope for the best."

In attendance at the London preview is the UK music journalist, Robert Brinton, who disapprovingly writes "Just imagine a seventy-minute bore. The film opens with John and Yoko strolling hand in hand engulfed in thick fur coats . . . mists swirl around, until you expect to witness Frankenstein pop from a hedgerow any second, then the couple gracefully disappear from view. Seventy odd minutes later, the same couple are frolicking around near the sea shore, writing their names in the sand, then they clasp hands again and slowly walk out along a ramp leading nowhere in particular but out into the dirty great ocean. An orchestra swells to a true Hollywood finale, then, thankfully, their film ends. Mid-way through, I found myself hoping the film would take some kind of turn to stop it becoming the crashing bore it is . . . If it was intended as a harmless bit of fun, then the only thing I could think about was why waste seventy minutes of everyone's time when there are more laughs in a *Tom & Jerry* cartoon . . ."

Also in the audience of this special screening is Chris Charlesworth of the *Melody Maker*, who writes, "Imagine a series of those meaningless short films they show on *Top Of The Pops* when they can't get the artist to appear and you're most of the way towards forming a picture of John Lennon's *Imagine* film, which had a press preview last week. If it proves nothing else, it dispels some doubts; Mr and Mrs Lennon are certainly very fond of each other. But it doesn't take seventy minutes to prove that point. For seventy minutes we have pictures of John and Yoko walking hand in hand and sailing in their lake in the grounds of Tittenhurst Park, playing chess, walking through doors, bathing, eating and entertaining some guests. After fifteen minutes, I was yawning, another fifteen brought in acute boredom and after the hour elapsed, I was dearly wishing that someone would turn the lights up. The film was shot, apparently, at the same time as the sessions for the *Imagine* album. How much more interesting it would have been to see a film of the actual recording sessions with Lennon making the music instead of wallowing in these supposedly arty sketches."

Friday, December 1
In the UK, Wings release their new single 'Hi Hi Hi' / 'C Moon'. The former, which is subsequently banned by the BBC for its apparent suggestive lyrics, was written in Spain before the mammoth Wings tour of the summer . . .

'Hi Hi Hi'

Paul "The BBC got some of the words wrong. But I suppose it is a bit of a dirty song if sex is dirty and naughty. I was in a sensuous mood in Spain when I wrote it. To me, it was just a song to close our act and since it went down well when we toured the Continent, I thought it would be a good single. I think it's the best single we've done as Wings."

'C Moon'

Paul " 'C Moon' was inspired by a line in a Sam The Sham & The Pharaohs single 'Woolly Bully', 'Let's not be L7', which, if you put L and a 7 next to each other, you make a square. Similarly, if you put a moon and a C together, they make a circle. This is something I worked out with my mathematical brain and wrote a song about it. I'm hoping to get the word started in the Oxford Dictionary of Language within two years, this is my ambition. I wrote 'C Moon' in London recently. Denny, our drummer, plays cornet on it, Henry plays drums, Denny (Laine) bass, I, the bass player, play piano and Linda, the pianist, plays tambourine."

Ringo "For me, none of Paul's records have been really great. I think, at this moment, he's getting his band together and no band is going to be the greatest group in the world when they first start. We can all play together but it takes more than just being able to play together to get into what The Beatles was. It's something else. It's the relationship and everything. Maybe later on, he will come out with something that's extraordinary, but at the moment, he's given me nothing that's really wiped me out."

Saturday, January 6

Disc & Music Echo reports "George Harrison's eagerly awaited new album is titled *The Magic Is Here Again* and was co-produced by him with Eric Clapton. No release date has been set. The black & white sleeve shows George working over a rainbow guitar. He has also written most of the material for Cilla Black's next album."

Monday, January 8 (USA)

Yoko Ono releases her solo double-album *Approximate Infinite Universe* . . .

Yoko "I wrote the material for this album in about a month. Usually I get the first line, then the lyrics and then the melody, which often come together. Many of the songs John wouldn't even hear until we were playing them in the studio. Sometimes I would go to the studio earlier than he would because he would be sleeping or something and then he would come in an hour later and we would show him what we were doing."

Monday, January 15

American newspaper reporter, Sandra Shevey "John Lennon wore a sweat shirt with AMERICA embossed on it, patriotic red-white-and blue shoes, and a peace button. The light in the small New York flat glinted on his gold granny specs and he was chain smoking. Lennon, now 36, gulps some coffee. He looks as though he needs a long rest from the social causes and protest songs, which have replaced Beatlemania . . . Yoko, who is 40, sits by his side. A white, cotton laced blouse clings kimono-tight to her small, round bosom and thick dark hair fringes an inscrutable, impassive face. On his first marriage, **Lennon** says, 'I am not putting down my first marriage, but what I found out when I married Yoko is that I never had a relationship with a woman before, that I had no idea how to have one. Lots of guys will probably snigger, but I'm admitting it. It was an impossibility because of the way I was brought up. In school we'd shout at girls on the bus, whistle at them in the park or perhaps have a bit of snuggling before we ran home. We were raised to have a relationship with other men, on the football field or whatever it was. So I had no idea how to treat a woman. I thought she was someone you met at a party, and whom you either dated or you didn't. Certainly you couldn't talk music with them, or even discuss rock'n'roll. Like most men, I was terrified of the opposite sex . . . Yoko was portrayed as the shrew who broke up The Beatles, the vamp who ruined John's music by making him turn away from images and humour, to be political and serious. It's almost a cliché, the bitchy wife. Even though Paul and I were shouting at each other long before, people would still say, "If it wasn't for Yoko and Linda, The Beatles would still be together." Well, that's idiotic. Paul and I were moving into musically different directions before Yoko and Linda arrived. I write music for my own sake, so if you don't like the music I'm making now, well, don't buy it and forget about it and don't bother me. It's only one album, one time, so don't let's defy it. But as soon as you rock the boat, try to be different, they try to put you in your place. Refusing to be the myth blows their minds. "Get back to your place, boy. You had your lucky break. You got your cash and we said you're a famous star. Now, what else do you want?" Well, that ain't good enough for me. I don't want to be an Uncle Tom, and they'll say nice things when you're dead. I'm still being told to grow up. Grow up means shut up, clean up, dress up and die. And then you're allowed to live. I refuse to live half dead, which is what most people do.' "

John's anger increases, 'I could go on repackaging my first big hit, but that doesn't interest me although I could probably get more cars and more money if I did that. But God knows I'm not interested in making money because I'm having enough problems with what I already have. The Beatles generated a billion billion, but it's all on paper or in a box or it's been spent or somebody has a business built on it. Nobody actually has it.' "

Sunday, February 4

David Blundy of the *Sunday Times* writes "Beatlemania began to twitch back into life in Liverpool last week as ageing fans campaigned to save The Cavern, birthplace of The Beatles and the tunes the world danced to in the Sixties. But the only new sounds to emanate from The Cavern in 1973 are the roar of bulldozers and the rhythmic rattle of pneumatic drills. British Rail, planning an underground loop line, will be sinking a waste disposal shaft through the place where John, Paul, George and Ringo strummed their first notes. The Cavern is a small, dark hole in the wall off Mathew Street in the centre of Liverpool. It smells dank, the bare walls are pitted with ancient slogans ((Up with CND, I Love Paul) and at least one rat scuttled out of the gents on Thursday evening. But the owner, Roy Adams, feels it ought to be a Grade 1 listed building at least on a par with Liverpool Cathedral. 'We get more visitors down here than the Cathedral does,' says Adams. 'We get Americans, Canadians, Japanese, French, Dutch, Germans. There's no justice in it.' He says he would have put up a more vigorous fight but British Rail's notice to quit was delivered a year ago to the wrong address and he received it only recently. 'The kids are signing petitions and they even offer to stage a sit-in when the demolition men start work,' he says . . .

"The Cavern still plays a nostalgic half-hour of Beatle music at midnight but most members prefer to rave to other Liverpool groups. The Beatles themselves are showing less concern than British Rail over the club that helped to make them rich and famous. Ringo has said that he might make a sentimental journey. Paul McCartney has expressed an interest. Not a word from George or John. 'British Rail have been very decent,' says Adams. 'They are trying to find a way of saving the club. The only possibility is shifting the disposal site and putting a concrete roof over the club. That could cost us £20,000.' 'All we need,' says Bob Wooler, the resident DJ at The Cavern for eight years, 'is a little help from our friends.' "

Monday, March 19
At Elstree Studios in Borehamwood, Hertfordshire, on the set of his new ITC television special, *James Paul McCartney*, **Paul** speaks candidly to reporters . . .

"I've been talking to John recently," he reveals. "I'm not sure what's going to happen to Apple, as everyone keeps changing his mind. But the only thing that has prevented us from getting together again has been Allen Klein's contractual hold over The Beatles' name," prophetically adding, "When he is out of the way, there is no real reason why we shouldn't get together."

Wings release 'My Love' as a single in the UK on **Friday, March 23** . . .

'My Love'

Paul " 'My Love' was the first song I ever owned. Someone else had always owned everything else I had written. 'My Love' was my definitive one for Linda, written in the early days of our relationship, and that came easily. We had an interesting moment on the session where we were going to cut it live at Abbey Road Studios, and the guitar player (Henry McCullough) came over to me right before the take. We knew what we were going to do as a band, and the orchestra was arranged and he said, 'Do you mind if I try something different on the solo?' It was one of those moments where I could have said, 'I'd rather you didn't, just stick to the script,' but I thought he sounded like he's got an idea, and I said, 'Sure.' He then came out with the really good guitar solo on the record. It's one of the best things he ever played. So that was like, 'Wow!' It was one of the best solos I had ever heard."

Saturday, March 24

Following the 'I'm The Greatest' session in Los Angeles, at the Sunset Sound Recorders Studio on Tuesday, March 13, featuring John, George and Ringo, the *New Musical Express* prints on its front page, "Beatles Denial – Reports elsewhere of a Beatles recording reunion were this week denied by a spokesman for John Lennon, George Harrison and Ringo Starr. He said the rumours that the trio was working together with Paul McCartney in Los Angeles were wildly inaccurate but that as has become common practice since The Beatles' split, Lennon, Harrison and Starr occasionally helped to back each other. 'All that's been happening this time,' he added, 'is that George joined Ringo on two tracks of Ringo's new solo album. John was in town and he helped out on a vocal track. The Beatles are definitely not reuniting. They just appreciate each other's music. That's all there is.' "

John "Only the report of it made it out to be something special. When you get down on your instrument you're playing, you're doing a take and when you look up and notice who you're playing with, it may be Ringo or it may be Jim (Keltner) and it's just like going to dinner with one friend and going to dinner with another. You might be closer to one friend, but when you're out to dinner with somebody, you are with whomever you are with at the time. But it just happened that the three of us were there and it wasn't anything incredibly significant. But it was enjoyable. I think it was more interesting or glamorous for the people around us who are saying, 'There are three of them there,' instead of just one or two. But we were just being ourselves. When it gets down to work, we are just musicians. We are not stars, we are just musicians."

Producer, Richard Perry "George had started to participate in the *Ringo* sessions before John came down. Ringo had played the tracks to John and he immediately wrote a song for Ringo. This turned out to be a sort of chronology of Ringo's life with The Beatles, as well as a brief history of his childhood through teenage years, onto becoming one of The Beatles. The song was called 'I'm The Greatest'. It was on that session that John came down. It was the first time I had met John, and to say that it was an exciting experience to work with him would be a gross understatement. It was really unique and quite special and something I shall never forget. We started to run the song down. It wasn't quite complete so there was also that very special thrill of experiencing a song being completed in the studio by John Lennon. We all sort of gathered around the piano and chipped in our ideas and helped complete it. Then the phone rang and it was George, who said, 'I hear there's a track going on. Is it okay if I come down?' So I said, 'Hold on a minute?' And I asked John if it was okay. I mean, here I am asking John if George can come down. So John said, 'Well, yes, of course. Tell him to get down here and help me finish this bridge.' And that was very much like John. It was on that session that the three Beatles played for the first time since the split. Paul, I'm sure would have been there, too, but it was at the time when he couldn't come into the country."

The subsequent 'Beatles To Reform' hysteria in the music press is soon quashed when **John** issues this slightly bitter, mock press release from New York. It is entitled 'Newswecanalldowithout' . . .

In part in reads "Although John and Yoko and George, and George and Ringo have played together often, it was the first time the three ex-Beauties have played together since, well, since they last played together. As usual, an awful lot of rumours, if not downright lies, were going on, including the possibility of impresario Allen De Klein of grABKCo playing bass for the other three in an 'as-yet-untitled' album called I Was A Teenage Fat Cat. Producer, Richard Perry, who planned to take the tapes along to sell them to Paul McCartney, told a friend, 'I'll take the tapes to Paul McCartney.' The extreme humility that existed between John and Paul seems to have evaporated. 'They've spoken to each other on the telephone, and in English, that's a change,' said a McCartney associate. 'If only everything were as simple and unaffected as McCartney's new single "My Love" ', then maybe Dean Martin and Jerry Lewis would be reunited with the Marx Bros., and Newsweak (sic) could get a job,' said an East African official – Yours up to the teeth – John Lennon and Yoko Ono."

Apple Records promoter, Pete Bennett "I first heard 'My Love' when a tape was shipped to me from London and my gut feeling was that Paul McCartney did not feel that it would be a No. 1 record. I was so excited about this record's potential that I had acetates made that were sent to every major radio station in the country. I received a phone call from the Eastmans asking me what I thought of the record. I told them that this was a No. 1 record and the record went to No. 1."

Saturday, March 31
From America, it is announced that Allen Klein will not be renewing his management contract with John, George and Ringo . . .

Paul "Let's get one thing straight, Klein did not break with John, George and Ringo. They broke with him. Afterwards, there was a little retraction on the sports page where each of them, in turn, just quietly and briefly said, 'Thanks for that. We'll save our money now.' That's about all I ever heard about it. John turns it round by saying, 'But you're always right, aren't you?' I came from Liverpool, I thought the idea was to get it right and it was surprising to find out that if you did get it right, people would turn it around and say, 'But you're always right, aren't you?' "

Monday, April 2 (USA)
The Beatles' *1962–1966* and *1967–70* greatest hits double-album compilations are released in the UK . . .

UK music reporter Roy Carr unflatteringly reviews the four discs "Listen kids and listen hard. It is alleged that the only reason why this brace of Beatles double-albums has suddenly been unloaded upon an unsuspecting public is purely a political manoeuvre. The prime motivation is to combat a similar American bootleg pack (*Alpha Omega*) that has been extensively advertised on US TV. Such is the structure of both American and International laws, it is apparently easier (and less costly) to bung out an officially endorsed compilation than take on the entire kit 'n' caboodle before a High Court Judge. And at just two pence under eight bloody quid for the whole four albums, what do you receive for such expenditure? I'll tell you, a shoddy and overpriced package of most of The Beatles and our greatest moments . . . If this is supposedly a 'definitive' Beatles collection, then someone somewhere has blatantly sold the lads and the public short. Taking into account the price of £3.99 per double-album, here was an opportunity to do a truly remarkable job of premium packaging, with photographs, notes, recording data and just about everything that would have made it more indispensable than it already is . . . The tracks are still as compelling as the day we first heard them. But the cardinal sin about these albums is that in the illustrious name of The Beatles, someone has seen fit to perpetrate the ultimate industry rip-off. All I can add is if George Harrison could see his way to release two three-album sets of newly recorded material at a reasonable price, and The Rolling Stones could put out their *Hot Rocks* collection at a reduced retail price, why not The Beatles? Considering that all these tracks have recouped their original production costs a thousand fold and that there is a minimum of overheads, how come such an inflated price? The Fat Man lives."

John "Allen Klein knocked out the basic list for the *Red* and *Blue* albums and then we'd just look down it and say, 'Yes, no,' and so on. I made sure they put that picture which I got Linda (McCartney) to take of the same pose as our very first album . . . No one can release old Beatles product without an okay from each of us. I like packages, you know. I approve of anything I would buy myself. I'd buy The Beatles' one . . . I asked for George Martin to reproduce the tracks. I was involved in that respect, just checking on the condition of them, because I didn't want lousy versions going out. I wanted them to be as it was. I asked Capitol/EMI, 'Please ask George Martin to take care of this . . . at least he knows what to do. I don't want some strange guy, you know, making dubbed versions of it and putting it out . . .' I want to talk to George Martin, why were we always putting drums on the right and why wasn't it in the middle? I was surprised. I was always thought in terms of mono. Anyway, I wasn't that sold on stereo."

Ringo "People who had the old records bought the double-albums, because their old copies were scratched. But I think a lot of new people bought them as well. To the kids of today, we are just like a myth, like some legend of the past. That's what is going on. It's a new crowd every year."

Paul "I had a new record out and the old re-packaged records were out. I knew they were good but I didn't actually know they were going to do *that* well. So when both records were up at the top, obviously I was chuffed to see mine did even better than The Beatles' stuff, which I knew was great stuff, so I was pleased with that, not from a competition thing, knocking The Beatles off the top spot, or anything. But just the danger that our new record wouldn't do as well because of the new (Beatles) one, that was a bit of a hang-up, you know, your past catching up with you."

Tuesday, April 3

Following the announcement of John, George and Ringo's split with Klein, in an interview conducted at his home in St John's Wood an optimistic Paul, completely unaware of John's previous statement, announces to the journalist Murray Davies . . .

"The Beatles could reform now that the manager Allen Klein is no longer involved," **Paul** says. "When Klein was there, the road was closed against the four of us ever working together. Now, as far as I am concerned, the road is open again. I saw Klein as a sharp operator who could only do harm with The Beatles. The others disagreed. Now they have come round to my way of thinking . . . There's no reason why we should not all work together again now. Klein was one of my main worries. He promised The Beatles the earth but the only one to make any real profit was Klein. At last the others have decided that it was simply not in their best interest to have him as manager . . . Klein takes a percentage and if he could have had his way he would have owned The Beatles lock, stock and barrel. As it is, the money we earn goes into a central pot. Even some of the money I get with Wings goes into the pot. Every time we say we'd split the pot, Klein would say, 'Think of poor old Ringo, he'll get far less than anyone. You'll have to give him some of your share.' Now I hope it's possible we can all own our own out of what we have earned and divide the pot between the four of us. We've all lived well but we have never touched a penny of the lump of money we have earned as Beatles.

"I felt Klein was a shrewd operator and I felt The Beatles were important enough to have a confrontation about him. It was far too important to keep quiet. He's had up to five million dollars out of The Beatles. I know he's had one million dollars recently because he's just been paid. His presence stirred up bad feelings between the other Beatles and me. It just wasn't true that I was trying to take over Apple . . . Klein kept us apart for two years. I was on strike against performing with the others while Klein was in charge. I was staging a boycott. But I was doing a session with Ringo last night for his new album. He said that they simply didn't think that continuing was in their best interests . . . This doesn't mean that The Beatles will go back together as a solid entity but it does mean that the main obstacle has been removed. There are no personal reasons between the four of us why we can't work together. There were some bad feelings between George and I when I sued the other three but that was natural and it has blown away now. There was a lot of publicity about the row between John and myself what with John making up songs about me, but we are happily talking to each other now. That was just John. Now that Klein has gone, the air is clearer than it has been for the past two years. There is a chance that we will do an album or single together but nothing has been discussed. No one is holding up the other three and saying, 'Hey, let's do a gig together.' If we fancied it, if we were all in the right place at the right time, and in the right mood, then we might do something together. Now there is nothing to stop us . . . I did a concert recently and found that few people there had ever seen The Beatles. So if we did get together again, it would be for a generation older than most of the current pop fans. But then, I suppose, we could have the same impact on this generation as we did on the last."

Wednesday, April 4

Meanwhile, at the BBC TV Centre in Wood Lane, London, Paul and Wings appear for the third time on *Top Of The Pops*. Prior to the recording, an upbeat **Paul** faces the Press in his dressing room and reiterates his previous opinions on his former group . . .

"The Beatles thing is loosening up," he announces. "There's no kind of bitterness there anymore, so it means if everyone is really keen and fancied like mad getting a band together, you know, great! There are a few headaches, like where can you go? To Bangladesh? Do the Madison Square Garden big-return-of-The Beatles concert? Or are you gonna keep going on with Wings and keep Wings going on and do Wings concerts and do, like, Wings and Beatles concerts? I don't know. There are all possibilities there, but I can't put my finger on any plan. I haven't got any plans. By the way, I heard the *White Album* the other day, and it sounded great! But I thought *Revolver* was out of tune. I was really annoyed with it for a couple of days. Originally, I thought 'Hey Jude' went on too long. I thought they'd never play it. But you see, I never think I'm much good."

Sunday, April 8
In his New York office, Allen Klein talks for the first time about his management break-up with three of The Beatles . . .

"There were a number of reasons why I didn't propose a renewal of the management contract. But one was just a gut reaction that it was time to let it stop; not so much that I quit. I was going to make a proposal for a continuation of the management contract. Then I decided not to. My position has always been that if things didn't work out for us, we should split. There's no question that the four of us were a great combination in so many ways. I said all along that if I was the one standing in the way I would get out. I said it to George only three weeks ago. Let's see if, with me not there now, they get back together. McCartney would certainly like to. But I would be surprised if the four worked together again as artists."

Klein continues "Paul rejected a £1 million offer by the other Beatles to buy him out of their partnership. But Paul turned it down. He wouldn't take it. He wasn't interested. He doesn't want to sell. He doesn't want to get out, and that's really the problem. Now you have a company with four partners, each of whom has a different interest, and to get each one to agree something, like whether Ringo should make a film, becomes almost impossible. How do they stay partners? It's very hard. I had hoped to arrange a take-over of Apple and The Beatles' interests, merging them with my ABKCO Industries. But my hopes were defeated by McCartney's attitude." Klein goes on to reveal that "ABKCO Industries earned about £2.6 million from its 20 per cent commission on Apple earnings over the four years. But in the last three months of 1972, the commission was only £100,000."

George "When John, Ringo and myself got rid of Allen Klein, our notorious manager, I was five years behind with my taxes and I needed someone to organise me out of all that mess. I wanted someone to help me with my present and future, but unfortunately he would have to get involved with my past. Anyway, a Hare Krishna friend of mine discovered this ruby mine in India and was wondering how he could use it to support the temple. He had met Peter Sellers, who put him in touch with Denis O'Brien, and the Krishna guy put us together."

The America lawyer and accountant Denis O'Brien "I was a fan of The Beatles but I didn't want to deal with one. The stories I heard of record people, I thought they had crawled out of the gutter. But George is an absolutely extraordinary individual. When we met, some kind of synergy occurred between two opposites. George was very centred and I walked away from that first meeting thinking, 'This is the most powerful person I've ever met in my life.' I've met the chairman of Shell, of RTZ, of IBM, of Ford, I've met all these people and I've never met anyone so together as George. I would do anything for this guy."

Monday, April 30 (USA)
Wings continue with their prolific recording output by releasing their new studio album, *Red Rose Speedway* . . .

Tony Tyler, music critic for the *New Musical Express* "*Red Rose Speedway* is certainly the best thing McCartney has done since the great demise and I also think it is the best thing he's likely to do with this band. Not, I hasten to add, because of any lack of talent, but simply because Wings' original briefing went no further than this. Paul makes his stand here, and as far as I am concerned, he's proved the point. And I also think that in the future, he's going to be able to look back on the last three years without cringing, which is more than I suspect Lennon will be able to do."

Paul "*Red Rose Speedway* was the live act. I mean, the album's okay. It has its moments, but nothing approaching the impact of the band in person. After I had heard *Wild Life*, I thought, 'Hell, we have really blown it here.' And the next one after that, *Red Rose Speedway*, I couldn't stand."

Linda "*Red Rose Speedway* was originally going to be a double-album. Denny wrote a song for that and I wrote a song, but then we narrowed it down."

Denny Laine "I thought *Red Rose Speedway* was good as a double-album and more of a showcase for the band. So when it came out as a single-album, I didn't like it as much as *Ram*."

Saturday, May 5
Beatles reunion fervour reaches fever pitch, prompting the music critic, Charles Shaar Murray, to paint a somewhat alternative view on The Beatles alleged get-together in today's *NME*. The piece is entitled "Beatles Reunion? Do We Really Need It?"

In part in reads "The Beatles reunion is the biggest non-story in rock'n'roll. Every day someone says that Paul was on Ringo's session or George was on John's or that the whole bunch of them are closeted somewhere in Los Angeles making, 'Wow', the next Beatles album. But basically, who needs it? We've already got the example of The Byrds hanging over our heads, remember? And once everyone got over the shock, and started listening to the actual outcome of the new venture, all that has happened was that the five people who used to make up the real original Byrds had recorded some songs they'd written (separately) plus a couple of things by their friends. It wasn't a group and it wasn't The Byrds. It was five people who used to be The Byrds, trying hard to pretend that they still were . . . Paul McCartney is doing it with Wings, John and Yoko are still into their political trip, Ringo's happier with his movies and that leaves Harrison. And Lord knows what he's up to, because we haven't heard anything from him since 'Bangla Desh'. John Lennon, Paul McCartney, George Harrison and Ringo Starr, for all practical purposes, have gone their own four separate ways. Let 'em be."

Monday, May 7 (USA)
George meanwhile releases his latest Apple single, 'Give Me Love (Give Me Peace On Earth)' . . .

'Give Me Love (Give Me Peace On Earth)'

George "I once read in the newspaper what Roger McGuinn, of The Byrds, had said. He was about the only one who spotted it, that 'My Sweet Lord' was a prayer, and that's all it was. I had a lot of letters from people saying, 'Oh, you're lost. Why don't you come to our church.' They missed the point. With 'Give Me Love', again it was a personal thing for me and if anybody else got off on it, well, there it was. But it was awareness of what we need, just give me love, thank you. So, at that period, I was really involved and doing a lot of chanting on these little wooden beads during the whole session. It was just a personal thing. Sometimes you open your mouth and you don't know what you are going to say, and whatever comes out is the starting point. If that happens and you are lucky, it can usually be turned into a song. This song is a prayer and personal statement between me, the Lord and whoever likes it."

Thursday, May 10
The 50-minute ITC Television special, *James Paul McCartney* receives its UK TV premiere across the ITV network. The American transmission had occurred on the ABC TV Network on Monday, April 16, but the sight of Paul, Linda and Wings in their first televised special does not sit well with some US critics . . .

New York music critic, Linda Solomon "Paul McCartney dealt a blow for liberty, and self expression, here when the ABC Network devoted an hour of television prime time to his special *James Paul McCartney*. This may be considered a television 'first', since there's always the possibility that solo specials from other former Beatles or big meaty rock groups may now be forthcoming . . . The show presents McCartney, the man and his friends, shown doing what they like best, and playing at being pop stars for fun and profit. But he seems to have lost respect, generally, for his music and he capitalises on and makes sport of The Beatles' at the same time. His only serious performances were material from his three solo albums and his theme song for *Live And Let Die*. I talked to at least half a dozen music absorbing friends, and they all agree that, although there were some fleeting musical diversions, the overall production was low level rubbish, a waste of time, energy and money."

Linda "The American critics were very square about it, I mean really square. They said Paul was too cute and what that has to do with it, I don't know! I think everybody expects God to appear whenever Paul does anything. Personally, I liked the show. But we had to compromise a lot in it, like a lot of our ideas were not in it. You see, it depends if you are going towards the critics or the people. The people loved it."

Paul "I think it worked for what it was. We wanted to do a drag sketch. Do you remember the bit at the end with the dancers? At that point, I was going to come on stage dressed as Diana Ross and Linda was going to be dressed as a man. But they didn't think that was a very good idea. It was a kind of Chevrolet show, and you couldn't go too far or they wouldn't show it. As far as we were concerned, it was a start. We all got on telly and we all got some experience working with cameras and stuff. But I think we could do better . . . I lot of people liked it. Elton John had it showing on his last plane trip. Although he had a choice, he wanted to watch our movie."

On **Friday, May 11**, Wings begin their first British tour, starting with a show at the Bristol Hippodrome . . .

Paul "I've deliberately avoided doing the old numbers, because we didn't want to turn into a second-rate Beatles and be compared to all the groups up and down the Costa Brava. I mean, we've come away from all that, although the others are more keen on The Beatles thing than anyone. Old Denny Laine there is a total Beatles freak! In fact, one night onstage, he suddenly comes out with 'When I was young and so much younger than today,' and I thought, 'God, there's me trying to get away from it.'"

Saturday, May 12
The second night of Wings' first UK Tour reaches Oxford with a show at the New Theatre . . .

The music reporter, Beverley Legge "Paul McCartney's Wings have got off to a tremendous start to their current British Tour. The group gave an extremely tight performance and was able to dramatically raise the pulse rate of an already enthusiastic audience at Oxford. I was among a party of press specially driven out to the city's New Theatre to witness the historic occasion. The set started off slowly with a few unremarkable numbers, during these songs Linda plays organ one-handed while Paul handles bass . . . Paul, always playing the dominant part in the proceedings, suggests that couples may like to cuddle one another during 'My Love'. Henry McCullough's advise that they 'Get 'em off' is greeted warmly, but not carried out . . . All this time, audience reaction has been building. Now comes the grand climax, two wild rock numbers. 'This is one they banned,' says Paul. 'I think it's because it's dirty.' A large selection of the audience knows it, and he's into 'Hi Hi Hi'. People are now on their feet and coming forward, clapping hands above heads. A group of girls leap onstage, but are neatly sidestepped and return looking slightly embarrassed. And so to the final song, 'Long Tall Sally'. This gives Paul a chance to do his cute Little Richard imitation and also winds up the show in a suitable exciting manner."

After the concert, at the nearby Randolph Hotel, Paul, Linda and Wings face thirty members of the press in a sixty-minute conference . . .

One waiting music reporter remarks "Journalists sit waiting for Paul, discussing the show they've just witnessed. 'Incredible,' remarks one. 'Nothing special,' remarks another. 'If it hadn't been for Denny Laine, they'd have been lost.' While another reporter adds that he thought the show was 'Dreadful!' Paul and Linda, arm in arm, then arrive."

Julie Webb, *New Musical Express* "It is as if no one's eaten for a week and the McCartneys have entered bearing a T-bone steak . . . Paul looks like Paul, he doesn't seem to have aged any. And Linda, she looks quite different, really. Better than you might expect, younger, skinnier and prettier."

"The Oxford gig was great," Linda admits. "Even though it was noticeable the crowd didn't get off at the beginning, a challenge is a good thing. I don't worry because we've done enough to know that we always get them off at some point. Like last night in Bristol, they were buzzing all night, but you can't expect them to buzz before you've done anything. Paul's attitude is to go out and fight it. His whole thing is that he wants the band to be good and play well and fight it."

Reporter "Will The Beatles get together again?"

Linda "That's like asking Elizabeth Taylor if she's getting back together with Eddie Fisher."

Reporter "Do you think there will be any more Lennon & McCartney songs written?"

Paul "No."

Reporter "Could Wings ever make it like The Beatles?"

Paul (after pausing) "Obviously not . . ." (After another pause, he continues, now becoming agitated) "Not obviously not. We *could* do it again. The Beatles were four guys, just like any of you. We wanted the lot. We got the lot. Remember that it took The Beatles three years as a professional group to break through and have a hit. Wings have got this far after less than two years."

Reporter "Do the critics bother you?"

Paul "It used to upset me being slagged, but not anymore. I just play what I play. If you like it, you like it. If you don't, you don't. I think I'm good. That's where I leave it. I can dig me. The rest is up to you."

Reporter "What do you think about the present pop scene?"

Paul "I think The Osmonds/Cassidy thing is nice. I like them for what they are. I can see it through the eyes of my daughter or my cousins in Liverpool. But I don't like the intellectual side of pop. Pop has got too intellectual recently."

Reporter "Have you seen Ringo's film *That'll Be The Day*?"

Paul "No, but we did watch the old Beatles film *Help!* at Christmas on TV."

Reporter "What about the future?"

Paul "There are no plans for the future. I just intend to keep on singing."

The gathering concludes and the journalists and accompanying friends climb back into a coach, which takes them back to London. Accompanying Wings on the tour is a juggler and the pub-rock band, Brinsley Schwarz.

Friday, May 25
The Wings tour reaches London, with three nights of performances at the Hammersmith Odeon. Watching the performance in the sold out crowd are the critics Adam Wall, of the *Evening Standard* and Robin Denselow of the *Guardian* newspaper . . .

"The compere, presumably chosen by Paul, prattled away inanely as if it was the kiddies show at the Saturday morning pictures," Wall writes, "and the main act was preceded by a notably unspectacular juggling and balancing duo, complete with an obediently disobedient poodle. One waited for the Tommy Cooper style punch line, but it never came. Perhaps it was all supposed to be kitsch or perhaps Paul had anticipated playing to a theatre of weeny-boppers. In fact, the audience was a fairly typical Rock cross section, although possibly more clean-cut than usual. But after such a dismaying start, it was all the more pleasurable when it quickly emerged that Paul McCartney and Wings are a superior pop group, honest, full of spark and eager to please. After absorbing some recent reviews of Paul's music, I quite expected him to come across as a longer-haired version of Val Doonican. The first number dismissed that notion. While the sound may not have been wild enough to satisfy the heavy-metal freaks, Wings can certainly punch out a solid Rock number. They never get hysterical and after repeatedly high doses of Alice Cooper and David Bowie, seem almost quaintly mid-Sixties by comparison. With little glitter to distract the attention, it was the music that counted. By and large it stood up well. Paul still has a knack of writing songs that resolve satisfyingly and become instantly familiar. Echoes of The Beatles at their melodic best could be heard in a song like 'My Love', Wings' current single . . . But what was rather disappointing was the band's lack of instrumental finesse. Apart from Henry McCullough's astringent guitar work, most of the playing was unambitiously sparse and, on occasion, barely adequate. It wasn't until right at the end of the show, beyond the point where the group could be concerned with making an impression that they worked up a sweat and began to play as a tightly knit unit. The show stopper was that rock'n'roll classic, 'Long Tall Sally', which is surely where we all came in more than a decade ago at a small Liverpool club."

"When it was announced that Paul McCartney had chosen the Odeon, Hammersmith to give his first London concert for eight years, there was a great shaking of heads throughout the rock world," Denselow writes. "The hall has poor sound and there is a gulf between audience and performer. Worse still, it was there that The Beatles held their triumphant Christmas shows in the mid-Sixties. Comparisons would be inevitable, and considering the track record of McCartney's new band Wings, they would be embarrassing. Yet, surprisingly, the scenes at the Odeon were enough to make any ageing teenager choke with nostalgia. Halfway through their set, Wings moved into The Beatles' concert formation, with McCartney and the lead guitarist, Henry McCullough, yelling face to face into one microphone, Denny Laine looking like a solitary Lennon on another, and Linda McCartney standing discreetly aside. From that moment, on one of Laine's two excellent songs, the hall erupted into a standing ovation, while a few hysterically minded young ladies tried to rush the stage. McCartney's painful comeback has succeeded at last. By bashing out rock'n'roll he can still get an audience to their feet, and by crooning a sloppy ballad he can still get into the top ten. It is a pity that he has, so far, written only three songs ('Maybe I'm Amazed', 'C Moon' and 'Single Pigeon') to match his best Beatles material and it is a pity that McCullough and Laine are under used."

At the end of Wings' tour, Brinsley Schwarz recalls . . . "The tour was a good experience for us. We learnt a lot from it. We all got on well together and we really enjoyed it. I had never seen Paul McCartney play, so that was a treat. It was quite amazing, everywhere we would go, everyone who saw him would just smile. There just seemed to be a good feeling throughout the tour. The last date was at Hammersmith Odeon and there was a party afterwards. We played our own set at the Kensington pub later and went to the party. When we arrived, there was no one on stage. So we thought, 'Right, let's set up the gear.' It was really insane. By the end, we had Elton John on piano, Denny Laine on bass, Henry McCullough on guitar and Keith Moon on drums."

Paul "When we toured Britain, there were a lot of very young kids in the audience. Maybe it's partly because we did 'Mary Had A Little Lamb' as a single. But grown-ups said terrible things about us and I did get very depressed. Everything I did was so slagged off by the critics. I began to believe all those people who were saying I wasn't very good and that I could not make decent records. I began to think I had lost the knack. I thought, 'That's it, I've lost it and it won't come back.' Before that point I had thought very seriously about jacking it all in and spending the rest of my life just farming or something."

Friday, June 1
Paul and Wings release the single 'Live And Let Die', the soundtrack to the latest James Bond film, the first to star the former star of *The Saint*, Roger Moore . . .

Paul (during the film's production at Pinewood Studios in Iver, Buckinghamshire) "I'm really chuffed to be doing the theme for Roger. I think he'll be great in the Bond role and I'm working on the right music for him. I'm also doing two or three songs for the film. Maybe we'll be using music played by Wings. I'm not sure about writing the whole film score – we'll just have to see how it goes . . . I read the *Live And Let Die* book in one day, started writing that evening and carried on the next day and finished it by the next evening . . . I sat down at the piano, worked something out and then got in touch with George Martin, who produced it with us. Linda wrote the middle reggae bit of the song. We rehearsed it as a band, recorded it and then left it up to him . . . I wouldn't have liked it if my music was going to replace John Barry's, that great 'James Bond' theme. I know I'd miss that. I go to see him turn round and fire down the gun barrel. Our bit comes after he's done that and after the three killings at the beginning. I'm good at writing to order with things like that. I'd like to write jingles really, I'm pretty fair at that, a craftsman. It keeps me a bit tight, like writing to a deadline, knowing I've got two minutes three seconds with a definitive story theme."

Paul, shortly after the film's release in July, "I enjoyed not being able to get into the cinema in Jamaica because it was sold out. You know, I told the guy at the door, 'But I wrote the bloody tune!' But the man said, 'No use, man. Get out!' "

Hot on the heels of 'Give Me Love', George's new studio album *Living In The Material World*, is released in the UK on **Friday, June 22** . . .

Tony Tyler, *New Musical Express* "There was a time when I considered George Harrison the finest packaged object since frozen pizza. I marvelled at the economy of his guitar breaks and I gasped at the uncanny way his phrases neatly underscored a subtle vocal point that either Jowl (John) or Porn (Paul) had just made . . . All this has changed. All things must pass. I'm not sure when I first began (mentally) to assign George the title of 'The World's Most Boring Man'. The suspicion may have crept in with the dire ennui-making *All Things Must Pass* . . . *Living In The Material World* is George's second solo album. It is an improvement on *All Things Must Pass*, pleasant, competent, vaguely dull and inoffensive. It's also breathtakingly original and, lyrically at least, turgid, repetitive and so damn Holy I could scream . . . I doubt very much if *Living In The Material World* would ever do well if it weren't for George's antecedents . . ."

George "Sometimes they (the critics) feel threatened. They feel threatened when you talk about something that just isn't 'Be-Bop-A-Lula'. Not all of them, but a lot of them. They don't want to hear anything and if you say something that is not just trivia, then their only way out of that is to say, 'You're lecturing us,' or, 'You're preaching,' which it isn't either. And if you say the words God or Lord, it makes some people's hair curl. They just can't come to terms with the words, or with the idea that there may just be something else going on apart from their individual egos. So a lot of people had a bit of trouble with that album . . . I don't know why, but for me, I felt something else in my life. There is a very strong positive alternative to just living a mundane existence. I have always been one for taking opportunities and the biggest opportunity in any of our lives is to become realised; to find out what it is all about and the point of what we are doing here, but it takes a lot of effort to do it. I mean, that's the whole thing, is that each soul is potentially divine and the goal is to manifest that divinity. Each living being is entitled to be Christ Conscious and actually had to become Christ Conscious in the end. And that is why we are all in these bodies. We are given the senses, which we experience through our senses, our experience becomes knowledge, and our knowledge liberates us from the tedium of just being boring ignorant people."

Friday, June 29
John and Yoko meanwhile spend time attending the senate Watergate hearings in Washington DC. For this rare public appearance he is seen wearing a newly cut, extremely short hairstyle . . .

John "I only went once to see Watergate but it made the papers because I was recognised straight away. I thought it was better on TV anyway because I could see more. When it first came on, I watched it live all day, so I just had the urge to actually go. I had other business in Washington, anyway. The public was there and most Senators have children, so every time there was a break in the proceedings, I had to sign autographs. I was looking like a Buddhist monk at the time because all of my hair had been chopped off and I thought nobody would spot me. They spotted Yoko before me and assumed, rightfully, that I must be with her. It was quite a trip."

Thursday, July 12
Meanwhile, back in the UK, the British tabloid newspaper, the *Daily Mirror*, interestingly writes about the discovery of an archive live Beatles tape from 1962 . . .

"Today, the long-parted Beatles will be offered a slice of their raucous, glittering past for the small consideration of an extremely large chunk of money. And if The Beatles turn down the offer, a part of their life, when it was all beginning for them, will be locked away, maybe forever. The slice of life, unedited, raw, vital, is a two-hour tape recording of their appearances before the boozy, late-night crowds at the Star Club in Hamburg during the winter of 1962 . . . It was there that The Beatles, hammering away twelve hours a day into the bleary-eyed dawn, evolved their music. And it was there that the million-dollar tape was made with toughie Lennon screaming at the Germans to 'Shurrup' and loosing the odd four-letter word just to keep the party atmosphere going. The recording was made by a friend of The Beatles, King Size Taylor, who ran a group called King Size Taylor & The Dominoes . . . King Size, now out of show business and well into the butchering business in Southport, Lancashire, forgot about the tape for ten years and then turned it up at his home the other day after he'd read all about the revival of rock . . . King Size Taylor says he bought the rights to the tapes because at the time, he asked The Beatles permission and they said sure, as long as he bought them a few drinks. The financial potential is tremendous. There is enough material for two albums and if they sold only 2,000,000 each, an easy thing for The Beatles, the revenue would amount to about £8,000,000.

"I sat in at a special hearing of the tape in a small backroom in Holborn, London. I was prepared for a scratchy recording, maybe of interest to hardened Beatles buffs and no one else. Not so. I found it to be one of the most exciting sounds I've ever heard from the group. Their hard driving rock'n'roll from the golden period of 1962 was all there and more. John, George and Paul all have vocals and Lennon is heard shouting for his girlfriend of those days, a barmaid called Bettina. Lennon, leaning into the mike and full of the joy of all mankind at the Festive Season, shouts at the ho-ho-ing German tipplers, 'I don't know if you can understand me or not, but piss off! You got that? Christmas or no Christmas.' Allan Williams (The Beatles' first manager) will be contacting Neil Aspinall, the managing director of Apple. He will ask for a down-payment of £100,000 for the tape recording and a cut of the record sales. 'It would be ironic if I made some money out of these boys at last,' Williams says."

Sunday, July 29

Syndicated news report "John Lennon, who has settled in New York with his wife, Yoko Ono, is planning to sell Tittenhurst Park, the Ascot estate he bought in 1969. Mr Lennon, who bought the white-walled mansion and 72 acres for £150,000, is likely to ask £500,000 for it. Last week, Lennon possessions at the house were being crated and removed for shipping to the US. A young, long-haired American called Peter Bendrey was supervising the work. Says Mr Bendrey, who is living in one of the cottages on the estate, 'Negotiations are under way for a sale and John will definitely not be returning here. In fact, he has no plans to return to England. Tittenhurst Park is a beautiful place and I am sure he is sad to part with it, but it takes so much to keep going.' Tittenhurst Park, once owned by Westward TV chief, Peter Cadbury, used to be open to the public at certain times of the year. When John Lennon bought it, he was asked if he would allow the public in. He said, 'Will I open the grounds? Will I hell!' "

On **Wednesday, August 1**, the UK tabloid columnist, Graham Saunders reveals that "Yoko Ono, on a telephone from New York, told me that she has been to see doctors in Britain and America about a problem, which is worrying her and John. They are concerned that after three years of marriage, they are still failing to have a baby . . ."

Yoko "At one time we thought there might be a problem, but now we have been told that there is nothing physically wrong with either of us. I have always been a nervous sort of person and John and I have had a lot of problems, which have caused tensions. Such as John's continuing battle with the American authorities over his application to stay there, the considerable hate mail we receive and my own battle for the custody of my daughter, Kyoko. The doctors have told me that too much worry and tension could easily affect me and we have reached a time in our lives where we would like to have a family."

Saturday, September 1

The *Disc & Music Echo* reports "McCullough Quits Wings". The article reveals that "Henry McCullough has left Wings. A spokesman for the band this week gave 'Musical differences' as the reason for the guitarist's departure and added, 'He has left by mutual agreement with the rest of the band and the move is considered by all to be the best.'

Wings leave to record in Lagos on September 1 and so far nothing has been said about a replacement."

Paul "Henry was asked to play a certain guitar lick on one of Denny (Laine)'s songs and he refused. Next morning, he phoned up and said he wanted to quit. Henry left over what they call 'musical differences' and it was actually that. We were rehearsing and I asked him to play a certain bit. He was loath to play it and kind of made an excuse about it couldn't be played. I, being a bit of a guitarist myself, knew it could be played. And rather than let it pass, I confronted him with it and we had a confrontation. He left rehearsals a bit choked and then rang up to say he was leaving. I thought, 'Fair enough.' So it was exactly the stereotyped 'musical differences'. "

Linda "I must own up, I think it's better. I know we had far more fun recording *Band On The Run* than any previous one. There was no row when Henry left. Somebody picked that up, but it's not true. It was all over a silly musical thing on Denny's song. Denny had a song and Henry was asked to play this little bit but he didn't. Then he rang up and said, 'I'm quitting!' We haven't seen him since. When Henry left, we thought, 'Right, fair enough.' "

Also departing from Wings at this time is the drummer, Denny Seiwell, who announces his decision to quit an hour before Wings were due to fly out from Gatwick Airport . . .

Paul "Denny Seiwell left about an hour before the plane took off. I think he was just uptight about recording in Africa. It was as simple as that. So we just went aboard, had a few drinks and waited till we got to Nigeria."

Linda "Denny rang up five minutes before we were leaving to record in Lagos and just said, 'Hey, man, I can't make the trip.' I don't think he wanted to go to Africa. I think it was a bit much, but then again, I think everybody should do what they want. That's what we said Wings should be. If anybody fancies leaving, great . . . We knew Denny (Laine) would come to Lagos. I think Denny has always been very happy in Wings. I don't think he's considered doing anything else. He was, after all, part of the nucleus."

Denny Laine "When Henry and Denny left, we knew we had to be better than what we had done before, so we came up with *Band On The Run*."

The now depleted Wings line-up of Paul, Linda and Denny continue with their journey from Gatwick to record in Lagos, Nigeria . . .

Paul "The idea to go to Lagos was originally just to have some fun, because I didn't fancy recording in London. I fancied getting out and EMI have got studios all over the world, including one in communist China, but because that was so far away, we decided to go to Lagos, because it would be sunny and warm. Then when we got there, we thought, 'What are we going to do?' So I played drums, Linda played piano and mellotron, Denny Laine added some extra guitar parts and between us we managed to make the sound a bit fuller. They were even building the studio when we got there."

Linda "On the album, I play piano and moog and Paul plays the drums. He's quite fantastic. Through the whole Beatles thing, he is very involved with drums. He played on *McCartney* but didn't get into it. That was like a one-off. But with this one, he thought,

'Right!' Denny has written one song on the album, which is just lovely. Paul wrote little bits with him."

Paul "We thought that it would be warm and sunny out in Africa. We thought it would be like a fab holiday place but it's not the kind of place you'd go for a holiday. It's warm and tropical but it's the kind of place you'd have monsoons. We caught the end of the rainy season and there were tropical storms all the time. There were power cuts, too and loads of insects. It does bother some people but we're not creepy-crawly freaks. Linda doesn't mind lizards. But someone else, for instance the engineer we took out, who did *Sgt. Pepper* and *Abbey Road*, he couldn't stand them. So a couple of the lads put a spider in his bed. It was all a bit like scout camp. The worst a lizard can do is bite you. So we're not freaked out by that, not like Ringo's wife, Maureen, who can't even stand a fly in her room. If one comes near her, she freaks out.

"Over there, they don't have many swimming pools and stuff, just a couple of big ones because they're frightened of malaria. What's more, we went there intending to use some of the local musicians. We thought we might have some African brass and drums and things. We started off thinking of doing a track with an African feel, or maybe a few tracks, or maybe even the whole album, using the local conga players and African fellows. But when we got there, and we were looking round and watching the local bands, one of the fellows, Fela Ransome Kuti, came up to us after a day or two, and said, 'You're trying to steal the black musicians' music.' We said, 'No we're not! Do us a favour, Fela. We do all right as it is, actually. We sell a record here and there. We just want to use some of your guys.' But he got heavy about it, until in the end we thought, 'Blow you then, we'll do it all ourselves.' So we did and the only guy from Africa we used, Remi Kebaka, was someone we met in London, then we discovered that he came from Lagos. But that was purely coincidental."

Linda "It was a lot of misunderstanding. We met Fela through Ginger Baker, who has a studio over there, and one night we went down to The Shrine, a club that Fela has. Anyway, he used to come by the studios and it was all very friendly and then one day, he came by with a lot of heavies and sort of sat Paul down and said, 'You're stealing our music.' And Paul said, 'I'm not. Come and listen to the tracks. I haven't used any of your musicians.' The trouble was, Hugh Masekela went there and used an African band and they did the same thing to them, you know, 'You're going to take our music and exploit it.' Hugh said no and he did."

Paul "Then, after we had been in Lagos a couple of weeks, we were held up and robbed at knife point. Linda and I had set off like a couple of tourists, loaded with tapes and cameras, to walk to Denny's house, which was about twenty minutes down the road. A car pulls up beside us and goes a little bit ahead. Then a guy gets out and I thought that he wanted to give us a lift. So I said, 'Listen, mate, it's very nice of you, thanks very much, but we are going for a walk.' I patted him on the back and he got back in the car, which went a little way up the road. It stopped again and Linda was getting a bit worried. Then one of them, there were about five or six black guys, rolled down the window and asked, 'Are you a traveller?' I still think that if I had thought really quickly and said, 'Yes, God's traveller,' or something like that to freak them out a bit, maybe they would have left us alone. But I said, 'No, we are just out for a little walk. It's a holiday and we are tourists,' giving the whole game away. So, with that, all the doors of the car flew open and they all came out and one of them had a knife. Their eyes were wild and Linda was screaming, 'He's a musician, don't kill him,' you know, all the unreasonable stuff you shout in situations like that. So I'm saying, 'What do you want? Money?' And they said, 'Yeah, money,' and I handed some over. Shaking, we walked on home and we were just sitting down having a cup of coffee to try and recover our nerves and there was a power cut. We thought they had come back and cut the power cables. We had a lot of trouble sleeping that night and got back to the studio the next day to be told, 'You're lucky to be alive. If you had been black, they'd have killed you. But, as you're white, they know you won't recognise them.' I wanted to call the police, but everyone said it would do no good there at all. With that we had to carry on and make the record, adding to the pressure, which we had already got. It seemed stuffy in the studio, so I went outside for a breath of fresh air. If anything, the air was more foul outside than in. It was then that I began to feel really terrible and had a pain across the right side of my chest and I collapsed. I could not breathe and so I collapsed and fainted. Linda thought I had died."

Linda "I laid him on the ground and his eyes were closed and I thought he was dead!"

Paul "The doctor seemed to treat it pretty lightly and said it could be bronchial because I had been smoking too much. But this was me in hell. I stayed in bed for a few days, thinking I was nearly dying. It was one of the most frightening periods in my life. The climate, the tensions of making a record, which had just got to succeed, and being in this totally uncivilised part of the world finally got to me . . ."

Paul concludes, "We were there three weeks and we recorded seven tracks. We didn't use anyone. We ended up working with just the three of us. We did the whole thing with just the three of us."

The album, *Band On The Run*, will become their most successful and critically acclaimed record to date . . . Also in September, on Tuesday, the 18th, after five years of being together almost every minute of the day, John and Yoko sadly separate. While she stays in New York, he heads off to Los Angeles, California with their assistant, May Pang . . .

May Pang "Those were enchanted days and their charm was broken only once in the morning and once at night. That was when Yoko would call. She had wanted to report the events of her day and hear how we were spending our time."

Yoko "It was all part of the process of giving each other space to see what John and I meant to each other."

John "First I thought, 'Whoopee! Bachelor life, whoopee, whoopee, whoopee,' and then I woke up one day and thought, 'What is this? I want to go home.' But she wouldn't let me come home. That's why it was eighteen (*sic* fifteen) months instead of six. We were talking all the time on the phone and I kept saying, 'I don't like this. I'm out of control. I'm drinking; I'm getting into trouble and I'd like to come home, please.' And she's saying, 'You're not ready to come home.' And I said, 'What are you saying?' 'Well, okay,' I thought, 'back to the bottle.' "

The Beatles' former roadie, Mal Evans "I spent a lot of time with John in Los Angeles. We spent hours together and it was fascinating, because John was talking to me like I was a songwriter and that was incredible. For the first time, John and I really communicated, whereas, when it was the four of them, John was always the hardest to talk to. I always thought that when John stopped insulting me, we had fallen out of friends. The more he likes you, the more he takes the mickey out of you."

John "Los Angeles, that's a different pace, that's a different lifestyle altogether. New York and Los Angeles, they have a kind of Manchester/Liverpool thing going. In LA you either have to be down by the beach or you become part of that never-ending show business party circuit. The scene makes me nervous and when I get nervous, I have a drink and when I have a drink, I get aggressive. I prefer to stay in New York."

May Pang "My times with John were so magical times. Thank God no one can take away my precious memories. I count myself as a very lucky woman to have shared some of John's most tender moments, his private thoughts and most of all, his love. John brought me more happiness than I could hope to find in a lifetime with another man. I did not steal John. They had broken up before John and I became lovers."

Saturday, September 22
As a promotion for her new album *Feeling The Space* (released in America on September 2), an interview with Yoko in New York, carried out by Andrew Tyler shortly before the Lennons split, is published in today's *New Musical Express* . . .

Tyler "Yoko looked remarkably sad and small and vulnerable, cramped there in a corner booth at Downey's steak house. We were just around the corner from the Record Plant where John was re-mixing a track called 'Intuition'. Yoko ordered no food, she just drank coffee, smoked lots and talked in erratic bursts . . ."

"Paul seems to be doing very well," Yoko announces. "You see, he was the bachelor and now he has three daughters and four dogs, or something, you know, the whole family scene. Paul often calls up. I spoke to George and Ringo recently and they seem to be all right. George is overdubbing something on Ringo's album . . . These days I'm living a very insulated life, because of the recordings and everything. But now, I've decided to go out more, for a walk or something, which is a big thing for me to do. May (Pang) and I walk around in the early morning and it makes me realise what girls still go through with all the whistling and the catcalling and all that. It's just a drag, but it's just the way men think they should treat women."

Monday, September 24 (USA)
Ringo releases his new Apple single, 'Photograph' . . .

Ringo "I wrote it and then took it to George and he finished it and put a few more chords on it because I can only play three chords. So I gave it to George and now I sound like a genius."

Sunday, September 30
John, meanwhile, becomes a reviewer, when his appraisal of *The Goon Show Scripts* book appears in the *New York Times*. His piece is entitled, "You Had To Be There, And He Was."

"I was 12 when *The Goon Shows* first hit," **John** writes. "Sixteen when they finished with me. Their humour was the only proof that the world was insane. Spike Milligan's (may he always) book of scripts is a cherished memory, for me. And what it means to Americans I can't imagine (apart from a rumoured few fanatics). As they say in Tibet, 'You had to be there.' The Goons influenced The Beatles (along with Lewis Carroll/Elvis

Presley). Before becoming The Beatles' producer, George Martin, who had never recorded rock'n'roll, had previously recorded with Milligan and Sellers, which made him all the more acceptable. Our studio sessions were full of the cries of Neddie Seagoon, etc., etc., as were most places in Britain. There are records of some of the original radio shows, some of which I have, but when I play them to Yoko, I find myself explaining 'that in those days, there was no *Monty Python's Flying Circus*, no *Laugh-In*.' In fact, the same rigmarole I go through with my Fifties records. 'Before rock it was just Perry Como,' etc. What I'm trying to say is, one has to have been there! *The Goon Show* was long before and more revolutionary than *Look Back In Anger* (it appealed to eggheads and 'the people'). Hipper than the Hippest and madder than mad, a conspiracy against reality. A 'coup d'etat' of the mind! The evidence, for and against, is in this book. A copy of which should be sent to Mr Nixon and Mr Ervin.

"One of my earliest efforts at writing was a 'newspaper' called *The Daily Howl*. I would write it at night, then take it to school and read it aloud to my friends; looking at it now, it seems strangely similar to *The Goon Show*. Even the title had 'highly esteemed' before it. Ah well, I find it very hard to keep my mind on the BOOK itself, the tapes still ring so clearly in my head. I could tell you to buy the book anyway because Spike Milligan's a genius and Peter Sellers made all the money. (Harry Secombe got SHOW BIZ.) I love all three of them dearly, but Spike was extra. His appearances on TV as 'himself' were something to behold. He always freaked out the cameramen/directors by refusing to fit the pattern. He would run off camera and DARE them to follow him. I think they did, once or twice, but it kept him off more shows than it helped him get on. There was always the attitude that, he was 'wonderful but, you know . . .' (indicating head). I think it's 'cause he's Irish. (The same attitude prevails towards all non-English British.)

"I'm supposed to write 800 words, but I can't count. Anyway, Spike wouldn't approve. I could go on all day about The Goons and their influence on a generation (at least one), but it doesn't seem to be about THE BOOK! I keep thinking how much easier it would be to review it for a British paper. What the hell! I've never reviewed anything in my life before. Now I know why critics are 'nasty'. It would be easier if I didn't like the book, but I do, and I love you to love The Goons as I do. So take a chance.

"P.S. Dick Lester (of *Hard Day's* Beatles fame) directed the TV version of *The Goon Show, A Show Called Fred*. It was good, but radio was freer, i.e., you couldn't float Dartmoor Prison across the English Channel on TV (maybe the BBC should have spent more money). Also there is a rare and beautiful film (without Harry Secombe) called *The Running, Jumping and Standing Still Film*. Ask your local 'art house' to run it. It's a masterpiece, and captures the Goon 'spirit' very well."

John recalls the *New York Times* review, "It was a bit like doing a school essay. But like all my generation, I was really drawn to The Goons. In many ways, they influenced The Beatles as much as rock'n'roll, Elvis and Little Richard. They were to my generation what we were to the next. I admire them all, but I've always reckoned Spike was the real lunatic."

OCTOBER

In Los Angeles, at the Record Plant Studios and the A & M Studios, John begins work on a new album, a set of rock'n'roll tracks with Phil Spector . . .

John "I have always loved old pop songs. Even in the Beatle days, we used to record old pop songs between making album takes. We had some amazing things on tape, but then one day we wiped them all out. We were afraid that we would all be killed in an air crash and somebody would release them!"

Paul agrees, "With The Beatles, we were always a bit aware of this idea of having all this unreleased stuff in the background. I suppose we always thought that if anything happened to us, like Buddy Holly, that the inevitable thing was that they would be bringing out all the old tapes, rehashing them, putting strings on them, doping all that, so we were always really careful never to have anything unreleased. And I think that, by the time we had finished, we had actually put out everything we had recorded, very nearly. There were a couple of Hamburg things and a couple of little things that we never meant to record."

John "I had just finished *Mind Games* and I thought, 'What can I do for fun?' . . . The *Rock 'N' Roll* album was a collaboration with Phil Spector . . . It took me three weeks trying to convince him that I wasn't going to co-produce with him, and I wasn't going to go in the control room. I just wanted to be the singer. I said, 'Just treat me like Ronnie (Spector). We'll pick the material, I just want to sing.' It's so relaxing. I go in and play around and sing 'Oo-ee', and not have to worry about whether they've got the snare drum right and it's nice to know that at the end of it, people won't be saying, 'Oh, he can't write anymore'.

"The album started off as *Oldies But Mouldies*. Around twenty musicians have been playing on the album, including Steve Cropper, Jesse O'Davis, Jose Feliciano and Leon Russell, it's been mad! There have been five electric guitars, two drummers, two basses, three pianos and five acoustics. There's been a nucleus of people around, and whoever else has been around has dropped by. Nino Tempo played sax. I mean, I never even knew he played sax! None of the songs are later than the Fifties. They're the ones I'd always liked to have done and things we did in Hamburg and The Cavern . . . When we started recording, we did about five of them and then we started writing a few so it will probably have a bit of everything on it."

But shortly after its conception, the recording sessions come to an abrupt halt . . .

John "One day, when Spector didn't want to work, he called me and said the studio has burnt down. So I got somebody to call the studio and it hadn't burnt down. Then I heard that Phil had been involved in a car crash. One never knows with Phil. The least you can call him is eccentric, and that's coming from one who is barmy! He then ran off with the sixteen tracks and locked them in his garage or somewhere. I couldn't get at them."

There's bad news for John's first wife, Cynthia, when, on **October 1**, it is announced that her marriage to the Italian restaurateur, Roberto Bassanini is over and she has moved back to Liverpool. Reports reveal the couple's marriage first ran into trouble three months ago . . .

Friday, October 19 (UK)
As a taster for his new studio album, Ringo releases the single 'Photograph', a collaboration between him and George . . .

UK music critic, Ian MacDonald "We all like Ringo, don't we? Of course we do. And we'd all like him to make a really good single about now, wouldn't we? You know, just to allay those nagging suspicions that he is, after all, just a likeable lunk who got lucky, I mean, wot an unfool thort, brother. The problem is, Ringo doesn't seem to want to give us any help in the matter. He just keeps slinging out terrible record after terrible record and, I'm telling you, the strain of keeping this fixed grin of expectancy on my face is beginning to give me earache. 'Photograph', yet another triumph for earache rock, is a totally undistinguished composition from the twin pens of Starkey and Harrison, although calling it a composition is stretching a point. It sounds as if it's been written the way those two aged sisters paint. One starts at the nose and paints backwards while the other begins at the tail and works forwards. However, they always seem to meet and make the joint convincing . . . 'Photograph' is a wash-out, let's leave it at that."

Saturday, October 20

Meanwhile, the Thrills *X For Breakfast* column in the *NME* reports, "As a result of an appeal for funds to continue the campaign to save Michael X from the death sentence he faces in Trinidad, John Lennon has given the International Defence Committee his piano, on which he composed, amongst others, songs for the *Sgt. Pepper* album. The committee, working in London, is looking for a buyer who they hope will offer a considerable amount prior to the auction in a few weeks. The piano, a red and black Edwardian upright, carries a brass plaque inscribed with Lennon's name and several of his song titles."

Friday, November 2 (USA)
Ringo releases his album *Ringo*, which features contributions from his three former Beatles colleagues . . .

Ringo "By chance, I did the *Ringo* album with Richard Perry, because I was going to Nashville with Harry Nilsson. I had just been working with Harry and Richard in England on Harry's album so I thought, 'Well, I'm going over there, I'll call Richard,' and I did and I told him we should do something. I said, 'Look, while we're in Nashville,' because that's where the Grammy's were that year, I said, 'Why don't we get some studio time, some players and do a few tracks.' So he said, 'Great.' But then he called back and said, 'Why don't we do it in Los Angeles?' So I said, 'Okay, we'll come down to Los Angeles for a week,' and I thought that we would just do a couple of tracks, but in a week we had eight backing tracks and we only needed two more for an album. So we felt that we had to carry on. The tracks were sounding good, we had four good songs, and John was in town and so was George. They wrote me some songs and then I didn't want to leave Paul out, so I phoned him and we flew back to England to do Paul. It just came about like that. I never thought, 'We're going to plan this one.' The album went on to sell a million copies in America alone. We had handled so many Beatles Gold records that we got blasé. 'Oh, another Gold record,' but suddenly I had got my own Gold record and I wiped all the others off the wall and just put mine up."

John "I really like the album. I played on the *Ringo* album, playing the piano and singing along with him. I sounded a bit like Reg Presley . . . I enjoyed working with George and Ringo again. Unfortunately, Paul could not come to the States to work on the album because he could not get a visa. But I think that we will play together again . . . The album leapt into the *Billboard* charts at No. 4, two better than mine. I sent him a telegram saying, 'Congratulations. How dare you. Write me a hit song.' It's the first real pop album he's made and it's a good album. He deserves it. He's going to need all the royalties he can get to wallpaper Ascot. He's going to need that hit just to keep up the garden."

(As part of a settlement involving an unpaid loan between John and Allen Klein, Ringo takes up ownership of John's lavish Tittenhurst Park mansion in Ascot, Berkshire.)

'I'm The Greatest'

John "It's the Muhammad Ali line. I couldn't sing it, but it was perfect for Ringo. He could say, 'I'm the greatest', and people wouldn't get upset. Whereas, if I said, 'I'm the greatest', they'd all take it so seriously."

'You And Me (Babe)'
(A song co-written by George and The Beatles' former road manager, Mal Evans)

Mal Evans "We were in LA at the time and George and I were sharing a house and Ringo was doing his album. It was late one night and I had this song going round my head. It was a meditation song of mine I had written when I was in New York previously and I asked George if he would help me out with the chords, because I don't play very well. He started playing on the piano, it developed and this is what it turned out to be. Ringo was surprised by it, I suppose."

Simultaneously with Ringo in the States, John releases his new album, the curiously titled *Mind Games* . . .

Music critic, Neil Splinter "When handed the latest John Lennon album, the concerned reviewer is faced with a singular dilemma. It is nobler in the mind to suffer the slings and arrows of outrageous bullshit or should he take arms against a sea of paranoid plastic platitudes and, by opposing, end them? At one time, I would have said that *Mind Games* is a terrible album because it in no way reflects Lennon's capabilities. But after four solo albums, each one lousier than the last, I'm no longer sure that Lennon is capable of anything other than leading a friendly corner superstar existence, facing nothing more challenging than whether to watch *Sesame Street* on the living room or bedroom TV set . . . There are some good tracks. 'Tight Ass' gives one hope that, after the turgid opener, 'Mind Games', this is gonna turn out to be a fine album after . . . The rest of *Mind Games* is instantly forgettable. I've already forgotten it."

John "I am happy with the album. The moods of the songs go up and down, just like my moods. I think it all works out quite well. For the cover, Yoko took the picture of me with a Polaroid just after I had all my hair cut off, standing outside an army induction post. My signature in Japanese is on the cover . . . I recorded it two months ago and took eight weeks over it. I always record first; I can't stand being in the studio. I recorded it all over the place in America. Some of the things I had only just finished writing when I went in. I used the same group Yoko used on her album. I heard her finished product and said, 'Hey, they're good,' so I used the same ones exactly. I could have gone in with half recorded ideas and written the rest as I went along. I have worked like that. But, as it was, only a couple of lyrics needed finishing."

'Mind Games'

John "It was originally called 'Make Love, Not War', but that was a cliché that you couldn't say it anymore. So I wrote it obscurely . . . When it came out in the early Seventies, everybody was starting to say the Sixties was a joke."

'Aisumasen'

John "This is Japanese for 'I'm Sorry'. It's a bit personal, it's a bit political . . ."

'One Day (At A Time)'

John "That says it all for me. You can only deal with one thing at a time, no matter what you think. So that's what I am singing. I don't want to spend too much time on the future or the past . . . I get bored singing in the same voice all the time, so I'm singing falsetto. I'm proud of that."

'Nutopian International Anthem'

John "It was an old idea of Yoko's, written after Immigration did a nasty! That was our answer."

Saturday, November 24
Meanwhile, Paul and Linda continue with their *Band On The Run* promotions by appearing on Capital Radio's Dave Cash/Kenny Everett radio show. But before they can appear on the show, they are presented with a writ outside Capital's London studios . . .

Dave Cash (holding the writ) "What is this bit of paper, this amazing piece of paper from the Supreme Court in the state of New York? Is this for me?"

Paul "No, this is for me. On the way in, just now, I got handed it by a man who didn't want to embarrass me. It's a writ for $20 million."

Cash (humorously) "Is that all? Hold on, we've got petty cash out there . . . That's amazing! Is that what it looks like, a writ for $20 million?"

Paul "Yes."

Kenny Everett (changing the subject) "Can I have a sip of your coffee, Paul?"

Paul "Yes, Kenny."

Everett "Just so I can say my lips have touched the bowl."

Paul "Oh, shut up!"

Everett "I'll never wash my lips again. So, tell us about your new LP."

Paul "It's called *Band On The Run*, Kenny. I haven't come here to plug it."

Everett "There's a bit on one of your old albums, which I keep playing and I keep wondering why he doesn't make it into a single. It goes, 'Boom, boom, boom, boom, boom, suicide.' "

Paul "It's a song called 'Suicide', which I had the first verse of and no more and that's all I've still got of it."

Everett "I suppose you'll be on the news in a minute, after being slapped a $20 million writ."

Paul "I should think so, yes."

Linda "By the VATman."

Cash "You heard it first on Capital. That's our exclusive . . . and our last."

Everett "What do you think of Capital radio, Paul?"

Paul "Super, Ken!"

Cash "You read that beautifully."

Paul and Linda then take calls live over the air . . .

Caller "I'd like to ask Paul a quick question if I may. I have some tapes of you on *Pop Go The Beatles*."

Paul "Oh yeah."

Caller "You're singing completely unreleased stuff. Can I make a record of it, please?"

Paul "Yes, certainly."

Caller "Thanks very much."

Paul "It's okay."

Cash (to caller) "We can send you a writ for $20 million any time."

Friday, December 7 (UK)
Wings release their highly acclaimed album *Band On The Run* . . .

Paul "Most of the songs on the album were actually written in Scotland, at the McCartney retreat. It's a collection of songs and the basic idea about the band on the run is a kind of prison escape. At the beginning of the album, the guy is stuck inside four walls and breaks out. There is a thread, but not a concept."

Charles Shaar Murray, *New Musical Express* "*Band On The Run* comes on as one of the best albums of '73 and the best solo performance of anybody who used to be in The Beatles . . . For a real revelation, listen to Macca's synthesiser work. He uses it like an instrument and not like an electric whoopee cushion. *Band On The Run* is a great album. If anybody ever puts down McCartney in your presence, bust him in the snott and play him this. He will thank you for it afterwards."

John "It's a good album. I think it's the best he's done."

Paul "It was fun to make and it's fun to listen to. I defy anyone to listen to *Band On The Run* and then say 'He's finished,' or even 'He's losing his knack.' Paul McCartney won't be finished until he's dead and even then his music will live on."

While Denny Laine admits, "I'm kind of an odd-job man in this group. I look on *Band On The Run* as definitely *their* album. We're not a group anymore. I'm one of the three or I'm an individual. If it was Wings, I'd feel more a part of it. But it's not my songs and I'd like to feel more involved and contribute as much as they do. I did write one of the songs on the album and Paul helped me out with it. I'd like to do more like that."

'Band On The Run'

Paul "This is the title track. It goes with that picture of all the stars 'on the run' on the cover. But apart from that, there was nothing special about it."

'Jet'

Paul "I originally got the idea for the title from a puppy, a small black Labrador puppy from a litter one of our dogs had. I'd gone off on my own to get away from everything and there I was sitting in the middle of a field when it came bounding up. The pup's name gave me a spark of an idea, and out came this song about a girl called Jet."

'Bluebird'

Paul "We wrote it in Jamaica when we were on holiday. In the recording, we used a bloke called Howie Casey who we've never used before. I know him from way back, when we were in Hamburg. Then he used to be in a group called Derry & The Seniors. At that time he looked about 40, with his porkpie hat and long drape jacket. Now he looks about 25 and is your groovy session player. He played a blinder of a sax solo. Helping us on percussion is a guy called Lenny Kabaka, the only African we used. When we were back in London, he just turned up at the studio and we found out he was from Lagos."

'Mrs. Vanderbilt'

Paul "This was recorded during a power cut in Lagos. Suddenly everything went black and eventually we found ourselves doing it on EMI generated power and just hoping that the hum wouldn't come over on the record. There's a phrase on this track that is also on a song I wrote for Rod Stewart, one he's just recorded. It fitted so well into this one, too, that I pinched it. So the phrase is in both songs."

'Let Me Roll It'

Paul "I was up in Scotland one day, on a nice day, I was sitting outside, plonking on a guitar and I got this idea for a song. We took it off to Lagos and put down a backing track, with Linda playing organ, me playing drums, Denny playing guitar. And then we overdubbed the big guitars you hear right the way through it, going through a vocal PA system to get the unusual guitar sound on this one, not through a guitar amp but through a vocal amp. It was a big powerful amp."

'Mamunia'

Paul "This was the first one we did in Lagos, recorded in the middle of a tropical rainstorm. I don't know if that had any effect on the final result. It's a name I came across a couple of times in my travels. First, it was the name of a hotel in Marakesh, where the whole band went to for a holiday. But it was spelt slightly differently in that case. Then we went to Lagos, Nigeria, recording *Band On The Run*, and we saw it on a plaque on a wall. The funny thing is, there was a plaque next to it, which advertised a local carpenter. It read, 'Son of always'. We nearly called *Band On The Run, Son Of Always*, but in the end we plumped for the title of the track."

'No Words'

Paul "That's one I did with Denny, he had half and I kind of finished it. A McCartney/ Laine composition, sounds good doesn't it? That's a favourite of mine. I think it grows on you and it really works as a record."

'Picasso's Last Words'

Paul "We met Dustin Hoffman when we were in Jamaica and went to have dinner with him one night. We were talking about songwriting and he pulled out a copy of *Time* magazine. He said, 'Here's a piece that I thought was really lyrical.' It was the story of how Picasso had toasted his friends one night, saying how he couldn't drink any more, and the next morning he was dead. So I plonked a few chords and out came the song. Dustin was very excited about it. When we came to record it at Ginger Baker's studio, the idea was to fragment it, make it sort of cubist. It's very disjointed, but that's the way it's meant to be."

'Nineteen Hundred And Eighty-Five'

Paul "This was originally a little thing I couldn't get words to, except for the first phrase. But the words just came to me the day we were due to record, and I think it's turned out quite well."

Paul is asked how he got the famous celebrities to appear on the front cover.

"I just rang 'em up and asked 'em," he replies. "We had an idea of what we wanted, then drew up a list of names and, to our delight, they all said, 'Yes, we'll do it.' The first person I rang up was Michael Parkinson and he was very nice about it all and said, 'Sure, I'll come along.' Then I rang up James Coburn, who was at his hotel and he said, 'Sure, Paul. I'd love to do it,' in his deep American accent. John Conteh is on there because he's a fellow Liverpudlian. We chose all the other people because they looked the part, and because we thought it would be more interesting than just having unknown faces, we thought we'd give people something to look at."

Paul "We've not had a great big hit single in Britain for a while and the British market is a bit funny at the moment. I mean, one week it's 'Eye Level' by The Simon Park Orchestra and then the next, it's Gary Glitter or Donny Osmond. So, with *Band On The Run*, I was going to do the old Beatles thing and not release a single. Everybody does that. Everybody pulls bloody singles off. So I was thinking, 'We'll not do that. We'll just release an LP. That's good enough.' So we released it and it didn't get much notice. A few people heard it, and said it was nice, it went up to No. 7, and then it started to plummet and I thought, 'Well, blimey, it's better than that. It could just be the fact that people haven't heard it.' You suddenly realise that everyone is housewives. A lot of your buyers are housewives or clerks or average people. The majority of people aren't people from the record business, like we'd think, but the majority of people are housewives. They don't know that *Band On The Run* is out unless there's a single. We say, 'This is the single from *Band On The Run*.' Someone says that and everybody knows it is out and that's the power of the single. Let's face it, everyone who makes an album is trying to sell as many copies as possible and any trick they can use to do it, they will."

Recently, a photo of John, accompanied by his and Yoko's assistant, May Pang, had been splashed across many newspapers. During a transatlantic phone call interview with Radio Luxembourg, on **Sunday, December 9**, the show's host, Tony Prince, confronts John about the girl in the picture . . .

Prince "Would you like to clear that up, John?"

John "We have a couple of people working for us and some of them are male and some of them are female. There are a couple of females and a couple of males and May happens to know about copyright and she handles the copyright situation. So, I was given May and Yoko was given John and Nadya. I've got May and Mal, the old Beatles road manager and so, when I'm being seen around, it looks like I'm going dancing, or something."

Prince "Yeah, people are putting one and one together and making 98!"

John "Over here, I was seen hanging around with half a dozen Japanese groupies. Also, I was supposed to be in a gay bar with Gilbert O'Sullivan."

Prince "Were you?"

John "I've never met Gilbert."

Prince (changing subject) "The Stones wanted to tour Russia and it was cancelled. Would you like to go behind the Iron Curtain to perform?"

John "I think I'd enjoy it, you know, simply because they don't see anything. It'd be really weird. I don't know how the Chinese would react, you know."

Prince "Did you see Princess Anne get married?"

John "I saw the replay. I saw the single. I didn't see the album. It was on very late at night. It looked pretty good, though."

Prince "There has been a lot of discussions on TV and radio over here, John, about the Royal family. Some people think we should dispense with it and some people think it's a good thing. What are your feelings on the Royal family?"

John "Well, my personal feelings are that, maybe, they are a little expensive for the country. But, I think, they don't have it that easy. I know they've got a lot of money but I get torn between it, you know. I think we should have them but not pay so much. I think the whole country should decide. I think it's up to the people of Britain. If they want 'em and they want to pay for 'em, that's their choice. Talking about Her Majesty, I think it's about time that she gave me a pardon."

Prince "Do you want your MBE back?"

John "No, I want a pardon for being bust in England. That's the cause of the whole problem, the whole immigration problem. So listen, Her Majesty, I think I've done more good for Britain than harm. Will you just give me a nice pardon, okay, and then I can just travel around again."

Prince "Well, thanks John. We look forward to the rock'n'roll thing, the album."

John "Okay, I should have it out in the New Year, I think."

Wednesday, December 26
In their regular *Beatles At Christmas* slot, BBC1 screens The Beatles' 1964 movie *A Hard Day's Night*. Watching the re-broadcast at their home in Scotland is Paul, Linda and the kids . . .

Paul "The kids saw The Beatles film on telly and were very excited about their dad being in it. Then they asked me who the other chaps were and if they were mates of mine. I assured them that John, George and Ringo were precisely that. You know, it's quite nice being old. When kids come up to me these days for my autograph, I feel more like their Uncle Paul than their idol."

Thoughts of the movie almost a decade on and memories from his public rows with John just two years ago . . .

"In *A Hard Day's Night* there were the stereotypes," **Paul** recalls. "John was the thinker, Ringo was the loner and Paul was the happy-go-lucky chap. I didn't mind that and I still don't. I was in the film and I didn't care what they pictured me as. As far as I was concerned, I was just doing a job in a film. If the film called for me to be a cheerful chap, well, great. I'd be a cheerful chap. It does seem to have fallen in my role to be a bit kinder than the others. I was always known in The Beatles thing as being the one who would kind of sit the press down and say, 'Hello, how are you? Do you want a drink?' and make them comfortable. I guess that's me. I'm not really tough but I'm not really loveable, either, but I don't mind falling in the middle. My dad's advice was 'Moderation, son.'

Every father in the world tells you moderation. So, to me, that's always been the way. I mean, there's nothing wrong with that. Why should I go around slagging off people? I really didn't like all that that John did. But I'm sure that he doesn't now. But I know John, and I know that most of it was just something to tell the newspapers. He was in that mood then and he wanted all that to be said. I think now, whilst he most probably doesn't regret it, he didn't mean every single syllable of it.

"I mean, he came out with all that stuff like I'm like Engelbert Humperdinck and I know that he doesn't really think that. But I hated it as you can imagine. I sat down and pored over every little paragraph, every little sentence. I thought, 'Does he really think that of me?' And at the time I thought, 'It's me. I am. That's just what I'm like. He's captured me so well. I'm a turd, you know.' I sat down, at my home in Scotland and thought, 'I'm just nothing.' Linda said, 'Now, you know that's not true. You're joking. He's just got a grudge, man. The guy's just trying to polish you off.' So gradually I started to think, 'Great, that's not true. I'm not really like Engelbert. I don't just write ballads.' And that kept me kind of hanging on, but at the time, it hurt me deep.

"In the music press, they really wanted me to come out and slam John back and I used to get pissed off at the guys coming up to me and saying, 'This is the latest thing that John has said,' and they'd say, 'What's your answer?' And I'd say, 'Well, I don't really have much of an answer. He's got a right to say.' You know, it was really limp things I'd answer. But I believe in keeping it cool and that sort of thing, and it soon passes over. I don't believe if someone kind of punches you over, you have to go kind of thumping him back to prove that you're a man and that kind of thing. I think, actually, you do win that way in the end, you know."

Saturday, January 19

News Survey "Beatles hint at reunion: **John Lennon** and **Paul McCartney** have both stated, independently of each other, that the four ex-Beatles may soon be playing together again. Lennon commented in Los Angeles, 'I think anything is possible now and, if it happens, I'm sure we will all do something wonderful.' While over in New York, McCartney declared, 'We wouldn't get together as The Beatles but I'd like to see us working together, possibly for recording, and I think we will.' Reasons for the enthusiasm is that all legal problems involving the four are expected to be finally resolved this month."

Also on this date, a telephone interview with John in Los Angeles is published in the *New Musical Express*. The interviewer, Andrew Tyler, discusses with John the subject of a Royal pardon from his 1968 drugs conviction . . .

"I was thinking of writing to the Queen," **John** jokingly remarks. "I hope she reads the *NME*. I was after a pardon for being planted by the cops and being hassled for three years and everything that happened. That so-called bust has left me with a criminal record. That's the legal reason they're trying to throw me out. If that was taken away, there'd be nothing they could do."

Tyler, like most interviewers, then asks John to reveal how he spends his spare time . . .

"I can move around a bit more freely now, for meals and odd visits to the movies," **John** announces. "I still get recognised, though. I think it's me nose. But I can generally go to the movies. The last film I saw was *Behind The Green Door*, which was a very rude film. The first 45 minutes were interesting but then it got a bit boring. When you've seen one cock, you've seen them all."

Thursday, January 31

An interview with Paul is published in the latest edition of *Rolling Stone* . . .

Rolling Stone "Could you write a song or songs with John again?"

Paul "I could. It's totally fresh ground right now, because I just got my visa too, about two or three days ago, and until then I couldn't physically write a song with John. He was in America; he couldn't get out; I couldn't get in. But now that's changed, so whole new possibilities are opening up. Anything could happen. I like to write with John. I like to write with anyone who's good."

Rolling Stone "Now that you're in New York, I suppose the rumours will start again, that there'll be a Beatles reunion of some sort."

Paul "Well, I must say, like as far as getting together as we were, as The Beatles were, I don't think that'll ever happen again. I think now everyone's kind of interested in their little personal things. I kind of like the way we did *Band On The Run*. It was something we've never done before and it's very interesting. But I do think that I for one am very proud. I am proud of The Beatles thing. It was great, and I can go along with all the people you meet on the street who say, 'You gave so much happiness to many people.' I don't think that's corny. Through all that kind of bitterness, I tended to think like John a bit, 'Oh, The Beatles . . . naww . . . crap.' But it really wasn't. I think it was great. So I'd like to see that cooled out and restored to its kind of former greatness, agree that it was a good thing and continue in some kind of way."

Tuesday, February 26

Frank Goldsworthy, of the *Daily Express*, writes "Split-Up Beatles Want To Patch Business Break, QC Tells Judge". The report reads "Yesterday, all their troubles seemed so far away . . . Three years away in fact, as the split-up Beatles yesterday revealed they were close to making up their business row. Mr Justice Megarry was told in the High Court, 'Happily, it is hoped the partners are on the point of resolving their differences.' But whether that means John, Paul, George and Ringo are ready for a real get-together is still in the air. **Ringo Starr** said last night, 'The four of us ask ourselves that quite a lot. I can't see it right now, but I wouldn't rule it out. It's a possibility.' He added, 'We are still tied to each other, which isn't fair. We are trying to sort that out. We signed all those silly pieces of paper, which keep us together until 1976, when we were lads.' The good news came from Mr Thomas Bingham, QC for the Receiver, Mr Stephen Gray. Mr Bingham said, 'A very high degree of agreement had been reached in The Beatles' affairs. A degree of harmony has been restored to The Beatles in this limited sphere.' Mr Bingham added that the four pop superstars, Paul McCartney, John Lennon, George Harrison and Ringo Starr were already agreed on some matters. On others, they were anxious to avoid arguments, which could cause more difficulties . . . And yesterday, the judge was told the three Beatles, John, George and Ringo, had now started their own legal battle with Mr Allen Klein. ABKCO, Klein's company, had also started proceedings against the group. Mr Andrew Leggatt, QC, said Paul maintained neither Mr Klein nor ABKCO were entitled to any of his money . . ."

On **Tuesday, March 12**, **John** finds himself back in the news when, at the Troubadour Club in Los Angeles, during an opening night performance by The Smothers Brothers, John is famously ejected from the club for being rowdy . . .

Los Angeles columnist, Chris Van Ness "The occasion was a special opening night at the Troubadour to celebrate The Smothers Brothers' 15th anniversary in show business. The evening marked the first time Tom and Dick Smothers had worked together in several years and a lot of their friends had turned out to lend support. The first show went well and I was sitting in the front bar between shows talking to some friends when John Lennon, Harry Nilsson and their party came in for the second show. Lennon was with his new oriental girlfriend, or as a colleague remarked, cruelly, 'The 1974 Yoko,' and we spoke briefly before he went into the show room. He was cordial and seemed in reasonably good spirits, hardly like the man who would be carried out kicking and swinging less than half an hour later."

John "I've never drunk so much in my life, and I've been drinking since I was fifteen. I was with the heaviest drinkers in the industry, who were Harry Nilsson and Bobby Keyes and all of them, and we couldn't pull ourselves out . . . It was, 'Let's all drown ourselves together.' Looking at it from where I was sitting, it was like, 'Let's kill ourselves. But do it like Errol Flynn,' you know, the macho way . . . Everything got so exaggerated. All the Tampax story was that we were in a restaurant drinking, not eating, and I just happened to go to the gents to have a pee. There was a brand new, fresh, Kotex, just on the toilet. And you know that old trick where you put a penny on your forehead and it sticks, well I just saw the thing (Kotex), picked it up and slapped it on my forehead and it stayed. So, for a gag, I walked back from the toilet, sat down at the seat and everybody went, 'Ha, ha, ha,' and I left it until it fell off, that's all. Harry and I were drunk. I was drinking Brandy Alexanders for the first time, they taste like milk shakes, and I was knocking them back . . ."

Chris Van Ness "It seems that Lennon began drinking rather heavily, singing before The Smothers Brothers show began and generally insulting the waitresses with obscene remarks. After the show started, he refused to quieten down and began throwing insults at the performers."

John "Suddenly I was in the fourth dimension. In the fourth dimension I noticed what I'd always secretly thought; that Dickie Smothers was an asshole, even though I always liked Tommy, and so that's what I said. But because I was drunk, I said it out loud. I yelled, 'Dickie, you're an asshole.' Tommy tried to cover it up. I always thought Dickie was a wimp and Tommy was all right. So then somebody said something to me, and I shouted sarcastically, 'Don't you know who I am?' They were then throwing me out!"

New York columnist, Lisa Robinson reported "According to the LA rumours, Lennon was heckling the Smothers Brothers during their act and repeatedly shouting obscenities at them. Peter Lawford, the actor, who was sitting behind Lennon, tried to quieten him. Ken Fritz, The Smothers Brothers' manager, also tried to dissuade Lennon from cracking audible remarks. Fritz remarked, 'He swung and hit me in the jaw. I hit him back.' Apparently, Lennon, who was sitting with May Pang, hurled a glass at the wall."

Chris Van Ness "At one point, actor Peter Lawford, seated near Lennon, complained to the management about the former Beatle's conduct, so John was politely asked to quieten down. Instead of complying, Lennon persisted with his heckling. His conduct apparently became so obnoxious that Tommy Smothers stopped the show and commented, 'There's a narrow line between bad taste and vulgarity, and you've managed to cross it.' And that was when the real trouble began. The Smothers Brothers' manager, Ken Fritz, allegedly rushed over to Lennon's table, grabbed him by the lapels of his Scotch plaid jacket and told him rather succinctly that he'd better be quiet. In rapid response, it's claimed, Lennon hauled off and punched Fritz in the face. Fritz returned the blow while Peter Lawford tried to pull a waitress out of the way, but not before she took Lennon's second punch in her ribs."

The waitress, Naomi "It's not the pain that hurts, it's finding out that one of your idols is a real asshole."

Chris Van Ness "Then Lawford entered the scuffle momentarily, retiring after five Troubadour employees charged in to carry Lennon out of the club, but not before his glass smashed against the wall, cutting several people. The show had come to a complete standstill, with all eyes focused on the former Beatle. John Lennon was, by this time, raving like a maniac."

John "If I died the way Dylan Thomas died, they'd be saying, 'What a wonderfully colourful way to go!' But because I'm alive, it's not so wonderful . . . It was the worst time of my life . . . That bloody fan with the Instamatic who sued me for hitting her. I never touched her; I never went near the girl. She sued me and I had to pay her off to shut her up . . . She just wanted money. I was not in the best frame of mind and I was wildly drunk but I was nowhere near this chick. She's got no photographs of me near her . . . I definitely didn't hit this fat broad who just wanted to get her name in the paper . . ."

Chris Van Ness "Lennon's behaviour, as I witnessed it last night, was that of a spoiled child throwing a tantrum in order to be acknowledged. It's no secret that his career has sagged since *Imagine* and even Yoko has received more press recognition than he has in recent months. Yoko was the stronger of the two. Now, John's ego-anchors have gone, his marriage appears to be on the rocks and his career appears to be at its lowest ebb for ten years . . . When legal charges are brought against Lennon, as they almost certainly will be, he will probably be asked to leave this country. Lennon is living here on probation, with an expired visa based on an appeal of his immigration status."

MARCH

John remarks, "Yoko and I are still very good friends. I still love her, but we're two artists and we found it hard living together. We talk on the phone every day, whether she's in Britain or here."

During her time in John's home country, Yoko pays a visit to Paul and Linda at their London home . . .

Paul "Nobody knows how much I helped John. Yoko came through London while he was in LA with Harry Nilsson having a crazy time. He was fighting, haranguing The Smothers Brothers and being quite crazy. Yoko came through and visited us, which was nice. Yoko came by at our home in St John's Wood and we started talking and the important subject for us was, 'What's happened? You've broken up. You're here and he's there. What's happened?' And she was nice and confided in us that they had broken up. She was strong about it and she said, 'He's got to work his way back to me. He's got to work at it.' And I said, 'Look, if I see him, are you still in love with him?' and she said, 'Yes.' So I said, 'Would you think it is an intrusion if I said to him, "Look, man, she loves you and there's a way to get back." Would that be okay? I might see him around and I'd like to be a mediator in this, because the two of you have obviously got something really strong.' And she said, 'I don't mind.' So Linda and I went to California when they were doing *Pussycats.*"

Thursday, March 28
At the Burbank Studios in California, John begins work on the Harry Nilsson album *Pussycats* . . .

John "I was in the middle of working on the *Oldies But Goldies* (*Rock 'N' Roll*) album with Phil Spector and he had a few car accidents, so that was the end of that. But I kept waiting and waiting for months and months and I was just hanging around with Harry Nilsson and people in LA, and getting into trouble. Whenever we were getting into trouble, it was my name in the paper, so I thought, 'Forget this,' you know. Every time we went out for the night, I ended up in the paper. So, I said to Harry one hungover morning, 'What are we doing? We're wasting our time here. We might as well put all of this energy into work.' I knew he was going to make an album, and I didn't feel like starting a new one, because I already had one half finished, so I said to him, 'Look, I'll produce you.' Which means that, I will sit behind the desk and make sure they get the drums on and things like that and keep them together as they take off. We had a good time making it. We had to a lot of friends in of there playing, half of them are on my album, half of them are on Ringo's, you know, that usual crew, with a few added extras, like Keith Moon. Some tracks are beautiful, some tracks are a bit too weird, but Harry Nilsson and John Lennon together is a pretty weird combination. Harry wanted to do certain tracks, like he wanted to do 'Loop De Loop'. He also wanted to do 'Rock Around The Clock', 'cos we thought it would be good fun. He said, 'Nobody has ever covered 'Rock Around The Clock', and then we open *Billboard* and there it is, at No. 108 by Billy Hayley!"

Two of the many visitors to John's rented beach house in Malibu are Paul and Linda, who drop by on John on **Sunday, March 31**. After an impromptu jam session this evening, Paul and Linda then return to the beach house the following day, where he takes the opportunity to have a word with John about his estranged relationship with Yoko . . .

Paul "It was weird meeting him. He was in the house with Nilsson, Keith Moon and a few other guys and it was a crazed house. It was pretty wild days. So I said to him, 'Look, come here. Come in the back room. I want to talk to you privately.' So I took him in the back room and I sat him down and said, 'I feel like a matchmaker here, but this girl of yours still loves you. Do you still love her?' And he said, 'Yeah, I do but I don't know what to do.' So I said, 'Well, I've talked to her and she still does love you but you've got to work your arse off, man. You've got to get back to New York. You have to have a separate flat; you have to send her roses every fucking day. You've got to work at it like a bitch, and you might just get her back,' which is sort of what he did but you'll never hear that story. We told him to go back to Yoko and not long after, he did. You won't hear that from them, because I'm too much in the story then. He never gave an inch, but he took so many yards. He always suspected me. He was always thinking I was cunning and devious."

Saturday, April 13

The *New Musical Express* features in its Teasers column, "What price now for a Beatles reunion? Betting stepped up to a new briskness this week at the news that Lennon and McCartney were buddying it around in Los Angeles together, just like old times. However, odds began to lengthen again on McCartney's denials of a working partnership and his return late last week to London. The way we heard it, trying to sift facts from garbled West Coast rumours, was that McCartney had been expressing worries about Lennon's current somewhat anti-social behaviour. Also that the pair of them were refused admission to the Whiskey A Go-Go because they were unrecognised at the door."

Friday, April 19
In Atlanta, Georgia, the world premiere takes place of *Son Of Dracula*, the Apple-financed comedy musical horror film . . .

Ringo "12,000 kids were there and as soon as we left, they took the movie off. It was the first movie to open in Atlanta since *Gone With The Wind*. We had marching bands and Harry and me went there and we thought it would be a nice place to open. Later, *Son Of Dracula* could only play in one-cinema towns, because they hated competition."

The movie is directed by Freddie Francis and stars, amongst others, Ringo and Harry Nilsson . . .

"I produced that film and it taught me one thing, never to produce again. It's a headache," **Ringo** announces at a press conference for the film. "I think it's the first musical horror film I know. I don't know any more . . . I met Harry when I was invited to play a few tracks on his album. That's when we met. Then I invited him to work on the movie. When I asked Harry, I had no idea about the cover of his album . . . I play the part of Merlin. I wanted to work with Harry but Harry's taller than me and Dracula has to be taller so I couldn't have his part. It was very hard becoming a 3,000-year-old man, but I enjoyed doing it. But I don't think it is the best thing I ever did. We asked for a director of horror but I felt it got lost when it got to the rock'n'roll part and the comedy. He's a famous English horror director. We filmed it all on location in England. It's not the greatest movie in the world but I've seen worse. To get it released we went round the usual circuit and had a lot of patting on the back saying, 'Yeah, it's wonderful, but what are we going to do with it?' So we got in with Cinemation and they were the only ones who thought like we did and they said, 'We'll try and get it out.' Their idea was to put it out in a college part of the country because the film is really for people in colleges."

Saturday, April 20

In this week's *Disc & Music Echo*, Paul is asked by one the paper's readers, "Did you ever recover the Hofner violin bass you played in The Beatles? I heard you had it pinched." Paul replies, "No! Ever since the early days, even before The Beatles I've had three violin basses. One was stolen and I was very upset indeed. I had a sentimental attachment to it. But I've still got the other two."

Wednesday, June 5

In London, **Ringo** tells reporters, "I'll bet anyone £1,000 that The Beatles will never play together again. Not this year, or for that matter, ever. We are all doing our own thing apart from everyone else, we are too busy to get together again."

When told of this remark, **Paul** replies, "I'd bet as much, but I wouldn't raise his ante."

On **Thursday, June 6,** at approximately 8.30pm, **Paul**, his manager, Linda, family and Wings fly into Nashville, Tennessee at the Metropolitan Airport. Despite a publicity blackout, a crowd of fifty fans is waiting, alerted by the presence of reporters and television cameras . . .

Jerry Bailey and Eve Zibart of *The Tennessean* newspaper "The McCartney group was the last to deplane, and the entourage was headed by Brian Brooly, who carried their second daughter Mary off the plane. Behind him McCartney, in a jade green battle jacket and bright picture shirt, emerged smiling with his hand extended in a familiar two-finger salute. He paused at the bottom of the flight steps to answer questions and pose for photographs before moving on through the terminal to the limousine parked out front. He answered questions briefly, but willingly . . ."

Paul jokes to waiting reporters "I am here to brush up on my three Rs: rehearsing, relating and riding. I may record here, I don't know. It depends on how things go." He continues, "I chose Nashville as a rehearsal base for an upcoming tour. I rather fancy the place. It's a musical centre. I've just heard so much about it, that I wanted to see it for myself. I also plan to enjoy myself while I'm here, socialising with the community and doing some horseback riding. We didn't come here to hide out. I plan to make myself available to newsmen for interviews. Maybe we'll have you reporters out some evening for a party."

A reporter then asks Paul if he likes country music. "I love country music," he replies. "I was raised on it!" Replying to a question about the lawsuits, which have been flying about between The Beatles, **Paul** replies, "We're getting them all worked out. Further legal action will be unnecessary."

Reporter "Will you be writing again with your former collaborator John Lennon?"

Paul "You know, you break up, you break up!"

Reporter "Ringo Starr recently said that The Beatles would never be reunited. Can you comment on that?"

Paul "I don't know what Ringo said . . . He's probably right."

Paul announces to the Nashville press that Geoff Britton and Jimmy McCulloch are the newest recruits to Wings . . .

"We have a new drummer, Geoff Britton. He's a karate expert. He has a black belt. I figure with those credentials he'll be able to whip the band in shape," he jokes.

The drummer, Geoff Britton, a keen fitness fanatic and martial arts expert "I took up martial arts when I was with my band East Of Eden. Some thugs set about us when we were in Hamburg so I thought I'd learn karate and give myself a sort of invisible shield. This led to teaching at West Wickham Karate Club in my spare time. One of my pupils was Clifford Davis, who managed Fleetwood Mac. He told me that McCartney was looking for a drummer for Wings. I called MPL and was told the audition list was closed, but I managed to talk them into giving me a listen. They had stacks of drummers wanting the gig and it took a long while and lots of practice sessions and auditions to whittle the contenders down."

Guitarist Jimmy McCulloch "I first saw Wings in Leicester last year. A friend of mine was the sound engineer and he had some tickets. So I went along and I was really knocked out by them. The first thing I was most impressed with was how much like his records Paul sounds; there aren't effects on his voice or anything. It's just him. I met him and the band too. They are really nice. I first met him professionally when *Band On The Run* was being mixed. Then he asked me over to Paris where Linda was doing her Suzy & The Red Stripes thing. Then he took me up to Stockport where Paul was going to do his brother

Mike McGear's album. While he was working there, Paul asked me to join his band and I said, 'Yes, Why not?' It's a great opportunity."

Friday, July 12
In Nashville, Paul, Linda and Wings hold a press conference on the front porch of his rented $2,000 per week plantation home, belonging to Junior Putnam . . .

Paul, to the gathered press "I've got a farm in Scotland. You're not the only people who have farms, you know. Back home, we have country people in our own way . . . Most of my time here was spent rehearsing with Wings, jamming with musicians and just enjoying the countryside. We did manage to put something on tape a few days ago, 'Walking In The Park With Eloise'. I was talking to Chet (Atkins) about it one night when we were over at his house and I said, 'Why don't you do it?' Then Chet brought along Floyd Cramer and some boys and there was my drummer, Geoff, and me and Bobby Thompson, the banjo player."

'Walking In The Park With Eloise'
(A song written by his father, James Paul McCartney)

Paul "I did it because Chet Atkins told me that he had once recorded one of his father's songs. The whole thing has turned out so well that it now looks as though we may have a hit on our hands. Fancy cashing in on my dad after all these years."

Paul's Nashville press conference continues, "Originally we were not going to record here. We were going to rehearse and then the members blended with a view to going on tour, possibly to Australia. I hope to go on an American tour next year and if it develops, there will be a concert in Nashville. We couldn't skip Nashville. We have to play here."

Reporter "Do you have plans to settle in Nashville?"

Paul "No, thank you. I'm British to the core. We're always being advised to move out of England because the taxes take 90 per cent of your money, but I'm British and Linda's kind of honorary British."

Reporter "What have you been to in Nashville?"

Paul "We've visited the homes of Chet Atkins and Johnny Cash. Also we've been to the new Grand Ole Opry House, several Nashville restaurants and taken in several drive-in movies. We've been to the drive-in a couple of times. We're very drive-in type people."

Nashville . . .

Geoff Britton "Along with the other guys in the band, I was promised wonderful things, percentages and so on, but certain members of the group screwed it up in Nashville when they went over the top with booze and certain substances, so we ended up on a flat wage . . . Paul always treated me well. It was a very tough time for Paul. His wife was in the band learning the ropes and he was trying to get over the loss of friendship of the other three Beatles, with whom he'd been so close. I got on well with Linda; she was having a hard time, too. She was finding her feet in the music business and was having to fight her corner against the people, inside and outside Wings and the MPL organisation, who were putting her down. What's more, she was trying to be a good mum as well as a rock musician . . . The problems lay with Denny Laine and Jimmy McCulloch, who just wanted to live the wild life."

Denny Laine "In Nashville, it got to the point where we used to rehearse every day, which we had never done except perhaps for a couple of weeks before a tour. We almost had to keep working to keep out of each other's hair; but that was the best thing we've done and from now on, we're always gonna work that way. Nashville was great for us because we were surrounded by all these musicians who were great. After Nashville, I felt I had more to say in the group because it kind of turned out to be Paul and I telling the others what was wanted."

AUGUST

An interview with **Paul** is published in the American *Redbook* magazine, in which, he confesses, "I prefer marriage to the wild sex like I had when I was with The Beatles. I do not yearn for the rip-roaring days of Beatlemania. I prefer the straight-and-narrow life with Linda." Talking about sex, he remarks, "Groupies, chicks, it was fabulous. There was no stopping me. I was the biggest raver out but got thinking, 'What am I doing with my life? What chick do I know as a pal?' And there weren't any. Knocking around is knocking around. It's du-du-du-boom and you're gone."

On marriage, **Paul** reveals, "Once we were married, it was marvellous. We have a marriage where I say, 'All right, I'm not going with anyone else.' And she says, 'I'm not going with anyone.' But if Linda did go with some guy, I would consider it an insult."

Friday, August 23
Still in the States, from his New York apartment, John catches sight of an Unidentified Flying Object . . .

John "I was in New York, in my apartment, standing by my roof and I looked left and there I saw this thing, about a hundred yards away. I could even see it without my glasses, and I was looking at it and thinking, 'What is it? What is it? Is it a helicopter?' And I realised it couldn't be because it wasn't making any noise. I thought, 'Is it a balloon? Is it the police?' It had all these lights around the bottom of it, flashing on and off and I said to myself, 'That's a UFO, you know.' Sometimes you just don't want to believe it. I didn't want to admit it. I imagined the papers, 'Lennon Sees UFO'. I was going to take the mention off the (*Walls And Bridges*) album because I knew people were going to say, 'He's crazy!' But I saw it and I don't care what people said. Nobody is going to explain what it was. I say it's a UFO. I got a friend to call the police and it was in the newspapers the following day. A couple of people saw something in the same area at the same time as me. It was just luck that I saw it."

Wednesday, September 18

In a conversation with the UK pop columnist John Blake, **Paul**'s recent success encourages him to announce, "I think now I am happier than I have ever been," adding, "there is no animosity between me and John, George and Ringo any more. We just keep in loose touch and I wouldn't object to us playing on the same stage again if the time was right."

Monday, September 23
John meanwhile releases in the States his new single 'Whatever Gets You Through The Night'/'Meat City', a taster of his new album, *Walls And Bridges* . . .

'Whatever Gets You Through The Night'

John "That was the last thing I wrote, virtually as I was walking in the studio. I heard someone saying it on the radio, on a late-night talk show, talking to someone on a phone, saying, 'Well, whatever gets you through the night.' And there it was, the whole tune came to me in my head. It was going to be like 'Rock Your Baby', but I often have an idea what it is going to be like but it never turns out anything like it. It's a very loose track. I call it the 'Crippled Inside' of the album, you know, or the 'Oh Yoko' of the album, which are tracks I made, which people say I should put them out as a single and I always fought it. But this time I swayed with the people who told me to put it out. I think they were right. It's almost the first or second take and the musicians are ragged, but swinging. We tried to cut it a few times again but it never got that feel.

"I was fiddling about with it one night and Elton (John), who was in town, walked in with Tony King of Apple, and the next minute, Elton said, 'Hey, can I put a bit of piano on it?' I said, 'Sure! I'd love it!' So he zapped in and I was amazed at his ability. I had never seen him, I knew him but I had never seen him play. He's a fine musician and a great piano player. I was pleasantly surprised at the way he could get in on such a loose track and keep up the rhythm and then he sang with me. He did the harmony on that and when Elton sang along with me, it was like having George or Paul there again. It was the same good feeling. He also sang on a track called 'Surprise, Surprise'. We had a great time. In fact, some people thought we had speeded the track up, but we didn't. Jokingly he was telling me he was going to do this Madison Square Garden concert, and he said, 'Will you do it with me if the ("Whatever Gets You Through The Night") record is No. 1?' And I did not expect it to get to No. 1 at all. I didn't think it had a chance in hell, because I wasn't being very well received on any level, you know . . . Well, I said, 'Sure I would. Sure I will.' "

'Meat City' . . .

John "When I go through tracks in my head, I think, 'Well, if I was in the countryside, it'd be better.' And when I'm in the countryside, I think, 'Well, if I was in the city, it'd be better.' I'm really saying, 'I've been all over the place so it's all the same.' People are never satisfied. The grass is always greener . . . 'Meat City' is just a vague impression of one part or one side of America. It could also apply to Glasgow, London or Paris."

Thursday, September 26 (USA)
John releases *Walls And Bridges*, his latest solo album . . .

John "It's amazing but still my biggest kick is making the music. I still surprise myself sometimes. There was a period when I was thinking that maybe I'm getting bored with music. I asked myself, 'Is this all I will be doing for the rest of my life?' I was going through all that dialogue. But for the last six months, my biggest buzz was still writing songs and trying to make them say exactly what I wanted them to say. I still get my rocks off exactly like that. Sometimes I say, 'I was 34 yesterday . . . You're not supposed to do this.' But then, one voice says, 'Don't be dumb!' You see, great artists like B.B. King or some of the old blues guys, like Ray Charles, are still performing and getting their rocks off. I think, 'That's what I wanted to do, you'll probably be doing it for the rest of your life.'

"I think *Walls And Bridges* is more commercial and more light-hearted than *Mind Games*. I enjoyed this one more. The title I picked for the album, I think I heard it on a public service announcement here in New York, they're the things that advertise Bangladesh or Drug Rehabilitation. I just heard someone say something about walls and bridges and it registered as something to do with communication and maybe walls that keep you in or separate people and bridges bringing them together. I liked it. "

'Bless You'

John "I like 'Bless You' from that album as a song. I'm not particularly enamoured of my performance, but then I never am, so I'll have to live with that. As a song, I think it's the best piece of work on the album, although I worked harder on some of the other tracks. In retrospect, that seems to be the best track, to me . . . In a way, it's about Yoko and I. And in a way it's about a lot of couples or all of us who go through that, whatever it's called, love experience. You know, the way love changes, which is one of the surprises of life that we all find out, that it doesn't remain exactly the same all the time, although it's still love. It comes in mysterious forms; it has wonders to perform. And 'Bless You' expresses one side of it"

'Scared'

John "I am scared a lot of the time, I think we all are, but I'm not always scared. I do have vindictive sides as well. But when it comes to writing down how Yoko and I feel about each other, that's how I feel about her, and I know that's how she feels about me, and we're as close as you can get."

'Steel And Glass'

John "That's one of the modern punk tracks for me. It actually isn't about one person in particular, but it has been about a few people and, like a novel writer, if I'm writing about something other than myself, I use other people I know or have known as examples. If I want to write a 'down' song, I would have to remember being down, and when I wrote 'Steel And Glass', I used various people and objects. If I had listed who they were, it would be a few people, and you would be surprised. But it really isn't about anybody. I loathe to tell you this, because it spoils the fun. I would sooner everybody think, 'Who's it about?' and try and piece it together. For sure, it isn't about Paul and it isn't about Eartha Kitt. It has a few licks like the saxes are playing the guitar licks from 'How Do You Sleep?' I like to compute variations of my own music in the music I do. I steal from myself."

Saturday, September 28
John guests with the DJ Dennis Elsas on his WNEW-FM New York radio show . . .

Dennis "Can you go about your life easily, like can you have dinner in a restaurant?"

John "Oh yeah. That goes for LA, 'Frisco, anywhere. But I think people are a bit cooler in New York. I've been here for three years and people sort of wave and taxi drivers say, 'Are you still here?' Or 'Good luck,' or whatever, about the immigration. One of my biggest kicks is just going out to eat or just going to the movies and doing things I couldn't do when I was in the middle of The Beatles, and I really get off on that. People occasionally ask for autographs or just want to shake hands, which is cool for me. I'm just known enough to keep ego floating and I'm known enough to get myself around, which is nice."

On the subject of his deportation from America, **John** replies . . .

"Every now and again, I suddenly hear that I've got thirty days to get out of the country. The last time was when I was on my way to the Record Plant, and I was in a taxi and the radio was on and I heard it announced over the radio. So, with me being rather jocular, I said, 'Drive me to the airport fast!' We were laughing about it. My lawyers hadn't told me, because they didn't want to depress me in the middle of the album, but I got it over the airwaves instead."

Monday, September 30
In a photo shoot for the *Evening News* newspaper at his St John's Wood home, **Paul** displays his love for riding a motorbike, an item he was photographed riding whilst in Nashville in July . . .

"It's more fun than the Rolls, isn't it," he says to the photographer, David Thorpe. "I still have my red Lamborghini and my Rolls Royce convertible, but I still prefer the bike. I started riding it in the States and I had it whipped over because it was so much fun. And another good thing is that no one recognises me when I've got the face screen on."

OCTOBER
This month in Los Angeles, **George** finishes his *Dark Horse* album and joins his band to begin rehearsals for the forthcoming North American tour . . .

Ravi Shankar "At the rehearsal, during the first run-throughs, it took about two hours and eighteen songs before George would do a Beatles song. I had to go to George to urge him to consider audience expectations and give people a couple of old songs. He says people expect him to be exactly what he was ten years ago. He's matured so much in so many years. That's the problem with all the artists . . . people like to hear the old nostalgia."

Tom Scott, a member of George's band "George is one of the few guys with the prestige and the resources to do something good and is willing to do it and put his neck on the line. By that I mean presenting a show with so much new material when people expect him to do a Beatles."

George "I had no control over the rehearsal and recording schedules, I don't have control over anything. I believe in God and he is the supreme controller even down to the rehearsal . . . It's more like I am right at this minute. I'm talking about the emphasis that gets put on a thing. People expect so much. If you don't expect anything, life is just one big bonus, but when you expect anything, then you can be let down. I don't let anybody down."

This month . . .

John remarks, "When I last saw Paul, we talked about the very early days a lot and we had a good couple of nights reminiscing about Liverpool and Hamburg. Now, it's so far away we really do like it. I even collected Beatles memorabilia from the recent *Beatlefest* held in New York. They had this rally with five or ten thousand people, in fact. It was very good. I got old Beatles posters and badges, all the jazz, and Beatles bootlegs. I'm a Beatles fan. I hardly listen to the albums but I listen to the stuff if it's on the radio. They are always still playing Beatles stuff, and if I've got the radio on, I'll listen. When they put the re-packaged stuff out (*1962–1966, 1967–1970*), I listened to that. I have favourites but there are too many to list favourites."

Thursday, October 10

John meanwhile continues with promotional appearances for his album *Walls And Bridges*. His time today is taken by being interviewed by the radio DJ Jim Ladd. The feature is recorded on the fourth floor of a New York office block. The microphone used in the interview is taped onto a coffee cup, which stands on a pile of books, because Ladd had forgotten his microphone stand. Ladd begins by asking John about his typical day . . .

"Well, there's two kinds of days," **John** replies. "In general, there's the days when I'm working in the studio, recording and when I'm not doing that, I like to wake up at eleven, eleven-thirty, inject myself with caffeine, a gallon of it. I always get the papers and put the TV on, whatever I'm doing, even if I'm not watching it. I hang out, take a walk to the office, see what the letters are, see what's cooking there, or I'll just stay in. My favourite occupation is staying in. I have to go out to appreciate staying in a lot, because I tend to be a homebody."

Ladd "After being hassled for so long by this country, I'm really interested to know what it is about America that makes you want to stay here so badly."

John "I think if there's hope in the world, America is it, however much bad side it has. And if there's anything cooking, or there's any hope in the world, America has it. It has the energy and everything else. That's why I want to be here. I feel comfortable here, luckily I speak the same language almost, so I really feel at home here. I've never felt a stranger. The music is international and American music is what I was brought up on. It feels quite natural for me to be here. The only unnatural thing happening is that they keep telling me to leave."

Ladd "What's your vision of the future at this point?"

John "It's hard to see the future. I'm not a good futureologist. I believe that we get whatever we project, somehow. It's putting it simply, but somehow I believe that. As an example, Leonardo Da Vinci projected that we would fly in machines or go under the water and we did that. I think a lot of the human race projected flying so that's why I always felt that projecting love and peace, even though we're all human and I get violent and I'm not always peaceful, that's what I want. So I think if I project that, then we're going to get that. And when I get depressed about any hope for the future, whatever that means, maybe it's never going to be any different and it's always going to be like this, you know, that's what it is. We've got to settle for this. If there's any change to be made, I think it has as much to do with attitude and projection of thought as it has with actually psychically changing things and when you get down to the nitty-gritty, it's all another clique. It's almost the battle between good and evil, for want of a better word. It's going on anyway, but if you don't do anything about it, however slight a way, then one side gets a slight advantage."

Ladd "How are George, Ringo and Paul doing? Are they happy and productive now?"

John "Well, you can tell by the charts how well they're doing. Ringo I've spent more time with in the last two, two and a half years, than any other ex-Beatle, because he comes to this country a lot. We get on fine; I don't have to say that. I've seen a lot of him. The next one I've seen a lot of is Paul. He travels more than George does. George I've seen maybe twice in two years and we've talked on the phone a couple of times and Ringo, Paul and I were together in LA and Paul and I were together in New York for a couple of nights. That's a couple of months ago. We just drunk wine and said, 'Remember this? Remember that?' We did all that trip and we had a jam session on the West Coast, too. It's the first time I've been in the studio with him since . . . George, I'm expecting to see when he's on tour. I know he's coming to rehearse on the West Coast . . . I know he'll kill me for saying this, I thought about zapping out to see him before the tour, but I don't think he'll be too much fun before he goes on tour, because he's going to be wound up. He's the first one of us to go out on the road. He's carrying the whole ball game. We get on fine. We all had our little pains when we split up, but that was possibly down to fear, you know. It's hard to be independent after ten years, after being locked in each other's arms, and then suddenly you're on your own. It was frightening for me and I'm sure it was for the others. But I think we've got over it."

Monday, October 21

Paul announces, "Through Wings, Linda and I have some pretty young fans these days. Youngsters call around and bring Linda flowers. Boys mostly and we treat them just like neighbourhood kids. I keep reading things that say how much happier I must be now that I am an old family man. Well, I am happy. But I have always been pretty happy. Leaping around the world with The Beatles and really raving it up did not exactly depress me, you know. I would never knock raving. I did it and enjoyed it. But these days I am happy on a warm, family level. Two of our kids are at school. But the littlest one, Stella, is not. She comes in every morning and gets into bed with us when the others have gone. And nothing can beat that, I suppose. Not all the raving in the world."

With the first batch of recordings for the *Rock 'N' Roll* album now regarded by John as a disaster, today he sets about finishing the disc at the Record Plant in New York . . .

John "We got the *Rock 'N' Roll* tapes back from Spector two days before I came to do *Walls And Bridges* and I couldn't stand to listen to them because I didn't want to even remember what was going on in LA, never mind listen to the tapes. When I put *Walls And Bridges* out, I thought, 'Now I'll listen to those tapes.' Only about four of the tracks I could save, in my opinion. Twenty-eight guys are out of tune and it's pretty hard to mix 'em down. There were twenty-eight guys playing live on the Phil Spector sessions. It was a fantastic experience in a way. Anyway, I decided I'd either throw these (tapes) away or I could make an EP out of it and so I thought, 'The best thing is to just finish it off and make enough tracks to have an album.' So, I started recording again and I finished the *Rock 'N' Roll* thing in five days. I did about ten tracks in all, one after the other. I really had more fun. In fact, I took it very relaxed. If it works, it works. All the words to 'Stand By Me', 'Be-Bop-A-Lula', I knew them all from being fifteen, they all just came back like that. So it was simple . . . I would do more albums of that stuff, but then I would get slagged off, 'Oh, he can't write anymore.' "

Wednesday, October 23
In Los Angeles, at the Beverly Wiltshire Hotel, **George** breaks from rehearsals to attend an 11am press conference announcing his forthcoming North American tour, his first since 1966. Unfortunately, he does not arrive at the hotel until approximately 11.45am, to the annoyance of the disgruntled American press . . .

Syndicated news report "Former Beatle George Harrison, launching his first Canadian and American concert tour in eight years, said he could not imagine The Beatles reuniting professionally unless 'we're all broke'. He says, 'Having played with other musicians, I don't even think The Beatles were that good.' The comment drew gasps at the news conference, the first time that Harrison has spoken out about the future of the former top rock group. 'It's all a fantasy, this idea of putting The Beatles back together again. The only way it will happen is if we're all broke.' Even then, Harrison said, he would not relish playing with Paul McCartney . . . 'To play with The Beatles, I'd rather have Willie Weeks on bass than Paul McCartney. Paul's a fine bass player, but he's sometimes over powering . . . Ringo's got the best backbeat in the business. He'll play a great backbeat 24 hours a day. He hated drum solos . . . John has gone through his scene, but feels to me like he's come round. I'd join a band any day with John Lennon, but I wouldn't join a band with Paul McCartney. That's not personal; it's from a musician's point of view.' "

George remarks at the press conference "I realise The Beatles did fill a space in the Sixties and all the people who The Beatles meant something to, have not given it up. It's like with anything, you grow up with it and become attached to it. That's one of the problems in our life, becoming too attached to things. But, I understand The Beatles, in many ways, did nice things and it's appreciated that people still like them. The problem comes when they still live in the past and they want to hold onto something and they are afraid of change . . . Now, all four of us are enjoying being individuals. We don't miss the cult adoration that caused riots when we appeared . . . With all respect to Paul, The Beatles was like being in a box. We'd been boxed up together for ten years. The biggest break in my career was in 1963 getting in The Beatles. The biggest break since then is getting out of them."

When hearing of George's remarks, **Paul** snaps back, "I don't agree with George. I don't think that The Beatles weren't any good. I think he's quite wrong on that. I think he has been taken out of context. Willie Weeks, I reckon, is a better bass player than me. I don't like to say that. It doesn't make me very happy to say that, but he has got all the finger techniques off and all that. But I still think The Beatles has an even better thing. I think we had more of an excitement, a more of a kind of joy. That was what people picked up on, actually. The whole kind of buzz of it was always coming out with a different record from the last one."

Reporter to George at his Press conference, "What do you think of Lennon's solo material?"

George "His new record, I think is lovely."

Reporter "Looking back, what do you consider to be the crowning glory of your career as a musician?"

George "As a musician I don't think I've done that yet. As an individual, just being able to sit here today and be relatively sane, that's probably my biggest accomplishment to date."

A reporter asks George about his estranged wife, Patti "I am now separated from Patti. She is now dating Eric Clapton."

Reporter "Do you intend getting a divorce?"

George "No, that's as silly as marriage . . . I'm pleased about her and Eric. I'm pleased about it. He's an old friend of mine and I would rather have her going out with someone like him than some other dope."

Reporter "Allen Klein is suing The Beatles. How is that affecting you? Do you have to sell more albums now?"

George "No. To tell you the truth, there's a whole lot of money which is in Receivership since Paul McCartney sued us and actually it's fortunate he did sue us, because the money's in Receivership, so at least nobody can spend it. There's a lot of millions of dollars from The Beatles' partnership, and we can either give it to the lawyers or we give it to the Revenue."

Reporter "What are the hopes of Dark Horse Records?"

George "I want it to be reasonably small. To tell you the truth, I've been here just over a week and if I signed all the people who gave me tapes, I'd be bigger than RCA, but fortunately, I don't have time to listen to them."

Reporter "I'm writing for women's pages, and you are married. May I ask you, does your wife cook for you?"

George "First of all, as I've just said, I don't have a wife anymore, but when I did, she used to cook sometimes and I learned how to cook myself. I cooked vegetarian Indian food, although I like other food as well. I'm a vegetarian. I don't eat fish, I don't eat chicken and I don't eat meat. That's why I'm so pale and thin."

Reporter "Are sales down for the concerts?"

George "Oh no!"

Reporter "What's your relationship now with John and Paul?"

George "It's very good actually."

Reporter "Do you see them often?"

George "I haven't seen John because he's been in the States, although I've spoken to him quite a lot on the telephone, and he sounds to me like he's in great shape. It's as if we've gone right round the circle and we're back at the beginning again. I just met Paul recently and he's . . . Everybody's really friendly. But it doesn't mean we're going to form a band."

Reporter "Do you still meditate?"

George "It's too difficult a question to answer, really. I must say there's a state of consciousness, which is the goal of everybody. I haven't sat down and done meditation like that for some time, but at the same time, I constantly think of the Lord in one fashion or another. My thing is just to remember and try to see him within all of you, and that feeling itself is a meditation."

Reporter "There's a paradox there between lifestyles."

George "It is difficult, yeah, but the point is it's also good practice in a way. As they say, 'To be in the world, but not of the world.' You can go to the Himalayas and miss it completely, and you can be stuck in the middle of New York and be very spiritual. I mean, I noticed in certain places, like Switzerland, I find a lot of uptight people there, because they're living within themselves. If you're stuck in New York, you have to somehow look within yourself; otherwise you'd go crackers. So, in a way, it's good to be able to go in and out of both situations. Most people think when the world gets itself together; we'll all free ourselves from the chains we ourselves have chained ourselves to. But I don't think that suddenly some magic happens and the whole of us will all be liberated in one throw."

Reporter "Do you pay much attention to what critics say?"

George "I cancelled all my papers five years ago, to tell you the truth, so I don't really know what people say. If I do see a review of an album, I'll read it, although it doesn't really make too much difference what they say, because I am what I am whether they like it or not."

Reporter "Would you ever want to live permanently in India?"

George " Yes."

Reporter "When?"

George "When I get through with all this madness. There's a word called karma and it means that whatever we are now we cause by our previous actions. Whatever is going to be in the future is what we cause by our actions now. I'd like to be able to cause my actions to lead me to end up sometime in India."

Reporter "How is it you don't want to do personal interviews?"

George "There's nothing to say, really. I'm a musician, not a talker. I mean that if you just get my albums, it's like *Peyton Place*. It'll tell you exactly what I've been doing."

Reporter "Is it conceivable that you could get together The Beatles to generate some money for charity?"

George "Well, if you're a promoter, I'd say no. I wouldn't rule anything out in life. People think we plan, but we don't plan anything. It's all at the mercy of the Lord and

I'm sorry to keep talking about the Lord to you all, but he's there. I have experienced something in my life and I know he's there."

Reporter "You said you had an experience which made you believe in the Lord. Was this a specific experience?"

George "Just certain things happened in my life, which left me thinking, 'What's it all about, Alfie?' And I remembered Jesus said somewhere, 'Knock and the door shall be opened,' and I said, 'Knock, knock, hello!' It's very difficult. From the Hindu point of view, each soul is potentially divine. The goal is to manifest the divinity. The word yoga means union and the union is supposedly between the mind and the body, and spirit, and yoga isn't lying on nails or just standing on your head. I mean, there are various forms of yoga, and they're all branches on one big tree. The Lord has got a million names. Whatever you call Him, it doesn't matter as long as you call Him. Jesus is on the mainline, tell Him what you want. Going back to self-realisation, one guru said he found no separation between man and God saving man's spiritual unadventurousness, and that's the catch. Everybody's so unadventurous. We're all conditioned. Our consciousness has been so polluted with material energy that it's hard to try and pull it all away in order to really get at our true nature. It's like everyone of us has within us a drop of the ocean, and we have the same qualities as God, just like a drop of the ocean has the same qualities as the whole ocean. Everybody's looking for something and we are it. We don't have to look anywhere. It's right there within ourselves."

Friday, October 25 (UK)
Wings release their new single 'Junior's Farm' . . .

Paul "Sometimes, we are a bit lazy about what should be the next single. If there's a good tune around, we'll say, 'Yeah, let's get that out,' but 'Junior's' was just a track we did. It wasn't going to go on the next album and it didn't fit in with the tracks we did and it was just there and it just seemed like a good single. If I thought, 'Yes, definitely the new single,' I think I'd have made sure we did a lot more with it, probably . . . Afterwards, people ask, 'What were you trying to say in that song?' And, do you know I wasn't trying to say anything, I was just trying to write a song. I just get hold of a guitar and the chords just come out. 'Junior's Farm' was quite an easy one; there are only a couple of chords. The tune came first. I wanted a bit of a bopper, not as Linda is supposed to have said, a real rocker. It has silly words and basically all it means is, 'Let's get out of the city. Let's go down to Junior's Farm or Strawberry Fields,' or whatever. As for reading deep meanings into the words, people shouldn't bother, there aren't any."

Promotional adverts for the disc feature the group surrounded by a rather motionless seal . . .

Paul "It looks very sedate in the picture, but you should have seen it in reality. The table was all neatly arranged with stacks of cards until Julie, who was the seal, decided to rearrange things. What's more, we had to keep her and her boyfriend, who was also there, apart. We got them from some people who just happened to have some seals for hire. They came along with this enormous van full of water and loads of fish. Throwing fish to them was the only way we could get the animals to do what we wanted. They weren't really trained at all and they had to be kept wet all the time. No seals next time, I think we'll put a bull in the next song or something easy like that."

... Its B-side is 'Sally G' ...

Paul "I wrote 'Sally G' after an inspiring visit to a country music club in Nashville."

Friday, November 1

In an interview with the UK music reporter John Blake, **John** announces, "I would like The Beatles to make a record together again. I am still asked almost every day about The Beatles getting together again, by waitresses and almost everyone else I meet. If we feel like it, we might make a record together some time soon. I mean, I am a Beatles fan. I realise now that I do like The Beatles. When I hear them on the radio, I think to myself that some of the songs are really, really good. I personally would like The Beatles to make a record together again. But I don't really know how the other three feel about the idea. We have all established ourselves separately now. We have got over the pain of breaking up. We have done whatever it is we wanted to do. The trouble is that Paul and George still have so many hassles getting into the States, that even the four of us have never even sat down in one room together to talk, let alone record. It is feasible though that we could all find ourselves in the same recording studio, and that could be fun."

Blake "How do you regard the work that the four of them have produced by themselves since The Beatles?"

John "Well, when I hear the records played on the radio, I still tend to think of them as individual Beatle songs. They still have that Beatley sound to them. I mean, if you took the best tracks from each of our albums, and put them together, you would have a great Beatles album. There just happens to be four albums instead of one now."

Blake writes, "The biggest single barrier to a Beatles reunion is John's drawn-out battle with the American immigration authorities. They want to deport him as undesirable because of a drugs conviction in Britain six years ago. Lennon, fearing for his visa, has pumped hundreds of thousands of pounds into fighting them."

John "About eighteen months ago, it really started getting to me and it was dragging me down, interfering with my work and affecting everything I did. My lawyer doesn't even give me the details any more. He thinks it will worry me or something. I think it could easily drag on for years yet. I'm not going to get kicked out in the next few days."

Blake "Why do you want to stay in America?"

John "Well, I don't necessarily want to stay here all the time. I would like to be free to travel anywhere. I like to think of the world as a kind of global village. And the one thing my money gave me was freedom to travel about that village. But the thing is that, just as Paris is the place every artist wanted to be in the last century, America is the centre of the rock world today. This is where it all began. This is the place where rock started and there is still so much energy here. I don't want to become an American citizen or anything. I just want to be allowed in and out like most other British people. Of course there are times when I miss Britain badly and I feel like climbing on a plane and going home. It's the little things you miss, like decent sausages, or a pub I know in London, or seeing the autumn in beautiful places, like Surrey or Wales. I still consider myself as an Englishman and I'll stay that way until I die."

Blake writes, "It is estimated that Lennon's fight to stay in the States has cost him well over a quarter of a million pounds. I ask him, 'Are you growing short of cash?' "

John "No, I'm still earning a bit from my songs so I'm not hard up and I know that if I needed money I could go back on stage again. The offers get higher every day. For a full Beatles reunion I have been offered seven million dollars and I could get about two million just for myself."

Blake "As he spoke, John smiled at his girlfriend, May Pang, a Chinese and American girl who was his former secretary and comes from the tenements of New York's East Harlem . . . 'What,' I asked, 'has become of your marriage to Yoko Ono?' "

John "Well, it sounds corny, but Yoko and I are just good friends now. We speak to each other almost every day."

Saturday, November 2
While John is openly optimistic about a Beatles reunion, George remains noncommittal and prepares to begin his North American tour . . .

George "I've just been so busy working this year, that if I had sat back and thought about it, I would have been petrified! I would not have been able to do it . . . I've felt, probably for three years, that this tour, subconsciously, I've felt the presence of this tour in my subconscious and it's been bubbling deep down and it's been slowly bubbling up to the surface and it's like a lot of forces and energies. In a way, I decided to go on tour, I suppose. But in reality, it was outside energies and maybe subconscious desires, or I don't know. But whatever it was, I felt it coming for three years, and when it finally came, I thought, 'What am I doing? It's mad. It's bloody mad!' It was such a big tour. I did think that if I was to tour America again, I certainly didn't want to do the same again as those hectic, really crazy tours like in the old days, where you'd be left in a room for eight hours. I thought we'd do a tour, maybe playing ten cities and take a lot of time to go to those ten cities, and maybe take two or three days off in between each city where I'd see a little bit of America, maybe going by train or something like that. Instead, it got to the point where I thought, 'Well, if I'm doing it, I might as well do it in one shot,' because once you get into the motion, I thought I might as well do as many as possible. I had no idea who wanted to see me, who doesn't want to see me, which cities to play, which cities not to play. I just had a lot of concepts, which I wanted to get rid of . . . There have been moments where I have thought, 'A little bit of negativity has crept in, and I had to try and squash it immediately. It's like what Lord Buckley said, relating to what I've said, he's said, relating to love, 'Love is like a beautiful garden. You use it and it just grows and blossoms, but when you don't, it recedes.' So positive and negative is like that. When you use the positive thoughts, it just blossoms and it seems to uphold and when you get negative and doubts come in, it comes like creepers to strangle you."

The tour begins tonight with a show at the Pacific Coliseum in Vancouver, Canada. Backstage after the concert, **George** talks to Ben Fong-Torres of *Rolling Stone* "There's been bad moments in the show, but I mean it doesn't matter, because of the spirit of everybody dancing and digging it. And if you get fifty drunkards who are shouting and bad-mouthing Ravi, or whatever, and you get 17,000 people who go out of there relatively pleased, some of them ecstatic and some of them who happen to get much more from it than they ever thought . . . I'm taping the audience every night and asking them about it, and I know we get ten people who say the show sucks and we get a hundred who, when you say, 'Did you get what you wanted?' say, 'We got much more than we ever hoped for.' "

Ben Fong-Torres "What about those who scrounged up $9.50 wanting, at least, a taste of Beatle George?"

George "Well, why do they want to see if there is a Beatle George? I don't say I'm Beatle George . . . I certainly am going to control my own concept of me. Gandhi says create and preserve the image of your choice. The image of my choice is not Beatle George. If they want to do that, they can go and see Wings. Why live in the past? Be here now and now, whether you like me or not, this is what I am . . . Fuck it, my life belongs to me . . . It actually doesn't. It belongs to him. My life belongs to the Lord Krishna and there's me dog collar to prove it. I'm just a dog and I'm led around by me collar by Krishna . . . I'm the servant of the servant of the servant of the servant of Krishna. I'm just a grovelling lumberjack, lucky to be a grain of dirt in creation. That's how I feel. Never been so humble in all my life, and I feel great."

Don Stanley, music columnist "Elton John's recent concert tour sold out in hours. George Harrison announces a sell-out after three weeks, but there were still empty seats in Vancouver's Pacific Coliseum, a newish concrete hockey rink that can hold 17,500 people. Outside in the cold, foggy, November air, ghostly scalpers were down to five and even four dollars for tickets set at $9.50 . . . In spite of window displays in record shops, which showed the three solo albums and action photos of the star, and in spite of hundreds of free tickets dispensed by a radio station, there was a noticeable lack of enthusiasm. And the press, arriving at the Coliseum on Saturday night, was surprised to find no waiting press conference. Smooth and fast talking PR men announced there would be no interviews during the tour, no backstage access and that the photographers had better be equipped with the telephoto lenses. All this sounds as though Harrison wants to stay out of touch and Saturday's concert was the result . . . After the 'My Sweet Lord' encore, his final words were 'Good night and God bless you.' He was an appealing figure on stage, obviously, even stupefyingly sincere, but it seemed he will need all the blessings that God can rant on the rest of the tour."

Joining him on stage are the chosen musicians Ravi Shankar, Tom Scott, Willie Weeks, Robben Ford, Emil Richards, Chuck Findley, Andy Newmark, Jim Horn and Billy Preston . . .

"He was definitely inspired after Bangla Desh," Billy Preston tells *Rolling Stone* magazine. "He wanted to do it again, right away. But it took some time. Bangla Desh was an exceptional show because everybody was there. He had to do a lot of thinking on this one because he had to get out there and be the one."

George "People always want to have their picture taken with you. I remember I was in America, on the tour, and I got a note from Henry Kissinger saying he wanted to meet me. So I thought, 'That's strange.' But I went along and he said, 'Glad you came. Why did you want to meet me?' And I thought, 'Well, I didn't want to meet you, you wanted to meet me.' He said, 'I met another one of your lot once, what's his name? The one with the Japanese wife?' Then he pressed this buzzer and a photographer appeared. He got up to have his photo taken with me and he was standing there with one half of his trousers stuck halfway up his leg. He was just like a pop star, really. He just wanted to have his photo taken with famous people."

Sunday, November 10
Long Beach Arena . . .

George "When I toured the States, in a way, it was pathetic. There was a lot of violence, just a lot of violence. After one concert, I stayed on, at the end, instead of running out and escaping. I waited until the whole hall had emptied out. I had to wait a couple of hours, because I was meeting somebody off a plane. This was Long Beach and what they call festival seating, which means there are no seats. You stand up and festival seating is where they open the doors and everybody has the same priced tickets for the main area in front of the stage. They all queue up and they open the doors and they run, and the first people in the queue get to the front and so on, until they fill that section. When all the audience had gone, I went out into the stadium. Sometimes, you don't really know where you are playing. Those stadiums are so big and with the stage lighting, you don't see much. So I went out to have a look, and it was such a mess! There was a bulldozer, a huge bulldozer, just moving this stack of garbage, people's trousers and coats and shoes and broken bottles of whiskey. That is one thing I noticed the kids are getting really into. I mean, they were all smoking reefers, for a while, but now they are really hitting the booze. They are all drinking whiskey and gin. They are all spaced out, anyway. You play a concert, and half of them don't even know who they are watching."

Monday, November 11
At The Los Angeles Forum, during the first of three shows, George introduces the song 'Maya Love' with a poor response . . .

George (to the unmoved crowd) "I don't know how it feels down there, but from up here, you seem pretty dead."

Later, a member of the audience screams out a request for the song 'Bangla Desh' . . .
George replies: "I have to rewrite the song. But, don't just shout 'Bangla Desh'; give them something to help. You can chant Krishna, Krishna, Krishna and maybe you'll feel better. But, if you just shout about Bangla Desh, Bangla Desh, Bangla Desh, it's not going to help anybody."

Robert Kemnitz, the *Herald* newspaper "Opening with 'While My Guitar Gently Weeps', the band was cooking so fast and hard that Harrison's vocal shortcomings were easily overlooked. But, as he tore into 'Something', shouting the lyrics of a most tender ballad like a possessed Bob Dylan on an off night, you realised the voice was almost gone."

Billy Preston "George didn't want to do 'Something' at all. I knew he was going to have to do it, and he started rebelling against it by doing it a different way, rewriting the lyrics. But, at least he's doing the song."

Friday, November 15 (UK)
Ringo releases *Goodnight Vienna*, his latest studio album . . .

'Goodnight Vienna'

Ringo "John wrote the title track. It's an old sort of saying, 'It's all down to goodnight Vienna.' You know, you can't do anything about it. Also I like science fiction and on the cover, we cut Michael Rennie's head off, because that is from *The Day The Earth Stood Still*, and they put mine on. It was like, 'Well, it's all down to goodnight Vienna, I'm leaving for a while.' You feel like that occasionally, you know, stop the world and let me off. I enjoyed the sci-fi cover and the title. It all seemed to tie in."

'Only You'

Ringo "That's an old song. When John came over during the recordings, we were just singing it and we said, 'Let's do that.' And I did it and it turned out, as far as I'm concerned, very good so we put it out as a single. We had this film clip with me and Harry Nilsson on top of the Capitol Tower. Stanley Dorfman, from the BBC, did it and while we were doing that, later that night, I did a laser show off my chest, reflecting lasers off my silver star. It went for 200 miles and it went right down town. It was a great day. We had marching bands and it was great fun to do."

Saturday, November 16
Meanwhile, with his throat continuing to give him cause for concern, George's North American Tour reaches Salt Lake City . . .

George "We were playing Salt Lake City and during the intermission or between the two shows, somebody said, 'President Ford's son is here, is it okay to bring him backstage to meet you?' And I said, 'Sure, I'll meet anybody. They don't have to be the President's son.' I don't have any ideas about the first family. The only impression I had of President Ford was that he was a person who was put in a job, which he didn't particularly want and maybe he didn't really need it at all. In fact, he probably would like to say he needs it like a hole in the head. When I met President Ford, I could look him in the eyes and I felt he was a decent human being, and it gave me hope. It gave me hope because, not only is America one of the heaviest places in this planet, but America has such an influence on the rest of the world. So I met his son and his son was just fantastic. His son was just a really nice, very, very good guy. I got a really good feeling for him the first time I met him."

Away from George's tour, the *Daily Mail* in the UK reveals on **November 19** that, "For fees that potentially could add up to half a million dollars, **Mr Paul McCartney** has accepted a commission to write an advertising jingle for the McDonald's hamburger chain."

Friday, November 22
George's tour reaches Texas with a concert at Fort Worth . . .

George "When we (The Beatles) went to Dallas or Houston on the old Beatles tours, I remember both years. The first year we went to Dallas and we almost got killed and the second year we went to Houston and again we almost got killed. So my concept of Texas has been wherever I go, I'm not going to Texas because they're all so mad! I just remembered what happened then, and so I played Fort Worth and Houston and it's amazing, the change, you know. It just blows me out, the change in five years of the people's consciousness. It's incredible! It's like, say, four or five years ago in San Francisco or Los Angeles, it's like that now in Texas, the feeling of the people and the way they look and what they liked. It's great! Fort Worth was really nice and so was one of the shows in Houston. I didn't have any of the old fears that I thought I may have . . ."

Wednesday, November 27

George performs at the Mid-South Coliseum in Memphis and announces, "I've just met David Bowie, who they call 'Boowie' in America. I know Ringo thinks he is great, and John does too. But I don't have any concept of whether he's great or not great. I met him in Memphis, and he was in the shower room with the band just before he went on for the second show and, I hope he wasn't offended by it, I pulled his hat off from over his eyes and said, 'Hi, man. How are you? Nice to meet you.' I pulled his hat off his eyes and said, 'Do you mind if I have a look at you to see what you are, because I've only ever seen those dopey pictures of you.' In every picture I've seen of David Bowie or Elton John, they just look stupid to me. I think he (Bowie) looks dopey. I want to see who the person is."

Meanwhile, back in England this evening, during a night out in the capital, Paul and Linda are the surprise guests onstage at Rod Stewart & The Faces' concert at the Odeon Cinema, Lewisham, South London . . .

Paul "It was just a night off for Linda and me. We turned up pretty much as audience, except that we were backstage and had just come along to see Rod and The Faces. I just had an old jacket and clothes on. I wasn't thinking of being in public. I had forgotten that there would be kids outside the stage door who would recognise me. Anyway, we went backstage and had a few drinks; I had a few more than Linda. Eventually Rod said, 'Look, why don't you come on?' He does one of our songs, 'Mine For Me'. We were joking around and said, 'Yeah, sure, we'll come on,' and thought nothing more about it. Next thing I know, we're watching from the side of the stage and Rod says, 'Now, my brother and sister are coming on to sing a song with me.' Linda just clenched my hand a bit and said, 'This is us,' and we went wandering on. I think it was good, we enjoyed it. I think it was nice for the audience, too. I think they enjoyed it. It was a nice perk for them."

Thursday, November 28
Back in the States, as the result of a bet, **John** agrees to join Elton John on stage during his concert this evening at New York's Madison Square Garden . . .

Elton John "We worked on 'Whatever Gets You Through The Night' and I said, 'If it reached No. 1, you must play onstage with me.' John was amazed at the advance in the PA systems. He said, 'Oh, so this is what it's all about, eh?' He was so nervous, he even threw up before going on stage."

Music journalist, Lenny Kaye "After Elton ran through his usual hit-laden repertoire, surprise guest John Lennon came out on the opening night to join him as the audience bounced politely off the ceiling. Chewing gum, cautiously nervous, Lennon was in fine shape, 'Whatever Gets You Through The Night', passing to 'Lucy In The Sky With Diamonds' and revelling in 'I Saw Her Standing There'. John admitted he had his best time on 'I Saw Her Standing There'. Why? Because it was Paul's domain. He was still wearing a white gardenia in his lapel, half of a matched set Yoko had sent to him and Elton and which they wore on stage."

Yoko "John came to New York a few times and asked me to go back to him. I wouldn't. I was going out with other people, several others. One of these young guns persuaded me to go to that big concert of Elton's and suddenly, John walked out on to the stage. I didn't know he was going to be there . . ."

John "I didn't know she (Yoko) was in the audience. I couldn't have gone on if I'd known she was there."

May Pang "Even though in the future John would tell the press that he did not know who was going to be there that night, he not only knew but Yoko also complained a number of times about her seating location."

Yoko "I was in the audience and Elton came on and he performed. This was the first time I saw Elton perform. He's such a fantastic performer, you know, the performer of the century. When John came out, the whole hall was sort of shaking . . ."

John "Performing is not my greatest kick. I had fun with Elton, but that's just because it was Elton. He was really more nervous than I was, because he was nervous for me. I think he felt, 'Poor bugger, maybe he'll collapse.' It was a weird feeling being up there alone, but I knew Elton and I knew the band and it was just a one-off thing . . . I was quite astonished that the crowd was so nice to me. The crowd was so nice."

Yoko "The audience gave him a terrific reception . . . Everybody was just jumping and applauding and screaming and shouting. It was an amazing scene. That floor was shaking. I thought it was like an earthquake. So, John came out . . . he was standing there, but the John I observed was a different John. I thought, 'Oh, he looks so lonely,' you know, 'he looks so lonely up there.' I began crying and somebody next to me said, 'Why are you crying?' 'I'm not crying,' I remember saying . . . When he bowed, it was too quickly and too many times. The young guy I was with wanted to go backstage. I didn't want to, but I said, 'Okay.' "

Elton John "The audience gave John a ten-minute standing ovation. It was one of the best nights I have ever had on stage."

John "I came off stage and there she was . . . We looked at each other, like the Indica Gallery scene again . . ."

Yoko "John, of course, was there with a young chick. He said, 'Oh, I'm so happy to see you,' and we sat there, talking and holding hands. His young chick and my guy were still standing there, getting more and more uptight. After that, John asked me out. We went to an art show together and we started dating all over again."

John " . . . and that's when we got together again . . ."

In reply to questions about his future after the show, **John** replies, "I might do odd TV or TV specials where I can control the thing, like in the studio. I like to see it. I like to have something afterwards. After the concert you don't get anything, you either get cash or a headache. I hate live albums really, even though I've put a couple out."

Saturday, November 30
Meanwhile, backstage in Chicago, during George's American tour, Ravi Shankar collapses with a suspected heart attack. Thankfully, it later proves to be incorrect . . .

George "I found out later, because Ravi and I both have the same doctor in London, that Ravi's heart, with these Indian time signatures, happens to beat in seven and a half beats, or something, and it has a slightly different rhythm cycle because the way he has to sit with the sitar and all his life he's sat like that. The organs inside his body are slightly at an angle, but there's nothing wrong with his heart, it's healthy, but the doctor said he was supposed to carry a card with him, in case anything happens to him, and he can just show a card. Then they'll know that his heart is OK. When he collapsed, the doctors listened to his heart and decided to shoot him up with a lot of stuff, thinking he was having a heart attack. So he had to spend a lot of time recovering from the hospital."

Friday, December 6
Back home, George's festive single 'Ding Dong Ding Dong' is released . . .

George " 'Ding Dong Ding Dong' was the quickest one I ever wrote. It took me three minutes, except it took me four years of looking at the thing, which was written on the wall at my home, 'Ring out the old, ring in the new. Ring out the false, ring in the truth,' before I realised it was a hit song. It makes me laugh because it's so simple. That song evaded me for four years."

Monday, December 9 (USA)
To coincide with his first major solo tour, George releases the album *Dark Horse* . . .

'Dark Horse'

George "I wrote that at five in the morning on my way to bed. I was just playing my guitar and I just thought of the line, 'I'm a dark horse'. When I was a kid, I always remember them saying, 'Oh, have you heard about Mrs Penguin from the Co-op? She's knocking off Mr Jones. Oh, she's a dark horse.' It was always that sort of thing. I was brought up knowing that dark horse was a phrase like that. So I thought, 'I'm a dark horse. Okay, I'm running on a dark racecourse,' but that just cracked me up. I thought, 'No, I can't use that. It's crummy.' Then, the next day, it was still on my mind and I thought, 'A dark racecourse? It may be silly, but it's so silly, it's fantastic, because that's the way it is. I'm a dark horse, but I'm running on a dark racecourse, you know.' What else do you expect? I was just born into it. Don't blame me, I'm a victim of circumstance.

"That album I made called *Dark Horse* was on Apple and distributed by Capitol. What I did was I wrote the song and then we were forming that company and my business manager said to me we've got to have a name for the company and I couldn't think of one. I had been thinking of so many different company names and he said, 'How about one of the songs?' So I said, 'Oh, 'Dark Horse'. That sounds good.' Most people thought I called the album *Dark Horse* after the company but it was the other way round. I called the company after the song."

Sunday, December 15

Meanwhile, George's tour moves on to Nassau with a concert at the Coliseum. Present in the audience during the second shows is John who is accompanied by May Pang . . .

John "I saw the one without Ravi because he had a heart attack. That night the band really cooked. The show I saw was a good show. My personal opinion was that even though I know what George was trying to do, I don't think it worked with Ravi. I mean, I'm no one to say what works and what doesn't work really, but my personal opinion just was that he would have been better without. I think Ravi's great, but it might have been better to keep Ravi separate. I want to see George do George. I'm with the kids, whether it's George Beatle or George ex-Beatle . . . He's cut off, really. It's easy to get cut off. If you're surrounded by people who aren't rocking, then you just forget what it is and he is so involved in the Eastern trip. If you don't listen to the radio, if you switch off from that, you don't know what people are listening to, which happened to me in England. I just suddenly decided because 'Whatever Gets You Through The Night' didn't even crawl around in England, I said, 'Send me a tape of the Top 10,' and it's nowhere like America. I was just 'My God, three years.' I had no idea what was going on there. Now I get them to send it over every few months . . . "

Friday, December 20

George's North American Tour concludes with two performances at Madison Square Garden . . .

Lenny Kaye, New York columnist "George Harrison opened the final engagement of his North American Tour at Madison Square Garden with the jollity of *Monty Python's* 'Lumberjack Song' played over the loudspeakers. But after the initial excitement of seeing an ex-Beatle on stage, it had to be contemplated whether the whole show wouldn't have been more appropriate on the *Flying Circus*, replete with 'Nudge, nudge, wink, wink, say no more'. It was a marathon night of, 'Thank yous'. Harrison would thank the audience and would thank Billy Preston. Uncle Ravi Shankar would come out and receive his thanks, turning to the crowd to thank them again. The band receives a round of thanks. Interspersed with thanks were blessings, 'God bless John, Paul, Ringo and all the x-x-x-x-s' . . . By the way, John Lennon was scheduled to appear at the concert, even going so far as to announce it on television, but he had a falling out with George during the soundcheck. This, however, didn't stop Harrison from wearing his 'Free Lennon' button, a reference to John's immigration problem, alongside the 'Win' badge, given to him by President Ford."

The non-appearance by John is down to his decision not to sign The Beatles' dissolution papers, an action that angers George and comes on top of many crazy happenings at the time . . .

John "Allen Klein was chasing George all over New York. George was even running down back elevators. Ringo won't come to New York. I live here so I get all the papers, and I'm always doing depositions. At the time George was doing his concerts, we were also finalising the Apple papers and what actually happened was that at the last minute I wouldn't sign it. Actually, my astrologer said it wasn't the right time to sign it. George got a little angry with me for not signing it and he decided to finish the tour as he started it. That was cool by me because I had just done Elton, but I didn't want to do George because it was expected. But he probably made the right decision. I saw him afterwards at the party. I love him; we're all right. The thing is that the business was always interfering with pleasure. It was hard to deal with each other anyway, because I had seen a lot of Paul and Ringo in the last two or three years. Paul always comes to New York or I see Ringo in LA, but I hadn't seen George. And not only were we trying to talk to each other not having seen each other in three years, all that time only vaguely communicating through lawyers, we tried to communicate in a hotel. I hung around the hotel for a few days but it was hard. And then I didn't turn up on the day that I was supposed to sign this agreement."

Paul "We had all arrived for the big dissolution meeting in the Plaza Hotel in New York. There were green baize tables, like the Geneva Conference it was, with millions of documents laid out for us to sign. George had just come off tour. I had flown in especially from England . . . and John wouldn't show up. He wouldn't come across the park! George got on the phone, yelled, 'Take those fucking shades off and come over here, you!' John still wouldn't come over. He had a balloon delivered with a sign saying 'Listen To This Balloon'. It was all quite far out."

Linda "The numbers weren't right. The planets weren't right and John wasn't coming. He said he was not coming and that was it. Had we known there was some guy flipping cards on his bed to help him make his decision, we would have all gone over there. George blew his top but it didn't change anything. It's beyond words . . ."

Paul "Later, at another meeting, everything was going swinging. We all settled and, at the last minute, John asked for another million pounds. That's all he wanted, an extra million pounds. So, naturally, that meeting went all into disarray and that finished that particular meeting. Later, when we got a bit friendlier, I said to him, 'What was that about? Why did you demand another million?' And he said, 'I just wanted the cards in my hands. I wanted cards to play with.' It's good standard business practice and he was quite open about it."

John "But I finally did sign it, in Disneyland. I wanted to go over it one more time. I had already seen the concert (by George) in Nassau so I wasn't really planning to go to Madison Square Garden anyway. I don't really enjoy sitting in shows, whoever they are, because you either have to go backstage with all that hassle or sit in front where you get all that looking at you. I know Mick (Jagger) and everybody's always doing it, but it wears the shred out of me. There are not many people I want to see in concerts. I only go because they're friends, you know. I prefer the records, I always did. It's like watching a painter paint, just give me the painting."

At the end of his tour, **George** reflects, "At the time I did that tour, it was a very difficult period because the audiences were like 'Wacko!' They were drunk and disorderly and I was thinking, 'Most of these people, half of them may come to see you and the other half come because that's what's happening in town or they're with somebody who's coming to see you.' And I thought, 'Well, maybe it's better to play to 200 people who like you instead of 17,000 who are just going somewhere to get loaded.' A lot of the people watching my concerts had more of a problem than I did. Although when you read it in the papers, it sounded as though I had it. There were a couple of really negative reviews from *Rolling Stone* and then, in all the other cities we played, the reviews were not bad. It balanced out about forty per cent was not so hot, but some of them were only because they said I didn't have a throat. I was singing like Louis Armstrong. And a lot of people came to see The Beatles. I don't know why, because I'm not The Beatles! A lot of people were a bit uptight about the Indian music section. But then, a lot of people, who came without any preconceived ideas, really loved the show. And it wasn't that bad. The audience response was really good. Every show had a standing ovation, but when you read about it, and the further we moved, it got like a rumour. By the time I came back to England, and I saw a few things in the papers, I said to somebody, 'I get the feeling that it did not go down well with the British people.' And he said, 'Oh no, it was the biggest disaster you've ever done in your life.' But actually doing it, it was not like that. Someday, maybe I can get some of the videos shown on TV of the concert. We took a lot of the audience by surprise because it was a heavy rock band for a start. I mean, two drummers, three horn players, Billy Preston, two guitars, bass and a crazy sort of percussion player, who plays marimbas and xylophone and all kinds of stuff. Then, at another point in the show, another fifteen Indian musicians join the rock band. So you get a band of over thirty people, playing some compositions that were written especially for that combination of people. As I said, a lot of people in the audience without preconceived ideas really loved it. I found out that the people who didn't like us were the ones who, first of all, don't listen or who were coming to see The Beatles. And there is no way that I can be The Beatles."

1975

JANUARY

John reflects on the last fifteen months "No more 1974. I don't want to go through that again . . . To me, '74 was hell and I was glad to be alive and out of it. A lot of my friends thought it was hell too, actually. I was on a 'lost weekend' and without Yoko I would probably be dead. After I split with Yoko, I was depressed with the separation and the things expected of me. So I spent most of my time boozing and drug taking in Los Angeles. I think I was suicidal. Night and day drinking, taking whatever, Librium or whatever. The goal was to obliterate the mind so I wouldn't be conscious. I didn't want to see or feel anything. While I was drinking at least a bottle of vodka a day, I would jump out of moving cars. It was a kind of crazy teenage game I had. What I was ignoring, of course, was that the car behind could have run me over . . . You can't believe how tired I was. I was absolutely depressed. For years I have been under pressure to produce, produce, produce and my head was cluttered. I was trapped and saw no way out."

. . . This month, and with his life showing signs of normality, John is invited to join the Glam Rock star David Bowie in a recording session at the Ladyland Studios in New York . . .

John "Bowie was around, and he was doing 'Across The Universe'. That was an old song of mine. I gave it away because we had made a lousy version of it, and then Spector made an improved lousy version of it and it ended up on the *Let It Be* LP, which none of us would have anything to do with . . . Bowie said, 'Come down.' I had sort of met him once in LA and met him again here. He's fiddling around, he writes them in the studio. He goes in with about four words and a few guys and starts laying down all this stuff and he has virtually nothing. He's making it up in the studio. The guitarist, or he, had this sort of a lick, and we made a song out of it called 'Fame'. So I just contributed whatever I contributed, which is like backwards piano and 'Ooh', and a couple of things, a repeat of 'Fame' and then we needed a middle eight. So we took some of Stevie Wonder's middle eight and did it backwards. It's an interesting track."

Thursday, January 16
Meanwhile, Paul, Linda and Wings begin recording their new album at Allen Toussaint's Sea Saint Studios in New Orleans . . .

Paul "I had never been to New Orleans, except on tour, when we never saw anything except the inside of a trailer. The only thing I remembered about New Orleans was the vibrator bed in the motel and it was sweating hot. We went down to New Orleans in search of a musical town and the weather, and then we found out that the Mardi Gras was on while we were there . . . I had written most of the tracks before we got there and Jimmy had written one of the tracks with a mate of his. We had been to Jamaica before we went to New Orleans and, for the first time ever, I had got all the songs together. I wrote them all out and stuck them together like a scroll that went from one room to the other. So I had them all together and we just turned up and started playing . . ."

At the start of the sessions, the American-born Joe English, is invited to become the third Wings drummer . . .

"I was working with Buddy Brown and he was going on tour," Joe recalls. "We were rehearsing and I got a phone call from New Orleans, asking if I would like to come and record the album. That call came from Tony Dorsey, who was working as an arranger for the horns on the album. So I found a replacement for myself. I had the phone call at 3pm that day and I left at 10 that night. It was amazing how everything clicked."

Geoff Britton, Wings' former drummer "I completed half the tracks for the album and then a local drummer called Joe English did the rest. My wife and I were talking about separation and a divorce. I came home to sort it out and Joe English was brought in and I was out. I suppose it would have been better to try and keep both things going but I had to consider that Wings would one day be over and my marriage was a life-long thing. In the meantime, I've had an offer to appear in an Italian spaghetti-kung fu film and I'll be going to Rome and Turkey next month for filming. I'll be a karate stuntman and I'm also writing the percussion score for the soundtrack. After that, I expect I'll be looking around for a new group. It's a funny band, Wings. From a musician's point of view, it's a privilege to do it. But from a career point of view, it's madness. No matter how good you are, you are always in the shadow of Paul."

Paul "In New Orleans, I just thought we'd do a new LP. I had these songs on my scroll and I thought it would be better than *Band On The Run* and I think it *is* better. With *Band On The Run*, a couple of the lads left just before we started and I felt, 'This new album has really got to work.' "

Paul had invited John to accompany them to the Mardi Gras country . . .

"I was supposed to be going down to join Paul in New Orleans," **John** recalls. "But my personal life sort of interfered with that. I was just too busy being happy. I reconciled with Yoko . . . we're happier than ever before. It's like the old, old story, when you get someone back that you've lost, it is better than ever. We were so wrapped up in each other that I just never made it to New Orleans, sorry Paul . . . This is no disrespect to anybody else I was having relationships with (May Pang), but I felt like I was running around with me head off and now I got me head back on. Yoko and I were always in touch, either on the phone or in one way or another. I just sort of came home is what happened. It's like I went out to get a coffee or a newspaper somewhere and it took a year, like Sinbad. I went on a boat and went around the world and had a mad trip, which I'm glad is over. Yoko and I have known each other for nine years, which is a long friendship on any level. We knew we were getting back together and it was just a matter of when. We knew, everybody else might not have, but we did . . . We had a mutual separation and a mutual getting back together. She ain't no chick that you'd say, 'Okay, I'll see you Friday or I'm coming back Monday.' You're dealing with a fully aware human being. There's no dealing with her like you'd treat a chick, you know."

John had returned to Yoko on **Saturday, February 1** . . .

May Pang "My fling with John effectively ended after John had bumped into Yoko backstage at Elton John's Madison Square Garden concert. She suggested that he should improve his health by cutting down on alcohol, losing weight and stopping smoking. An appointment was made for him to visit a hypnotist who treated chronic smokers. After his first session in the hypnotist's chair, John walked almost spellbound back to Yoko's flat. From then, the two were inseparable. When John went back to Yoko, I knew it was finished between us forever, because he was a loyal and honourable person. He was faithful during our time together and as he had returned to Yoko, there was never any question of him looking at another woman."

Yoko "When John and I got together again, we went to see the film *The Way We Were* because we had both seen the film independently while we were apart. The lyrics of the song reminded me so much of our life together. Naturally, 'The Way We Were' became John and mine's song."

One week earlier, on **Saturday, January 25**, the UK music journalist Lynne Thirkettle reviewed 'No. 9 Dream', **John**'s new single . . .

"Taken from the lovely *Walls And Bridges* album, this is a really beautiful song," she announces. "It's soft and has a lovely melody. John's vocals are tip-top and the backing is excellent. Everyone should be ashamed of themselves if this doesn't soar high in the charts."

While Colin Irwin reviews the same single in *Melody Maker* . . . "John, we love you very much," Irwin writes, "but why have your recent records sounded as if they've been recorded in the bathroom with the shower running and a mike in the wash basin? This is an excellent song, a relaxed melodic piece and one of the best he's written in the last couple of years but it stands an admirable chance of sinking without trace with this lush over arrangement. Lennon has one of the most potent voices in rock but its effect is lost here along with the lyrics. There's no punch and if we didn't know better we might think he was auditioning for The Mike Sammes Singers. It sounds okay on the *Walls And Bridges* album, which I think is excellent, but it doesn't stand alone. Miss."

Thursday, February 13
John meanwhile continues with his *Rock 'N' Roll* album promotions by appearing with Scott Muni on his WNEW-FM New York radio show. John, naturally, spends some of the time talking about tracks from the album . . .

'Be-Bop-A-Lula'

John " 'Be-Bop-A-Lula' was one of the first songs I ever sang and the first day I ever sang it in public was on the day I met Paul in a church hall garden party. 'Be-Bop-A-Lula' has always been one of my all-time favourites."

'Stand By Me'

John " 'Stand By Me' was one of my big ballads. I used to score a lot of groupies on that one."

'Ain't That A Shame'

John "This has a lot of special meaning for me. There were a lot of Fats' tracks I would have loved to have done. I did 'Ain't That A Shame' because of my mother, she taught me to play banjo and she bought me my first guitar and this was the first song I ever learnt. I used to do Johnnie Ray, but this was the first song I ever learnt where I could accompany myself and it's a pretty simple song. That's probably why I learnt this one. It has a lot of memories for me and I thought I'd do it for that reason."

'Do You Wanna Dance'

John " 'Do You Wanna Dance' is the only one that I messed around with a bit more. I tried to make it reggae. We'd been doing some jam sessions on the West Coast and I'd always try to do this song with a reggae feel. This one makes you feel happy, but I don't know if it makes you want to dance, and that's the problem. It's definitely different from the original."

'Slipping' & Slidin' '

John "The first time I heard this Little Richard track, a friend imported it from Holland. It came out in Europe first. The A-side was 'Long Tall Sally' and this was the B-side. I also liked Buddy Holly's version."

'Peggy Sue'

John "The next one on side two is the great Buddy Holly's 'Peggy Sue', and what a cosmic joke! Paul McCartney has bought the catalogue of the late great Buddy Holly, which is one of the best buys that one could make in this business. Now, I wasn't sure if he had this song or not, but he'll be making more out of this than I will . . . This is virtually as Buddy Holly did it. In fact, when I was doing it, I had deja vu. It came back to me. I didn't even have to read the words, which I did on most of them. I was singing this one when I was around sixteen. It's virtually how Buddy did it. Well, not quite, but it'll have to do."

During the broadcast, **John** remarks about The Beatles' audio recordings . . .

"I have stuff from The Beatles that I didn't even know existed," he reveals. "I have one that is very important, and nobody knows how important it is. I'm not going to say what it is until I can find the sources of this amazing bootleg. I don't even know where they got it from. It's been out a few years, but nobody knows the story behind it, but I do! It's gonna blow a few minds when they find out what it is!"

Scott Muni (to John) "By the way, someone called and said that the current price of the *Yesterday . . . And Today* 'butcher' cover you mentioned is now $250!"

John "My God!"

Scott "Speaking of rarities, the Christmas messages that The Beatles used to issue are also hard to come by."

John "Yeah. I have that set as well. That's why I'm schizophrenic about pirates. I'd get a copy of something and say, 'I didn't know they recorded this in Sweden.' "

To wrap up the interview, Scott prompts John by saying, "You have some news, which I'm sure our listeners are not really aware of."

John replies, "Yeah, I'd like to dedicate this whole album to my very special friend and wife, Yoko. As I put it, our separation was a failure."

Scott "You're back together again."

John "We are. Those two inimitable loonies are back together again and we're very happy . . . It's not really been out. It came out in England, I can't remember how it got there, but our separation was a failure and John and Yoko have got back together in their bag, as it were."

Scott "I'm certainly delighted, and I speak for my audience when I say that. This and the album then will be for Yoko from John . . . I know that you have to go and I must say that the three hours that we've spent together on the show seems about thirty minutes. But it's been such a sheer pleasure and a lot of fun. I know how the listeners feel as each time this happens, they respond. And I think that they are going to respond too to help you with your immigration problem."

John "Well, thanks to all of them either intending to or wishing me well. Wishes are useful too . . . I'd like to thank you, too, Scott. I like DJing."

Scott "Will you come back?"

John "I'll be back, yeah. You're always good to me on the station. I appreciate it and thanks a lot for having me."

Scott "God bless you and Yoko, too."

John "John and Yoko are back together again. Our separation was a failure. Goodbye, folks, keep listening."

Monday, February 17 (USA)
After months of problems and delays, Apple Records finally issue John's album *Rock 'N' Roll* . . .

John "I stuck all the tracks together and I thought, 'Now what do I do with it?' They had all been waiting for this Phil Spector/John Lennon thing and whatever they expected, it's not going to be good enough. So, at one point, I thought, 'I'm not going to put it out.' And then I got away from it a bit and played it to people who hadn't been involved and weren't expecting heaven and they said, 'Hey, it's all right,' and so I said, 'It's all right, is it? Oh, it's not bad at all. I quite like some of it myself. Okay, let's put it out,' and it went out . . . Quite a lot of the cuts I was singing when I was 15 in 1955. Some of them are the first songs I ever learnt that were rock'n'roll on a guitar. They are some of my all-time favourites. There are 14 on the album but I could have gone on forever. I would have done it years ago but I was always in awe of the records which I wouldn't cover and when

I came to the end of the album, I realised that there were so many I didn't cover. I didn't touch Jerry Lee (Lewis), Carl Perkins, early Presley and so many people. I could go on forever. I'd often thought of doing old Beatles numbers again myself, I've thought about it many, many times in the last five years. It all depends on how much time there is to it. I'd love to do a couple of Dylan's and I'd love to do 'Your Song' by Elton. I love that song, but whether I could do it or not is another point . . . The cover of the *Rock 'N' Roll* album is a picture of me taken in Hamburg in 1962. I've had it around for a long time and I thought it was the perfect time to use it and there are some mystery people on the front of it . . . But this album has been such a drama. It just went on. I'll be glad when it's out and I can get on with my next album."

'Ya Ya'

John "I like Lee Dorsey. There are other tracks I prefer but I just knew 'Ya Ya'. It's so easy that whenever you sit down to jam, everybody could just fall in with it. The Stones did it . . . This has my son, Julian, playing drums on it, with me playing piano. I brought him over here to New York because I can't leave the country, so he comes to visit me and I was in the middle of this album and I thought, 'Oh God, he's going to be bored.' The last time he was here, I took him to Disneyland and stuff like that, in LA. But this time, I was in New York, and I thought, 'He's going to be bored stiff,' but he loved the studio. He loved the knobs; the controls and he ran round all the instruments all the time. So we slyly put the tape recorder on and while he was drumming, I started singing 'Ya Ya' and we just taped it. He doesn't know he's on it yet. I'm going to ship it to him. I haven't told him. I'm just going to let him find out. He'll love it."

'Just Because'

John "At the end of *Rock 'N' Roll*, on a track called 'Just Because', which Phil (Spector) wanted me to sing, I didn't know it that well, you hear me saying, 'And so we say farewell from the Record Plant West.' And something flashed through me mind as I said it, 'Am I really saying farewell to the business?' "

Monday, March 3
In Los Angeles, shortly after midnight, during a journey back to their temporary base in Malibu, Paul, Linda and their children, are stopped after **Paul** was caught driving through a red light on Santa Monica boulevard. But there is trouble ahead when a patrolman starts writing out a traffic ticket . . .

Syndicated news report "Paul McCartney's wife Linda was on a drugs charge after the couple were stopped in their car by Los Angeles police. She was said to have had marijuana in her handbag. The California Highway Patrol swooped on the McCartney car after the former Beatle drove through a red light. Also in the car were their children, Mary, 5, Stella, 3 and Heather, 12, Linda's daughter by a previous marriage. Police said, 'As one of our officers was writing out a ticket for McCartney, he smelt burning marijuana in the car and ordered the McCartneys out. He then found a partly smoked marijuana cigarette on the floor of the car and more of the drug (16oz) in a plastic bag in the 33-year-old Linda's handbag.' The police statement said that Linda told them, 'It's my grass. Paul does not have anything to do with it.' She was freed on £200 bail after being charged with possessing the drug. She will appear in court next Monday."

After landing back in England at Heathrow airport, **Paul** announces, "The police stopped us and found a tiny bit of stuff in Linda's bag. It was hardly anything at all, only enough to make about four cigarettes. They took us down to the station and charged us with a misdemeanour. We said that we were sorry and they let us go. In Los Angeles, it is different from over here (in the UK). Out there, it is not a big deal. In fact, very shortly they are going to legalise the stuff, because so many people smoke it."

Monday, March 17 (USA)
The Who's drummer Keith Moon releases his solo album *Two Sides Of The Moon*, which originally featured production from The Beatles' former roadie, Mal Evans . . .

"We were doing Ringo's album *Goodnight Vienna*," Mal recalls, "and Keith Moon was at the session and we drove him back to his hotel and we carried all our drinks into the hotel. We were a bit stewed at four o'clock in the morning and he was moaning, 'All the others are doing solo albums. Ringo's doing a solo album, and I've been trying to get a producer for years.' Then he said, "Hey Mal, won't you produce me?' So I said, 'Sure, I'd love to do it.' So that very day, we called up all our friends, got them into a studio at the Record Plant and we did 'Don't Worry Baby' that first day, which was his single. That's how it started. We had a falling out towards the end of the album so I only did about eighty per cent of it. One of the tracks on the album I'm really pleased with is 'In My Life', the old Beatles song, which was **John**'s song. We did two of John's songs, the other was 'Move Over Miss L', so I sent rough mixes of those two songs to John and I got a beautiful little card back from him, saying 'That's the best version of "In My Life" I have ever heard in my life.' So, for me, that was the ultimate in compliments."

Monday, March 24
In Long Beach, California, **Paul**, Linda and Wings hold a lavish, star-studded launch party for their new album *Venus And Mars* aboard the land-locked Queen Mary Liner . . . The event also serves as a "cheerio" to their American show business chums before they return home to England . . .

The *Daily Mirror* reports, "Parting is such sweet sorrow, especially when the farewell comes with a big binge, as ordered by former Beatle Paul McCartney. But even at a farewell, there is a time, too, to say hello to old friends. Among Paul's guests was his one-time music partner, George Harrison, sporting a be-bop haircut. Paul, of course, now has his own group, Wings and George, too, is doing his own thing. Singer Davy Jones got in on the old pals act, as well. Between drinks with Cher, he renewed acquaintances with one of his old Monkee partners, Micky Dolenz. In the words of The Beatles' song, the party was just a case of 'Hello . . . Goodbye'."

Linda "Someone was introduced to us and came up and said, 'Hello Venus, hello Mars.' I really was horrified! It wasn't meant to mean that at all."

Paul agrees, "At our LA party, someone came over and said, 'Hello Venus, hello Mars,' and I thought, 'Oh my God, no!' It never even occurred to me."

Thursday, April 10
Meanwhile, back in the UK, Capital Radio in London broadcasts *An Evening With John Lennon*, a special programme to help promote the *Rock 'N' Roll* album and features an

exclusive interview with **John** carried out in New York by the station's DJ, Nicky Horne . . .

Horne "What is the latest news with your elusive Green Card?"

John "The latest is, I'm appealing. It's just about there, I don't know, you know. It goes on, I'm in court. I don't go, the lawyer goes and then he sends me a note saying this happened, or this didn't happen, this is good, this is bad, there is hope, there isn't hope. I try and be positive about it and I think I'm going to get it this year. But I've got no rational reason to think that but I think I'm going to get it."

Horne "What is life like in New York?"

John "It's not dissimilar to life in England, because one's life, anybody's life, revolves around your personal family, friends that you either live with or hang around with, the business or work that you do. So my life, for the last few years, say, has been basically a bedroom, a studio, a TV, a night out, back home, you know. And, apart from the fact they talk the American version of English on TV, and it goes on a bit longer in New York, there's not that vast a difference. It's not a culture shock. I imagine that this place is like what London must have been in Victorian days when Britain was at its height of power or on the decline or whatever the peak was. The American Empire is now what the British Empire used to be . . . I just felt at home here, as soon as I relaxed. I just fitted in and one doesn't feel like an American because, when you try and point out what an American is, you come over here and it's pretty hard to find one because they're all Italian Americans, or Irish Americans, African Americans, Afro Americans . . . you know. Everybody is from somewhere else. It's pretty hard to find out what an American is. It's just a bunch of people from everywhere else who came over here. So I just feel quite at home here."

Horne then directs John's attentions to the current state of Apple, The Beatles' company . . .

"Apple has not been officially closed down yet," **John** reveals, "although it doesn't operate a talent contest. Don't send your tapes to Apple, folks, because there all there is is an accountant, probably, in London. It virtually has no function; it's more like a bank now, which was what it was set up to do. It was set up to deal with the money coming in, you know, pay the tax or do some business. It was a good thing and a lot of fun. But now it's over, let's get on to the next round."

Horne asks John "What is your relationship like with the other three Beatles?"

"Our relationship is as close as it can be," **John** replies, "considering that we are not working in the studio together or doing anything else of that kind together or seeing each other as infrequently as we do, which is like when Paul was here last. He came to see me and we go to eat, to drink or we sit around, whatever, and I see them whenever they are in America. I don't travel because of the Green Card thing. I've seen Ringo more because I'm on his albums all the time and he's always in LA. George I only saw on the tour and he flashed through in a mad fuzz. But I did get a few moments with him. We're all right, you know. We've all got over the separation."

Horne "What do you think of the critics who say *Imagine* is your best album?"

John "Up them! As far as I'm concerned, the best piece of work I put out is the 'Mother' album (*John Lennon/Plastic Ono Band* – 1970). I call it the 'Mother'/'Working Class Hero' album. I think it's my best piece of work. That's my personal opinion. But I don't know much more than anybody else. I'm just making it as best as I can. Some are better than others, that's the way of life."

Horne "If we can go back to some of the things you created, four or five years ago, is there something still there that still grabs you, and you say, 'Yeah, great!' "

John "Yeah, lots of it. There are lots of stuff I like."

Horne "Like what?"

John "Well, of my own, I like 'All You Need Is Love', 'Walrus', 'Strawberry Fields'. I like 'Hey Jude', what the hell, there are so many of them I like. I like 'Yellow Submarine'. They all have meanings for me, objectively as well as subjectively. There are just too many to mention. I like lots of Beatles stuff. What do you want, a list?"

To conclude the interview, **John** sends a message to all the listeners back in England . . .

"This is John Lennon in New York. The crazy one. I'm saying 'Hi' to all of you, to the folks who are interested, the fans and otherwise. I miss a lot of you. I don't miss the ones who don't like me; you can go and eat a banana. The others I miss and I'd like to see you all and talk to you more often. But I want this Green Card, you know and you know I'm a bit of a pig so I want it and I'll stick around until I get it, then I'll see you. I appreciate all of you who are still listening to me and I haven't been home since Capital Radio had begun so it's strange, isn't it? But I know England won't float away, Britain won't float away so I'll see you when I see you. I'll just look a little weirder, probably. Bye, bye."

While in another interview, this time with the UK Arts & Entertainment reporter, John Walker, **John** replies to the question of what he would like his epitaph to be. This is his reply . . .

"I'd like, 'He was the instigator of world peace', and not only the instigator but also part of it. Music to me is part of the peace campaign. People who try to misuse power have short-lived lives. They can do a lot of destructive things, like Hitler or Napoleon. I think it's those people who try to manipulate and use an abstract power and it only lasts a short time. The bigger they are, the harder they fall. So any power I have is abstract and I couldn't misuse it. I'd like to be perfect, like Christ, but the music is always imperfect. That's why you keep going on. The image of The Beatles became more a museum than a reality. And I don't believe in museums. The Beatles were in danger of becoming the Establishment, which I don't want to know about, so I woke up, which was when I met Yoko. I don't regret anything. I don't think there's any time for regret, any more than I'd want to know about the future, unless it's going to be a peaceful one. But I wouldn't have missed anything."

MAY . . .

Paul "At the moment we are rehearsing to go out and play as a band. We are learning a lot of numbers and the band is myself on bass, and I change to piano. You've got Denny

Laine on guitar and Jimmy McCulloch. It's funny with the line-up of Wings. We got rid of Henry McCullough, or rather he got rid of himself, Henry left and we get in Jimmy McCulloch, which is spelt differently. We get rid of a drummer called Geoff Britton, who is English and get in a drummer called Joe English, who is American, so it's a bit amazing! So, at the moment, we're just enjoying ourselves, having a play and seeing if it's coming to anything. It seems to be getting very nice. We seem to be getting a few numbers together, and then we'd like to take the band out in Britain."

Saturday, May 10

Melody Maker reports, "Apple Records, the company formed by The Beatles, closed down last weekend. Neil Aspinall, who with The Beatles was one of the founders of Apple in 1968, will stay on as head of a small staff handling accounting."

Friday, May 23

UK columnist, Christopher Ward "**Paul McCartney**'s press agent telephoned me on Tuesday evening and said, 'Paul's very worried about Britain. He's not at all happy about the way this Common Market thing is going and he would like to talk to you about it.' Well, if Harold Wilson's private secretary had announced that the Prime Minister was forming a rock group, I couldn't have been more surprised. And next morning, at 11.30 sharp, I turned up at Mr McCartney's office in Soho. At 12.10, Mr McCartney breezed in, wearing a pair of jeans, a tee shirt and a £150 Savile Row jacket. He explained that he had been out to dinner at the Savoy the previous evening with Twiggy and her boyfriend and they had all gone on to the nightclub, Tramp. Mr McCartney came straight to the point, 'The Common Market is like The Beatles' partnership . . .'

" 'When I wrote a hit, the money was shared among all the group, and no one ended up getting anything. Now that the partnership has been dissolved, I'm much better off in every way.' Mr McCartney goes on to announce he felt that the Government had failed in its duty to explain the issues to the voters. 'What we need is someone like Linda's dad as chief advisor to the public. I mean, I fall asleep at accountancy meetings, so I couldn't explain all this Brussels stuff, but my father-in-law could.' The way that the Referendum was being conducted didn't please Mr McCartney very much either. 'They could have held it at no extra cost by bunging a question at the bottom of the Census form that came round a few years ago,' he said. 'Instead of asking how many lavatories we all have, they could have put, "Do you fancy the Common Market?" '

"Mr McCartney sat back with all the satisfaction of a politician who had made his point. Next, he turned his attention to the economic crisis. 'Britain's assets,' he said, 'were seriously underestimated. For a start, we don't have earthquakes or hurricanes here as they do in America. That's definitely a plus and it's real cool these days to own a bit of oil.' He only wished he had more confidence in our leaders. 'I don't think Harold (Wilson)'s the boy. I don't think Maggie (Margaret Thatcher)'s the girl. "Wedgie" Benn (Anthony Wedgewood Benn), on the other hand, was a right loony. Clever blokes hold no wonder for me. Basically, they're just swots.'

"He admitted that it was perhaps a silly point when so many more important issues were at stake, but he felt that metrication was extremely unpatriotic. 'Why should we change miles to kilometres? English is a beautiful language so if we have to change the system, why can't we call them "new miles"?' Mr McCartney said he had felt compelled to speak out on these matters, just as he had felt compelled to send a telegram of protest to President Ford recently. 'It was a protest against an American army plan to kill hundreds of thousands of blackbirds. They ought to have tried to shoo them away, but instead they showered the buggers with detergent from the air and killed them.' He had also opposed the war in Vietnam, although he had never sent a telegram to the President about it. I wonder whether our conversation was a prelude to Mr McCartney launching himself on some kind of a political career, but he vehemently dismissed the suggestion. 'I am a songwriter, a musician,' he said. 'That's what I'm good at, but I feel that these other things needed saying.' Mr McCartney's new album, *Venus And Mars*, comes out shortly. It's a very pleasant record, as one might expect from McCartney and his group, Wings. But I have no doubt that when Mr Wilson and the Cabinet hear it, they will believe they could have produced something better."

Tuesday, May 27 (USA)
Wings release their new album *Venus And Mars* . . .

Paul "Although we recorded it in New Orleans, it doesn't sound very New Orleansy to me."

Linda "It's just another album I really like. Of course, it's the first album with the new band and aren't they great? This album's a bit looser than the last. We weren't under such pressure this time and we worked in some great places, such as New Orleans, with some great people. Their music was *my* music . . . A lot of people are asking what *Venus And Mars* means. But all I can say is that it means nothing and everything. We had a pool table in the house that we rented and there was one in the studio, too. The comparison between the balls and the planets were noticed, so it was decided that was what to call it."

Paul "I never really liked *Venus And Mars* until I heard it at a party one night and saw everybody leaping around."

'Venus And Mars'

Paul "I was just sitting down and I started to sing anything and some words came out. The song 'Venus And Mars' is just about some fellow, an imaginary person who's got a friend. I just imagine he knows some girl who's into astrology, you know. The kind who asks you what your sign is before they say hello. You know, 'A good friend of mine, studies the stars.' In fact, in the first verse, it's, 'A good friend of mine, follows the stars,' so it's a, kind of, ambiguous groupie or astrologer . . . I just thought it is a nice opening to an album. He's sitting in the stands of a sports arena, waiting for the show to begin, so you've got this feel going. He says, 'A good friend of mine, follows the stars, says Venus and Mars are all right tonight. It's going to be a good show tonight.' It sums up all this, 'Your star's in ascendant tonight,' so I just bunged it in and all these other things came in later. Someone said, 'You did know they were the Gods of love and war,' and I said, 'Oh, yeah, yeah, I forgot all that.' It's only later that I find out about all this."

'Rockshow'

Paul "I started off with this idea, 'If there's a rock show,' and then Concertgebouw came in my mind, because that's one of the places you play in Amsterdam. We played there. So I rhymed Concertgebouw with Rockshow, and then long hair, what else but Madison Square. Then rock'n'roll, what else rhymes with that? Hollywood Bowl, you know. Often, these little things turn out to be great afterwards but often you're just searching for a rhyme. That's the only song Allen Toussaint played on when we were in New Orleans."

'Love In Song'

Paul "I sat down, I had my 12-string and I started to write this thing. I thought, 'That's a nice opening,' you know, 'My heart cries out for love'. I thought, 'That'll do for a nice opening for a love song.' I liked one of the other lines, 'My eyes cry out as a tear still born in misunderstanding'. I thought, 'That's a nice little line.' Otherwise, it's just a tune that, sort of, came forth. I feel I don't have a lot of control over some songs but some songs I do. But with this song, I just started playing my guitar, singing those words, wrote them down and I said to Linda, 'How do you like that?' And that was it."

'You Gave Me The Answer'

Paul "When I started listening to music, when I was a kid, the radio was on and in 1942, the only music on was the music they were harking back to, like Fred Astaire, *The Billy Cotton Band Show*, all that kind of music. I liked the Fred Astaire films. I thought, 'Boy, can he dance. Boy, can they arrange things.' So on this LP, I thought, 'I'd like to get a bit of that in,' and so 'You Gave Me The Answer' is kind of real fruity. It's me imagining that top hat and tails thing. I'm going back to that Fred Astaire era."

'Magneto And Titanium Man'

Paul "That's all about a comic book. It's *Marvel* comics. When we were in Jamaica on holiday, they have a lot of comic books in the supermarkets and we'd go in, every Saturday, and get a new stack of comics to read while we were on holiday. I didn't seem to read comics from when I was eleven onwards because I thought I had grown out of them. But then I came back to them a couple of years ago, just thinking, 'Wow, the drawings are great.' I love all that stuff. I love all the names and all the comic book stuff and I've been reading a little bit of science fiction. The whole vision of it all is a great vision to do a song because you can write anything."

'Letting Go'

Paul "I think 'Letting Go' is one of the better songs on the album. I think it's a nice track. It's a nice tune and kids sing it all the time. I think it works as a track. It's my favourite track."

'Medicine Jar'

Paul "I said to the others, 'If you've got anything, let's hear it, to see if it fits in with my stuff. We'll see if we can work it in.' Jimmy had been playing it in Nashville and I had heard him playing it in the corner of the studio on an organ and I thought, 'That's a nice one. That's a nice little one.' And he said, 'Yeah, I wrote that with Colin Allen,' who is playing with Focus. So I thought, 'Great, let's have a go at that one.' So we had a go and it fitted."

'Call Me Back Again'

Paul "I wrote that about a year ago in Los Angeles and I was in The Beverly Hills. There was a little electric piano in there and I was banging away this tune and I thought, 'I'll develop that, put a few more words to it.' But I never did. So while we were in New Orleans, we thought, 'Well, let's just have a go at it.' And I ended up just sort of ad-libbing a bit, stretching it out a bit. I like that myself. I had a chance to sing and then we put the brass on it. I like the brass on it, it's nicely arranged. Tony Dorsey helped me on that."

'Listen To What The Man Said'

Paul "All of the tracks, except for three or four, were done in New Orleans. 'Listen To What The Man Said' was done there. That was a song I had hanging around. You can say the song is a religious song but when I was writing it, I never thought of it as that, that the man could be Jesus, or it could just as easily have been your father, or your best mate. It could be anybody, you know . . .

"We did the sax bit, with Tom Scott when we were in Los Angeles. We did the basic track in New Orleans. When we were recording that, it was one of the songs that we had come in with, with high hopes. Whenever we played it on the piano, people would say, 'Oh, I like that one.' So I thought, 'This'll be a good 'un.' But when we first did the backing track, everyone thought, 'Oh no.' We really didn't get that together at all. But we let it stand and put a couple more things on it. Dave Mason dropped in and we did a little bit of overdubbing on it with guitars one evening and the thing was, what do we do for the guitar solo? And we thought, 'Oh, it'd be great to get someone in to do a great lyrical solo or one of the great technical musicians, a great ad-libber.' Then someone said, 'What about Tom Scott? He lives near here in LA.' And we said, 'Oh yeah, give him a ring. He might turn up.' So he turns up within half an hour. There he was, with his sax. He walks into the studio, sat down, he's playing through and the engineer was recording him and his first little notes that he was playing through, casually. We kept them all. He came in and we said, 'I think that's it.' And he said, 'Did you record that?' And I said, 'Yeah, listen to it back then.' Nobody could believe it. He went and tried a few more but they just weren't as good. All the feel was on this early take. The first take, in fact. So we sat around for two hours, but there isn't a session anymore, he has finished it. So we sat around and chatted for a couple of hours. I think it's lovely what he plays on that. The voice introduction on the track is me. I did that in New Orleans."

'Treat Her Gently'/'Lonely Old People'

Paul "I wrote the 'Treat Her Gently' bit as it fell into the key of D and once I was in D, I thought, 'Well, how do I get out of this?' And so I wrote the second half of the thing. It just fell together. It wasn't two separate songs put together. They just fell into each other and I wrote it as I was practising the other, almost."

'Crossroads'

Paul "This tune was Tony Hatch's. It's a bit of a British joke, that. When we were working on that, I thought, 'Well, maybe it's a little too British but I'd still like to put it out. I don't care. It doesn't matter if some people don't get it.' I think if you don't get the joke on it, it sounds like a closing theme. But if you do see the joke, coming after 'Lonely

Old People', which is, 'Nobody asked us to play. Nobody gets involved with lonely old people.' They just sit there, wondering what's going on. Well, one of the big things with lonely old people, or a lot of people in England, is watch *Crossroads*, which is this soap box. Originally it was this joke. It doesn't even sound like the *Crossroads* thing. I think they're going to have it on the British series. They're going to use our tune on it, which will be great."

Saturday, May 31
Meanwhile, the first part of John's interview with the music journalist Rosemary Horide is published in the UK in the *New Musical Express* . . .

"It's 99 to 1 that if I came to Britain, I'd come to London," **John** reveals. "I probably wouldn't have time to go to Liverpool. My idea of fun is to travel from London to New York to Paris. I may even go to Germany. I don't know why but I just fancy going there. I like travel actually, but luckily this country is big enough to occupy me so if I get the urge, I can get on a plane and think I'm going to the moon, but actually land in LA."

Rosemary asks John about his plans for the future . . .

John "I'll probably do a TV special, which I've got in my head, if I can find the right front man. I know what it should be, but you have to have someone that convinces the people. It's also better for the people who are putting it on to think that they have a professional looking after it, so I'm just sniffing round for a sympathetic professional."

Rosemary Horide "Do you miss the Abbey Road studios?"

John "No, we got bored with it because we were there all the time. In fact, we went to Olympic and other places towards the end. We even tried to build one. In fact, we did build one, which they've pulled down, I understand, while I've been away. It was at 3 Savile Row, which is now only a shell and I haven't seen it, I'm glad to say. I don't want to hear about it."

Rosemary Horide "You went to the *Sgt. Pepper* musical opening?"

John "Peter Brown asked me to go and he's been a friend for a long time and he was involved with it. So I thought, 'I'm in town, so I might as well go.' I didn't go to the *Tommy* opening, although I was invited, because I couldn't face another one. You've got to get out of the car and get clawed, like it was *A Hard Day's Night*. I've had enough of that, really. With the *Sgt. Pepper* thing, it was deja vu because they'd built this thing up saying, 'He's going to be there.' It was pretty wild. Most of the audience was watching me. I enjoyed *Sgt. Pepper* because I'd never seen that guy's work before. I think they reproduced the music well, very well in fact . . . It makes me feel like I'm dead, if you want to know. What with that and *Stardust*, which was written by Ray Connolly . . . You bum! White house indeed with white bedrooms! Guess where he got that from? Ascot, where he always visited me and Yoko."

Saturday, June 14
John and Yoko's fortunes appear to be on the up when it is announced that, after years of disappointment, they are expecting their first child together . . .

Syndicated news report by Piers Akerman "Ex-Beatle **John Lennon** and his wife Yoko Ono are expecting a baby in December, a close friend revealed in New York today. Neither John nor Yoko was available to speak about the happy event, but a neighbour in their apartment block said, 'Yoko told me she was expecting the child at about Christmas. She said she was taking special care of herself because she'd had a series of miscarriages and didn't want the same thing to happen again.' "

Bob Mercer, managing director of EMI Records Group Repertoire Division, "I was with them when Yoko had her pregnancy confirmed. They were absolutely ecstatic about it and John turned to me and said, 'Well, that shelves the work for some time now.' John's concern then was to look after Yoko, who was then 39 or 40 years old, quite old to be having a baby. She'd had attempts before and had miscarriages. So John was really going to devote the next few months to looking after Yoko, to make sure she was okay."

This news corresponds with the announcement made by the American columnist, Jack Anderson, who claims that "John Lennon may be allowed to stay in the United States indefinitely. Lennon has a better than even chance of staying in the States." The report continues, "Watergate-like tactics had been used against Lennon. They involved a smear campaign by a Senate sub-committee that falsely linked Lennon with militants alleged to be plotting to disrupt the 1972 Republican Convention. Now the Federal prosecutor has said that the Immigration Services will undertake to review the case. An attorney has persuaded the prosecutor that hundreds of aliens with worse drug records than Lennon have been allowed to stay."

SEPTEMBER
In the States, this month's *Modern Hi-Fi & Music* magazine prints an interview with the 57-year-old Hal Fein, the man who, apparently, "really discovered The Beatles". The article is written by Robert V. Weinstein . . .

"The man who discovered The Beatles is not Brian Epstein," Weinstein insists. "The man who discovered The Beatles lives quietly in a New York suburb with his family, spending his days at a Manhattan brokerage firm. The man who discovered The Beatles, the man who handed them over to Brian Epstein, wanted to cut their hair and change their name, but never got the chance. 'I discovered The Beatles, yes that's right, before Brian Epstein even entered the picture. I discovered the boys,' Hal Fein insists. 'For the first time, the story of The Beatles' beginning is being told. I'm the one who gave them to Brian Epstein. Everyone thinks that they were discovered in England. Well, that's not true. The truth is that Bert Kaempfert and I actually discovered The Beatles and made their first record in 1961, in Hamburg, Germany. I was in Hamburg for a recording session with Kaempfert and I asked him if there were any rock'n'roll groups in Hamburg. I also wanted to see how the kids were dancing there. Kaempfert said he had heard about this club on the Reeperbahn called the Top Ten Club, where there was supposed to be a good band. American and British bands would always wind up on the Reeperbahn; it was the only place where they had entertainment. And it was also a big red-light district.

"Kaempfert, I and our wives visited the Top Ten and all it took was a sixteenth note to tell my well-trained ears that I was hearing something unique and remarkable, a future sound. I stopped dead in my tracks as soon as I heard them. I couldn't believe it. They sounded so good. I was out of my fucking head. I knew it! They were terrific! Sure, they didn't have the polish they had after playing together a long time, but they did have something nobody else had. Those boys were giving a definitive white performance of black music. At that time there were no white musicians in the States who could play race music with any sense of conviction or authenticity. During the course of the evening, I learned that the boys did not have a recording contract or any other ties, and that was all I needed to know. The next day, The Beatles and Tony Sheridan, the singer the band was backing at the time, were signed to Bert Kaempfert Productions. The contract was simply for recording and involved no publication rights or personal management. Sheridan and The Beatles first recorded 'My Bonnie' and 'When The Saints Go Marching In'. It was just a single. On the record it said Tony Sheridan & The Beat Brothers. They didn't use the word Beatles because they thought it sounded strange, like an animal. After they were signed, I had to leave for Copenhagen. My parting words to Kaempfert were, 'Give the boys some money and make sure they get haircuts.' If it had been left up to me, I think they would've been called The Oxford Four instead of the avant-garde Beatles. When the record was released, the initial sales were about 180,000 copies, a fair sized hit for Germany. Due to its success in Germany, it was played on Radio Luxembourg, beaming in all directions, into Germany, south into the Continent and north into England.

"Brian Epstein began to get enquiries about the record from his customers who had either heard the record on the air or had seen The Beatles at a local club. Brian Epstein contacted Bert. He said he was interested in the boys and could do a lot for the boys. Kaempfert released the contract with no strings attached, lock, stock and barrel . . . From my own sources, I learned that Epstein was shrewdly manipulating the group. I never met him, and I only had one conversation with him on the phone. Whatever I know about Epstein is pure hearsay, but I've heard a lot. Essentially, he was a prick! When he signed the boys, they were hungry. He made a deal with them where each one got ten per cent of their earnings and he took sixty per cent and paid for their expenses. That went on till Epstein died. It's never been publicised, but I think that was one of the reasons The Beatles broke up. They were completely dissatisfied with the financial arrangement and his estate took over the contract. The boys refused to work under those conditions. He was a real prick! Taking 25 per cent is usurious, but this prick went one step further and took sixty per cent. This is what Paul told me. Epstein was also a big fag and a junky! He took advantage of four hungry kids who just wanted to say something musically. The Beatles were mature enough to realise that they had made a bad deal and there wasn't anything they could do about it. They had signed an agreement in good faith and made a bad deal for themselves. Not being businessmen, not being conversant with business procedures, they didn't realise exactly what they were doing. Although we let go one of the Twentieth Century's greatest show business phenomena, I have no regrets. George Harrison and Paul McCartney were just super young men. The only thing I ever disagreed with them about was their advocation of legalising the use of marijuana in England. I am a hard-hat where drugs are concerned. I went up to Paul and I told him it was disgusting that a group with such a huge following and with such an incredible impact on young people all over the world, should be advocating something as dangerous as the legalisation of marijuana. He didn't say anything."

When the article is published, **John** promptly types out a reply. It reads, complete with typing errors . . .

"Dear Robert Wein-stein

Bert Kaemfert I remember him well. Hal Fein must have been one of the people working with him . . . but he no rings da bell (too much). Brian (Epstein) didn't hear the record over the air . . . he rana record shop in Liverpool . . . near the Cavern . . . the local club we played at . . . one of the kids went to his shop to see if he had our record . . . he didn't . . . so he checked it/us out.. he prided himself on being able to get any record that was asked for. We cut a few tracks for Kaemfort.. My Bonnie.. was one in which the Beatles backed a London singer, who was 'big' in Hamburg, Tony Sheriden.. the first real Beatles single, was Aint She Sweet . . . meaning we/I sang it. Bert K et al thought the Beatles wer TOO BLUESY! Thats why we ended up as Sheridens' backing group. Sheriden was very good actually, and he definitely knew what the Germans wanted . . . he'd been working Hamburg for years!

Those were the days mein friend!
Very corderoy,
j.l.

p.s. Ther's a very good book on those says called "The Man Who gave the Beatles Away (Alun Williams) *I've forgotten which publisher . . . it's new, but available
*he was our first manager . . . he took us to Hamburg..tra la la . . ."
"excuse the typing!"

SEPTEMBER

Meanwhile, Paul and Wings' gruelling 1975/76 world tour begins in Britain and is soon scheduled to continue in Australia, Japan and end, the following year, in America . . .

Paul "We did rehearse a lot for this. We rehearsed more than we had rehearsed for anything, because we thought, 'We had better know the numbers. That's one requirement, to know how the things go.' So we took the albums apart to find out what we played on the records, because you make the record and, by the morning, you've forgotten about it and it's out. So you've got to listen to the records again to see what you've played. We listened to them and we took them apart, worked on what everyone should be singing and how to cover this or that. Joe English is not only a good drummer, but he's also a great singer. He's got a great falsetto range. It's ridiculous. When he gets carried away, he starts singing falsetto throughout all the tunes. So occasionally I have to turn to him and say, ' No, just the thumping, Joe.' We decided that most of the people in the audience wanted to hear the records exactly like the records, so Jimmy had to learn up how the records went on the tracks he didn't previously play. He plays a lot of his own, and he's a good player . . . The eventual Beatles line-up of John, George, Paul and Ringo took something like six years of trying out everyone, hustling around and working for eight hours a day for next to no money in Hamburg. We had all the experience but we, in Wings, felt a little small-time, or 'bush league' as the Americans would say, especially compared with other bands like Led Zeppelin who had been together for a long time. But I felt we had better get up there with them. We had to get a reputation, to show our faces, to let people know who we were and dare to do it, and do it big, and commit everything. We went on holiday and got really fit. By the time we came to do that world tour, I could have done a marathon in the Olympics."

The marathon series of shows begin on **Saturday, September 6** with a preview concert at Elstree film studios in Hertfordshire for the members and staff of EMI . . .

Paul "I thought we were terrible! Everyone was so nervous. I swear our trombone player, Tony Dorsey, who is black, went white. Nothing could be as bad again as that night. The funny thing about being famous is that people don't think you get nervous. But I am nervous every time I go out. Sometimes more than others."

The UK leg of the world tour opens with a concert at the Gaumont in Southampton on **Tuesday, September 9** . . .

Beatles fan, Peter Doggett "What no one realised at the time, probably not even **Paul**, was that the Southampton Gaumont show would be the first date on a world tour that would stretch, on and off, for another thirteen months. Initially, Paul announced a series of just twelve British concerts, starting in the South, working up via Cardiff to the North, skipping back to London for two shows at the Hammersmith Odeon, and then heading North again for three final gigs in Scotland. But after another couple of weeks, another set of concerts was confirmed, this time on the other side of the world, as Wings trekked across Australia, via Adelaide, Sydney and Brisbane . . . Outside the Gaumont that opening night, on that mild summer evening, there was an understandable air of excitement. I had expected the show to sell out and what I hadn't bargained for, in my innocence, were the ticket touts doing healthy business, and the hundreds of ticketless customers who had turned up on the off chance. Most remarkable of all was the group of fans who had jetted in that day from California without having tickets for any of the shows. Knowing that Paul was effectively banned from playing in the States, they reckoned that coming to England was the only way they'd ever get to see him perform in concert, and they were willing to pay whatever it took."

Wings' 130-minute performance, which includes tracks from both *Band On The Run* and *Venus And Mars*, and a choice few Beatles numbers, is considered by many to be a vast improvement to their 1973 shows . . .

Ray Fox-Cummings, UK music reporter "Most of us emerged from the opening night of the Wings' tour elated. We had heard all 29 songs, loved 'em all and seen two hours fly by as if they were but 40 minutes. We felt we had been invited to a musical at home, to meet the family and watch our hosts perform a selection of their well-known party pieces. The party's scheduled to begin at 8pm – and it does, prompt! The lights are low and we can scarcely see our hosts and Linda leads us into 'Venus And Mars' . . . Thanks very much for a super evening. I enjoyed myself very much, can I come again and will you please treat this as my 'thank you for having me' letter?"

Paul "Afterwards, when it's worked out and it has been a great show, there's no feeling like it. It takes me at least half an hour to come down because two hours singing, virtually non-stop, makes me get the stamina very much higher."

Wings' tour reaches the Cardiff Capitol on **Thursday, September 11** . . .

Wendy Hughes, the *Sunday Times* "Ticket holders for the gig in Cardiff queued for hours before the doors of the Capitol Theatre opened and a small army of security men stood on guard. Teeny-boppers, their noses glued to the glass doors hoping to get a glimpse of their idols, the Wings group, were frequently squeezed out by pinstripe suited gents and matronly looking ladies eager to see McCartney. Screams and applause for tracks from Wings' long-playing records, *Band On The Run* and *Venus And Mars*, were marginally exceeded by the response to Paul McCartney's most famous hit from The Beatles' days, 'Yesterday' . . ."

Backstage at the venue, **Paul** declares to the Press, "That was the best show so far on the tour. The audiences are getting better as we are warming up. But audiences are always good in Wales and Scotland. They are the barbarians that the Romans did not get to and they are all good rockers. Age does not make any difference as far as our fans are concerned. Even in The Beatles days, we had older fans. Our aim is that everybody should like us. After all, I am exactly thirty-three-and-a-third years old, and I look forward to speeding up to forty-five and eventually seventy-eight."

Reporter "Paul, what else do you intend to do?"

Paul "I am hoping to break into the film world, but not on the acting side. It has been an idea of ours for many years to make a *Disney* type film of *Rupert The Bear*. We have bought the film rights from Sir Max, boat racing, Aitken. This doesn't mean I will leave Wings, in fact, I want Wings to provide the background music for the film."

On **Monday, September 15**, the Wings UK Tour rolls on to Paul's hometown in Liverpool . . .

Record Mirror "McCartney mania erupted in Liverpool when Wings played Paul's hometown. More than £2,000 worth of damage was caused to the McCartneys' Rolls Royce as it battled through nearly 1,000 fans blocking the backstage exit. Earlier, the Monday night show had to be stopped after the very first number when hundreds of fans rushed the stage. The manager appealed for order but before the end of the show, the same thing happened. During the disturbances outside the theatre, there were scuffles with police."

Wednesday, September 17
The Wings Tour reaches London with two nights of performances at the Hammersmith Odeon. In the crowd is Derek Jewell of the *Sunday Times* . . .

"Wings gave a continuous two-hour show, which was rapturously received and a model of what one kind of pop concert should be. It was presented with the minimum of thrills, a touch of Bondsome strobe flicker during 'Live And Let Die', smoke and soap bubbles cascading from the ceiling at the start. No time was wasted. It was all music which, whether quietly reflective or barrel housing, totally involved the audience. McCartney, of course, is the centre of it. His band revolves sensibly around him. There is solid support from Denny Laine, powerful lead guitar from Jimmy McCulloch, drive from drummer Joe English, flickers of keyboard from his wife, Linda, and a superb horn section, but McCartney remains the sun. And what a rich programme he presents. Flitting from bass guitar to acoustic guitar or piano, he lays it out. Heavy sounds like 'Letting Go', past Wings hits like 'C Moon' and 'Blue Bird' and, best of all, his expressive voice looking tenderly backwards through 'Blackbird', 'The Long And Winding Road' and 'Yesterday'. His tonal range has developed too. He cuts and carves now, as well as soaring lyrically. If 'Yesterday' movingly reminded us of what we've lost, Wings tell us what we've gained and McCartney himself promises us still more. For even Wings, good as it is, can't be the end, can it?"

Also in attendance is Dave Gelly of the *Observer* . . .

"The packed crowds flocking to the current Wings tour, range from early teenage to mid-30s and beyond. They come knowing that Paul will play for them, and that, for two hours, they will be given the fruits of weeks of careful preparation and that the aim of the whole thing will have been their delight. Although Paul keeps insisting that the band should be known simply as Wings, his personality, his musicianship, and, above all, his sheer style dominate the evening. As a natural stage performer, McCartney exudes the kind of energy that draws an audience to him even when he is simply playing the accompaniment to one of the others. Wings is his creation, and his signature is stamped on every note they produce . . . The shows are enormous fun and two hours' high-grade euphoria is a valuable commodity these days."

Monday, September 22 (USA)
George, meanwhile, releases in the UK his new album, *Extra Texture (Read All About It)* . . .

"I had to record it in Los Angeles," **George** recalls, "because of other work I was doing at the same time and, from a technical point of view, it was very limiting to what I wanted to do. At the same time, I was going through a very heavy period, for many reasons, like personal things, you know, and business things. So, in a way, it was a very heavy album."

The opening track on the album is 'You', a song originally recorded back in 1971 . . .

George "I was working with Phil Spector, around the *All Things Must Pass* period, and we were trying to do an album with his wife (Ronnie) and I wrote the song especially for her. At the time, we put down six tracks and all we did was finish the one that was a single and we never got round to doing the album. I wrote 'You' in The Ronettes flavour and, years later, I suddenly remembered I had this track and it had such a good backing track, and when I came to sing it, it was so high! I know my vocals have been dropping over the years, but I couldn't believe how high it was . . .'"

George "It just seemed a really good track, except that it just seemed to be going so fast. What I did was one drummer on the original track, who was playing double-time, I added Jim Keltner again, playing half-time against it, which gave the impression that it was slowed down a bit. You can still hear Ronnie Spector in the background. I left her in. I wrote it especially for her."

Ronnie Spector, recalling the original 1971 Abbey Road sessions with George and John, "I had known them from The Beatles days when The Ronettes had toured with them. George liked my voice and asked if I could write a song for me. He came up with 'Try Some, Buy Some', and we all liked it. It's a kind of weird song but I'm not in it that much. It's kind of like a movie with a star but the star only appears now and then. I really don't know how much I like me not singing so much. I was very nervous in the studio to start with but I got to feel very good, eventually. Phil (Spector) did the orchestral tracks first. He used about 40 strings and I don't know how many mandolins. He had Leon Russell on piano and Klaus Voorman on bass. George played guitar. He had a lot to do with the single as well. In fact, he and Phil had about equal time on it. The B-side of the single was 'Tandoori Chicken'. We were in the studio one night and we were real hungry so Phil sent out for some Indian food, from a place called Tandoori Chicken. Listen to the words, that's what it was about."

'The Answer's At The End'

George "It came from a Victorian thing written on the wall at the house I live in. I've got a lot of songs off the wall. This comes from a Victorian poem, or something. It stuck in my mind and it seemed like a song to me."

'This Guitar (Can't Keep From Crying)'

George "It's son of 'While My Guitar Gently Weeps'. I decided to write this one because of the popularity of 'While My Guitar . . .' It really is a cheap excuse to play a bit of guitar and that song, 'Gently Weeps', was really more popular than I realised. And it was one of my favourites from the old Beatles albums, so I thought I'd write another one, a son of . . ."

'Ooh Baby (You Know That I Love You)'

George "For ten years or so, I've realised one of my favourite singers has been Smokey Robinson. He was a songwriter also and has written some of the most fantastic tunes. Although I'm not anywhere in his league as a singer, this song reminds me of Smokey's kind of mood. So, I dedicate this song to him."

'World Of Stone'

George "I wrote that a couple of years ago and I've only just got round to recording it. There's not much of a story to it, other than it's really down to saying everybody has their own opinion and right to be. It's a nice melody."

'Can't Stop Thinking About You'

George "I wrote that at Christmas time two years ago and I was just sitting round the log fire. Joe Cocker could sing that song. It's a very commercial song and the middle bit kills me. I don't know what it is but I have a tendency to write dramatically or mellow dramatic melodies and that one makes me think it should be sung by someone like Al Jolson or Mario Lanza. It's a very interesting melody. The beginning is my impersonation of John Lennon. It was hard to sing that first chorus."

'Tired Of Midnight Blue'

George "I wrote this and sometimes I just think of titles and write them down on a piece of paper and then, sometimes, I get round to writing a song about it. I always thought of 'Midnight Blue' as a title, so I wrote the song and, about three weeks after I recorded it, Melissa Manchester's came out and so it's now 'Tired Of Midnight Blue'. It's a story of when you go out and wish you hadn't. It's one of those."

'Grey Cloudy Lies'

George "This is one of those deep, depressing, four o'clock in the morning kind of songs. I don't know where these songs come from half the time. That one was a piano song. Sometimes I write on a piano, but I can't play the piano so I'll play certain chords, which

I probably wouldn't bother with on guitar, because I know them too well and they always sound different on piano. This was written on the piano and the rhythmic thing about it got me and it tends to miss beats every so often. I think it was one of those songs after talking a lot. That's a song about being quiet."

'His Name Is Legs (Ladies And Gentlemen)'

George "It's the craziest song, both lyrically and musically and the story on this one is 'Legs'. It's actually Legs 'Larry' Smith who was the drummer with The Bonzo Dog Doo Dah Band, and he's a very nice person who is very eccentric and I'm very partial to eccentrics. I met him two years ago and I had this piano by the fire and I had just met Larry. He kept coming and coming and he just amazed me with the things he was saying, so I just decided to write this song about him. The lyrics are just crazy, just like Larry. 'Everything is dinkey-doo. Everything that you do. Are you the king of la-de-da?' He sings the first part of every bridge. I've never seen him since."
(Excerpted from a conversation with Paul Gambaccini, September 1975)

George "The album marks the end of Apple as a label, unless somebody else forms a company called Apple. Paul's already done a deal for his future, which puts him on Capitol for the world. It doesn't look like Ringo or John will be doing another album this year so I look like being the last one on Apple. Funny, the first Apple record was the music from *Wonderwall* (1968), which I wrote. Quite a coincidence. I feel a bit of sentiment about it because Apple did a few good things, you know. But we were always bugged by business, though, right from the start. And business as opposed to the artistic side is always a problem for everybody. I was never really in Apple shops or anything else. During the whole Apple period I was always mainly interested in working in the recording studio. John, Paul and Ringo would have some great ideas but at that time I couldn't be bothered to follow them through. I suppose my attitude didn't help. The business ending up becoming an incredible headache. Everything that could go wrong for us did go wrong. Yet it was a great boom for some people, like Badfinger and the Billy Prestons of the world. But it went crazy at the end and that's why I am here now with Dark Horse Records. Apple didn't shake my faith that much. Good musicians are really worth encouraging."

SEPTEMBER

In the States, as promotions for his new album, radio stations syndicate a pre-recorded interview with **George** in their *Rock Around The World* series. The piece was conducted by the UK DJ Alan Freeman, and originally broadcast on BBC Radio One back on December 6 last year. During the fascinating piece, Harrison reveals that, "It was Ravi (Shankar) really who helped me get back into being a pop singer and also my association with Eric (Clapton). He really helped me. I had no confidence in myself as a guitar player, having spent so many years with Paul McCartney, because he really ruined me as a guitar player."

Freeman naturally asks, "In what way?"

George replies, "I don't know. I think it's easier just to read what . . . He also seemed to have done the same thing to Henry McCullough. I remember reading something Henry said, that he 'left Wings because I don't know if I'm good or I'm bad. If I can play this or if I can't play anything.' . . . Eric, who I rated as a guitar player, treated me like a human and gave me a guitar, which was the best guitar I've ever had. It went from there and I just decided, 'Okay, I'm going to become a pop player and a guitar singer again.' "

Freeman "Do you ever think, because of the magnitude of The Beatles, Beatles songs were ever overrated at all?"

George "I think, probably, eighty per cent of them were overrated but then, the twenty per cent that weren't, were exceptions. I think The Beatles were fantastic, John and Paul were fantastic. You see, the funny position I was in was that, in many ways, this whole focus of attention was on The Beatles. So, in that respect, I was part of it but from being in them, an attitude came over, which was John and Paul, of, 'Okay, we're the grooves, and you two, just watch it.' They never said that, or did anything, but it was over a period of time . . . In a way, I felt like an observer of The Beatles, even though I was with them. Whereas, I think, John and Paul were the stars of The Beatles . . . I've been meeting Paul again, you know, Paul McCartney. We drifted off away from each other, suing, suing, sue you blues stuff. I've just met Paul and I just know that whatever we've been through, there's always been something there to tie us together. We've had a big dog collar and we've come through the other end and we've really picked up to be friends again. I know with John Lennon, John Lennon's an amazing person who is brilliant, is brilliant. There is no question about it. John Lennon is a saint and he is heavy duty and he is great and I love him. But, at the same time, he is such a bastard. But that's the great thing about him. You see, I don't feel I owe John anything or I don't owe Paul a thing or I don't owe Ringo anything. I've certainly given them whatever I could and I've taken from them whatever I could. But I don't think any of us owe each other a thing and at this point in our time, you know, I'm really ready with John Lennon, in particular, to get down and kick down a few doors and let's get going together."

While on **Tuesday, September 23**, **John** is told that he could stay in America because Yoko is expecting their baby. Immigration officials decide to temporarily suspend moves to deport him on "humanitarian grounds". Mr Oswald Kramer, acting commissioner for the Immigration and Naturalisation Service in the North-Eastern states, grants an administrative stay of the deportation order.

Tuesday, October 7

For **John** meanwhile in New York, he has two reasons to celebrate, beginning today with the announcement that he has "virtually won his long-running legal battle to work and live in the United States". This stems from the news that the Court of Appeals has instructed the Immigration Department to consider John's application for residence. They also tell the department that "they cannot use the musician's British drug conviction as grounds for refusal." John's attorney, Mr Leon Wildes, says in New York, "That's complete victory. There's no way in which the Immigration Department can reject him now." When told of the news, John replies, "This is a great birthday gift from America. I'm absolutely delighted."

And on **Thursday, October 9**, there is further good news for **John** when, besides celebrating his birthday, Yoko gives birth to Sean in a New York hospital. It is her first child with John . . .

A reporter on the scene is Mark Dowdney, who files this report "John Lennon was celebrating his greatest hit tonight after his wife, Yoko Ono, gave birth to an 8lb 10oz boy on his 35th birthday. It was the baby the couple had longed for. The one they feared they might never have. For 42-year-old Yoko has had several miscarriages since they married in 1969. The baby was born three weeks premature by Caesarean operation in a New York hospital. But both mother and baby, who will be called Sean Ono Lennon, were doing well. An overjoyed Lennon, who was at his wife's side throughout the labour, said proudly, 'Yoko's fine and the father is pretty good too.' John was so delighted that he insisted on giving the baby its first feed. Yoko underwent a major operation to make it easier to have what was thought to be her last chance to give birth. She spent the whole pregnancy confined to the couple's luxury apartment overlooking Central Park. John remained devotedly at her side, cancelling all public appearances, and doing everything he could to make life easier for her."

John "We worked hard for that child. We went through all hell together, through many miscarriages and terrible, terrible things. Doctors in England told us that we could never have a child. We had almost given up, 'Well that's it, we can't have one, then.' She was forty-three. They said she had had too many miscarriages and when she was a young girl, there were no pills, so there were a lot of abortions and miscarriages. The prognosis was, 'She's too old and you've abused yourself too much.' What happened was a Chinese acupuncturist in San Francisco said, 'Heck, have your child. Just behave yourself. No drugs, no drink, eat well and you'll have a child in eighteen months.' So we had Sean and I sent him a Polaroid of the baby just before he died. He died right after Sean was born."

Yoko "When I discovered I was pregnant, I agreed to go ahead and give birth only if John and I totally reversed our roles. I would take on the job of the breadwinner while he became Sean's full-time mother to the child. John was so delighted at the prospect of becoming a dad again that he actually stayed in hospital after the birth of the new arrival to feed him. I dropped an emotional curtain between Sean and myself. As a mother I had opted out. You might say I was playing the part of a typical father. I came home from the office at night, blowing a kiss to Sean and saying, 'How was your day?' I must confess I had not wanted to have a baby. I wanted an abortion but John wouldn't hear of it. So I told him, 'Okay, I'll have the baby. But after that, though, he's definitely got to be your responsibility.' "

Bob Mercer, EMI Records "I was with John and Yoko when Yoko came out of hospital with the baby and again John reaffirmed that he intended to spend the foreseeable future, which I imagined meant the next five years or so, bringing up the baby. He wanted to have a close paternal relationship with the child, which is laudable. And given his state of health and wealth, he can afford to do that. He's very interested in parenthood and he is very interested in the way children grow up and their impressions of the world, basically what maketh the man. I suppose it would be fair to speculate that Julian didn't see very much of John because John was on the road and the whole Beatles thing was happening. I also think it would be fair to say that John regrets that now and has no intention of letting it happen again."

Friday, October 24 (UK and USA)
EMI Records in England and Capitol Records in America simultaneously release John's greatest hits compilation album, *Shaved Fish* . . .

John "Hits and misses, I think, and nears . . . When I went to look for the 'Cold Turkey' master tapes, nobody knew where they were. I had to use dubs of 'Power To The People' because the tapes had gone; nobody could give a damn at the record companies . . . I thought, 'If I don't put this package together, some of the works are going to be lost forever.' So I just put it together, at least it's there now for anybody who's interested."

Tuesday, October 28
Meanwhile, Paul and Wings' departure for Australia on the world tour doesn't go quite to plan, when he keeps 200 other Jumbo Jet passengers waiting by arriving for the flight twenty-one minutes late . . .

Syndicated news report "When Paul was asked why they had arrived late for the 10.45am Qantas flight at London's Heathrow airport, the unflappable ex-Beatle replied, 'We overslept a little. What's the panic?' While his wife Linda chipped in, 'Oh, the eggs would not boil.' Daughters Stella, Heather and Mary were still breathless after the dash from their home in St John's Wood, London. Airport officials had waited anxiously for the McCartneys' Rolls Royce and another vehicle loaded with luggage. Inside the waiting Jumbo, tempers began to rise among other passengers. But a Qantas official insisted that the plane stay on the runway until McCartney and Wings were traced. By 11am, people inside the plane became increasingly angry. Five minutes later, the pop stars arrived, with twenty cases of luggage still to be put aboard. McCartney and his group are booked for a concert tour of Australia and Japan. Qantas spokesman, John Ford, said after the group's jet had taken off, 'The plane was delayed twenty-one minutes, partly due to waiting for McCartney and partly because of a fuel delay. Seventeen of his party had checked in and it seemed reasonable to wait for them.' "

OCTOBER
The Willy Russell stage play *John, Paul, George, Ringo . . . And Bert* plays in London . . .

Melody Maker "**George Harrison** went to the celebrated play *John, Paul, George, Ringo . . . And Bert* in London last week. He left the theatre at the interval. He could not stand the pain of seeing himself and The Beatles' years being re-enacted so uncannily, and he questioned the fundamental need for the show. The first ex-Beatle to view the play, he had been persuaded to go by close friend, Derek Taylor . . ."

Derek Taylor "George found it hard work to watch and I found it hard work sitting with him. It was a genuine form of suffering for him. It was hardly surprising that George didn't enjoy it, after all, he was hardly in love with The Beatles' story while it was happening."

Paul "I never saw that, but I did see clips on the telly and I thought it had me down as being the one who broke the group up. I just saw one little scene out of context where the character who was playing me was saying, 'I've got to leave,' and John's line was, 'All right, Paulie, for the good of the group, stay.' And that got me really angry! I thought, 'Bloody hell!' If there ever was any way, it wasn't that way. It certainly didn't happen like that. But I've seen since the fellow who wrote it, Willy Russell, and he said, 'No, it's out of context.' He's since given me the thing to read so I can really understand it."

Saturday, November 1
The Wings world tour plays Australia and, following their show at the Perth Entertainment Centre, **Paul** holds his first press conference down under . . .

Reporter "McCartney appeared to prefer to talk about the future rather than The Beatles' past. 'The Beatles are gone forever,' he announced. 'But Wings are now on the scene. Nothing is left of The Beatles, memories only.' "

Paul, at the press gathering, "My remaining ambition is to be happy and I am happy with my new group. The good thing about this group is that it is new. It's just at the start of the life. That's always the best time. Some other groups that have been playing a long time, get a bit jaded because they get a bit fed up with it, playing the same gig for years. The only worry was trying to follow The Beatles. When you're in a group called The Beatles, and people see you in another group, they say, 'It's not as good.' But I think it is. It is a progression. Everything in music is a progression."

Backstage at the Entertainment Centre, Wings are interviewed by the Australian television personality, Mike Walsh . . .

Linda reveals, "I had a song written about me, a Jan & Dean song, when I was about five. It was sung by a guy called Buddy Clark, who was very big in America but got killed in a car crash and it was No. 1 and then Jan & Dean recorded it and it was No. 1 again."

Paul takes up the story; "Her dad was the lawyer for the songwriter. He said, 'Instead of a fee, why don't you write a song for my little girl?' Which he did and she got dragged onto television when she was five and she got stuck on top of a piano and they said, 'Now sing, Linda.' But she didn't know the words. She was only five and she cried."

On **Thursday, November 11**, plans for Paul's world tour with Wings are thrown into disruption . . .

Syndicated press release "Tokyo, November 11 – The Japanese Government has banned Paul McCartney, the former Beatle, from entering Japan for a series of concerts because of a British drug conviction two years ago, the promoters said today." (Japanese concerts were due to take place between November 19 and 21.)

Paul on this announcement, "It's a bit tough. It's a pity because we were ready to go but some places are more old-fashioned than others. The offence is two years old. It's a bit much. It's been cleared in America. We're allowed to go into America and Australia. It's a bit of a drag but if the man says we can't go in then we can't go in. We'll just have to wait until next time. The funny thing is that we had the visas for Japan. It's in the passports. It's there. It's stamped but there's one man in Japan, the Minister of Justice, who hadn't actually approved it, and he's the man who has decided not to approve it. He's no friend of mine."

Saturday, November 29

Back in the States, Mal Evans is interviewed by Laura Gross on KCSN Radio. During the interview, The Beatles' close friend and former roadie discusses his forthcoming book on his time with the group. Provisionally titled *Two Hundred Miles To Go*, this is a cryptic Beatles reference to the distance between London and Liverpool . . .

"The book is my whole life," he explains. "There was a monthly magazine called *The Beatles Monthly*, which ran for six and a half years and I used to write articles for it, called Mal's Diary. I used to take a lot of pictures for it. So I was always a part of their whole environment. You know, bashing chains on 'Yellow Submarine' for some sound effects and shuffling sand. You got involved in it. I was there basically. I want the four of them to love my book. That's my whole dream. My whole dream would be realised if they said, 'I love what you're doing.' I was talking to Ringo about the book and I said, 'You know, I wouldn't put you down,' and Ringo said, 'Look, if you don't tell the truth, don't bother doing it.' It will be the truth. There will be a few things they'll be mad about, but it'll be the truth. It's not meant as a derogatory thing, it is just what happened. The book is going to be a good book because I only had a good time."

Publication is expected to be in early 1976.

DECEMBER

An exclusive, rare, interview with John, conducted by Lisa Robinson, is published in the American *Hit Parader* magazine. She begins by asking him about the history of his now distinctly promising deportation case . . .

"I don't know where to start," **John** announces. "It's going on the same as before, for me it's the same. It's been going on since 1971. The first conviction came down in 1973, when they said I had to leave. I couldn't be a permanent resident of the United States with a British conviction. They've taken the stance that I have to leave. They always say 'Thirty days', but that passed a month ago. They say that once a year. It's so complicated. It started out because I had a British conviction for possessing marijuana, which was planted by Sgt Pilcher, which everybody in England knows now because the guy's in jail . . . You know, incidentally, there was a CBS documentary I saw last week about Nazis in America, allowed known Nazis who are here. The guy who was prosecuting me got taken off my case and put onto this Nazi thing. On TV he said that someone in his office, in the immigration department, had stolen his file on Nazis from the file in his office. Meaning that someone in his own group is protecting these people. They're so busy protecting them, but they're attacking me. I mean, there was a list of Nazis as long as your arm and one of them was holding a service in Congress at one time. It's just ludicrous. It's Kafka . . . They keep falling on back on that law about misdemeanours, and it's some trip to change the law here, even though in England that law has reversed."

Robinson "But they could get around it?"

John "Of course they can. My lawyer has a list of people, hundreds of people in here who got around the law for murder, rape, double murder, heroin, every crime you can imagine. People who are just living here."

Robinson "Why then do you want to live here?"

John "Because it's the same everywhere. Name somewhere where it's different. It's not as if it's a choice between living here or in England where it's different. It's the same in England on a different level, and the Americans and the English are hand in glove. Whatever the game is, it's the same game. It's really a choice between living in the West or the East, but I'm West and I don't want to live in the East. America and England to me are almost very similar places. Maybe you can't see it if you're living in England . . ."

Robinson "Would you want to become an American citizen?"

John "I'm too involved with this to think about citizenship. I'd prefer to do a PG Wodehouse. I found out before he was knighted that he was living here and I thought, 'Well, that's cool.' Nobody thinks PG Wodehouse is not English. He was English until his last breath and he lived on Long Island and that suits me fine. I'm English and I want to live here. And the funny thing about America is that there's almost no such thing as American. You go on the streets and everybody's Italian or Israeli or English or Jamaican or Nigerians . . . My ideal is to be able to travel, that's the thing I really miss most. I miss England, Scotland, Wales, all that sentimental stuff, but I also miss France, Holland . . . Germany I haven't been to for years. I'd like to go to South America. I've never been. I'd like to be based there, and just travel."

Robinson "Do you ever think you'll be so overcome with all the legal hassles that you'll get like Lenny Bruce and become obsessed with learning the law?"

John "No, I got obsessed with the politics for a while, but law is, well, I could never take it that seriously. At a certain point, I would see the funny side of it and say, 'Fuck it!' The worst that happens with most of these lawsuits is that they'll take more money off of me and the worst that would happen with immigration is that I'd have to move."

Robinson "Let's say that there's a happy ending to all this, and there comes a day when you're knighted, or the Academy Awards bring you back to receive a special award, what would your reaction be? Would you tell them to fuck off?"

John "Well, there will be a happy ending. But I have no idea what I'll do at age 70 or 80 like Charlie Chaplin or PG Wodehouse. I don't really know his story but there was something weird about him and being captured in France by the Nazis and doing broadcasts. And I think that's one of the reasons why he left, although he was forgiven. But the real forgiveness was when they knighted him last year, and he died happy, right? So, I'm not really interested if I get knighted when I'm 70. I'll deal with it when it comes. If they give me a knighthood at age 70, I'll deal with it then, Sir John . . ."

Robinson "Do you think that there would be tremendous excitement if you went back to England now?"

John "No, there was no hysteria when I was living there so why should there be now. I mean, The Beatles nostalgia and getting back together bit goes on as much here as it does there, maybe more. All hysteria is manufactured anyway. At the *Sgt. Pepper* opening, it was announced, 'He's going to be there,' so it was bloody Beatlemania going on. I got a fright because I didn't know what I was letting myself in for . . . It was bloody *Hard Day's Night*, but that's because it had been manufactured and they expected all four. Ever since George done Bangla Desh, they expect everybody to come on with him."

For most of this period, **Ringo** had been dating the 24-year-old Californian beauty, Nancy Andrews...

Andrews storms to the US press "I am not a marriage wrecker. I'd hate to be thought of as a marriage wrecker. Everything between Ringo and Maureen was finished a year and a half before we met on a blind date in Los Angeles."

Christmas Week...
Paul and Linda are the surprise guests of John and Yoko at the Dakota building in New York...

Paul "Linda remarked for some reason that, when she was a kid and her family had company, she had to go to bed. I said, 'Oh, it wasn't like that for me. I grew up in this big Liverpool family and the only company we had were aunts and uncles. There were always plenty of them around, with us kids jumping all over them. It was a very warm sort of upbringing I had.' And John and Yoko just looked at each other and said, 'We never had company.' They had this very sparse upbringing, with maybe one visitor once in a while. That would really have made me a different person."

On **Sunday, January 4,** the year begins badly when The Beatles' former roadie, the friendly and gentle Mal Evans, is killed by a 30.30 rifle fired by Lieutenant Charles Higbie of the Los Angeles Police robbery and homicide division. The tragic event takes place in Mal's motel apartment situated at 8122 West 4th Street . . .

Syndicated news report "Mal Evans has been killed by police in Los Angeles. The incident happened, claimed the police, when they were called to a house owned by Evans' girlfriend. They found Evans armed with a rifle, which he refused to drop. The police then shot him."

When told of the news, Laura Gross of KCSN radio, the reporter who interviewed Mal just five weeks ago, announces her protective, emotional tribute to the man on air. She will speak for many . . .

"The press reports that have been coming out about Mal since he died, have been very negative," she announces, "besmirching his character, claiming he was depressed because of a lack of work, and that he was fighting with Fran (his current girlfriend). Obviously he just had his book to come out and he was contracted to produce the group, Natural Gas, so he wasn't out of work. He wasn't fighting with Fran and I think those type of reports are not only sensational and tacky, but also a blatant lie. Ask anyone who knew him, or talked to him. He was a fabulous person and I think you can tell it from his own words. He's gone and it is a terrible fact that we have to accept. But I know he will live on in the memories of those of us who knew him and loved him."

Ray Coleman, music journalist and friend of The Beatles "Mal Evans was much more than The Beatles' roadie, even though that was the official title he shared with Neil Aspinall during the group's rise from the Liverpool Cavern. A huge and strong man, Mal was rarely argued with by promoters and he developed a warm and winning way of getting precisely what The Beatles wanted. He had a passionate belief that roadies were badly written off and once formed a road managers' association, which guaranteed that roadies would not be 'sat on'. He believed that The Beatles were second only to his idol, Elvis Presley, whose every record and piece of paraphernalia he possessed and about whom Mal had made a life's academy study. When I met Mal about a year ago in Los Angeles, after many years, he said, 'I've met him, you know. The King! I want him to record one of my songs.' A true character of the Sixties pop scene, and a Beatles fan at heart, Mal will be missed."

On **Saturday, February 21,** with news that John is about to win his Immigration 'green card' case, rumours are rife that, "John Lennon Is To Re-Open The Rainbow." The story, which appears in today's *Record Mirror*, reads, "London's Rainbow looks likely to be reopened for rock this year and John Lennon is planning an appearance for the new season. The way is now clear for Lennon to come to Britain, knowing he can return to the States when he wants to. An American court has ruled that a visa should not be denied to anyone because of a previous drug charge, Lennon's present circumstances. His case, which he is expected to win, has not yet been heard, but is due to go through within the next few weeks."

Tuesday, March 16

American LA based promoter, Bill Sargent, again offers The Beatles $30 million to re-form for just one concert appearance . . .

Paul "One day, I work up and reached for my morning newspaper, as usual, and read the story in it, which said, 'The Beatles To Re-form, Sargent Offers Millions And Millions Of Money', you know, and I thought, 'Oh, that's going to bring the questions up.' And, just like the rest, I thought, 'I wonder what the strength is in that.' So I just waited around for something to happen and then I got a telegram from Sargent in LA and it put the offer out, straightforward. So I knew what I read in the papers and I had a telegram saying it was official. But the thing was, what I was waiting for was some of the group, you know, somebody to do with the music, to ring up and ask me, 'Are we going to do it? Aren't we?' It's been a few weeks now and the truth of the matter is that no one has actually rang up to talk about it.

"I got a telephone call saying that John has rang and he wants me to ring. So I rang him in New York and I said, 'What is it?' And he said, 'What do you mean, "What is it?" You're ringing me.' And I said, 'Oh, no, I thought I was supposed to ring you.' He said, 'Oh no, no, no,' and I said, 'Oh, blimey, we've got it wrong there.' So we just nattered on for about an hour and a half. We were just chatting and we ended up talking about politics and the state of Britain today, you know, the taxes, and all that kind of stuff, like a lot of people and we were just having a laugh. I hung up the telephone, at the end of the conversation, and said, 'Ta la, then, it was great speaking to you,' and suddenly I thought, 'I'm sure there was something we were supposed to talk about there.' If everyone could realise, that's how it is. That's all the problem is, really. Even though it's masses of money, I think it's the wrong motive with something like The Beatles. For me, it was never really for the money that we would do anything. Obviously we did stuff to get paid, but we did it for the music or for the group, or for the enjoyment. So that's the only way we'd get back together. If we did do it, to be done ever, in my view, it must be done because the four of us want to do it and obviously we'd have to talk, but we haven't even talked about it. But everyone gets asked in different parts of the globe. When Ringo was in Los Angeles, somebody asked, 'What do you think?' And he said, 'Well, I don't mind, I'd do it.' And then they ask me in Europe, and I said, 'Well, I don't mind, I'd do it.' But it's a positive maybe at the moment."

George "That was a sick offer. It's putting pressure on us in a way and I don't like that. I'm not saying a Beatles reunion is never going to happen, maybe in the future. It's not beyond the bounds of possibility but we're so diversified now. We've gone separate ways. To make us play together now is like expecting us to go back to school or something. I mean, how would you like to go back to doing what you did eight years ago? Maybe it'll happen sometime, but I don't see us ever getting together just because of people bringing pressure on us. It's not our responsibility to live up to demands like that."

Wednesday, March 24

American newspaper correspondent James Johnson anticipates **Paul McCartney**'s second American invasion when he writes; "Excitement mounts in the United States as Paul McCartney prepares for his first American tour since the days of The Beatles. With talk of a possible Beatles reunion concert still in the air, McCartney and his group Wings next week embark on a nationwide series of dates that is likely to break box office-records across America. On the jaunt, he will be taking his wife Linda, who plays keyboards, and his three children, Heather, 14, Mary, 5, and Stella, 3. A strong believer in family life, McCartney always takes his children to concerts and appears to believe that they benefit in an educational sense. The tour begins deep in the heart of Texas at Forth Worth on April 8 and continues for five weeks before closing at Madison Square Garden in New York . . ."

Thursday, March 25
McCartney mania continues to grip the States . . .

Syndicated news report "Los Angeles: More than 36,000 tickets to ex-Beatle Paul McCartney's two concerts next month were sold out within three-and-a-half hours. 'The old magic is still there,' said Larry Solters, the spokesman for McCartney's group, Wings, which will tour twenty US cities. 'We didn't even have time to announce the concerts,' Mr Solters said. 'It was all done by street rumours. People started queuing up at the box office two days ago.' "

Also today, Wings' new studio album, *Wings At The Speed Of Sound*, is issued in the States . . .

"It turned out less of a McCartney production and more of a Wings effort," **Paul** announces. "It wasn't intended like that. There was one of the songs that I had sung but I just let Joe, our drummer, sing it because he's got a very nice voice, and he sang it great. Denny is a natural for a couple of tracks because he is, after all, a lead vocalist. So I wrote one track for him, which I called 'The Note You Never Wrote' and he wrote one track himself, 'Time To Hide' and then Jimmy, who writes a bit with Colin Allen, did one track this time, 'Wino Junko'. It seems he can't get off the plonk!"

'Cook Of The House'

Paul "We were in Adelaide, in Australia on tour (November 1975) and we rented a house there to stay in, instead of hotels all the time. We felt more comfortable in a house and we were in the kitchen after a show. We had driven back and Linda was cooking up some grub for dinner and I was just playing my guitar, just sitting around as usual, and around the kitchen there were all these little pots of sago, macaroni and various other things, and I just read them all off, you know, rice, sago, macaroni and put them down into a song. I was looking around for a second verse because I wanted to do it exactly with the things in the house and not make things up of my own. Then I noticed a little plaque on the wall. It was one of those little wooden plaques you see in the kitchen, where you see 'Welcome To Cornwall' or something. This one said 'No Matter Where I Serve My Guests, They Seem To Like My Kitchen Best', so I had the second verse and then, for the middle of that, I was watching what Linda was doing. She had some rice cooking, and some beans, some salads, and stuff, so I just wrote it into the tune. Afterwards, I said to Linda, 'That would be a good song for you.' So we just decided to try it and if it didn't come off, well, I guess I would have done it or somebody else would have done it, or we wouldn't have done the song. But we went in to do the session, and I took in an old stand-up bass I've got, which used to be owned by Bill Black, and I think it's the original bass he played 'Heartbreak Hotel' on. I've got it as a collector's piece. So I took it into the studio, and I was just banging it and playing it terribly and it gave the record this kind of interesting old Fifties sound. Linda sang it great and it turned into a track."

Wings release 'Silly Love Songs' as a single off the album . . .

Paul "Over the years, people have said, 'Aw, he sings love songs, he writes love songs, he's so soppy at times.' So I thought, 'Well, I know what they mean, but, people have been doing love songs forever. I like them, other people like them, and there are a lot of people I love.' So the idea was that you may call them silly, but what's wrong with that? The song was, in a way, to answer people who just accuse me of being soppy. The nice pay-off now is that a lot of the people I meet, who are at the age where they've got a couple of kids and have grown up a bit, are settling down and they'll say to me, 'I thought you were really soppy for years, but I get it now. I see what you were doing.' "

But the countdown to the American visit, entitled Wings Over America, has to be shelved when there is an unforeseen accident within the ranks of the group . . .

Samuel Justice, *New York Herald Tribune*, **Tuesday, March 30**, "Ex-Beatle Paul McCartney and his group, Wings, have postponed a 31-concert tour of the United States because their guitarist, Jimmy McCulloch, 22, slipped in his Paris hotel room and broke his hand. Wings ended a European tour in Paris on Friday night. The US tour was to open in Fort Worth on April 8. It has now been rescheduled for May and June."

Paul, Linda and their family take a holiday in the South Seas . . .

In **April**, the build-up to Wings' rearranged American tour continues. This month in the magazine *Rock Around The World*, staff writer Mr Curt adds to the excitement in his piece entitled, *Paul McCartney And Wings, The Second Band . . . On The Run . . .*

"After years of varied preparation, **Paul McCartney** & Wings are due to start their first American tour," Curt writes. "It begins in May and criss-crosses the States for two months, playing in large halls and arenas, mostly in big cities. This man, who hasn't set foot on an American stage in almost ten years, is demanding the respect only playing bass in The Beatles could possibly accord someone. As one of the modern architects of present-day rock'n'roll, Paul has carefully constructed his newest version of Wings, making it tougher, more confident of its stature, and more committed to rock rather than pop. Performing up to twenty-nine songs per show, Paul has wisely inserted some old favourites, including five Beatles songs, 'Yesterday', 'Lady Madonna', 'Blackbird', 'I've Just Seen A Face' and 'The Long And Winding Road', for the sake of long-time fans who would certainly be disappointed at the absence of past hits. Having finally maintained a proper balance of musicians, Paul is able to offer a diverse show, complete with a solo section for different Beatles tunes. His concert is probably a perfectly planned, well-staged show. No wonder Paul has felt it possible to tour the world. Already, Wings have scored huge success during their recent Australian tour. The American tour had to be postponed a month because Jimmy McCulloch broke his left hand after a concert in Paris. Delayed, but undaunted . . . Nostalgia buffs can only revel in the aura of Beatlemania – a joyous mood that swept the world for three full years. Such total abandonment to a group seems increasingly improbable today. Cynicism has become a foundation of the fan phenomenon. The search for 'the next big thing' is a false premise, one that creative musicians and artists have no control of. The immediacy of the modern world inhibits musical ideals and promotes only visual idols. The Beatles won't get back together for money, even though twenty-five million intergalactic-credits is a hefty incentive. Groups should (re) unite for musical expression-progression and this is part of the reason Paul formed Wings; to create music and play it live before a true audience (a task The Beatles were reluctant to do from '66–'70).

"Paul enlisted the aid of his wife, Linda, guitarist Denny Laine, and drummer, Denny Seiwell to form Wings I . . . Wings II brought Henry McCullough to the band as lead guitarist and prompted a 1973 tour of small concert halls in England. Paul had insisted on small venues because he believed a new band couldn't demand top status. The thrill of playing live didn't overcome McCullough and Seiwell, both of whom quit the band just before a trip to Lagos to record a new LP. The tight rapport of the remaining trio, Wings III, is evident in their most famous and respected offering *Band On The Run*. Remember that this LP set a precedent. It was the first time that an album became No. 1 on two different occasions, just weeks apart. Paul, Linda and Denny were able to meld their musical growth toward a mastery of the recording studio . . . Wings IV introduced Jimmy McCulloch, a spunky lead guitarist with grit, able to spur Paul on unlike any previous soloist. His debut track, the magnificent single 'Junior's Farm', stands as one of Wings' finest emotional and technical releases. Then, in early 1975, Paul added Joe English, to replace Geoff Britton, whose work on *Venus And Mars* is limited to only three songs, a drummer of enormous potential and flexibility. Wings had roosted . . . With this important final addition, McCartney was finally satisfied with a band, one that gave him the confident spark to plan a worldwide tour. Each member of the band is highlighted with assists on lead vocals or song composition, further demonstration of the democratic tendencies Paul has always insisted on – and actively reluctant for Wings to become his vehicle solely. With the release of *Wings At The Speed Of Sound*, his wish has been achieved. He is lead vocalist on only six songs, though writing nine of eleven. These are the motivations that have made Paul's post-Beatle resurgence so compelling. He has never strayed from his designs for a collective outfit. He has ignored critical slagging (of wife & band), choosing to explain, simply, that Wings hadn't reached a level of rapid maturation. Rather, they evolved assuredly and slowly . . . Okay the time is now here. This month, Wings open their tour in Fort Worth, Texas on May 3 and conclude in Los Angeles on June 22. Don't forget to scream, applaud, and cheer. Wings need the encouragement. If anyone else has been keeping track, one might note that Paul saved America for last – reserving the U.S. tour as a mark of conclusive professionalism. Come on, America, let's welcome Wings and Paul McCartney in a really grand way . . ."

Monday, May 3

After the aforementioned short delay, the Wings Over America tour begins at the Tarrant County Convention Center Arena in Fort Worth, Texas . . .

Paul "I told the others, 'America will be okay. It's nothing to worry about. John was the best with the smart answers but any jokes go down well.' I told the others that they would ask you, 'What brings you here?' And you reply, 'We came on a Jumbo,' and they go, 'Ho, ho, ho, ho.' You don't have to be an Oscar Wilde. But really, it's the tired old questions that get me. 'Do you ever see John Lennon? Are The Beatles getting back together?' I'll go mad if I have to hear them again. I'm really happy with Wings. I'm as happy as when I was playing with The Beatles. Not happier, as happy, no more, no less."

Reviewing Wings' first stateside show is John Rockwell of the *New York Times* . . .

"**Paul McCartney** has long since proved himself the most steadily professional, commercially viable of the former Beatles. But that was all through recordings. But last night, in beginning an American tour at the Tarrant County Convention Center Arena, here with his first performance in this country in ten years, Mr McCartney established himself and his band, Wings, as concert artists in their own right. And he did so triumphantly. Fort Worth crowds are reportedly reserved about most pop acts and indeed before the concert, the clean-cut, denim-clad crowd seemed quite subdued. But when the lights went out, the audience suddenly came to life, standing and cheering and remained enthusiastic for the whole two-hour, 15-minute set. People liked the five Beatles songs Mr McCartney included, needless to say. But they also responded warmly to his many post-Beatles efforts and that is, of course, the real key to his continued health in the music business. They had good reason to like the Wings material, for on the whole, it sounded better than it does on records. Last night's performance sounded tougher and more overtly rock'n'roll than the recorded versions. The concert may have been the first American date but extensive touring in Britain, Europe and Australia has preceded it. The result was an impressively polished, yet vital performance. Wings is a good band. Mr McCartney plays bass and a good deal of piano, during which time Jimmy McCulloch or, more often, Denny Laine switched from guitar to bass. Both guitarists are excellent and sing decently well. Joe English is a perfectly decent drummer and there are four first-rate wind and brass players with unusually tasteful arrangements to play. Linda McCartney has suffered through the criticism that inevitably befalls any strong Beatle wife. In Wings, her main function (other than moral support for her husband and visual appeal) is to provide back-up harmonies, which she does adeptly. She has no solo songs, and noodles away functionally but discreetly at the keyboards . . ."

Associated Press "Smoke filled the stage and bubbles cascaded from the ceiling during the opening number, the theme from 'Venus And Mars', before the satin-clad McCartney, backed by wife Linda on keyboards, Denny Laine and Jimmy McCulloch on guitars, and Joe English on drums, started a long set of rock'n'roll with 'Rock Show' and 'Jet'. The tour was delayed a month because McCulloch had broken a finger on his playing hand, but he was showing no ill effects. There was only one minor incident during the show, when a youth rushed on stage to shake hands with Paul. He was quickly ushered off by security men."

John Rockwell, the *New York Times* "The programme, which Mr McCartney said later backstage would likely remain fixed throughout the tour, consisted of twenty-six McCartney songs, one by Mr McCulloch, one by Mr Laine and a Paul Simon song, 'Richard Cory'."

Associated Press "Paul drew ovations for 'Maybe I'm Amazed', The Beatles' rocker 'Lady Madonna', two fine acoustic ballads that McCartney soloed on, 'Blackbird' and just about everyone's favourite, 'Yesterday'."

John Rockwell, the *New York Times* "The five Beatles songs, which Mr McCartney later insisted had been random choices, were 'Lady Madonna', 'The Long And Winding Road', 'I've Just Seen A Face', 'Blackbird' and 'Yesterday'."

Associated Press "Everyone in the band took a turn in the spotlight as they ran through a set that included hits like 'Listen To What The Man Said', 'Silly Love Songs' and the closing number, 'Band On The Run'. They returned to the stage twice for encores, which were 'Hi Hi Hi' and 'Soily', a song McCartney later said backstage remains as one of their favourites."

John Rockwell, the *New York Times* It was, in all, a spiffy show, nicely paced with a clear, solid sound system and some pleasing special effects, including one spectacular bit with lasers at the end, in which a thin sheet of light was deployed over the audience and marbled smoke patterns reflected off it. Afterwards, the performers were ebullient . . ."

Linda "Not bad for an opener."

Denny "Great, fantastic, frightening."

Paul "I was a little bit nervous but I pretended I wasn't. I used to get more nervous with The Beatles. I was younger, I guess. I love American audiences. They're just great. The response to 'Live And Let Die', it was ridiculous. The Beatles songs? We didn't want to be too precious about choosing them. That's the trouble with The Beatles thing that people will think it's all we came from. Some of the younger kids like the new songs better than the old ones."

John Rockwell, the *New York Times* "He may be right, but you couldn't prove it by the response here. Without question the greatest applause, a welling up of screams and emotion that closely approached the old Beatlemania, came for 'Yesterday', and deservedly so. Mr McCartney's version of that haunting ballad, sung alone in the spotlight, accompanying himself on acoustic guitar, was the high point of the evening. Its success symbolised Mr McCartney's inevitable fate. No matter how much pleasure he gives audiences with Wings, people will never forget The Beatles and nor should they. One certainly hopes that The Beatles do get together again, at last briefly. For many, Mr McCartney has confirmed that he has something distinct and individual to offer us in the meantime."

An American reporter remarks, "When kids were buying tickets for the McCartney concert, they were asked, 'Did you know that Paul was in The Beatles?' Many replied saying, 'Yes, we understand that Paul was in a group before Wings.' "

Paul "Anyone connected with the Wings tour could not fail to be impressed by an incredible team spirit. Linda and I decided to take our three children, Heather, Mary and Stella, with us. Our decision, and that of hiring a special jet to transport us between concert halls in America so that we could always be together, attracted world Press attention. I thought that either the kids were going to be with me and influenced by me, or with some babysitter or nanny. So they came to all of our bases. They only came to four shows as treats, special nights, so they would not be camp followers. We treated it as if we were on holiday and us parents would go out during the evening. We also thought we would always see the bright side of everything and we communicated to everyone on the tour. When something went wrong, one of us would say, 'Never mind, eh?' And instead of going to soundchecks until the early hours of the morning and saying, 'You're no bloody good. You're no use and you're fired,' we tried to keep it very straight. The results were fantastic."

Saturday, May 15
Wings perform in Washington at the Maryland Capitol Center. Watching the show is Jeanette Smith of the *New York Herald Tribune* . . .

"The other night," Smith begins, "ten years after The Beatles last toured America, six years after The Beatles broke up, **Paul McCartney** introduced the girl he married to more than 22,000 roaring fans in Washington. He and his group, Wings, are two weeks into a US tour. 'I'd like to introduce you to my missus,' he said. 'My better half, Linda.' There's nothing like the chagrin an ageing hippie feels knowing that the Woodstock generation is fighting flab instead of a revolution. That generation didn't have to flaunt its dope the other night because nobody would have been arrested anyway . . . 'They don't scream like they used to,' McCartney said, when asked how this generation of American audiences differed from those of ten years ago. 'But then I looked out at the audience tonight and they were going potty out there, weren't they? This was a crazy audience, one of the craziest we've had on this tour.' Only two were treated for fainting at the first aid station. Only eleven arrests were made, most for possession of alcohol, and one for interfering with an officer. There were no drug arrests. Some waited all night to get first-come first-served festival seating. They stampeded the barricades. 'He is the most important person I'll probably ever see,' as one Woodstock generation oldie put it. But they didn't dance on their seats, in the aisle or on the ceiling. If that's the pottiest crowd he's had, then this is an old generation of young people. 'People don't want to lose their seats,' said a 17-year-old Alexandria girl with braces and jeans. 'Most of them are drunk or stoned.' By the end of his second show, McCartney was still exuberant. He had every reason to feel that way. The Wings Over America tour may well be the most polished and professional rock show ever mounted. He is with Wings now, not The Beatles, but twelve years after it all began, it's still Paul McCartney ascendant."

Also viewing the proceedings is Larry Rohter of the *Washington Post* "Paul McCartney can rest easy. His place as one of the greatest rock'n'rollers of all time is assured. That's not as obvious a statement as it may seem. Back in the days of The Beatles, McCartney got stuck with a reputation as the 'pretty' one, the Beatle whose cuteness often seemed to spill over into syrupy ballads that infuriated fans of the quartet's harder stuff. 'Wimpy' was the word that, in the high school slang of a decade ago, when the great John versus Paul debate raged, was sometimes used to describe him. But when McCartney played in Washington, he was the consummate rock'n'roller. There's still a sugary streak in his music, but in live performance, he showed a toughness that's missing in much of his recorded music."

Monday, May 17

To coincide with the rearranged Wings tour of the States, an interview with Paul and Linda, carried out in New York the previous week, appears in *Newsweek* magazine . . .

"It has been six years since the break-up of The Beatles," Maureen Orth writes, "but their magic lingers on. If any proof of that was needed, it came last week when ex-Beatle **Paul McCartney** and his hard-driving, four-piece band, Wings, opened a sell-out, seven-week, twenty-city tour of the US, to the screams of thousands of fans, old and new . . ."

Orth "Do you think you've finally made it on your own?"

Paul "When we first went on tour in England, we were worried the audience would be more enthusiastic for The Beatles songs. But we found that there were many people in the audience who were not that keen on the old stuff. I love that, because it means you don't have to live in the past. It means you can really keep moving."

Orth "How did Linda become part of the band?"

Paul "We were up in Scotland and I just happened to say to Linda, 'Do you think you'd enjoy to be with me in a band?' So when the curtain went up, she just appeared. She's got good fingers."

Linda "I love it now, but I used to be scared stiff. And if I thought it wasn't working out, I'd say it's not for me."

Paul "I remember John Lennon, he's an old singer, saying, 'I didn't think that was your taste in women!' But when your wife comes along, it doesn't matter what your taste for women has been before, if it's someone you love. Mind you, I could have said to John, 'Well, look at you. You must be joking, aren't you?' Now we are all older and wiser."

Orth "You are one of the few British superstars who still chooses to live in Britain and pay the country's enormously high taxes. Why is that?"

Paul "I've always hated the idea that you had to live where it's convenient for your money and secretly disliked people who kept their money in Swiss banks. And we like it in Britain. We love the country. But it's getting to be a near thing. I mean, 98 per cent taxes is just too punitive. I'm thinking of writing a letter to Mr Callaghan. When we were all together as The Beatles, we got an MBE and the biggest perk from an MBE is that you can go to St Paul's Cathedral and not have to pay the sixpence fee to go into the whispering gallery. That's what we got for doing all we did for Britain."

Orth "The big question that remains is when do The Beatles plan to do something for the world by getting together again?"

Paul "I personally doubt very much that it would happen. As someone once said, 'You can't reheat a soufflé.' The only basis that I could see anything like that happening would be if the people involved are really hot to do it, if they have a lot of ideas and very genuinely want to commit themselves. The offer of The Beatles thing ($30 million reunion offer) came up and in about the two months that followed, none of us happened to ring each other and talk about it. So that's how committed everyone was."

Orth "Do you rule out any kind of onstage reunion?"

Paul "The real truth of the matter is that none of us wishes to close the door. We're all good friends still. We all know that possibly something may happen. Two weeks ago, for example, I was talking to John about this exact point and I was pleased to hear that his feelings were exactly the same as mine, which is, if anything really happens, we won't close the doors on it. But until it does, we'll all go on opening doors."

On **Saturday, May 22**, Wings' concert tour reaches The Boston Garden. Accompanying them is the *Sunday Mirror* reporter Alastair Buchan . . .

"At the end of each gruelling two-and-a-half-hour concert, Paul and Linda relax in their dressing room," Buchan writes, "sipping whisky and Coke and chatting to friends. After a while, they may drop in to the press hospitality room. With patience and professionalism they fend off the same Beatles questions they have been answering for six years. Then, a quick drive in a hired Cadillac, behind a police motor-cycle escort, to the airport and on to the privacy of one of the three houses they have rented in the States for the duration of the tour. Not for them nightly parties in hotel rooms until dawn and bleary lunchtime breakfasts, which suits Linda fine. 'Our job is playing music and recording,' she says. 'But I don't believe that means you have to live the part every hour of the day. The reason so many groups split up is that they try too hard to live up to the role others decide they should play.' While I was with Wings, I felt I was part of the family rather than an observer."

Tuesday, May 25

The biggest concerts on the Wings Over America tour take place at New York's Madison Square Garden. On hand to preview the successful event is Robert Palmer of the *New York Times* . . .

"**Paul McCartney** and Wings, who will be performing their second and last Manhattan show in Madison Square Garden tonight, come complete with all the trappings of a major rock band on the road. Clever lighting effects illuminate the musicians, a huge 'state of the art' sound system bombards the hall with decibels and the audience dutifully tosses firecrackers, sets off Roman candles and roars. But the Wings show isn't just rock. It's also music-hall vaudeville, middle-of-the-road pop and sheer schmaltz, all the ingredients that made The Beatles the most popular group of the Sixties. The trouble with the show from a rock standpoint, and it is as a rock group that Wings asks to be judged, is that Mr McCartney's hardest-hitting music is also his most ordinary. But when he wants to, Mr McCartney can sing in a convincingly gritty fashion. He turns 'Call Me Back Again', which is not very spectacular on the *Venus And Mars* album, into a gospel ballad with considerable conviction and power, and saves 'Maybe I'm Amazed' from the treacly fate it has suffered at the hands of lesser vocalists . . . When heard one after the other, Mr McCartney's songs do not indicate the presence of genius. A handful are enduring pop standards and they deserve to be. Quite a few more are memorable. The rest are well crafted but forgettable, like Loggins and Messina songs. One enjoys them while they are going on and forgets them as soon as they are over. The popular wisdom concerning The Beatles has long had it that their diversity was their strength. With John Lennon and George Harrison to balance his tendencies towards cloying sweetness, and to make his hard rock even harder, Mr McCartney was able to use all his talents to their full potential, to be wholly effective in all his guises. Alone, he is chameleon-like, and even with his wife, Linda, lending support on keyboards and backing vocals, and the rest of Wings thundering behind him, Mr McCartney is alone on the stage. His rock fails to generate the sort of communal ecstasy The Rolling Stones and a handful of other bands create, and his ballads, which would be affecting in a more intimate environment, sound frail and disembodied in a hall as cavernous as Madison Square Garden . . ."

Also covering the concert is the American reporter, Dan Bennett . . .

"Paul McCartney filled his lungs with the expensively conditioned air of Madison Square Garden and savoured his coming triumph. Ten years ago, at Shea Stadium, in this city, he scored a historic victory in front of 55,000 people, with a group called The Beatles. But tonight, his triumph would be even sweeter. For tonight, the group Wings was his own creation. **Paul**, aged 33, but looking more like 23, sat in one of this mighty auditorium's 20,000 empty seats and told me, 'This is what I have been working towards. This is what I wanted the band to do when it was good enough.' Every seat was sold. Touts were getting

$150 for $10 tickets. Wings have proved with this, their first tour of America that they are a rock act to be reckoned with. An hour from concert time, everyone was asking, 'Would John Lennon take the stage with Paul?' He didn't, but the audience who heard a flawless collection of the best of Wings, helped along with some Beatles classics, hardly cared. The reception was hysterical."

Paul "On the night of Madison Square Garden, people were saying how relaxed I was and I should have been nervous. But what they did not realise is that a few months before, I had been in a taxi driving past Madison Square Garden and I thought, 'We're not going to play that, are we?' I had got over all my nerves in that taxi because I was actually shaking at the thought of coming to this huge city and being the only attraction on the night. My God! It worried me stiff. So I imagined when I actually got there I would be terrified. Thinking that made me quite relaxed. I have a joke, which I do when I'm nervous, by saying, 'I'm not going on,' and I walk around panicking people by saying it. I know that I am going on, but it is just something to relieve the nerves."

Saturday, May 29

Back in England, The Who's drummer, Keith Moon, tells the UK pop columnist Pat Moore "I like to swap crazy presents with my best friend, **Ringo Starr**. He gave me a ten-foot high rocket filled with bubble gum for my birthday. I got him a six-foot panda he calls 'The Chairman'."

Monday, June 7 (USA)
Beatles-related compilations continue when Capitol Records in America release *The Beatles Rock 'N' Roll Music*, a two-album set comprising previously released recordings . . .

Ringo "We've left EMI and Capitol now so they're going to put everything out. They're going to capitalise and get as much bread as they can out of us. They don't even ring us up and ask what we think of them putting out this or that. They just do it. I don't even like the album cover. John told me that he rang them up and asked if he could draw them one, or get them designed a good cover, and maybe he could design it himself. John told me that he was told to, 'Piss off!' All of us looked at the cover of *Rock 'N' Roll Music* and could hardly bear to see it. It was terrible! We have come to terms with this now, with the realisation that the songs are EMI's but you think we would get a hand in the way we are recycled."

Paul "If I was still in The Beatles, I would still be worried by it. I would care how they repackaged it and how they did it all. But I'm not in them anymore. They've split up and the record company has all the tapes and they are allowed to do what they want. I'm more interested in the new stuff and I can't be bothered. I don't knock the old Beatles stuff, I love it, I love to hear it on the radio, but as to actually bother about repackaging, looking at the cover, seeing what the price is, that's the record company's business so I don't really bother. I do that on all our own (Wings) stuff, but of the repackaging, I let them do that. There's nothing I can do about it, short of suing them all."

Tuesday, July 27
Finally, after a five-year fight, there is good news for **John** . . .

Syndicated Press Release "New York: John Lennon Gets His Ticket To Ride. John Lennon has won his five-year battle against the Immigration authorities in the United States. At the end of a 96-minute hearing in New York's Immigration Bureau, Lennon was granted his 'green card'. Effectively this means that Lennon can remain in the US indefinitely without fear of deportation and, more significantly, he is free to travel outside the US and re-enter again without any problems. As Judge Ira Fieldsteel announced his verdict, Lennon embraced his wife, Yoko Ono, and the packed courtroom burst into spontaneous cheering."

United Press International sums up, "New York: The US Immigration and Naturalisation Service announced today that it has granted permanent residence status to British musician, John Lennon. Mr Lennon entered the United States as a visitor in August 1971. His application for permanent resident status was denied in March 1973, on the grounds he had a previous conviction in England for possession of marijuana. In October of that year, the Court of Appeals concluded that the conviction in England did not make Mr Lennon ineligible for permanent residence. After further review, the service dropped its opposition to the charge in Mr Lennon's Immigration status."

While, back in England, the UK tabloid reporter Ian Robertson writes, "I have news for ex-Beatle John Lennon as he celebrates his new status as permanent resident in America. Cynthia, the wife with whom he made his Sixties success, has secretly married once more. Cynthia is now living in the wilds of Wales with her new husband, John Twist, a 30-year-old engineer from Prescot, Lancashire . . . Shortly after her divorce from John in 1968, Cynthia, a talented artist, fell in love with the Italian Roberto Bassanini. But, unlike her much publicised divorce from John, her quiet break-up with Roberto did not make headlines. Her marriage to Mr Twist has been a quiet matter."

Cynthia Twist "It doesn't worry me to be married to another John. Only occasionally, when people call us John and Cyn, do I catch my breath slightly. It is a phrase I heard so very often in the old days. But apart from that, I'm not bothered."

Friday, September 17 (UK)
Ringo releases his new album, featuring the unusual title *Ringo's Rotogravure* . . .

"*Ringo's Rotogravure* is like a colour supplement of the *Sunday Times* or the *Observer*," he explains, "and it just means a book of photos and I also think the tracks on the album are like photographs anyway. Also, in *Easter Parade,** that's where I first heard the word Rotogravure and at first hearing, I thought, 'Why is she speaking Russian?' I had never heard the word, and suddenly in the middle of this song, this crazy word comes in. So it stuck with me a long time and it's a nice match, *Ringo's Rotogravure*. It flows, and I think it's all pictures, even the tracks are pictures if you close your eyes."
(* *Easter Parade* is a 1948 musical film, starring Judy Garland and Fred Astaire.)

The album features contributions from his three former Beatles colleagues . . .

"With John and Paul and George, I asked them to write a song," **Ringo** reveals. "John wrote me a song, which is called 'Cookin''. Paul wrote 'Pure Gold' and with George, I said, 'Write me a song,' but I really liked this song from five years before that he had written that no one had ever put out. People have recorded it before but no one had ever put it out, and it's such a good song. So I said, 'It doesn't matter if you don't write me one, I'll do that one.' The song was called 'I'll Still Love You' and that's what I'll still call it. I don't know if that's what he wants to call it in the end."

During promotions for *Ringo's Rotogravure*, he is asked, by an LBC Radio reporter, the expected question as to whether or not The Beatles will ever reform . . .

"I would find it more interesting if someone else came along," he announces. "I really thought that Queen, for a moment, would take it somewhere. They did a fine album and I thought, 'At last, there's a new group coming up that's really going to go somewhere.' But they went somewhere else and just stopped. Elton's doing a lot of good stuff and so is Eric Clapton, but they are only covering it. There's nothing amazing! So I would really love someone else to come along. Why do they keep asking us to get together? Of course we are special, it was a monster situation. The drag is, at the age of 85, they are going to wheel us on a TV show and they are going to say, 'Here he is, ex-Beatle.' It doesn't matter what I've done since . . . But I would like some band to top us, but, of course, there hasn't been anyone."

The "Will The Beatles reform" questions continue to haunt Ringo throughout the album's promotional interviews. To another reporter, he replies . . .

"If you say anything with a possible 'Yes,' in it, then it's across the world, 'Ringo says they're getting together.' But all I say is, 'No,' because it won't be this year, I doubt if it will be next year. It could be in ten years; it could be in five years. We could get together, there's nothing stopping us, really, barring the time and what we're doing ourselves. I'm not too interested in getting together now. But I am interested in going into the studio. We could try and do something."

The LBC reporter asks Ringo, "Do you do any live performances these days or are all your efforts mainly put into recording?"

Ringo replies "The responsibility of fronting a show, well, up to this year, I have been adamant that I will not go out. I'm not going to go out there and sing 'Back Off Boogaloo' or 'Photograph'. Fronting is something that I can't do. That's not me. But this year, I've been thinking of a format that may go out next year, which is more of a circus situation, not with animals, it's a revue. It's a Rotogravure, right, of a crowd of artists and we go out and the audience doesn't have to put up with me for two hours. When we (The Beatles) went out, we did twenty-five minutes. We did thirty but if we didn't like the place, we played everything fast so we could get out after twenty-five minutes. But now, they're going on for two-and-a-half hours. You're bored with seeing the act, so I'm going out with a two-hour show but with things coming in and out, other people, other artists. I can't mention them because I'm still talking to them now, so I may go out next year if we get it together."

Ringo's *Rotogravure* promotions continue when an interview with Ringo is published in the *New Musical Express* on **Saturday, October 16**, a piece conducted in the playroom of his Hollywood Hills house. The interviewer, Lisa Robinson, begins by asking Ringo, "How long have you been in this house?"

"This is our second year," he replies. "I live here for about six months of the year, but not continuously, a month here, a month abroad. I am going to Europe this week, on the Concorde."

Robinson "Tell me a little of how you got together with Arif Mardin and the way *Rotogravure* came about?"

Ringo "Well, it started last year. I was going to record with Richard (Perry) and then that went out of the window and I was getting into new contracts after leaving Capitol. Then, when we eventually signed with Atlantic for the US and Canada, and Polydor for the rest of the world, we thought that since we were trying another label, we'd try another producer. Richard was busy, so I decided to look for someone else, and since I was on Atlantic, it was suggested to me to work with Arif, because he's like the house producer. And since he had just won the Grammy, I figured great. He flew to London for a day to say hello, just to see if we could do that together. He said he'd like to do it. And at the end, I said, 'Well I'd still like to do it, too.' Then I said, 'I want to do it in Los Angeles,' and he said, 'Oh dear,' because he likes New York or Miami. But I knew everyone here (in Los Angeles), the players. But for the next one, I'll go anywhere he wants. I now feel totally secure with him. I'd go to Nebraska if necessary. And we had a great time doing the album. It was very fast, three weeks, that's fast, right? And we did three or four tracks that we're not using . . . We had Peter Frampton and Eric Clapton on guitar. Frampton just came in for a visit. On my sessions, if you visit, you're on. I have a party atmosphere if we're working well. We all sit around and drink and really have a good time. John played on his track 'You Got Me Cooking' and Eric (Clapton) came down to play on his track. Then, the other night, who should come to town but Paul and Linda! Just as we were finishing. We went to dinner, and I got them on the track. It's nice to have the people who wrote the song do it with you."

Robinson "Did you write anything?"

Ringo "Yes, I wrote a country number with Vinnie Poncia and we wrote another one that we didn't use and that's a drag when you have to throw one of your own away. Nancy (Andrews – Ringo's current companion) and I wrote one in Mexico and I put a mariachi band on it. Just a mariachi band from a restaurant and me. No other players and I played maracas. It's great, with Mexican and Spanish words."

Robinson "How did you find the mariachi band?"

Ringo "We looked around all these Mexican restaurants and found this band who were sensational. They don't actually dance while they play but they're great players. I don't think they had ever been to a recording studio in their lives. So, I walked in with my mirror shades on, real paranoiac shades and they're all tuning up. No one says hello or anything. Then I take my glasses off and all of a sudden, 'Hey, one of The Bottles . . . Hey! De Bettles . . . Bing-A-Loo! Pappa-lay, one-a-da-Bodles.' Only one of them spoke English and there was all this Mexican ra-ra-ra-row, I just fell on the floor."

As he said, *Ringo's Rotogravure* features a contribution by John. It will be his last musical release for over four-and-a-half years. John, now free from EMI's record contract, will then voluntarily go into pop seclusion, but why?

"Everything was crazy," **John** will announce. "I realised that I wasn't making records for me anymore but because people and record companies expected me to. It was hard for me to admit that I was allowing some illusion to control me. After all, wasn't I the great pop seer? Hadn't I written 'The Dream Is Over'? Was I not the great John Lennon who could see through all the world's hypocrisy? The truth was I couldn't see through my own. It's easy to see thy neighbour and say, 'You and your phoniness,' but the trick is to see your own. Finally, Yoko said, 'You don't have to do it anymore.' And I was shocked. I had never thought of that. Could the world get along without another John Lennon album? Could I get along without it? I finally realised that the answer to both questions was yes. So I just shut up and learned how to cook and be with the baby and allow the feminine side of myself to exist rather than crush it out in fear of insecurity that I wasn't manly enough. I cut through all that macho ritualism that we all go though. I kept reading (in the newspapers) that I had become a lunatic or something who sat in a dark room all day with his long hair and long fingernails. It was hysterical."

Bob Mercer, managing director of EMI Records Group Repertoire Division, "I tried to persuade John to renew his record contract. He just said that his own feelings were that he didn't want to have his signature on any pieces of paper. He'd had enough of contracts, and so forth."

Yoko "It was wrong for us to turn our backs on the world but, really, it was the other way round. Both of us were people who couldn't really get understanding from others. In the end we were just driven into each other. Maybe we were too exclusive. John said we didn't need friends and that it was great to be self-sufficient. We didn't socialise at all and that created tension and hatred from other people."

Stephen Birmingham, author of the book, *Life At The Dakota* "The Lennons created their own world within the Dakota. They bought up six apartments and set each of the 50 rooms aside for a special interest in their lives. For these, they paid an amazing £26,000 a month in maintenance alone. In one of these apartments, John had a giant 14-foot-high playhouse built for Sean complete with life-size doors and windows. Their plan to install a full-size swimming pool in another apartment was scrapped only because the old building could not support the weight. The kitchen in the main living flat, bought from the actor Robert Ryan, is spacious. They have just about every conceivable gadget you can imagine. They have four dish washers and several hotel-sized stoves. It is quite incredible when you consider that John and Yoko don't entertain."

Tuesday, October 19

In an interview with the UK magazine, *Woman*, Cynthia (Lennon) Twist, now aged 36 and living an idyllic life in a remote corner of North Wales, recalls her life living with her former husband, **John Lennon** . . .

"In many ways he was quite Victorian," she recalls, "very much the man of the house and 'I'm in charge'. Everything had to be just so. When Julian, our son, was two or three years old, if he wasn't perfect with his knife and fork and table manners, there'd be a terrible scene . . ."

In the magazine article, she reveals her memories of The Beatles . . .

"The four of them always seemed to me very vulnerable," Cynthia admits. "I was older than all of them and I felt like their big sister. I thought they needed one, although I'm pretty sure they didn't think they did. The Beatles were married to each other and, in many ways, the girls were superfluous . . . Nowadays, people always want to remind me of The Beatles. They can't understand that, for me, it's all over. It's eight years since my divorce from John."

She admits that their marriage began to flounder the night (in April 1965) they went to a dinner party at the home of a friend of George Harrison, and saw a row of sugar cubes on the mantelpiece . . .

"It was a lovely dinner," she recalls, "and afterwards there was coffee galore and the host kept saying, 'Have more coffee,' so we did, in our innocence. The next thing, everybody sort of disappeared. The stupid, stupid man had put LSD in our coffee. It was terrifying. We finally came out of it eight hours later. It was John's first time, as it was for all of us. He thought it was wonderful. John had so much enthusiasm. I tried to pull him back, but I couldn't. There were so many people around him trying to influence him. They would say they could invent an island where there was sunshine all the time and John believed them. I always hoped he would understand that you don't have to do these things to be yourself. But it didn't work. I could see John being sucked away into a dream world."

Woman magazine "Cynthia gradually became aware of John's friendship with the Japanese artist and film maker, Yoko Ono, and she tried to escape to Italy."

Cynthia continues, "Before I knew where I was, there was a detective following me. John was having me tailed while he was back in Weybridge, sleeping in our bed with Yoko Ono. I moved out and as far as I was concerned, it was all finished. But the people I met wouldn't let it be finished. I would be introduced to complete strangers and it would only be a matter of time before they brought the conversation around to my personal life. Eventually I met John Twist and we married earlier this year. I swear he has brought me back the peace I have been seeking since I divorced John Lennon. But it can be sad when you're talking to someone and you regard them as a friend and you think that's how they regard you. And, as you walk away, you hear them saying, 'You know who that was, don't you?' But they'll get used to me, and then they'll let me forget."

In New York, **John** reads the article and, true to form, promptly decides to reply. In full, his letter reads:

"Dear Cynthia,
As you and I well know, our marriage was long over before the advent of LSD or Yoko Ono and that's the reality! Your memory is impaired, to say the least. Your version of our first LSD trip is rather vague. And you seem to have forgotten subsequent trips altogether. You also seem to have forgotten that, only two years ago, while I was separated from Yoko Ono, you suddenly brought Julian to see me in Los Angeles after three years of silence. During this visit, you didn't allow me to be alone with him for one moment. You even asked me to remarry you and or give you another child for Julian's sake. I politely told you no and that, anyway, I was still in love with Yoko (which I thought was very down to earth). There were no detectives sent to Italy. Our mutual friend, Alex Mardas, went to Bassanini's hotel to see how you were, as you said you were too ill to come home. Finally, I don't blame you for wanting to get away from your Beatles past, but if you are serious about it, you should try to avoid talking to and posing for magazines and newspapers. We did have some good years, so dwell on them for a change and as Dylan says, it was 'a simple twist of fate.'
Love and good luck to the three of you from the three of us.
. . . John."

Helen Seaman, John and Yoko's secretary "I advised him against sending this letter, but it is a measure of his anger."

In reply to John's letter, Cynthia Twist replies, "All I can say is that the whole idea of the letter is so stupid. I wrote the article to kill a lot of birds with one stone. When I wrote about our marriage break-up in the magazine, I had no intention of hurting him."

Also on **Tuesday, October 19**, while Cynthia's controversial spread is gracing the news stands across Britain and Europe, **Paul**'s group Wings are preparing to begin a run of sell-out shows at the Empire Pool in Wembley. Covering their performance for the *Guardian* newspaper is Robin Denselow . . .

"Just over four years ago on a hillside near Toulon, in the south of France, I watched one of the most depressing, almost embarrassing concerts I can remember," Denselow writes. "Paul McCartney was launching a new band called Wings, which included his much-criticised wife, Linda. Her nervousness and her obvious lack of talent seemed contagious, for the band was out of tune, awkward and generally dreadful. But last night, Wings, still including Paul, Linda and Denny Laine, but with a couple of the other personnel changed, started a sold-out run at the cavernous Wembley Pool. They played non-stop for more than two hours and gave one of the happiest, most exhilarating and most brilliant rock concerts London has seen in recent years. It was a show so well executed, so well performed, so well lit, and with such excellent sound, that one came out with all the old enthusiasms for McCartney as one of rock music's few real geniuses rekindled. Above all, he was to be admired for his courage in sticking with Wings while they slowly built up to this peak. This concert was remarkable because almost all the material was post-Beatles and all of it compared well with the few, inevitable, Beatles classics he threw in. It was the climax of a world tour that had included McCartney's first performances in America for a decade, and it was the ultimate confirmation that he can still match his early success. Most concerts have their long sections of padding between the peaks or the hits. But with McCartney's repertoire of songs, Wings could play hits all the way."

While John Collins, of the *Daily Telegraph*, has this to say . . .

"It is all very well Paul McCartney insisting that a certain four-headed ghost must be laid and his second incarnation, Wings, should be allowed to stand alone for judgement. He knows the power of legend and when the Empire Pool, Wembley, threatened to crumble about its foundation last night, it was, of course, the hallowed 'Yesterday' that had initiated a sort of sonic nostalgic boom . . . 'Lady Madonna' thundered out of a truly tremendous sound system and from then on, McCartney could do what he willed to the disarmed legend with the aid of his superb group, now improved beyond recognition."

The three nights of performances at the Empire Pool in Wembley concludes Wings' mammoth thirteen-month world tour. The group, who had played in sixty-six cities, watched by more than two million people, had travelled approximately one hundred thousand miles . . .

Paul reflects, "We were very lucky throughout the thirteen months of touring. And success leads to more success and my confidence grew. I need this inner strength to develop, otherwise I find myself closing in to my shell again. Our greatest triumph was in Zagreb, Yugoslavia, behind the Iron Curtain, which is not very 'iron' curtain these days. The Communist audience wanted autographs and silver boots and they love all these things. They are not at all grey. The band played so well that night. I did an encore for 'Yesterday' and they knew every word. It was a blinder of a show . . . By the time the tour ended, everyone wanted it to go on. The crew was working so hard; it was like the James Hunt world motor racing championship pit team. We all had so much fun."

Monday, November 8 (USA)
Capitol Records release the compilation album, *The Best Of George Harrison*, which comprises a mix of George's tracks from his Beatles days and solo years.

George "One side was all Beatles and I think that's a bit chintzy. It's tacky and the cover is tacky. We were with Capitol/EMI for so many years and they have the right, apparently, to do just what they like, but at the same time, you would think that after all those years and all that music that we did, they would at least have a bit of discretion."

Sunday, November 14
At his home in Beverly Glen Canyon, Los Angeles, at the start of a five-day promotional tour for his new album, which takes in LA, Chicago, Boston, Washington and New York, climaxing in an appearance on NBC TV's *Saturday Night Live*, **George** talks about his former group to the American reporter, Lisa Robinson . . .

"The Beatles weren't a very good band," **George** announces, "and a few years ago, I never wanted to play with Paul McCartney again. I just couldn't see it. Musically, for John, Ringo and me, we're no problem. But Paul and I had a terrific problem in the Sixties and later on, he wouldn't even allow me to play. I would come to The Beatles' session, be taking my guitar out of the case, and he'd say, 'No, no, I don't want any guitar yet. Let's do that later.' Over a period of time, he really stifled my feelings and I just had to get out. Being with The Beatles was stagnating. We weren't a touring band and it was just studio work at that point. But even in the studio, I had such little freedom to play. The Beatles were a good band when we were playing together but if you took each of us individually, compared to the level of other musicians around, we were amateurs. Ringo is a great rock'n'roll drummer, he's not technical at all, but he happens to be the best. John was a lousy guitar player, really, but he'd play certain things that nobody else could play, and his singing was fantastic. Paul had amazing charm and could write those sweet melodies. I don't know what I did but all together it was The Beatles. Anyway, it's all past and I'm happy now and the only way I could see us getting together again is if we wanted so badly to be in each other's company and to play music together. It's really hard now, because we're all such strong people. You put the four of us in one room together and it's really a heavy crew."

Tuesday, November 16
Shortly before catching his aeroplane flight, George gives a telephone interview to a Chicago radio station . . .

DJ "I had a chance to talk to Paul and Linda when they were here for the Wings tour and I asked him how Wings would compare to The Beatles. Paul said The Beatles would blow Wings away, or anybody else."

George "Did he say that?"

DJ "He did."

George "That's very nice of him."

DJ "Look, Sinatra's come back, Muhammad Ali's come back, Elvis has come back, the magic of The Beatles would be bigger than ever . . ."

George (interrupting) "Yeah, I know. I suppose there's a chance. Who knows? We never really knew it was going to happen then and I don't know if it is going to happen again. I think there's a chance sometime in the future. The biggest problem would be if we decided to make a decision, we'd have to set a date, ahead of when we'd decided it, because we'd all have to get out of what we were doing and make arrangements. If we did get together, there would be a lot of time needed to remember each other and remember the songs, and decide what songs to do, then rehearse before we even get to the concert. Then, if we did get it down, and say it was pretty good, it'd be no point in just doing one show. Maybe we'd end up on the road again, doing another tour."

DJ "I love the idea. Listen, Capitol has just put out George Harrison's greatest hits. They forgot to put in 'I Need You'."

George "Yeah, I know, yeah."

DJ "How could they leave that out?"

George "Really there's a lot they left out. I personally thought they were going to put together just the songs of mine since the band split up, because Ringo's *Blast From The Past* album was just his solo stuff and John's *Shaved Fish* album was him solo. I didn't know why they had picked up on all the other (Beatles) stuff. In a way, I thought this was a bit cheating. But I didn't have a say in that."

DJ "The song we've been playing for a while in Chicago is 'This Song'. In it is a little riff from your last single 'You'. Well, at least I thought it was."

George "You're starting to get like me, listening to every bar and beat."

DJ "Well, I've got one more thing to lay on you. I have a four-year-old son who swears that there is a little bit of the Captain & Tennille record 'Love Will Keep Us Together' on your record. That's what he told me."

George "Maybe he should become a musicologist. He can make a lot of money."

Wednesday, November 24 (UK and USA)
In contrast to the heavy themed *Extra Texture (Read All About It)*, George releases the relaxed and more pleasant sounding album, *Thirty Three And A Third . . .*

George "I had got myself more together, in both business and the personal side, and I got myself more relaxed and I think it shows on this record. I tried to get Tom Scott to co-produce the album with me, but Tom is really busy. He writes and records all the music for the *Baretta* and *Starsky & Hutch* American TV shows and he's making his own albums and produces his own albums all at the same time, and playing on mine. Tom is really good to work with. He's a very technical musician, whereas I'm more like a jingle musician. When I was working on the album, I found out that I didn't have a piano player. So what happened was that this guy, David Foster, who is in the band Attitudes, arrived in London and I collared him and he plays on three tracks and then Billy Preston came over after The Stones' Earls Court show. He played on this one song, one take, and drunk out of his mind. He went straight into it. Billy came back again and put some synthesiser and piano on the album. Gary Wright passed through one day and he played on a song called 'Beautiful Girl'."

'Beautiful Girl'

George "I started 'Beautiful Girl' back in 1969. I had been working on a Doris Troy record and Stephen Stills had a very good twelve-string guitar, which he loaned me for the evening. I couldn't get past the first verse with the lyrics and so the song sank back into the distance. But I remembered it during 1976 and finished the lyrics. I related them to Olivia . . . I can see all around beautiful girls in one way, ones who look good, and sometimes you see ones who don't particularly look good but have such beauty within them. And when you get the combination of both, then it's fantastic. Beauty to me is something, which comes from within and is not limited to the physical body, although that is helpful. I was watching Elvis at Las Vegas on a videotape and you know how Elvis does his karate chops, and has a big orchestra and backing singers, that tune he could do like that."

'Woman Don't You Cry For Me'

George " 'Woman Don't You Cry For Me' was really like one of my first influences as a kid, when I was about thirteen, fourteen, that period of time when I got my first guitar and the big craze in England at the time was skiffle. It was easy to play and there was a lot of bands, skiffle groups, and you only had to know two chords, which really got people off the ground playing. That song 'Woman Don't You Cry For Me' is really like that style. Eric Clapton was a big influence on me in the late 60s and he gave me this great guitar and I started to try and play slide guitar. Because I had been playing sitar for so long, I really wanted to try and catch up with my guitar playing because we (The Beatles) had given up playing live dates and I was really rusty. Little kids were coming up and playing the best licks you had ever heard, so I sort of felt a bit behind and so I got back into the guitar due to Eric. I admired him as a guitar player and as a friend and that song, 'Woman Don't You Cry For Me', really goes back like the old skiffle days. It's only got a couple of chords but played more in the country rock sort of thing, with slide guitar from my old pal, Eric."

'Dear One'

George "I dedicate 'Dear One' to Paramahansa Yogananda, who is a swami from India who left his body in 1952, as opposed to dying, he left his body and he's been probably the greatest inspiration to me from all of the swamis and yogis I've met. I've met a lot of the really good swamis and yogis and I like their company whenever I get the chance to spend some time with them. Yogananda I never met personally in this body, but he had such a terrific influence on me for some very subtle reason. I can't quite put my finger on it. I just dedicate this track to him because it's like a lot of my feelings are the result of what he taught and is teaching still in his subtle state and I wrote this. This song was one of the newer songs I'd written and it's like a prayer, really. It's a prayer and again just a realisation of that appreciation."

'This Song'

George "In the film clip for 'This Song', the famous Jim Keltner was the drummer with attitude. He's the judge in the film clip. That song came about because, after I had been sued and I went through this sequence in court, it was a joke. They were suing me for three notes in effect. At first I got into it and I was a bit depressed and then, as it went on, I was thinking, 'It's a joke! What are they talking about? It's a record; it's nothing to do with those three notes. It's a song, it's just a record.' I was getting very depressed and I was getting a bit paranoid about writing songs. I didn't even want to touch a guitar or a piano. So I then suddenly thought about 'This Song', there's nothing tricky about it. It's no big deal. I'd be willing if, every time I write a song, somebody will have a computer and I could just go up the thing and sing my new song into it, and the computer would say, 'Sorry,' or 'Yes, okay.' I'm willing to do that because the last thing I want to do is keep spending my life in court.

"I produced the record using session men. I got a friend of mine to put in a bass line so it's got that Tamla sort of bass line. I also got Eric Idle, who is one of the *Monty Pythons*, to throw in the funny lines, 'Could be sugar pie, honey bunch,' and, 'Naaaoo, sounds more like "Rescue Me".' But I do admit there are times when I have a hankering to work with John, Paul and Ringo. I definitely do miss it in some ways. When you have a band there's a certain amount of knowledge you have about one another and you can fit right into a slot. There's a certain starting point that's already established that you don't have to spell it out, as you do with new musicians. I like having the instant situation we got into with The Beatles, but at the same time, I don't think I could stand it again. It was too confining. The good thing about being on one's own is all the time being able to use other musicians."

'See Yourself'

George "The original idea in the first verse came about in the 60s when this thing happened with Paul McCartney and the Press (1967). There was a big story in the press where somewhere they had found out that Paul had taken the dreaded LSD and they came hounding him, saying, 'Okay, have you taken it? Have you taken LSD?' And he said, 'Well, look, whatever I say, I'm gonna tell the truth and whatever I say, I just want you to know that it's you, the media, are gonna be the people who spread out what I say,' and they were saying, 'Did you take it?' And he said, 'Yeah, I took it,' and then they put it all over the papers. 'Paul McCartney took LSD.' Then the press came after us saying, 'Have you had it? Have you had it?' And we said, 'Sure, we had it years ago.' And then there was an outcry saying, 'You should have said you didn't take it.' In effect, they were saying, 'You should have told a lie.' The press pushed the responsibility onto Paul, saying, 'You're going to influence other people to take it,' and he had said out front like, 'It's gonna be your responsibility, whatever I say,' and so I just thought of that. It's easier to tell a lie than it is to tell the truth. It's easier to criticise somebody else than to see yourself because people won't accept responsibility for themselves and it's very often that we all, and I included, point our fingers at people and criticise or pass judgement on others when first what we should do is try and see ourselves."

'It's What You Value'

George "One person can have an opinion about something and something can be very important to one person and it can be of no importance whatsoever to somebody else. It can be a big deal to one person and no deal at all to someone else. It's really a matter of values; it's what you value. They always talk about having sets of values and so for me, it was just that. This all came about from my 1974 American tour, and a friend of mine who did this tour with me. Everybody got paid really well on the tour and I was trying to get this friend to play and he wouldn't do it. But I really needed him to play and I was saying, 'Come on, come on, please play,' and he finally said, 'Okay.' I begged him to death until he agreed to play and he said, 'Okay, but look. I don't wanna be paid for the tour but I'm sick of driving that old Volkswagen bus,' and I said to him, 'Oh, well, okay. I'll get yer a car.' So we got him a car. I bought him a Mercedes 450 and then some of the other people, I later heard, were saying, 'How come he got a motor car and I only got a . . .' You know, it was one of them. So I just thought that in song. To one person, it's a big deal, but to somebody else, it's just like a throwaway thing."

'True Love'
(Originally a song by Cole Porter)

George "You know Cole Porter got the chords wrong? I don't know. He wrote some fine songs. I think we might have sung that tune in the past. We, The Beatles, used to play this in Hamburg, Germany. We had to play like eight hours a night, so we used to play every song we would ever imagine. We used to do whatever we heard and whatever we could come up with in order not to repeat ourselves. So, I think that somewhere down the line we might have done that song. I don't know why I did this this time, but it just stuck with me. This summer, I was just playing it one day and it sounded good and I put down the track and the track sounded even better and the track sounded comical. The song to me is a comedy. It depends on what way you want to take it. It has a very simple melody and simple words. There's only about four words in it. I liked the tune and I started fiddling with it, and then I heard that arrangement. But it could be done anyway, really."

'Pure Smokey'

George "A while back I was thinking about personal records that I just like to hear, and when I was in the Sixties we were really into Tamla Motown just around the time it was first breaking. And I always liked Smokey Robinson & The Miracles from that period. I found myself playing a lot of his records and I dedicated a tune on my last album to Smokey but I had written this one at the same time as that song, which was 'Ooh Baby'. This song is called 'Pure Smokey' and that was the title of one of Smokey Robinson's albums and it was really just like an idea that I had. Sometimes when you like something, you never get to say to somebody that you appreciated it. So I thought I'd use this way of getting across a point. I didn't want to be late. I didn't want to die and realise that I hadn't told my dad that I like him or whatever. It's like that. So I try and make a point. If I really like something now, I want to tell the person I like it, rather than to find out that I should have done something and never did. I try and live like that now. So the song just says, in the past I would hesitate. I would feel some joy but before I showed my thanks, it became too late and now, all the way, I want to find the time to stop to say, 'Thank you, Lord for giving us each new day,' so it's really just to say thanks for certain things. And then it just gets into Smokey, because I get a lot of pleasure out of his records and so it's a big thank you."

'Crackerbox Palace'

George "First of all, the idea of 'Crackerbox Palace' was, as in the third verse of the song, where it says, 'Some times are good, some are bad. That's all a part of life, standing in between them all, I met a Mr Grief.' Now Mr Grief isn't just to rhyme with life, as people will think. He was and is a real person. I met Mr Grief at MIDEM. He used to manage the singer, Barry White. I met this guy and I was talking to him and the way he was talking, I said to him, 'Hey, you really remind me of somebody. You remind me of, I don't know if this is an insult or a compliment, but you remind me of Lord Buckley, who is my favourite comedian. But this guy is now dead.' Lord Buckley was one of the first very hip comedians. When I said this, this guy nearly fell over, and he said, 'Hey, I managed him for eighteen years.' And so I was talking to this guy about all these Buckley things and he told me that he lived in a little old shack, which he called Crackerbox Palace and I thought, 'Wow, Crackerbox Palace.' It just sounded so good and I wrote it on my Gitane cigarette packet. I just loved it, the way that it sounded. Then, at a later date, it stuck in my mind and I thought I'd write a song called 'Crackerbox Palace', and there it is. It could be the place where you live but I turned it more into the world, the physical world."

'Learning How To Love You'

George "The main thing I felt from the result of the LSD thing and then later getting involved with meditation, was the realisation that all the goodness and all the strength and things that can support life is all coming out of love and not just as simple as one guy saying to a chick, 'I love you,' you know. So often we say, 'I love you if,' you know, or, 'I love you when,' 'I love you but,' and that's not real love. Love is 'I love you even if you kick me in the head and stab me in the back, I love you.' Or, 'I love you, unconditionally,' and that goes beyond everything, and that is a pretty far out love to try and conceive and when I realised a little bit of love, then I realised how shallow it was. It's like with everything, it's like saying, 'Okay, I'm a singer now,' and then you start thinking, 'How good, how many notes can I hit, where's my limitations?' And you realise, 'I wanna be the greatest singer in the world, but I'm not because I'm limited by something,' and with love, it's like that. Okay, 'I love you,' but how do you measure it? How do you live with it? How do you be it? And then you realise how limited you are and then it's a process of learning how to develop that. It's all right saying, 'I love you,' but let's see it manifest. I just don't wanna hear the word, I wanna feel it and see it and be it.

"It was just after we had laid some basic tracks down that I got some sort of food poisoning. I went yellow and that put me in bed for two months. When I got a bit better, I finished the album. It left me really weak. It was a sort of jaundice. I had a good rest, though. It was a good excuse to stay in bed and not answer the phones. But I actually got out of bed when I was still all yellow. In fact, that guitar solo on 'Learning How To Love You', I went and played that because it was boring lying in bed. So if you listen to that guitar solo, it's a yellow guitar solo."

The album's curious title?

George "The title seemed so simple. I was thirty three and a third at the time the album was recorded and it is also the speed that the LP is played. I thought that somebody must have used that title before, but apparently they hadn't. When The Beatles were still together, we used to travel along on tour, in the car, when we had a new album, and just think of album titles for hours and hours. I remember specifically on the *Revolver* album, we were happy with the title because it suggested the record going round and round. It's almost surprising that we never came up with *Thirty Three And A Third* then. Maybe, somewhere down the line, we thought of it. Every time we'd have a new album, we must have gone through thousands of titles, some of them were ridiculous and some of them had potential. We would just keep throwing out titles until one of them would stick."

Speaking at the time of the album's release, **George** remarks, "Things seem to go in phases. For a while, things were bad but now I feel really up and my health's fine. But there was a time that I felt really run down. When I started cutting the new album, I felt really awful. I put in a lot of late nights and wasn't eating right and then there was that episode with the Bull's Blood. The guy who played piano on the album kept bringing in this horrible red wine called Bull's Blood and I drank a lot of it. I think that's what really did me in. Then I got food poisoning and jaundice and liver trouble and I turned all yellow. So now I've quit drinking. I never liked the stuff much anyway, though I used to drink wine and sometimes go crazy and drink brandy and tequila. I think cigarettes will be the next thing I'll try to give up. It's hard trying to balance your life between the rock'n'roll existence and the sort of straight life and the east Indian philosophy and meditation I've been into for so long. Now I think I've found the balance."

In New York on **Wednesday, December 1**, in light of the recent 'My Sweet Lord' plagiarism suit, **George** announces his paranoia over recurring threats of legal action . . .

"My biggest worry was facing possible litigation over my new compositions," he reveals, "on the grounds that someone might come forward and say they were stolen. There are so many songs that are similar to some degree. I started to get really worried about writing songs after I testified in court earlier this year. I'd pick up a guitar and say, 'Well, I can't use those chords, those chords have already been used. And I can't use those words because I've heard those words before. Before you know, it becomes a problem and you start to get really paranoid about it. In the end, I thought, 'Oh, I'm going to get hung up about this.' My fears started shortly after the gruelling three days I spent in court, testifying about a charge of plagiarism . . .'"

Harry, George's father, "The action was wrong. 'My Sweet Lord' was George's work. He got cynical and wrote songs about it, as if to say, 'Well if this is what you think of me, this is what I think of you.' There were times during that business when he got very fed up. While he never thought of quitting, he wanted to break away for a while because the pressure was getting too much."

Friday, December 10 (UK and USA)
Wings release the live triple album *Wings Over America* . . .

Paul "That had to be a triple album in the end, because we were doing two-hour shows and there was no other way to get two hours of music on record. This album just called to be a triple album. If we could have made it a double-album, we would have made it a double-album. I don't like releasing huge price items; I prefer everything to cost fifty pence. I'm not in just for the profit, in spite of what some people might think. This bloke who works with handicapped children wrote to us saying the album was the one that really lifted the children and he wanted to thank us for that."

Saturday, December 18
Europe's first Christmas Beatles Convention takes place over two days at the Alexandra Palace in North London. The event is sadly a disaster . . .

Syndicated news report by Angie Errigo "Over the stage, four giant models of The Beatles hang, deflated, by their plastic necks. They are sadly symbolic of Europe's First Christmas Beatles Convention. Held at the barn-like Alexandra Palace, the convention was probably the most embarrassing fiasco ever linked with the name Beatles. Twenty-three-year-old organiser, Dave Chisnell, head of Whamm Enterprises and Secretary of Britain's Beatles Appreciation Society, seemed a very pleasant, honest, untogether young man. Financed for this operation by his dad, he candidly admitted he'd made several boobs. Naively responsible for what he thought was to be 'the best Beatles Convention', Chisnell failed to obtain the originally hoped-for hotel conference room for the gig, rejected The Roundhouse as too small, opted for the most inaccessible venue in town and booked it for the last shopping weekend before Christmas. *Get Back, Jojo!* Disappointed, Chisnell estimated the number of ticket holders present over the Saturday at 1,500. On Sunday afternoon, I saw about 100 people, and by Sunday evening, the doors had been thrown open free of admission to any comers.

"Looking pathetically lost in the vast floor space, just over a dozen dealers flogged their wares to listless takers. Brand new T-shirts, badges and posters sold pitifully, as did overpriced Beatles import LPs and the terribly poor quality selection of bootlegs. Completely irreverent street junk such as chokers did little better. A record dealer from Paris lamented the worst sales he'd seen in three Beatles conventions. He'll have been lucky to cover his stall rental costs of £12 per day. Besides the bootlegs, dealers were selling gold Beatles records – £15 for singles, £35 for LPs – and unaccredited photographers' rough prints stamped 'not for reproduction'. All of which are, as Chalkie Davies put it, 'totally illegal, unethical and nasty'. Chisnell conceded that, 'We asked them all what they were selling and warned them if they were selling bootlegs and anyone came, it was their lookout.' Allan Williams busily autographed paperback copies of his book, but the 2,500 extras optimistically stacked in the office where he was kipping down in a sleeping bag, didn't look like being required. Derek Taylor begged off appearing and Faron's Flamingos played for two grisly hours on Sunday night. A pirated copy of *Magical Mystery Tour* was shown without permission, along with some *Star Trek* out-takes.

"Also on Sunday night, Allan Williams irritated the pants off the 300 or so people present when he acknowledged that he did have the legendary 'Hamburg Tapes' with him, but wouldn't play them because, 'I'm not going to spoil a million dollar deal.' According to Williams, WH Records will release the tapes as a double LP in America because, 'nobody in England has got any money!' Angry Beatles fans questioned Williams' rights to use the tapes, to which he responded with, 'I'll be laughing all the way to the bank.' That's something that Dave Chisnell and his dad certainly won't be doing – the hire of Ally Pally alone cost them something like £1,300. One imagines that those who paid £2 for admission or £3.50 for a weekend ticket to this ride aren't laughing either."

1977

January
The year begins with George suffering from hepatitis, result ing from jaundice. George experiences the first two-and-a-half months of the year laid up in bed . . .

George jokes, "I needed the hepatitis to quit drinking."

Monday, January 10
In New York, the long-standing feud between John, George and Ringo and Allen Klein ends with an out-of-court settlement. Apple Corps Ltd. will pay £2,946,588 to Klein's American-based Industrial Corporation, ABKCO. Upon reaching the agreement, the tough-talking Klein pays tribute to the "Kissinger-like" diplomacy of Yoko Ono . . .

Allen Klein to reporters camped in his New York office "Shall I tell you how it all ended, after all these days, years and weeks? Well, Yoko Ono came up to me and said, 'I have two questions. One, if we settle now, is that an end to it all?' 'Yes,' I said. Then she asked, 'And secondly, will you come and have dinner with John and myself tonight?' Well, as you can imagine, we went off and got very merry. That was how we boiled it all down. But it would never, never have happened if Yoko had not been there to calm us all down and be a total diplomat when the going got hot and tough. That woman is extraordinary. She said to me simply and so sweetly, it was disarming, 'Allen, we used to be on one side of the table and now we are on opposite sides.' She talked for 45 minutes. She gave such a brilliant discourse on why we should all be friends again that I didn't say a word for a whole quarter of an hour. For me, that is unheard of . . . The negotiations went on for three days, non-stop at New York's Plaza Hotel, and do you know, never once did Yoko complain or say she wanted to go home. There was no way she was going to quit until everything had been straightened out. There were all these lawyers there, some of them very Machiavellian and devious, who just wanted money, money, money.'"

When told of what Klein had said about her, Yoko replies "That's the first time I ever got any praise for anything."

Linda "It is true she settled with Klein for $5,000,000 but it wasn't her money, really. Each Beatle gave a share, Paul included and he never wanted that man as manager in the first place. Five or six million! When you think that they were pulling bloody cards to see what they could do. If only we had known what they were doing back there! All I know is, with all the advisors and lawyers and parasites, we're putting a lot of kids through prep school and buying a lot of swimming pools. And all Paul has been saying all this time is, 'Divide it four ways, please.' Instead of it staying in one kitty, where only the lawyers make money, divide it four ways and let's get on with life."

Chris Hutchins, **the former writer for the** *New Musical Express*, recalls a chance meeting with John at the start of the year . . .

"The man in the smart three-piece suit could have been a Manhattan executive," says Chris "Happy and smiling in the New York sunshine, he certainly didn't look like a one-time member of The Beatles. But it *was* John Lennon. Had he not spotted me, I would probably not have recognised him. John had been out of circulation for a couple of years and the last time I had seen him, he had long hair and more than a drop of drink. 'Hello,' he said cheerfully. 'Didn't know you were in New York. Why didn't you call me?' I told him that I didn't have a number for his apartment. 'I'm in the book,' he replied. Despite the fact that he had to use an alias derived from his early Beatles days, John was thrilled to be on the phone, just like millions of other New Yorkers. Unrecognised by passers-by, John chatted about the old days and then about his son, Sean. 'He's incredible,' John remarked. 'I should know, I'm his mum.'

"I told him, 'You certainly seem like a changed man.' 'Well, of course I am,' he replied. 'You know what it was like. The pressures, the threats. Well, all that's gone, now. I just look after Sean and give my money away. I actually gave $25,000 to a bloke the other day for a New York down-and-outs hostel and it made me feel great. Just look at me, I'm out on my own.' True enough, it was the first time in the sixteen years I had known him that I had seen him out of doors without company. As we walked the short distance to an art shop, John told me of plans he and Yoko had to move west and buy a ranch so that Sean could grow up in the country.

"John was shunning publicity at this time and I was not surprised, because I had sensed his growing need for seclusion years earlier. It was in Las Vegas in the summer of 1964, during The Beatles first American tour. There were three of us standing by a dusty roadside, looking up at the Desert Inn Hotel. Lights blazed from every part of the building except the heavily curtained top floor. 'That's it?' asked John. 'That's it,' said Irving Kandell, The Beatles' buddy and concert programme seller. 'That's where Howard Hughes lives.' While thousands of fans were gathered outside the Sands Hotel where The Beatles were staying, it had been John's one wish during the group's visit to the gambling city to see at least the outside of the building of the man who fascinated him more than any other on earth. 'Impossible,' pronounced The Beatles' security guards. No way could they be responsible if any of the four ventured outside their heavily guarded suite. But Mr Kandell had other ideas. He borrowed a doorman's uniform for John to wear and a catering van, and together we smuggled him down a fire escape, through the kitchen and into the forbidden world outside. For days afterwards, John talked about nothing but Howard Hughes and his strange lifestyle, quizzing everyone he met in search of further information about the eccentric billionaire hermit. 'That would suit me,' he said. 'In one place forever instead of this constant travelling. Total privacy, nobody to bother you, scream at you, poke your hair or ask what your favourite colour is.' At last, it seems that John has got his wish."

FEBRUARY

A young New York couple discovers the sharp edge of **John**'s tongue when they walk into The Sensuous Bean, a tiny coffee and tea store on Columbus Avenue in Manhattan . . .

Eye witness, Steven Wright "John and Yoko had just bought 1lb of Colombian and 1lb of Haitian coffee at a total cost of about $7 and they were discussing whether to buy a coffee pot costing $15 when this couple spotted them through the window . . ."

The Sensuous Bean store co-manager, 28-year-old Joe Pumphrey continues, "They obviously recognised John and Yoko. They walked on, walked back and then came into the shop. The couple made this big pretence that they were looking for some herb tea and kept speaking very loudly about the relative merits of the various teas. I knew that they had no intention of buying anything. All the time, they kept edging towards John, almost begging him to join in on the conversation. I saw John's face and I could see he realised what was going on. Suddenly, he whipped round on this couple and he had a sort of strange look on his face. It was a smile but not a nice sort of smile. 'Herb tea?' John said. 'You want herb tea? Well, in my opinion you'll want this.' Then he picked up the most expensive brand of herb tea, in the largest container, that we had. It must have been about $20. 'Here, buy this,' he said. The couple looked terrified. It sounds when you repeat it as though it was a recommendation, but it wasn't. It was an order. The couple took the tea, paid for it and hurried out of the door."

John's behaviour, this time more of a kinder nature, features in a story told by Nelson Segal, a 61-year-old furniture maker who sells his wood products from a sawdust-covered store near the Dakota apartment block . . .

"One day last year," Segal recalls, "a young woman walked into the shop and ordered $450 worth of cupboards for the Lennons apartment. I gathered she was the nanny and I think the cupboards were for her quarters. 'Lennon is paying,' she said. I established that from the beginning. In my business, you've got to know who is paying and that they can. I figured Lennon has got to be okay for a few bucks, right? So I finish these cupboards and I ring the Lennon household. They gave me a number I should call. Some woman, maybe it's Yoko, maybe it's the nanny, I don't know, says, 'We don't want them yet.' So I says, 'Lady, you may not want them yet, but I want the money now.' So I take them round, with an assistant, and they let us in and we are fitting these cupboards. Next day, I get a cheque signed by John. That's the sort of customers I like, good payers."

Sunday, April 10

Back in the UK, the *Sunday Mirror* reports, "Ex-Beatle **Paul McCartney** has given his hens a ticket to ride. The pop superstar paid out more than £100 for a taxi to make a 500-mile trip with the hens aboard. And he didn't even cock an eyebrow at the cost. In fact, he reckoned the fare was chicken feed. Paul found himself in a fowl dilemma when he took wife Linda and their children on an Easter trip to the family farm at Campbeltown in Argyllshire. There was no one left at their house at St John's Wood, London, to feed the pet hens. And the strike by engineers at Heathrow Airport last week ruled out an immediate airlift to get the birds to Scotland, so Paul hired a mini-cab to drive the hungry hens over the border. The back seat of the car was removed to make space for their baskets on the 518-mile journey. A friend of Paul said later, 'It seemed the only way to get round the problem.' "

Friday, May 6

Coinciding with the release of The Beatles' legendary 1962 Star Club tapes, EMI and Capitol issue *The Beatles Live At Hollywood Bowl*, a single album featuring a compilation of the official Capitol Records recordings made at the venue in 1964 and 1965 . . .

Paul "I haven't heard it. Geoff (Emerick) keeps telling me to, because he did it. He thinks it's good, but I'm just not that bothered. I've got a lot of those tapes anyway in my private collection. I've got original demos and original tapes so I've heard a lot of them. But I *must* have heard it, because I'm on it."

Voyle Gilmore, retired A&R man at Capitol Records and producer of the original Hollywood Bowl recordings, "Capitol called me a few months back and asked if I could help find the tapes in the library and, of course, I knew right where they were. They wanted to get permission to put them out and thought it would be useful if George Martin was involved, since he knew the boys and had made all their other records."

The Beatles' former producer, George Martin "Bhaskar Menon, the President of Capitol Records, is an old friend of mine. He mentioned these tapes to me and asked whether I would listen to them because Capitol was thinking of releasing an album. My immediate reaction was, as far as I could remember, the original tapes had a rotten sound. So I said to Bhaskar, 'I don't think you've got anything here at all.' There have been an awful lot of bootleg recordings made of Beatles concerts around the world and they've been in wide circulation. But when I listened to the Hollywood Bowl tapes, I was amazed at the rawness and vitality of The Beatles' singing. So I told Bhaskar that I'd see if I could bring the tapes into line with today's recordings. I enlisted the technical expertise of Geoff Emerick and we transferred the recordings from three-track to 24-track tapes. The two tapes combined twenty-two songs and we whittled these down to thirteen. Some tracks had to be discarded because the music was obliterated by the screams."

Voyle Gilmore "George Martin made such a speech. It sounds like he changed it but I doubt it. There's not much he could do. It was recorded on three-track machines with half-inch tapes. The Hollywood Bowl has a pretty good stereo sound system so we plugged our mikes right in there. I didn't do an awful lot. There wasn't much we could do. They just played their usual show and we recorded it. It wasn't that bad. I kept thinking, 'Maybe we'll get permission to release the tapes.' So I took them back to the studio and worked on it awhile. I worked on the applause, edited it down, made it play and EQd it quite a bit. The Beatles heard it and they all wanted tape copies. I had five or six copies made and sent over. That's where the bootlegs must have come from. We had a system at Capitol and we knew where all our copies were. The Beatles said they liked the tapes, that it sounded pretty good, that they were surprised but they still didn't want to release it."

George Martin "Once the technical work had been completed, EMI needed approval from the four Beatles before the album could be released. I had to go to New York anyway, so I rang John Lennon and told him about the recordings. I told him that I had been very sceptical at first but now I was very enthusiastic because I thought the album would be a piece of history, which should be preserved."

Voyle Gilmore "I thought the first concert was a little better than the second. I don't know if I would have put them together like they did because doing it that way they have sacrificed an album. They really could have made two albums."

George Martin "I said to John, 'I want you to hear it after I've gone. You can be as rude as you like, but if you don't like it, give me a yell.' I spoke to him the following day and he was delighted with it. The reaction of George and Ringo was much cooler."

George Harrison "I have an acetate of it, right from '64 and I had the tapes in the studio in England a few years ago. The thing is, it's only important historically, but as a record, it's not very good. While each of The Beatles was on EMI/Capitol, the LP wouldn't have been released because we didn't like it. But as soon as we left, and we lost control of our material, it was released. The sound quality on the album sounds just like a bootleg, but because Capitol is bootlegging it, it's legitimate."

JUNE

John, Yoko and Sean, currently on holiday in Tokyo, Japan, send a series of postcards to John's Aunt Mimi at her bungalow home in Poole, Dorset. The first reads . . .

"Mimi: Are up in the mountains, really very nice. Love John, Yoko and Sean."

The second reads: *"Mimi. Still up in the mountains. Here is the number in case you wanna give us a call. Love Da-da, mom-ma and Sean-chan."*

Aunt Mimi "You would think he could have written a bit more than that, wouldn't you? I think 'chan' means son. That really is typical of him. He gives some telephone number in the middle of the Japanese Mountains. I don't know where and he expects me to call him. I don't know what time it will be there, whether he'll be in or anything. If he wants to talk, he can jolly well call me."

During the Tokyo holiday, John announces to the gathering press that he has let his professional career take second place to baby Sean . . .

"We've basically decided to be with our baby as much as we can until we feel we can take time off to indulge ourselves in creating things outside the family," **John** says. "Maybe when he's three, four or five, then we'll think about creating something else other than the child."

Thursday, June 2

At Heathrow Airport, London, Paul returns to England following *London Town* recording sessions in the Caribbean and a brief stay in New York. Accompanying him is a pregnant Linda, and their three children. Their homecoming features in a report in the *Evening News* . . .

"We'll never leave England, despite tax problems," a patriotic **McCartney** said as he flew into Heathrow from New York. "We plan to stay here and so does the Wings pop group. There's no point in living somewhere just for convenience sake, so far as money is concerned. I like it here, so does Linda and so do the children. It's the best place to bring up the kids. I've even taught the missus how to make a cuppa. I am also pleased that our new baby will be a British citizen. I don't mind which it is, but we're expecting another girl. We're used to girls."

Sunday, June 12

George meanwhile partakes in a phone conversation with the Australian 2SM Radio station. "I saw Paul about a month ago," he reveals, "he's out in the Caribbean recording. I haven't seen John for over a year. I believe he's in Japan . . . I think that, like all the other three, The Beatles are like something else. In fact, sometimes, I look at the old pictures, the records, and it's like a past and distant memory. I can't really feel that close to it anymore, you know. The Beatles were bigger than all of us. It looks like, because it happened to be at that point in time, The Beatles sort of covered the kids to the grannies. But I don't see us getting together because it was that period and I don't know what would happen in order to make us get together."

Monday, September 12
At the Avenue Clinic nursing home in London, Linda gives birth to Paul's first son, James Louis . . .

Paul "I was waiting outside the door at the nursing home when the baby was being born. Linda had him by Caesarean, so I was the first to tell her we'd got a boy. She was pretty drugged up but I knew she was as pleased as I was. I knew in my heart I'd have been just a bit disappointed if we hadn't had a boy but I didn't think it would be fair to tell Linda."

Outside the home, **Paul** tells waiting reporters, "I'm over the moon! When I knew the baby was a boy, I really flipped. I was waiting outside the door when he was being born. The baby weighs 6lb 1oz, has fair hair and looks like Linda. Linda is still a bit tired, but otherwise she's smashing. I don't know how she does it."

Paul talks about the baby's name. "Though my first name is James, too, we are really calling him after my late father. The 'Louis', as in Armstrong, is after Linda's late grandfather. We have called all our children after people we loved, who have died. We don't go in for crazy names. If our son wants to be a 'straight' guy, James sounds great, and if wants to abbreviate it, he will be simply Jim."

Paul "The Apple thing is very complicated, as it has been for many years. Ringo came to see us when we had the baby and we were chatting and polishing off a bottle of wine. We were having a great time until we started talking about Apple and the minute we did, it was like, 'Uuuuugggggghhhhh!' So we thought, 'Christ, we'd best start talking about the light things again.' So this is the situation and as soon as anyone brings up the word Apple, there are incredible rows. It's like a divorce."

Saturday, October 1
Back in New York, shortly after returning from their holiday in Japan, John and Yoko are among 400 guests at a party thrown by Rod Stewart's record company. On this rare night out for the Lennons, John and Yoko share a table with the singers James Taylor, Carly Simon and actor Peter Boyle and his wife, Lorraine . . .

New York newspaper columnist, Judith Simons "This was John Lennon as you've never seen him before, sober suited, clean cut, and looking just like a bank clerk. There was a time when a short back and sides haircut would have made the ex-Beatle twist and shout with anger. But there he was, the former rebel, at Rod Stewart's party. His hair neatly clipped, wearing a dark grey suit and a tie! And there was his wife, Yoko Ono, conforming in a patterned black velvet cloak and matching dress. Was she the same person who once directed a film composed entirely of naked bottoms? What lies beyond The Beatle fringe for quiet, serious looking Lennon? He said, 'I have made my contribution to society. I have no plans to work again.' The Lennons were on their first outing since returning from six months in Japan. But they have no plans to visit Britain. Said Lennon, now 37, 'We have been away for eight years (*sic*). New York is now my home. I love it here. I smoke American cigarettes.' In New York, one thing was sure . . . Yesterday, all John's Beatle fringe seemed so far away."

John "I didn't say that, 'I have made my contribution to society.' The fun of when we weren't doing anything was all these amazing stories. They had me in the *Daily Mail*, the *Daily Express* that I had gone bald. They showed before and after pictures. Another story that went round was that I had made this extraordinary statement. Can you imagine me saying that? 'I've made my contribution to society.' I never said that because I didn't talk to any reporters or radio people or anybody for five years. I don't know where they got that from . . . I wasn't underground. I was overground. I was all over the place; travelling and we were doing all kinds of business. We were pretty damn active. We just weren't in the papers and we weren't available for comment, that's all."

Ringo "John said that he just feels like having a year off, with no contractual obligations to anybody, no record companies or anything. He is his own man for twelve months and he has never been that."

There are several Japanese restaurants on Columbus Avenue in New York, and John and Yoko are frequent visitors. Shortly after their return from Japan, the couple pay another visit to their favourite restaurant, Lenge, where they take their usual favoured corner table in the dimly lit bamboo walled dining area. Their bill rarely exceeds $20 . . .

A waiter at the restaurant "Yoko orders in Japanese and I think it's a pleasure for her to speak. Sometimes we chat about things in our language. John just sits there and smiles politely. I think he only knows a few words of the language like, 'Thank you,' and 'Please.' He is a very polite man. Not like Americans. He is very considerate."

Sunday, October 9
At his Dakota department, John celebrates his 37th birthday . . .

Aunt Mimi "He's like a child about his birthday. He likes cards and presents, and he's particularly keen that he gets one from me. But John is so absent-minded. He always forgets mine. So, last year, I thought, 'Okay, if you can forget mine, I can forget yours,' and I didn't send him a card. It was unforgivable, really. Well, about a week later, I got a letter from New York. It just said, 'Mimi, you forgot my birthday. John.' He didn't phone for weeks. I'll never do it again. I know just how much his birthday means to him. He made a point of making me not forget his birthday again because he sent me a birthday present. The postman knocked on my door and there was this small parcel from Japan. It was a beautiful set of Japanese pearls. They must have cost the earth. It was his birthday and he sent *me* a present. That's typical of the real John."

Friday, October 21

Back in England, the *Daily Mail* controversially reports, "The Beatles! 'They're A Disgrace To Their City.'" The article reads "The Beatles have been disinherited by heads of the city, which once celebrated them as its favourite and most talented sons. Councillors in Liverpool branded John Lennon, Paul McCartney, George Harrison and Ringo Starr as a 'discredit' to their birthplace. And the city's General Purposes Committee refused to allow the erection of a lifesize statue of the group. 'They aren't worthy of a place in our history,' said Tory councillor Roy Stoddart, the committee chairman. 'They made a lot of money and we have never seen them since they departed from the scene.' The Tory councillor, Tony McVeigh, added, 'The Beatles couldn't sing for toffee. Their behaviour brought tremendous discredit to the city. John Lennon returned his MBE medal to the Queen. It was an absolute insult. They turned down requests to appear in the city for official functions. I am dead against having the statue.'

"Yesterday, 29-year-old John Chambers, a joiners mate, attacked the committee's 10-8 vote not to provide a public site for the statue. He hit out, 'It's an insult to the people of Liverpool. The Beatles were the biggest thing to come out of the city this century. They are folk heroes.' But Councillor McVeigh will not be silenced. 'I'm not an old fuddy-duddy and I know more about music than The Beatles ever will,' he said. 'I've had a lot of people congratulate me on what I said. I couldn't care less about The Beatles and they couldn't care less about Liverpool. We should leave it at that.' Support for the group came from Mike McGear, brother of Paul McCartney. 'Liverpool without The Beatles is like Pisa without its leaning tower,' he said. 'One solution could be to erect two separate statues. Rotten tomatoes could be thrown at one, and bunches of roses at the other. People could express their own feelings.'

"Allan Williams, The Beatles' first manager, declared, 'The councillors don't seem to realise just what a world phenomenon The Beatles are. There should be a complete museum and tourist industry in Liverpool, let alone a single monument. They will be recognised as the greatest composers of the century.' Paul McCartney said he had no wish to comment. There is still hope for the statue. The final say will rest with the full council. Consolation for any Beatles hurt feelings came with the announcement of Thames Television's Britannia Awards, which celebrate the centenary of the first human voice recorded. The Beatles were voted the 'Best British Group', and as making, 'The most outstanding contribution to the British record industry'."

Paul "I don't really care. I've never wanted a statue put up to us. When it got in the papers, and the fellow started saying, 'They can't sing for toffee,' I just thought, 'Oh God, that's typically council, isn't it?' You know, 'These rock'n'roll groups coming and playing in our nice halls, they should have a nice British Legion do,' you know, all that rubbish. They've got to realise that there is a younger generation and we were it then. I don't agree with him, that's all. I don't think he's that much. I just read about it in the paper, like other people and I thought the remarks saying, 'They can't sing for toffee,' or 'They're no good, anyway,' is a bit daft coming from a council in Liverpool. I saw a little photo of the statue in the papers the other day and I don't like it. It's horrible! And it's certainly not the guitar I played. The people who make these statues tend to be people who don't really know about it, but at least he's got me being left-handed. I was looking out for that because they forget that kind of thing. But, anyway, I wasn't too big on that statue."

Sunday, October 23

Stuart White of the *News Of The World* writes a report on the increasingly quiet John Lennon, "In the fifteen shattering years since The Beatles first burst upon us, John Lennon's sad, sometimes tragic face has not been much of an advertisement for success. It isn't only love that money can't buy. 'I enjoy the security of knowing I've got it,' **John** says. 'But I've still got that lower-class fear. In life, it doesn't make me happy, but it's like what my Auntie Mimi said, I'd sooner be miserable in luxury. That for me is a bed, a carpet and some food . . . If they took the TV away, I'd call that suffering.' "

White "Life is almost that simple for millionaire John. For he is, if anything, the Beatle who was trapped by success. He has become the prisoner of 72nd Street, New York, where he lives in a vast apartment in a Colditz-like mansion block. He rarely goes out. He rarely entertains. His circle is close and he almost never gives interviews. It is Aunt Mimi who can tell us most about the most secret of the ex-Beatles . . ."

It is 3am and the telephone rings in the Poole, Dorset seaside home of 65-year-old widow Mimi Smith. A world-famous voice booms down the line from New York, 3,440 miles away. "Allo Mimi, 'ow are yer?" The accent is unmistakably Scouse. But there is more than a hint of what years of Manhattan living have etched into the nasal Merseyside tones of ex-Beatle John Winston Lennon. Aunt Mimi, who brought John up from childhood, scolds gently; "Do you know what time it is here? Well, do you?" He laughs off the five-hour time difference that makes it only 10pm in New York and says, "Never mind that, Mimi, how are you? How are things? How are you going?" She props herself on her pillows and for up to an hour, the man once known as the Cruel Beatle, the master of the acid remark, shows a side to his character few people believe exists. Tenderness . . .

Aunt Mimi "Oh, John can be very tender. I know he has this reputation for being cynical and sharp, but I know him better. I know that beneath all that, he can be very warm. He asks how I am, how my health is, what the weather's like. You know, all the little things that people seem to want to know when they're living abroad. Then we'll start to talk about the old days. The last time he was on, we started talking about his schooldays and the time he came home on the last day of term with his school report. He just rode up to the kitchen window on his bike, threw the report in and shouted, 'I'm off out.' I knew it must be a bad report, so I chased after him, shouting, 'You come back this minute, John Lennon,' but he was off. We had a good laugh about that over the phone. I think, in a way, he's a little bit lonely. I've not seen him for over five years and though we talk regularly on the phone, it isn't quite the same. We'll talk on the phone for ages and ages, and it costs a pound a minute or something. The last time he rang, we spoke for over an hour and I said, 'John, this is costing you a fortune. You put the phone down this minute.' He sounded just like a little boy again. He said, 'Oh, Mimi, I haven't finished yet. Besides, I can afford it.' I give him a good telling off sometimes. Well, I can. Can't I? He's not famous to me and he knows it."

Cynthia Twist "Mimi is right about John. He's an extremely tender person, or rather he's capable of tenderness. This tough, bitter side he has is a kind of protection. I feel sad for him because a lot of people seem to get satisfaction out of hurting him. I'm only sorry that with all his health and with all his fame, he doesn't appear to be happy. One thing I really wish for him is happiness."

Stuart White "Rarely do John and Yoko venture out of the Dakota mansions on Manhattan's West Side, home of film actress, Lauren Bacall, and husband and wife pop stars, Carly Simon and James Taylor. And no one gets in unless the security guard in his entry box has written instructions. The security guard on duty is a former Panzer crewman, Heinz, who was born in Berlin . . ."

Dakota security guard, Heinz "That John, you know, you hardly see him. Even now, there are girls, teenage girls, they wait on the corner for him. It's hard for him to go out, getting pestered all the time for autographs. He's a strange chap, John. When he comes out and passes me, he always says, 'Morning.' It doesn't matter whether it's afternoon, or evening, always the same. I suppose that is an English sense of humour. But when the Lennons do come out, they push Sean in their English-made baby carriage through Central Park, braving photographers, autograph hunters and well-wishers. Almost all their needs can be met in less than a 400-yard walk from their home and they go no further."

Stuart White "Next door to the Dakota building is an underground car park, open to the public but only if they can afford the prices, which are up to $100 a day. That is where John leaves his old-style Rolls Royce. It stood in an inch-deep pool of oily water while John and Yoko were in Japan. The Rolls rarely leaves the garage . . ."

The Puerto Rican attendant in charge of the Dakota garage "John's Rolls is always there. I bet the battery is flat. If there was a fire here, we would never get it out. The Beatle, John, he never comes out of that apartment. I'm a poor man, but I bet I'm happier than he is. At least I can walk down the street in peace."

Wednesday, November 2

Pete Townshend of The Who recalls, "John Lennon's 'roadie' once told fans to clear off because they were jumping on his Rolls Royce. Lennon wound down the window and said, 'It doesn't matter. They paid for it.' But *he* paid for a bit of it, too!"

Wednesday, November 9

In New York, while **John** confines himself to life in their apartment tending to Sean's every whim, 32-year-old Frank Sinatra Junior controversially announces that "The Beatles have ruined the world!" During his hysterical outburst, which is published in a New York newspaper column, he blasts, "The Beatles are to blame for almost everything that's wrong with the young generation. You name it and it's their fault. I rue the day that The Beatles were, unfortunately, born into this world. They are, in my mind, responsible for most of the degeneration that has happened, not only musically but also in the sense of youth orientation and politically, too. They are the people who made it first publicly acceptable to spit in the eye of authority."

Meanwhile on **Friday, November 11**, Wings release their new single 'Mull Of Kintyre' c/w 'Girls School'. It will soon become the biggest selling UK single ever, even outstripping the phenomenal sales of The Beatles . . .

'Mull Of Kintyre'

Paul "It's just this place in Scotland. It's about seventy miles of land, a big peninsular called the Mull of Kintyre. It's just one of those bits of Scotland, and this bit sticks out into the sea a bit. Our place is on the Mull of Kintyre, but there's about a hundred miles of the Mull of Kintyre. I was never sure, I just heard about it, and so I had to ask somebody, 'Where exactly is the Mull of Kintyre?' So I was sitting at my piano, up in Scotland, and I thought I would like to write a song with a Scottish flavour. Most songs you hear nowadays are old tunes that people re-do, or comedy songs, like 'Up Your Kilt'."

Denny Laine "Paul and I sat with a bottle of whisky one afternoon outside a cottage in the hills of Kintyre and wrote the song 'Mull Of Kintyre'. Paul had written the chorus and we wrote the rest of it together."

Paul "At first I got the melody and you can't help seeing the mist rolling in from the sea because it does it quite often. I got the melody together, had a verse and then I got together with Denny on guitar. The pipes on the track are the local pipes band, the actual Kintyre pipers. They all live there now. They are all farmers, farmer's sons and an ex-copper from Glasgow. They are a nice bunch. We had done the song so I gave them a tape and a fellow came up to my house with his bagpipes. He was going to play them but he decided it would be a bit too loud indoors so we went out into the garden and he starts tuning up. I took my guitar out and found out what key he was in, 'cos I don't know anything about bagpipes. I still don't, actually. So we worked it out, I gave him a tape, he went back, rehearsed it with his lads and then came up a couple of weeks later. I said, 'Are you having any problems with it?' They said, 'No, no problems.' When we finished it, all the pipers said, 'Aye, it's got to be a single that.' It was up to them, really, to do it. I thought it was a little too specialised to bring out as a single, you would have to bring out something that has something with more mass appeal. But they kept saying, 'Oh, the exiled Scots all over the world. It'll be a big single for them.' Yet I still thought, 'Yeah, well, but there's maybe not enough exiled Scots,' but they kept telling me, after a few drinks."

'Girls School'

Paul "The other side is a rock'n'roll thing and that's to compensate for the people who will knock me for doing the romantic song. As you get older, you realise the romantic stuff is inside and there's not much point hiding it. If people want to dance or leap around, they can just turn the record over and you've got it. I suppose a few people will prefer the more rocking B-side. You see, B-sides get swallowed and hardly anybody plays them, so this time around we did a double A-side, so everyone can hear the varied sides of Wings."

Paul on 'Girls School' . . . "I was on holiday at the time. We had just finished touring Australia (1975) and we were coming back the scenic route via Hawaii. We had just been told we couldn't play Japan, following the two-year-old drugs bust. The Japanese Minister Of Justice decided we couldn't go in because we had been a bit naughty. So we were on holiday, an enforced holiday and I was in Hawaii and I picked up one of those American newspapers and I looked at the back in one of those entertainment sections, where they've got the big page full of porn movies, and they're all called great titles. So I just took all the titles, and if you read through the lyrics to the song, it is nearly all just porn titles . . . *School Mistress, Woman Trainer, Kid Sister, Oriental Princess, Spanish Doll,* and all that kind of thing. So it's supposed to be like a pornographic *St Trinians.* I must see them sometime."

At a lavish party in London to launch 'Mull Of Kintyre', **Paul** announces that his 14-year-old daughter, Heather, is the latest to join the ever-increasing band of punk music fans. "Heather's really into punk," he reveals to reporters. "She loves the music and the fashions. At first, I thought punk was a bit weird and I was worried that she was just following the herd. I suppose I could have played the stern father and stopped her, but I like punk. It's a young people's thing and young people's music. Heather used to have lovely long blonde hair right down to below her shoulders, but now we've cut it all off for her so it's short and spiky. She wears the safety pins and all that. Her favourite bands are The Stranglers and The Clash. She saw The Stranglers recently and she thought they were great. But she doesn't think that her dad's old-fashioned. She's not blinkered like that. She's open-minded about music and she's very loyal. She likes our music too. I like punk. I think young people can still rebel. They do things we never did; they spit for a start. They also swear more freely and they look scruffier than we did."

Around the time of 'Mull Of Kintyre's release, **Paul** engages in a conversation at Abbey Road Studios with the UK Pop Plus columnist, Alasdair Buchan . . .

"A look of weary disgust appeared on Paul McCartney's face when the subject of his mate's 'retirement' came up," Buchan writes. "Paul made no attempt to hide his feelings about John Lennon's recent statement, 'I have no plans to work again.' With a sigh and a shake of the head, Paul said, 'He's full of wind, isn't he? Maybe he isn't going to work anymore, but it's no skin off my nose. It's really up to him. I've heard him talk like that before. He says he wants to write the great novel. He did books and stuff, that makes you literary. I think he must be bored.' "

Buchan "It's ten years, several million records and a musical era on from the recording of *Sgt. Pepper's Lonely Hearts Club Band*, and Paul is still active. After a late-night recording, he breakfasts on shepherd's pie and chips. He is determined to carry on. More importantly, he revealed that Wings would be on the road next year. For he, Linda and Denny, after the departure of Jimmy McCulloch and Joe English, are considering playing the small clubs and basement dance halls of Britain . . ."

Paul "I have an ambition to play Joe's caff and sing the requests from the audience. It's the atmosphere of the man in the street."

Sunday, November 13
The UK tabloid reporter Stuart Robertson files a report about **George**, concerning his property, lifestyle and beliefs . . .

"The Bhakhvedanta Manor, in the Hertfordshire village of Letchmore Heath, is worth a conservative £300,000 but George Harrison, the generous one, rents it out for a nominal amount. He bought it for the Hindu-style Hare Krishna sect, who use it as their British headquarters. A colony of more than 100 men, women and children live at the HQ. And at the manor, George Harrison is revered like a holy man. Sect leader, Gyanadas, aged 33, told me, 'We owe so much to George. It is almost impossible to gauge the extent of our debt to him. He is a kind, warm and very spiritual man. He still contributes money to our religion and has helped people to know more of what we are. There is great love for George Harrison here.' "

Gyanadas' wife, Lilaveta, who comes from New York, said, "Unhappily, George does not devote as much time to the religion as he used to. But we understand that he has many things he must be doing. He is a very questing man. We all love and respect him for the help he has given us. We pray to Krishna for him." While a business colleague from George's Beatle days, said, "Anyone who came to him with a plausible story was always all right for a few quid, but now it's thousands."

George's father, Harry, added, "People exploited him during his Beatles days but I don't think he's quite as easy these days. He's a lot more cynical. But with things he believes in, or people he knows, he can still be very, very generous."

George's own home is just half a mile away from the centre of Henley-on-Thames. A Gothic lodge guards the entrance to the mansion. A sign warns, "Beware of guard dogs – trespassers will be prosecuted". On your right as you approach the house is a massive Japanese style area of lakes and gardens with little bridges and linking islands, flowers and shrubs overhang the lakes with water-lilies floating in the water. Rumour has it that there are stones set in the lake with their surfaces just below the water. Those who know the layout can give the appearance of walking on water. The story goes that a favourite trick of George's was to call a member of staff to bring drinks for him and his friends at the other side of the lake. Harrison would say to the unsuspecting guests, "Marvellous bloody bloke, he can walk on water." Then the guests would watch in amazement.

George's youngest brother, Peter, has a full-time job looking after the house and estate. Peter tells Stuart White about his famous brother. "There's very little to say," he reveals. "To me, George is George. He always has been and always will be. He's not a bit like he is made out to be." White naturally asks, "Which is what?" "Well," Peter replies, "as though he's a weirdo or something. He's just an ordinary bloke."

The extensive report goes on to feature **George**'s view on romance. "Romance for me is an extension of my religious life," he announces. "When you love a woman, it is the God in her that you see. The only complete love is for God. The goal is to love everyone equally but it doesn't necessarily work out that way." The South American-born Olivia Arias, George's current companion, continues the subject, "We have a nice relationship. When you strive for something higher in the next world, you have a much easier time in this one."

George, who was brought up as a Protestant, reveals that he almost chose to become a Catholic when he was eleven years of age, "But I couldn't relate to Christ being the only son of God, like he was it and there was nothing more."

George's father, Harry, "When he first became interested in Indian religion, it caused some problems. Being brought up as a Christian, and then having a totally new kind of religion being brought in, doesn't go down all that well at first. We often had long talks about it and I found quite a lot that I could go along with and I discovered that there was a lot of real truth in other religions. It was all heading the same way, towards the one God. It was just that there are various ways of getting there. It was George who taught me that."

Harry continues, "In the evening, George might curl up on the sofa and watch the massive colour TV, *Monty Python* is his favourite. Wherever he goes, his guitar goes with him. One day, I was in the middle of talking to him when George said, 'Excuse me, but I've just thought of something.' He got up, went out of the room and came back about half an hour later. He said, 'Something you were saying gave me an idea for a song, so I had to write it down.' That's typical of him. He may appear as though he's not taking an interest, but in fact he's following everything that you're saying."

On **Saturday, December 10**, Paul, Linda and Denny give their first television performance in three years by appearing on BBC TV's *The Mike Yarwood Show*, where they naturally mime 'Mull Of Kintyre'. Denny Laine recalls, "When Wings did *The Mike Yarwood Show*, Paul was working in front of an audience for the first time in a long while, and they had to stop filming halfway through to wipe his face because he was sweating so much from fear."

Paul "We went on *The Mike Yarwood Show* and Linda was great. But I was terrible. I fluffed my lines and I was saying, 'I'm supposed to be the pro here.' She was just so cool under pressure and kept getting it right, but I kept getting it horribly wrong. They had to do re-takes on me."

But, nevertheless, 'Mull Of Kintyre' becomes a monster hit . . .

Tabloid reporter, Robert McGowan "The record 'Mull Of Kintyre' is a pop legend. It has been No. 1 for seven weeks and has already outsold any other record in Britain. But more than that, it has sold Kintyre . . ."

Lachie MacKinnon, of the Mid-Argyll Kintyre and Islay Tourist Organisation "Normally we get about 500,000 to a million visitors a year in Kintyre. But from the letters we have had already, that total will be up by about twenty per cent, and the letters are still flooding in. It's even sold the pipes to the Arabs, Libya, Saudi Arabia and Abu Dhabi. They are offering the Scots £30,000 a year to go out and teach their military bands the bagpipes."

Pipe major, Tony Wilson, "It's magic. All the boys are proud to have played on the record. McCartney's a genius. The pipes are part of Scotland and there is nothing new in that. But now the Arabs are making this offer to teach them how to play, it's tremendous! I won't be going because we're recording soon. Aye, 'Mull Of Kintyre' will be on it and it would be disloyal for me to leave the boys now. They're grand boys . . . Paul's song has done wonders for Kintyre but we won't be earning royalties from the song. We were paid as session musicians for the job. We did the job and got paid for it and that's that."

The single's success is tainted with the rumour that **Paul** did not write 'Mull Of Kintyre'. There was another song, also called 'Mull Of Kintyre', which was written in 1973 by the composer, Archie Duncan . . .

Archie Duncan, speaking from his home in Campbeltown, emphatically dismisses the story, "The two tunes are as different as The National Anthem and 'Rock Around The Clock'. Mine is a jig for the pipes and nothing like Paul's."

December - 'Mull Of Kintyre' era promotional interviews . . .

Paul "I keep winning things like '*Playboy* Bass Player Of The Year' and I keep writing back to tell them, 'You've got it wrong, folks. I'm not the best. You people just put my name on the form because you know I'm a bass player in a band.' Lately, there was this thing saying, 'I got my name on more hits than any living writer.' Of course I love it, but I don't go mad about it. I don't really bother about polls. All I bother is whether I like the music I put down on record."

UK pop columnist, Keith Dalton . . .

"Nothing irks **Paul** more than questions of a Beatles reunion. Is it because Paul plays Beatles numbers in the live set that people are so insistent on asking about a Beatles reunion? Paul thinks for a while, then calmly replies, 'I was reading one of those books about us and you've got older quotes from us over various periods of time when each of us was feeling good, saying, "I don't see why we shouldn't record together." Then John said, "We might easily get together again." So now I think the main basis for reunion rumours is that in any given time, one of us will say, "Yeah, I wouldn't mind doing it," and that will start the rumour rolling again. Really I don't think it will happen and we always come back to that. So it's us to blame in a way. The Beatles' situation went full circle and came to an end, so it's very hard to revive that. It's like trying to revive a dead person.' "

1978

Thursday, February 21
John and Paul's sons feature in a report by James Erlichman in tonight's *Evening News* newspaper . . .

"The Beatles' sons have become the apples of their fathers' eyes," Erlichman writes. "Since his son, Sean, was born over two years ago, John Lennon has lived a hermit's existence. He seldom leaves the towering bastion of a tower block overlooking New York's Central Park and rarely lets the toddler out of his sight. He has not written a song since his wife, Yoko Ono, gave birth to Sean. And according to Ringo Starr, even Ono is barred from changing the boy's nappies, that is John's work now, and John's alone. Back in Britain, Paul McCartney is equally ecstatic about his wife Linda's latest child, their first son, James, who is four months old . . . But here the similarities between the two proud fathers end. While John hides with Yoko in his fortress home with Sean, Paul and Linda are said to keep 'open house' for their friends in their St John's Wood home. 'We like to keep our family life straight and normal,' says **Paul**. 'So, as we're not members of the aristocracy, there was no reason why I should consider putting James down for Eton or Harrow. I'd far sooner he went to a council school down the road than any snob place. We will never leave their upbringing to other people. We don't believe in nannies and that kind of thing.' "

Friday, March 31 (UK and USA)
The three-piece Wings line-up of Paul, Linda and Denny release their latest studio album, *London Town* . . .

Paul "This one, we did a couple of weeks in London, a month in the Virgin Islands and about a month at my studio in Scotland. So it took about three months. We started this album in London and Geoff Emerick, who was working in the studio with us, started telling us tales of how he had been working in Hawaii with the group America, and how he had had a fabulous time in the sun and sea, and he got us a bit jealous. So we hired three boats and went out to the Virgin Islands. We kitted out the main boat with recording gear and we were worried that the studio wouldn't work but we were dead jammy and on the first day, the engineers had worked it all out. We recorded a track on the very first day. The captain of the boat wasn't too pleased, though, because we remodelled his lounge a bit, to make a studio. At first we thought we were going to have problems with salt water going through the machines.

"We didn't work much in the mornings. We would just get up and swim, and stuff, and do all nice kind of holiday things and then we'd have something to eat and then bop across to the boat to record a little bit and then leave it for the afternoon and go back for the evening. On holiday, I always find there are parts of the day when you've got to find something to do. I always end up going for dinner, but instead of going for dinner, we went to the studio. We got nine tracks done out there and we like 'em. We didn't want to rush this one, because that was all we did last year, just making that record. Linda was having her baby and so we didn't want to do any live stuff, because it's a bit hectic to be doing that. On this album, I've written five tracks with Denny and we did it piece by piece to build it up. We mainly did the backing tracks on the boat in the Virgin Islands, just to get the performance feel and those worked well. We got the tracks down and came to my home studio in Scotland to finish them off."

Denny Laine "I've been writing with Paul on his farm in Scotland. There's no pressure there, just peace and quiet. Sometimes he'll write a verse, then I'll write a verse. Or I might just play him a fragment of a song idea I've had, he'll react well to it and so we build an entire number from it. We are very critical of each other. One has to be. Of course, neither of us is inspired all the time. If things don't work out, Paul will say, 'Shall we call it a day?' and then we'll have a walk around the farm."

'London Town'

Paul "This track was started in London when we first started to record the album and then we went to the Virgin Islands, where we did the rest of the tracks, and then we finished it up when we got back to London town. It was written in Perth, Australia."

'Cafe On The Left Bank'

Paul "This song 'Cafe On The Left Bank' is reminiscent of all the times I've been to Paris, when we'd go walking round the streets."

'I'm Carrying'

Paul "When we recorded this in the Virgin Islands, I was on the back deck of a boat, just myself and a guitar. And with the lovely blue water and blue sky, I just recorded the backing guitar and vocal and later we finished it by putting on strings and a thing called the Gizmo, which is an attachment you can have on a guitar. So we had half strings and half guitar. It's a load of fun."

'Backwards Traveller'/'Cuff Link'

Paul "That's a track I played drums on and I like to do a bit of drumming, occasionally. We recorded this late in the album. Joe, our previous drummer, had left us to go back to America, so I decided I had better drum it myself and I had a bit of fun with this one. It's a song I wrote in Scotland and it goes into a song called 'Cuff Link', which is just a little jam we had in the studio one evening, and we put the two together."

'Children Children'

Paul "This was written mainly by Denny. He originally had this idea to do a kid's song and it's all about fairies. You can imagine a cartoon going on with fairies playing flutes, violins and stuff. It's a good one to animate."

'Girlfriend'

Paul " 'Girlfriend' was written when I was on holiday in Switzerland. I was amongst the mountains there, in my hotel room, and I started writing this song and it's got this souly type of influence. We did a lot of work in London on this one and eventually finished it up in London after getting back from the Virgin Islands. I like this one."

'I've Had Enough'

Paul "I was just sitting in the studio one day, just working on some chords and I didn't have any words to it. I just had the chorus, 'I've had enough, I can't put up with anymore.' This was the only bit I had. We recorded it on the boat in the Virgin Islands but we still didn't have any words until we got back to London and then I wrote a few. I overdubbed the vocals in London and it's just one of those 'fed-up' songs. It doesn't mean that I'm fed up but it applies to anyone who is fed up at this moment."

'Famous Groupies'

Paul " 'Famous Groupies' was a sort of joke song. It's about anyone who had ever been in a rock'n'roll band, and they'll know about groupies, and one or two of them have made themselves pretty famous. So this is a send-up of that kind of thing."

'Deliver Your Children'

Paul " 'Deliver Your Children' was a song that Denny wrote most of the words and tune for and I just helped him out a little bit on it. He takes the lead vocal on this one and I help him on harmonies. Denny plays the Spanish guitar you can hear coming in and out. We recorded most of this one on the boat in the Virgin Islands."

'Name And Address'

Paul " 'Name And Address' is a song I wrote in London and it was an affectionate half-tribute to Elvis Presley, but I hadn't completed it before he died. I was hoping to be able to send him the track and say, 'Here we go, Elvis. This is the kind of thing I think of you. Here's a little tribute to you. I hope you like it.' But unfortunately, he died, which was a drag for all his fans and that includes me. It'll do as a tribute now, anyway. It's done in the style he used to do back in the old Sun days."

'Don't Let It Bring You Down'

Paul "We were on tour in Scotland. I think we were up in Aberdeen, sitting in our hotel bedroom, just before we were going to turn in for the night and I had my 12-string guitar with me and I started plonking out a little tune and it became 'Don't Let It Bring You Down'. We did most of the backing track on the boat in the Virgin Islands and then, when we got back to London, Denny and I overdubbed quite a bit of the stuff. I play the little bit of lead guitar you can hear and Denny and I play the tin whistles."

'Mouse Moose And The Grey Goose'

Paul "This one started on the boat in the Virgin Islands. One of the electric pianos we were working with had a funny sound on it and I was just hitting it and it sounded like a crazy Morse code. When we started, we made six minutes of this funny sound and we had nothing else. We had no idea for a song at all, and we later overdubbed little bits and pieces on it, making it all up as we went along. This was one of those songs that we didn't know how it was going to turn out. In the end, we got it back to London and we wrote a little bit called 'The Grey Goose' in the studio. It's a sort of mad sea epic, all about those in peril on the sea. We put that in with the first song and the song became 'Mouse Moose And The Grey Goose'."

Wings release 'With A Little Luck', the first single from the new album . . .

Paul " 'With A Little Luck' was the first single from the album and this was a song we started on the boat, in Watermelon Bay, in the Virgin Islands. We just had the backing track, a very rough version of it and we later finished it all up when we got back to London."

Linda "Paul's actually incredible. On Friday he decided he needed a new single, on Saturday and Sunday he messed about in the house writing it, on Monday he explained to the group how it should go. On Tuesday we recorded it and there he was, on Wednesday, re-doing the vocals. He just never stops. Ideas seem to come to him all the time."

Appearing at the same time as *London Town* is *The Rutles*, an American-financed Beatles parody television special written by *Monty Python's* Eric Idle and featuring music by Neil Innes, formerly of The Bonzo Dog Doo Dah Band . . .

Eric Idle "In 1975, I was sitting writing and I wrote a joke about the camera pulling away from someone, and leaving them helplessly running after it. I liked the idea very much, and I knew that it was funny. But I wasn't sure though what he should be talking about. At the same time, I was writing for a BBC TV show in England called *Rutland Weekend Television,* which I did with Neil Innes . . ."

Neil Innes "I was in the London Drury Lane shows with the *Pythons* when Eric Idle asked me if I would be interested in doing music for his BBC2 TV series, *Rutland Weekend Television,* which was still in the planning stages. The idea was that he'd do sketches and I'd do musical comedy numbers."

Eric Idle "Neil had a couple of Beatley songs, and there was one on a Bonzo album, which was very Beatley. And so I thought that it would be a good idea to combine these two elements, so that the joke would lead into a song, and that's virtually what happened on the show."

Ian Keill, producer of *Rutland Weekend Television* "*The Rutles* were born out of something we did for the TV series. We were making a sketch about people suffering from lovesickness and Neil had written a song to go with it, 'I Must Be In Love'. It was a miserable day (November 24, 1975), and we took a crew down to Denham Memorial Hall in Buckinghamshire, which we had hired for £6.75, to film what turned out to be the very first Rutles song."

Eric Idle "We shot *A Hard Day's Rut* in black and white, and I played the George character."

Neil Innes "I had the idea of doing it in that black-and-white, semi-documentary style that Dick Lester had used in *A Hard Day's Night,* mainly because it was cheap, which perfectly fitted the idea of Rutland Weekend. The song, 'I Must Be In Love', was quite Beatlish and Eric coined the name The Rutles, which I hated. For this clip, it wasn't quite the same group that appeared in the full-length Rutles movie. Instead of Rikki Fataar, we had David Bately as Stig, and John Halsey, who is Barry Wom in the film, was originally called Kevin. Soon after that, Eric was asked to host *Saturday Night Live,* and he started a running gag about getting The Beatles back together, so they showed The Rutles' clip and they got a huge postbag response to it. That's why Lorne Michaels, who owns *Saturday Night Live,* agreed to finance the film as a prime-time NBC TV special."

Eric Idle "When I first hosted *Saturday Night Live,* in October 1976, we ran this clip from my TV show and it worked really well and everyone seemed to like it. I had the idea to do it as a TV show, just a one-off, and follow the mythical career of The Rutles. I was going to do it with the BBC, but Lorne Michaels, of *Saturday Night Live,* offered me a chance to do it with him as the producer for late-night TV on NBC, and the offer of American money, while still filming in England, was too good to miss. He suggested that Gary Weis and I direct it together, since we had worked on a couple of silly little films for *Saturday Night Live* (*Drag Racing* and *Body Language*), and the combination of my writing and his shooting worked pretty well. So I wrote *The Rutles* in February of 1977 and Neil set about writing thirty tunes and we set about filming in July."

Neil Innes "The next thing I know is, I'm being asked to write sixteen songs by next Thursday lunchtime in the style of The Beatles. I made a conscious decision not to listen to any of the records. I did everything from my memory of how it ought to sound. The psychedelic lyrics were easy; you just rhymed anything with anything else. But the earlier songs were difficult to get right, because one of The Beatles' trademarks is that the tunes and the words were always just a little bit unpredictable, so I was constantly throwing out tunes because they were too ordinary."

Eric Idle "Pretty soon after the original synopsis, NBC wanted to move the show to prime time and we said, 'No,' since we didn't want to compromise what we wanted to do. Later, when everything was shot and there was nothing to compromise we were happy to move to prime time to get our money back. *The Rutles* was a magic project; some things are like that and this was definitely one. Everyone enjoyed working on it, everyone from make-up to wardrobe. Even the minicab drivers would come and watch the rushes. It was great working with Neil Innes, whom I always thought was absolutely wonderful, so it was good being his pal, and conspiring together. Neil wrote all the songs and had a perfect freedom in them. I would just comment on what I thought we needed. Obviously, I preferred some to others, and would put them in or feature them more strongly. Then again, he can write to order. I remember calling him up from the US from my hospital bed and saying we needed a sitar, George-type number to cover a short piece of film, and he called me back in a couple of days with it already recorded. Neil really has an incredible ear, a great gift for melody.

"Neil was always set to play the John character, Nasty. Rikki Fataar was the closest emotionally and spiritually to the George that I knew and he too would just listen to the music. John Halsey was Barry Wom. I had originally played the George part, and I wanted to avoid being a Rutle so I was looking for a Dirk. I searched hard, but never found anyone. The difficulty was finding someone to balance Neil, someone who could hold his own in the comedy, and these people are not easy to find. I liked Ollie Halsall, but though he was left-handed and played and sang wonderfully, he wasn't really a comedian. Plus he shut his eyes while singing, which is what Paul McCartney does. So in the end I was forced into playing it. Time ran out but I kept hoping someone would turn up. Even though, some people say I have a respectable singing voice, I had my Dirk singing voice dubbed over. This was because Neil was already working with Ollie Halsall on the music. They rehearsed and played together and it was a tight band and working very well. And secondly, I was in hospital. I had just had my appendix out and then I had to go back in for unpleasant complications, and I had only just made the filming. It was a lucky break really, as I lost a lot of weight and had more chance of looking as the young man as he started out. I staggered along to one recording session, but could hardly stand, so they just carried on, and I think were much better than I could have been. Ollie is a great singer-guitarist and he did a great job. It was lovely miming him."

Neil Innes "The whole Rutles group could play. Ollie Halsall, who did a lot on the songs but is only in the film as Leppo, the fifth Rutle, was an incredibly underrated guitarist and singer, as was John Halsey. Rikki Fataar was a very accomplished all-rounder who had played with The Beach Boys. The best thing I did was to insist that we all rehearsed together, playing live several times before filming started, so we became a proper band. Ollie did most of the Paul-type singing and Eric had to mime his vocals. He never quite forgave me for that."

Eric Idle "I found some other very funny people to act in the film. For instance, Gwen Taylor (who played Chastity and Mrs Mountbatten), Terence Bayler (Leggy Mountbatten), David Battley, and Henry Woolf (Arthur Sultan), etc. etc. And it's good to work with other actors, because later when you're sitting around wondering who to put in, you know what they're like and their strengths and weaknesses, and it's nice to write especially for people. Gwen Taylor is a wonderful actress. I think in the class of the American actress, Diane Keaton and Terence Bayler was always the perfect Leggy. The filming of *All You Need Is Cash* was great fun. It's very interesting dressing up and pretending to be other people. Especially if you've seen the other people go through their lives. You get a strange perspective. It's almost more interesting when you know that they were real people, rather than when you just make up some crazy character. So, yes it was interesting being dressed in that gear and swanning up to Buckingham Palace and watching the tourists having heart attacks like they were time-tripping. We were actually mobbed on the Mersey ferry, although the reasons for this are obscure. Someone said he thought we were the Mafia. It was interesting to find out just how unpleasant it is having people scratching and chasing you. But basically the weather was lovely, and we got to film in the North of England, which is much more friendly than the South, and everyone was very happy. It was just one of those projects."

Roger Simons, production manager "We started shooting in the summer of 1978 and it was fraught with problems. We had a very small budget, under £100,000 I think, a crew of about 35, and we had only about four weeks in total to shoot it. To make matters worse, a lot of the actors were taking part purely as favours to Eric, so we had to fit our shooting schedule around when they happened to be available."

Dick Strickland, the stills photographer, "Working so cheap and fast brought all kinds of headaches. On the very first morning of shooting, we did the Apple rooftop sequence on top of an editing suite in Dean Street. They had all grown their hair and beards to look like The Beatles in that era and once we had it on film, they had it all cut off because they were going on that same afternoon to film the Buckingham Palace shots. The next day, we saw the rushes of the rooftop stuff and there was a lens hood showing in loads of the shots so it all had to be done again, this time with wigs and false beards."

Eric Idle "The only problem we had during filming was a technical one. The first day, we filmed 'Let It Rot' on the roof of a building in Wardour Street, London, I had grown a beard for it, and had it shaved off for the rest of the filming. But unfortunately there was something wrong with the camera, so we had to re-shoot it. So I had to have a false beard for the re-shoot. If you are very quick, you can see the back of Ronnie Wood of The Rolling Stones sitting on the parapet."

Gary Weis, the co-director on the film, "We used up a lot of favours. Paul Simon, for example, is a friend of Lorne Michaels. He even lives in the same building in New York, so it was a simple matter to go and film him and Mick Jagger had connections with Eric Idle. The great thing about Mick is that he was simply recalling the real story of what happened between The Beatles and The Rolling Stones and substituting The Rutles names at appropriate moments. Mind you, it took him quite a few takes to get them all right."

Chris Sargent, the second unit cameraman, "Everybody doubled up doing extra things. While we were shooting in Morecambe Bay, I was dragged in to be a member of another imaginary group, Les Garcons de la Plage. Ron Wood's wife was on the set and she got drafted in as a groupie. Everybody's brothers and girlfriends got parts."

Neil Innes "Mick Jagger's wife, Bianca, was absolutely brilliant. She supplied her own dress, a beautiful antique lace thing made in 1849, and at one point Eric accidentally trod on it. She said, 'Mind my 1849 dress,' and Eric shot back, 'Is that all it cost?' They both saw the funny side. As filming went on, John Halsey and I started ad-libbing a lot of our lines. There's a scene where my character, Nasty, is in a shower with our version of Yoko, Chastity. Eric was a reporter asking us why we were in the shower and I ad-libbed this line about civilisation being an effective sewage system. Eric totally cracked up, laughed so much we had to re-shoot it several times, with us getting progressively wetter and wetter."

Chris Sargent "The Ratkeller in Hamburg was actually a basement in Westbourne Park and we had to get in loads of live rats from an animal supplier. The Che Stadium sequence was cobbled together from several sources. The exterior shots were done outside the real Shea Stadium in New York, the shots of the group going on stage were done in Queen's Park Rangers' football ground, and the scenes on the stage were done in Shepperton studios with a black backdrop. They came down the same fire escape at the Hammersmith Odeon that was used in *A Hard Day's Night*, then ran around in the next shot in a field near Shepperton."

Chris Sargent "When we went to West Malling airfield in Kent to do the shooting of 'Piggy In The Middle', I realised there was a big gliding school nearby so I suggested asking one of the instructors to fly over the set because it would make a good shot."

Neil Innes "Gary Weis, Eric's co-director, was shooting the sequence with the camera over his shoulder. The four policemen had clambered up on to the top of the wall and then suddenly, the glider shot into view over their heads, missing their helmets by about three feet. They all went white as sheets."

Eric Idle "One segment of *All You Need Is Cash* had to be altered because of censorship by American TV. That was the bit with Dan Akroyd as Brian Thigh. After a few questions I asked him, 'What's it like to be such an asshole?' One might well ask the same question of NBC. I did make certain changes, though, for English TV. Because there were no commercial gaps when it was shown in England and Europe, I snipped seven minutes out and made it flow much faster. I prefer the English version obviously, but you need the extra time on American TV. You're in and out of commercials so frequently you have to remind people you're back in your bit, and out of the selling parts. I had Brian Thigh commit suicide at the end of the sketch because that was the only alternative to not having the joke line that the censor cut. In England we had the asshole line. Basically Danny and I ad-libbed an alternative, but it was never as funny. In Europe the show was a terrific success. Thirty-five countries bought it, and many repeated it at once, including England. In the United States, if twenty-five million people watch the show then it's considered a failure. It seems to me that the failure lies with American TV thinking, because twenty-five million is a hell of an audience, larger than most films ever get until they are shown on TV. So, for me, I was really pleased that it was on prime time, but sorry that it was opposite *Charlie's Angels* and glad that it was re-run on late-night TV. I think it's really hard to programme one-offs and specials. On TV, audiences build, and the longer you have the better they build. If we had done twenty-six weeks of *The Rutles* we would all be extremely rich and extremely boring. I'm glad to have gone from a small cupboard on BBC2 to the vastness of American TV without having to alter more than one 'asshole'. Within two hours of *The Rutles* album being released, there were rumours around about The Beatles really being on it. People very much think what they want to. But the truth is often less interesting. Incidentally, the second time I hosted *Saturday Night Live* in April 1977, Neil Innes was my guest and he came out in a Lennonish wig and sang 'Cheese And Onions' and the song appeared on a bootleg album claiming that it was a John Lennon demo. But it's obviously taped from that show. Mind you, I don't suppose even John could tell the difference at times. Neil has a great John Lennon-sounding voice."

Neil Innes "The official thing I heard was that John was fascinated by The Rutles and kept watching it. When the soundtrack album came out, I sent it to him. He was worried that the song 'Get Up And Go' was too much like 'Get Back' and that Paul might sue me. Allen Klein actually owned up and said, 'Yes, I do talk to myself in the mirror.' Ringo liked the happy bit but not the sad bit. It was too close. That was the big thing about *The Rutles*. The real story was too sad to tell. I feel very sorry for Neil Aspinall, who actually put together a very informed and balanced, well-made film of the whole Beatles period called *The Long And Winding Road*. I don't know whether it's seen the light of day or not, but George had a copy and showed it to Eric and I. And after Leggy [Brian Epstein] dies, it's miserable. You feel, 'What a downer,' and so it was a way of telling the story without downing the audience, skipping over the sad bits. So I think Ringo was too much reminded of the real break-up. Paul had an album out at the same time as *The Rutles* came out and was forever saying, 'No comment' about *The Rutles*. He had dinner at some award thing at the same table as Eric one night and Eric said it was a little frosty. But they all agreed to release The Beatles' Shea Stadium footage and other things and things like that and said good luck to you, because I think they all wanted the record put straight a little bit, even if it was slightly cockeyed. Really, The Beatles were very good about it. They allowed us to use lots of their old footage and intercut it with newly filmed Rutles sequences to give it more authenticity."

Appearing in a cameo role as a television reporter is **George Harrison** . . .

Gary Weis "George Harrison was involved almost from the beginning. He was around quite a lot, even when he didn't need to be there. We were sitting around in Eric's kitchen one day, planning a sequence that really ripped into the mythology and George looked up and said, 'We were The Beatles, you know!' Then he shook his head and said, 'Ah, never mind.' I think he was the only one of The Beatles who could see the irony of it all. The most surreal thing for me was that when we were doing the bits outside of the Apple building, and George is made up as a TV reporter interviewing Ronnie Wood and Neil Innes, a teenage kid came up and asked George, 'Is that John Lennon?' It never dawned on him who he was talking to."

George "*The Rutles* were so important to my career. Everything I ever knew and wrote was due to *The Rutles*. Really, *The Rutles* sort of liberated me from The Beatles in a way. It was the only thing I saw of those Beatles television shows they made. It was actually the best, funniest and most scathing. But at the same time, it was done with the most love. But the sad thing about it is that the songs, which were so nice and such great parodies, written by Neil Innes, also got ripped off by Sir Lew Greed (Grade), because he couldn't afford to sue him back. That's the sad thing about *The Rutles*, but they're brilliant."

Eric Idle "It's a shame that ATV music in America took fifty per cent of all the copyright of all Neil's Rutles songs because some of them bear no relationship to Beatles songs, and are just good songs in their own right. Also it would have been stupid writing tunes that didn't sound somewhat like the Beatle originals, because that was the whole point. So I always thought they were very greedy in their demands, and showed no kindness or understanding or tolerance and I hope that one day their factory burns down, and they all have upset stomachs on their holidays and their children are unpleasant to them. I'm sure the Fab Four don't know they own half of The Rutles' music, and I'm damned sure they won't see any money from it. It's just the usual corporate greed, or corporate Grade, as it's known in England. So The Rutles songs are officially by Lennon-McCartney-Innes and Harrison-Innes. I told Neil he should put out an album of these songs called *The Best of Lennon-McCartney-Innes* just to teach ATV a lesson. It wouldn't matter so much if Neil was extremely rich, but he lives off what he writes, unlike ATV, which lives off what other people write."

Sunday, April 9
With almost nothing being heard publicly from John for almost three years, fans, who are becoming desperate to know more about his latest activities, continue visiting the Dakota apartment building in New York hoping to catch sight of the now apparently reclusive former Beatle. Bill Goldsmith is one fan, who recalls his visit to the building on this day with his friend, Jimmy . . .

"My friend Jimmy and I were unspectacularly hanging out in the afternoon when it just occurred to us that it would be a great time to go to the Dakota and see how the other half lives," Bill recalls. "Undeterred by the very real potential stumbling block that John and Yoko might very well be out of the country, out of the city, or just not coming out, we boarded the next Long Island Railroad train that came along and were swept to Penn Station as if on the wings of angels. Upon our arrival in the Big Apple, we took an uptown bus and somehow we both knew we were going to see them. We didn't want to ruin the karma by talking out loud about it, but we couldn't resist anyway. We got to the Dakota and things were quiet. We didn't see any other fanatics in the area, only the usual blasé, jaded New Yorkers going to and fro, for instance, people walking eight dogs at once, and one man who was pulling a train of skateboards with a bunch of cats on them. I think we just waited a while, soaking up the atmosphere and deciding when to play 'interrogate the doorman'. When we did, we said, 'Is John Lennon here?' He didn't let on much, but we found no reason to be discouraged. He didn't say anything outright like, 'They're in Japan,' which was always a possibility, but he did say, 'Sometimes they stay in for days. People come from all over the world and wait for days, and as soon as they leave, they come out.' We shuddered.

"Soon, some other tuned-in Beatles fans came by and their radio was blasting out 'I Want To Hold Your Hand'. They told us that they had seen John recently and he was 'real skinny'! But after a while, they split. At one point, soon after, his nanny wheeled out Sean in a stroller. He was holding a red plastic baseball hat. Not to traumatise the child, we just hung out, coolly. This meant that they must be here and we were sorry we hadn't brought cameras. By the time Sean came back, we had resolved to hold out as long as it took. I was hoping John and Yoko would go out for dinner, or come in for dinner, or go out after dinner, or come in after dinner, or anything else that I hadn't thought of. After a while, Jimmy couldn't take it anymore, and had to run down the block into a darkening Central Park to . . . relieve himself! 'Stall them if they come out,' he said. Since it was dinnertime, and we were hungry, we bought some infamous New York City street hot-dogs and sodas from a vendor and ate while leaning on a parked car. The doorman, with whom we had struck up such a good rapport, said he was going out for a few minutes, and Jimmy asked him to buy some cigarettes. The doorman came back with them.

"It grew darker and cooler, but our spirits remained high. The pivotal moment came when this long black and grey limo pulled up into the driveway of the Dakota. Now we knew that many celebrities lived in the building, as well as a few rich people, but 'Ah-ha!' I said, 'The licence plate number is 101 and that's the catalogue number of the *White Album*. What an omen!' We knew. Now it was around 7.00pm, and it was very calm and quiet and the only people there were Jimmy and I, the doorman and the chauffeur. It's hard to believe, but Jimmy, the same person who was wily enough to find his way into the Wings' soundcheck at Nassau Coliseum and get Linda to pose for a picture at the keyboards, was inexplicably looking out at 72nd Street at the big moment, while I was correctly staring at the south-east door, past the office booth. 'There's Yoko,' I had to say to get him to turn around. Yoko had come out by herself and was dressed up all in white. She had on a white dress and a white 'Yoko hat' and her hair was down on her shoulders. She looked great. I said, 'Hi, Yoko,' for lack of anything else to say, but she didn't seem to hear. Now she was standing there, staring at the door, too. Now you can imagine how we both felt at this point. Hours seemed to go by, even though it's hard to gauge times in these situations. Was John doing this for our benefit? We were freaking out. I think he was probably tucking Sean in. But finally, John *did* come out! He was also all dressed up, in a grey suit, with maybe a light brown tie. His hair wasn't too long but it was combed down, kind of like *Magical Mystery Tour* times. And he wore his round rims. Since we only had the distance it took for him to walk from the door to the car, I only had time to say, 'Hi, John.' And John said, 'How are you doing?' in our direction and got into the car. Yoko had circled around to the left side of the car. What I remember most was the way that he walked, kind of loping, with his shoulders bobbing up and down. Despite total paralysis, and the inability to talk, we both shuffled over to John's side of the car to have a look, but of course not to bother him. John was holding a book and playing it cool. He had been through this many times before. After those golden moments, the car started pulling away, so I said, 'Might as well follow it till we lose 'em in traffic.' Like true Beatlemaniacs, once we started losing it, we started to run after it. It was heading south down Central Park West, so I was kind of sorry I hadn't asked them for a lift to Penn

Station. Anyway, we were so excited, we ended up running practically all the way back to the train station, non-stop."

On **Thursday, May 11**, the *Evening News* reporter, Cliff Wayne announces that "John Lennon is back in the New York recording studios making a new album at his expense. And I understand that Elvis Costello was dragged out of the legendary Maxie's Kansas City club by one of Lennon's friends to go and see the former Beatle. Lennon is currently without a record deal although he is reported to have been offered several million pounds by both CBS and WEA."

In June, Cynthia Lennon releases *A Twist Of Lennon*, her book of memoirs from her time with John . . .

"After my marriage to John Twist was over, I wrote a book called *A Twist Of Lennon*," Cynthia says. "I even moved to Ireland to write it because there it is a writer's tax haven. Actually, I need not have bothered because the book was not a success. But really, it was a message to John. I wrote at the end of it, 'In the words of the I Ching – no blame'. Meaning that I didn't blame him for what had happened. But the way it was treated in the papers upset John and he took me to court over it. Eventually three High Court judges decided that there was no case to answer, no reason to make such a fuss over the book."

Thursday, June 29

Paul, meanwhile, begins recordings for his next studio album, soon to be titled *Back To The Egg*. During the sessions, which begin at Paul's Spirit Of Ranachan Studios in Scotland, he is joined by Steve Holly and Lawrence Juber, ultimately to become the latest full-time additions to Wings. Paul explains how they came to join the band . . .

"What happened was Denny knew Steve and he recommended him when we were looking for a drummer," **Paul** says, "and Denny had also run into Lawrence on a TV show, so he talked about them both. He had played with them a couple of times and got on really nice and easy. Then we started playing with them and we started doing an album and by the time we had finished the album, it was really easy to work with them, which is a very important thing to do. So we were quite chuffed to find these fellows who were very easy to work with and that helped the music, I think. We actually enjoy playing together."

The drummer, Steve Holly "I didn't know Paul, but I knew Denny, because I live in the same area and we tend to congregate in the same areas. We had a few jars (drinks), went to a few parties and I went back to his house one night, there's a drum kit in his front room, and everybody started jamming. I think it was a while before he realised that I played drums."

Paul "The first time we got together with the new line-up, whenever we played, everything we put down was a bit more rocky, unlike things like 'Mull Of Kintyre' and stuff. Three of the tracks on the new LP appear a little bit like what people wouldn't be used to from Wings."

Steve Holly "At first, I was a bit intimidated by Paul. When he had a song, I'd say, 'What do you want me to play on it?' When we started out we were doing that, but then we,

Laurence and I, started to have a lot of scope. I play drums so I know, roughly, what I'm doing all the time. So if I've got an idea for something, and I play it and it doesn't work, I'll come up with something that does work, otherwise I wouldn't be here. It's good to play with someone like Paul because he'll play a melodic bass line whereas most bass players would just thump their way through."

Recordings for *Back To The Egg* will also continue at the more relaxed surroundings of Lympne Castle in Kent . . .

Paul "We got bored of recording in a studio so we thought we'd record some of the album in an old castle in Kent, which was where Thomas A-Becket and the old monks used to live in the old days. The vibes there are different from the normal studio so when you go in there, it kind of tweaks you up a bit. Your imagination gets a little freer."

While in **July**, there is a change of direction for George when he gives the go-ahead to the financing of the new *Monty Python* film, *The Life Of Brian*. It marks the launch of HandMade Films . . .

George "The name of the company came about as a bit of a joke. I'd been to Wookey Hole in Somerset and when you come out of the cave you go through an old paper mill, where they show you how they make old underpants into paper. So I bought a few rolls and they had this watermark 'British Handmade Paper'. I said, 'Let's call our company British HandMade Films.' But when we went to register it, we were told, 'You can't call it British!' You can only call things British if everyone is on strike the whole time and it's making huge losses. So we said, 'Sod it! We'll just call it HandMade Films.' "

Newsweek magazine "Harrison started HandMade Films with his business manager, Denis O'Brien, less as a conscious decision to move into films than as a way to help his friends in *Monty Python* finance *The Life Of Brian* after everyone else refused. The film, budgeted at $4.6 million, went on to earn more than $35 million and, as Harrison puts it, 'The thing (HandMade) took on a life of its own.' "

George "I was friends with Michael Palin and I was very excited when EMI took on *The Life Of Brian*. I had followed it all the way and I had heard all the gags. In 1978, when Lord Delfont stopped the film, I asked Denis if there was any way I could help out the Python team myself. I thought he had forgotten about it, but a day or two later, he came back to me and said, 'I've found a way to make it. We'll be the producers.' I had watched that Mel Brooks film *The Producers* hundreds of times, Peter Sellers introduced it to me, and it was a hilarious idea."

Denis O'Brien, George's partner in HandMade "I have to say that if the script of *The Life Of Brian*, which Lord Delfont saw, had been made it would have been a total disaster. I persuaded the Pythons to re-write it."

George "Before HandMade Films, I was slightly involved in pictures through The Beatles, with the ones we made with Dick Lester and then with Apple, which was the non-happening event of the late Sixties. 'Come all ye faithful and we'll give you all our money.' I was a personal friend of John Hurt and I saw him in the play *Little Malcolm And His Struggle Against The Eunuchs*. Apple Films had been set up to make them and I thought, 'Let's do this as a movie.' So we did and we had a fantastic cast, John Hurt,

David Warner and John McEnery. It was so wonderful we didn't even get a distribution deal. It was very depressing. It's difficult enough to get a record distributed, let alone a film . . . I don't profess to know anything about the business, except that it's very confusing. Denis is the one with no hair on his head. As for the Pythons, let's face it, there are certain things in life which make life worth living and one of those things is *Python*, especially for someone like me. When you've gone through so much in life, and you're supposed to decide what is real and what isn't, you watch the television and you see all this madness going on and everyone is being serious and accepting it, and you're ready to bang your head against the wall in despair, then someone says, 'And now for something completely different'. That saves the day. Laughter is a great release . . ."

The *Monty Python* comedy star, Eric Idle, talks openly about his close friend, **George Harrison** . . .

"He's one of the few morally good people that rock'n'roll has produced," Eric reveals. "He's one of the few people who have turned their attentions into goodness and being good, and he's extremely generous and he backs and supports all sorts of people that you'll never, ever hear of. He's a wonderful bloke. He's simply interested in goodness and spiritual values and whatever is of worth and merit in the world. And he does a lot of things, which are good, which are certainly missed out by the Mary Whitehouse form of Christianity that passes for Christianity in this part of the world . . . When he heard, for example, that another friend, Barry Sheene, was trying to raise £150,000 sponsorship to race Formula One cars, George promptly offered to pay £150,000 for Barry *not* to do it, because he was worried about the risk to Barry's life. On another occasion, George heard that it was the birthday of Dot Mitchell, who was then the landlady at The Row Barge, his local public house. He called her to one side and, teasingly, told her to hold out her hand and close her eyes. Then, he dropped three perfect, impossibly valuable rubies into her hand. 'Have a nice birthday,' he told her . . .

"One time, I got a phone call from Australia asking could I come over and promote a new chocolate biscuit, called Nudge, named after our famous *Monty Python* sketch. I told George I was going, and he asked me if I'd be flying over India on the way. I asked, 'Why?' and George said, 'No particular reason, just asking.' So I was on the plane and I had got a parcel from George, covered in OM signs and the message, 'Not to be opened until flying above India.' The time comes, I undo the package and I find the immortal message, 'Shag a Sheila for me!' "

The Formula One racing driver, Jackie Stewart, joins in the praise of **George** . . .

"I guess I must have been the world's biggest Beatles fan," Jackie announces. "I mean, I would have given my right arm to meet any of them. And when I met George, he was very modest, and that was one of the first things that really impressed me. He seemed to be more knowledgeable about my racing career than I was. Maybe I was more knowledgeable about his career than he was. It was very nice. Nobody had to try to impress anybody else. And he's a man who appreciates people. I think that's what I like about him. He's one of the most well-balanced men that I know and he has dealt with success and is still enjoying that success in a highly moderated way . . ."

Filming on *The Life Of Brian* begins in Tunisia on **Saturday, September 16**, and on **Friday, October 20**, George is forced into filming his cameo role in the movie . . .

George "I went out to Tunisia where they were shooting *The Life Of Brian*. It was the place where they shoot all these Biblical kind of films. I believe that they had just shot a Fellini film there. So, I was meant to be leaving one night and I got shoved into wardrobe and make-up and before I knew it, I was dressed up as an Arab. There's a scene where Brian comes out in the morning and he's surrounded by people saying, 'Put your hand on this, Brian,' and, 'I'm afflicted by a bald spot.' And John Cleese is saying, 'Will all those afflicted by the Devil form a group on the left and all those with gifts form a group on the right.' And as he's going through the crowd, he says, 'Oh, Brian, I'd like you to meet Mister Papadopolous who's going to loan us the mount for Monday afternoon.' You'd have to stop frame the film to see this was me. We ended up investing five or six million pounds in *Brian*. We made a bit of money on it, which we then put into the next one. Terry Gilliam had this idea scribbled on a piece of paper, and it was *The Time Bandits*."

Ringo also continues with his film career by filming *Sextette*, his latest solo film. The star of the project is the legendary actress Mae West . . .

Ringo "I thought it would be fantastic to play with Mae, just to see what the legend was really like, but on the first day of shooting I got really uptight. I felt completely left out of things. But by the end of the second day's filming, I would have stayed on as long as she wanted me. She's old enough to be my grandmother, so it's sort of embarrassing to say, but she's bloody attractive. And Mae's no (Greta) Garbo. Mae doesn't want to be left alone."

Friday, July 28
The second part of an interview with Paul, carried out by Paul Gambaccini, is published in *Record Mirror*. In it, Gambaccini **asks Paul,** "Do you ever wish or do you wish now that the McCartney ones from the Lennon and McCartney songs had said McCartney and the Lennon ones had said Lennon?"

Paul replies, "You asked me if I ever wish that. Yeah, I do and not just out of a personal thing for me. I sometimes feel it for John, things getting called Lennon and McCartney, things like 'Strawberry Fields', 'Norwegian Wood', certain ones that John wrote and I just helped a little bit. And there are certain ones that I wrote. There's probably only about, say, 20 that are really our own. On the rest, there's quite a lot of collaboration. I suppose you do get a little niggled, you wish that people knew that was mine, but hell, how much credit do you want in a lifetime?"

Gambaccini "Do you ever hope that John records again? Do you think he should?"

Paul "I hope that if he would like to record again, he will record again, but I hope that if he doesn't want to, he doesn't. This is something totally down to his own feeling. Whatever gets you through the night."

In **August**, controversy spreads when *Sgt. Pepper's Lonely Hearts Club Band*, a big-screen musical starring Peter Frampton and The Bee Gees, opens in cinemas across America . . .

Rock star Peter Frampton, who plays Billy Shears "I see Billy Shears as Mr Clean, the naive, virginal farmer's wife's son who has a magical grandfather and becomes a big star. In a lot of ways, the character and I are very similar, though I'm not as goody-goody as Billy. It's a send-up of me, the whole rock business and the idea that the money is the essence of life. The hardest thing I had to do, the only real acting I had to do, was the suicide scene. I did everything but jump off the building. I had to cry all the way through 'Golden Slumbers' and 'The Long And Winding Road'. I thought about the Lynyrd Skynyrd plane crash, which happened about the time that we were filming that scene. All my road crew died on that crash . . . There's a scene with Lucy In The Sky where I get stoned at this party and she drags me off. We've got to kiss but with twenty people watching, I was scared stiff about this scene. I wound up kissing her while she was singing."

Barry Gibb, of The Bee Gees, who play The Hendersons "The great excitement for us has been re-recording The Beatles' songs with George Martin. The fact that we've been doing Beatles harmonies since we were kids helped. It was easy for us to become a foursome with Peter Frampton. We didn't really know him, just an on and off acquaintance since we first met him in 1968 with The Herd. George Martin was in complete control all the time. But more than anything, we'd like the boys, The Beatles, to like it."

Paul is somewhat more relaxed with the idea of the film "I've heard George Burns sing 'Fixing A Hole', which sounds interesting and The Bee Gees do a few, Frampton does a couple. Geoff Emerick was working on it and he likes it. He says it's great . . . The film doesn't worry me. They're plugging my songs and because they're using the songs they just have to ask the publisher of the songs, which was Northern Songs and that means Lew Grade and that means he has the rights. They had to ask him to make the film."

But a most disgruntled **George** remarks, "They say, 'Oh well, The Beatles are these old people. They're so familiar to us all. Let's use them. I've got a great idea, let's get together 30 Beatles songs, make up characters based upon characters in the songs and we'll come up with a flimsy idea and make a 90-minute movie.' This is about how to make a project and sell it based upon The Beatles, rather than based upon their own talent . . ."

Paul "I haven't seen it yet, so I can't talk about it. I thought that, at the time we were making the *Sgt. Pepper* album, 'They can't make a film out of this.' We used to be stoned all the time and say, 'Hey, what a great film this would make,' but the trouble was that people were all freaking out on acid on the album and you'd never be able to get those big elephants in that were coming through their heads. We thought, 'You just can't capture it.' Once it gets to be a film, it's always going to be a bit plodding compared to the album. Those days it was a fantasy thing. It all took place in your mind, and it will be harder than anything to capture that feeling. And from what I hear about the Stigwood thing, it doesn't seem to have captured it."

Thursday, September 7
Meanwhile, sadness surrounds the death of The Who's drummer Keith Moon, who is found in Harry Nilsson's London apartment. His final night alive was spent with Paul and Linda whilst attending a party to celebrate the opening of the movie, *The Buddy Holly Story* . . .

Ringo "I always loved him very much. And a few of my other friends have gone, and some that were acquaintances, like Jimi Hendrix and Janis Joplin, all those people . . . It's always a tragedy. Mainly I get annoyed because they're not playing anymore. But I'm a fatalist, you see and I really think that our time comes, whatever we're doing. That's the only way I get through most of my friends dying, I think. I won't go to funerals because I don't believe in them. I totally believe your soul has gone by the time you get into the limo. She or he's up there or whatever it is, I'm sure. I can't wait to go half the time . . ."

On the other musicians who have passed away?

Ringo "What a band! I mean it would be nice if you could visit. But, yes, I get sad because, you know, I go through those times being crazy, thinking that it's a waste that they do go. And then I pull through, well God's called together his fold, you know. But I miss Marc (Bolan) and Keith. You look through your phone book and it's no good calling anymore. So that's the end of it."

Saturday, September 9
Newspapers around the world announce that **George** has wed his long-time companion, Olivia Arias, at a Henley-on-Thames registry office six days ago . . .

Daily Mirror "Beatle George Weds In Secret: Ex-Beatle George Harrison has had a hush-hush wedding. His marriage to Mexican beauty Olivia was so secret that even his family were kept guessing. And when the news crept out yesterday, six days after the wedding, the honeymooners were far away, somewhere in Tunisia. The witnesses, and the only guests, at the wedding were Olivia's parents. It took place at Henley-on-Thames registry office, just a few hundred yards from George's country mansion."

Daily Express "George, 35, obtained a special licence so that the usual bans need not be posted making the ceremony public. He even managed to drive in his Rolls Royce the 200 yards from his mansion in Friar Park, Henley, Oxfordshire, to the local registry office without anyone spotting him. George became a father for the first time five weeks ago. George's brothers, Harry and Peter, who live in the grounds of his stately home, were not even told about the wedding last weekend until it was all over. Olivia, who comes from a strict Roman Catholic background, has now, like George, converted to Hinduism. Warner Brothers say George is now busy working on a new album, which will be released in time for Christmas."

1979

FEBRUARY . . .

Sean "Even though I was so young, I remember John always being around, always doing something, dressed in a kimono and looking relaxed. I also remember watching TV with him. We'd watch *Doctor Jekyll And Mr Hyde*, which was scary, but it didn't matter because *The Muppets* came on right after. I remember him singing to me when he put me to bed. He'd sing a song about 'Popeye The Sailor Man' who came from the Isle of Man, and he'd take me to Central Park zoo, and make up characters for all the animals, like Mister Polar Bear."

Ringo spends most of his time living as a tax exile in Monte Carlo . . . "It's very nice here," he announces. "I can see three countries from my apartment, Italy, France and Monaco. It has its advantages. Most of my days in Monte Carlo are spent sleeping, although I like sunbathing in the summer. And in the evenings, all you can do is eat and gamble. There are a lot of friends down here now. There's a lot of English people gone to live here."

The UK reporter, John Blake, asks **Ringo** how he would describe his life now . . .

"Semi-retirement is a good way to describe the way I live now," he says. "I work for a bit, then I don't. And I love the position of being able to do what I want to do. I used to have to go to the factory every morning. I don't want to do that anymore. I've done that and it's more fun this way. But a lot of people have to do it . . . I am a jet setter. I am on planes half the year going to different places. Wherever I go, it's a swinging place, man. It's a crazy kind of world . . . I have a son of 13 who wants to be a drummer, who is a very good drummer already, has his little band, and I can only tell him. I can give him encouragement, which I do."

As expected, Blake then asks Ringo about his former band . . .

"That band? They were the best band in the world. I've never played with finer players. It was wonderful. I couldn't say I enjoyed every minute but even the bad times were good. I always loved that time. When you reflect on it, you always remember the good times. There were hard times. Some periods with not much joy at all. But, overall, I think it was a wonderful period of my life. Specially with those three adorable chaps."

Blake "Why do people throughout the world still care about them?"

Ringo "Well, who else is there? There's nobody else . . . Everyone can relate to The Beatles. You know, children who weren't born then relate through the music. Well, if you listen to the records, they related to everybody, from children's songs to songs for our parents and grandparents . . . When I go out, I usually go to the same places and they know never to put anything of ours on while I'm there. You can't relax if they do because everyone looks at you and you're expected to get up and mime. But yes, I am a big fan. I think we made some of the finest records, still, today."

In **February**, **George** passes through Brazil for the first time, and attends the Brazilian Grand Prix. He is asked by a reporter, "Will The Beatles sing together anymore?" He replies, "I don't think so. I don't think there's any chance at all. I haven't even seen John for over two years. It's like saying to people when they've grown up, 'Will you go back home to the same family?' "

Wednesday, February 14 (USA)
George releases his new album, entitled simply *George Harrison* . . .

'Love Comes To Everyone'

George " 'Something there in my heart, something is never changing.' Well, that feeling *is* there in my heart. Actually, the heart is the part of the body where God resides. That's the psychical position in the body. If you look at the chart in yoga, there's these energy centres and there's the jacra at the heart and that is where the feeling of love comes from. If you feel sick, you feel it in the jacra in the stomach and if you feel love, you feel it in the heart and that's unchanging. The only thing that changes is the bodily condition, from the womb, to a baby, to a boy, to a young man, to middle-aged, to an old man and then you die. You come out of this foetus shape, bent over, you straighten up as you grow up, and then you bend over and then you die. But the one thing that remained the same, all through it, is the soul and the heart. That thing goes from life to death, from life to death. As Krishna says, 'There's never a time when we weren't and there'll never be a time when we cease to be. The only thing that changes is the bodily condition.' "

'Not Guilty'

George "I wrote that right after we got back from the Himalayas and the Maharishi (1968). I got back a bit later than everybody else because all the others had split and started Apple. I got back and it was like a mad house. John and Yoko had some guy throwing the I Ching every ten minutes. They'd say, 'Oh, we're having a business meeting, well, let's throw the I Ching.' The place was just full of lunatics and 'Not Guilty' was really about John, Paul and Apple."

'Here Comes The Moon'

George "It isn't true that my lawyer called me up and advised me to sue myself over this song. The two tunes, this and 'Here Comes The Sun', aren't alike anyway. But things like that can happen. That's like *The Rutles*, you know, he sues himself by mistake."

'Soft Hearted Hanna'

George "It's an ode to the mushroom, I must admit. But you have to be careful because it's so good. The difference between that and acid is that when you feel that half of you is elated, the other half of you is feeling physically rotten. That stuff is very organic, you know. You feel that everything's great, everything's in perfect focus and even the physical body feels good. And because I felt good, I just kept on eating them all day. I nearly did myself in because I had too many, and I fell over and left my body. I fell over and hit my head on a piece of concrete."

'Blow Away'
... Written by George when he was sitting in his garden in the hut looking at the water as it was pouring with rain.

George, in his book *I Me Mine* "We were having leaks in the house because some drain had blocked and I had gone out in my hat and raincoat and was down there in the hut, getting away from it all."

'Faster'

George "I did 'Faster' to write about something specific as a challenge. Since I was a kid, like twelve years old, I got into motor racing and motor cycle racing. Not actually racing myself, but as a spectator. There was a racetrack in Liverpool where they had Grand Prix races from time to time so I got into that just before I got into the guitar. And it was always interesting to see in what other areas of life who was wearing their hair long. In motor racing, Jackie Stewart became the world champion in, I think, 1968, and he was the first guy with long hair who had opinions and he was a big Beatles fan.

"I got the title 'Faster' first. I took it from Jackie Stewart's book. I thought, 'Good, that's a title,' so I lifted the title and once I had got the title, I was away. I then wrote the chords 'Faster than a bullet from a gun', and later worked out the rest of the song in a way that doesn't limit it only to motor cars. The story can relate to me or you or anybody in an occupation who becomes successful and has pressure pressed upon them caused by the usual jealousies, fears, hopes, etc. The only thing that limits it is the sound effects I put on later."

'If You Believe'

George "Pray, give up and it all recedes away from you. Lord Buckley did a thing called 'God's Own Drunk', and he was talking about love. 'Love is like a beautiful garden. When you use it, it spreads, But when you don't, it recedes,' and it's true. It's really that in its simplest form, positive versus negative. If you apply positive thoughts, that energy is there. But if you apply negative thoughts, that energy drains you, and it is that simple. If you think, 'Oh, God, what can I do? Life's a misery,' and you're thinking that, you're actually putting fuel onto that negative, draining aspect. When you realise it, you can at least try and correct yourself all the time. And when you make an effort, get up, you have all your needs. Give up and it all recedes away from you."

Wednesday, February 28
It is announced that George is to sue the makers of the new musical film, *Sgt. Pepper's Lonely Hearts Club Band*. On the same day, the UK columnist, Mick Brown files a report on him in an article titled "The Driving Force Behind The Silent Beatle" ...

"The young girl at the reception desk did not turn a hair when **George Harrison** walked past," the piece reads. "Not a matter of short-sightedness, simply of non-recognition. Once upon a time that would have been unthinkable. Nowadays, Harrison will probably take it as a compliment to his efforts to maintain the lowest of all possible profiles. Up from his home in Oxfordshire for the day, he had spent the morning with Paul McCartney, not, he hastened to add, with any view to a Beatles reunion. 'There is no likelihood of them ever playing together again,' Harrison says emphatically. While McCartney proceeds smoothly on to his next million, Ringo Starr commutes from one country to the next to avoid the taxman and John Lennon lies low in New York, Harrison has opted for the peaceful life at his Oxfordshire home.

George "There comes a time when you say, 'I don't have to be mad all my life,' and when you realise that happiness is what should come first. I am as happy as I have ever been. The birth of my first child Dhani last August and marriage to Olivia Arias have transformed me . . . I would like to devote the next part of my life to putting more effort into spiritual work. I'd like to make a couple more albums before I call it a day, but I'm not going to die for rock'n'roll. The music business is like any other in that the more time you spend in it, the more you come to believe that the world can't exist without it. But when you stand back, you realise that life would go on even if there was never another pop record played again."

Friday, March 9
George is seen passing through Los Angeles airport, en route to a holiday in Hawaii. Onlookers are greeted with the sight of the former Beatle being confined to a wheelchair with his ankle heavily bandaged . . .

"I was driving a tractor around the garden and couldn't find the accelerator," **George** explains to reporters. "I flipped it out of gear and began to roll down a hill. I put my foot on the brake, but there were no brakes! I turned up a bank to stop it, rolled it over and it went over my foot. X-rays showed it was just a bad sprain, but I've been in a wheelchair for a few days."

Then, in between ordering afternoon tea and crumpets, George begins by answering the inevitable questions about The Beatles from the reporters . . .

"I can only answer the 'Come Back Beatles' call by saying it's just a trip, a fantasy," **George** announces. "People tell me The Beatles saved the world in the Sixties. What rubbish! We couldn't even save ourselves. Maybe it's true that we created a lot of love by writing and singing songs with feeling and meaning. That was wonderful but suddenly around 1969, the love suddenly stopped and the hate set in again. People around the world began kicking each other again and stabbing each other in the back. Where did all the love go that people say we created? I hope someone else will come along with some more positive music. It's why we went into the meditation bit. I found I was like a cork bobbing on the ocean, anchored nowhere. I know Ringo said that when The Beatles broke up it was like losing a steady job. I didn't agree, I said, 'Thank God.' I was glad that little factory burned down. It became too stifling. Now I can deal with my life on a happier level. It would be just great if the four of us could sit down like this over tea and crumpets and chat. I haven't even seen John for two or three years but it couldn't be like that. If we met, the world would want to be there and that would spoil it."

Sipping on his tea, and munching on his second crumpet, **George** continues "Everything is really nice for me now. Life is really great and I'm really happy. I'm working with other people. That was a problem for me, John and Paul wrote their music together. One of the few times I worked with someone was when Ringo got stuck on some songs he was writing and I helped him to finish them."

A reporter asks George if would consider going on tour to promote his latest album. "There's always the chance," he replies, "but I would say not. For a lot of musicians, being on tour is just escapism. It's a way out from the taxman, telephones and your mother-in-law. You have to be a workaholic."

Thursday, March 15 (USA)
Wings release their new single 'Goodnight Tonight', but only after a slight delay . . .

Paul "We had a meeting and decided that it would be nice to have a single while the TV show, *Wings Over The World*, was out, because it had been something like seven months since we'd put a record out. 'Goodnight Tonight' was going to be the B-side and 'Daytime Nightime Suffering' was going to be the A-side. So we sat around for years, well it seemed like years, discussing it, you know, the normal soul-searching you go through, and we decided, 'No, it isn't all right. We won't put it out.' So we scrapped the whole thing and about a week later, I played the record again and I thought, 'That's crazy! We've made it. It's stupid, why not put it out? Just because people are going to pan it.' I liked it and other people had taken it home and played it to people at parties. So we decided to do it."

'Goodnight Tonight'

Paul "When I was writing 'Goodnight Tonight', I was basically just trying to write a dance record. I would call it a disco record because I wrote it after going to a disco one night. I had listened to everything that night that was going down and went away with that kind of thing in my mind and I happened to write that particular tune. I was just thinking of dance records."

Its B-side is 'Daytime Nightime Suffering'

Paul "That's a pro-women song, you know, 'What does she get for all of this?' It's like the plight of women. My stuff is very humanistic and I say that's what I would be most proud of, as would any artist."

Ringo "His new single's bothering me, I must say. But he always has growers does Paul. First time you always say, 'What's this?' But then they grow on you."

On **Sunday, April 8**, BBC2 transmits the documentary *Wings Over The World*, a special about Wings' 1975/76 concert tour of the world . . .

Paul "It was my idea to take a film crew across America and Australia when we went on tour. I also wanted to show what happened to us after The Beatles broke up, so I've also included all kinds of bits and pieces of films of us at home on the farm in Scotland. The most difficult thing was trying to follow The Beatles. People were bound to say we were not as good as they were. Really, the only drawback about the film is that the music is not right up to date. It's not our new stuff. I know it's confusing for some people because we have a different line-up now, but I had to make a decision about the film. I either present it late or the alternative is to do nothing with it, at all! I don't know why the film is being screened on BBC2. I would have preferred BBC1, obviously, with a simultaneous broadcast on the radio."

Denny Laine "We spent an unbelievable amount of time making the *Wings Over The World* film because Paul kept changing his mind. It took three times as long as it should have done."

Reviewers of the show remark that the programme was unusual in the way that very few back-stage and off-stage shots, commonplace in other similar documentaries, were shown. **Paul** explains . . . "I don't like a lot of back-stage stuff in films myself. I prefer music in films, whether it's onstage or in the studios. I mean, if I see a Stones documentary, I wouldn't be interested in seeing Jagger going round from club to club."

Saturday, April 28

There's a bad time for Ringo when he is rushed from his Monte Carlo home to hospital where, during a long operation, surgeons remove five feet of his intestines because of a blockage. It is believed to have been caused by the long-delayed effects of peritonitis, an illness he suffered when he was a child . . .

Ringo "I reckon I had a good look at death's face that day. I would have died if they hadn't done it. But it still blows me away to think of all the stuff they have taken out of me."

Saturday, May 5

Paul's interview with Ray Bonici is published in the *Record Mirror* . . .

"We may be playing some concerts," he announces. "We'll probably do something in a couple of months' time but we want to do something this time, like playing smaller halls and clubs. We want to turn up and offer them a gig for the evening. We want to have that kind of freedom. We have also been approached to play Russia some time next year. We were asked to play in the Red Square a week before the Olympic Games, but as yet nothing is definite. We had an album there released last year."

While on **Tuesday, May 8**, from her Dakota apartment, Yoko Ono delivers the news that many millions of his fans have been waiting years to hear, "John Lennon is considering returning to work after more than four years in retirement," she announces. "I think John will have a great deal of work to talk about in the fall. For the moment though, he still doesn't want to see anyone. He is happy to be a private person."

Saturday, May 19

George's first wife, Patti, had married the guitar legend Eric Clapton in a ceremony in Tucson, Arizona on March 27. Today, during a reception held in the grounds at Eric's baronial hall home, Hurtwood Edge, in Ewhurst, Surrey, the high spot for the specially invited guests, who included Mick Jagger and David Bowie, is an end of evening jam session, which involves Paul, George and Ringo, performing together for the first time since January 1970 . . .

Paul "It didn't feel strange at all. It was all pretty straightforward. We were having a bit of a booze-up and a laugh together and we were with each other again. It felt pretty normal.

It was only the next day when everyone was making a huge fuss about it that I realised that our playing together was half-way important to anyone else. We were invited to the reception, which was held in a large marquee . . ."

Denny Laine "There was a large marquee in the grounds and the party went on for a day and a half. The highlight was when all the musicians were up on the stage jamming together. The only Beatle missing was John Lennon and Mick Jagger took his place."

Paul "It all started with all the grown-ups sitting around having a drink and chatting. Some of our kids got bored so they started playing with some of the musical instruments that had been left lying around on the stage. Eventually, one of the adults got up and then we all did. So there was George, me and Ringo on stage and suddenly everyone was joking about whether this was a reunion. Ginger Baker, Robert Palmer and Chas & Dave were also there. The jam was mainly just to get the kids off the mikes, because they were making such a row. So we adults got up there and thought, 'We'll make an even worse row.' "

Denny Laine "God knows what the music sounded like but The Beatles were almost together again. The stage was heaving with people singing the old Beatles hit 'Get Back'."

John tells Ringo the following week, "If I had have known about this, I would have come along."

On **Tuesday, May 22**, Reuters reports, "Ex-Beatle **Paul McCartney** yesterday signed what is believed to be the richest recording deal in history. McCartney and his rock band Wings signed up with Columbia Records to make nine albums over the next three years, for an annual advance of $2 million and royalties of up to 28 per cent."

Monday, June 11
In Liverpool, the made-for-TV Dick Clark film, *The Birth Of The Beatles*, begins shooting. The technical advisor on the production is The Beatles' original drummer, Pete Best . . .

Paul "I can't keep up with all these old Beatles nostalgia things. It all happened so long ago. But it does seem weird to think that I'm living and someone else is going to be up there playing me on the screen. As for Pete Best being advisor, that should prove to be very interesting. I haven't seen him for about 15 years!"

George "They didn't wait for any of us to die before they started making these silly docu-dramas."

Tony Bishop, the film's producer "The film will take a hard but fair look into their lives and why they became what they did."

On the same day, the new Wings album *Back To The Egg* is released in the UK . . .

Paul "It was a kind of back to the beginning kind of feel to us while we were making it where we were trying different things. The title just seemed to sum it up, *Back To The Egg*, Back To The Beginning. We recorded most of it in a medieval castle in Kent (Lympne). For a whole month we took over this fortress and proceeded to record in the kitchen, the stairwell, the spiral staircase and the main hall. What's more, the owner found herself narrating a story called 'The Poodle And The Pug' on a special track. It was good. It was interesting. We like to record in unusual places because it gives the recordings a healthier and brighter approach. I personally don't believe in acoustic myths. I think that, as long as you have good mikes and good songs, you can record anywhere."

Linda "It started off being a concept album. It had a travelling idea, where somebody got into their van on a rainy night and was heading towards the gig, but in the end it just ended up being just songs."

Paul "When we put the new album together, we used just about the best 24-track tape machines and all that. But I don't know that what we are doing is really any better than it was in the old days when four tracks were the maximum. It's easy to lose sight of what it's all about and I don't want to . . . I saw a thing on telly the other night. It said that there are three million copies of *Back To The Egg* waiting around in a warehouse, which sounds as if it is the world's greatest flop. But for any other group to sell a million, which the album has, it is a major success. It is a good album; it's the band's first album. Those copies that they didn't sell were mainly because the record company produced too many. They just thought that it was going to sell in huger quantities and they got stuck with them, which I think is a daft idea anyway. I think they should wait until somebody orders them, and then print them up."

'Old Siam, Sir'

Linda "I wrote a bit of a melody on 'Old Siam, Sir' and Paul and Denny were there and they just started making up the song. They later brought it into the studio. The whole riff came about when we were rehearsing to go live."

Paul "It came from a riff that Linda was playing one day and we kind of fitted in all little bits and pieces. The middle bit was a riff that we used to jam on when we were just jamming together, and then I wrote the words to it and I had this idea about this girl coming home from Siam to get a fellow in the UK. But in the end, she just ends up back in Siam. It's a long story."

'Again And Again'

Denny "That came about in Rude Studios. We hadn't seen each other for a while and it was just a song that I got up and played. I started singing it and Paul and Linda seemed to like it and I thought, 'I'm in here.' That's more or less how it came about. If somebody picks up on it, you record it."

'Baby's Request'

Paul "That came about because we were on holiday in the South of France, last summer, and we saw The Mills Brothers, the famous old Mills Brothers. Everyone thought that they were dead but they were in cabaret down there, and they were 73 years of age and rotund. They were great and sang exactly like they used to and they are still an amazing group. I went to see them backstage and one of them said, 'Hey, Paul. How's about writing The Mills Brothers a song?' So I said, 'Yeah, Herbie, okay.' So I went back to the hotel and spent the next day writing a song for them and when we got back to London, we demoed it, sent it out to them and, unfortunately, there was a slight cock-up on the management front. For some reason, their manager got the idea that we were going to pay them to record it. So they ended up not doing it, and we ended up doing it ourselves."

'Rockestra Theme'/'So Glad To See You Here'
(Recorded at a session in Abbey Road Studio Two on Tuesday, October 3, 1978)

Paul "If you sit around musicians, quite often you'll hear them dreaming about a project that they would just love to get together, like (John) Bonham (Led Zeppelin) and Ringo drumming at once. It's a kind of dream that many have, but I just decided to try it instead of just talking about it. So I rang up a bunch of people, like John Bonham to play drums. I spoke with Keith Moon, actually, and he was going to do it but he died a week before. So we just waited to see who would turn up, who could make it and we thought, 'Well, if no one turns up, the Rockestra Orchestra will be just Wings.' I really was expecting no one to turn up. Setting it up, I had to go through all those, 'Oh, he'll never turn up,' or 'What if it doesn't turn out good?' A few people did say no when I asked them to come over. Jeff Beck said no and Clapton had flu . . . Well, that's what he said. Anyway, everyone else did turn up and it was an amazing day. I didn't tell them what I had in mind till the last minute, like a surprise. There was Pete Townshend, Dave Gilmour, Hank Marvin, Bonham and many others. Together we did two tracks, 'The Rockestra Theme' and 'So Glad To See You Here'.

"We filmed it as well. They turned up and we had it on film, like a candid movie, from behind a partition, and we'll probably use it for a future documentary. I said to everyone, 'Look, if there's anything you don't like, or there's anything you're unhappy about, we just won't do it.' But no one said that. I had written this piece and I was a bit worried in case it was a bit too simple because everyone there was a monster musician. There were five lead guitarists playing and it was hard to record. I thought, 'I'm not letting Dave Gilmour do a big solo, because he'll want to do one.' We did two tracks in the day and everyone seemed to enjoy it. We had a blast doing it. Pete Townshend said we should do it every Christmas . . ."

Back To The Egg is unfavourably reviewed in the *Daily Mail*, labelling Paul as a "jaded genius" . . . "Paul McCartney is Britain's most successful entertainer. Last year he earned over £26 million. And he has just received the ultimate show business accolade. He has been asked by EMI to star in a major film, about his own life. McCartney has been one of the most financially successful and artistically creative pop writers in the last 25 years. But today, millions of former McCartney admirers are asking just where has his talent gone? What is happening to his career? Is he suddenly losing interest? After hearing his latest, highly publicised album, *Back To The Egg*, the music critics and general public alike have been surprised by the sudden erosion of the poetry and melody that has been the hallmark of all his work. The vivid lyricism and subtle wit that he invented in pop classics like 'Yesterday' and 'Eleanor Rigby' are virtually absent from the new LP. Instead, the long-awaited record, with advance orders exceeding one million, is a disappointing collection of ersatz new wave, second-rate rock and roll, and a camp number that sounds like second-hand Manhattan Transfer. McCartney always used to be the innovator, but today he obediently follows trends instead of setting them. The most disturbing feature of his current work is the lack of real invention. The message that is clear from this, and indeed permeates all his work, is that McCartney will not take risks. He has lost the courage to gamble. Ironically, as McCartney gets older, he is writing for an increasingly younger audience. The generation that originally made him famous is bitterly disappointed with what he now has to offer . . ."

Saturday, June 30

The *Daily Mail* exclusively reveals that "Paul McCartney is to make a multi-million pound movie about his own life, and star in it himself. The former Beatle will appear in the film, *Band On The Run*, the title of his biggest-selling album, as an international rock star who escapes from the pressures by leaving his band and setting up an unknown group. Starring with McCartney in the film will be his wife, Linda, playing herself, and the members of Wings. Filming by EMI, McCartney's record label, will begin early next year. Willy Russell, the man who wrote the successful West End and Broadway musical about The Beatles, *John, Paul, George, Ringo . . . And Bert*, is writing the script. A show, ironically, McCartney refused to see. Although it is his first picture since he appeared with the other Beatles in frothy pop films like *A Hard Day's Night* and *Help!*, *Band On The Run* seems likely to establish him as a new name in the film world. Before McCartney starts filming, probably on location in England and Scotland, he will tour Britain with Wings."

Paul "We're working on a script of a kind of acting film. We play something near to what we are, something like a band on the run. It's very much like what we are. It's something we'll get into this autumn, I think. It'll be a laugh to do."

. . . The project fails to materialise.

JULY . . .

Reporter "Most people in the record business estimate that you still earn more than one million pounds a year from royalties on The Beatles' records. Would you agree with this figure?"

Ringo "Apple does. Apple certainly does, yes. Sometimes more, but things are so expensive these days. Have you seen the price of bread? I couldn't afford to live here in the UK, I tell you. No, but seriously, it depends on the sales really. Every year we sell a million records anyway. And, of course, with Capitol and EMI, they re-release everything, and the money goes to Apple. That's a problem, you know, Apple is still not sorted out. It's a problem in one way; it's not a problem in another. So we're trying to sort it out. We've been trying to sort it out for ten years. And it has taken all of those years for The Beatles to come to terms with one another. At the time, we were all angry with each other. Not because of the split-up, that was not a problem, that was a natural progression in our lives. But then we all got to court and we all acted like big girls. But we all wanted our own way and that's how people are. I'm sick of saying 'Paul took us to court,' but he did because he had his reasons. I can't put him down now for it. At the time, of course, I hated him. Well, I never really hated anybody, but I was really angry. Of course I don't hate him now. He's a fine lad and the last time I saw him, in fact, was when they had the last baby. I went into the hospital to visit Linda . . . John's baking bread and minding the child. Yes, I love that man. Last time I was in New York, I phoned him. The time before that we saw each other. Yet again it's the same. George is the same, still trying to make records, like we all are. So when it's comfortable, we just meet. That's it. Today, I'm in

London, but I'm not phoning Paul to say, 'Well, let's meet each other and say hello.' He's probably busy and so am I. Of course we all went through that amazing period of our lives. But it doesn't mean we have to live together forever."

Friday, September 21

New York reporter, Fred Wehner misleadingly writes "The Beatles are on the brink of a glittering one-night comeback, to help the Vietnamese Boat people. John, Paul, George and Ringo are said to be 'fully considering' a charity concert invitation from UN Secretary General, Kurt Waldheim. Earlier reports had ruled out a reunion of the Fab Four at New York's General Assembly Hall or Madison Square Garden. But UN spokesman, François Giulane said, 'It looks on. The Beatles are reacting positively. There are small problems still to be ironed out.' Since the group split in 1970, John Lennon has been the member most opposed to a Beatles reunion. And UN sources see his change of heart as a personal victory for Mr Waldheim . . ."

The man chiefly behind another reunion idea is again Sid Bernstein . . .

"I just couldn't reach The Beatles individually," Sid reveals, "so I figured this was a way to go over the heads of their managers, advisors, agents, and all the other people who wanted to have a say in what The Beatles did and didn't do. The only response I got was from John Lennon. He wanted more details on how the money was going to be raised and how the concert was going to be conducted. After I had given what I thought was enough information over the phone, John then asked me to put this information down in writing. So I typed it all out, and rushed over, with my secretary, to his apartment at the Dakota. I told the doorman that Mr Lennon was expecting this package and he said that he would get it to him straight away. But we never heard from him again. That was it."

Paul "George rang me up to talk about it. I said I'd told the guy that Wings were rehearsing and we didn't want to do anything yet, but that we'd try to do something sometime. And George said, 'I thought that if you were doing something maybe we'll get together and do something, or whatever.' So that was just left. Then, I got a letter from Kurt Waldheim, the UN Secretary General, when he was in London, saying that the guy who approached us hadn't been authorised to do so. Kurt suggested in his letter that I do a concert simply as Paul McCartney & Wings. The next thing I knew, it was all in the newspapers as a Beatles reunion. The whole thing was quite unbelievable. But it would obviously be a great idea to do something, particularly in Cambodia now."

Ringo "They think that I can just pick up the drums and drive out to Sheffield or somewhere and play. It would take us months to get an act together if we wanted to. Anyway, I personally don't want us to get together . . . They can get together, but I'm not getting together. If there's any chance of us getting together, we'll tell you, not somebody from outside. It's just these people who like to make themselves famous. And it's easy to do, you've just got to mention The Beatles."

Paul "None of us really wanted to do the show, really, because The Beatles are over and finished with. So there was absolutely no chance of it happening. It would have been the kind of thing that would have been impossible to organise even if we had all wanted to do it. To tell you the truth, I never think in terms of The Beatles because that was ten years ago and I'd be living in the past if I did. So I tend not to think about it unless someone asks me or something like Eric's wedding just happens. But I'd still be prepared to do a show with Wings for the Vietnamese Boat People or the International Year Of The Child. The trouble is in finding a promoter who is prepared to give up a free evening to put it on."

Wednesday, September 26

Philip Finn, *Daily Express* "The Fab Four are back together again. They are suing the *Beatlemania* exploiters to the tune of £30 million. John, Paul, George and Ringo tonight began a court action in Los Angeles to collect the staggering amount. Although The Beatles broke up almost ten years ago, the group's legend is doing incredible business in America. The main target of the action is a series of shows called *Beatlemania*, which have been drawing capacity audiences from Los Angeles to New York. *Beatlemania*, featuring Fab Four lookalikes, is due to descend on London next month . . ."

George "The *Beatlemania* stage play was on Broadway and everywhere, it became a free-for-all. People were just thinking that The Beatles were like public domain, like Mozart or something and that's what has been happening to us. With *Beatlemania*, we had to sue them and the funny thing is that we were going to settle with them out of court for a million dollars and they refused or they had an insurance company who refused to pay the million dollars. So it went to court and the judge awarded us 11 million dollars! We settled with them for some figure below that. We did that to say, 'Look, you can't just go round pilfering The Beatles' material.' "

Thursday, October 18
Even with the lawsuits now starting to fly about, the West End musical extravaganza, *Beatlemania,* starring four John, Paul, George and Ringo lookalikes, still opens in London at the Astoria Theatre . . .

Paul "I think it's a bit weird when somebody is going around impersonating you while you're still alive. At least you feel that somehow they should have asked us, or you should have a say in it. But then again, I've been coping with weirdness for years."

Daily Mirror "John, Paul, George and Ringo are together again, and looking just like they did in the good old days. But hang on a minute . . . Is it really them? Didn't Paul McCartney play guitar left-handed? Yes, you've guessed it. They just look like the lads from Liverpool except that the protégés are not from these shores. The man behind it all is American rock impresario, Steve Leber . . ."

Steve Leber "I spent a month searching for English Beatles and I just couldn't find any. I auditioned 2,000 would-be Beatles. So I returned to America and after scouring Hackensack to Miami, I came up with some real life photo fits. This is no reflection on British musicians. I just think that the youth of America are more Beatles-orientated. Paul's double is a 22-year-old from Tucson, Arizona, called Tony Kishman, but unfortunately, he can't play bass left-handed. Mike Palaiskis, from Hackensack, New Jersey, does a good impersonation of John Lennon. Jimmy Poe, a guitarist from Miami, Florida, is George Harrison and Ringo is played by a 28-year-old lightbulb seller, Louis Calucei, of New York's Bronx district."

The long-time British bedroom comedy farce actor, Brian Rix, stages the lawsuit-threatened production . . .

Brian Rix "The show will go on in London in spite of action by The Beatles, who are against people cashing in on their image. We have been in touch with our lawyers and we are happy that we will be able to go ahead. Providing we do nothing to hurt their image or damage their reputations, we have nothing to fear. We are paying them the greatest compliment anyone can imagine."

But Mr Bert Fields, the man who has brought the landmark case to Los Angeles's courts for Apple Corps, says, "It's like putting a Coca Cola label on your own drink and claiming that it is a tribute to Coca Cola. They are trying to do something very similar."

George agrees, "It's a bit of a liberty isn't it? These people should think of original ways of making money, instead of riding on our success. The four new Beatles? They should use their own talents, if they've got any, instead of using ours. I hear it's not even a good show. As for Brian Rix, he probably didn't even like The Beatles in the first place. He should know better. What does he think we are, another farce?"

Ringo "We don't get anything from any of those shows, or anything from one of those wigs. But people seem to like imitations."

Further problems befall the London version of *Beatlemania* when the actors' union Equity begins protesting about the show. "We now realise that American actors are portraying The Beatles and their accents," a spokesman for Equity remarks. "This work could and should be undertaken by members of the British Equity."

Thursday, November 20

The *Evening News* show business correspondent reports, "Predicting Beatles reunions is a dangerous game to play, but it is beginning to look more and more as though John, Paul, George and Ringo will all be playing on the same stage at the Hammersmith Odeon on December 29. The occasion is a concert in aid of the people of Kampuchea and the official line-up so far is Wings, Elvis Costello, Dave Edmunds' Rockpile and Billy Connolly. McCartney has made no secret of his wish to see the Seventies out with his erstwhile mates and, I understand, approaches have been made to George, Ringo and John. The Beatles would not open themselves to possible criticism by playing alone on stage so instead, they will appear as part of a huge superstar jam session. I understand that George and Ringo have provisionally agreed to play the show, unless they are too busy. And now even John Lennon is considering returning to London from New York to step out of the mist and play a few chords. Though tickets for the concerts were sold out within minutes, the whole event is being videotaped and will almost certainly be televised."

Paul, at the time of these rumours, "I've provisionally agreed to play a show with Wings at the end of December to raise money for the United Nations. If we're lucky, and if he'd like to do it, there may be a chance that George will play with us. But I've still got to ring him up. If Ringo is in town when we are playing places and feels like doing it, then there is always the chance he'll play, but I wouldn't come to any show expecting it. I like to keep quiet about it because if anyone is going to be there, the last thing we need is a load

Paul and Linda in January 1984, pictured on their farm at Peasemarsh near Rhye in Sussex. *(Rex Features)*

Paul on stage with Wings during the American leg of their world tour in 1976. *(Hulton-Deutsch Collection/Corbis)*

John celebrates New Year's Eve 1976 at the Shun Lee Dynasty restaurant in New York with Yoko and friends. *(Pictorial Press)*

The Rutles – Ron Nasty, Dirk McQuickley, Stig O'Hara and Barry Wom, alias Neil Innes, Eric Idle, Rikki Fataar and Ollie Halsall – in March, 1978. *(Rex)*

George with his good friend Eric Idle, holidaying together after the competition of the film *The Life Of Brian*, in which George had a small part. *(Rex)*

Paul on stage with Denny Laine during Wings' last ever performance at The Concert For Kampuchea, Hammersmith Odeon, London, December 29, 1979. *(Pictorial Press)*

John and Yoko outside the Hit Factory in New York, August 4, 1980. *(Corbis)*

John, wearing his Quarry Bank High School tie, and Yoko in November 1980. *(Corbis)*

John and Yoko listen to a playback of songs from *Double Fantasy* inside the Hit Factory, New York, November 1980. *(Corbis)*

They came in their thousands...

America stops to mourn John Lennon

by Fred Wehner in New York

AMERICA stopped for 10 minutes yesterday.

It was the largest tribute ever afforded a dead hero —something the Americans had not done for their beloved John F Kennedy, perhaps more than anyone ever did for a king.

Such was the impact of John Lennon's death.

In Central Park, they stood, heads bowed, some with lighted candles, most wiping away the tears.

It was a massive tribute to the man who, with his music and his thoughts, became a Messiah to a whole generation.

In the streets of New York too there was silence. Traffic halted and people stopped in their tracks to offer their thoughts, just as Lennon's widow had asked.

And then, when the silence ended, the crowds chanted Beatles phrases from their best known songs. And they waved their hands in the air in unison, displaying the wartime victory sign that had been adopted by the 1960s peace movement.

But near freezing temperatures kept thousands

Crowds at St George's Plateau yesterday pay their final tribute.

Pictures by Derek Wright and Geoff Roberts

15 DEC 1980

The silent vigil

Coverage of the St. Georges Hall Memorial Service for John in the *Liverpool Echo* (above) and the crowds that gathered in New York's Central Park (below). Both events were held on December 14 1980. *(Liverpool Echo/Rex)*

Ringo with future wife Barara Bach on the set of *Caveman* in 1980. *(Rex)*

Paul with George Martin at AIR Studios, London, in 1984, recording tracks for *Give My Regards To Broad Street*. *(Rex)*

George, suitably dressed in Fifties fashion, with Carl Perkins on the set of the TV show *Blue Suede Shoes*, October 21, 1985. *(Rex)*

George accepting a *London Evening Standard* film award from the Duchess of Kent at the Savoy Hotel, January 26, 1986. On George's right is Dennis O'Brien, his former partner in HandMade Films. *(Rex)*

George with Madonna at the press conference they convened to dispel rumours of trouble on the set of *Shanghai Surprise*, at the Kensington Gardens Hotel, March 5, 1986. *(Rex)*

Paul with artist Peter Blake at the party at Abbey Road Studios to celebrate the 20th anniversary of the release of *Sgt Pepper's Lonely Hearts Club Band*, June 1, 1987. Blake designed the original sleeve. *(Rex)*

of people saying that this is a big, special reunion. I've never ruled out the possibility of The Beatles playing together for a show. I've always said, 'Yeah, if everyone said we really want to do this, and the four of us were really keen to do it, then yes.' I've no idea if John wants to do anything again. I haven't spoken to him for quite a while because he's been keeping himself quiet. But, if you think about it, there's a fella whose father left home when he was a little kid, who lived with his aunt and his uncle. Then his uncle died, then his mother remarried and used to come to visit him but lived with another man. And while she was coming to visit him one night, when he was 16, she got knocked down by a car and killed. So that guy has grown up in a world where basically he's never had any family. He then got married to Cynthia, but he was in the middle of all the Sixties dope and everything and he never really got with that family. And now he's married again to Yoko, who, for him, is the love of his life. He believes he's found it and they now have a son. And I think he's just taking every second that's left to him to enjoy that, and there's nothing wrong with that."

John's disappearance from the public gaze continues to enthral the world's press. America show business reporter John King writes this month . . .

"For nearly five years (*sic*), John Lennon has lived the life of a recluse," King states. "He has no recording contract, does no work of any kind and simply spends his days sitting around his New York flat or his Catskill Mountain farm, playing with his four-year-old son, Sean. Most days, he bakes a loaf of bread for his family. Occasionally, he writes or paints a little. He has taught himself to speak fluent Japanese and, several times, he has booked recording studios to make records, which he takes home and plays to Yoko, and Yoko alone. He could, of course, command a fortune if he was to desire a comeback. One top record company executive suggested to me that an advance of $20 million would not be unrealistic. But money no longer has any real meaning to John or to any of the other Beatles. Even without doing any work whatsoever, it is estimated that John is currently picking up more than £5 million a year in assorted royalties on the songs he wrote and the records he made both alone and with The Beatles. The money comes from all sorts of different directions. John and Paul were recently earning approximately $40,000 a week between them for the use of their songs in the three simultaneous American stage productions of a show called *Beatlemania*. Every one of their records is still available, still selling steadily. In Britain alone, 30,000 Beatles albums are still sold every month, from which The Beatles themselves share round about $15,000 of the profit. Yet, with so much money pouring in from so many different sources, it has proved difficult to keep tabs on exactly what is going where, and occasionally, John has lost many millions of pounds over the years to lawyers, accountants and sharp businessmen."

NOVEMBER
Paul, Linda and Wings return to live performances after a gap of three years. He explains how their time was spent . . .

"We were doing other things like making albums," **Paul** explains. "We took about a year off because Linda was having a baby, so rather than leap around on tour, we took a year out. Then we were making an album with the new members so that they didn't have to come on stage and play parts that others had played. Some of the songs (in concert now) they copy other people's parts but a lot of what we do now is them on the record."

Friday, November 23
The UK tour begins with another nostalgic homecoming concert, a dress rehearsal show in Liverpool . . .

Syndicated news report "Paul McCartney was back in his home city, Liverpool, to launch his first nationwide tour for four years. The ex-Beatle and his group Wings began with a curtain-raiser at the city's Royal Court Theatre for 600 pupils from his old school. Paul wanted to play for youngsters who could not get a ticket for the three shows the group is doing at the theatre. Tickets were sold out within hours of going on sale and were changing hands at up to £100 on the black market, twenty times their face value. The boys, from Paul's old school, the Liverpool Institute, were joined by 300 girls from a nearby school and hundreds of the city's underprivileged children."

UK newspaper columnist, James Johnson "Paul McCartney celebrated a triumphant return to Liverpool with a boisterous family party. Underlining his position as the happy family man of rock music, the ex-Beatle invited nearly seventy relatives to a show and then to, what he described as, 'a traditional family knees-up'."

Paul "My father came from a family of seven children. I suppose you could say they all bred like rabbits. That means there's quite a few of the McCartney clan about."

James Johnson "The collection of aunts, uncles and cousins, loudly welcomed back their most famous relation into the early hours. There was even singing in the traditional vein of 'Bye, Bye Blackbird' and 'I'm Getting Married In The Morning'. Paul chatted enthusiastically to elderly relatives while his wife, Linda, took family photographs. Towards the close, the atmosphere suggested a Merseyside public bar on a night when Liverpool had won the cup. Said Paul's cousin, Kathy, 'Paul's always been close to his family and tries to see everybody whenever he comes home.' McCartney and his group held the party during a series of Liverpool concerts that have successfully launched the first British tour by Wings for four years. In Liverpool, tickets were changing hands for £100. At the Royal Court, the audience naturally squealed with delight when he launched into old Beatles numbers like 'Yesterday', 'The Fool On The Hill' and 'Let It Be' . . ."

Paul "For a long time after I started this group, I was embarrassed to do Beatles songs because it seemed like a cop-out. But that's long gone, now. I wrote the songs after all and everybody has been saying to me, 'Why not do them?' "

James Johnson concludes, "During the concerts, Paul played straightforward rock'n'roll with as much vigour as his romantic ballads . . . Meanwhile, in London, six-deep queues stretching for more than 300 yards formed outside Wembley when the box office opened."

Michael Nally of the *Observer* newspaper reports "Middle-aged Merseyside pop fans are celebrating the twenty-first anniversary of the Liverpool debut of a briefly noted teenage duo, The Nurk Twins, who have achieved more lasting fame as Lennon and McCartney of The Beatles. Happily for the fans, Paul McCartney, now 37, is in the city again to join in the celebrations and sing. With his band Wings, he opened a national tour tonight after a lively dress rehearsal on Friday in front of a specially invited audience from his old school, the Liverpool Institute, where he first teamed up with John Lennon. A flourishing black market trade in tickets for the concert at the Royal Court Theatre continued until the doors opened. In pubs on Lime Street, just round the corner from the theatre, touts were asking between £40 and £100 for tickets, which cost £4 at the box office last week. A barman said, 'I know somebody who can do you two for £150, but you'll have to skate. He's due at a card school and he might need the money.' Two schoolgirls congratulated themselves on paying only £20 each for their tickets. They shrugged off an invitation from a taxi driver to name their price. One said, 'I've waited years for this. He's lovely, like mam said, and the music's great.' McCartney, his wife, Linda, and the other members of the group relaxed before the concert with relatives and friends, leaving last minute arrangements to a press agent . . ."

Daily Telegraph "Taxi drivers in Liverpool took their vehicles off the road for three hours last night. The trouble started outside the Royal Court Theatre as the audience was leaving a concert given by ex-Beatle Paul McCartney's Wings band. One driver was arrested and charged with obstruction."

While back in the United States on **Wednesday, November 28**, further problems befall Ringo when his rented house in the Hollywood Hills goes up in flames. He is at home when the fire begins . . .

Ringo "Suddenly I saw a great belch of smoke through the window. When I got outside, I saw the whole roof was going up. I managed to bring out quite a few things but a lot of irreplaceable stuff from the old days was destroyed. The attic where I stored most of my Beatles mementoes, including gold discs awarded to the group, was totally wrecked."

Monday, December 17
Before the final performance in the current Wings concert tour, **Paul** is interviewed backstage in Scotland by Radio Clyde, where he talks about the tour so far . . .

"The tour is smashing. We started out in Liverpool, did Manchester, we went down south to the South East, London and then Birmingham, and then Newcastle. Down south the audiences tend to be a bit quieter. Nothing wrong with that but up north, they are a bit wilder!"

Paul also announces the immediate future for the group . . .

"We finish tonight here in Glasgow," he says, "and then we've got time off for Christmas and New Year. In between Christmas and New Year we are doing one concert in London, which is for the Cambodia, Kampuchea people. We're doing something for those refugees, a lot of groups are getting together to do these concerts, and then, about the second week in January, we've got a big Japanese tour coming up. So, we go to Japan, spend three weeks out there and there's no plans after that. Maybe when we get back from that, we're going to write or record something and we're going to have to leave time. We've got no plans after February."

Tuesday, December 25
. . . Christmas Day with the Lennons . . .

From her £100,000 bungalow in Poole, Dorset, John's Aunt Mimi recalls another phone conversation, "John rang up and announced, 'Hi, it's Father Christmas here.' He's the same old jokey John. He really seems much more settled and happy now than he used to be. He'll be doing something; just you wait and see. Something that will surprise everyone. I only hope he doesn't go poncing about on stage any more. He's nearly 40 now and if he went back on stage, he'd be doing exactly what he was doing when he was 19. You must go on. When he phones now, he wants to talk about Sean and about when he was a little boy himself. When he phoned the other night, he was talking about the time when I wrapped him in a blanket because it was cold and I brought him downstairs. He can't have been more than five then. He just amazes me with the things he remembers."

Patrick Walker, astrologer for the *Evening News* "I saw John at Christmas and he was fantastic, very relaxed and joking that he was the highest paid house-husband in the world. For John, the ego trip is over. He's been to hell and back. He's been searching for something and he thought he would find it in meditation or by going to India and by gurus and astrology and drugs, or whatever it was. But now he is back. For me, he is exactly the same as he started and has found himself again."

Friday, December 28

The *Evening Standard*'s show business correspondent reports, "Whether the reclusive John Lennon shows up in Hammersmith tomorrow night or not, fans of the bespectacled former Beatle can take heart. I hear from New York that he has just started work on a new album, his first for four years and a complete reversal of his protestations some time ago that he had retired for good. The sessions in a downtown Manhattan recording studio have been shrouded in secrecy. John and Yoko Ono, who manage to live in seclusion with their children (*sic*) in several different apartments in the exclusive Dakota building, arrive in separate cars under heavy disguises. However, the results should apparently be released late next year and secrecy is only typical of Lennon's recent behaviour. He was recently spotted walking down one of New York's avenues by a leading British news waver who flung himself uncharacteristically at the ageing Liverpudlian's feet. 'Out of my way,' snarled Lennon and walked on."

Saturday, December 29
As expected, Wings perform at the Concert For Kampuchea charity show at the Hammersmith Odeon in London. Although not billed as such, it will turn out to be the group's very last performance together . . .

Philip Norman, the *Sunday Times* "The endlessly imminent rebirth of The Beatles failed to take place as expected at the Odeon, Hammersmith. It was McCartney's agreement to play on the final night that provoked rumours about a Beatles reunion. It was widely believed that the sorrow of Kampuchea would do what no multi-million pound offer has yet accomplished, put McCartney, John Lennon, George and Ringo Starr on the stage together for the first time in 11 years (*sic*) . . ."

James Johnson, *Evening Standard* "In the end, The Beatles were not especially missed at the Hammersmith Odeon on Saturday. The rumours in circulation concerning a reunion that surrounded the last of three concerts in aid of Kampuchea seemed largely based on hopeful but slightly misplaced nostalgia. If The Beatles had turned up, it is hard to imagine what they could do after all these years, apart from shake hands. Indeed, young and dedicated rock aficionados might wonder who needs The Beatles when Elvis Costello is available. As it turned out, Paul McCartney staged a spectacular climax with the giant 24-piece Rockestra he first put together on the last Wings album. The McCartneys, a dishevelled Pete Townshend, Robert Plant and a score of others bounded noisily through the 'Rockestra Theme', 'Lucille' and 'Let It Be'. Earlier, Wings had played through most of the show they had performed on their recent tour, proving once again how they can adapt almost any form of contemporary music for the McCartney style . . ."

Paul "We had a disastrous concert for Kampuchea. It actually wasn't too bad but we thought it was dreadful . . . At the time, we hated it so much, it just put us off being in a band for a couple of years and this led to the break-up of Wings."

Linda "I think Paul was very frustrated. He wanted it to work with Wings, but we just picked the wrong people. He needed the best to work with, but he had to carry almost all the weight."

Denny Laine "Paul is too easy-going at times. He allows things to ramble along and he doesn't expect anything more than good musicianship and dedication. But I expected a great deal more and as a result, I have become the hatchet man when the musicians have not been giving enough."

With his concert appearances for this year and, indeed, the decade concluded, **Paul** reflects on the UK tour . . . "I always thought that I would be giving up a lot sooner," he reveals. "But I don't seem to have done. The motivation is simply that I enjoy it. I also thought that I would have slowed down a bit and played at a more sensible pace for my age group but that doesn't seem to have happened either. When I was 18 years old, I thought that 25 was about as far as you could go."

Linda "I'd love him to give up touring altogether. But it's a bit like being married to a husband who is mad about golf. You might be able to talk him into giving up golf, and stay at home with you and the children but you'd be taking away a part of him. And marriage should be a give-and-take thing; you should each share in the things your partner wants to do. But, in our case, it's more than just the fact that we have to go away from home that I don't like. It's also about me playing in the band. I mean, if you had a scale of musicians, Paul would be at the very top and I'd be right at the very bottom."

Paul "If we didn't tour, my whole life would be just at home with the animals, Linda and the kids. That would be very nice, but I think everyone likes to feel they have something other than just their home. I still really don't know why I want to go out and play concerts. I haven't got a real answer. But we have just had a few months off and now we feel that we have got a new band and we really want to get out with that new band and play."

Wednesday, January 16

Upon Wings' arrival in Tokyo, Japan for an eleven-date concert tour, **Paul** is arrested at Tokyo's Narita Airport after customs men find half a pound of marijuana in his suitcase. The first concert on the tour was due to take place at Tokyo's Endokan Theatre on January 21 . . .

Daily Mirror "The rock star was arrested and handcuffed when he arrived at Tokyo Airport. If convicted he could face a five-year sentence, but more likely banishment from Japan. McCartney's troubles started as he was passing through airport customs with his wife and four children. An official stopped him and searched his luggage. His arrest was seen by millions of Japanese television viewers. Wings' 11-date tour is due to start next Monday. One hundred thousand seats have been sold. But now all the concerts will almost certainly be cancelled."

Miss Haruko Minakanoi, Wings' Japanese publicist, "Paul was coming through customs when officials stopped him and searched his luggage. In his suitcase they found 220 grams of marijuana. He was detained but Linda and the band were allowed to go."

Laurence Juber, Wings "After a 14-hour flight with the family, they had to wait on the plane for three hours for Paul's visa to be validated. Then they had to wait in line to go through customs like everyone else. There was no preferential treatment. I was right behind Paul and the customs man was as totally surprised as anyone at what he found. He looked at it hoping it was tea. Paul didn't think that they'd make it public."

Paul "We had gone to Tokyo from America and I had the choice of throwing it away or just being silly and packing it in my suitcase in the States. But, for some reason, I didn't register that it wasn't so easy to go into Japan with it. In New York, where I had been staying, the attitude is casual. The atmosphere in America suggests to me the prohibition years when alcohol was driven underground. Shortly before I left, President Carter had been asked what his attitude was about cannabis and I think he replied that it ought to be decriminalised and made a misdemeanour. That affected me too. So I just put a bag of the stuff in my suitcase without thinking.

"I'd just had 14 hours on the plane and then the customs men went through all the bags at Narita Airport and there, lying right on top of the last one, was this packet of grass, more than I could have got through in months. I didn't even try and hide the stuff. When they found it, I thought, 'Fair cop, nice nick.' The customs man held it up and I think he was more embarrassed than me and I was blushing. They have different cultures over there. I last went there 14 years ago with The Beatles and that's a long time ago. I didn't realise that Japan's drug laws are very strict and that is what I told the Japanese officials. It was a stupid goof."

Linda "People certainly were different out there. They took it so very seriously. We had a good lawyer who was on the case and we contacted the British consul. It seems to me that as soon as they get someone like Paul they make a field day of it. Paul was put in some kind of detention place and I was not allowed to see him at first."

But Denny Laine is not happy about the incident . . .

"I was bitter and resentful when our tour of Japan turned into a fiasco because Paul was caught with marijuana in his luggage. I didn't go to Japan to sit in a hotel or for a publicity stunt," Laine admits. "It was then that I realised how vulnerable Wings were. The tour was cancelled and that was the total end for me. I had worked so hard towards the tour and I didn't get paid. Japan made up my mind for me to do other things, because I didn't want to spend the rest of the year sitting around twiddling my thumbs. Paul was put in jail for ten days and I jumped on a plane and left."

But for **Paul**, "On the first night, after I was taken in handcuffs to the narcotics detention centre, the vice-consul visited me and I thought, 'Fantastic, good old consul, he is going to get me out.' I thought that I would be on the first plane out of the country but he just sat down and said, 'Well, Paul, it could be eight years, you know.' That was quite frightening. I thought, 'Well, this time they're going to lock you away.' Then they began interrogating me. At first, I thought it was barbaric. They put handcuffs on me twice a day when I went to see the interrogator. There seemed to be a different lot every day. I made a confession on the night I was arrested and apologised for breaking Japanese law but still they wanted to know everything about everything."

Paul is thrown in a jail, where he will stay for ten nights . . .

Paul "It was hell, but I only remember the good bits, like a bad holiday. My arrest was on every bloody TV set. When they hustled me into jail, I was dazed, not drunk. And then, for three days, I virtually couldn't sleep. I had a song of Dave Edmunds going round and round my head and all I could think of was how I had dropped Linda and the kids right in it. Then there was the culture shock. I eat toast and eggs and corn flakes for breakfast. But next morning, there it was, seaweed and onion soup . . . My days started at six o'clock in the morning. The guards woke me up and I had to roll up my bedding, a thin mattress on the floor of my unheated cell. Then I had to clean and wipe my cell with a wet cloth. I washed myself in the water from the cistern from the flush toilet in my cell. I was allowed one bath a week. After breakfast, at ten o'clock, I got thirty minutes of exercise with the other prisoners, during which I could smoke. Lunch at noon was bread and jam and Japanese tea and the afternoon was usually for interrogation. I returned to my cell at five where I had rice and soup. The lights were turned off at eight.

"Everyone knows that you don't bring grass into Japan, so some people assume I was arrogant. I wasn't. I was just being dumb. I had got some good grass in America and I was loath to flush it down the toilet and I was silly enough to think that I might get past the customs men. I was daft! Looking back, you could say why didn't I pay someone? Then they would have got busted. I didn't want anyone else to take the rap. It was dumb, that's all. We all make mistakes and that was one of mine. The joke of the matter is they haven't changed my opinions on the marijuana thing at all, because they didn't make any attempt to rehabilitate me. They didn't, of course, in jail. They lock you in a box and hope the experience will be so horrible you won't do it again. I was held in jail for nine days and the other prisoners all knew who I was and asked me to sing. I didn't have any instruments but the world's press would have loved to have had cameras rolling as I was doing drums with hands. Well, I had seen *The Bridge On The River Kwai* and I knew what you had to do when you were a prisoner of war. You had to sit cross-legged and be inspected by 12 guards who looked like they had come from a submarine. You had to laugh a lot and keep cheery and keep yourself up because that's all you had . . . After three days, I got my humour back, and began tapping on the cell walls and communicating with the other prisoners. We talked pidgin English. I had no papers so I made my own calendar. I picked bits of plaster from the cell walls and made a kind of abacus to keep a record of the days. After a week, they asked me if I wanted a bath and enquired whether I would like it privately or with others. I thought that to go to the prison bathhouse was the nearest I'd get that trip to being a tourist so I went. I ended up sharing a bath with a man who was in for murder. All the guards stood at the door grinning and we had a McCartney sing-a-long with the prisoners and the fans outside.

"When I was in jail, I really got scared when I was told that the maximum sentence on conviction of drugs possession was seven years. I feared missing seven years' worth of my kids growing up. I had visions of Linda and the kids getting a house and living in Japan. I was sweating all the time for the first few days, worrying about what might happen."

Linda tells *Playboy* magazine "The kids and I were in a Japanese hotel, not knowing what was going to happen. I was so frightened for Paul; I can't even describe it. Your imagination takes off. I didn't know what they would be doing to him and for what? A bit of nothing. Marijuana isn't like bombs or murder of the Mafia. I don't think pot is a sin, but I didn't want us to be a martyr for it."

Tuesday, January 22
Linda leaves her £500-a-night penthouse suite at the Okura Hotel and visits Paul in the bare, yellow visitors' room of the Metropolitan Police Jail . . .

Paul "When she came visiting, she was so warm and I was so cold."

Linda "Paul is in good spirits. He's still got his sense of humour and he cracked a few jokes. I found myself laughing, which I haven't been doing much in the last few days. The really hard part about all this is being separated from Paul. We've spent every single day with each other since we've been together, which is ten years now . . . He hasn't been allowed a guitar or a tape recorder so I don't think he'll be writing any songs. He'd like to write his autobiography but he is not even allowed pencil and paper. He isn't allowed any visitors except by special permission of the examining magistrate, so I was grateful for the chance to see him. I made him a cheese sandwich and the rest of the time he's been eating Japanese food. He wants to do it like everyone else."

On **Friday, January 25**, Paul is released from jail . . .

Paul "When I was released, it was a sad parting scene. I was shaking hands with all the prisoners through the letter boxes of their cells."

Evening News "Paul McCartney was today deported from Japan, ten days after being arrested for possessing marijuana. The Tokyo prosecutor's office has dropped its investigation and the former Beatle was taken to the city's Narita Airport and put on the 12.30pm flight for Paris. He was smiling and gave the thumbs up sign to crowds of teenage girls as he was taken from jail. 'I'm okay,' he told reporters at the airport. He said life in jail 'wasn't too bad' and added that the 'Japanese fans are just so great. I want to come back again if I'm allowed.' He is expected to arrive in London tomorrow morning with his wife Linda and four children. 'Linda is delighted,' said a spokesman. 'She left her hotel in such a hurry she didn't even pack.' The prosecutor's office decided to drop its investigation because McCartney said he brought in marijuana purely for his own use, an official said. He said that since McCartney did not intend to sell the drug during his stay in Japan, and was scheduled to stay for only a short time, it was decided he should be released. 'He's been punished enough,' said an official. Paul will get a big welcome when he returns home, according to his brother, singer Mike McGear. His tightly knit relatives are planning to push the boat out with a party to celebrate his freedom."

Mike (McCartney) McGear, speaking from his home in Liverpool, "This is excellent news about our kid. It is what we have all been waiting for. I'll be on the phone straight away. Everyone was very worried about the way he was treated. There will be some celebrations in Liverpool tonight. Paul is a very resilient person and I would imagine he stood up to the ordeal very well. But everyone has had a rough time, particularly Linda and the kids."

During a stopover in Holland, Paul naturally faces interrogation from the Dutch press. To gathering reporters, **Paul** remarks . . .

"All of us are on drugs, cigarettes, alcohol, women, and in the middle, there is marijuana. Society thinks alcohol is terrific, yet it kills. Cigarettes can kill. They are worse than marijuana. It is just not true that marijuana can kill. What about all the little old ladies on Valium? Think of aspirin's danger to the stomach. But I do not intend to start preaching again for marijuana to be legalised. I don't care that much about it, but I do believe that an unbiased, thorough medical report is needed. I can take marijuana or leave it. It's not as though I was craving for it on the floor in prison. I spent my time making a mental list of all those drugs, which are legal but dangerous. Marijuana is like homosexuality, you don't have to like it, but if it's not doing any harm, what does it matter?"

While to another journalist, Paul shows that he is now clearly agitated . . .

Reporter "What happened, Paul?"

Paul "What happened? I was in jail for ten days. Didn't you hear? It was on the news."

Reporter "How did you get out?"

Paul "How did I get out? Walking, on foot."

Reporter "What did the authorities do?"

Paul "They dropped the charges."

Reporter "Why?"

Paul "Well, why don't you ask them?"

Reporter "Don't you know?"

Paul "It was because it was considered . . . I don't know! I don't know! They just told me today that I could get out, you know."

Reporter "Do you have any idea of the consequences of the whole thing?"

Paul "How do you mean?"

Reporter "Well, financially?"

Paul "Well yeah, it's a bit of a drag, financially."

Reporter "Do you think you'll ever go back to Japan?"

Paul "I don't know. I don't know."

Reporter "Do you want to?"

Paul "Maybe. I'm not sure."

Reporter "There must be a lot of disappointed fans over there?"

Paul "True, but I'm disappointed, too. So that makes two of us."

Reporter "Were you aware that the drug laws were so strong there?"

Paul "No, I didn't realise that the laws were so strong over there, you know. I thought it was more like America."

Reporter "Do you always take drugs abroad?"

Paul "No, do you?"

Reporter "Isn't it usual that somebody else carries drugs for you into the country?"

Paul "No. Do you do that?"

Reporter "No, but that's what I heard."

Paul "No, no, you hear a lot of things in newspapers that aren't true, and on television."

Reporter "How was your treatment in Japan?"

Paul "It was okay. It was not bad. It was all right, but it was a drag being in there, for such a thing as this. It's a very stiff law, you know. These days, in some countries, it's not thought of as quite so serious as the Japanese think of it. But it's their law; it's the way you have to take it. But I'm glad to be out, anyway."

Reporter "Last question, what are you going to do now?"

Paul "Sleep, okay, and go home."

Back home . . .

Paul "I wanted to write it down (his time in jail), just for the record, because I know how I am. I forget things very easily. I haven't got the world's greatest memory. Anyway, I wrote it all down immediately I got home. I thought, 'God, this is like writing an essay for school. I can't do it, I'm frightened of the piece of paper.' But because I knew I had to write it down to remember the incident, I forced myself to write it. In the end, I had written 20,000 words . . . I wrote it in case anybody ever asked, 'What was that like?' But really, I did it for my children. I thought, 'One day, when they're all older and my son is a great big 30-year-old, he'll say, "Dad, what about that Japanese thing?" ' Then I'll be able to say, 'There you are. Read that.' I've just got one copy at home, it's called *Japanese Jailbird* . . . If I think hard, I can remember that the first thing I expected was rape. That was my big fear. So I slept with my back to the wall. I didn't know what was going to happen. I slept for a week in the green suit I was arrested in. I didn't even know you could ask for fresh clothes."

Ringo "After Paul was busted for carrying pot in Tokyo, I found I didn't even have his new phone number so I just sent flowers and a packet of candy."

Sunday, February 3
Eager to put the misery of Paul's Tokyo jail exploits behind her, Linda describes her typical happy family life and general day-to-day activities to the UK columnist Glenn Gale . . .

"We live in a two-bedroom house so as soon as our son James, who is two, starts calling, 'Mummy, Mummy,' around seven every morning, he wakes everyone up," Linda reveals. "Being his mother, I like to be the first to greet him, so I get up. I take him downstairs and start getting breakfast early. If Paul isn't working, he gets up at the same time as us and joins the kids. We're all vegetarians, so breakfast is eggs laid by our own hens, home-grown tomatoes fried, vegetarian sausages, cereals and whole-wheat bread. During the bread strike, Paul baked the most beautiful bread. He's an excellent father, very involved and very protective towards them. Quite often, Paul comes with me when I drive the girls to school. Mary and the kids travel everywhere with us. When we were playing up north during the last British tour, we all stayed at Paul's dad's house in Liverpool. And when we were playing down south, Paul and I commuted from home for each concert, which, in the case of the Wembley gigs, meant a two-and-a-half-hour car journey before and after each concert, with Paul driving. Mary and Stella go to a local primary school and Heather attends a nearby art school. I drive a Mini because being American, I'm used to wide roads, so with a small car, I've no fears about scraping it.

"I buy most of the kids' clothes at Mothercare. I look at their catalogue or go into the shop and pick out things that are made from natural fibres. I feel most comfortable in jeans and T-shirt. I don't really spend that much. Paul pays all the bills. Because we have a big breakfast, and a big dinner about six in the evening, we don't have lunch. So about that time, I'm doing jobs around the house. Paul never helps me. He likes tidiness but is not too tidy himself. If I'm working or going out, I have a woman who comes in to do the cleaning. But I always do the cooking, because I enjoy it. I cook for six every day! For dinner, I usually cook things like quiche Lorraine, without the bacon. Paul's favourite soups are pea soup or cream of tomato soup made from home-grown tomatoes and onions. If I'm lucky during the day, I go for a ride on my Appaloosa stallion called Lucky Spot. He's got a lovely temperament. Horse riding is a marvellous form of exercise, both physically and spiritually. One other interest Paul and I share closely is football. We rarely get to see matches but we always watch it on television. Paul is a great Liverpool fan but I support Liverpool and Everton. We don't socialise that much but I think that's also partly because I'm too lazy. There's so much I'd like to do, especially in the photographic field, but I'm loath to leave the life I lead in this country unless I absolutely have to. I get various offers to take photographs and sometimes I might find one particularly attractive. But when it comes down to it, I just can't bring myself to leave the kids and go and take pictures. So I stay at home and take pictures of them instead. Most of the evenings are spent in front of the television. I like *Dallas, Top Of The Pops, The Old Grey Whistle Test* and some quiz shows. Before I turn in for the night, I always go to the kids' bedroom and give them each a kiss. But the trouble is, James often wakes up and doesn't want to go back to sleep."

Sunday, February 17

While in Durango, Mexico, following an unpleasant strip search for drugs when he arrived in Mexico, a spin-off from Paul's drugs bust, Ringo begins shooting his latest film; a zany comedy called *Caveman* in which he is cast in the role of Atouk . . .

Ringo "I don't have much to say in the film just a few dozen words of gobbledegook. I'm spouting stuff like 'Ool' (food), 'Harakah' (fire) and 'Folls' (children)."

Caveman's veteran producer David Foster, famed for the 1967 Dustin Hoffman film *The Graduate* "Ringo is potentially a comic genius. In the past he never really attacked an acting career seriously enough, perhaps. But now he's determined to do just that."

On the film set, **Ringo** holds a conversation with the tabloid reporter Paul Connew. "To my mind, I've already proved I can act," he says. "The trouble was that I used to approach acting like a rock'n'roller. I was getting parts simply because of who I was. Geezers would say what a great idea it was to have a Beatle in their movie. And the fact that I wanted to act, that I felt I could act, wasn't really the issue. But no one is going to offer Ringo Starr a top role these days just because I used to be one of The Beatles. I've got to be able to do the job. That's much more demanding but much better too. That's the way I like it . . . I could end up with egg all over my face but succeed or fail, it's all down to me standing on my own two feet as an actor . . . Maybe *Caveman* is the dawn of a new era for me. I have already lined up my next film, a modern comedy in which I play a way-out psychiatrist. But my big ambition is to play a real, sadistic villain. Acting is going to be my main career priority from now on, although I do want to make one rock'n'roll album a year. Once a rock'n'roller always a rock'n'roller . . .'"

Co-starring with Ringo in *Caveman* is Shelley Long and the James Bond *The Spy Who Loved Me* actress, Barbara Bach, starring in her twenty-third feature film . . .

"We were filming *Caveman* for three months," Barbara reveals. "Durango was the best location because the location was so beautiful, even though it took us two hours to get there and two hours to return in the evening. When I first went for the part, I was going to do it because I have always been typecast. But at least this time I was typecast with comedy and they said to me, 'We are going to get a really big comedy star to play the lead.' I said, 'Great,' because it was Warner Brothers and so forth. And then, about a week before, they said, 'Okay, we are having a meeting at the director's house and the star is going to be there, and it is Ringo.' One week into the shoot and we realised that we had got the right star."

Barbara on Ringo . . . "I saw Ringo first in 1965 when I took my younger sister, Marjorie, to The Beatles' Shea Stadium concert. We watched them arrive in a helicopter. I was about 19 then. I wasn't really interested. All I can remember about their performance was that it was rather short and rather loud."

Filming begins . . .

"We had an on-camera love affair," she will reveal, "and somehow it just spilled over nicely into real life. It wasn't quite love at first sight but it began to grow within days of meeting each other."

Ringo "We were close friends through the movie and, two weeks before the end of shooting, we fell in love."

Ringo, who for some strange reason will call Barbara 'Doris' "I was first attracted to her by photographs in *Playboy* magazine, which left little to the imagination. Then, during breaks in the filming, I told her a lot about the South of France. I explained about the Monaco Grand Prix and asked Doris to come with me. I said I'd be upset if she didn't and I'd miss her very much. She said she would feel the same way, so we went off . . . It might sound soppy but when you're this happy, you don't care."

Barbara "When Ringo invited me to the Grand Prix, I didn't hesitate. You know, despite that '007' film image, James Bond isn't my kind of man. To me, he is arrogant and selfish. I like a man who is quiet, intelligent and sensitive, as well as being attractive, of course. Like Ringo. It turns out that not only do we like the same things, we like the same places. We intend to spend the summer in France. There are a lot of out of the way places we want to show each other. We'll be quite happy driving up and down the coast and through the French countryside."

But Ringo and Barbara's romance does not please Nancy Andrews, Ringo's current companion . . .

"I was furious at being abruptly dropped by Ringo for Barbara," Nancy blasts. "He had already proposed to me and I wanted to settle down with him and raise a family. I was very hurt and angry at the way he treated me. He did not behave at all like a gentleman. I had been his 'wife' for the best part of a decade and he suddenly dropped me without warning. It was like being slapped in the face. I considered Barbara a close friend and I felt humiliated that their love affair had started behind my back."

(Twelve months after their acrimonious split, Nancy will begin a palimony action against **Ringo**, details of which will not become public until October 1989.)

Thursday, March 6

Simon Kinnersley, *Daily Mail* "Paul McCartney is set to go into semi-retirement following his 10-day spell in a Japanese jail, after being arrested in Tokyo for carrying half a pound of marijuana. Plans for his band Wings' world tour later this year have been shelved and the musicians have no idea when they'll appear together again. McCartney, meanwhile, is retreating to the kind of secluded lifestyle he adopted shortly before The Beatles split; recording a solo album and spending time with his family . . ."

Meanwhile, in light of **Paul**'s apparent retreat from activities, his Wings partner, Denny Laine, admits to the press that he has "just completed my own solo album and I'm forming a new band. I'm setting up a group because I've got so much time off. I've really got no idea at the moment when Wings will be getting together either to rehearse or tour. Wings have got to the point that they only need to do a little bit. We only have to record an album a year and do just a couple of concerts for friends and to keep our hands in. The role of the group has changed. We used to be a touring rock band that made the occasional record but now we're a studio band who tours occasionally. Now, it seems as though Paul's drug bust is forcing him still further from the concert hall and encouraging me to get out on the road again. I've come to realise that there is a lot of other things I want to do."

Tuesday, March 11

Meanwhile, a day spent by John and Yoko in Florida's West Palm Beach features in a report in the *Evening News* newspaper. "Henpecked recluse John Lennon is most unimpressed with his new neighbours in Florida's West Palm Beach where he and Yoko have just moved into a £1 million mansion by the sea," the piece reads. "On a recent stroll through town, elderly blue-rinsed ladies who wanted to touch their clothes mobbed the two of them. 'Will you give us some space?' begged John. 'Please, please, we're just window-shopping,' shrilled Yoko. The couple made their getaway through a nearby Gucci store but on their next outing, they were accosted again, this time by a girl who wanted to know when The Beatles were going to re-form. An exasperated John rolled his eyes to the heavens and said, 'Why are you doing this to me? Have I ever done anything to aggravate you, love?' "

Friday, May 16

While the Lennons are having their tranquillity shattered, Paul releases *McCartney II*, his first solo album in almost a decade . . .

Paul "After we had done the last Wings album, *Back To The Egg*, I was fed up with the idea of making albums, you know, just churning them out. So I hired a 16-track machine and got an engineer friend, Eddie, to fix me up a thing where I just took one microphone into the back of the machine direct and I put it into the front parlour of my old farmhouse . . . We didn't use a big console. It's very difficult if you're trying to work on your own with a big console, so we bypassed it. People said *McCartney II* was McCartney fiddling the knobs and twiddling, but it wasn't in my mind. It was me experimenting. It was me getting into synths and me seeing what I could do. I wanted to have some private fun and I thought I'd produce a cassette we could play in the car. I was in total control. I had no echo chambers, no drum machines. I'd play the snare drum in the tiled kitchen to get an echo or fiddle with the machine and guess what interval was needed on my voice to do the effect. I made everything up, except for one song. I'd go along on my bike and a song might spring out of what I had seen on TV the night before. It was like being a sculptor, chopping and changing as I went along . . . It wasn't an amazingly successful album, I don't think. It was definitely an experiment. It was me at home, multi-tracking, like *McCartney* had been. But I'm glad I did that . . . I started it down in Sussex, then during the summer I went up to Scotland so I just carried on doing it up there."

'Coming Up'

Paul "I originally cut it on my farm in Scotland. I went into the studio each day and just started with a drum track. Then I built it up bit by bit without any idea of how the song was going to turn out. After laying down the drum track, I added guitars and bass, building up the backing track. I did a little version with just me as the nutty professor; doing everything and getting into my own world like a laboratory. The absent-minded professor is what I go like when I'm doing those; you get so into yourself it's weird, crazy. But I liked it. Then I thought, 'Well, okay, what am I going to do for the voice?' I was working with a vari-speed machine with which you can speed up your voice, or take it down a little bit. That's how the voice sound came about. It's been speeded up slightly and put through an echo machine I was playing around with. I got into all sorts of tricks, and I can't remember how I did half of them, because I was just throwing them all in and anything that sounded good, I kept. And anything I didn't like, I just wiped . . . I always thought the single was going to be the solo version. We did the song on tour because we wanted to do something the audience hadn't heard before. The live version on the B-side of the single was recorded on the last night of the tour in Glasgow. In America, a lot of the disc jockeys on the Top-40 stations picked up on this side and so it became the A-side in the States. It's the B-side in the rest of the world. I heard a story from a guy who recorded with John in New York, and he said that John would sometimes get lazy. But then he'd hear a song of mine where he thought, 'Oh, shit, Paul's putting it in, Paul's working!' Apparently 'Coming Up' was the one song that got John recording again. I think John just thought, 'Uh oh, I had better get working, too.' I thought that was a nice story."

'Temporary Secretary'

Paul "It's like a disposable secretary, and it struck me as being funny. The song is written from the point of view of a fellow who just wants a disposable secretary, and he's writing to a bureau to try and get one. I just like the idea. I just thought it was funny, you know, asking for a temporary secretary rather than a secretary . . . That sound on the track, which is like a space typewriter, is a sequence machine. I used that to give me a tempo and, again, I just made the song up as I went along. It was a little influenced by Ian Dury."

'On The Way'

Paul "I put down a drum track and some bass and that was that and it sat around for a month or so. The day before going back to it, I had seen Alexis Korner on a TV programme about the blues, and I thought, 'Oh, I've got to do something like that because it's the kind of music I like.' So that's how that one came about."

'Waterfalls'

Paul "The only song that was written before I came to record was 'Waterfalls' . . . 'Waterfalls' could have been called 'I Need Love' but that would have been too ordinary. I just had this waterfalls and lakes idea, from the notices you see in American tourist resorts, and it stuck. Halfway through the album, making it all up as I went along, I got a bit bored. I had finished about eight tracks by then and I thought I would do something different. So I decided to do a song that was already written, a track left over from the last Wings album, and that was my favourite at the time. That's why it's included. The original lyrics were just working lyrics, gut lyrics, just spewed out. I thought I'd have to get serious and sensible and change them. Lyrics like that I don't trust. But in time, I got to like them and I thought I should add electric piano and a distant string synthesiser like a mad Swiss orchestra on a mountaintop. And it worked! A lot of people have rung up about that one and said that it's their favourite. So when you get such a good feeling, you think that perhaps it should be a single."

'Nobody Knows'

Paul "That also came about after watching the blues series. I'm a big fan of a lot of the blues players. One of the many funny things for me is that in blues, you'll get what is supposed to be a 12-bar blues, and then you get odd timings come in. On many blues records, they're never exact so, on this track, I do the same thing. That was the basic inspiration behind it."

'Front Parlour'

Paul "That was the first thing I did on the album and it was done in the front parlour of an old farmhouse. It was empty at the time so we just brought the recording machinery in and used the kitchen as an echo chamber. It was a big echoey kitchen so I didn't have to use echo or any gimmicks on the sessions. I had to make do. If I wanted any kind of echo, I'd just have to stand in this big kitchen with a snare drum and belt it. That's how I got an echo snare. This little front parlour, which has still got the old wallpaper on it and a little fireplace, was where the main track was recorded. So I called it 'Front Parlour'."

'Summer's Day Song'

Paul "I had heard a piece of music that I liked, which was a very classical sounding piece. So, that day, when I went into the studio, I thought it would be a nice change if I tried something, sort of, classical. I built it up, wrote a couple of words, and put a few vocals over the top, so it does sound like something classical-cum-something else."

'Frozen Jap'

Paul "It was recorded in the summer of 1979 and originally I was working around on synths, again, experimenting and I suddenly got something which sounded very Oriental. When the track was finished, it seemed so Oriental to me and I thought, 'I'd better get a really lyrical title.' I tried to think of a suitable title and things came to mind, like 'Crystalline Icicles Overhang The Little Cabin By The Ice-Capped Mount Fuji,' or 'Snow Scene In The Orient,' but all the titles sounded clumsy. So that I wouldn't forget, I scribbled down a working title of 'Frozen Jap', you know, frozen being the ice bit for the snow scene idea, and Jap meaning Oriental and somewhere over in that part of the world. And the title stuck. I found that the 'Crystalline Fuji' bit just didn't work. Now, I'm sure people will think it was recorded after that incident in Japan. We decided to change the title to 'Frozen Japanese' for the album release in Japan, since we didn't want to offend anyone over there. But when the Japanese were told of the album's track listing, they went spare. They thought it was connected with the fact that I had been busted there. They regard it as an incredible slur."

'Bogey Music'

Paul "There's a book called *Fungus The Bogeyman,* for kids and grown-ups, too, which was sent to me by some fellow who's making it into a film and who wanted me to do some music in it. The story is a bit strange, and the basic idea is that the bogeymen are people who make bumps in the night. They live beneath the ground and come out at night and frighten people and they like everything that is opposite to what we like. If we like warm dry clothes, they like wet slimy ones. And they've got all sorts of crazy books in their library, like

Lady Chatterley's Bogey . . . It's just a great book, but it's crazy and it just tickled my fancy when I got it. Anyway, I had that book in the studio one day and opened it to a page where the young people in Bogeyland rebel against the old people who hate music. They all start to get dressed in warm clean clothes and then they start to actually take baths, which is unheard of, and get into rock'n'roll. So I just took that page, looked at it a bit, and just thought, 'Well, it looks like a bit of rock'n'roll.' So I made up the track and called it 'Bogey Music'. It's a crazy fantasy, really, but that's what I was thinking of when I did it."

'Darkroom'

Paul "It wasn't anything to do with Linda, and the darkroom where she develops her pictures. Actually, somehow I just heard the word 'darkroom' and thought it had lots of connotations. It could be a dark room, a photographic darkroom, or just a room, which is dark. You know, a fellow saying to a girl, 'Come to my dark room,' is a bit like a 'Come, let me take you to the Casbah,' kind of thing. So I thought of this double meaning and it's just a chant that says, 'Comma, come along to my darkroom.' And then I added a sort of atmosphere thing in the background and that's it. It's supposed to sound like a sort of freaky darkroom or something. Originally 'Darkroom' wasn't going to be on this album because we had to knock off about eight or nine tracks at the beginning. We had planned a double-album, but then it came down to a single album. I was going to lose 'Darkroom' because the original version is a very long track and goes on through all sorts of little crazy noises. But I edited it down because I liked it, and now it's on the album."

'One Of These Days'

Paul " 'One Of These Days' all happened when a Hare Krishna bloke came round to see me. He was a nice fellow, very sort of gentle. After he left, I went to the studio and the vibe carried through a bit. I started writing something a bit more gentle that particular day. The song seemed right as a very simple thing and it basically just says, 'One of these days I'll do what I've been meaning to do the rest of my life.' I think it's something a lot of people can identify with."

At the time of the release of *McCartney II*, in a conversation with Paul Gambaccini, **Paul** is asked what the other members of Wings were doing when he recorded this album. "When I started on this last year," he replies, "we were all taking some time off. Denny started to get a solo album together, I started on this and Laurence did his own solo album. And now, with Wings not touring, and the solo albums beginning to emerge, it appears as if no one is doing anything. But it doesn't mean that Wings are going to split up, it just means that, for the time being, we're doing solo things rather than a group project. The way it works with a group, is that sometimes you're playing with the group and rehearsing with it, sometimes you're not and you're just doing your own stuff. Most people do it, you know. Townshend does it with The Who and Gilmour does it with the Floyd. We just each got into these solo things . . ."

Gambaccini also asks Paul about unreleased Beatles and Wings recordings . . .

"With The Beatles," **Paul** replies, "we were careful about not having unreleased tracks lying round. We used to dig into all the old tracks, like 'You Know My Name (Look Up The Number)', which was an unreleased track for a long time. We dug it out and finished it and released it, so that by the time The Beatles finished, there weren't any unreleased things hidden away. But with Wings, there are quite a few, a few from the *Ram* sessions, which, strictly speaking, wasn't Wings, and quite a few off *Red Rose Speedway* that didn't get released. And there have been the odd songs that just didn't fit for what people wanted them for, like a film or something. I still say that I'd like to get it all together, finish it all up, and release an album called *Cold Cuts*, which would just be all the things that didn't get released. Some of them are pretty good tracks, some of them are almost better than the ones that did get released!"

To coincide with release of *McCartney II*, **Paul** and Linda travel to the Cannes film festival, in the South of France, to promote the album and Linda's short animated feature, *Seaside Woman*. Covering their appearance at the prestigious event is Michael Zwerin of the *International Herald Tribune* . . .

"Beatles do not appear in public often and gourmet food was wolfed down at McDonald's tempo in the journalist crossfire. His record company told him that, this one afternoon, his album could sell more than 100,000 copies in France alone, and since it was probably the closest thing to work he would have to do this year, he said he would do it. He said he had made up his mind to be a good boy this afternoon, a decision he may make too often . . ."

At the mediocre press conference, Paul and Linda face the questions, many of which are inevitable . . .

Reporter "How did you like Japan?"

Paul "I didn't get to see much of Japan."

Reporter "What do you two like most about each other?"

Paul "Her legs."

Reporter "Paul, as you know, Roger Daltrey is in town. Are you planning to steal his show?"

Paul "No, I'm not going to steal Roger's show."

Reporter "I met some 12-year-old kids who have never ever heard of The Beatles. How does that make you feel?"

Paul "Older."

On **Monday, May 19**, in Roehampton, south-west London, Ringo and Barbara are involved in a horrific car crash . . .

Syndicated UK news report "Ringo's Mercedes, with him at the wheel, skidded on a wet road near Kingston, Surrey. In the chaos of ripping metal, the car rammed two lampposts, somersaulted 50 yards and ended up on the opposite side of a dual carriageway. The couple escaped with minor injuries but so shocked they hardly knew whether they were alive or dead."

Ringo "After that car crash, we agreed never to be separated. It was a miracle that we both got out alive and that Barbara's beauty wasn't scarred . . . As soon as I could, I went and played the drums to see if I could still play. I'm still the best."

MAY
Meanwhile, in the States, in an attempt to just be by himself and rediscover who he is, Yoko sends John on a trip around various parts of the world . . .

John "The actual moment of awareness when I remembered who I was came in a room in Hong Kong . . . I hadn't done anything by meself since I was 20. I didn't know how to check into a hotel . . . Whenever I got nervous about it, I took a bath and in Hong Kong I had about 40 baths! I was looking out over the bay when something rang a bell. It was the recognition, my God! This relaxed person is me from way back. He knew how to do things. It doesn't rely on any adulation or hit record. Wow! So, I called Yoko and said, 'Guess who? It's me!' I wandered around Hong Kong at dawn, alone, and it was a thrill. It was rediscovering a feeling that I once had as a youngster walking the mountains of Scotland with my auntie. 'The heather, the mist,' I thought, 'Aha! This is the feeling that makes you write or paint.' It was with me all my life, and that's why I'm free of The Beatles, because I took time to discover that I was John Lennon before The Beatles and will be after The Beatles, and so be it."

Paul "We all got postcards from Yoko saying, 'Go round the world in a south-easterly direction. You are allowed to stop in four places.' George Martin got one of those and said, 'Would it be all right to stop in Montserrat?' I said, 'No.' John did the voyage. John went in a south-easterly direction but we all went, 'Um, sure, sure, we'll all go round the south-east.' "

Wednesday, June 4
John's foreign jaunts continue when he goes on a sailing trip to Bermuda, and makes a fascinating discovery . . .

John "I went with Fred (Seaman), the guy who works with me . . . and I went there (a nightclub) and upstairs they were playing disco and downstairs I walked in and they were playing 'Rock Lobster' and I said to him, 'She's finally made it! I mean, they've studied her.' So I called her on the phone and I said, 'You won't believe this, there's a group called The B-52's, they're doing your act here.' "

On **Thursday, July 3**, a syndicated New York news report reveals that "John Lennon, the songwriter, and his wife, Yoko Ono, have sold one of their Holstein cows for the world record price of $265,000 at the Syracuse State fair."

The *International Herald Tribune* "John Lennon and his wife, Yoko Ono, disclosed the sale of one of their Holstein cows for $250,000 on June 23 at the Syracuse NY State Fair, breaking a world record. The previous record price for a Holstein was $235,000 set in 1976."

Wednesday, July 9

In an interview for the BBC, **Paul** rather prematurely tells the BBC Radio One DJ Paul

Gambaccini, "I do not think John Lennon will ever record again. I asked him about music and he said, 'No.' At the moment he didn't feel like doing that anymore. For Lennon fans this adds to the mystique, but I've a feeling he may not even bother to record again."

Monday, August 4
John and Yoko enter the Hit Factory recording studios in New York where they begin work on their first studio album since 1975. An event summed up perfectly by . . .

The International Herald Tribune newspaper, which writes, "Lennon hasn't been a recluse. He and the family travelled to Japan and elsewhere, but he stayed away from the music business and the media. Lennon began writing again last summer during a vacation with Sean in Bermuda. Excited by the new material, he called Yoko and played her a tape on the phone. She responded by writing reply songs of her own, which she would then play back to him a few days later. With the songs forming a man and woman dialogue, the Lennons went into the recording studio here in August."

John "What I realised during the five years away was that when I said, 'The dream is over,' I had meant the physical break from The Beatles, but mentally, there was this big thing on my back about what people expected of me. It was like this invisible ghost. During the five years, it sort of went away. I finally started writing like I was even before The Beatles were The Beatles. I got rid of all that self-consciousness about telling myself, 'You can't do that. That song's not good enough. Remember you're the guy who wrote "A Day In The Life". Try again.' "

Thursday, August 14

In the UK, the Evening News reports "Lennon's Planning British Concerts: John Lennon is planning to play British concerts to promote his forthcoming comeback album . . . After more than five years in seclusion, Lennon has secretly booked unlimited recording time at the Hit Factory recording studios in Manhattan. He is working intensely with Yoko and a few close friends on an album of love songs and hopes are high that the album will be ready for release early next year. Lennon, who is 40 in October, said five years ago that he would not work again until his son Sean started school. Sean, now five, starts school this autumn. Such is the interest in a new album from the ex-Beatle that he could demand an advance of several million pounds from almost any major record company."

Friday, August 29

Stories originating from the Double Fantasy sessions in New York continue to feature in the UK press when the Evening News runs the following story headlined "Lennon Bans The Boss". The short piece reads: "John Lennon is behaving in his usual neurotic fashion. He has banned all visitors from the recording studio where he is working on his solo album, and that includes friends and top record executives who have been queuing up to get Lennon to sign on their labels. When the boss of Atlantic Records arrived to call on John, Yoko physically barred his way into the building. But the eccentric ex-Beatle is quite happy and he's told friends he's very pleased with the tracks completed so far."

Monday, September 29
John's great comeback continues when his first major interview in five years is

published in the American magazine *Newsweek* under the title "The Real John Lennon". The interviewer, Barbara Graustark, asks John to give her "a typical day in the life of John and Yoko."

John replies "Yoko became the breadwinner, taking care of bankers and deals, and I became the housewife. It was like one of those reversal comedies. I'd say (jokingly), 'Well, how was it at the office today, dear? Do you want a cocktail? I didn't get your slippers, and your shirts aren't back from the laundry.' To all housewives, I say I now understand what you're screaming about. My life was built around Sean's meals."

Graustark "Yoko, why did you decide to take over as business manager?"

Yoko "There's a song by John on the album called 'Clean-up Time', and it really was that for us. Being connected to Apple and all the lawyers and managers who had a piece of us, we weren't financially independent, we didn't even know how much money we had. We still don't! Now we are selling our shares of Apple stock to free our energy for other things. People advised us to invest in stocks and oil but we didn't believe in it. You have to invest in things you love, like cows, which are sacred animals in India. Buying houses was a practical decision. John was starting to feel stuck in the Dakota and we get bothered in hotels. Each house that we've bought was chosen because it was a landmark that needed restoring."

Graustark "How do you look back on your political radicalism in the early 1970s?"

John "That radicalism was phoney, really, because it was out of guilt. I'd always felt guilty that I made money, so I had to give it away or lose it. I don't mean I was a hypocrite, when I believe, I believe right down to the roots. Being a chameleon, I became whomever I was with. When you stop and think, 'What the hell was I doing fighting the American Government just because Jerry Rubin couldn't get what he always wanted, a nice, cushy job?' "

Saturday, October 4

Ringo and Barbara feature in an interview in the UK magazine *Woman*. He uses the piece, conducted in their apartment overlooking France, to display his evident pride in the fact that his 14-year-old-son, Zak, plans to follow his father's footsteps in the music industry . . . "Zak plays drums in a heavy metal rock group and already he wants to leave school and do it full time. I'm having to play the heavy father and say, 'No, you'll stay at school until you're older or else daddy will have to go to jail.' "

Conversation changes to Maureen, Ringo's first wife, "For the first few years after the divorce," he says, "my relationship with Maureen wasn't easy. Now the two of us can talk together again. We've become sort of friends and I can go into the house in London to see the kids without feeling odd."

Ringo also talks about his current love, Barbara Bach. "We're shopping for a house," he reveals. "We have asked Los Angeles estate agents to look for something in the £1 million bracket."

Barbara "Until I met Ringo, my stability in my crazy kind of job lay in my children. If an actress doesn't have some kind of responsibility she can very easily go off the deep end. Ringo is part of my stability now. He has given me even more than I already had and that's what I want for our future. We have no intention of losing each other. We're taking each step at a time, knowing deeply that what we want is to spend a lot of time together. We're sharing something very special. We don't care if people think we are acting like teenagers in love, the feelings are good and that is all that matters. Both of us have decided to hold on to them for as long as possible. Who knows where it will end? We can't tell that so we're going to enjoy each other while we can."

On Ringo, Barbara announces that "He's the nicest, kindest, funniest, most sensitive man I've met."

Ringo on Barbara "Something special clicked. She's a beautiful, sexy, funny, warm-hearted person. I'm not with her because she's the most beautiful woman in the world. She's just the sweetest, most sensitive woman I have ever known. I haven't been as happy as this in years. She's the only star in my life."

Friday, October 24 (UK)
With great anticipation, John and Yoko issue the single '(Just Like) Starting Over' c/w 'Kiss Kiss Kiss', the first tracks from the *Double Fantasy* album sessions . . .

'(Just Like) Starting Over'

John "I wrote 'Starting Over' for Yoko, but afterwards I realised it's a message to all women, a plea for all of us, men and women, to start over. Sexism is such a big issue and we haven't even begun to deal with it. There are all kinds of inequalities in the world, this race vs. this race, this country vs. this country, but it's always women at the bottom."

. . . Almost immediately, critics begin sharpening their knifes, preparing their attack on **John**'s musical comeback . . .

Ian Pye, *Melody Maker* (**Saturday, November 8**) ". . . In February 1975, his majestic album of standards, *Rock 'N' Roll*, came onto the streets and was followed later in the year by the *Shaved Fish* compilation. Then there was silence. Five years as a virtual recluse ensued. Time was spent with the family, he was now re-united with Yoko on one of his dairy farms or at their various holiday retreats or simply in the bowels of the Dakota building. Lennon had made a significant and lasting contribution to rock but people still wanted more. Whether to satisfy their demands or to see if he could still cut it at 40, Lennon decided to return and one can only hope that the rest of the album is better than the cloying sentimentality of his new single. Ironically, he once said this of George Harrison, before his self-imposed exile. 'Well, he's just cut off really. It's easy to get cut off. If you're surrounded by people who aren't rocking, then you just forget what it is.' What's happened musically over the last five years seemed to have bypassed Lennon completely. His latest single is abundantly inferior to any of his previous solo work. It was painful enough watching another of the last heroes getting pummelled to death by his old sparring partner earlier this year. To quote one of the man's own lines, 'If you can't stand the heat, you better get back in the shade'. Let's hope the sight of another sagging champion, out of breath and on his knees, won't come round so soon."

Monday, November 17
Simultaneously in both the UK and the USA, John and Yoko release *Double Fantasy*, their first studio album in five years . . .

Yoko "I have two concerns in this album. First, I hope that it reminds people of John's talent. Second, I hope the fact that I am working with him enhances the man-woman dialogue . . . People laughed at John for being a cissy and dedicating songs to their loving family life on his *Double Fantasy* album. John was risking a lot with that record. It was an act of great courage because he was supposed to be a hard man. But really, he was soft and gentle, too. A complete man."

'Woman'

John "That's to Yoko, and to all women in a way. My history of relationships with women is very poor, very macho, very stupid but pretty typical of a certain type of man, which I was, I suppose, a very insecure, sensitive person acting out very aggressive macho."

'I'm Losing You'

John " 'I'm Losing You' was actually written when Sean and I were in Bermuda and I couldn't get through to her (Yoko). She was in New York and was coming for the weekend. We were like, 'Mummy's coming! Mummy's coming!' We were thrilled to see her but she was on the phone the whole time she was with us. So she went back home and I was trying to call her but I couldn't get through. After that weekend, I was so frustrated . . . I wrote the whole thing about that. The direct feeling was of not being able to reach her, of not being able to get through, that she was slipping away."

Friday, December 5

Yoko Ono "Just days before his brutal death, John was making plans to return to England for a triumphant Beatles reunion. His greatest dream was to recreate the musical magic of the early years with Paul, George and Ringo. That dream depended on the success of 'Starting Over'. John was always an Englishman at heart. He wanted to return to his roots but he wanted to do it in style. John discussed the possibility of returning to England if 'Starting Over' made it to No. 1. If it had, John, Sean and I were going to sail back to England on the QE2. John was very excited about the idea. John never really fell out with Paul, George and Ringo, despite what people think. There were differences, sometimes intense, but none that totally destroyed those friendships. They just grew apart because each had families of their own to care for. Finally, John felt that they had travelled different paths for long enough. He felt they had grown up and were mature enough to try writing and recording new songs."

On **Saturday, December 6**, at the Hit Factory studios in New York, John and Yoko consent to an interview with the BBC Radio One DJ, Andy Peebles . . .

"We, the BBC producer Paul Williams and I, had met Yoko on Friday at the Dakota apartment where she and John combine their home with their offices," Andy recalls. "We spent an hour with Yoko and she told me that John was nervous about the interview because it had been a long time since he faced a radio microphone. We arranged to meet at the Hit Factory Studio at noon the next day. It would be the Lennons' first interview for BBC Radio in five years. On the Friday, the temperature in New York was minus four. We went to see David Bowie in *The Elephant Man* at the Booth Theater. His performance was brilliant. I felt proud to be British. Later, back at the hotel, I found it hard to sleep because I had never met John Lennon but my memories are many. Visiting Hereford for a family holiday in 1963 and the first album from the Fab Four in the window of the local record store; the race to become the first person locally to buy the group's latest; and my school friend Richard Rowe, whose father Dick had, on behalf of Decca Records, said no to The Beatles in 1962. On Saturday, at noon, we arrived at the Hit Factory but there was no sign of John and Yoko. They had been recording all night and won't be available until 6pm. I feared that it would all fall through. After spending the afternoon Christmas shopping at Macy's, we arrived back at the studio at 5.50pm and the engineer smiled as he lets us in. John and Yoko had arrived twenty minutes ago. We walked into the control room and there he was. Slim, bespectacled, wearing tight trousers and thin sweater. He looked very fit, very healthy. He had lost an enormous amount of weight but I thought he looked good. We talked for well over three hours. I was impressed by his honesty. He didn't duck one question. He was very relaxed and seemed elated to be telling me the stories he had bottled up for so long. He was willing to talk about anything and everything, right back to the days when he first met Paul McCartney, when they were The Quarry Men. He was totally at ease and he didn't express any worries about his security. Afterwards, I felt that I had known the man all my life. His warmth and desire to please quite astonished me. Then we went off to dinner at Mr Chows. John held court over a meal and we were all spellbound . . ."

Producer Paul Williams, who was present throughout Andy's interview, "John said he liked the atmosphere in New York now and felt at peace with the world. He had become totally a family man in love with his wife and child. He had got out of the whole pop scene, hanging around with the Jaggers and so forth. That was obviously all behind him."

Monday, December 8

During the morning, in their Dakota office, **John** and Yoko give a lengthy interview to RKO Radio. Radio reporter Laurie Kaye recalls, "John told me that if Yoko died, he wouldn't know how to survive. He couldn't carry on. He stressed, 'I hope I die before Yoko.' John also spoke about how he hated the cult followings of dead rock stars like Buddy Holly and Jim Reeves."

Dave Sholin, RKO Radio "I spent three hours with John and it was the best and the happiest interview he had ever had. Lennon was so looking forward to the next few years and getting back into music."

The New Jersey freelance photographer, Paul Goresh, who had become a regular visitor to the Dakota apartment block, "When I arrived at the Dakota apartment building at about 12.30pm, there were two other people already waiting to see John. One of them was a tall, husky guy. The other was a blonde girl who looked about 20 years old. About two hours later, Sean Lennon arrived home from a two-day vacation with Helen Seaman, his nanny and a nurse. The girl, who claimed that she knew Helen, approached the child with the tall man. They talked for several minutes and then Sean, the nurse and the nanny, went inside. The man then approached me and asked, 'Are you waiting for Lennon?' I said I was. We started talking and he told me that his name was Mark and that he was from Hawaii. We stayed outside the Dakota for two more hours and then I decided to go. I explained to him that I could get Lennon's autograph another day. He said, 'I'd wait. You never know if you'll see him again.' "

Later, after returning from recording at the Hit Factory, shock spreads around the world when Mark David Chapman tragically shoots **John** dead outside the Dakota apartment block . . .

Donald Zec, *Daily Mirror* "One shattering moment of madness on a New York street and a Liverpool man who helped to change the world is dead. John Lennon, the undisputed inspiration and pathfinder of the most celebrated foursome in the history of entertainment, cut down at forty."

Yoko "It was so sudden, so sudden. We had planned to go out to eat after leaving the recording studio but we decided to go straight home instead. We were walking to the entrance of the building when I heard the shot. I didn't realise at first that John had been hit. He kept walking. Then he fell and I saw the blood."

Tom O'Leary, a neighbour of the Lennons, living just across the road opposite the Dakota building, "I was watching football on television and then I heard, 'Bang, bang, bang, bang,' I grabbed my jeans and ran outside to see what had happened. It was bedlam. I could see a commotion around the entrance to the Dakota. Yoko was there. She was shouting, 'Help me. Help me. John has been shot.' I thought some crazy nut had shot him. I felt my stomach shrivel. I thought my legs were made of jelly. It was as though I had been shot myself."

Reporter Philip Finn "Within minutes of the shooting, police officers Stephan Spiro and Peter Cullen from Manhattan's 20th Precinct were racing into 72nd Street in their blue police cars. Lennon, bleeding from five direct hits and seven wounds, had been hit by a man firing a .38 in a crouched, military stance from close range. The officers picked up his body and carried it into their car. Their car almost came off the road as it roared the five blocks to the side door emergency entrance at Roosevelt Hospital. There a big fat woman was asleep in the waiting room and a Hare Krishna follower touched the strip of hair on his otherwise bald head and said a silent prayer. Doctors and nurses surrounded Lennon. The covers on the trolley were stained with blood. They wheeled him into a curtained area and through the gap I could see them all working frantically. They were pumping and prodding."

New York reporter, Michael Leapman "Hundreds of mourners, chanting 'All You Need Is Love' and other songs of The Beatles, clustered outside the Dakota apartment building in New York where John Lennon was shot dead. Mark Chapman, a 25-year-old visitor to New York from Hawaii, was charged with killing Lennon with a .38 revolver as the singer and his wife, Yoko Ono, returned from a recording session just before 11pm. Mr Chapman had been lurking around the building for days and earlier in the evening had asked Lennon for his autograph. Lennon shouted, 'I'm shot,' and staggered into the building's entrance booth. He was driven to a hospital nearby in a police car, but was dead when he arrived."

New York columnist, Dave Conmist "John Lennon, the legendary singer, songwriter and Beatle, was dead by the time his body had been rushed by patrol car to Roosevelt Hospital in New York late on Monday night. Four bullets had shattered the 40-year-old Beatle's back and left shoulder, leaving fans the world over in a state of shock. The media likened it to the assassination 17 years before of President Kennedy."

Michael Leapman "Mr Chapman made no attempt to flee the scene and when the doorman of the Dakota asked him whether he knew what he had done, he is alleged to have said, 'I just shot John Lennon.' When Mr Chapman was formally charged this afternoon, Miss Hogrefe, the assistant district attorney, said that he borrowed money to come to New York specifically to kill Lennon. Miss Hogrefe said that Mr Chapman had $2,000 (about £800) in cash on him when he was arrested a few minutes after the shooting."

Melody Maker "The most morbid news came from police who said they could not locate the *Double Fantasy* album Lennon autographed for Chapman only hours before he was killed. In the confusion following the shooting, police think the autographed record was snatched up by a souvenir hunter."

Dave Conmist "By the early hours of Tuesday morning, hundreds were huddled at the Dakota building, quietly respectful, some weeping, turning the gates of the luxury Dakota block into a garden of remembrance. Close on 1,000 kept a tearful and occasionally tuneful vigil throughout the following drizzling day."

American reporter, John Heilpern "The high forbidding iron gates into the building, guarded by police and surrounded by barricades, have been festooned with wreaths, poems and photographs of Lennon, giving the appearance of a shrine. Some among the crowd kneel in prayer before the entrance. While others stand crying in the bitter cold or sing Beatles songs in sad muted voices. A mourner, perhaps speaking for his generation, said, 'I just felt I had to come here, to leave a flower or something. He represented my youth and I wanted to somehow pay my respects for all the pleasure he gave me.' At one moment, a school bus passed the Dakota and all the children inside leaned out of the windows, waving and calling, 'John, we love you! John, bye!' "

Yoko "On the night of the murder, I came back here, to the Dakota, and went into our bedroom, which faces 72nd Street and all I could hear, all night, and for the next few weeks, was the fans outside singing and playing his records. It was so excruciating, just spooky. I asked my assistants to beg the fans to stop it. Of course they didn't mean anything except good thoughts, but for me it was unreal, listening to his voice after what had just happened."

Playboy reporter David Sheff and his wife, Victoria, write in their article, 'The Persecution Of Yoko Ono' . . . "It is just minutes after midnight and the horror will not sink in. John Lennon was murdered just over an hour ago but those who have been part of his everyday life cannot comprehend it, cannot do anything but try to find a way into the first floor apartment at the Dakota. Yoko had been sneaked into the building through the rear entrance and is in the kitchen of her apartment. Speaking numbly, she asks Rich De Palma, office manager of the Lenono company, to make only three calls, to Julian Lennon, John's aunt, Mimi Smith and to Paul McCartney. De Palma is unable to contact any of them. By the early morning hours, Elliot Mintz, one of the Lennons' closest friends, who had flown in specially from Los Angeles, and De Palma are exhausted, still manning the phones in the dimly lit offices. One of the calls features the news that a photograph of John lying on the mortuary slab is being offered for sale to newspapers. Mintz immediately makes calls to head off the sale, but it is too late. One of the morgue photographs will shortly appear on the front page of the *New York Times* and later, in colour, in the *National Enquirer*. A Dakota investigation later discloses that the attendant was paid $10,000 for the photographs. He becomes, Mintz observes, 'The first to make a buck off John's death.' "

Tributes to John immediately begin pouring in from musicians and celebrities who had been inspired by John's music . . .

Mick Jagger, who is making a new Rolling Stones album at his Studio in the south of France, remarks "It's a barmy world, isn't it? I'm absolutely stunned! I knew and liked John for eighteen years, but I don't want to make a casual remark about him now at such an awful moment for his family and his millions of fans and friends."

The Beatles' producer, George Martin "I am deeply shocked and saddened to hear of the death of John Lennon. I'm also extremely angry that this violent world should do this to one of the great people of our time."

Roger Daltrey, The Who "It's terrible. My heart goes out to his family, wife and sons."

Liverpool singer, Cilla Black, who is currently in Abu Dhabi on tour "I'm shattered. To me, he will always be the eternal rocker. John was a man of brilliance and I think he was reserved and shy. He was a do-er. He was the one who went up to Brian Epstein and said, 'She's good.' I wouldn't be where I am today if it hadn't been for John Lennon."

Scottish singer, Lulu "I had quite a crush on him and we used to get on very well together. I found him very appealing. He had a tremendous sense of humour and he was a fascinating character. But we were just good friends, nothing more."

Bob Geldof, lead singer with The Boomtown Rats "Imagine no John Lennon. It is very hard to do. That guy with the gun stole away our childhood when he shot Lennon. His music was the background to our growing up. I feel his death more keenly than say Presley or Hendrix. He wasn't a hero. He transcended that. His music was omnipotent. He was playing your thoughts back to you. He was so close to me and the people of my generation that it feels like someone has just raped your mind to have this happen."

Jeff Lynne of The Electric Light Orchestra "Lennon was the greatest influence on my life and probably on everyone else's as well. He was my idol. He was the one person I always wanted to meet. I saw him once but I never met him. What can you say? It's terrible. Absolutely terrible!"

Pete Townshend, The Who "I'm too upset to talk about it. I can't find words to express how I feel."

BBC Disc Jockey, Alan Freeman "I haven't stopped crying since I heard the news and I doubt if I will for some time."

Fellow BBC Disc Jockey, John Peel "I was very distressed when I found out that John had died. I'd probably still be a computer programmer if it hadn't been for The Beatles. In 1964 being British, especially if you could claim to come from Greater Merseyside, which I do, was enough to get you on the radio. I had to cultivate something like a Liverpool accent in order to convince them. I wouldn't have done it except for The Beatles."

The actor John Junkin, who had co-starred with The Beatles in *A Hard Day's Night*, remarks "I will always remember John's kind side. I once showed him six songs I had written. He listened to them and asked if I had written them to make money. I said I had and he said I should write what I liked and hope that the public would like it. He said, 'That's what Paul and I had done, and waited for the world to catch up.' "

Bill Harry, the founder of Liverpool's *Mersey Beat* newspaper, recalls another time with John: "He gave me a bundle of papers containing his early stories and poems. But they were accidentally dumped out of my desk. I told John and he broke down and cried. He never blamed me but it was obvious something of great personal value had gone out of his life."

Former Apple employee, Peter Brown "John Lennon was a genius. He was The Beatles. Think of all the things he did. John wrote books, there was a Foyle's literary luncheon in his honour. He wrote poetry. He made films. He had a play produced for the National Theatre and it was John who created the most phenomenal and influential music history. Paul McCartney was the easy, charming one but John was the brilliant one and he knew what he was doing. He consciously worked at creating what became The Beatles. Yet, underneath Lennon's cynical, calculating exterior, there lurked a shy and very sensitive man. The remarkable thing is that he was unable to communicate on a social level with people. He was very insecure. He would only go to places where he knew people. He was always desperately intense about himself and that intensity nearly killed him and it was only the appearance of Yoko Ono that saved him from becoming yet another rock'n'roll casualty. She is the most extraordinary woman. She did a magic thing for John. She turned him on both mentally and psychically. It was Yoko who kept him alive. He was very close to killing himself by his craziness. She pulled him back from the brink."

While John's first wife, Cynthia, has this to say in a statement, which is read out by her third husband, John Twist, at their home in Ruthin, North Wales . . . "I would like to say how terribly upset we are at the sudden and tragic death of John Lennon. Julian is particularly upset about it. It came so suddenly. Julian remained very close to his father in recent years and is hoping to follow a career in music. I have always had the deepest affection for John since the divorce and have always encouraged his relationship with Julian."

John's former lover May Pang recalls the fateful day, "I was at a friend's flat a half a mile away. The disc jockey suddenly interrupted, saying, 'John Lennon has been shot.' At first I thought it was some kind of a sick joke. The initial news flash said that John was wounded but a few minutes later it was announced that he was at the hospital being operated on. I began shuddering and held my breath. I prayed that it wasn't true, but the third bulletin revealed the awful truth, that John was dead. I screamed hysterically for several minutes. I stayed in bed for two days, sobbing and just thinking of John. I couldn't eat or sleep. My body was just too numb from shock. The only thing I managed to do was put a call through to Yoko. One of her aides answered the phone, saying she was too upset to talk to me. I could understand her feelings. Perhaps she cannot forgive me for loving John as much as her, and feel I have no right to intrude into her sorrow. I left a message that I would gladly do anything to help her or Sean."

While **Paul** announces through his Press Officer, Tony Brainsby, "John was a great guy. I won't be going to the funeral. I'll be paying my respects privately. I want everyone to rally around Yoko."

The UK columnist John Chartres writes from Liverpool "John Lennon's death aroused deep emotions not only in Merseyside but throughout North West England where The

Beatles were regarded as symbols of cheerfulness and hope for the future in an area which has always suffered a lack of this form of joy. All four of The Beatles were regarded as homespun Merseyside lads, perhaps John Lennon especially who came from a working-class background in south Liverpool and was labelled as a natural rebel from his early schooldays onwards. His former art school teacher, Mr Arthur Ballard, said yesterday that he had recognised him as a genius from the start and his former headmaster, Mr William Pobjoy, went so far as to say that John Lennon would not have disapproved of the manner of his death because he could not imagine him enjoying any sort of long-term geriatric state.

"Both BBC and commercial radio stations in Liverpool and Manchester devoted hours of time to his death and tributes to The Beatles, including a one-hour phone-in programme by Radio Manchester during which scores of listeners in their late thirties and forties expressed their feelings with much emotion. But one relatively happy spin-off now seems certain to materialise. Liverpool City Council has, for some time, accepted that there ought to be a permanent homage to The Beatles, but there has been a problem in finding the £40,000 needed to erect it on a selected site in Williamson Square, not far from where The Cavern used to be. Today, it was being confidently predicted that the money will now flow in."

Meanwhile, back in New York, Dave Conmist continues with his report, "Teenagers and punks, wearing newly manufactured John Lennon buttons huddled together, talking. 'We are all his brother and sister. It's what he preached . . . I worshipped him. He was my life, man,' they said. Suddenly the crowd caught sight of Ringo Starr surrounded by bodyguards. The crowd screamed and shrieked, becoming a mob trying to touch the body of the grey and frightened legend. A limousine passed in front of the Dakota and many in the crowd, hoping for another celebrity, surrounded the car, rocking and beating on the roof. 'Is it George?' someone yelled. 'It has to be someone.' Inside was John's first son, the 17-year-old Julian . . . Many fans who had left the Dakota building headed for the record stores in a panic to clutch at the final remnants of a passing generation, John's most recent album *Double Fantasy,* which had been only a modest seller since it was released last month. Within minutes of opening, many of New York's record stores had sold every available copy. *Double Fantasy* is now expected to head America's Top 20 album chart list next week."

George "At that point I was lying low. It was funny really because the press in England were saying I was like Howard Hughes and I never left the house. But really, I went out all the time. I visited friends, I went to dinner, and I went to the movies. I just didn't hang out in places where the gossip columnists went to. When the thing happened to John, it wasn't a nice thing to think about. It made us realise just how vulnerable you are. We'll never know when our life is to be taken away from us and so John's death certainly influenced all of us, but it certainly wasn't the reason why I was lying low. I was asleep at the time and Neil Aspinall rang me about three or four in the morning and he told me that John had been shot. But, at that point, the first thing I thought was, 'How bizarre! Is he okay?' I thought it was just a flesh wound or something."

Paul "My manager rang me early in the morning. Linda was taking the kids to school. It was just too crazy . . . it was all blurred. It was the same as the Kennedy thing, the same horrific moment, you know. You can't take it in . . ."

Linda "I had driven the kids to school and I had just come back in. Paul's face, ugh, it was horrible . . . I knew something had happened."

Paul, in a 1984 interview for *Playboy* magazine "When we heard the news that morning, strangely enough all of us, the three Beatles, friends of John's, all of us reacted in the same way, separately. Everyone just went to work that day. Nobody could stay at home with that news. We all had to go to work and be with people we knew. We just had to keep going. So I went in and did a day's work in a kind of shock . . .

"We were very surprised to go to work that day, and that was a shock. I wasn't going to sit at home and watch the television and watch the news. So we went into AIR London. George Martin rang me up and said, 'Do you want to cancel? I'll understand if you do.' And I said, 'No way. I've got to walk through this day.' So we came to AIR and it wasn't too bad getting in there and we did our work, of sorts, it was a track called 'Rainclouds'. Paddy, the pipes man from The Chieftains, was there. He was just the right kind of character to see that day because he is like a magical leprechaun. It was nice to have a magical person around. It was as if he was a guru somehow, sent to help that day out. So we just beavered on and occasionally people would do jokes, not meaning it, saying, 'We'll do a film next week. We'll shoot it.' And when you heard the word 'Shoot', everyone would go, 'Ugh!' Everything you said seemed to be 'Shoot' or 'Don't kill me'. Every time you spoke, you seemed to say all these terrible things. And eventually I said, 'It's time to go home now. There's no more work to be done now. I can't stay here all night. I can't hide here any longer.'

"As I was coming out of the studio, there was a reporter and as we were driving away, he just stuck the microphone in the window. I was man enough to have it open. I was telling the fans, 'Thank you.' I was the Fab Macca, thumbs aloft character and, to me, that's just being nice. It's ordinary to me. I'm not taking the can for that shit. The reporter stuck the microphone into the car and said, 'What do you think about John's death?' I had just finished a whole day in shock and I said, 'It's a drag.' I meant drag in the heaviest sense of the word, you know. But when you look at that in print, it says, 'Yes, it's a drag.' Matter of fact . . . I should have lengthened the word 'drag' by about a thousand years, just to get the meaning in it. But the minute that appears in print, in black & white, when the editors have been to it, it reads, 'Paul McCartney said, "It's a drag." Hey-ho, onto other matters.' We just went home and we just looked at the news on the telly and we sat there with all the kids, just crying all evening. I just couldn't handle it, really . . . Hunter Davies was on TV that night giving a very reasoned account of John. He sprang right up there, the puppet sprang right up and I thought it was well tasteless. We all did, actually. 'Jesus Christ, we're ready with the answer, aren't we? Aren't we just ready with the summary.' Mind you, Hunter had admitted to us years ago that he already had our obituaries written. We were already on file at the time. He obviously pulled his obituary out on John and went to it."

Naturally, television and radio station schedules all around the world are rearranged to broadcast their own tributes to John. One such station is BBC2 in England, who transmit a special edition of *The Old Grey Whistle Test*, which is hosted by the BBC Radio One DJ, Anne Nightingale . . .

"Everyone remembers where they were and what they were doing when they heard that John Lennon had been shot dead in New York," Anne says. "It has become one of those 'where were you then' dates, just like the day when President Kennedy was assassinated. Old friends telephoned each other, while others just sat over a sobering pint in a quiet corner of the pub. For all of us in the UK, because of the time difference across the Atlantic, it was the next day before we heard what had happened. I was awoken by a phone call from my Radio One colleague, Richard Skinner, who was a member of the station's *Newsbeat* team, asking me if I had Paul McCartney's home number. Andy Peebles, who had just flown from New York overnight with the tapes of John's interview, was told at Heathrow Airport that John was dead. I was the presenter of the long-running BBC2 music show *The Old Grey Whistle Test* and the show's producer, Mike Appleton, decided that we should do a live tribute programme that evening. It was, naturally, a day of intense activity, with chasing film and video clips, checking facts and trying to persuade people who had known John to come into the studio to talk about him. Few would agree to do so. They were too upset. One of our regular production team waltzed into the *Whistle Test* office in the mid-afternoon and cheerfully threw herself into helping out in any way she could. She had not heard the news. She thought our sudden interest in John Lennon was because he was coming in to the studio that evening to do a live interview. We were, in fact, scheduled to have filmed an interview with him in New York two days later. Gradually it began to dawn on her that she had misread the facts. 'Has something happened I don't know about?' she asked. The programme went ahead and there was no time for hair styling, make-up and attention from the wardrobe department. Anyway, it would have seemed indecently trifling under the circumstances. It was just a matter of trying to do the job as well as possible and reflecting how people all over Britain were feeling, without sinking into any cheap emotional display. While a film clip of John was running, Mike Appleton called me into the control room to say that Paul McCartney was on the phone. On the phone he said to me, 'Please say thank you to everyone from me, George and Ringo.' I was never quite certain what he meant, but Paul, George and Ringo had an awful ring about it. No more Fab Four. I went back in front of the cameras with this thought in my mind and must have communicated it much more than I realised."

Paul "The last phone conversation I ever had with John was really great and we didn't have any kind of blow-up. It could have easily been one of the other phone calls when we blew up at each other and slammed the phone down. It was just a very happy conversation about his family, my family. I remember he said, 'Oh God, I'm like Aunt Mimi, padding round here in me dressing gown,' robe, as he called it, because he was picking up the American vernacular . . . 'Feeding the cats in me robe and cooking and putting a cup of tea on. The housewife wants a career.' It was that time for him. He was about to launch *Double Fantasy* . . . In a way, I'm kind of expected to say, 'He was a saint, he was always a saint, I remember him as a saint,' but it would be a lie. He was one great guy and part of his greatness was that he wasn't a saint. He was a great guy but he was pretty sacrilegious. He was pretty up front about it. But it was half the fun."

The terrible deed naturally features prominently in newspaper headlines right around the world . . .

Daily Mirror (December 10) "Millions Mourn An Idol Who Changed Their World – Grief for John Lennon was shared yesterday by everyone who knew him and by countless millions who did not. One of the first people in Britain to learn of his killing was his former wife, Cynthia, the mother of his 17-year-old son, Julian. The news was broken to her before dawn by Ringo Starr's ex-wife, Maureen, after the ex-Beatle drummer phoned her from the Bahamas. Cynthia, who had been visiting Maureen in Surrey, left immediately to be with Julian and her husband, restaurateur John Twist, at their home in Ruthin, North Wales . . . Later, Cynthia and her husband took Julian to Heathrow Airport and he flew to New York. Julian, who was clearly showing his distress, told reporters he wanted to follow in his father's footsteps as a musician."

Cynthia Lennon "I couldn't bear to watch television for a year after John was shot because when there was any shooting, it reminded me of his death. I would have liked to have been at his funeral but I knew it wouldn't have been right, so Julian went."

Immediately after John's death, newspaper houses and magazine companies around the world begin preparing their own special John Lennon tribute editions. Reports soon emerge that a "rash of unreleased John Lennon and Beatles recordings will soon be released by EMI and WEA", the two companies responsible for issuing John's back catalogue of recorded work. But the companies are quick to quash their rumours. WEA, Geffen's parent company in Britain announces, "It seems certain that there was no more material recorded for the *Double Fantasy* album that didn't appear on the record and John and Yoko were only working on demos of new material at the time of his death. As far as we know, there is no more unreleased John Lennon material."

EMI Records in England announces that "despite the widespread speculation that there is a certain amount of unreleased John Lennon/Beatles material in our vaults, we have nothing in hand that has not already appeared on record. If The Beatles or John Lennon had material that didn't appear on their albums, they retained it rather than the record company."

Melody Maker "In the days following Lennon's death, Beatles and solo Lennon music could be heard everywhere. Radio stations devoted most, if not all, of their needle time to Beatles records. At local rock clubs, deejays played Beatles and Lennon records in between acts. In an appearance at Irvine Plaza on the day after the shooting, Captain Beefheart opened his show with a brilliant, almost transcendental, sax solo, which he then dedicated 'From John, through Don, to Sean.' On walls and telephone poles around Greenwich Village and Soho, someone pasted up mimeographed posters with Lennon's picture and the lyrics from Television's 'Little Johnny Jewel'. John Lennon and Beatles albums literally disappeared from record stores as fans snapped up every note Lennon ever laid on vinyl. Some stores sold as many as 200 and 300 copies of Lennon's latest album *Double Fantasy* the day after the tragedy. One record store, King Karol Records on 42nd Street in New York, reported selling out its entire Lennon stock. At Colony Records on Broadway, someone bought a copy of The Plastic Ono Band's *Live Peace In Toronto* for $40. Many of the smaller rock record shops around New York pulled out all their posters and advertising from their show windows and simply put up a picture of Lennon or a Lennon album cover, sometimes with a handful of flowers."

Wednesday, December 10
From her Dakota apartment, Yoko talks with quiet sorrow . . .

"This is not a time for hate or disillusionment. The future is still ours to make," she says. "The Eighties will blossom if only people accept peace and love in their hearts. It would just add to the tragedy if people turned away from the message in John's music. People say that there is something wrong with New York but John loved New York. He would be the first to say that, that it wasn't New York's fault. There can be one crank anywhere . . . John and I had planned so much together. We had talked about living until we were 80. We even drew up lists of all the things we could do together for all those years. Then it was all over. But that doesn't mean the message should be over. The music will live on."

Thursday, December 11

American reporter, Philip Finn writes, "Mark Chapman, the man accused of killing John Lennon, was taken to a New York court in a bullet-proof vest today so that his lawyer could ask to be taken off the case. Family man, Herbert Adlerberg, 50, who was appointed by the court on Tuesday to represent Chapman, denied he had received threats but said the case was 'an albatross round his neck' . . ."

Herbert Adlerberg "Constant telephone calls from hundreds of people about the case has disrupted my practice and I could not properly represent my other clients. Was I frightened? I can't say that but in handling something like this, you have to deal with a lot of wacky people. I understand the man who sold the gun to Chapman has already had his life threatened. I have been involved in many top criminal cases but I'm too old for this. It would be all right for some guy about 29 or 30 who wants to make a name for himself. I'm relieved to be out of it."

Friday, December 12

New York reporter, David Fricke files this report "As John Lennon's body was secretly cremated on Wednesday during a ceremony at a crematorium thirty miles from New York, a massive assault by Lennon fans started on record shops the world over. In Britain, EMI, The Beatles' record company, geared up its pressing plants to full output and started a rapid search for spare capacity in other pressing factories, including those run by their rivals. Just three full days after the shooting of Lennon in New York, more than 300,000 copies of the 'Imagine' single had been shipped out to Britain's shops. Another 300,000 or more of 'Happy Christmas (War Is Over)' singles had been shifted and more than 100,000 copies each of 'Give Peace A Chance' and 'The Ballad Of John And Yoko' were in the racks. The demand was so heavy that the sales of 'Imagine' and 'Happy Christmas' lodged the singles into the lower reaches of the chart. They seem certain to feature in next week's charts. As well as the massive boost Lennon's death has given to his most popular singles, his recent single, 'Starting Over', has done a U-turn and is going back up the charts, with WEA, which distributes Geffen Records, reporting "a considerable increase in demand for both the single and the *Double Fantasy* album.""

From London, John Orme writes "The mass emotional groundswell that followed the tragedy has also meant a resurgence of four Lennon/Beatles albums. The *Beatles Ballads* album, *Imagine* and The Beatles' *Red* and *Blue* albums have all started appearing in the British charts."

Meanwhile, the *Melody Maker* reveals that "Lennon's killer, Mark David Chapman, had several days of psychiatric examination at New York's Belle Vue Hospital under a 24-hour suicide watch before being moved to Riker's Island jail to a more secure cell for his own protection from other prisoners. He spent his first two days refusing food following a threat from another prisoner scrawled on a prison wall."

Sunday, December 14

Around the world, millions of **John Lennon** fans honour Yoko's wishes for a ten-minute period of silence . . .

New York columnist, Philip Finn "Millions of people from all generations paid a remarkable worldwide tribute to John Lennon. They gathered in parks, streets and churches to pray for him sing his songs of peace and love and to shed their tears. The climax in a day of international sorrow was at 7pm, London time, the start of a ten-minute silence widely observed in Britain, America, Scandinavia and Australia. The dramatic vigil was given the distinguished support of the Archbishop of Canterbury, Dr Robert Runcie. He joined in the silence alone in Canterbury and was said to feel the loss of the murdered former Beatle. 'I gladly associate myself quietly with many young people across the world who sincerely long for world peace. Of course I liked John Lennon. I was born and brought up in Liverpool, so there is a connection, which I do not underestimate and it is a part of why I take seriously what young people are doing today in response to his death.' The world prayers were requested by Lennon's widow, Yoko Ono, who stayed home all day with their five-year-old son, Sean, where the rock star was shot last week."

UK reporter, Paul Eccleston "There were moving moments in Liverpool. Beatles songs blared from pub jukeboxes throughout the city and 20,000 people gathered for an open-air concert on the steps of St George's Hall. The Lord Mayor, Councillor Jimmy Ross, said of John's death, 'We don't know what treasures the world has been deprived of.' Recorded musical tributes were by locally born singer, Gerry Marsden and local songwriter and poet, Mike McGear, Paul's brother, and Frank Sinatra. Sporting personalities John Conteh, Bill Shankly, Henry Cooper and Liverpool playwright, Alan Bleasdale, sent messages. The Rev David Arnott, Anglican Chaplain of Liverpool Polytechnic, which incorporates the Art College where Lennon started, led a candlelight vigil. Mr Arnott told the crowd, 'For John's sake, mankind's sake and for God's sake, give peace a chance. Tonight pray for it. Tomorrow go out and do it.' In London's Trafalgar Square, 500 stood in silence near the giant Christmas tree. Candles, flowers and a picture of Lennon were placed at the foot of Nelson's Column."

Philip Finn "The biggest turn-out was in New York's Central Park. More than 100,000 people paid their tributes in bitterly cold weather. The police said, 'It just shows a measure of the love and respect John Lennon held.' Among the mourners were the peace worker and actress, Jane Fonda, who stood gripping the arm of her husband, Tom Haden. Like many in the park, she was in tears. She said, 'John was such a lovely, lovely man.' New York's Mayor, Ed Koch said, 'The city, the nation and the world have been saddened by this assassination. He was a natural, cultural treasure.' The silence in the park ended with the voice of John on the loudspeakers singing his haunting song 'Imagine'. Hundreds lined 72nd Street, outside the Dakota building, the scene of Lennon's murder. Inside, away from it all, sat Yoko Ono, comforting a little boy who had lost his dad."

Yoko "Since John died, I've had so many long, loving letters that I don't know how to take it. I find it distressing and grotesque. I wish they could love me for what I am. It's sad that so many people are warm towards me because of the death. I feel like saying, 'Please don't love me. Let's go back to the days when you hated me, then John might be here.' I'd rather have him around than the whole world saying nice things about me. You know, I'm not the devil they all thought I was, but I'm not particularly angelic either. I don't want people to think I'm claiming that."

Monday, December 15

The American reporter Paul Connew writes in New York "John Lennon's self-confessed killer, Mark Chapman, ended a 48-hour hunger strike today. He began eating only after officers at New York's tough Riker's Island jail hired a civilian cook and agreed to sample his food first. Chapman was convinced that fellow prisoners were trying to poison him. Death threats have been daubed on some of the walls. Chapman became hysterical after reading one, which said, 'You don't have much time left.' When he has to be moved from one part of the prison to another, he is dressed in a bullet-proof vest."

One of the first to rush to see Yoko and Sean is John's look-alike first son, Julian, who had flown from his home in Wales just hours after John's death last week. He will temporarily move in to the Lennons' Dakota apartment . . .

New York columnist, Fred Wehner "Residents at the plush Dakota building on Manhattan's Upper West Side where John Lennon lived, and died, see Julian and Yoko holding hands as they go out together. Deena Bernstein, a neighbour in bustling West 72nd Street said, 'It's uncanny. It's as though John Lennon had never died. His boy looks just like him. You can tell by looking at them that Yoko and Julian need each other right now.' Said one member of Yoko's staff, 'They seem to be very close. For days after the killing, Mrs Lennon was in shock but now she's laughing again.' "

Tuesday, December 16
An interesting **John Lennon** mystery is revealed in today's *Daily Mirror* . . .

"This morning, we present the Tittenhurst Tapes Mystery," the report reads. "The stars, Freddie Starr and Ringo Starr (no relation). Just after John Lennon's tragic death, we revealed that some of his tapes had been found at Tittenhurst Manor, a mansion he once occupied in Berkshire. We then heard from one John Hemmingway. He acts for Ringo Starr, the owner of the Manor. Hemmingway says there are no John Lennon recordings at Tittenhurst Manor. However, the comedian Freddie Starr told us that, while recording at Tittenhurst, he had actually seen and played John Lennon's tapes. So what is going on? Back to Freddie Starr. 'When I went back to Tittenhurst the other night, after John's death, the tapes were gone and somebody there said they had been sent to America.' "

Further mysterious tales about John's archives are revealed when the film director Franco Rosso publicly reveals that "A film based around John Lennon recording the *Imagine* album with Phil Spector in Ascot, back in 1971, is lying uncut and forgotten in a film laboratory's vault in Britain. Around 70,000 feet of 16mm colour film, or around 35 hours, was shot during the week." He continues, "The project started after the *John Lennon/Plastic Ono Band* album and was originally going to be based around the 'Working Class Hero' track, but the idea expanded to include a portrait of Lennon in opposition to the music business through interviews and the *Imagine* sessions. John was very pissed off with the music business at the time. He could see through the whole thing. The aim of the film was to put his point of view. The future of the film became confused when the then Beatles manager Allen Klein wanted a slick TV film on Lennon for America, but Lennon, myself and another director, Nick Knowland, preferred our concept. As far as I know, Lennon, who personally paid for the filming, took a small part of the unfinished film with him to New York. But the rest went to Rank's processing laboratory in Denham, Bucks, and as far as I know it's still there, all thirteen miles of it."

Sunday, December 21

Aside from the stories about John, **Paul** features in a report in today's *People* newspaper . . .

Harry Warschauer writes, "Paul McCartney paid a total of £5,897 to hush up a German girl's claim to have borne his illegitimate daughter. Legal documents revealing part of the ex-Beatle's secret were handed over to the daughter, Bettina Hubers, in Hamburg on Friday, her 18th birthday and coming of age day. Lawyer Jurgen Wehlen produced the documents in my presence and Bettina showed them to me. They helped me piece together the full story of an astonishing chapter in McCartney's life. He met Erika Hubers in Hamburg where The Beatles were appearing in 1962, early in their careers. According to her, there was a love affair. And when Erika gave birth to Bettina, officials of Hamburg's Juvenile Department went to see her in hospital. Legal proceedings against Paul were in fact begun in 1964, but they were stalled because McCartney had long before that gone back to Britain. A spokesman for McCartney said in London yesterday, 'Paul is not contactable for comment.' "

On **Tuesday, December 30**, the *Evening Standard* reports "Los Angeles: A 1956 Bentley S1, once owned by John Lennon and featuring the definitive psychedelic paint job, is being prepared for auction next month. Mr Rick Cole, the professional auctioneer who will sell the multi-coloured Bentley, says Lennon's car may bring in £25,000 to £50,000. He will donate his commission to Lennon's Spirit Foundation."

Tuesday, January 6

The Times' New York correspondent reports, "Mark Chapman, accused of murdering John Lennon, the former Beatle, pleaded not guilty in a short court appearance here today. His lawyer said his defence would be insanity. The judge appointed two psychiatrists and a psychologist to examine the prisoner's state of mind. He has already received long psychiatric examination and supervision at Belle Vue Hospital in Manhattan since his arrest. Wreaths and flowers are still being placed outside the New York flats where Lennon lived."

Thursday, January 8

Andy Peebles, the Radio One DJ who interviewed John just two days before his slaying, announces that he has turned down offers for his story, which could have netted him around £100,000 . . .

Andy Peebles announces, "I just feel that it is morally wrong for me to make money from John Lennon's death. I turned down fat cheques offered by newspapers and magazines and I plan to give the substantial royalties from a book, which the BBC are publishing of his interview, to a charity of Yoko's choice. People have told me I am missing the chance of a lifetime. I must admit the temptation was there, but when I see some of the extraordinary people who crawled out of the woodwork to sell stories about John, I'm very glad that I didn't succumb. I carried out my interview as part of my work for the BBC. They pay me very well and that is enough."

Thursday, January 22

Another BBC Radio One deejay, Anne Nightingale, writes in her *Daily Express* column, "It is now 44 days since John Lennon was shot dead in New York. Yet there is no sign that the overwhelming reaction to his death has abated, especially in terms of record sales. EMI report that sales of John Lennon and Beatles records since his death on December 8 are approaching two million in Britain. 'Imagine' tops the charts this week, for the third week running. Since Lennon's death, only at Christmas did his records slip from the No. 1 position. 'Woman', another single taken from his last album, *Double Fantasy*, went into this week's chart at No. 3. It is expected to take over from 'Imagine' at No. 1 next week or the week after. There are three John Lennon singles in the top 20, and nine altogether in the top 200, including 'No. 9 Dream', 'Power To The People' and 'Give Peace A Chance'. Even 'Hey Jude', a Paul McCartney Beatles composition, has re-entered the charts. Eight Beatles and Lennon LPs appear in the album chart, including *Double Fantasy*, at No. 2. In America, it stays at the top, with '(Just Like) Starting Over', a Lennon single, as the No. 1 there. In other countries such as Spain, Germany, Holland and Japan, Beatles and Lennon records are best sellers . . ."

A spokesman for EMI Records in London adds "We had orders for half a million Lennon records within three days of his death. There was no way in which we could meet the demand until after Christmas." He says, "The Beatles' original record contract specified that none of their records were to be deleted, which means that they have been available since their original release. This removed what would have been a terrible decision for us to make. Of course, it could have appeared tasteless in the extreme if we had deliberately re-issued any Beatles or Lennon records after his death. But we have one never-released Beatles track, recorded at the same time as the *Revolver* album in 1966. But we have no plans to release it at present, though we were discussing the possibility before John's death. There is also a possibility that we shall release a tribute album at a later date, provided this is in agreement with the wishes of those concerned. It's possible that the unreleased Beatles track could appear on it."

Anne Nightingale "Public reaction to Lennon's death is reflected elsewhere than record sales. Heavy Metal fans are adding John Lennon's name in large letters to adorn their denim jackets. Yoko Ono is still receiving mail in truckloads at her home in New York. Record companies are being inundated with tapes of tribute songs written about John and many have been deluged with letters and poems referring to his death. In America, gold souvenir mementoes were on sale within a week of his death. Fortunately Britain has been a little more restrained in its marketing of the death of a Beatle."

Thursday, February 5
From her villa home by the sea in Poole, Dorset, John's Aunt Mimi speaks out protectively about her beloved John Lennon . . .

"It makes me livid when people make snide remarks about John's millions and ask what he ever did for Liverpool," Mimi blasts. "To set the record straight, he gave away one-tenth of his income every year secretly to a charity for spastic children. He didn't make a big fanfare about it. It was just something he wanted to do without fuss. If people have the chance to make money, they would be mad not to. The secret is to make sure it doesn't ruin your life and make you swollen headed. John still cared deeply about people and about the world. In his last letter to me, there was one paragraph that summed it all up. It read, 'So many people are dying so young from getting cancer or some other such horror. I count my blessings, Mimi. Believe me.' Sometimes it worried me that he cared so deeply about things. I had his MBE on the mantelpiece but he got so angry about Britain's role in the Biafran War, that he sent it back. It wasn't done lightly, but out of deep conviction."

Saturday, February 28
In light of the news that John left two-and-a-half million pounds in Britain, his first son, Julian has, according to UK tabloid reports, become a millionaire . . .

Julian remarks, "It doesn't make any difference to me. I know I am included in my father's will, but I don't know the details. The whole thing has been left in the hands of my lawyers and I am not really questioning what they have to say about it. I just want to improve my drumming and make the right move in my career. I have no idea whether my mother will benefit from it or not."

UK columnist, Dan Smiley "Julian heard the news on a radio bulletin, then went off to play pool at his local pub. Julian is likely to have inherited half of John's two-and-a-half million British fortune. The remaining goes to John's second wife Yoko Ono, who holds probate over the will, dated November 1979. His total fortune is estimated at £125 million and worldwide royalties boost it by £100,000 a day."

But, according to the *Daily Mail* "The division of John's total estate, estimated at £125 million, will not become known until next week in a New York court room. However, it was disclosed yesterday that the murdered singer's will includes a clause to avoid squabbles over the fortune. It stipulates that if any beneficiary petitions to increase his or her portion of the estate, they shall receive nothing at all. Julian denied any suggestion that he and his mother might contest the will. Cynthia, 40, has had several meetings with lawyers in London over the contents of the will. Yesterday, she was staying with friends."

MARCH ...

Yoko "It's still hard for me to take John's death in. For three months afterwards, I could eat only chocolate cake and mushrooms. What was there to stay healthy for? I spent nearly all of those three months in bed and when I wasn't, I was at the recording studio. People who wanted to see me had to come to see me in bed. A lot of people also invited me to parties, which they said would soothe me. But I was horrified at the thought of that. I'm not a cocktail party person. I'm too shy. In the first two months since John's died, I had about 200,000 letters. One day, I was looking in my drawer for a ring and found a little note that John had written, which I had never seen before. The letter said, 'Mother, don't forget the clocks are one hour fast, Daddy.' He always wrote funny little notes to me like that. Can you imagine what it was like finding that after what happened last December?"

Monday, March 30
Just three months after John's death, the acknowledged *Sunday Times* writer Philip Norman publishes *Shout! The True Story Of The Beatles*, one of the most groundbreaking books on the group ever written. It will instantly become an international best-seller . . .

Paul on *Shout*'s author Philip Norman . . . "Norma Philips, as I prefer to call her. I met him at a reception, a *Guinness Book Of Records* thing and he said, 'I'm doing a book, Paul. I've talked to all the people in Liverpool, Bob Wooler and all of them.' And I said, 'Oh, yeah, great,' and I didn't really like the look of him. He didn't seem the man to me to go and do the big story. I had a lot of stuff on so I wasn't keen to be interviewed, and the others weren't either. Nobody agreed to be and so he turned it all around and tried to do that clever thing at the end of the book, 'Unfortunately, I asked to see The Beatles, but they wouldn't see me and people have told me that I've got a better book because of it.' It's rubbish, you know. He's taken some very accurate moments and written them well. He's got a little bit of class attached to his name so people tend to believe in anything to do with the *Sunday Times*. It's not like the *Sun*. He just put some stuff in there that's just crazy, you know. But it's written very well and also set in a lot of true facts. But Brian Epstein and the hit man, Mafia, well, I think that's a lot of old crap! I really do. I don't know where he has got it from and the evidences about the merchandising set-up, I just think he's made it up for sensationalism. I really do think it's myths but it is true we did get screwed for all that merchandising. But in the end, it wasn't worth suing everybody. We knew most of them would still get away with it in the end. It was all Brian's fault. He was green. I always said that about Brian, he was green. We knew he was gay but it didn't matter. For a while he didn't know that we knew and we pretended it that way. And all these things about John being gay that's in the book! I just think they're old fruits these guys. They're just old fruits who are out to make a buck . . . The crime is for Norman to call it *The True Story Of The Beatles*. He never interviewed any of us for the book."

Paul's anger towards the book continues in an interview in the *London Times* newspaper, "I hated *Shout* for the way I am portrayed in it. The contrast between myself and John, so assiduously cultivated by journalists, was fabrication. I wasn't brilliant at school; I was trouble just like John. I got caned practically every day and the only exam I ever passed was Spanish. John and I weren't black and white, although people took John, for all his aggression, to be the good guy, because he showed his warts. It makes them sympathetic. I'd always thought that, in order to be liked, you had to be unwarty. What the book says about me being the great manipulator simply isn't true. Nothing happened in The Beatles unless everyone wanted it to happen. But when there was a decision to be made, somebody had to say it out loud and that usually turned out to be my job. I accepted it. I certainly wasn't responsible for splitting up The Beatles, as some people think. In fact, I was the last one to come to that view. I had wanted us to tour, to bring us closer together again . . . From a purely selfish point of view, if I could get John Lennon back, I'd ask him to undo his legacy he's left me. I'd ask him to tell everybody what he told Yoko in the privacy of his own room. Yoko and I talk on the telephone a lot nowadays and what she says, tells me something very important. John still liked me after all."

Monday, April 27
Following months of speculation, Ringo and Barbara finally marry, in a service at the Marylebone Registry office . . . After the ceremony, the contingent attend the reception at the Rags club in Mayfair . . .

The UK reporter, Danny McGrory files this report "With just a little help from his friends, Ringo Starr turns his wedding reception into a Beatles reception. It's back in the old routine for Ringo, George Harrison and Paul McCartney, together again for the first time in 12 years. George on guitar, Paul on piano and Ringo on drums, or rather Champagne bucket, were back in the Mersey Beat accompanied by percussionist, Ray Cooper. It was a party night to end all party nights at Mayfair's Rags club. Ringo's bride, American actress Barbara Bach, screamed with delight at the impromptu singsong. Silver spoons in hand, Ringo and Ray beat out that old rhythm and booze. The years rolled back as they launched into a medley of old hits that even Ringo's mum, Elsie, knew and joined in. There was 'Whole Lotta Shakin' ', 'Lawdy Miss Clawdy' and a rock version of the bride's favourite song, 'She'll Be Coming Round The Mountain'. The very private family party ended with two of their classics, 'I Saw Her Standing There' and 'Twist And Shout' and a brief return to Beatlemania as the guests went wild. And as Ringo and his bride left, someone was humming, 'She loves me, yeah, yeah, yeah'."

Paul "At Ringo's wedding, I was told that (Aunt) Mimi was upset that I had never contacted her after John's death. But I had never even thought of it. I probably haven't even seen Mimi for about twenty years . . . And I was saying to Cilla (Black) that I liked Bobby (her husband). That's all I said, 'Bobby's a nice bloke.' And she replied, 'Ah, but what do you really think, Paul? You don't mean that, do you? You're getting at something.' I was being absolutely straight but she couldn't believe it. No one ever does. They think I'm calculating all the time. Also at Ringo's wedding, I happened to go to the toilet and I met Ringo in there, at the same time, just the two of us. He happened to say that there were two times in his life when I had done him in. Then he said that he had done himself in three times. I happened to be spitting something out and by chance, the spit fell on his jacket. I said, 'There you go, now I've done you three times. Now we're equal.' I laughed it all off and it was all affectionate. It wasn't a row, but since then, I keep thinking, 'What are the two times that I put Ringo down?' I suppose we all do that. George told me recently of a time when I had hurt him. But he's done worse. He said he would never play guitar with me ever again."

On the same day, Paul announces that his seventies supergroup, Wings, were no more and had disbanded . . .

Paul "With Wings, with so many changes in the line-up, it wasn't easy. That often distracts you from the music and you start thinking a whole load of other things. You're thinking about the whole group image. Anyway, I got bored with the whole idea and I thought, 'Christ! I'm coming up to 40 now. I don't really have to stay in a group. There's no rule anywhere that says I have to do it that way.' At that time, Denny was staying with me and we were writing together. He was going to stay on but we had a bit of a falling out. There were little personal things here and there, little things that were just niggly. In the end, it blew up a bit. It was a bit of a number. We didn't part shouting at each other or arguing. It was his decision to part. It was his decision. He rang up saying that he was going out on his own to get his own stuff together. He thought he'd be happier that way. I just said okay . . . 'The group busted up! Wow!' It was nothing madly serious, but he did decide to go his own way, saying that he wanted to go on tour . . . He hasn't been on tour since."

Denny Laine "I left Wings for two reasons, one was money and the other was my missus, Jo-Jo. Paul and Linda didn't like her. They didn't want her around and that smashed my marriage. The McCartneys made her feel like an outsider. But I wanted my family involved. Paul used to have little digs about her, saying, 'I can't work with people around.' Jo-Jo used to send Paul love letters when she was a kid. She was in love with him. Linda totally misinterpreted it when I met Jo-Jo in the south of France when we were touring in Wings. She thought, and so did Paul, that Jo was after him. She was fascinated to meet him, but that soon wore off. Paul's not Jo's type."

Thursday, April 30

One month before the release of George's tribute to John, 'All Those Years Ago', the *Evening Standard* reports, "The Beatles sing their hearts out together on record for the first time in more than ten years. In a single to be released next month, they pay a poignant tribute to John Lennon. Soon after Lennon was gunned down outside his New York apartment four months ago, the three surviving Beatles put together their song, 'All Those Years Ago', written by George Harrison. It features the voice and guitar work of George, with Ringo on drums with Paul McCartney and his wife Linda harmonising. They recorded separate tapes, which were then mixed in the sound studios of their former musical director, George Martin. Harrison's lyrics credit Lennon with soldering The Beatles into the supergroup they became and adds, 'You were the one who imagined it all.' The guitarist tells his dead comrade, 'Living with good and bad, I always looked up to you.' The three Beatles' first record in over a decade does not mean they are back together, according to friends. It is a one-off recording and will be featured on Harrison's forthcoming album, *Somewhere In England*, due to be released in the summer. The single will be issued on May 15."

One of the tracks on *Somewhere In England* (released in the USA on Monday, June 1) is 'Blood From A Clone' . . .

George "It's all about when, in everybody's career, you take your album into the record company and they say, 'Oh, it's very nice. It's very artistic but piss off and go and do it better.' It's about that kind of thing."

MAY
Playboy reporter David Sheff and his wife Victoria write in their *Persecution Of Yoko Ono* article . . .

"Fred Seaman, still a trusted aide at the Dakota, is sent by Yoko Ono to Wales to visit Julian (Lennon). She wants Julian to have some gifts from his father. Arriving in Wales, Seaman begins courting Julian. He drops hints of his growing feelings of disillusionment with Yoko. He gives him the gifts and, as a personal token, a copy of the cassette of John's final songs recorded in Bermuda in 1980. Seaman's journals suggest that his aim is to draw Julian into his plan, to persuade him to claim he knew of his father's diaries and that Lennon intended his eldest son, not Ono, to be the guardian of the (John Lennon) diaries. Julian knows nothing of this but is thrilled at the gifts."

Monday, May 18

The *International Herald Tribune* newspaper in America run an advert selling the tiny, two-bedroomed terraced house at 9 Newcastle Road in Liverpool as "The house where John Lennon was born and lived during The Beatles' early days." But this claim upsets greatly John's Aunt Mimi, who remarks, "It has nothing to do with John Lennon. It was my mother's house and John was only there for a couple of months as a small baby. The Beatles never even saw the place. I'm so tired of all these lies. They're untrue and downright wicked."

But Richard Hunt, estates manager for Sullivan Management Control, the company who placed the advertisement, is unrepentant. "The address on John Lennon's birth certificate is 9 Newcastle Road," he states, "and the woman who lives next door remembers John Lennon quite well throughout his youth. People have suggested that we are selling the property for up to £50,000, but it's mad, considering we only paid £18,000 for it." Richard insists, "We will sell the house without any profit, as long as we are given assurances that it will be used for appropriate purposes."

On **Monday, June 1**, the respected UK columnist Peter Blake remarks on the continued, unashamed cash-in on John's tragic death . . .

"The tasteless rush to cash in on the death of John Lennon seems to be far from abating. Phillips are holding an auction next week (June 10) of items that include thirteen lots of Beatles memorabilia. A mere sheet of paper with a dedication to a fan signed by the Fab Four is expected to fetch between £60 and £100. And if you have about £500 to spare, you can snap up a folder of scripts, notes, photographs, press cuttings and other items relating to John Lennon. Phillips tell me, 'Most of the vendors were obviously autograph hunters who think they might now have something of value. We are basing our estimates on previous sales. We have got £280 for just the four autographs. If there are people who are collectors of Beatles memorabilia then they are prepared to spend a lot of money.' "

While one week later, on **Monday, June 8** in the States, Yoko releases *Seasons Of Glass*, her first solo album since 1974 and her first work since John's death . . .

Yoko "People are offended by the glasses and the blood on the cover. Well, there was a dead body, you know. I wanted the whole world to be reminded of what happened. The album is like a psychological diary for me. As for shouting 'Bastards!' Well, John would have added a few stronger words. It was mild compared with the event. Do people want to close their eyes to that? John and I stood for peace, but that doesn't make us holier than thou. We're human beings and by no means am I a totally peaceful person. I wanted that side of my emotion to come out on this album. If people can't take the picture of glasses because they're bloody, I'm sorry but I'm not sorry. John had to stomach a lot more. His whole body was bloody. There was lots of blood all over the floor. That's the reality. The glasses are just a very tiny bit of it, a mild suggestion of his death. I want people to see it and face up to what happened, that he did not commit suicide. He was killed!

"Going back to the studio where we made our final album together was like going back home and sustaining our relationship. It was like John was there. The musicians were right behind me and they shared the same rage and sorrow at what had happened. They were inspired and helped me a lot. There was this empty chair that John used to sit on and I couldn't somehow sit there. I felt him all around. It was hard when it came to singing. The strain was concentrated in my voice. It was a few weeks before I could get my voice anything like good enough to record and there are still traces of the cracking and croaking, which showed my feelings about being in the same studio, especially on 'Goodnight Sadness'. Making the record was the only way I could survive."

'Goodbye Sadness'

Yoko "We, John and I, separated for eighteen months (*sic* fifteen) around 1973, which was when I wrote 'Goodbye Sadness'. But I couldn't write the final line. It came to me only when he died. I don't believe things are written by me. They come from above. John and I believed in the psychic. So obviously I wasn't meant to complete the song until what happened last December happened."

'I Don't Know Why'

Yoko "One of the reasons why I had to scream in the middle of 'I Don't Know Why' was to show my hatred and resentment for what happened to John. It was a scream towards the world, not towards any one person. I don't regret doing it because I felt the presence of John when I did it."

Thursday, June 18

The *Daily Mirror* reports "Ex-Beatle Ringo Starr is believed to be planning to leave America and settle in Britain because of the death threats he and his bride, actress Barbara Bach, have received. Ringo is also said to be tired of the expense of hiring bodyguards to watch over them since last December's murder of fellow Beatle, John Lennon."

While on **Sunday, June 21**, it is announced that Ringo's previous love life is to be portrayed on the big-screen in a feature film . . .

Syndicated press release "The film is to be made this autumn by the jet-set playgirl, Stephanie La Motta, and it will be based on her love affair with the ex-Beatle . . ."

La Motta, the 23-year-old daughter of the American boxer, Jake *Raging Bull* La Motta, announces "My film will be a love story, but it is based on the fabulous times I spent with Ringo. My affair with Ringo ended two years ago, but I'm not trying to cash in on the romance. I told Ringo what I planned to do when I last saw him in London. He wished me luck. I wrote the script myself. The film is to be called *Goodnight Vienna*, which is also the title of Ringo's solo album . . . Ringo and I had a wild time in Vienna with Harry Nilsson, the singer, but while I was there, I noticed my sight wasn't so good. At first I thought that maybe we had been partying too hard, so I didn't say anything to Ringo. Then we went on to Greece and there my sight got worse and by the time I got back home to New York, I was completely blind. I was blind for a month and spent most of the time in hospital. It was then that I would write my story. After a month I got my sight back, although I still can't see out of one eye. The hospital told me that I had multiple sclerosis but my mum, dad and I refuse to accept that."

(Note: Stephanie's planned film, *Goodnight Vienna*, fails to materialise.)

Sunday, July 5

Stephen Pile, in his Atticus column of the *Sunday Times*, writes "Paul McCartney is desperately keen to buy the long-forgotten first-ever Lennon – McCartney recording, which has just come to light. So far, he has had a £5,000 offer turned down for the unknown disc, of which only one copy was ever made. It was recorded in 1958 by the pre-Beatles Quarry Men group. The A-side features Lennon singing 'That'll Be The Day' but the real interest is the B-side, which is an unknown love ballad written by McCartney and George Harrison called 'In Spite Of All The Danger'. It was McCartney's first recorded composition. While still at school, Lennon arranged for the recording to be made in a small Liverpool studio. Only one disc was cut and the tape was destroyed within 24 hours."

The seller of the unique disc is John 'Duff' Lowe, the piano player in The Quarrymen, "The record was passed around the group and it ended up with me."

Paul "I had it for a week, John had it for a week, George had it for a week and John Lowe had it for 23 years!"

John 'Duff' Lowe "I had forgotten about it and then, just recently, I remembered it and realised that it must be worth a fortune. I approached Sotheby's and they told me it should fetch a five-figure sum. The record has some background scratches but Sotheby's were surprised at its clarity and the instantly recognisable sound. Over the phone, Paul offered me £5,000 for it but I turned him down. He then invited me to his home to discuss it but I declined because I am a softy and I don't want to give it to him for old times' sake. I would love him to hear it or to have a recording but he wants the original disc for a Beatles museum he is starting. I was in the same class as Paul at school and one day he said, 'Do you want to be in a band?' We used to go round to his house to practise and on Saturday nights, we'd play gigs. After a bit, Paul suggested the recording. It was done in the back room of a house. At one point on the record, John goes very sharp and then he comes in late. He was very embarrassed by it. I sometimes wonder what would have happened if I had stayed with them. But with a pianist, they might not have become The Beatles. Actually, I never thought they were anything special, even later when they played at the Cavern."

Thursday, July 23

But, over two weeks later, the *New Standard* newspaper reports "Paul McCartney won a High Court order today to stop the sale of the only copy of the first record he made with John Lennon. John Lowe, who played piano with Lennon and McCartney's original band, The Quarry Men, on the record, put the record on the market earlier this month. Lowe said he planned to auction the disc, which was cut in 1958. It is probably the most valuable single in the world and could be worth £100,000. Lowe said McCartney wanted to display the record in a planned Beatles museum and tried to buy it. But his offer was not high enough. The disc features the songs 'That'll Be The Day' and 'In Spite Of All The Danger'. Mr Justice Falconer ordered that Lowe should disclose the whereabouts of the record and deliver it to McCartney's solicitor. He also banned Lowe from attempting to sell it. Though the record was amateurishly recorded, the quality is said to be very high and friends say McCartney is desperate to own it."

Monday, August 10

Syndicated news report "Paul McCartney is to release an album dedicated to John Lennon after all. He is to release an album dedicated to John in the New Year, which will include contributions from most of the world's top rock stars . . ."

Paul, at the time of the press release, "Every superstar there has ever been will be on it. The only two we couldn't get were Elton John and George Harrison. But there will be Stevie Wonder and Ringo Starr, and a host of others. We've been recording the album most of the year and it should be out in the New Year. So far, we have no title for it. George wasn't left out deliberately. I think he was doing something else at the time."

Monday, August 24
The US reporter, Terry Coleman, reports from New York . . .

"Mark Chapman, who had pleaded guilty at a previous hearing to the murder of John Lennon, was sentenced here to twenty years to life. While two psychiatrists gave evidence on his behalf, and while prosecution and defence lawyers made final addresses, Chapman sat in a blue T-shirt holding a copy of J.D. Sallinger's book *Catcher In The Rye*, with whose identity he claims to identify. When the judge asked him if he had anything to say before sentence, he stood and read a short passage from the novel. Chapman arrived at the New York State Supreme Court escorted by guards carrying shotguns. On the 13th floor, outside the courtroom, notices informed spectators, 'All persons will be frisked', and, 'No weapons permitted in the courtroom' . . ."

NOVEMBER
Playboy reporter David Sheff and his wife Victoria continue to write in their *Persecution Of Yoko Ono* article . . .

"In a London newspaper, Yoko Ono reads that Julian Lennon has entered a recording studio intending to record some of his father's last unreleased songs, the ones intended for the *Double Fantasy* sequel. But Ono is dumbfounded. 'How could he have gotten John's songs?' she asks aloud. Seaman is sitting nearby in the Lenono offices and shakes his head sympathetically. 'Didn't I tell you that Julian was a bad seed?' he says. Ono calls Julian in England and asks him about the songs. He explains that Seaman gave him a cassette. Ono is confused but tells him that his father intended the songs for his own album and Julian apologises. There is a call a day or two later from MacDougall (Sean's former bodyguard). Elliott Mintz takes the call. 'I'm owed back pay,' he tells Mintz. 'Yoko will take care of it,' Mintz replies. 'Well, I'm holding some stuff until I get my money.' MacDougall says that when he quit his job working for Yoko, he took with him, for safekeeping, amongst other things, a pair of Lennon's glasses and a love letter from John to Yoko including the original version of his song 'Dear Yoko', and he'll be glad to return the items when he gets the pay he feels he is owed. Mintz takes MacDougall a cheque and retrieves the items."

Thursday, November 19

The *Daily Telegraph* reports, "Lord Grade, chairman of Associated Communications, said yesterday he has had five different offers for the group's music publishing business, which includes the copyright on the songs of The Beatles. Talks with lawyers of the former Beatle, Paul McCartney, have been going on during November for the sale of Northern Songs for a reported $25 million . . ."

Friday, November 20

John Moore, *Financial Times* "Former Beatle, Paul McCartney has had his attempts to buy back 'Yesterday' and the copyrights of all the hits he wrote with John Lennon turned down. Lord Grade, chairman of Associated Communications, said that he had rejected an offer of £21 million from Mr McCartney for the copyrights. 'If I sell,' Lord Grade said yesterday, 'I sell the whole business. But they only wanted part of the catalogue of the music publishing division, Northern Songs. They know what price I am looking for. I have a bad memory and I hope it is a nice round figure. I have had no approach from Yoko Ono for The Beatles' songs. Maybe she's thinking about it.' "

Wednesday, November 25

Neil Darbyshire of the *New Standard* writes, "Paul McCartney and Yoko Ono, thwarted in their attempt to buy the rights to all the Lennon-McCartney-Beatles songs, are to sue Lord Grade's ATV Music corporation. ATV Music, including Northern Songs, which holds The Beatles copyrights, has been put up for sale at an estimated £25 million. Lord Grade recently turned down an offer from McCartney of £21 million. Today, McCartney said that he and Yoko 'wish to make it clear that contrary to recent reports, we are not engaged in a battle with each other over the proposed sale of Northern Songs. We are, in fact, united in our intention to sue ATV for breach of trust.' New York sources have suggested that five offers have been made for ATV Music from such business giants as Warner

Communications, BC Records and Paramount. Despite the age of the songs, Beatles albums are still selling at a rate of a million a year in the United Kingdom alone. Lord Grade's decision to sell ATV Music was made in the light of disastrous losses of the company's films division . . ."

Lord Lew Grade "If Paul and Yoko do sue, we believe we have a settlement signed by Paul McCartney. It is to do with royalties and nothing to do with the copyrights. We own all the copyrights. They are saying they should get more money for their share as writers but a settlement was reached some time ago. I really don't know what they are looking for. They made me an offer to buy Northern Songs but I don't want to sell Northern Songs. I want to sell the whole company if I sell it at all."

DECEMBER . . .
Shortly before the first anniversary of John's death, a letter, bearing the return address of Attica State Prison, is delivered to Yoko at her Dakota apartment. It reads:

"Dear Yoko,
You may remember that I wrote to you previously regarding how sorry I was that I murdered your husband, John Lennon. My new attorney, Marshall Bell, may have contacted you concerning a possible agreement that would consist of seeking to use any funds, earned by the release of certain materials, towards charitable purposes. Yoko, if you feel that what I might enter into, even though all funds would be given to charity, is against your wishes, I would honour this completely. And if you do not wish me to proceed with the release of my story, you can be assured of my co-operation in this delicate matter.
Sincerely,
Mark David Chapman"

David and Victoria Sheff "The implication is immediately clear to Yoko. Her husband's assassin is proposing that she assent to his participation in a book. He assures her that all funds would go to charity. Sick, Ono heads for her bedroom."

Monday, December 7

On the eve of the first anniversary, Yoko gives an interview in the lounge of her Dakota apartment to the respected British reporter, Ray Coleman . . . "It has been a viciously emotional year for Sean and me," she admits. "I cry a lot and this has been the year of crying in this place. But I tell Sean it's better not to repress it. Let it all come out, sooner rather than later. He's an amazingly mature little boy and he understands. We talk about John quite naturally."

With Yoko still residing in the Dakota, the scene of John's senseless murder, Coleman naturally wonders why she stays here . . .

"This is where John died and for that reason alone, I don't feel like leaving here," she explains. "I feel close to him here because this is where we spent many years of our lives together. I haven't changed anything. The paintings are where John put them on the walls. Nothing is different. It's almost like by still being here, I'm still close to John. I would feel very, very lonely if I left here. I really like this place. For a few days after the murder I'd tell myself I couldn't go out of my rooms and past the passage where it actually happened.

But now when I walk past the spot, I feel like I'm talking to John. I don't want to be thought of by the world as a grieving widow forever. It's not a nice image. But what shall I say? That's how it is and that's how I am."

Coleman "Do you talk to Sean about John or do you both try to avoid the subject?"

Yoko "We're both aware of him and often talk about him as if John was still here. He comes up in the conversation, naturally. When Sean has something to eat, I'll say, 'This is what your dad used to like.' We are not repressing our feelings. Sometimes we are very sad and we cry and I tell him it's better to cry. We're not hiding our feelings from each other. I cry at the drop of a hat."

Coleman "Do you listen to John's music? Or is it impossible to listen to his voice now?"

Yoko "I don't particularly want to listen to John singing now. On the night he died, they were playing his music outside my home, in the streets. I haven't been able to avoid it since then, even if I wanted to. But at home, I don't put John's records on. That would still be very hard. I'm still finding little notes and letters, which he would write to me and hide inside a book for me to discover suddenly. That was a very sweet game he used to play. That sort of thing about John was very beautiful."

Coleman "Looking back on John's last few years and particularly to his final songs on your duet album *Double Fantasy*, it seems as if he was making a final statement. Did he have a premonition he was going to die?"

Yoko "In hindsight, it's easy to feel that way, though I can't definitely say so. Twelve years ago, when we met, he'd say, 'I want all the tapes I've made to be burned, other than the ones that have been re-mixed and put finally on disc.' I'd say, 'Why?' He said, 'If I die, some engineer is going to remix the sound and put it out and I don't want to see that happen.' So he must have had some kind of feeling that he was not going to live until old age."

Coleman "Why have you joined forces with Paul McCartney to try to buy back the copyright ownership of early Beatles hits, which were sold in 1969 to ATV? Is it for sentiment or as a business operation that you want to own the copyrights?"

Yoko "Originally, John and Paul owned the company, Northern Songs. They are the rightful owners of those songs. I'm left with the job of asking myself, 'What would John have wanted me to do?' It is my duty to John now to recover his rights as the composer of songs, which are important to John and Paul, as part of their past."

Coleman "What song do you think of automatically when you remember John and what do you think is his best piece of music?"

Yoko "Oh, 'Imagine'. We were both very proud of that song and I think John will probably be known for that song most of all. It's a beautiful song."

Coleman "What is your summing up of John Lennon and his contribution to the world?"

Yoko "He was someone who was very human. He really tried very hard to become a good man. In his last year, he was very, very good, surprisingly so. Maybe people often get that way just before they die. He was almost angelic and I remember that fact painfully."

Mid-December

David and Victoria Sheff "Yoko Ono goes into her private bathroom and finds Fred Seaman taking a bath during working hours. He will be fired and given $10,000 severance pay. Seaman writes defiantly in his diary, 'My immediate regret is that I won't have any opportunity to go through the files and avail myself of research material.' "

Meanwhile, Ringo closes the year heavily promoting his new album, *Stop And Smell The Roses* . . .

"I had five producers on this album," **Ringo** announces. "I thought I'd make a change instead of just having one. Paul and George both produced tracks, so did Harry Nilsson, Stephen Stills and Ron Wood and it was an exciting project to get all those guys involved, individually . . . For the cover, it was hard to find an image that was instantly recognisable that portrays an attitude and the cop is one who'll stand in the middle of the street and say, 'Stop, sir!' There's no gun in my holster because I'm against guns. It was the idea to wear a uniform just to stop people and in England you don't have guns. You don't have to have a gun to be a policeman."

In one of his numerous newspaper, TV and radio interviews, Ringo announces that, like Paul, he was born left-handed . . .

Daily Record (December 17) "It wasn't until I came to this country (America) that I found out that other musicians admired my style. Drummers were asked to play like I played and that isn't easy. Why? Because I'm naturally left-handed but I play right-handed. I was born left-handed, but my grandmother believed that was a witch's spell and she made me write right-handed. Now, when I go from the trap drum to the tom-toms, I have to reach under . . ."

Ringo also gives an 18-page interview to the **December** issue of the American *Modern Drummer* magazine . . .

"I never like to let my kit out unless I know the person," he reveals. "The only two times I ever lent a snare, it was broken. And it takes a long time to get it to how you want it to sound. I could understand others not lending their kit, but I thought they were real mean. I remember a guy asking me if he could use my kit and I said, 'Well, can you play?' And he said, 'Yeah, I've been playing for years,' and, if you can imagine, a guy gets on your kit and puts his foot on the beater of the bass drum pedal and thinks it's a motor bike starter, kick starting. So I just went over and grabbed him off the kit and threw him offstage. It blew me away. The man had never played in his life and he thought it was a motor bike. That was one time I lent the kit out."

During the piece, **Ringo** naturally turns his attentions affectionately towards The Beatles . . .

"It's not even just that we were the best," he says. "A lot of it was telepathy. We all felt so close. We all knew each other so well that we'd know when any of us would make a move up or down within the music and we'd all make it. No one would say anything or look at each other, we'd just know. The easiest word is telepathy. The band worked so well and we were four good friends, a lot of the time. But like any four friends, we had rows and shouted and disliked each other for a moment. Then it ended and I started playing sessions and had a really good time, but I was playing. You can play with any band, but that band was something special to me and it's never been like that again. I've had great sessions, great tracks, but it's never been like that, and I think you can't expect that if you walk into a studio and play someone's session. You're strangers. We had all lived together so close; we knew each other so well; that it crossed over into the music. We knew exactly what we were doing. That's even the wrong way to explain it. We just knew that the chemistry, it worked! The excitement! If things were just jogging along and one of us felt, 'I'm just going to lift it here,' it was just a feeling that went through the four of us and everyone lifted it, or everyone lowered it, or whatever. It was just telepathy."

Tuesday, December 22
The day that Sotheby's in London reels under modern day Beatlemania. UK reporter John Passmore reports . . .

"Paul McCartney bought back his old postcards, John Lennon's tie fetched £700 and Sotheby's, the auctioneers, rocked under its first onslaught of genuine, antique Beatlemania. When the dog-eared past of the Fab Four came under the hammer in the shape of old fan magazines, grubby autograph books and what were originally nothing more than John Lennon's doodles, the collectors went wild. They exhibited all the symptoms of teenage girls at a 1963 concert. More than 300 packed into the sale room, another 250 craned their necks to watch by closed circuit television and the re-run of Beatlemania was complete when someone in the crush sat on a fire extinguisher, flooded the floor and set the whole lot screaming. In a sale that was supposed to encompass the entire rock era, Beatles memorabilia accounted for £81,634, more than 80 per cent of the business. And one man put up his hand for almost £37,000 worth of the bids. Terry Smith, managing director of Liverpool's Radio City radio station, arrived with instructions from his board to 'Pay what you like. But get the stuff.' He did. He got pins and needles from holding up his hands to take 50 lots ranging from old fan magazines to John Lennon's piano at £7,500 and George Harrison's guitar at £3,000. He bought John and Cynthia Lennon's marriage certificate for £420. He even bought a virtually valueless moped with John Lennon's name on the logbook for an incredible £2,000. The free-spending Mr Smith didn't get it all his own way. A certain Mr Paul McCartney spent £200 on a postcard, which he had sent to a fan from Hamburg, observing, 'The weather is not too bad here.' He also spent another £300 on a collection of postcards, circa 1968, sent during his days of meditation in India. A three-and-a-half-inch self-portrait by John Lennon was bought for £8,000. The buyer, Mayfair businessman, Mr Johann Bendlen, said, 'I just like it, and it is Christmas.' "

Wednesday, February 24
Back in the States, Yoko and Sean attend the prestigious Grammy Awards in America to collect the 'Album Of The Year' award for the *Double Fantasy* album . . .

Yoko "Whenever I do something in public, I always think, 'Do it right so you won't embarrass John.' When I went to the big Grammy Awards, I knew I had to appear before many of the people who had disapproved of me and laughed at John for being with me. If I were going as Yoko, I would have gone in just jeans and a sweater. But I was going as Mrs Lennon and I wanted to do it right. I kept hearing John say, 'Show it to them, Yoko, show it to them. Give it to them.' So I went out and bought an elaborate dress, put my hair up, wore jewellery and make-up, a whole routine I never go through. I think John knew I had done it. I know it's a silly idea because he's dead. But that's definitely the way I felt."

But the Grammy Awards presentation becomes the final straw in the fall-out between Yoko Ono and the *Double Fantasy* producer, Jack Douglas, with news of their split becoming official today, on **Sunday, March 21** . . .

Syndicated press report "There is a bitter twist to John Lennon's last album *Double Fantasy*. The album's producer, Jack Douglas, is taking legal action against the murdered Beatle's widow, Yoko Ono, in New York, claiming he hadn't received money due to him. The album was completed only weeks before Lennon was gunned down outside his New York flat in December 1980. Douglas claims he hasn't received all of his money and was prevented, on Yoko's orders, from collecting a Grammy Award the album won last month. Yoko, 47, who inherited Lennon's estimated multi-million fortune, collected the award with the couple's six-year-old son, Sean."

Monday, March 29 (UK)
On a happier note, Paul releases the single 'Ebony And Ivory', which features a duet with the legendary Motown recording artist Stevie Wonder . . .

Paul "I was in Scotland and, sometimes, one good time to write a song is when you're not in a very good mood. And, as I recall, when I wrote 'Ebony And Ivory' I wasn't feeling that brilliant. So I went into a little studio I've got there and sat at the piano. I'd had this title lying around for a while going back to when I heard Spike Milligan make this analogy with black and white notes on the piano. He'd say, 'It's a funny kind of thing, black notes, white notes, and you need to play the two to make harmony, folks.' He made a little joke out of it, and I thought, 'Yes, this is a good analogy for harmony between people.' If you've just got the black notes, then you're limited. And if you've just got the white notes, you're also limited. So, eventually, you've got to go into them both. So I was thinking, 'If I was going to write a song about that, what might it be called?' So I came up with the idea of 'Ebony And Ivory'. I wrote it paraphrasing Spike Milligan . . .

"I saw 'Ebony And Ivory' described as insipid and vacuous the other day. It is a very simple song. If you're looking for a thoughty verse, you won't get it. You better look to

Coleridge for that kinda gig. That was the best I could do . . . Who else has a number one record talking about the black and white colour problem? Who else has done anything else remotely like it? There were a few records a few years ago, you got anti-Vietnam, 'Give Peace A Chance' and stuff. There's not many people actually even bother to take issues like that . . . 'Give Ireland Back To The Irish' I just had to write and 'Ebony And Ivory' I just had the idea and thought, 'Yeah, well, that says something I wanna say.' One of the reasons why it says it so simply is because I tried forever to write the second verse and never could.

"One of the things we didn't do a lot of with The Beatles was work with black musicians. We admired them; we always loved all the Motown and Stax tracks. We went crazy for all that. But, outside of Billy Preston, who played on 'Get Back', we never really worked much with black artists and it had been one of my unfulfilled ambitions. Working with Stevie Wonder came about because I had written 'Ebony And Ivory' and that was about racial harmony and I thought I'd sing it with a black guy and we could show, physically, that there ought to be some harmony by the two of us singing it. So I gave him a call and asked him to come to Montserrat. I told him that he needs a holiday. He came down and we did that one song, 'Ebony And Ivory', first of all, and then he started jamming on this other tune. So I jumped on the drums, thinking, 'Well, he's playing a bass line on the keyboards so I won't go on bass, and I'll get in his way.' So I started drumming and eventually he started cutting me back because I was doing too much on drums. I was getting too busy and spoiling it, really. It ended up with me just doing bass drum and snare. When Stevie wasn't there, I re-did the drums. Then I put the bass on it and made up some words and it became the track 'What's That You Doing?' "

. . . 'Ebony And Ivory' is a track lifted from Paul's new album, *Tug Of War*, which is finally released in the UK and America on **Monday, April 26** . . .

Paul "Doing an LP like *McCartney 11* at home was an experience, but I didn't want to repeat it. I want to do something different every time. I wanted to work with George Martin again. I called him on the phone, asked him if he was interested, he accepted and we decided to make a very professional album. It was the first time that George Martin produced me since 'Live And Let Die'. I really like him as a producer, and when you work with people who are really good like that it makes it easier for yourself. So after 'Live And Let Die', I didn't do anything with George for a while and continued working with Wings and stuff, and on *Tug Of War*, I just thought that it would be nice to have a change. He was interested in working with me again and we got together and made the album. It was as simple as that. George also played on the album, blocking out chords on the Fender Rhodes. I ended up producing him on those bits . . .

"This album was, at first, heralded as a kind of tribute album by the press, which I hadn't thought of because, I suppose, John would have been the first one to laugh at that . . . As if it was a film, once we had decided that this wasn't going to be a Wings album, George and I chose the right performers for every track. I wanted to play with Stevie Wonder on one song and we did two together instead. I wanted Steve Gadd on drums and Stanley Clarke on bass simply because they're the best and I wanted the best. Why not? I wanted to play with Carl Perkins. I have loved him since I was a boy. His songs were the first 'blues' I ever listened to. 'Blue Suede Shoes', for example. We didn't cast him in a track. I just rang him up and asked if he fancied getting involved. He said, 'Why, Paul, I sure do,' and he came down to Montserrat. He came down on his own, no entourage. He just turned up off the plane. He came down late at night."

Carl Perkins "I stayed in Montserrat for eight days and they treated me as if I was just one of the bunch."

Paul "We were in the studio and he came down and said, 'My, it's real pretty round here, Paul.' He went to bed, got up the next morning and he obviously hadn't seen the island. So he came back later that day and said, 'Paul, believe me. This morning, I thought I'd died and gone to heaven when I woke up. It's so pretty here and so beautiful.' So while he was there, I wrote the track 'Get It'. We had a bit of fun recording it. I can always see Laurel & Hardy dancing to this track."

Carl Perkins "The night before I was supposed to leave, I thought I might run short of words telling Paul how much I appreciated him having me down there, so I wrote down some words and put a little tune to them. I called it 'My Old Friend', and sang it to him the next morning. Then I had to stay another day, because he said, 'This is one we have to record.' Linda told me, 'He doesn't cry a lot, but you touched him with that song.' I only meant the song to be from me to him, but it turned out that it sounds like John Lennon is talking to him."

'Tug Of War'

Paul "On the orchestra, we were quite happy with it, but we just weren't 'over the top' happy with it. So we decided to do it again. With George Martin, it was, 'Oh, come on, let's really get it right,' and that attitude really made the album enjoyable, because you know that by the time you finish the album, you're going to have an album that you started off wanting."

'Somebody Who Cares'

Paul "I played the album to my kids and out of all the hooks on this record, my four-year-old boy, James, sings 'Somebody Who Cares' and I don't know why he chose that hook from the whole album. He's a baby and he now knows 'Somebody Who Cares' and so he goes around humming it . . . We decided we wanted the distinctive Spanish guitar sound on the session. I had written it the day before, out in Montserrat. We used to have the weekends off, because I like to do that, otherwise you just work yourself into the ground. I like a break and then you come back so fresh. On this Sunday afternoon, I sat outside and just got my guitar and went off into a corner. I knew that Steve Gadd and Stanley Clarke were coming in the next day and we were going to do a session. So instead of just doing one of the songs that I had written, I thought that it would be really nice if I wrote something fresh and I'd play it fresh to them and we'll all be up to the same time on the thing. So I wrote 'Somebody Who Cares', took it to the session but I still didn't have a middle. So I said, 'Hang on a couple of minutes, I've got a bit of a song, it's gonna be good. Give me about an hour. Go and have a cup of tea.' So I sat around for an hour, got the middle bit, which I was happy about and went back into the studio. Stanley started ad-libbing a bit on his bass, and I started off on my acoustic."

'Ballroom Dancing'

Paul "Like most people, I've got memories that go back to when I was a teenager, like when George Harrison and I used to go to the local dance and neither of us would ever dare to ask a girl to dance until the last waltz. It was then that we thought, 'Oh God, we've wasted all our money when all we came here for was to touch a girl. We've got to do it. Okay, let's waltz, come on.' We were always too shy but we'd always try and grab someone for that last dance. But most times we'd get refused. We never really got into ballroom dancing but that was where you went if you wanted to dance. We'd go to The Locarno or The Grafton, all the big ballrooms. And with The Beatles, the ballroom circuit was a big circuit. We did a lot of ballrooms in our early career before we gravitated to the theatres. The song 'Ballroom Dancing' was just little images you have as a kid, flying carpets, playing Davy Crockett, going down the Nile in a china cup, all these childhood images mixed up with this ballroom. It's a lot of little images involved in growing up."

'The Pound Is Sinking'

Paul "When you are looking through the papers, you always see headlines saying, 'The Pound Has Moved A Quarter Of An Inch Today', and 'The Mark Has Made A Surprising Move Today In The Money Markets'. I see these pictures of all the hundreds of people on the phones saying, 'Did it go up? Did it go down?' But I've never really been into that. I'm not a big stocks and shares man, just because it all seems so crazy, it's just a big gamble to me. I think it's funny how you see how the pound is sinking, no it isn't, it's gone up and against the dollar, it's 2.000003 or whatever. I think it's funny how everyone gets serious about something that is obviously just going to keep on altering. The song 'The Pound Is Sinking' laughs at how everyone gets so serious about it."

'Be What You See' (link)

Paul "The idea originally was that I wanted a few moments on the album where, like on a Pink Floyd album, you'll get a sound developing into another sound, and I like that kind of thing, like where a radio play atmosphere develops. Carl (Perkins) and I had a joke at the end of 'Get It' and he started laughing. It was a nice way to end the track. It was genuine laughing but I wanted the laughing to go on into something more mystical. So I got on a vocoder, which Herbie Hancock, the musician, uses, where you play the actual notes with your mouth. And I got into this and it developed like the way you hear on the album, mixed into the next track. It's difficult because if you start a short track and it starts to sound good, how do you finish it? It's only a link you're making, but you've got to get out. You can't stay there forever, because it was only meant to be a link. We kept it like that with the laughing."

'Here Today'

Paul "I was kind of crying when I wrote it. It's like a dialogue with John. One of my feelings even when he used to lay into me was that he really didn't mean it. I could always see why he was doing it. There was this spectrum of me, which I understand because he had to clear the decks just like I did. In the song, John would hear me saying that and say, 'Oh, piss off! You don't know me at all. We're worlds apart. You used to know me but I've changed.' But I feel that I still knew him. The song is me trying to talk back to him, but realising the futility of it because he is no longer here, even though that's a fact I can't quite believe, even to this day. The 'I love you' part was hard to say. A part of me said, 'Hold on. Wait a minute. Are you really going to do that?' I finally said, 'Yeah, I've got to. It's true.'"

Paul "I think the main reason why the album took so long to make was because we decided that we wouldn't stick any limits on ourselves. We thought that if it was going to take a long time, then it would take a long time. It's like a film. If you dash it off, then you've got one kind of film, but if you want something like the flying saucer in *Close Encounters*, you've got to give it time. It didn't actually feel like a long time but actually we've been working on two albums, rather than one."

In the *LA Times* (on **Sunday, April 25**), on the eve of *Tug Of War*'s release, Paul talks about the reflective theme of the album with Robert Hilburn . . .

"At one time I didn't think life was a tug of war," he says. "Even when I wrote 'When I'm 64', I had the feeling that everything was possible. The age 64 seemed as far away to me as 150. It's not until you get into your thirties that you start seeing the other side of it. You see how your life can be affected by things that are irrational and beyond your control. You suddenly begin to realise how delicate everything is. I like to convey optimism, there already seems to be so much pessimism around that you don't figure the world needs any more of it. Besides, I don't like it when people around me are negative. I know death is there, but I don't like to sit around all night and talk about it. When I started making this album, though, I realised that these feelings are real too, and that I shouldn't try to ignore them."

Hilburn "Why did you decide to work with George Martin again? Do you think you may have avoided working with him before because of his ties to The Beatles days?"

Paul "Sure. I did 'Live And Let Die' with him, but never a whole album. I don't think I could have for a while. After The Beatles' break-up, everything was so weird. Everyone was warring and we didn't want to be around anything or anyone who reminded us of the pain. In my shows, I wouldn't even do Beatles songs at first. They almost had to break my arm to do 'Yesterday', which was silly because I loved a lot of those songs. The thing is I had to convince myself there was life for me after The Beatles, so I couldn't very well go back to George Martin because he was part of The Beatles. Eventually, though, you get over that."

Hilburn "What about touring? It's been since 1976 in this country?"

Paul "Before John's death, I had been thinking about it, but his death changed a lot of that stuff because it just, sort of, changed my plans. Now, I'm not really bothering to have any plans about it. But I do still enjoy performing. I'd eventually like to go out with some of the musicians I've been working with lately. They're so good that they challenge you to do your best, just like I used to get with The Beatles."

Hilburn "Why the reflective tone (on *Tug Of War*)?"

Paul "I think it's just something that happens naturally as you get older. You don't have to have a certain birthday to make you realise the changes in your life. One big thing is having children and being a parent. Your worry quotient automatically goes up with that. You can't help it. For instance, our doctor in London advised against giving a whooping cough vaccination to the children because there's reportedly a slight chance of brain damage. He said just let it go. So, of course, James got it. And it lasted for months. It was like something out of the Victorian ages . . . the baby was coughing and going blue. You're standing there helpless. It doesn't matter what you've done or what you've got. You're helpless. It's a terrible feeling. You can't go through too many episodes like that before you start asking yourself, 'Jesus Christ, what's this all about?' "

Hilburn "Did you resist writing a song about John at first?"

Paul "Yes, I worried that it might not be good enough and that someone might think I was trying to cash in on it or something. I was kind of crying when I wrote it. I'm sure you understand why without me going into it all. His death is something that the three of us find very difficult to talk about, even to each other."

While in the *New York Times*, in a piece by Robert Palmer, **Paul** again spoke about his relationship with John and the writing of 'Here Today' . . .

"Even though he put me down, I'm not going for it," Paul announces. "We were friends and we got it on, we got a lot on. Songwriting is like psychiatry, you sit down and dredge up something that's inside, you bring it out front. I just had to be real and say, 'John, I love you.' I think being able to say things like that in songs can keep you sane."

The reviews for *Tug Of War* start appearing . . .

Music critic, Karen Dyson "*Tug Of War* hit the streets only three days ago and I already find myself humming the tunes as I sit at my office desk, or on the road home from work. Each musical piece on *Tug Of War* is a special thanks to the brilliance of George Martin and, of course, Paul McCartney . . . There is so much to be said about the LP. If you listen to *Tug Of War*, you'll see (hear) that the album says it all. What stands out the most for me, though, is that Paul has finally come out of the closet. There actually is a real man behind the imagery he/we created. I feel he's finally being honest with us and perhaps himself. It seems many of McCartney's compositions have been written just for the sake of writing songs, not that they weren't great songs, don't get me wrong. I don't mean to say Paul has never been straight with us, but that he so rarely gives us a glimpse of what is really inside the man. *Tug Of War* gives us so much all at once."

The glowing reviews continue . . .

Jim McFarlin, the *Detroit News* "There are no 'Silly Love Songs' here, no hints of a bandsman on the run from his legend. In McCartney's 12-year solo career, only his 1970 *McCartney* can match this one for pregnant anticipation and only 1973's *Band On The Run* comes close to the new album in terms of aural complexity and consistent songwriting quality. To say that *Tug Of War* is McCartney's finest solo LP seems insufficient. It may be the 1980s' first classic rock album."

Steve Pond, *Los Angeles Times* "For the past several years, McCartney has been squandering all his talent so blatantly that, by all rights, most of his fans should have long since deserted him. His current No. 1 'Ebony And Ivory' can't be encouraging. It is as insipid a song as he's ever recorded, wasting another good McCartney melody with simplistic, simply dumb lyrics. That's why it's such an amazing, wonderful surprise to find that *Tug Of War* is a resonant and almost completely satisfying album. Maybe it's easy to over-praise *Tug Of War* simply because the album is so superior to anything McCartney has done in years. The record lacks the sustained eloquence of *Band On The Run*, and most of his Beatles work. But it's a delicious shock to find that Paul McCartney still is capable of that kind of work, to realise that he still can match his consummate craftsmanship with so much heart, soul and depth. So let's not worry about over-praising him. Let's just welcome him back."

Rolling Stone magazine "*Tug Of War* is the masterpiece everyone has always known Paul McCartney could make. The songs are far more substantial than the eccentric doodling of recent albums. A record with sumptuous scope that recalls *Sgt. Pepper* and *Abbey Road*. Of the many albums McCartney has churned out in his twelve-year solo career, only *Band · On The Run* comes close to touching *Tug Of War* in the richness of its style and the consistency of its songs. Paul McCartney has left the rest of his solo career behind in the dust."

C.P. Smith, *The Register* "Before deification is finalised, a dissenting view. Paul McCartney's newest album has received so much preliminary praise that it's important to state that this is not the perfect album it's being touted as. There are flaws here, flaws which may render it, with time, the same as all his other solo efforts. Nevertheless, *Tug Of War* is his one album which disproves the old 'Paul is dead' line. Though a pop songwriter of the purest sort, McCartney doodled his way through the 70s without making a dent. Okay, *Band On The Run* was a palatable album and some of those singles were catchy, but name one Seventies song that stands up to the perfection of 'Yesterday', 'Eleanor Rigby' or any of the other Beatles era McCartney gems . . . Far and away the best title on the *Tug Of War* album is the brief, unabashedly sentimental song about John, 'Here Today'. Only Paul could write something this naked and innocent and (no other word says it) right. Whatever problems there are with the album, this song puts McCartney in a place where one can say, without equivocation, he's making great music. Not great in the context of the current scene or his own career or any other context, just great music, once again."

Tuesday, March 30

The honeymoon period for Ringo and Barbara comes crashing to the ground when the columnist Suzy in the *New York Daily News* announces doubts about their fairytale eleven-month marriage . . .

"Bottles and punches were thrown during a violent argument between Ringo and Barbara," she claims, adding, "their marriage could crash anytime. Their rows take place in public as well as at home. Ringo and Barbara had one of their biggest fights during a recent holiday on the Caribbean isle of Antigua. Bottles flew through the air and slaps were administered. So far they have managed to kiss and make up but for how long?"

Monday, April 12

Meanwhile, the public attacks on Yoko continue when her former hairdresser and make-up man, Luciano Sparacino, claims in an American tabloid magazine that "Yoko Ono was planning to divorce John Lennon just before the ex-Beatle was assassinated. She had become bored with her 11-year marriage to the superstar. I spent a lot of time with her during the five months John was in the Bahamas writing music for their last album *Double Fantasy*. She told me, 'I'm bored with John and tired of living in his shadow.' Yoko had made a vow that as soon as the record was finished, the marriage would be over."

George, Olivia, Dhani and his nanny, Racheal, meanwhile, are to be found down under in Australia, arriving at Brisbane Airport and being quickly whisked away by private helicopter to a penthouse at Surfers Paradise on the Gold Coast. One local newspaper inaccurately announces that "The pot-smoking superstar was here to buy some land." George, in fact, spends his time in Australia visiting and staying with the former world motor racing champion, Alan Jones, at his vast ranch, north of Melbourne. In addition, he also makes a visit to the Hare Krishna hilltop headquarters in New South Wales. The Harrisons also make a trip to Sea World where George was, apparently, seen riding the dolphins! Besides filming an appearance on *Good Morning Australia*, George's only newspaper interview while he is in the country appears in *The Australian Women's Weekly*, dated **Wednesday, April 28** . . .

"He could have passed for a local fisherman," the report reads, "in his shorts, thongs and khaki bush hat. The only thing that might have given him away was the Liverpudlian accent. And that's the way George likes it. 'I've spent the last ten years trying to become un-famous. And I think that, just maybe, I have succeeded. Only two people have recognised me during my stay in Australia,' he says. For three weeks George, Olivia and Dhani had been trekking around Australia as typical tourists, visiting wildlife reserves, feeding kangaroos and koalas and picnicking in national parks. For George, it's his first return since the days of Beatlemania. 'This time round,' he said with a smile, 'I am here as a real person. I love Australia. Everywhere I go, I find myself thinking how happily I could live here. There's no tension. A lot of Australians don't know how lucky they are. It's a happy country. In Britain, one almost feels guilty for feeling happy. Winter is so depressing. Strikes and more strikes. Everyone is miserable. It's a constant struggle not to let the attitude of others rub off on you.' Because tropical plants cannot be cultivated with any great success in Britain's harsh climate, George is thinking of buying a home somewhere in the South Pacific. Back home in the UK, he loves pottering around the annual Chelsea Flower Show. Here in Australia, he has been visiting our botanical gardens, collecting ideas for the hideaway he may buy one day. About reincarnation? 'I wouldn't mind coming back as a grain of sand, at least I'd never have to worry about the press hounding me again,' George replies. Both George and Olivia are semi-vegetarians. 'We eat chicken and seafood,' he announces. But Dhani, by choice, is a total vegetarian. He is a bright, creative child, currently hooked on space toys. He speaks with a quaint upper-class English accent. Olivia spends hours each day playing with Dhani and George talks to him like an adult, patiently answers his never-ending stream of questions. Consequently, at three-and-a-half, the boy prattles away in a manner that would put to shame children twice his age. George feels they spoil Dhani, but admits he is drawing comparisons with his own childhood. 'We were lucky to get one present at Christmas time.' Dhani's toys are mostly educational and passed on to charities when he outgrows them."

Thursday, May 27

Meanwhile, the *Daily Express* reports "Ringo Starr plans to build a video and sound recording studio at his 72-acre Berkshire home. The former Beatle has asked Windsor and Maidenhead Council for permission to erect the two-storey studio at Tittenhurst Park, the Georgian mansion he bought from John Lennon. The application will be considered by the Council's planning committee."

Wednesday, June 23
Still in England, at the Elstree Film studios in Hertfordshire, Paul, Linda, George Martin, Eric Stewart, Paul Gadd and other assorted musicians, shoot a promotional film for 'Take It Away', Paul's new single. It is an event attended by selected members of the Wings Fun Club, Paul's official fan club . . .

Macca fan, Kathy Turner "My friend, Margaret Drayton, and I arrived at about 9.20am that day, and joined an already growing queue."

Paul McCartney fan Tracy Harris "My friend Bec and I both managed to get the day off from work. Our tickets for the filming said on them, 'Be at Elstree at 9.30am', but thanks to London Transport, we didn't arrive until 10am. The tube drivers would pick this week to go on strike!"

Kathy Turner "Eventually we were led to an enormous building, which turned out to be Stage 3. It was vast and almost devoid of anything, except some hideous green and blue plastic chairs. We waited with anticipation but at 10.30am we were told that we wouldn't be needed until 2pm and asked if we could come back later. As we stepped out of the studio, the rain came down in torrents!"

Tracy Harris "Then we were told that they, Paul's film crew, didn't need us until 4pm! So we spent six hours walking around Elstree in the rain."

Kathy Turner "When we came back to Stage 3, we waited and waited. At one point, we were told to go to the back of the stage, which we did only to find out it was for nothing. We were beginning to feel a little peeved at our treatment. Eventually at 4pm, we were told that everything was ready and the excitement began to return. We were led about one hundred at a time to Stage 4. We were in the second group. Some fans were already ahead of us in the studio . . ."

Tracy Harris "At 4pm, we were let in and we sat around the stage they were filming on. After memorising the set, I noticed a few girls going through a little door at the side of the stage. I dragged Bec with me and through the corridor at the end was a gang of eight girls, and through the open door at the end sat Paul having his make-up put on. Bec screamed, 'Hello!' The next thing I remember is Paul saying, 'I'll be out in a minute. Don't make too much noise, we don't want anyone else here, do we?' He came out and I flung my arms around him and kissed him on the cheek. Then he said, 'Better not kiss me as you'll ruin my make-up.' We said goodbye to him and went back into the studios. Then Paul and Ringo came onto the stage and we all stood and cheered. Paul said, 'Ta for coming and sorry for the wait.' "

Kathy Turner "When we got into Studio 4, Paul, Linda, Ringo and Eric Stewart were already on stage jamming. Paul introduced everyone and Ringo got cheers and ovations that lasted ages. When he got to the other drummer, Paul said, 'A Steve Gadd look-a-like called Butler.' "

Tracy Harris "People kept asking questions and he would shout back short answers. Ringo didn't say much, but seemed surprised that we wanted him to speak. Then we were given instructions of what to do, which was to stand up and shout, clap, scream for the end bit of 'Take It Away'. After each take, we kept clapping and the studio floor manager said, 'Shut up, for Christ's sake!' With that, Paul started pulling faces at him and sticking his fingers up and making us laugh. In between, he played little bits of songs, like 'Peggy Sue' and sang 'Heartbreak Hotel'. Someone shouted, 'Sing "Searchin'"' and he did. A group of girls wanted him to sing 'Yesterday', but he wouldn't. Ringo did though, and Paul sang about two words of it."

Fellow McCartney maniac, Tony Luscombe "The real interest was in the periods between shooting when they performed a number of standards and filled in with jams, including an improvised 'Elstree Blues'. They clearly hadn't rehearsed anything and the performance was surprisingly coherent. Paul's vocals were consistently impeccable, particularly on a superb Buddy Holly imitation of 'Peggy Sue'."

Kathy Turner "At one point, Linda started to sing 'Maybe I'm Amazed' and it sounded pretty good. Paul sang everything from Eddie Cochran, Buddy Holly, The Coasters and Elvis."

Tony Luscombe "Other songs they played around with were 'Twenty Flight Rock', 'Reelin' And A Rockin'' and something based around the 'Bo Diddley' riff. At one point, George Martin, who was on piano, played a muzak version of 'Here, There And Everywhere' and in one gap, Ringo jokingly suggested that they have a go at 'Mull Of Kintyre'."

Kathy Turner "We also kept having attempts at shooting the same bit of video with Paul only miming to the end bit of the record. But it kept failing for one reason or another . . . After we had been ushered out to Stage 3 and then back again, where the final phase of filming was completed, Paul said it was all over and added that if anyone wanted autographs they could come up, but he begged us to be calm, but, of course, people weren't."

Tracy Harris "To be honest, I think he looked very surprised at the reaction of the audience to him. At 8.15pm, it all ended and Paul did his famous disappearing trick. Heather (Paul's daughter) was in the front row, but said, 'I'm me, I don't give autographs.' Barbara (Bach) signed some but then wouldn't do anymore. We only got Paul's, but some people got nothing. It was, without a doubt, the best day, or afternoon, of my life!"

Thursday, September 23

The *Sun* prints a revealing interview with Ringo's son, Zak, who announces, "To be perfectly honest, being Ringo's son is the biggest drag in my life. I'm always being written about as Ringo's son, always classed in with him in every single thing I try to do. But I just don't always want to be in his shadow, always to be known as his son. I don't want to be known like Julian Lennon is, for being photographed in places like Stringfellows or Tramp with girls. And if I do get successful, I don't want to live like my old man, on a big estate and all that."

The article, by John Blake, goes on to report on his drum playing with his new band, Monopacific, an act managed by Peter 'Dougal' Butler, who worked as The Who's drummer, Keith Moon's personal assistant for ten years . . .

"This is a really, really good band," Zak says, "and I'd much rather be respected for my drumming with the rest of the guys than earn a million pounds."

Pete Townshend, of The Who, "Zak has the most accurate emulation of the late Keith Moon's style. Luckily, Zak has a style of his own, but many have been moved when listening to his explosive solos to say, 'Oh my God, it's him.'"

Zak recalls, "You see, my old man was never here. During my puberty, Moonie was always there with me while my old man was far away in Monte Carlo or somewhere. My old man's a good timekeeper, one of the best, but I've never thought of him as a great drummer, not really, at least not until the album he is working on now. But Moonie was the very best in the world. He was just amazing. Ringo gave me one lesson, just one, when I was young. Then he told me to listen to records and play along with them."

Zak on money "People might think I have a lot of money but they would be very wrong. Last Christmas, my old man gave me a hi-hat cymbal for my drums, which cost him about £40 and my mum, who I live with in North London, gave me a jumper."

Zak on The Beatles "They were obviously a really good band, but I don't remember them in the days when they were playing together. And, to be honest, their music doesn't really appeal to me. Now The Who's music, that was different. I've been into The Who since I was six."

OCTOBER

Appearing in the shops is the new compilation album *The John Lennon Collection* and *Gone Troppo*, the latest offering from George who explains, "Gone troppo is an Australian expression for someone gone a bit peculiar and, at that period of time, I had gone troppo. I just liked gardening and planting palm trees." But the album is a flop, largely down to the fact that George does not undertake any promotional work for the release . . .

George "Although there has always been a bunch of people who seem to buy my records, I didn't really seem to be getting them across all that well. There was so much pressure to have hits that I lost interest in even promoting my records. It's one thing writing a song, tape it, and make a record, but I wasn't interested in promoting myself. All that happened with The Beatles. I'm not into myself in that manner and I think you have to be quite a bit of an egomaniac to go touring and promoting yourself all the time. There was a bit of pressure once I started making my own records because everyone expected each of us to be as powerful as The Beatles, which was an impossibility . . . Sometimes you release an album and the record company just about ignores it and so many people don't even know it's out. And I'm not about to jump up and down and shout, 'Hey folks! Look at me! I'm cool and groovy.' No, that's not what George Harrison is all about."

Guesting on *Gone Troppo* is the former Deep Purple and now Whitesnake keyboard player, Jon Lord . . .

"He (George) simply chooses the musicians he will use on the new album, pays to fly them in, offers them five-star accommodation at his house, with resident chef, maid and cleaners, and rehearses and records for week after week," Lord announces. "Once he starts an album he becomes even more of a recluse than usual. George feels that he has said all there is to say about himself, but I don't agree. I don't want to build him up as a paragon of virtue but George is a charming, gentle man, in the truest sense, with a real Scouse sense of humour."

Friday, November 5

At Elstree studios in Hertfordshire, Paul begins filming *Give My Regards To Broad Street*, his first big-screen movie since *Let It Be*, some 13 years ago . . .

Paul "I was sitting in a traffic jam and I was bored and I had been trying to get together a film of some kind. At first, it was going to be based on the *Tug Of War* album, an anti-war film. We were working with Tom Stoppard, who's a great writer, but it wasn't happening. I think if it's someone else's idea, it's not as easy as if it's your own. I'd talked to a few directors and David Putnam, who did *Chariots Of Fire*, recommended Peter Webb. So I was trying to do this *Tug Of War* thing with him and Tom Stoppard, and it was all falling down, and I was stuck in this traffic jam, so I said, 'I'll write something then.' I wrote it first as an account . . . in the same way, really, that *A Hard Day's Night* was just these four guys going round from song to song and being chased by a lot of fans, which was a kinda parody of what was really happening to us. Well, this is a sort of *Hard Day's Night* of me solo. It's a kind of parody of me now . . . I wanted to do a movie because it was the only thing that I hadn't done in my life. We had very little to do with *A Hard Day's Night* or *Help!* Here I'm responsible for the script and play the lead part. When I was faced with making it, it was sort of like, well, should we get into this kinda space blockbuster and the first person I talked to was Gene Roddenbury, but somehow it didn't click. He had to go and do *Star Trek*. That was his baby and I came in second. Then I thought, 'Space films? That's Spielberg, that's Lucas, that's *Raiders*, that's those guys. They do it so well; there's no point in trying to compete with them.' . . . So *Broad Street* just ended up being a story about me and what happens to me and we decided to draw upon my entire composing output. We were trying to do the equivalent of a live show. When we began filming, I put up the first bit of money. I thought just over a million dollars would see us through but in the third week alone, we had spent nearly all that and I was ordering new cheque books."

Co-starring on *Broad Street* is Tracey Ullman, best known in England for her appearances in the BBC1 comedy series *Three Of A Kind* . . .

"Paul was lovely," she reveals. "I was so excited, I went hot and cold all over. It wasn't too long before the ice was broken and we were running around taking the mickey out of him and his Liverpool accent. But we were friends, really . . . The plot for *Broad Street* is incredibly complicated. All I know is that I get in and out of vans a lot and I never stop crying from the start of the movie till the end of it, and I look absolutely dreadful, as usual. I play this bird who can't stop crying. It's not a big part or anything. I enjoyed doing it and I got to know Paul and Linda quite well. Paul's excellent in it. He's a really good actor actually."

Tuesday, November 23

With *Gone Troppo* now languishing in the basement of the album charts, Garth Pearce files this report in the *Daily Express*, entitled "How George Harrison Became The Howard Hughes Of Rock". The article reads . . .

"The black Porsche 928 glides only momentarily to a halt as a pair of ornate green and gold iron gates swing open and close in an instant behind the car. George Harrison, former Beatle, ex-hippie, present-day businessman and multi-millionaire is home. Such glimpses are all that the outside world is now allowed of the shy, quirky musician who struggled to find an identity in the world's most famous rock band. But Harrison, nearly 40, and fast becoming a recluse behind the walls of a Gothic mansion called Friar Park in Henley-on-Thames, Oxfordshire, has slowly been building an entertainment empire like a Howard Hughes of rock. At this month's London Film Festival, Harrison's company, HandMade Films, launches three movies, *Scrubbers, The Missionary* and *Privates On Parade*, starring John Cleese. And a new solo album, *Gone Troppo*, has just slipped out with the strangest promotion, no interviews, no chat shows, no radio talk shows and no personal appearances anywhere at any time. Harrison's attitude is in total contrast to that of Paul McCartney, who is always enthusiastic to give wide publicity to every album he releases. Appearances on video, interviews and photographic sessions helped put his last album *Tug Of War* to No. 1 in the charts. But everything George Harrison is involved in these days, even his passion for motor racing, is operated in total, almost neurotic secrecy. All Harrison's income is protected and invested by Euro-Atlantic, a company set up by Harrison and headed by former Rothschild executive Denis O'Brien at a redbrick three-storey house in Knightsbridge, London. Over at HandMade Films, Ray Cooper, a 37-year-old former drummer with Elton John, is a director of the company and also producer of George's new album. Any comment from the luxurious offices with their pastel walls, beige carpets and oatmeal coloured sofas is as bland as the décor. 'We cannot do George's talking for him,' is the constantly repeated message.

"Those at Harrison's vast home operate on the same principle. Again he trusts only a handful of people. His brother, Harry, 48, is estate manager and lives in a Gothic gatehouse, complete with electronic surveillance equipment for the 42-acre garden, which would do credit to MI6. Brother Peter, 42, is in charge of 10 full-scale gardeners on the estate, more men than the local council employees for the entire town of Henley, plus a botanist, hired three weeks ago. Even Peter, who lives with his family in a modest bungalow, says, 'I hardly ever see George socially these days. I didn't know he had a new record out.' . . . Now, when George does emerge, it is usually to the garden or to play in the grounds with Dhani, wearing the sort of clothes seen on any Sunday morning at any pub in Britain, check shirt, jumper, jeans and anorak. Yet, in reality, all visits to pubs have long since ended. In a new book (*The Beatles' England*), there is a photograph of the Row Barge Inn, only 200 yards from the massive, electrically operated gates of Friar Park, with the caption 'One of George's favourites'. The truth is that the present landlord has been there since 1978 and has seen Harrison only once. 'He had a brown ale,' he recalled, 'about three-and-a-half years ago. He arrived in one of his cars, he has four Porsches, all black, and disappeared after just a few minutes.'

"As one friend of George's said, 'He has been through the mill before with The Beatles and now just wants the quiet life. What is wrong with that?' Behind the iron gates and warning signs of Friar Park, beyond the security scanners and up the quarter-mile red tarmac drive, there is no fool on the hill."

DECEMBER

The Beatles' former Press officer, Derek Taylor "At the end of the year, George and I drove to Liverpool and covered old haunts, Speke, Hale, the Institute, the Cathedral and the Philharmonic Pub. There was a nasty moment in Grafton Park, West Kirby, when a Securicor man drove up to my old house, number 27, where I had spent 25 years planning escape. Putting his camera away, George and I made our escape by fast car, not wishing to go into a long explanation of why one of the former Beatles was taking Instamatic pictures of someone else's house."

Thursday, December 30

The year ends with Ringo's eldest son, Zak, again featuring in the national press. This report comes from Alastair Campbell of the *Sun* "Ringo Starr's rebel-rousing son, Zak, has been banned from his local pub, after swearing at the landlord for playing a tape of Beatles hits. Seventeen-year-old Zak went wild when songs by his father's former group boomed out during a Christmas Eve party. He shouted for the music to be changed but the Fab Four sang on and Zak started hurling abuse at publican, Mike Gillings. The star's long-haired son was eventually hustled from the party at The Cannon, Ascot, Berks. Mr Gillings' wife, Sandy, 39, said, 'He was drunk and abusive and we won't take that from anyone, not even the son of a Beatle.' Mr Gillings, 36, revealed that Zak, has caused trouble in the past. 'I once had to put him to bed in the pub because he was drunk as a skunk. He'd been at a party in London and knocked us up after hours. He was legless, so the only thing I could do was let him sleep it off.' "

Sunday, January 23

The *Sunday Times* prints the following movie-related interview with **George**. The UK columnist George Perry conducts the piece in HandMade's headquarters, a tall, brown house in Cadogan Square, London, over some expensive claret from Denis O'Brien's special bin, with each bottle carrying its own special number . . .

"Making films is a frightening business to be in," he announces. "It's higher stakes than the record business. Both operate on paranoia, on the one hand you don't get something that's a hit, on the other, you get something that isn't a hit. Between that, everyone's tap dancing around, trying to be a success. The only people who have really got it covered are George Lucas and Steven Spielberg. They always come up with something new and original, and you don't even know it's been made until there are these lines around the block . . . Before HandMade Films, I was slightly involved in pictures through The Beatles, with the ones we made with Dick Lester and then with Apple, which as you know was the non-happening of the late Sixties, 'Come all ye faithful and we'll give you all our money.' . . . The good track record of HandMade is entirely due to Denis O'Brien. I'm a very bad businessperson. In fact, I loathe it. What with all the stuff with Apple. I was supposed to be a musician and I was forced into legal battles that went on forever. Consequently, now that I am free of a lot of the past, I know that if you can't control the situation, it gets out of hand. It needs somebody with a certain amount of weight. On the whole, HandMade Films have made more friends than enemies."

Denis O'Brien, HandMade Films reflects, "Newspapers keep saying I'm saving the British Film Industry but I can't deal with that. It's as though I sat down and said, 'The next thing I'm going to do is save the film industry.' I'm far too humble these days to think of saving anything; I can't even save myself! I used to go to the cinema when I was a kid, when it was very nice, Art Deco palaces with great curtains and goldfish swimming in the foyer. I remember seeing Walt Disney's *Bambi* when I was about four, it was the first film I saw on a big screen. The horror of the forest on fire, and that. Film is a fantastic medium, really."

Of course, the subject of George's former band appears in the conversation, forcing him to reply, "Bob Dylan said, 'How many times must a man look up before he can see the sky?' How long do you have to be a Beatle before you are satisfied with being on the front of every magazine in the world? It was just too much. Nobody should have to live a life like that and if I left it to the media to give me a break, I would never get it. They're not interested in me as a human; they're only interested in The Beatles, what guitar I played on *Sgt. Pepper* and all that crap. I'm a person. The Beatles are actually a small part of my life. I'm almost 40, and I was in The Beatles when it was a popular recording group for eight years, yet that eight years is all that anybody wants to know about. I can understand that but I'm not The Beatles. I have to try consciously to avoid being interviewed; I haven't done one for years. Yet the *Daily Scum* says awful things about me. If it was up to the newspapers, I'm Howard Hughes with ten-inch fingernails and Kleenex all over the place. When I do come out, I drive racing cars around a racetrack at midnight, or something . . . If I was sentenced to life imprisonment with The Beatles, it would not be that bad, because as Lennon said, 'We were a Trojan Horse. Everybody loved us, we were wonderful and they pulled us in there. Then we went, "Ha-ha" and revealed that it wasn't exactly like they thought. We were all a bunch of loonies, taking drugs and trying to be honest, yeah, yeah, yeah.' I think, with that, I'll get another bottle of wine. I know where Denis keeps it . . ."

Monday, February 14

UK reporter, Peter Sheridan writes, "Rock star Paul McCartney lost the rights today to at least £5 million worth of the royalties on some of The Beatles' greatest hits. A High Court decision ended a 14-year legal battle over such songs as 'Yesterday', 'Hey Jude', 'Eleanor Rigby', 'Penny Lane' and 'Let It Be'. The High Court in London decided to strike out the claim, first launched in 1969 by McCartney and his songwriting partner, John Lennon, for additional royalties on all their songs dating back to 1965. Although a second legal action, filed in 1980, is still being pursued for additional royalties, the Statute of Limitations binds these only to records made after 1974, eliminating the rights to nine-years' worth of hits from The Beatles' heyday. Lawyers for McCartney were unavailable for comment today but Michael Eaton, acting for Northern Songs, said, 'We are delighted. We always looked upon this claim as more of a nuisance than a real threat.' Multi-millionaire McCartney is unlikely to be too shaken by the judgement, however. He still collects royalties from the 20 or so hits he made with his group Wings up to 1979, plus their worldwide sales."

Sunday, March 6

Newsweek's Barbara Graustark writes, "Now two years after John's death, delicate Yoko, her face unlined despite her 50th birthday last month, is still adjusting at the Dakota apartment to life without Lennon and to bringing up Sean, now seven, as a mother. 'At first I was scared,' she said. 'Just looking at Sean was painful. He reminded me so much of John because he had been so close to him. And now, by this tragic twist of fate, Sean and I were left just with each other. I wondered, "How do you start a relationship from scratch?" ' Yoko's anguish wasn't eased when Sean wistfully asked questions like, 'Do you think daddy went away because he got tired of me?' But Sean helped Yoko through her miseries, too. Hiding his own tears, he would console her with, 'Don't cry, mummy, daddy's not the only man for you.' The worldly-wise little boy would later slip away to his room to cry and later perhaps to express himself with art. In poignant paste-ups he sticks pictures of himself beside those of his daddy. Giant tears run down John's cheeks as if to say, 'Daddy is sad because he can't be here.'

" 'I'm often afraid that Sean's not happy with me,' said Yoko. 'I'm not a mother who washes his socks and makes him chicken soup.' I asked her if another man could ever take John's place, as even Sean has suggested. Yoko was recently reported to have wed the interior decorator, Samuel Havadtoy, who bears a striking resemblance to John. He would have been her fourth husband. 'Sam's just a long-time friend who has been a good help,' said Yoko. 'But I'm just not interested in having any big smashing romance, like the involvement I had with John and I don't think that I ever will. No one can compete with the dead. If I'm crying about John, or Sean is, and our house is filled with his pictures, no other man could deal with that situation.' "

MARCH

In the States, the former Apple employee Peter Brown, and the American author, Steven Gaines, publish the controversial book *The Love You Make*, another inside view on The Beatles' famous story. Upon its American publication, the book is serialised in a US magazine, which leads to the following story in the *News Of The World* on **Sunday, March 27** . . . "Astonishing claims that Beatles manager Brian Epstein had a mad sexual passion for John Lennon have been made in a new book," the report reads. "The pair once even slept together so the young superstar could see what it was like, claim the authors . . ."

Angered fans rename the revealing tome *The Muck You Rake*, while the former Beatles are united in their anger at their one-time friend Peter Brown's betrayal . . .

Paul "The problem with Peter's book was that it was a betrayal because we thought he was a friend and he came round like a friend. If I see an old friend, they'll come round, I'll talk and I'll tell 'em stuff. I don't expect them to repeat stuff. Peter came over and said, 'I'm writing a book about the music of the Sixties,' and he brought a guy who was ghostwriting it with him and he was an American. I thought he was a bit of a drip but he's Peter's friend. 'All right,' I said. I invited them in, something we don't do, and was nice and hospitable. We gave them dinner, showed them the kids, it was all very ordinary. I know Patti (Harrison/Clapton) was furious because the same thing happened to her. We all invited him in."

Peter Brown "The attitude of everyone towards the book was, 'Yes, I suppose it's a good idea,' instead of, 'What a fabulous idea!' They were all totally co-operative. For the first interviews, we went down for the weekend to Paul's house in Sussex and he was super. In London, we did a long session with Paul that lasted for several hours. I had people coming over for dinner that night and Paul was going on and on and on. I kept hoping he would finish the interview so I could get home and start cooking."

Paul "We said, 'Peter, old buddy,' because he was such a friend. We said to him, 'We'll be able to see what the book is before it goes out, won't we?' And he said, 'Oh yes, don't worry, my dear. Would I?' And so we were all totally confident that we would see it all, and we'd all be happy and if there was anything that was a bit dodgy, something that was going to hurt somebody, we might ask him to ease it down. There's people like Brian Epstein's mum . . . she's an elderly lady, and she doesn't need that kind of stuff. Her son's died, and she doesn't need to hear stuff that puts down her son's memory, I don't think and it's very hurtful. So that was it and when it came out, we all thought, 'Cor, if we ever catch up with him.' It was a naughty one. He just brought the book out and he put in it every little bit of gossip he could find, including a lot where he has perpetuated some myths that just weren't true. That's really the tone of the book."

Linda "He was a friend. He was the one who introduced Paul and me. A man I trusted. When I was going to the hospital to have Stella, I handed him my baby, Mary, to hold. I wouldn't trust my baby to anyone but a friend but now it's like he doesn't exist. His book? Well, it doesn't matter what he wrote, because he betrayed a trust. We decided not to read it, but we have heard things. We put the copy he sent us in the fire and I photographed it as it burned, page by page."

Peter Brown "I think Patti and Maureen were nervous about having talked about the incest incident but I haven't heard anything from them. No one has called except Yoko, she's so sophisticated, so inscrutable."

Monday, April 4

The Times reports, "When the history professor, Jon Wiener, made a Freedom of Information request to the Federal Government for John Lennon's file, he could hardly have hoped for a richer pay off . . ."

John Wiener, lecturer at the University of California at Irvine, recalls "Every month or so, I would get a little package of documents from the FBI. Then, one day, 26lbs of material arrived. The entire Immigration Service files. Heavily censored, the FBI's records, as well as the hefty Immigration documents, told quite a story; details of widespread Government surveillance of Lennon and his wife, Yoko Ono, especially in the months before the 1972 Republican National Convention in Miami, Florida. According to the file, in April 1970, FBI director, J. Edgar Hoover, instructed some officers to watch John and fellow Beatle, George Harrison, who were then visiting the US. He advised his agents to look 'For information indicating they are using narcotics'. The bureau's wariness of Lennon mounted in December 1971 when he and Political Radical, Jerry Rubin, drew a crowd of 15,000 to a University of Michigan rally. Not long after that, the Senate Internal Security Subcommittee suggested in a report to Attorney General John Mitchell that Lennon be deported . . ."

Meanwhile, on **Tuesday, April 19**, the West Berlin judge, Ingrid Kuhla, orders that Paul must begin paying Bettina Huebers, his alleged child, $287 per month until the paternity suit has been decided, and a further $1,500 to backdate the payments to last September. The judge adds that if Paul is proven not to be the father, he can sue Bettina for repayment of the money. She responds to the news by sending a bunch of flowers to the judge, who just happens to be pregnant herself.

Paul "One thing I think is very unfair is that the judge is a woman and is pregnant herself. But I'm not going to ask for a different judge. I just want to get the whole thing settled. Never mind what the people say, or if the courts reject it. I know it was my blood. Professors tested it and it shows I could not be the father. It seems that the girl's blood contains something that is not in mine or the mother's, so it must have come from a third person and he is the real father."

Even Bettina's attorney, Bernd Guentsche, has to agree. "The blood test could have been anybody's," he says. "There is no real proof that it is his."

Paul "What I object to most is the effect this is having on my children. It's not fair on them. Why should they suffer? I have never met Bettina's mother, Erika, who claims we had an affair in Hamburg. People have said that Bettina looks like me, but the whole world is full of people who look like me. I mean, John Alderton (the actor) looks just like me but he's not my son, is he?"

Not surprisingly, the following day, **Paul** appeals against the judge's decision, insisting he will pay no money until his case is heard, adding, "I am willing to make myself available at any time to have as many blood tests as the German authorities wish."

While in the April 24 edition of the *Sunday People*, during a break from filming *Give My Regards To Broad Street* at Elstree studios, **Paul** speaks more openly about the case . . . "I am not Bettina's father," he insists. "I was virtually tricked into paying money to support her until she was 18."

Paul goes into how he came to settle the original maintenance claim without admitting paternity . . .

"It was (June) 1966 and we were due to do a European Tour," he says. "I was told that if the maintenance question wasn't settled, we couldn't go to Germany. I wasn't going to sign a crazy document like this, so I didn't. Then, when we were actually on the plane, leaving for the tour, they put the paper under my face and said if I didn't sign, the whole tour would be off. They said the agreement would deny that I was the father and it was a small amount anyway (approximately £2,700), and so I signed. I've actually seen a letter from Brian Epstein saying it would be cheaper to sign than not go to Germany where we could make a lot more money."

There was more unpleasantness and betrayal for Paul when, one week earlier on **Monday, April 18**, the former Wings guitarist, Denny Laine, features in a tell-all, television advertised, exposé about Paul and Linda in the British tabloid newspaper the *Sun* . . .

Amongst the many revelations, Denny says, "Paul McCartney is a dope. Why? Because he smokes much too much cannabis. I reckon he and Linda sometimes get through as much as two ounces a day, that's about £1,000-worth a week. Personally, I wish he'd just stop being so silly. I am having terrible trouble getting a visa to work in America and I am convinced that it is because I was a member of Wings and of all the publicity surrounding Paul and drugs. He and Linda did smoke a fantastic amount of the stuff by anybody's standards. They smoked joints the way ordinary people smoke cigarettes. Really, I don't think smoking that quantity of cannabis did Paul and Linda all that much good. Sometimes smoking a little cannabis helps to give you good ideas, but lots and lots of it makes you very indecisive and takes away your confidence. That's why Paul's albums take him ages and ages to make. He just cannot be decisive about anything. It is very frustrating for people working with him because he changes his mind so often. That's what smoking does to you, it opens up more avenues to explore."

While in another chapter, Denny claims that "Paul's influence over Linda is great. He is the powerful one and if he snaps his fingers, Linda has to jump. Paul has got that way with people. He takes them and turns them into the way he wants them. He can manipulate them. Linda should have stood up for herself instead of being so passive."

Linda "Denny Laine wrote two articles, one said I led Paul around totally, the other that Paul totally dominated me. But I thought that Denny came off badly. I could see some girlfriend or an ex-chauffeur writing such rubbish, but a musician?"

Sunday, May 3

In America, *The Globe* newspaper claims that "Record companies are hot after an alleged secret reel-to-reel tape, made when Elvis and The Beatles recorded a medley of their own hits in one of the greatest jam sessions of all time. Among the songs on this tape, supposedly, is a version of 'Hound Dog' by John Lennon and Elvis. The tape wasn't found among Elvis' belongings after he died, and was thought to have been lost or destroyed. But Elvis was a pack rat who never threw anything away, much less a tape like this. The hunt for this tape has only recently begun when it was learned that whole boxes of demos that Elvis had made in his hey-day had been shipped to warehouses around the country,

319

and forgotten. Record companies quietly began shuffling from Memphis to Los Angeles trying to get a whiff of the tape. And when it was learnt that competitors from Britain, Germany and even Japan were also hot on the trail, the Americans hired private detectives to give themselves the advantage. Rumours speculate that Paul has also joined the hunt for the tape. Of course, if the tape is found, it could take years to untangle the red tape prohibiting its release, since Elvis and The Beatles belonged to different record companies."

Sunday, May 29

The *Sunday Mirror* eerily reports, "John Lennon's ghost is said to be haunting the New York apartment block where the ex-Beatle was murdered. Several people claim to have seen his ghostly figure wearing familiar round glasses. Friends of his wife, Yoko Ono, say that John's spirit has spoken to her. Musician Joey Harrow, who lives nearby, is convinced that he saw John's ghost at the entrance to the Dakota building, the spot where he was shot three years ago. 'He was surrounded by an eerie light,' said Joey. Amanda Moores, a writer who was with Joey at the time, says she also saw John's ghost. 'I wanted to go up and talk to him,' she said. 'But something in the way he looked at me said, "No." ' Yoko, who still lives in the block with son, Sean, claims to have seen John sitting at his white piano and that, on one occasion, he said, 'Don't be afraid. I am still with you.' New York psychic, Shawn Robbins, says that she, too, saw Lennon."

Thursday, June 16
Paul records a BBC World Service interview at AIR Studios in London . . .

Question "Do you have any time for a domestic life?"

Paul "I have as much time as most people have, really. Most people work five days a week and take weekends off and mornings and nights off, and that's the same as what I do. And I can even take the odd day off as well. What happens is that I get a project on, like this album, and you can't leave it."

Question "So what are the things you would warn your children about out of your life and times and experience?"

Paul "Everything."

Question "Would you want them to follow you into entertainment?"

Paul "Not particularly. It's a tough business. You've got to be very good or you die real quick. Somebody like David Bowie, if he fails to have hits for one year, he's in trouble, or me. No matter how big you get, you are still proving yourself all the time. I happen to have been very lucky and happen to have learnt over the years how to do it. But kids coming into it, it's very difficult. The way we're playing it, is if one of the kids, when they're 15 or 16, is really keen to get into something like music or stage, then we'll help them. I don't think their heads can handle it before that age."

Question "Today, somewhere in the world, someone is going out and buying their first Beatles album . . ."

Paul (interrupting) "Yes, it's funny. You find a lot of young kids hearing it for the first time and seeing connections with today's music. And they see all the connections and buy it as if it's fresh again. You get young kids who know more about it than I do."

Question "Is there a Beatles track, which you particularly love?"

Paul "All of them. I'll pick out 'Love Me Do' as the very first one we recorded and I'll remember how I was scared stiff. We were standing down in the studio and there was George Martin up a floor at a big glass window at Abbey Road. We were in a different world. Nowadays we can go in that big glass control room, but we couldn't then. It was like Them and Us. If you happen to play 'Love Me Do', listen for the shake in the voice, that was all pure nerves. Then I remember 'Hey Jude' because that was great fun. 'Strawberry Fields' because that was crazy and amazing. I can remember so many of them. Some of the tracks I like are the little offbeat tracks that nobody has never heard of."

Question "Give us an example."

Paul "Well, not nobody, but a lot of you, won't have heard of a song like 'She Said She Said'."

Question "Looking back over the years, is there one hero that's remained consistent for you?"

Paul "I suppose John would have been one of the heroes. Although I never would have told him that, but when somebody dies like that, it's final enough and you can talk it all then . . ."

Question "People were surprised that John turned out to be quite mellow in songs."

Paul "That was only because his image was tough and like all tough images, it was because he was frightened behind it. He was insecure. He was as sappy as the next man, but you'd have to get him drunk for him to be sappy. He was tough as nails except when you started talking to him, then he was an old sappy."

Friday, July 15
A New York judge reveals the fate of Fred Seaman, the Lennons' one-time assistant, today . . .

Syndicated press release "A man who admitted stealing four diaries written by John Lennon was ordered never to reveal their contents. Frederick Seaman, 29, was warned by a New York judge that he could face seven years in jail if he made any disclosures. Seaman stole the diaries, along with stereo equipment and videotapes, from Lennon's New York apartment shortly after the star was shot dead in December 1980. The Supreme Court Justice Jeffrey Atlas in Manhattan had allowed Seaman to plead guilty to second-degree grand larceny on May 27 and put him on probation for five years. Later, the Manhattan district attorney's office said the diaries had been returned to Lennon's widow, Yoko Ono."

Monday, July 18

Meanwhile, in England, the world famous Abbey Road Studios in London throws opens its doors to the public for the very first time and presents the show, *The Beatles At Abbey Road* . . .

Gene Siskel writes for the *Chicago Tribune* newspaper "In a clever promotional stunt and genuine tribute, officials at Abbey Road decided to invite the public for the first time into Studio 2 to listen to some of the tapes, including one of the new songs, and to watch a two-hour film and video tape tribute, featuring many of the little known films The Beatles made, MTV style, to accompany the release of their classic songs. *The Beatles At Abbey Road* popped on the screen and the first thing you couldn't help but notice was the sound, the incredible sound, incredible to anyone who had never been in a recording studio before. What a treat! It would turn the film into a party. And there was plenty of information for the musical novice, too. The soundtrack compared many early versions of a popular song with the released version. We heard songs being built, listened to just the bass line and eavesdropped on Paul, who comes across as being very much in charge of the sessions, complaining, 'Where's the tempo, where's the tempo?' All fascinating stuff. And quite separate from the music as the film progressed, we noticed the physical transformation of The Beatles from mop heads to long hairs, to cite the most obvious change. In only the seven years of this film, they played a lifetime of roles. And on it went for the second hour, concluding with 'All You Need Is Love' and an early version of 'Hey Jude', which didn't sound like anything special, until we got to the final track. 'This is Ringo,' said the final voice. 'Everybody said everything else, so I'll just sign off by saying, "Carry on and best of luck from The Beatles."' The lights came up in Studio 2 and slowly but surely the sights and sounds of the Sixties slipped away, disappearing into the porous walls of the studio. The younger members of the audience were the first to leave. Staying behind for a minute, though, I noticed another member of the audience, a guy like me in his 30s. He was balding, too. We were the last to leave, and we caught each other's eye and we smiled."

Thursday, July 28

The *New Standard* newspaper reports, "Yoko Ono is fighting to stop an American porn magazine from publishing nude pictures of herself and John Lennon. *Swank* magazine say they got the pictures from a man who claimed to have found them in a dustbin, but Yoko says they came from her private collection and were probably stolen from her apartment before John was murdered in 1980. Yoko says the photos were taken for the *Double Fantasy* album but were never used. 'They were done very tastefully,' says Yoko. 'There was nothing dirty about them.'"

AUGUST

An interview with Paul appears in this month's *Breakout* magazine, today's equivalent of the 1960s *Mersey Beat* newspaper. He is asked for the latest news on the *Give My Regards To Broad Street* film . . .

"It's coming along great," **Paul** replies. "We've just finished the main bit. We started it in November last year and worked on and off till a couple of months ago. It was a big change for me. I did *A Hard Day's Night* and *Help!* and enjoyed the set-up of films. It's like a fantasy world but a lot of hard work is involved. I might make more films if this one works out. I think it's working out. I feel good about it and didn't even mind getting up early, which traditionally musicians don't like. It was great actually seeing the dawn again. I still prefer music, though."

Paul is asked what he thought of *Breakout* compared to *Mersey Beat* . . .

"Well, we were there when Bill Harry started *Mersey Beat*," he replies, "and for us it was just great to have anything, in truth, anything that was going to put our picture in it and have laughs. So, for that, *Mersey Beat*, for us, was great, and I'd say that, for the groups of today, having something like *Breakout* is great. *Breakout* is more professional. Well, actually, the cover is, but inside isn't . . . As for comparing it with *Mersey Beat*, it's like comparing a brown shoe with a black sandal."

Paul also gives a lengthy, heated reply to the question about the redevelopment of the Cavern Club site in Mathew Street in Liverpool . . .

"The redevelopment of the Cavern site is rubbish," he blasts. "They should never have pulled it down. It was the most maniac move and the one man who did it, one berk on the council, somebody must have said, 'It would be a great idea to have an underground railway coming this way. It doesn't matter about the Cavern.' I think there was a bit of an attitude going round at the time, which was, 'Well, The Beatles left us. They hate Liverpool anyway. They've deserted us.' We used to get an awful lot of that. I don't care. If someone's got to live somewhere else, it doesn't mean he hates Liverpool. Not for me, anyway. So I think a lot of the people at the time, maybe the council, were thinking, 'Well, sod it! Who needs the Cavern anyway?' And what's happened is you get all these tourists turning up now saying, 'Where is it that The Beatles were?' So you get the Cavern Mecca people and stuff trying to keep a little bit of that going. I just think it was a stupid move to close it down. They could have easily kept it. They would have certainly used it for this Garden Festival. They could have stuck a big thing up and said, 'Come on,' and charged 50p a go or something, like everywhere else in the world, Disneyland, Graceland. Instead, now they're having to go round all our old houses and do that trick whereas it would have been much better to leave it all in Mathew Street and they could have had Eric's. I don't know all the interior politics of it all but it just seemed to me stupid and the final irony seemed to me that now they don't need it. There's a car park now wherever the underground was going to be. Now they're trying to excavate it and it'll cost them much more. Typical bureaucratic crap. You know, where they fill in a thing and now they're excavating it, spending millions. Now they've found a pothole in the Cavern and they've got a little boat in the water, so I've heard, and there's a bank or some big building society putting money in and they're going to recreate it downstairs. I think it's stupid, myself. I'd rather just see all of that stuff go. I mean, I don't want to down the Garden Festival because it's happening, and so it's best to get behind it, I suppose, because I just think surely you could spend the money better in somewhere like Liverpool, where you've got so many people who need a break. Instead of all those statues they've put up, I'd rather see them put up one little plaque, 'This is where they're from' or something. I've always said that, you know, first they want to put statues up, then they don't want to put them up. Then they don't want to pay for it, and then they want the people to pay for it. I think it's stupid. I think there are much better things they could do, but you have to have a touch of class and touch of genius to know all this, see, and they haven't got it. Those councillors, whoever it was who filled the Cavern in, are just not bright, just not that smart."

SEPTEMBER

Interviews with Paul continue to appear. The latest appears in this month's edition of
Musician & Recording World. Paul Ashford conducted the piece at AIR Studios in
London. McCartney had agreed to the 50-minute interview because he just fancied
talking about his green Alpico Amp . . .

"The thing is," **Paul** explains, "in truth, it ends up that most interviews don't mean
anything. You just talk to everyone on earth about anything, toothpaste; you name it, just
blabbing off about anything they want to hear about. But with this magazine, I know the
musos (musicians) read it. It's a bit more satisfying than talking about what soap you use
all the time. I want to talk about what I'm interested in, which is music. That's how we
started, picking our way from guitars through pianos and basses and various other
instruments. Actually, playing the instruments is the important thing and the personality
thing is just what happens to come with it if you do your job well. You never get to like
that better than the musician bit."

Paul then proceeds to chat about his Alpico amp . . .

"This week," he reveals, "I've been using, on the new album, the Alpico, which is the first
amp I ever bought. It's a valve amp and I like valve amps. A little green Alpico and it's
brilliant, really good. We've just been using it on one of the tracks and it pokes like mad
because it's an old valve amp. Great, it's like an automatic buzz and, of course, it's fun
using the first one you ever had, again. I still have one of the old Beatles basses, although
I'm not sure whether it's the first. An old violin bass, and the great thing about it is that
it's still got the running order list taped on with sellotape. It starts with 'Rock'n'Roll
Music', and goes on to 'Baby's In Black'. You always have it on the guitar to tell you
what's coming next. I don't play it now; the Rickenbacker gives a better recording sound
and I also use a Yamaha."

Paul Ashford writes, "Arrangements and embellishments are, by and large, an important
facet of the way McCartney thinks about a song. He's not the only one who has an ear for
a good interpretation either."

Paul "People notice the arrangement even as something apart from what instruments are
playing. It's funny. A little while ago, we were invited to a Lennon & McCartney tribute
concert at the Royal Society for the Prevention of Cruelty to Birds, when they took a lot of
our songs and did them with the London Symphony Orchestra. In the interval we met the
Queen and there was an old feller with her, not the Duke, an older gentleman, and he
said, 'What do you think about these new arrangements?' And the Queen was amazing
because she said, 'Oh no, no, no, the arrangements are the same. These are basically the
same arrangements off the records.' And I was amazed to hear her say that, because it's
true. They were taking all the arrangements and putting them on cellos instead of guitars,
just giving all the lines to different elements of the orchestra, and she actually realised it."

Saturday, October 8

The *Daily Mirror* sensationally reports "Yoko Ono is set to release some John Lennon
songs never heard before. The six tracks, recorded just before he was tragically shot dead
in December 1980, form part of a new album. *Milk And Honey*, like the *Double Fantasy*
album they shared, will also include six of Yoko's songs. John's tracks are hard rockers

and highlight Lennon's good humour and self-deprecating wit. They include 'Steppin' Out', 'Grow Old With Me' and 'I Don't Wanna Face It'. The most poignant lyrics come in the reggae-styled 'Borrowed Time'. It's almost as if John Lennon had a premonition of his imminent death. Yoko meanwhile, has recorded another album, *Every Man Needs A Woman* (*sic*)."

Monday, October 24

With 'The Girl Is Mine', another duet recorded with Michael Jackson, currently sitting at No. 10 in the British singles charts, **Paul** talks about his latest duet with Rick Sky of the *Daily Star* . . .

"I love working with other people," Paul reveals, "because it fuels you into doing things you didn't think you were capable of. Since Wings broke up, I've worked a lot on my own, but at the back of my mind I felt I was missing the company of other people. These duets have been the perfect solution. But at first, I had my doubts about teaming up with another star. I wondered whether two so-called legends working together might inhibit each other. But luckily, when I met up with both Stevie Wonder and Michael, we forgot our reputations and status and just got on with making music. And it's worked out very well. With both of them, it's been a very relaxed and friendly atmosphere. Michael Jackson was a singer I had long admired. I told him I had written a song and sang it to him, there and then, while lots of people watched."

While on **Friday, October 28**, the current issue of the *Psychic News* magazine reports that "John Lennon is having a very jolly time on the other side and he has personally met Clark Gable, David (*sic*, Brian) Epstein, his former manager, John Wayne, the late president, Harry Truman and Jesus himself." The magazine also discloses that John is currently having an affair with the actress, Carole Lombard, who died in 1942.

On **Monday, October 31**, in both the US and UK, Paul releases *Pipes Of Peace*, his latest studio album . . .

'So Bad'

Paul "I sometimes worry about my songwriting, especially when it is a simple song like 'So Bad'. You worry that, because it came to me too easily, there must be something wrong with it. I used to play 'So Bad' around the house and I'd sing, 'Girl I love you, girl I love you so bad.' Suddenly, I thought of my son, James, who was feeling a little bit left out. So I started singing, 'Boy I love you, boy I love you so bad.' He got all embarrassed but it was great because I didn't want to leave my boy out of a love song."

Wednesday, November 9

In the current issue of *Titbits* magazine, **Paul** announces "If I had known that John was going to die, I would have made a lot more effort to try to get a better relationship with him. But when he started slagging me off, I was not prepared to say, 'Well, you're quite right,' because I'm human. My big regret was that I could have told John to listen and put my arms round him . . . But it still goes on, that's the terrifying thing. George and I had a barney the last time we talked."

Saturday, November 12
NBC TV in America airs the first part of *Princess Daisy*, a two part made-for-TV mini-series, which features Ringo and Barbara in a brief cameo role as the Valerians, two highly camp hairdressers . . .

Barbara "I'm a journalist assigned to interview Ringo."

Ringo "And I try to interview her . . . We loved doing *Daisy* because they paid us for four days and we only had to work three! We don't insist on working together but we don't want to be separated. If Barbara gets a job in Brazil, well, I'll go along for the holiday. I'm ready for more TV parts though not necessarily guest shots on *Love Boat* or *Fantasy Island*. I'm not putting any of them down, but we won't do walk-ons in *The Rockford Files* or any of those established series. I feel that I'm pursuing an acting role rather than a musician's role right now. That doesn't mean I'm not a musician anymore, but you have to put your energies in one direction and we're putting our energy into our acting careers right now."

Monday, December 12

An amazing discovery is made in Liverpool . . . the *Daily Star* reports, "Wall paintings by John Lennon and The Beatles' first drummer (*sic*) Stuart Sutcliffe have been uncovered by workmen in a Liverpool club where they used to play. Their former manager, Allan Williams, confirmed that the weird works of art in the Slater Street Jacaranda Club are genuine. He said the pair was paid £15 to decorate the walls in 1960. The new Jacaranda Club boss, Archie Walker, has called in experts to find the best way of preserving the weird works. 'I'm determined to keep them,' he said."

Monday, January 16
Exactly four years after Paul was busted for drugs in Tokyo, he, this time with Linda, again falls foul of the law after being caught with pot . . .

Paul Connew, *Daily Mirror* "Ex-Beatle Paul McCartney and his wife, Linda, have been caught in a drugs raid on the Caribbean island of Barbados. The McCartneys were each fined £75 after pleading guilty to possessing marijuana. Paul and Linda were seized on Sunday by police acting on a tip-off. The raid was at the villa rented by the couple and their four children who arrived on the island last Friday. Paul and Linda were taken to police headquarters while a nanny cared for their children. They were released later the same day on bail. The couple sat in court looking embarrassed as their lawyer explained to the magistrate that they smoked marijuana to relax and it helped their creativity. He said they bought the drug for their own consumption."

Paul "For me, pot is milder than Scotch. That doesn't mean that I've turned around and advocated marijuana, I haven't. I'm really only saying this is true for me. In Barbados, where I was on holiday, I was in a room miles away from anyone. It never interfered with anyone. No one was watching me except one manservant at the place. There are things that marijuana is more harmful than, air for instance. I advocate air every day. I'd advocate a good vegetarian diet any day of the week but in print, you're put in a corner and they make you sound like the bloody high priest of pot. It's stupid, you know, I can take pot or leave it."

Then, on **Tuesday, January 17**, as Paul and Linda return to London, customs men arrest Linda at Heathrow Airport after discovering a further stash of pot inside her handbag . . .

John Kay and Michael Fielder, the *Sun* "Superstar Paul McCartney's wife, Linda, was charged with having drugs again only hours after being fined in Barbados. Linda, 41, was seized by customs officers at London's Heathrow Airport as the multi-millionaire couple cut short their Caribbean holiday. A quantity of 'grass', the leaves of the marijuana plant, was allegedly found in her hand luggage. Last night, Paul blamed Barbados police who searched the bags for the 'mistake'."

Paul "It wouldn't have been there if they had done their job properly. Most of the time, Linda doesn't know what's in her bag anyway."

The *Sun* report continues, "His wife was arrested just minutes after the ex-Beatle, currently No. 1 in the charts with 'Pipes Of Peace', made a speech to newsmen saying the drug should be legalised. He claimed it was less harmful than alcohol, nicotine, or glue, 'All of which are perfectly legal. I don't think that, in the privacy of my own room, I was doing any harm.' "

An airport eye witness, "When Paul and Linda arrived at Heathrow with their children after a holiday in Barbados, they cleared customs with their heavy luggage through the 'green' channel. Shortly afterwards, a camera bag and a shoulder bag, which had apparently been left behind accidentally, were presented for clearance by a British Airways employee through the 'red', something to declare, channel. In the camera bag, cannabis was found inside a film canister together with a reefer cigarette. While in the shoulder bag there was another reefer and there were traces of cannabis at the bottom of the bag. Then, Paul and Linda, who were just about to leave the airport, were stopped."

Linda "Barbados, okay. That was a fair cop. Although everybody and his uncle buys a little gear there on holiday. I had bought cannabis a few times in Barbados and put it in a number of places. The police in Barbados had carried out a thorough search of all of our belongings and I had assumed that all of the cannabis had been confiscated. Anyway, it is horrible to feel like a criminal when you know you are not, particularly when there is so much horrific crime going on. But they always seem to catch the little people like me. They never seem to get the big guys, the heroin pushers, the Mafia and the murderers. I honestly didn't know the drug was there. But I decided to plead guilty to it and save all the hassle."

Paul "It might be quicker and simpler to plead guilty but she's not guilty. We feel we've got to stand up for ourselves. I think the case for decriminalisation of cannabis is pretty strong now. We have never smoked cannabis in front of the kids and never will. We prefer them not to know about any kind of stimulant. We just smoke from time to time to relax. It makes us feel good. It's no big deal for us. We don't consider we are breaking the law. We don't particularly want the kids to take it just like we don't want them to drink alcohol. But we have explained the situation to them, like we've talked about drink, racism, politics and sex. We tell them the truth. We don't tell them a stork brought them. We give them the facts so that they can make up their own minds. Linda and I are not crazy drug addicts. We never take heroin or cocaine like other people in the music business. We smoke in the privacy of our own home and we believe we are not doing any harm, not even to ourselves."

During this period of time, Paul challenges a report by doctors who have accused him of trying to bring in a "junkies' charter" . . .

"That's idiotic," **Paul** blasts. "We don't want to corrupt anyone. We are totally law-abiding. But I would like to make a call for a medical report proving that cannabis is not dangerous. So far there is no evidence at all. They wouldn't let you smoke it in some States in America if it was, would they?"

Linda's court appearance regarding her arrest takes place in Uxbridge at the magistrate's court on January 24 . . .

Guy Rais reports on the hearing for the *Daily Telegraph*, "Paul McCartney's wife Linda said after being fined £75 at Uxbridge magistrate's court for smuggling cannabis through Heathrow that it was 'Much ado about nothing.' Her husband, who sat in the public gallery during the 12-minute hearing, sketching his wife and the woman chairman of the bench, repeated his suggestion at the airport last week that cannabis should be decriminalised. Mrs McCartney, 42, who gave her address as Soho Square, London, pleaded guilty. Mr Alan Hughes, prosecuting for Customs and Excise, said the cannabis involved was a small amount, 4.9 grammes, with a street value of £4.90. Linda told the court that her take-home wage was about £50 a week from her business. When asked to explain her £50 income from singing, she said, 'That is money spent on food. I sing for nothing. I do it for the pleasure.' "

In court, Mr Edwin Glasgow, defending, tells the magistrates, "Almost anything I say by way of an explanation or apology is being written down and reproduced elsewhere, either as sneering hypocrisy or as an encouragement by my client to other people to use drugs. I want to avoid that. The suggestion that Paul McCartney's wife ought to grow up and set a better example is pretty puerile, ill informed and prejudiced judgement from people who have not met her. She is a thoroughly likeable and decent lady."

Meanwhile, one day before the trial, on Monday, January 23, Rick Sky of the *Daily Star* writes, "John Lennon is heading for the top of the charts again, three years after his death. His record, 'Nobody Told Me', looks certain to displace another ex-Beatle, Paul McCartney, from the No. 1 spot. And Paul says, 'I couldn't think of anyone better to knock me off the top. It's a great record and will help keep John's memory alive forever.' The track 'Nobody Told Me' is taken from the album *Milk And Honey*, the first album put out since Lennon's murder by a crazed fan in New York. His widow Yoko, who also included some of her own compositions, chose the material. The whole thing took her three years to put together . . ."

The *Milk And Honey* album is released in the USA on **Friday, January 19** . . .

Yoko "I was first listening to the tapes in 1982. These were the tapes we were working on just before John passed away. I felt very responsible to finish that album so I listened to the takes in the studio and I kind of nearly fainted. It took so long for me to do it because I found it hard for me to cope with all the memories that came flooding back every time I listened to those songs. That made me think, 'If I'm in a position where I can't listen to it, I'm sure a lot of fans will have difficulty listening to the songs also.' So I decided to postpone the album until 1984 . . . John's death was such a waste. I desperately wanted to put the album out because John's songs mean so much to so many people. John is still with us. I feel him all around me. His spirit is desperately alive. The things he left us, like his music, are going to keep on touching people's minds and their emotions. They always will, because John believed in the goodness of mankind and wanted to make music that would make the world a better place to live in."

Tuesday, January 24
Yoko and Sean make a pilgrimage to John's hometown of Liverpool. An eyewitness at the event is the British reporter Alan Dunn . . .

"For Yoko, it had been a beautiful and emotional day while Sean, aged eight, summed up his reaction to his visit to his father's home town as 'Terrific!' Both had been visiting the formative features of Lennon's young life in Liverpool, Strawberry Fields, Quarry Bank School, Penny Lane, The Liverpool Art School and the pier head. Only the birthplace of Beatlemania, Mathew Street, where the Cavern Club once stood, was crowded out after Yoko and Sean had spent longer than intended on a visit to the Wirral home of Mrs Mary Smith, the Aunt Mimi who raised Lennon after his parents died. The trip began with a morning flight from Paris to Manchester, then car to the Salvation Army children's home at Strawberry Field, in whose gardens Lennon played as a child. The home and the art school have been pledged money, some reports say up to £3 million, by Yoko Ono from the sale of land and art in the United States but talk of that was left for another day. Yoko, not much taller than her son, said that the visit had been promised to Sean since his father's death in December 1980. The two set off for their day trip like any Beatles fan, except for the hovering presence of two steely-faced minders. At the art school, they sent out for fish and chips at Yoko's request. To oblige photographers, two trips were made to the pier head but they did not take a ferry across the Mersey, preferring to go by tunnel to visit Aunt Mimi. Before that, they saw the mould for a statue of Lennon to be placed in the International Garden Festival this year."

Yoko "John's spirit lives on here. The visit is for Sean, really. It is his heritage and I want to show him as much of Liverpool as possible, especially places important to John."

Sean "I have been asking mum to come here since I was little and she kept saying we'll go in a couple of months."

Wednesday, February 29
Meanwhile back in the capital, a life-long Beatles fan recalls another chance meeting with Paul . . .

"What started out as just another day trip to London, turned into a pretty magical day," Stephen Rouse, a long-time Beatles fan, admits, "and one day that I shall never forget. I had seen Paul the previous December. He was busy recording the songs for his *Give My Regards To Broad Street* film soundtrack at AIR Studios with George Martin. It was a great thrill to meet them both. Paul was this man who I'd had so much respect for. You just want to say so much to him but you just go blank when you come face to face with him. I can remember thinking 'This is the guy who wrote "Hey Jude" and all those other great songs.' On that day, I couldn't believe that people who were also waiting to see him were giving him such a hard time, demanding that various items of theirs be signed. I felt so sorry for him, so I got what I had waited for, a couple of signatures and then I wished him a very happy Christmas and off I went on the way home on the train. I remember thinking to myself, 'I bet I never get to meet him again,' but I was wrong.
    "Three months later, I was in London chatting to a friend who worked in the Press office at Polydor Records. The label had just released both of John Lennon's new records, the single 'Nobody Told Me' and the album *Milk And Honey*, and were about to release the second single off the album, 'Living On Borrowed Time'. Polydor was always very happy to give you all the latest publicity material so I decided to pay them a visit and I was knocked out when I was handed a 12" promotional single of the track, a record still two weeks away from hitting the shops. They also gave me a huge *Milk And Honey* cardboard shop display. When I left Polydor, it was about 3.30 in the afternoon and, because of the size of the display, I decided that I would head back home on the train. I certainly couldn't carry this large thing around London for the rest of the day. So why I ended up in Oxford Street this day is still a mystery. But I did and I guess the reason for my action was so that I could head home via Oxford Circus tube and catch my train at Euston. But as I approached the tube station, I could see a few people I remembered from the previous December waiting outside AIR Studios. I guessed that maybe Paul was again recording there and so I decided to wait for him. The fans outside AIR told me that they couldn't wait any longer, and off they went. So there I was waiting, but the problem was where do I put this large cardboard cut-out of John and Yoko? I thought that even if Paul was there in the studio, he's not going to be pleased to see this cut-out. It was just over three years

since we lost John in such tragic circumstances and I thought the last thing I wanted to do was remind Paul of that. So what I decided to do was turn the cut-out towards the wall, and that way the only thing you could see was a large piece of blank white cardboard. I looked at my watch and it was 4.30. I decided that I would stick around for another five minutes. After all, all the others had gone and I was just left standing on my own. Then suddenly, the doors of the building opened and as I turned around, a huge gust of wind came bursting down Oxford Street, blowing my cardboard cut-out around and forcing it into the path of whoever was coming out of the studio building. I quickly caught hold of it, eager to say how sorry I was for the embarrassment and I could not believe who was standing there, having just come out through the doors, but Paul McCartney! He was really nice about the whole situation, even saying how much he liked the John and Yoko poster. But what was so amazing was the fact that it was just me on my own with Paul. It's the thing you dream about when you meet your musical hero. I was able to ask him anything and I think we spoke for about ten minutes. I showed him a Beatles magazine I had just bought, in which he showed a lot of interest. He asked me if this was the new *Beatles Monthly* magazine. Paul very kindly signed it for me and he said that he had to go. All I can say is that I heard an interview with Paul in which he said, 'The trouble is you never get to meet your greatest fans, because they are always at home playing your albums.' Well, Paul, I'm sorry to say this, but you do, because you met me."

Monday, May 21
In rather more sedate surroundings, **George** makes a surprise appearance at a preview for London's annual Chelsea Flower Show. He is followed everywhere by two heavyweight minders, who glare suspiciously at passers-by. Alongside George is a leggy brunette who refuses to give her name . . .

"After what happened to John, I'm absolutely terrified," George reveals to the gathering reporters. "I don't like being seen in public. I never know who might be around and I don't like being photographed." He then relaxes slightly to speak about the colourful show. "This represents real life to me. I love flowers and gardening and it is a wonderful treat for me to see such a display."

Wednesday, June 20
In a conversation with the UK reporter Jonathan Kirby, **George** speaks at great length again about Hare Krishna . . .

Kirby writes "George Harrison has been fascinated for 15 years by the bizarre, bell-ringing, chanting monks with shaven heads and orange robes. Although the reclusive former Beatle has never shaved his head to dance down London's Oxford Street, he claims that his life is ruled by the Hare Krishna movement . . ."

George "I chant whenever I get the chance. In fact, the more I do it, the harder I find it to stop, because I don't want to lose the feeling it gives me. It feels so nice and peaceful. I once chanted the Hare Krishna mantra all the way from France to Portugal non-stop. I drove for about 23 hours chanting all the way. It gets you feeling invincible. The funny thing was that I didn't even know where I was going. Once you get chanting, things start to happen transcendentally . . . When the first Hare Krishnas arrived in London in 1968, I welcomed them with open arms. I felt at home with Krishna, as if it had been something that was with me from another birth."

Kirby's report continues "Later that year, George met another 'spiritual master', His Divine Grace A.C. Bhaktivedanta Swami Prabhupada, who encouraged George to give up drink and drugs and to follow the Krishna's code of life. This included no illicit sex, no intoxicants, including tea, coffee and tobacco, no gambling and no meat, fish or eggs. Before his death in 1977, Prabhupada translated and organised the distribution of more than 50 million copies of the Bhagavad-Gita, the Hindu's bible, and watched the movement grow from a few thousand devotees in India to a worldwide movement. At the mention of Prabhupada's name, George speaks with awesome respect . . ."

George "A lot of religious prophets say, 'I'm it, I'm the divine incarnation so let me hit you,' but not Prabhupada. He told me, 'I am a servant, we are all servants of God.' Even though he was a great scholar, he spoke with childlike simplicity. He made me realise that we are not just physical bodies. We just happen to be in them but we really belong in the spiritual sky . . . I began reading the Bhagavad-Gita and started chanting the Hare Krishna mantra up to 1,700 times a day using a string of wooden beads. Chanting is a form of meditating, which helps me fix my mind on God. It doesn't stop you from being creative or productive, it actually helps you concentrate. Chanting is the answer to increasing our industrial output. Imagine a car assembly line where all the workers chant Hare Krishna. I'm sure it would help the industry and produce much better cars."

Kirby "Six weeks ago, George announced his retirement from the music business . . ."

George "I still write songs but they're just for myself. It's difficult for me to lead a spiritual life and remain in the music scene. The music world is often seedy."

Concluding, **George** announces "I live in hope. People should stop thinking about Britain or America or Russia becoming superior. The best thing we can do is to become God-conscious. If people would just wake up to it, there'd be no misery left in the world, and chanting Hare Krishna is a good place to start."

SEPTEMBER

On the run-up to the release of *Give My Regards To Broad Street*, Paul's first solo acting film, an interview with the former Beatle, conducted by Deborah Frost, appears in *Record Magazine*. The piece is entitled 'Once There Was A Way To Get Back Homeward' . . .

Deborah "How do you feel about the books that keep coming out about you and The Beatles? Does it bother you that people who were once friends and employees are trying to cash in by revealing all the trash?"

Paul "It's trash! Let's leave it at that. It is trash and they know it and they have to live with it. I think I'm pretty lucky to have got off like this, considering how bitchy and jealous people can be."

Deborah "Did you really play drums on a lot of The Beatles' things? At least one of 'those books' claims that, in your attempt to control the band, you sort of pushed Ringo right off his own drum stool."

Paul "Some Beatles things. On 'Back In The USSR' and I think I played guitar on 'Taxman' and 'The Night Before', a couple of those. But everything else gets exaggerated in The Beatles' case. People were reading so much into our lives and our lyrics that we found ourselves feeding 'em the crazy facts. Like me going across the Abbey Road crossing with no shoes on. I mean, that's all made up, that stuff. If you're trying to look for the truth of it, with The Beatles, you got four guys who were a good little band, a tight little unit, and for most of their working lives were really good with each other."

Deborah "Are you ever going to tour again?"

Paul "I don't know. I haven't ruled it out. I know in the back of everyone's minds when they ask this question, and they all ask it, in the back of everyone's minds is he won't tour again because John got killed. And no one mentions it. To me, I haven't been able to consider a tour in the last two years because I've been making this film and no way could I have taken one second off what I have been doing. I may easily do it after this movie. If I was some 24-year-old bachelor, I sure as hell would want to be on tour, just for the women, probably. But I've got four kids and they deserve most of my time, if they're to be brought up happy. They deserve for me to be around sometime."

OCTOBER
Paul and Linda spend the latter half of the month in New York, Chicago and Los Angeles promoting the film *Give My Regards To Broad Street* and naturally face the country's media . . .

Paul "The public will be the judges on the film."

Bob Lundegaard, *Mpls. Star And Tribune* "I asked Paul whether he still missed the glory days of The Beatles, and he replied, 'No, I don't, because I wouldn't like to be doing that still. At the Plaza Hotel (in New York) the other day, someone said, "Do you miss all the screaming?" And I said, "No, I'm really glad it's not like that anymore, because I'm mature and those things pale after a while." Then we come out of the Plaza, and they were all there again. There must have been 300 or 400 people. It was crazy. It seemed very much like the old days, except those were kind of gay bachelor days. When you get married you can't go down to the club looking for birds.' "

Steve Morse, the *Kansas City Star* "Paul has been dismissed as having his best work behind him. Lacking the stimulus of fellow Beatle, John Lennon, he has been accused of being bland, sophomoric and out of touch with the real world. 'What's happened to me is that I just tended to assume that the critics were right,' Paul said at a recent press conference. 'I tended to believe that, yeah, I'm not as good as I used to be. But I recently started to say, "Hey, wait a minute. Let's check this out. Is it really true?" And I don't think it is.' At age 42, McCartney is starting to stick up for himself. 'I've spent so long worrying about everything, never mind my image but just getting up in the morning, that I'm really now trying to approach that, "Look, I gave it my best shot with this movie and I'm just not going to worry about it." A lot of people said I shouldn't make this picture but I held on and went ahead,' noting that Richard Lester, who directed *A Hard Day's Night* was one of the sceptics. 'So I got used to rejection, but I remembered that *Star Wars* and *Bonnie And Clyde* were other pictures that no one would touch because they couldn't understand them. *Star Wars* was hated until they put John Williams' music on it. Then it all made sense. So I clung to that idea.' "

Sunday, October 21

The number of alleged sightings of John's spirit increases when the *Sunday Mirror* reports that "The ghost of ex-Beatle John Lennon is haunting a club where the group used to play, according to the licensee, 37-year-old Isabel Daley. She claims to have seen the spectre of the murdered star arguing with Stuart Sutcliffe, the group's original bass player, who died in Hamburg in 1962. Now Isabel is too scared to go into the cellar of the Jacaranda in Slater Street, Liverpool, where she says the apparition occurred . . ."

Isabel Daley "It was frightening. There were too shadowy figures of young men arguing. I recognised one of them as a young John Lennon from photographs I had seen. He said, 'Come on, Audrey. That's not right.' I shot up the stairs when I realised they were ghosts and I don't want to go back."

Sunday Mirror "The club's owner, Ray Hudson, who was a regular in the early Sixties, says The Beatles used to argue with teenage barmaid Audrey Reynolds. Audrey, who now breeds dogs in Egremont, Cumbria, said, 'It's uncanny. John used to row over everything.'"

Wednesday, November 28
Paul's big-screen film *Give My Regards To Broad Street* is premiered in the UK at the Odeon cinema in Liverpool.

Paul "I'm sure the acting world shouted in relief when they saw the movie. I'm certainly not a threat to any of them. Anyway, I like the movie. It has a lot of myself in it. I was criticised for how simple the script was. But the story in *Indiana Jones* isn't exceptional . . . I suppose my movie is strange because it's not like anything current now. I'd like people to say, 'What a wonderful movie,' but I know it's not a wonderful movie. But it's a movie that has a certain amount of worth, which will be proven in time. *Magical Mystery Tour* wasn't a good movie, but it's a worthwhile film to see now because John's in it. In *Broad Street* I knew I went against the golden rule of script writing. I put in dream sequences with no explanations. That confused the audiences of today. But I'm sure that, in a few years, it will be looked at differently."

Paul's historic return home for the premiere also includes an appearance at the Picton Library where he will be presented with the Freedom of the City award, an event not free from problems . . .

The *Daily Star* newspaper reported on November 27, "A political row has blown up over Paul McCartney's triumphant homecoming tomorrow. Left-wing Labour councillors were yesterday accused of 'hijacking' all the places at the Freedom of Liverpool ceremony. And, claimed angry political rivals, they have also grabbed all the tickets for the British premiere of McCartney's film, *Give My Regards To Broad Street*. 'What should have been a good news day for Liverpool has been hijacked by the militants,' said Liberal councillor Rosemary Cooper. 'Instead of jobs for the boys, it's now tickets for the boys.' All 57 Labour councillors will be at the freedom ceremony, with just two Liberals and two Conservatives. No opposition councillors have been invited to the film premiere. But Councillor Cooper said, 'To my knowledge, about 16 tickets have been commandeered by the Labour party.' Last night, a city council spokesman said, 'The invitations are a reaction to demand.'"

The American premiere for *Broad Street* had taken place on Thursday, October 25 at the Gotham Theater in New York and then opened in 319 cinemas across the country, apparently earning less than half-a-million dollars and closing everywhere within two weeks. Not surprisingly, the media attack on the film had begun . . .

Jim Washburn, film critic for *The Register* "Don't give much regard to Paul McCartney's film. *Give My Regards To Broad Street* is touted as depicting a day in the life of a pop star. Let's hope not, because any mind as empty as the one behind *Broad Street* could be rented out as a racquetball court. The problem seems to be Paul McCartney. The minute he appears up there on the screen, his mouth sat in its permanent oval of mild surprise; it's as if a monstrous vacuum begins sucking up every bit of razzle-dazzle. He's so enervating that nothing can help . . . The only good thing to say about the climax of *Broad Street* is it's safer than sleeping pills and cheaper than a lobotomy."

Tucson Weekly "All Paul needs is someone willing to criticise and add to his ideas who he is willing to recognise. John Lennon played that role once, and the partnership was brilliant. It's not that McCartney isn't a genius, he is, or that he's run out of good ideas. But, left on his own, Paul McCartney doesn't explore the potential of his material. *Broad Street* is a good example. It has a wonderful soundtrack, but it has a plot that is absurdly thin, even for a musical, no subplots and no characters. Anyone out there who isn't familiar with Paul McCartney will make no sense of the film. As it is, it doesn't make much sense to anyone and the film is a showcase for the songs. The problem is that the film has been made as if music videos don't exist. Most of the time we simply watch Paul play and sing. This needs either the plot of a traditional musical or the visual imagery and shorthand storytelling of a rock video. It has neither. The past irreverence of The Beatles is one of the reasons that this film stands in contrast to *Amadeus*. It may be hard to accept, but in a way, Paul McCartney is a Mozart of our times, he has been to popular music what Mozart once was to classical music. They were both bad-boy musicians and they were both undeniably brilliant. But Mozart died young, leaving classical music fans to mourn over what might have been. McCartney lives on, often frustrating and angering his fans, many of whom seem to feel that the creative genius he had is slipping. But it isn't true. While *Broad Street* isn't much of a film, it has some fine film moments. The new arrangement of 'Eleanor Rigby' is tremendous and at least two of his new songs, 'For No One' (*sic*) and 'No More Lonely Nights', are among the best things McCartney has written alone."

Bob Lundegaard, *Mpls. Star And Tribune* "What's missing is that manic, impish irreverence, the utter cheek that propelled The Beatles' films *A Hard Day's Night* and *Help!*"

The California-based *Sacramento Bee* newspaper "*Broad Street* is slow freight, overloaded with blandness. We give it a B rating . . . B for boring."

But good reviews do appear . . .

Janet Masling, *New York Times* "Director Peter Webb has no comparable flair to Richard Lester, who brought such exuberance to The Beatles' films . . . *Broad Street* is a home movie on an amazing scale. But it has enough good musical sequences to please Mr McCartney's many fans. It also shows the singer in a relaxed, unselfconscious mood that goes a long way toward making the film appealing."

Broad Street is released featuring Paul's covers of some classic Beatles songs, prompting the question from certain quarters of the media, "Do you think the songs you're writing now are as good as, for instance, 'For No One' and 'Paperback Writer'?"

"No," **Paul** replies in an interview with the Capital Radio DJ Roger Scott. "I don't. I think some are as good, but I don't feel like they're as good, because they don't come as easily. Basically speaking, I think 'Here, There And Everywhere' is probably a more complete song than some of the ones I'm writing now. But, because I've written so many songs, they just can't be as good as each other. You've got to have your ups and downs; you can't keep churning them out like a sausage factory. From time to time, I do like my modern stuff. I don't think it's as rich a vein as the goldmine we (The Beatles) were mining then, but I do think there's some good stuff and I wouldn't dismiss it all."

One of The Beatles tracks covered is 'The Long And Winding Road' . . .

"For this film we wanted to do a new version of 'The Long And Winding Road'," **Paul** announces, "but you're faced with the reality of then having to do 'The Long And Winding Road' and improve on The Beatles' version and it's not that easy. It isn't an easy thing to do. It's a bit of a daunting prospect, but it's silly never to play it again. That's how we thought until we said, 'But this is crazy, c'mon. It's my song. I like it. George (Martin) wants to record it. He's happy about doing it. So let's do it.' Ringo wasn't happy to get involved with it. We had some songs in the film where we wanted him to drum on them. But he didn't want to attempt a new version. I can see it from his point of view, actually, because it would have been, 'Did I drum good on version A or version B?' and he didn't even want a comparison. From my point of view, I'm looking at a song; I'm looking at one of my songs. I don't want to be ashamed of anything I've written. So we did a new version of 'The Long And Winding Road', which we liked. It turned out to be very easy in the end. We just sat down, while a couple of the kids played it. It was all done in about half an hour. It wasn't painful at all . . . I doubt if we could have sung something like 'Getting Better' without getting emotional. Sometimes you just remember the silly moments that to you are big moments. And in a song like 'Getting Better', I'd sing, 'It's getting better all the time, better, better', optimistic, and John would mumble, 'Couldn't get much worse.' "

One of the film's most memorable sequences is where Paul, in heavy disguise, plays a busker singing 'Yesterday' outside a London tube station . . .

"One or two people wandered up and looked a bit funny at me," **Paul** recalls. "You know, like, 'Aren't you Paul McCartney?' I said, 'Are you kidding? "Yesterday, jinga jinga, all my troubles seemed so far away, jinga jinga." ' You know, I am doing this ridiculous version of 'Yesterday'. I really enjoyed that. If what you do is play a guitar, then the most basic form of that is to be on the street as a busker. It's real live music and you are actually there, nose to nose with your audience. There were some people out there, like this great old Scottish fellow, out on a binge, who gave me all his change. But the joke was, I said to the assistant director, 'Now what's going to happen here is that I'm going to make some money, so whatever happens, this money has got to go to charity. I know someone's going to say, "Wouldn't you just know it, he's so tight, he took the money." ' I said, 'I'm going to get nailed for this.' So it went to charity and, sure enough, on the radio the next day, there was a woman saying, 'Wouldn't you just know it, Paul took the money.' So, you can't win."

'No Values'
(An original *Give My Regards To Broad Street* composition)

Paul "I dreamt this song. I dreamt that I was with The Rolling Stones. They were all there, Mick, Bill, Charlie, Keith, and Mick was up front. I woke up and said to myself, 'I really like that song that they do.' Then I thought, 'Hey, wait a minute, there is no Rolling Stones song called "No Value". They don't do that song.' My brain just created it. So I thought, 'Well, there it is. I've got this new song called "No Values".' But I won't be telling Mick, he'll probably claim the copyright."

In October, **Paul** gives an insight into working on the movie, for instance working alongside Ringo again . . .

"Ringo and I are good friends. After all The Beatles' years, and all the troubles of the break-up, we find it easy to get along. He's in England a lot and we see each other quite a bit. We can tell each other what we think. If he thinks something stinks, he tells. There's no messing with Ringo, you know. I saw him one night socially, and I was very excited. I said, 'I'm gonna do this film and I'm gonna get you involved. Will you do it with me?' For some reason, he got the idea it was like a Beatles film. Well, we'd had a few drinks. So he went home and imagined us in the old days, driving 200 miles through a freeze to play some gig and he came back the next day and said, 'OK, but I've got my line. I just want to say this line in the film.' And I said, 'Yes.' And he said, 'Have we got any agents, or are we practising to be Canadians?' And I said, 'Well, uh, yes . . . that's a terrific line. We'll work that one in.' And we did, it's a Ringo line. Ringo and I are like hams; we like to gag it up for the cameras. But I know George well enough to know he wouldn't want to be in this. He's not really reclusive, a Howard Hughes type, but because he won't see the press, they think he is. He has a busy social life, but he's shy in public and anyway, he's out of the country."

And working with the legendary actor, Sir Ralph Richardson . . .

"I was frightened to do it," **Paul** reveals, "because he's a big, famous old British actor and that's intimidating because a person's image does walk ahead of them. But he made it easy. He had a twinkle in his eye all the time. I thought my script might not be to his liking and I said, 'Look, this isn't Shakespeare or Chekhov, so we can change it if you like.' And he said, in his way, 'Not a comma out of place!' "

1985

JANUARY
The year begins with interviews with Paul appearing in various French-language magazines . . .

A journalist remarks "Despite his incredible success, behind his relaxed appearance, Paul McCartney is an anxious man with little self-assurance. He said that to me many times, and when I brought up the subject of punk music . . ."

"I don't feel threatened anymore now because all my life I've felt threatened," **Paul** replies. "In the beginning, in Liverpool, we were anxious because of a group called Gerry & The Pacemakers. Later on, in London, we used to feel threatened by The Dave Clark Five. In fact, as far as I was concerned, anyway, I didn't trust anyone. I remember one day, someone came into our office saying, 'Dave Clark is No. 1 in the charts.' There was dead silence. It was serious stuff. Today, it makes you laugh to think that The Beatles were scared of Gerry & The Pacemakers or Dave Clark. But we were! Then I remember I was scared of Alice Cooper, because of all that satanic side and all that and of the huge success he was having. I wondered, 'Is music really going in that direction?' Then I met Alice Cooper and realised that he was completely normal. He was just a guy with a drinking problem. So the punks didn't really frighten me musically. You can't say it was great music. What I didn't like was the destruction side with heroin and the murder stories with Sid Vicious. That completely disturbed me. When we were young, our parents were afraid to see us with long hair because they thought we'd associate with the scum of society. That was a ridiculous fear. I understand that today. One time, I saw my oldest daughter dressed like a punk and I was afraid that meant she was getting into something bad. When, in reality, she simply wanted to be different. You're always afraid of what you don't know. I learnt that from the Maharishi. I learnt a lot about myself from him."

Journalist "It was said that the Yogi was only interested in your money."

Paul "Yeah, it was said. But I don't think so. If that's true, then what is he doing with his money? Have you seen him dressed any differently than his white cheese bag he's always worn? He doesn't have jewellery, no rolls, and no playmate around him. If I hear that he bought Elton John's house in Beverley Hills or that he's got 50 bunnies stashed away, then I'll ask myself some questions. But that's not really the case. The man lives very simply. He taught me to relax. I stayed in India with him for a month and it was very good."

Journalist "And what is the truth behind the strange 'Paul Is Dead' story?"

Paul "Listen man, I always deny that. I'm not dead, believe me!"

FEBRUARY
Paul features in a cover story in this month's *Musician* magazine . . .

"Obviously, it's not easy to top something like The Beatles, to top that feeling, to ever recreate any of that," **Paul** is quoted as saying. "What I do is look to some of the things that have happened that have been successful. 'Mull Of Kintyre' in Britain, is the highest selling single record ever. I can't just dismiss that and secretly I have even had the kind of cheek to think recently, 'I can do better even.' I've begun to really go toe-to-toe with my consciousness and say, 'C'mon, man, this can be done.' That's how I deal with that one. It's a little too easy to just dismiss the critics, but it's very tempting, because they can be wrong and because you just couldn't get by otherwise. There are certain criticisms I read where I go, 'You clever bastard, you've got it right.' Somebody on the *Broad Street* tour said to me I'm bigger than any role I could ever play, well if that's the case, I'm finished. I might as well go and sit on the toilet and take Polaroids of myself. I just can't exist like that. I've just got to get out there. I've got to take all the knocks, all the chances, take John Lennon telling me I suck; I've got to accept all that crap full in the face. And if I still want to keep doing it, I've still got to ride through all that stuff, and it isn't easy, but I'm not pleading mercy. It just comes with the territory."

Friday, February 1
George appears in a pre-filmed, unexpected, interview during tonight's edition of BBC2's *Newsnight* programme, where he is interviewed by Robin Denselow. The conversation takes place in HandMade's Cadogan Square, Knightsbridge headquarters, a venue which also serves as Denis O'Brien's flat . . .

"It's silly," **George** says, "they make out I never leave the house, but I leave the house all the time. I just try to live the life of a normal human being. If I have a hit record, they'll be knocking on the door and phoning me up, but I don't particularly want to be on that side again. I've done that and it's boring. Now I like to live a quiet life. They think I'm this Howard Hughes character, with fingernails down to my toes. It used to annoy me, but now it doesn't bother me. I think it's quite a good image."

Denselow on HandMade Films "George plays an active part in the company, and as much in deciding the films that shouldn't be made as those that should. His own languid explanation is, 'I pop in and out. I hear what's happening day to day and make any suggestions I can. Ray Cooper (Elton John's percussionist) keeps me informed about what's happening on the artistic side and Denis tells me what's going on as far as the money goes. I'm lucky really, because I'm not trying to be David Putnam, that's to say I don't have to be there every day taking care of business.' It may seem a casual way to run a very risky, multi-million pound enterprise, but they do have two films in the London top five and their individual style is part of the attraction. . . . Over the past seven years, HandMade's films have ranged from the realism of *Scrubbers*, not a box-office success, to the gentle comedy of *The Missionary* and the fantasy of their biggest financial success to date, the low-budget *Time Bandits*, which grossed $45 million in the States. This summer, they are shooting their most expensive yet, *Travelling Men*, a thriller set in Scotland and Ireland, which will star Sean Connery and Michael Caine."

George on HandMade's films "I wouldn't mind being more involved but I don't want to be a film star. I don't want to be a pop star. After The Beatles, I was offered all sorts of parts, like the White Swami . . . I just want to live in peace, but I'd like to be involved in some way; that is to say I'd like to get more of my ideas on to film, ideas against killing, against blood and against noisy madness. *The Killing Fields* upset me because where there's a war that's limited to a certain area of the planet, it's filtered to us anyway, but then someone takes the thing and makes us all have to suffer. I don't want to have to shout to make-up to 'Put more blood on the babies'. There's enough blood on babies without film studios adding to it . . . I'd like to see a film that made you come out of the theatre feeling very joyous and very happy. I'm not sure what that film is, but I may end up making my own 8mm, which I'll show you . . ."

Denselow "In the meantime, George hasn't completely forgotten his music. He hasn't released any new material for a while but said he was 'Busy writing lots and lots of songs. I think that, because I don't have to make an album now, I can write whatever I like. I suppose that before I used to think I had to write whatever was saleable.' "

Saturday, February 2
George's private life is again the focus of attention when this story is published in the *Daily Mirror* . . .

"Ex-Beatle George Harrison has been living in fear since the murder of John Lennon and the threatened kidnapping of Linda McCartney," the report reads. "Now he is planning to move his family to an extraordinary Tenko style jungle hideaway. George's strange new retreat has been built into a perilous clifftop on Maui, one of the Hawaiian Islands in the Pacific . . . One of the few people who have seen George's new hideaway is Jamie Hammond, who also lives on Maui. 'George's homestead is surrounded on three sides by jungle,' he said. 'It's impossible to walk through. Even at midday, it's so dark you can't see where you're going. Anyway, your feet would be cut to ribbons by the razor sharp lava underfoot. George has a big Hawaiian guard who doubles as his caretaker. He's had a six-foot barbed wire fence built around his homestead, except for the clifftop. The cliffs drop sheer to the ocean. There are no beaches, only rocks. You can't even get a boat in. George's place isn't even on the map, he's about as far from civilisation as he can be.' George has told friends he will visit Britain each summer just to keep an eye on his successful film business."

Saturday, February 23
Three weeks after the *Daily Mirror* report, scandal breaks out in The Beatles fraternity when it is announced that Paul is being sued for £8 million by the other members of the group . . .

Andrew Golden, *Daily Mirror* "Ringo Starr, George Harrison and John Lennon's widow, Yoko Ono, have joined forces in what could be the pop world's most sensational court battle. The action centres on an alleged deal whereby McCartney, the richest rock star in the world, earns more royalties for Beatles records than the others. Details of the lawsuit, which has been filed in New York, are being kept secret, but the *Daily Mirror* can reveal that the summonses allege 'breach of position of trust, breach of contract and other wrongs'. The writ follows reports of renewed bitterness between Paul, George and Ringo over money. George and Ringo were said to be furious to learn that Paul has made a private business arrangement with Capitol Records to corner a larger slice of song royalties. Bob O'Neill, legal spokesman for Capitol/EMI records confirmed that McCartney, reported to be worth £400 million, did earn a higher share from The Beatles' smash hits. He refused to say what the difference is, but said the agreement was worked out after the fab four split up. Mr O'Neill added, 'Paul approached us seeking terms under which he will continue with us as an individual artist. The deal was that he would get an increased percentage on the company's Beatles recordings.' But Mr O'Neill claimed the extra money came out of the record company's cut and that the share-out to the other Beatles was not affected. The legal action also involves the firm of US lawyers run by the father and brother of Paul's wife Linda. The copy of the summonses was served on forty-year-old McCartney through a member of his personal staff, Sheila Jones. Miss Jones said last week, 'I don't think he was expecting such a move, but he has taken it in his usual calm fashion.'"

Sunday, April 7

Alwyn Thomas of the *Sunday People*, reports "The truth about John Lennon's secret family can now be revealed. For the *Sunday People* has tracked down John's two half-sisters. They have kept their background shrouded in secrecy for nearly 40 years. Not even close friends know of their connection with the dead superstar. The girls were born to John's mother, Julia, after his father Fred abandoned his family when he jumped ship in the United States during the war. One of them, 37-year-old Julia Baird, a divorcee with three children, now lives in a smart house in Chester. But the other, 35-year-old Jackie Higgins, is penniless and lives on dole money in a rundown Liverpool terrace. Now the sisters are about to break their long silence in a book."

Jackie's live-in lover, jobless Paul Higgins, said, 'We are penniless. God knows we could do with some money. I suppose everyone would expect John Lennon's sister to be comfortably off. But nothing could be further from the truth. We are not only broke, but we owe hundreds of pounds. Life is a real struggle. I lived with Jackie for two years before I found out that she was the Beatle's half-sister. I discovered it when her sister, Julia, called round asking if she had heard from John. I wanted to know who John was. I thought it was an old boyfriend. So she had to tell me it was John Lennon. I was staggered but she said she hadn't told me because she didn't want to be accused of cashing in on his name. She was just an ordinary girl and wanted her own identity. She just didn't want to be known as a Beatle's sister and she was very worried about the effect it might have on her ten-year-old son, John. She has always been afraid of this getting out in case the other kids at school teased him."

An old school friend of Jackie's recalls an event back in July 1964. "When The Beatles were given a civic reception for *A Hard Day's Night* in Liverpool, John invited Jackie and Julia and told Jackie off for staying at the back of the group when they went on the balcony to wave to the crowd. She knew her school friends were in the crowd and she didn't want to be recognised. Back at school, she insisted that it wasn't her up there with everybody's heroes. She insisted that she was in the crowd with the rest of the girls."

The *Sunday People* report continues, "When Lennon moved to the United States in 1971, the letters and phone calls from John gradually dropped away. And Jackie was too proud to keep in touch herself. She read in the papers that John was sick of being tapped for handouts. But after a five-year silence, in 1976, she received a letter from John asking her to ring him in the States. Paul Higgins recalls, 'She rang and Yoko answered. She said it was nice to hear from her but John was busy and she put down the phone. Jackie got the impression that Yoko wanted John to sever all connections with his family in Britain. That really hurt Jackie and then, years later, John was dead. It broke her heart.'"

But John's Aunt Mimi feels little sympathy for his half-sisters, Jackie and Julia. "The girls became a problem after their mother was knocked down and killed by a car," Mimi tells the *Sunday People* newspaper. "To help out, I had Jackie to stay at my house in Poole. She bought her clothes and I even got her fixed up with a job as a hairdresser. But one day she didn't turn up for work. I looked in her room to find her clothes had gone. No note, nothing to say where she had gone. After weeks of worry, Jackie turned up on the doorstep crying bitterly. 'I'm pregnant,' she said. After that, she stayed for a while but vanished again. I only heard from her when she got pregnant yet again and wanted more money."

Julia "I have always remained silent about my connection with John. I hadn't seen him for years, but when he died it was like having an arm cut off."

Sunday, April 14

One week after the revelation about John's lost half-sisters, the *Sunday People* features an interview with Aunt Mimi, headlined "Sometimes I Can Imagine I See Him. Is It Him? I Like To Think So," adding "I have never spoken like this before. But it's time the truth about John's kindness and generosity was known."

Reporter Len Adams writes, "The frail old lady sits alone in her mansion of memories overlooking the sea. It is the house that John bought her and for the 82-year-old Mimi it has become a shrine to the star she regarded as her son. There are Beatles photographs, letters from John from all over the world, paintings that he gave her, precious souvenirs of the days when the Fab Four had the world at their feet. And on one wall is a silver engraving, which reads, 'The guitar is all right as a hobby, John, but you'll never make a living at it.'"

Aunt Mimi "How wrong can you be? It was a remark I once made to him and he never let me forget it. He told me to read it every time the lads won yet another Gold disc . . . I'm not psychic, and I don't believe in spiritualism. But I do feel John's presence wherever I am in the house. When John was alive and far away, we both shared the same telepathic experience, knowing that one of us would be getting in touch. I'd ring John and he always expected my call. It was the same with me. No, John isn't dead in that sense. He is always with me . . . Do you believe in fate? Because I knew the moment I first saw John in the hospital that I was the one to be his mother. Not Julia. Does that sound awful? It isn't really, because Julia accepted it as something perfectly natural. She used to say, 'You're his real mother. All I did was give birth.' It isn't true that John was three years old when he came to me. I brought him up from a few weeks until he was 21. My husband George adored John just as though he was his own son. Sometimes when John had done something wrong, and I sent him up to his bedroom, I would find George creeping upstairs with the *Beano*, John's favourite comic, and a bar of chocolate. Sometimes I pretended I didn't notice but I could see George slipping the goodies under the door.
   "All this talk about John's hard upbringing in a Liverpool slum is fantasy. He wasn't pampered but he had the best of everything we could provide. I remember when John first started playing the guitar. I really couldn't understand it. Here was a nicely spoken boy attending church three times on Sunday of his own free will, in the church choir, who had suddenly taken to twanging and strumming a guitar. I told him it was awful and that it was distracting him from his studies as an art student. One day, a long-haired young boy knocked on my door in Liverpool asking for John. I asked him, 'Who are you?', I demanded to know as I caught sight of his winkle-picker shoes and gold chain. 'Paul McCartney, I'm a mate of your John.' Until John met Paul and the others, John spoke

what I call the King's English without a trace of a Liverpool accent. One day I complained when he lapsed into broad Liverpudlian. He turned on me, saying he felt embarrassed by his accent and suddenly ran upstairs in a fit of temper. Leaning over the banisters he yelled, 'Dat, Dese, Dem and Does,' mimicking the local habit of dropping their ths."

Saturday, July 13

Paul, making his first live appearance since December 1979, appears at *Live Aid* as one of the world's greatest rock and pop performers in a massive sixteen-hour concert, simultaneously running in London at Wembley Stadium and America to raise money for the starving people of Ethiopia. Bob Geldof, the lead singer with The Boomtown Rats, arranges the charity event. By the end of the two shows, the 1.5 billion people, who had witnessed the musical spectacle on TV all around the world, had pledged over £50 million . . .

Bob Geldof "I knew that if I could get Paul, millions who would not normally watch, would watch, and that would mean that extra money would come in, which would not otherwise come in. I thought that if he felt he really couldn't do it, there wouldn't be any pressure. But if he did decide to do it, it would be the crowning glory to the whole enterprise. When I first phoned Paul, he turned me down . . ."

Paul "I told him, 'I haven't got a band and I'm not touring. I'm not even in rehearsal. I'll make a fool of myself.' Then Bob said to me, 'It doesn't matter, we'll give you a piano. Come and do it on your own. Do "Let It Be". "Let It Be" is like a hymn to failed dreams. If you do that, the whole world will cry.' He convinced me to do it and the nearer it got to the concert, I thought, 'I've never been on stage on my own with a piano before, what the hell am I doing?' It was pretty nerve-racking. There were rumours at the time that the remaining Beatles would do *Live Aid* but they were only rumours . . ."

George "I didn't know anything about the *Live Aid* concert. I had flown back into England on the morning of the concert and everyone at the airport was saying to me, 'Are The Beatles going to get together for *Live Aid*?' But I really didn't know anything about it."

Paul "I'm sure that we weren't speaking to each other then, anyway. We'd had a lot of business problems and we weren't on good enough terms to do it. We couldn't have done it as The Beatles anyway. We were like a feuding family. You can't ask someone who's just divorced to get together with the ex-wife for a darts match down the pub. So I was on my own. When I arrived at Wembley, I just had a mate who drove me there. He doubled up as my roadie. I had started watching the *Live Aid* show on TV at home and seeing bands like U2 perform got me into the spirit of it all. Then, as we were driving in from the country, it seemed like it was one of those street party days, like the Queen's Silver Jubilee events. Everyone near the stadium had their windows of their houses open and you could hear that they were all watching the *Live Aid* concert. It was as if the whole country had become madly besotted with this good thing, everyone was taking part in this national event and that really encouraged me.

"When I used to play a concert, I usually arrived hours before show time and spend two hours checking my band, crew and the sound system but arriving for *Live Aid* there was no rehearsal or warm-up. I remember seeing Bob (Geldof) asleep backstage from exhaustion. So, when it was my time to perform, I wandered up to one side of the stage and asked, 'Where's the piano? Bob said that there would be a piano.' Then someone pointed to the one Elton John had left behind and said, 'There, that's it over there, and you're on.' I walked to the piano, thought, 'Oh, here we go,' and tried playing a few notes, but there was nothing! I couldn't hear a thing! I thought, 'Okay, just busk it. We're on the BBC and the sound must be heard somewhere. I'm not hearing it but maybe my monitors are out. Don't worry, the sound must be heard on the telly and anyway, I can't stop and say, "Uh, excuse me, millions of people, but my monitor's gone." ' So the moment when the world was meant to cry was not being heard. I remember seeing the sea of confused faces and I started panicking. And I thought that the only thing I could do was to keep on singing. I sang, 'When I find myself in times of trouble,' and I knew that it had all gone terribly wrong. In the middle of the biggest ever thing I had ever done, I find that my mike is not on. The crowd took a minute to realise what had happened and then suddenly, they all began to sing. There were no catcalls, just a huge, helpful singalong and that was the spirit of the day. It was the marvellous audience that saved me and then, halfway through the song, my mike finally came to life and, you know, I didn't care.

"Normally, if that happened on tour you'd come off stage panicking and sweating and thinking you had died. But that day, it didn't matter. The audience helped me out. I found out later that, because of the rush to get one band performing after another, roadies working for Queen's Freddie Mercury and Brian May, the act before me, had accidentally pulled out my microphone plug. But it didn't matter, it was a brilliant day for Britain, for the whole of the world and for the people we were doing it for. We finally did something and it took someone like Mad Bob to get it all together. But what gets me is when people moan at the likes of Bob, Sting, or myself when we try to do something for the starving or the environment or Amnesty. It was a day I'll always remember and I'm proud to have been a part of it."

Friday, August 23
Meanwhile, the filming of the new American, Johnny Carson produced, made-for-TV film, *John & Yoko – A Love Story*, is disrupted with further spooky goings-on . . .

UK reporter Dick Blair reports, "Everyone on the set is aware of them. First there was the strange case of actor Mark Lindsay, who was originally picked to play John Lennon. He was born Mark Chapman, the same name as Lennon's murderer. When the bizarre discovery was made, Liverpool actor Mark McGann, who played Lennon on stage four years ago, replaced him. Then, when he wanted to listen to a tape of a radio programme on Lennon's death, his recorder would not play. Assuming the machine, which had been going fine before, had broken, Mark tried the tape on a friend's cassette player . . . 'It just ate it,' says McGann. He and Kim Miyori, who plays Yoko, are so like the couple that people have asked them for their autographs. Recalls Mark, 'Two women in Coventry came up to us and said, "We've got all your records," but when I signed my real name, they looked really disappointed and turned to Kim and said, "Can we have yours too, Miss Ono?" They didn't realise that John is dead . . .' The film should be the most accurate portrayal of John and Yoko's life together from the time they met in a London art gallery in 1966 until John's murder in 1980. The reason is that Yoko Ono has helped the director and writer, Sandy Stern, with the research. He spent five days with her as she reminisced about the events in their colourful lives. Yoko invited Sandy to her Dakota home and showed him her private collection of home movies . . ."

Sandy Stern recalls, "That was hard on her. It dredged up so many memories. She's a strong lady but she's very vulnerable inside."

Monday, October 21

At the Limehouse Television studios in London, George and Ringo along with Eric Clapton and Dave Edmunds, appear as guests on *Blue Suede Shoes – A Rockabilly Session*, a musical all-star tribute to the rock'n'roll legend, Carl Perkins . . .

George "Carl was a big influence on me as a kid. I first met him, of all places, in Alma Cogan's flat in Kensington, back in the Sixties and he was so very nice."

Perkins "I was ready to retire, thinking that my best days in music were behind me. Then came the idea for the rockabilly special. I videotaped personal invitations to George, Ringo, Eric and others and I went to great lengths to see that they were hand-delivered."

George "He sent me this special video of a little hot rod coming down the road with 'Matchbox' playing in the background and then he pulled up, got out of the car and said, 'Hey, George Harrison. Hi, Carl Perkins here. I'm going to do a TV special and I want you to be on it. In fact, it won't be a TV special unless you're on it.'"

Perkins "Enclosed with each video was a self-addressed card. If the recipient was interested, they were to sign the card and return it to me. They signed the cards and returned them so fast. I just couldn't believe it! In ten days I had Ringo, Clapton and Edmunds."

George "I sent back my card and then I never heard any more about it for about five or six months and then, once Dave Edmunds really got involved, it came together really suddenly . . . The Carl Perkins show was really for me. It was done because I like Carl and I ought to do something, otherwise I'd get so out of it, I might never want to do that kind of thing again. It's hard to step back out after you've not done any shows. So I did it thinking, 'Well, Carl Perkins' music is so enjoyable and such fun, it's the kind of thing I should be able to do without too much worry.' The night before we did the show, Carl came over to my house with Dave Edmunds and a couple of guys from the band. We had dinner and a couple of bottles of wine and started playing guitars. I said to Dave Edmunds and Carl, 'It's a pity that these days there's not the kind of songs that are so simple and yet really classic tunes.' So Carl started playing some new songs he had written and they were killers! I mean, if they could be recorded like his Sun Records, just done really nicely, up-to-date with that sound, those songs are as good as the original hits."

Perkins "Playing with George was a particular thrill. He got really excited because he hadn't played in front of an audience for so long. Before we went on, George was real nervous and I felt him freezing up right after he walked up there and I pitched him a guitar break that he wasn't expecting. I could tell by the grin on his face that his fears were leaving."

George "It was nicely presented. Did you hear what he said? 'Look at you guys, all in your nice, clean shirts and little shirts.' He was so blown away. There was one point where he was almost in tears, saying, 'It's been thirty years since I wrote this tune and I've never enjoyed it so much as with my rockabilly buddies.' He's so sweet."

Perkins "His wife, Olivia, was just so happy. She told me in the dressing room after the show, 'Carl, I don't know what to say to you, because I saw my old George so happy tonight. I saw something there that I hadn't seen in a long time.' After the special was taped, I received a nice hand-written letter from Ringo. He said it was just one of the magic nights in his life to get to play the kind of music that they cut their teeth on in the early years."

Saturday, November 9
A 1981 interview with **Paul**, conducted by the authorised Beatles biographer, Hunter Davies, is published in today's *Woman* magazine in the UK. The piece features Paul again trying to defend himself against John's legacy . . .

"No one ever goes on about the times John hurt me," he insists. "When he called my music Muzak. People keep on saying I hurt him, but where's the examples, when did I do it? Could I have hurt John more than anyone in the world? (A reference to a recent comment made by Yoko.) More than the policeman who ran down Julia in his car? We were always in competition. I wrote 'Penny Lane', so he wrote 'Strawberry Fields'. That was how it was. But that was in compositions. I can't understand why Yoko is saying this. The last time I spoke to her she was great. She told me she and John had just been playing one of my albums and had cried. There was only one incident I can think of which John has publicly mentioned. It was when I went off with Ringo and did 'Why Don't We Do It In The Road?' It wasn't a deliberate thing. John and George were tied up finishing something and Ringo and me were free, so I said to Ringo, 'Let's go and do this.' I did hear John later singing it. He liked the song and I suppose he'd wanted to do it with me. It was a very John sort of song. Perhaps I have hurt people by default. I never realised it at the time that John would mind . . . I was never out to screw him, never! He could be a manoeuvring swine, which no one ever realised. Now since his death, he's becoming Martin Luther Lennon. But that really wasn't him either. He wasn't some sort of Holy Saint. He was still really a debunker . . . But I idolised John. He was the big guy in the chip shop and I was the little guy. As I matured and grew up, I started sharing in things with him. I got up to his level. I wrote songs as he did and sometimes they were as good as his. We grew to be equals. It made him insecure. He was insecure with women. You know, he told me when he first met Yoko not to make a play for her . . . John and I were really army buddies. That's what it was like, really. I realise now we never got to the bottom of each other's souls. I didn't hate John. People said to me when he said those things on his record about me, you must hate him, but I didn't. We were once having a right slagging session and I remember how he took off his granny glasses. I can still see him. He put them down and said, 'It's only me, Paul.' Then he put them back on again and we continued slagging . . . That phrase keeps coming back to me all the time. 'It's only me.' It's become a mantra in my mind. Until I was about 30, I thought the world was an exact place. Now I know that life just splutters along. John knew that. He was the great debunker. He'd be debunking all his death things now."

JANUARY

George's company HandMade Films continues with their film production by financing *Shanghai Surprise*, a romantic adventure movie starring the singer Madonna and her husband, Sean Penn. Filming starts this month in Hong Kong . . .

"The movie had been in HandMade for some time," **George** recalls. "We had considered making it and most of the people in HandMade didn't want to make that film and then there was some talk about that Madonna may be in the lead part because the film's producer happened to know Sean. That film got one day away from being elbowed out and then we had this phone call, saying that Madonna really wanted to be in it and she's told Sean that, 'If you want to see me for the next few months, then why don't you be in it, too?' So suddenly it was on, and it seemed like a good idea at the time . . ."

Chart star, Madonna "When the idea of doing *Shanghai Surprise* came up, it sounded like a great joint project, with Sean and I. We didn't actually plan on working on the film together. When I was given the script, I read it and liked it. I asked Sean to give it a quick read and he liked the main male role and the concept of working together seemed like a natural career progression. I liked the script, but when we got there, the director (Jim Goddard) just had no knowledge of what he was doing, and it was downhill from the second day."

The *Sunday Mirror* reports (March 2) "Beatle turned film boss, George Harrison, had a heart to heart chat with rock star Madonna yesterday as rows on the set threatened to wreck his £10 million movie. Moody Madonna and her surly husband, Sean Penn, spent more than an hour with him. Later, a worried George appeared on the steps of the mansion at Virginia Water, Surrey, where filming of *Shanghai Surprise* is running behind schedule, and said, 'I want everybody to cool it, things have been getting way out of hand. I'm not blaming anyone in particular but I cannot let the situation continue. Unless everyone cools it and gets on with their work, it could have a very serious effect on HandMade.' The on-set wrangling reached a peak when Penn demanded to know the 'mole' who kept leaking information about him and Madonna to the press. George said, 'He is obviously upset because it seems to him that Colonel Gadaffi and President Marcos have been getting a better press than him. I feel terribly sorry for Sean. It's very difficult to go out and act after all this trouble. I really like Sean but I cannot give him advice all the time, I'm not his father. He is paid to be an actor.' "

Denis O'Brien, HandMade Films "We could have all warned him not to get involved with the likes of Madonna but we all felt for poor old George when he was dragged out of his magnificent garden to patch up with the press on account of her behaviour."

On **Thursday, March 6**, in an attempt to help publicise *Shanghai Surprise*, George joins Madonna in a London press conference, an event reported in the *Daily Mirror* by Christena Appleyard . . .

"It was an extraordinary double act and between them, George Harrison and Madonna put on quite a show," the report reads. "George played the ageing superstar coming out of retirement and Madonna played her usual role of the misunderstood but terribly talented superstar. George looked gorgeous but the world's hottest superstar was a bit of a disappointment. Dressed from head to toe in black, with not a glimpse of her famous flesh on show, she looked more like a novice nun. Topped off by an old-fashioned Hollywood style hairdo that looked like a slightly limp, peroxide halo. But she only looked saint-like."

Madonna, at the press gathering "What is a trained actress?" she hisses at someone who dares suggest she wasn't. And on the subject of George, "He has given me more advice about how to deal with the press than how to make a film," she responds.

Christena Appleyard "Every time a really tricky question came up, George took over and managed to get everyone laughing . . ."

Reporter "Where's Sean?"

George "He's busy, working. I don't think he's talking to the press. I happen to like Sean very much, and apart from all the bullshit that's been said, he's actually a human being. He's very nice and he's a very talented actor."

Reporter "Madonna, are you a fan of George Harrison?"

Madonna "I wasn't a Beatles maniac. I think I didn't really appreciate their songs till I was much older. But he's a great boss, very understanding and very sympathetic."

Reporter "Do you fight with Sean?"

George (interrupting) "Do you fight with your wife?"

Christena Appleyard "When Madonna laughs, you can tell she's been practising in front of the mirror. She rolls her eyes and curls up a bit. It's a slightly familiar pose and all becomes clear when you read the publicity bumph, which hails her as the Monroe of the 80s. She does have a lot in common with Marilyn Monroe, everything in fact except talent, warmth and real sex appeal . . . Just as she got up to leave, someone asked her if she thinks she is coping well with all her sudden fame and success. 'Yeah, sure I am,' she said and George said nothing."

George "The press was a bit unkind to them. I had experienced it with The Beatles, you know, they love you and build you up to the point where the only thing left is to knock you down. So there was a lot of attitude. A lot of stuff they wrote in the British press was just terrible. It was really nasty and a bit over the top. But, at the same time, their attitudes didn't help. The Beatles had a sense of humour and that's one that she (Madonna) didn't seem to have, which was a pity, because it was a comedy movie. Nevertheless, they were treated unfairly. The press kept getting in the way of the making of the film. Sean would come in, read the papers, go crazy, hit the wall and then he would take it out on the film crew and the film crew would get to the point where they didn't like the pair of them. And what I did was like a, sort of, Henry Kissinger job, just trying to get it finished. So I said to Sean, 'If they're going to write this about you, you just can't read it. Don't read it! And if you are going to read it, don't let it affect you.' I must say, Sean, when he's not going crazy, is absolutely brilliant. The scene when he's up, he's a good actor, but when he's down, it shows, and he's got a good sense of humour. He's a real funny fellow. I had some good times with him."

Speaking in March 1987, by which time the £8 million *Shanghai Surprise* had sunk without trace, **George** announced "What went wrong with *Shanghai Surprise*? Well, we got the wrong script, the wrong director and the wrong stars. It was more a case of, 'Where did I go right?' It turned into a bloody nightmare. We were damn lucky to get our money back and not lose our shirts . . . It's pointless to pretend that we didn't have any problems but *Shanghai Surprise* does have some good points. It's quite entertaining, it's good to look at and it works as an action film where you can see Madonna and Sean together for the first time. But . . . let's just say that Madonna and Sean could have been much better if they had not been hounded by the press and hounded by their own minds. It was a combination of her thinking she's a star and the way the press was gunning for her. The British press went after them like dogs chasing a bone. If there are dogs barking at your heels, it's much better to throw them a bone to keep 'em happy than totally ignore them. All this aloofness and star stuff, it's just bullshit. I'm not trying to be nasty, she's probably got a lot in her that she hadn't discovered yet, but she has to realise that you can be a fabulous person and be humble as well . . . I haven't seen 'em from that day to this. I still think Sean Penn could eventually become a big star, because when he's good, he's great. But he needs to lighten up instead of being heavy all the time. It's a bit immature."

While Madonna will reflect, "*Shanghai Surprise* was edited as an adventure movie and they cut all my major scenes down to nothing, which made me look like an air-head girl without a character."

Shanghai Surprise will become HandMade Films' biggest box office disaster, opening in four hundred cities across America on Friday, August 29, 1986, and reaching the important cinemas of New York on September 19. *Rolling Stone* will describe the film as "Madonna's first flop." While Fred Schruers, of the *US* magazine, will be propelled to describe the movie as "Shockingly amateurish!" Needless to say, almost instantly *Shanghai Surprise* will disappear from the US cinema circuit . . .

Friday, June 20
Tonight and tomorrow, George and Ringo perform as special guests at the Prince's Trust gala concert at the Empire Pool, Wembley. It is George's first UK concert in twenty years . . .

"It was the first time I've done anything in England since 1966," **George** reveals. "It made me nervous. I liked the show, I liked the tape and the record of it, but it was a bit like going to the electric chair waiting to go on. After a long time, you forget how to stand up in front of the audience. But you get used to it by the middle bit. When you get into it, your mouth dries up. With the Prince's Trust, there were only two shows. The first show had an electrical problem and they didn't record anything. So it was the only show recorded. Take 1 and that was going to be a video and a TV show and a record and a tape and that's pretty hard, you know, just to expect a brilliant performance in one take, having not performed in forty years! Eric (Clapton) asked me to be on the show. He said, 'Would you do this show? They've asked me to ask you.' They're pretty clever, really, because I suppose there's more chance of me saying yes to Eric than to some guy I don't know. My thoughts to him (Eric) was, 'What would I do, you know?' I'm so out of touch. He said, 'Well, do "Here Comes The Sun", you know.' I always think that that stuff is so passé and to hear him request that, I think, 'Oh, it must be okay.' The funny thing was, at the end of the show, you could look across the stage and see all these young new groups like Curiosity Killed The Cat doing the latest dances. And then, if you looked down the line, the musicians got older and older, and there was less and less hair until you got to the real old guys, like me and Elton (John) and Phil (Collins), all looking a bit arthritic."

But shortly afterwards, George will admit that his concert comeback will be marred by cold terror. Not from playing in front of Princess Diana and Prince Charles, but from a crazed fan standing just feet away in front of the stage . . .

"It suddenly struck me that it was somebody like the guy who had murdered John Lennon," **George** announces, "and it scared the hell out of me. Before I even took to the stage I was petrified. I had looked down into the first few rows and immediately it struck me that this guy was going absolutely bananas. He was jumping up and down, waving his arms about and screaming my name. He was so fanatical and kept staring at me with this manic glint in his eye. He really freaked me out. Every time I looked over, he was going a little crazier. Even if I had been considering coming back to do large shows, the sight of this guy made me think twice. I couldn't get it out of the back of my mind that this was the sort of person that had probably killed John. That creep that killed him really affected my life . . . it made me very wary of fans spotting me on the street. It scares me when fans recognise me and come up to me. I just don't like it. Having laid low for all those years means that, thankfully, today's generation really doesn't know much about me or what I look like. Now I reckon I could walk down the High Street and there would be very few people who would recognise me. Certainly not many of today's generation would be able to point me out in a crowd, and that's a great feeling. Unlike most stars, and it seems like many of the new ones, I'm not interested in fame and being a celebrity. During those mad Beatles days, I got my fame and fortune at a very early age and after that I lost my fascination for it. Those days were really hectic and I have no desire to relive them again."

Tuesday, July 29
George's recent surprisingly high profile continues when he again features in tabloid reports, not for his thriving HandMade Films organisation or his appearance at the Prince's Trust concert, but for his attempts to save the historic 740-seater Regal cinema, situated near his home in Henley-on-Thames and built in 1936 . . .

Richard Wallace, the *Standard* "Beatle turned film producer, George Harrison, has lashed out at 'faceless bureaucrats' who plan to pull down his local cinema. Harrison is leading other showbusiness celebrities in the fight to save the Regal and described the move by a supermarket chain as 'Orwellian cynicism'. Years in the limelight have made Harrison wary of public attention and he is now rarely seen and never gives interviews. But when retail giant Waitrose said they were buying the cinema in the centre of Henley to build a large supermarket, Harrison decided to go public . . ."

George "The fight for the cinema personifies the state of British towns and cities. For years, planners have pulled down buildings of value and put up concrete monsters. I have felt since my days back in Liverpool that the planners and architects are getting away with too much. I go round to towns I used to visit and I don't recognise them at all. You don't know where you are. Henley is a little town with a whole mixture of designs and periods. During the time I've been here, one building after another has been torn down. The sense of community and place is being destroyed. We are being choked to death with cars and lorries crashing through the narrow streets that were originally built for the horse and cart. Waitrose have the largest store in the town, just 200 yards from the Regal. Why they need to pull down this fine building to build another even bigger supermarket is beyond me. The council owns the site and I understood a council represents the people. We, the people, want to keep the cinema. There is a huge industrial estate not far from here where you can build a hypermarket and have loads of space for car parking. Let them go there. Waitrose say they are buying an empty building. This sort of Orwellian cynicism will not do. We want to see these people who change the face of England and ask them some questions."

His attentions return to the cinema "I'd love to redecorate this place. You just don't find places like this anymore . . . I'm not doing this for an ulterior motive. I genuinely want to preserve this town. These faceless people who make the planning applications and those who give permission should come out of the shadows. Let us see the faces of the assassins."

Summing up, a spokesman for Waitrose says, "We are not faceless people, but we can make no comment at this stage about the allegations being aired. Perhaps those matters will be more fully aired when the public inquiry is held."

(Note: George's protests were in vain and the cinema soon closes for business and becomes the supermarket as threatened.)

Wednesday, December 31

As the year draws to a close, Andrew Stephens of the *Daily Express* writes, "Superstar Paul McCartney has written a secret love song just for his wife, Linda. Unlike all the golden hits the ex-Beatle has written in the past, his latest composition hasn't a chance of making the charts. For, on his emphatic orders, only one disc has been cut, and the song won't even be heard outside Paul's Sussex farmhouse home where he presented the record as a surprise for Linda's 45th birthday back in September. Paul warned all sixteen top musicians he hired for the recording not to breathe a word about it. And as far as publicity was concerned, every player kept mute. But last night, the news was trumpeted when proud mother, Mrs Glennis Beachill couldn't refrain from talking about her son, 25-year-old, trombonist Peter . . ."

Mrs Beachill, of Barnsley discloses to reporters, "Peter was staying with the family over Christmas and we naturally asked him what sort of session work he had done in the past year. He told us casually about the special recording he had made with Paul McCartney, who had wanted to keep it all a secret. Our Peter wouldn't tell us any white lies to boost himself. He wasn't even showing off when he told us. It came up because of something that reminded him of Paul McCartney. He told us that Paul was great to work with and he is sorry that the song would never be heard in public. Peter said it was one of those classic McCartney compositions."

Thursday, February 19
George makes a surprise guest appearance at The Palomino Club in Los Angeles, performing alongside such musical greats as Bob Dylan, Taj Mahal and John Fogerty . . .

George "I had gone to America and Bob rang me and said, 'Do you want to go out for the evening and see Taj Mahal who is playing at The Palomino Club?' I did so we went there and had a few Mexican beers and then a few more. Jesse Ed Davis, the guitarist, was in the audience and Bob said, 'Hey, why don't we all get up and play? We've had a few beers, right, and you can sing.' So we get up there and I'm in the spotlight, Bob's hanging in the back and I start singing. Every time I got near the microphone, Bob comes running up and starts singing all this rubbish in my ears, trying to throw me. It was really funny, really."

Friday, March 20

George announces to the UK journalist Fay Egan "There are good things about being a celebrity. If I phone up a hotel and ask for a room, they're more likely to give me a good one. There are perks but it all balances out. Other times you're out just being a normal person, having a walk and suddenly everyone's pointing at you and taking photos. Then you feel like a monkey in a cage. Generally, I feel very fortunate. It's been a good life. I mean, if you're going to be in a rock'n'roll band, you may as well be in The Beatles."

Monday, June 1
The world goes *Sgt. Pepper* crazy on the twentieth anniversary of the release of the classic album. Coinciding with the anniversary, EMI issue The Beatles' *Sgt. Pepper's Lonely Hears Club Band* on CD for the first time . . .

George "*Sgt. Pepper*? It was a surprise to see it on top of the album charts in England but I was frankly a bit disappointed about it. I don't know exactly what happened with the mix itself, you know, the balance that we had, because everything is really down to a mix. It became one thing in the mix, but on this CD, somehow you can see behind it and you can hear things sticking out too much. To me, it just sounds like a rough mix. It seems that some of the hard work we did to get them to sound like they sounded has been undone and I don't know if that's just the result of the digitising of these songs or not. Because you have to remember most of them were either done on two- or four-track machines . . . I heard a strange story that Geoff Emerick had one CD mix and somebody at EMI had a cassette copy of them and the copy was faulty and they listened to it and said, 'Oh, these are terrible!' So somebody went in and redid them, but actually Emerick's mixes were good."

Paul "I think *Sgt. Pepper* translates perfectly to CD and it sounds great."

George "I still prefer the old versions, how I remember them on vinyl. On *Sgt. Pepper* I keep hearing this horrible tambourine that leaps out of the right speaker. It was obviously in the original mix, but it was never that loud. I don't know where that came from. Some things jump out a bit too much. I think CDs are good on all this new stuff, but I don't know about the old stuff being put on them."

Friday, July 24
The subject of the long-time non-appearance of the CD releases of The Beatles' back catalogue reaches the courts of New York . . .

New York correspondent for *The Times*, Charles Bremner "Ringo Starr, George Harrison and Yoko Ono, widow of John Lennon, have filed a $40 million (£25 million) law suit against The Beatles' former record company, claiming that it had tried to punish them for a drawn-out legal battle by delaying the release of their recordings on compact disc. In their action, filed in the Manhattan Supreme Court, the two former Beatles, Yoko Ono and their defunct company, Apple, allege that Capitol Records and its British parent company, EMI, held up the compact disc release in the United States for two years to try to force them to drop a long-standing claim over royalties. They are also demanding the return of the master tapes of their Sixties albums. Mr Leonard Marks, The Beatles' New York lawyer, said the record company was 'cheating The Beatles out of millions and they are very upset'. The compact disc versions of The Beatles' hits went to the top of the record charts when they were first released in the US in February, three years after Capitol had begun releasing compact disc versions of other artists' Sixties hits. Mr Marks has been waging a battle for eight years to win about $50 million in damages from Capitol for what the claimants saw as an attempt to camouflage the sale of 19 million copies of *Abbey Road* and other record albums by claiming they were scrapped, so denying them royalties. As well as alleging delay in releasing the compact discs, the claimants say Capitol deprived them of royalties by charging 25 per cent of the price of the discs for 'repackaging' when the true cost was one-sixth of that."

Sunday, August 30

Jonathan Ashby, *Sunday Mirror*, reports, "Paul McCartney is to form a new group and go back on the road. The former Beatles and Wings star is looking for chartbusters of the Eighties to tour with him. One of his associates said, 'Paul is interested in getting together with some of Britain's younger rock musicians who he met for the first time at the *Live Aid* concert.' In recent weeks he has held recording sessions with numerous artists including The Smiths' former guitarist, Johnny Marr and Simple Minds' singer, Jim Kerr. The final line-up will not be decided until later this year. But it will *not* include his former Beatles partners, George Harrison and Ringo Starr. The only Wings star in the band is likely to be Linda. McCartney has been writing and recording songs for the new group at his lavish studios in a converted mill overlooking the sea at Rye in Sussex, near his home. But Paul won't blast off with his new band until he's tested his popularity by releasing a double-album of his Wings' hits. His colleague said, 'When he unveils the new group, you can bet he will put other pop stars half his age to shame.'"

Tuesday, October 20
The build-up to the release of George's first studio album in five years continues when a pre-taped interview with the former Beatle appears in the States on NBC TV's *Today Show*, where he is interviewed by Rhona Elliott . . .

Rhona "How do you feel about putting a new entry out into the market place?"

George "Putting it out into the market place is strange for me, because I've never been that competitive. I mean, you won't find me on your sixteen-minute videos dancing and shaking my fist. I just can't do that kind of thing."

Rhona "As recently as last month, as I know you're aware, there is a phenomenal interest in Beatles memorabilia. As an example, John Lennon's handwritten lyrics went for $22,000."

George "It's ridiculous, yeah. It's got out of hand, actually, if you ask me. Sotheby's, Christies and Philips in London have a sale every month, and a lot of it is stolen property or stuff that disappeared, and a lot of it is phoney. There are some autographs and stuff that we did sign on aeroplanes, but there are a lot of autographs that our road managers used to sign. He used to sit there with all these pictures and they learned how to do all our autographs or we'd be doing them all our lives. So there are a lot of our road managers' autographs. Actually, they're probably worth a lot more than the real Beatles autographs. But there is a lot of junk in there, but they're selling it. I get a little bit annoyed by it. I think, I can really clean up. It's nice to know that if we are ever short of cash, I can sell up and go on holiday. I've got lots of bits of paper. I've got all kinds of things, Paul's underpants from the Shea Stadium, very cheap, $60,000."

Wednesday, October 21
An interview with George is published in the UK tabloid newspaper, the *Sun*, during which the formerly "quiet Beatle" takes an opportunity to again dismiss his image of being an "eccentric recluse" . . .

"If you believe everything you heard," **George** says to the reporter Rick Sky, "you'd think I sit in a darkened room all day, grow long, curling fingernails and pick up the telephone using tissue paper. I don't take ten showers a day either and the toilet in my Hawaiian home doesn't play 'Lucy In The Sky With Diamonds' every time it's flushed! But there is a bizarre side to my 100-year-old, 30-room Friar Park home. Beneath the 15-bedroom, eight-bathroom mansion runs an amazing maze of caves and tunnels built by a previous owner. I've spent a lot of time and money cleaning and renovating the caves. The guy who built them was a complete loony. He spent a fortune modelling them on the Blue Grotto in Capri . . . Gardening is a real passion; I love being close to nature. It makes me feel very peaceful."

Later, George and Ringo join Paul for a quiet evening at his home in Cavendish Avenue in St John's Wood, London . . .

Paul "I'm just getting back with them now. It's just all business troubles. That's what spoils the whole thing for us. If we don't talk about Apple, we get on like a house on fire. The minute anyone mentions Apple, something comes up and they'll say, 'Well, you wouldn't show your records to the accountants,' and I say, 'But I did! Your man is, at this moment, in my office,' and they'll say, 'Like hell he is!' And we have major misunderstandings over things like that. But I do bend over backwards to try and not to be crazy. So I am starting to see them again. In fact, George came down to visit me and, for the first time in years, we had a nice time."

George "When we got back to his house, I started trying to sing 'She's Leaving Home' and I suddenly thought, 'This must have been really interesting if you were trying to write this song,' and I suddenly said to him, 'Now who wrote that bit? Was that you or was that John?' And he said, 'I think what probably happened was I wrote the first bit then John came in.' Then I suddenly thought, 'This is stupid! I'm asking Paul who wrote which bit of "She's Leaving Home" twenty years later.' "

Paul "He was my original friend in Liverpool. We were quite big buddies then, so that's something I've missed through all these years. We had got all professional, Beatles and everything, and you lose that. He came down the other day and we didn't say anything about Apple and we didn't play together. We didn't touch an instrument. We didn't do anything. It was back as mates, like on the bus in Liverpool. We talked about trees and it was really great just to relate as two people, and to get all that crap out of the window and to put it to one side for once. We did brush off The Beatles at one time but now we're all coming to. Obviously it was a huge deal, and The Beatles were a huge deal. But I don't think half of us know what happened to us, really. I mean, I can never tell you what year a thing was. They just all go into a haze, you know. I keep seeing pictures of myself, like shaking hands with (the American celebrity) Mitzi Gaynor and I think, 'I didn't know I had met her.' It's that vague! But life was speeding. I'd meet Mitzi Gaynor and then I'd go and meet Jerry Lewis's kids. I keep seeing myself with people I didn't know I'd met. It's quite embarrassing, but a laugh."

Monday, November 2 (UK and USA)
After a five-year wait, George releases his new studio album . . .

Michael A. Lerner of *Newsweek* magazine writes, "In terms of post-Beatle identity, George Harrison always posed a problem. John became a househusband to the dominant Yoko, Paul grew Wings and went pop and Ringo made bad movies and married a Bond girl. But George stayed aloof, dabbling in music, movies and Nirvana, and keeping the press as far away as possible. Until now. After five years of total silence, the 'quiet Beatle' is going public. He has a new album coming out, *Cloud Nine*, his first since 1982 . . . *Cloud Nine* features some of the best music Harrison has written since his Beatles days . . ."

Bob Merlis, head of publicity, Warner Brothers Records "It was twenty years ago today that *Sgt. Pepper's Lonely Hearts Club Band* hit the stands and America has been drowning in a wave of Beatles nostalgia as a result. Released for the first time this year on compact disc, Beatles albums have sold exceptionally well. I think anything George Harrison puts out is going to get some kind of listen, but it's true, people are definitely into Beatleness."

Soon after *Cloud Nine*'s release, George is asked why he had taken so long with releasing a follow-up to *Gone Troppo* . . .

"I think I just got a little tired of making records by myself," **George** replies, "because most of the records I've made since *All Things Must Pass*, I've tended to write the songs, arrange them myself, produce them, perform them and mix them. And I found that I was getting a bit bogged down by the end of it. I was getting really tired of that. So I thought I'd just have a rest because I'm not really enjoying it. But I continued to write songs throughout the years between *Gone Troppo* and *Cloud Nine* . . ."

"While you were a recluse?" a reporter stupidly asks.

"I never became a true recluse," **George** snorts. "It's all gossip and rumour and the press always exaggerate, especially here in England. You want to know the truth? Simple, I didn't want to end up like some famous people, always living in a goldfish bowl with no real private life of their own. So I just decided not to do all these television talk shows every five minutes . . . Next thing I know, they started saying, 'George Harrison is just like Howard Hughes, he never leaves his house, ever.' It simply wasn't true, I go out all the time, I visit friends and I travel all over the place. They love to make out that I'm this weird eccentric but I was never really weird. I mean, I always had a sense of humour about things, even during my really heavy religious period. . . .

"*Cloud Nine* was the most enjoyable thing I've done in years and I'm really pleased with the way it's turned out. 'Cloud Nine' and 'Just For Today' are two songs from the winter of '83/ '84. Maybe eighteen months ago I felt just right, I felt good enough to make a record. Being away from it, I thought, maybe absence makes the heart grow fonder. It was mainly my decision to get a producer to help me work on it. The idea was who I could get to work with. I wracked my brains because I don't really know a lot of producers. I'm sure I could put an advert in the paper, but then I thought, 'Jeff Lynne!' If I figure him out, meet him and then I could see if we got on well. I know that musically we could get on well because he's a guitar player, songwriter and producer . . . So through Dave Edmunds, I got to meet Jeff Lynne. This happened about eighteen months ago now. We started hanging out a bit over a period and then I said, 'How about you helping me make an album?' I think it really worked out well . . . Working with Lynne reminded me of when I was in The Beatles, when you had the support. You think of one idea, it bounces off the other person and turns into something else. I really enjoyed working with Jeff and I think he enjoyed it, too. I'd like to hang out with him in the future and write more pop songs."

Summing up, **George** admits "I won't say I won't care if *Cloud Nine*'s a hit, because I do! After all that work I would like it to do very good. I think it's a great album. There's a place for it in the charts. I think the people should like it . . ."

Asked as to whether he would consider touring to promote the album?

George replies "Everyone is trying to get me back on the road but I'm not keen on it. Touring can be hell and I don't relish the thought of people coming up to me, trying to shove drugs up my nose. Yes, I've taken drugs in the past, but these days the most I'll do is a reefer and a few puffs of that and I'm out of it. I just can't handle it. I can't understand the craze for heroin; I never wanted to try it. But heroin is not the only killer in rock. I think booze is just as bad, if not worse. It may be legal but it's ruined so many people's lives."

George talks about the musicians who perform on the album . . .

"Fortunately, most of my friends tend to be stars," he announces. "It's not that I chose stars for the album. Eric Clapton and Ringo are friends. Elton (John) was calling me while he was in Australia with the Melbourne Symphony because Ray Cooper, who was in Elton's band, is actually working for HandMade Films. They call me periodically, and Elton was saying, 'Oh, I hear you're making a new album. If you want me to play on it, just give me a call.'"

'Cloud Nine'

George "The track seemed a good opener. Later, when I saw the album cover, which had clouds on it, I just used that song as the album's title. It's the kind of song that is not expected from me. There's Eric Clapton and me on that one. I play some slide and Eric plays regular guitar."

'That's What It Takes'

George "We (Jeff and George) started writing 'That's What It Takes' together and we did about five middle parts but weren't sure about any of them. Then Gary Wright was over at the house and I said, 'Gary, have you got a middle bit for this?' He said, 'Oh, I've got these funny chords and I don't know what to do with them.' He played these strange chords and we sort of welded them into the middle of this song. It's like a little Beach Boys bit in the middle."

'Fish On The Sand'

George "I wrote this on the night before we started the basic sessions. I wrote it in the mood of an old rock'n'roll song. On the track I used my old Rickenbacker twelve-string, which was probably last heard on 'Ticket To Ride' or 'A Hard Day's Night'. Fish on the sand is a phrase I read somewhere that was very descriptive. It said, 'If I can't be with you, then I'm not so much a man. I'm like a fish on the sand.' Ringo plays drums on it."

'Just For Today'

George "I wrote this in the winter of '83 or in early '84. I have a couple of friends who were at the house and they had been to Alcoholics Anonymous and they had given up drinking. One of them had this leaflet that he was showing me that AA give out to help them get through the day. It's called *Just For Today*. I wrote the song based upon that. It says try to live through this day and not deal with all of life's problems. That's where the song comes from. The first part of the song is just me and a piano. I've haven't really done that before. It's like being naked. The backing parts on the song, which sound like a Welsh choir, are actually just Jeff and myself."

'This Is Love'

George "When I decided I was going to write with Jeff Lynne, I said, 'Will you write me a tune?' I thought it might be interesting for me to sing one of his songs. So he came back with a cassette, and on it were the makings of this song. He had the chorus all set, but he had four different versions of the verse part. So it was a matter of just playing them and saying, 'I think I'd like it to go this way.' So 'This Is Love' was basically his, but I helped put it together and I wrote some of the lyrics."

'When We Was Fab'

George "I started writing that song when I was with Jeff. We happened to be in Australia and I just had that thought that I'd like to write a new song that's like reminiscent of that period, 1967. I heard it in my head. I could hear Ringo counting it in, and I just started right there, I started writing that song. Jeff was around and we got on piano and he came up with all those little bits like the catchy little piano parts. The title of the song and the original intention was that we should have that kind of sound. We got crazy little backing voices, little touches of phasing, little background bits, all those little goodies. I think the track worked out well. The word 'Fab' was, at first, a joke word. It became a tongue-in-cheek sort of thing. In that period (1967) everyone was fab! It wasn't just The Beatles. We were tagged the fab four, but everyone was fab . . . I decided to write about The Beatles after all this time because we all go through cycles. For years after The Beatles, I didn't want to talk about it. It was all too close, the pain and the suffering, 'cos that was what was in my mind at the time. Then after the years away from it, I thought, 'No, we had fun and had a good little band and had more laughs than misery. It's just that the misery got broadcast more than the fun.' So I forgot the unhappy times. It was part of exorcising all that and bringing it back to a positive thing. Then, the Fab Four song just popped out. We also wrote 'This Is Love'."

The clever promotional video for 'When We Was Fab', which features cameo appearances by Ringo and Elton John, is shot at the Greenford Studios in Greenford, London and is directed by Kevin Godley and Lol Creme, formerly of the chart group 10cc . . .

George "It was fun making it. But I was a bit nervous because Godley and Creme are a couple of loonies, especially Lol. They are sweet but I wasn't sure if they knew exactly what they were doing and I found out that they knew ninety per cent of what they were doing. But it was still very good and very funny. I asked them to come up with an idea for the video. I said, 'Go home and smoke something and come up with an idea,' and they came up with that idea. But after a few days, they started panicking. They said, 'It's not going to work. It's not going to work,' and they tried to get out of it. I said, 'Don't panic now,' because I *had* to do it. I had three or four days before Christmas and it had to be done. So I said, 'Just go for a walk in the garden, have a cup of tea, calm down and I'll talk to you in an hour.' And then I talked to them in an hour and they said, 'Yeah, we think it'll be okay,' and I said, 'Good!' They built a street in the studio so that we could have action going back and forth. There's Ringo carrying the synthesiser at both ends."

'Devil's Radio'

George "I passed a little church and on the outside of it was a small billboard. It said, 'Gossip . . . the Devil's Radio. Don't be a broadcaster.' So I took it from there. The song is all about gossip, gossip, gossip and there's a lot of it going on. There's even little bits in the background going, 'Hey, you wouldn't believe what I heard.' Ringo's on drums, so it's very much a rock'n'roll song and, to me, the only thing missing off this song is Bob Dylan. It reminds me very much of something that he would have done back in the late Sixties or Seventies."

'Someplace Else'

George "I did the music for *Shanghai Surprise*. I wrote some songs for the soundtrack and since they never came out on a soundtrack album, I re-cut them for this record. One of them was 'Someplace Else'. The producer of the film at the time, said, 'I want you to write a song like "Stardust".' And I said, 'That would be nice. Who wouldn't like to write "Stardust".' So this isn't exactly like 'Stardust' but it was an attempt at a very melodic love song."

'Wreck Of The Hesperus'

George "I wrote this a couple of years ago but I didn't actually make a demo. I just sang it onto a cassette with an acoustic guitar."

'Got My Mind Set On You'

George "I don't know when it was written but I've had a copy of it at least since 1960 or 1961 (*sic*, 1963). That version was very strange and old-fashioned, but I thought it was a really great song. It's always been stuck in the back of my head . . . A guy called Rudy Clark, who I know nothing about, wrote it. The drumming on 'Got My Mind Set On You' is all machine."

NOVEMBER . . .

George travels to New York where he holds a press conference to promote *Cloud Nine* . . .

Reporter "When will you next perform live in concert?"

George "I haven't really played live. It's very difficult. I mean, I do enjoy it. Once you get into it, it's really enjoyable. There's nothing nicer than being in a band when it's all rocking, but to actually get to that stage . . . It's the sort of thing you must do permanently. Even Eric Clapton said to me, 'God, I'm getting so I can't play. My fingers are jamming up.' It's the kind of thing you've got to do all the time, and he takes gigs in between his own albums and tours. He plays on everybody else's stuff and plays in everybody else's band and I admire that because he's never lost his touch by stopping. Yet, at the same time, to just go on stage after not doing it is very hard. I did two nights of the Prince's Trust this year and I was so nervous. On the actual record, it didn't sound bad. I liked the TV show except that I really don't like watching myself. It was nerve-racking."

Reporter "Someone told me you were working on a whole batch of old rock'n'roll classics for a possible album, rather like John's *Rock 'N' Roll* album."

George "It's not true, actually. But I've tried to write those kind of tunes because years ago Leon Russell always used to say to me, 'That's the kind of record you should make, a rockabilly album.' Because that's the kind of music I'm good at playing."

Reporter "Are you still playing the sitar?"

George "I just play it for my own amusement. It's such a great instrument with a wonderful sound."

Reporter "Are you nostalgic about those days?"

George "I'm able now to really see the fun that it was and I think more about the good things that appeared. As opposed to maybe ten years ago, when I was just thinking about all the lawsuits and the negative stuff. A lot of that has just gone away with time. It's quite enjoyable to think about the things we did and the things that happened."

Reporter "How do you like the CD versions of the old (Beatles) albums?"

George "Well, I know there's a big controversy over whether they're any good or not. I know that the first batch of CDs, as George Martin said in *Billboard*, they were only made in mono, so you can't really make them sound like digital things. That's it, they were mono . . . I'm out of touch really with the old Beatles stuff, because we no longer have that deal with Capitol/EMI. They no longer consult us about anything and so we just know what we read and hear."

Reporter "What about all the press reports that there are lots of unreleased Beatles recordings still in the vaults?"

George "It's not true because there were only ever a couple of songs I can remember that weren't put out. Like there was a song I did with John and Yoko called 'What's The New Mary Jane'."

Reporter "That's on the *Sessions* bootleg."

George "There are some things which people may regard as being performances, but they're really not and shouldn't have been released. I know there's a version of 'While My Guitar Gently Weeps' with just me and an acoustic guitar."

Reporter "That's on *Sessions*, too."

George "Well, I haven't heard that. Someone I talked to yesterday has put it on a cassette for me."

Reporter "Are you still interested in Formula One motor racing?"

George "Yeah, I am, actually. I follow the world championship. In fact, I got to my hotel last night and I was really tired. I was going to have an early night and I was just going through the channels and heard Jackie Stewart's voice. It began with the Portuguese Grand Prix from last Sunday. So I ended up sitting until 2.30 in the morning watching all that."

Reporter "What originally interested you in racing?"

George "I don't know. When I was a kid, they used to have races at a place in Liverpool called Aintree and I used to go there and watch the motorbike racing and car racing. There was a World Championship Grand Prix there, I think, in 1954 won by Manuel Fangio, who was one of the greatest racers of all time. I was always into watching racing."

Reporter "What did you think of all the nostalgia surrounding the summer of 1967? I mean, you personally seemed to be in the eye of the hurricane of that whole thing."

George "I don't suppose you got to see the TV show that was made about the summer of 1967? It's quite interesting as a historical piece. I suppose it was to be expected, because nostalgia is a big part of our lives. I know, because ever since I can remember they're always showing Hitler on television in England. I think it became more romanticised as time goes by."

Reporter "Do you look at that (1967) period and say, 'Boy, we were young and stupid?' "

George "Yeah, we were a bit. But at the same time I think there was a lot of good came out of it, too. Although people considered us to be the leaders, we were just as much caught up with what was happening as the rest of the people. Although I suppose we were being innovative, a bit more so than others."

Reporter "You were quoted as saying you'd had enough fame for one lifetime. Do you still think that way?"

George "Yeah, I do, really. This is the conflict I have. I like making records and writing songs. When you do that and go to all that trouble, it's nice to get people to hear them. It's such a huge business now that, unless I make a video, unless I do an interview, the public just doesn't know it exists. So somewhere, you have to make a compromise. I would really prefer just to make records and put them out. I don't really enjoy the self-glorification, or whatever you call it, because I had my fill of ego fulfilment during all those years. Although now it's easier because I think I'm more mellow. I can handle that and I enjoy doing it. But sometimes it gets too crazy when you're talking about yourself and your past all the time."

Reporter "Do you have any regrets?"

George "I don't have any regrets. If we could do it all over again, maybe we'd get more royalties and not sign up with all those greedy managers but apart from that, I wouldn't change a thing."

During his time in Los Angeles, **George** is asked by Dave Herman of the radio station WNEW-FM about the state of play with the much-delayed official Apple-produced Beatles documentary . . .

"That is still waiting to come out," he replies. "We have had all this footage for a long time and been trying to get it out. It's gone dormant for a while and now it's gone back again. The only problem at the moment is that Yoko wants to make her version of The Beatles story. And so she, being John's heir to the Apple stuff, she won't agree to that (documentary) because she wants her version of it where The Beatles probably didn't have much to do with anything."

Denis O'Brien, rather prophetically "George is a very private person. After this (promotional tour), the five years he's taken may be ten years next time. He will most likely return to Friar Park and indulge in his favourite hobby, gardening."

Also in November . . .
The tug of war in the bidding over the rights to own The Beatles music finally ends with Michael Jackson successfully outbidding Paul. Besides the classic tunes by Lennon & McCartney, the early songs of George are captured as part of the deal, including his 1966 track, 'Taxman' . . .

George "I'm not blaming Michael Jackson. For him, it was just a business deal, like investing in a Picasso, but as far as I'm concerned, it's only right that I should own the songs I've written. It was theft, really, robbery with a fountain pen. I also thought it was a bit off, the way Michael Jackson bought up our old catalogue when he knew Paul was also bidding. He was supposed to be Paul's mate."

Paul "Michael came to me because he wanted some advice on how to invest his profits from his *Thriller* album. I suggested that he should try music publishing and he promptly bought up the rights to The Beatles' song catalogue from under my nose! He paid more than double the asking price of £20 million, crushing the deal I was putting together with Yoko. Did I wince about Michael Jackson buying my songs? Yeah I winced and I'm still wincing. Jackson used to be a family friend, staying at our home and joining in with games with my kids. He had made a lot of money and he came to me for advice on how to invest it. I said he should try going into music publishing and then explained to him how all that works. Then one day he said, 'Paul, I'm going to buy all of your songs, you know.' I said, 'Yeah? That's a great joke, Michael. That's really funny, man.' So when I got the call saying that he had actually gone and bought the songs, I was just stunned! I was not only hurt but I am angry that Jackson used my own advice to plot against me. And I am also furious that he is allowing the classic Beatles tunes to be used to sell products in America. When John and I started out, we didn't know that anyone could actually own songs. Then, when they went on offer for £20 million, Yoko and I thought we could buy them. But Yoko thought she could get them for £5 million and in the end Michael paid £50 million for them. To be fair, the songs were up for grabs. It was a business deal for Michael. But I'm still angry. I'm planning a showdown with Michael next July when we meet in Los Angeles."

Tuesday, November 3
For Ringo, meanwhile, his ten-year-old divorce from his first wife Maureen is the subject of a London High Court case . . .

The *Sun* "Beatle Ringo Starr was branded 'a sodding great Andy Capp' by his ex-wife because he wouldn't give her enough money, a court heard yesterday. Maureen Starkey claims she had to beg him for cash just like the wife of the boozing, brawling cartoon slob. Ringo is said to have paid her £500,000 when they divorced in 1975 after ten years. His yearly maintenance payments are running at £70,000. But 41-year-old Maureen never wanted a divorce and says the alimony is not enough. She is suing her former solicitors in London's High Court, accusing them of failing to win her enough cash. Maureen's counsel Thayne Forbes said the ex-hairdresser was still 'devoted' to Ringo when she divorced him for adultery. Her husband gave her cash whenever she needed it during their marriage, often as much as £5,000 at a time. Mr Forbes said, 'She lived a lavish lifestyle.' And when she saw solicitor Charles Doughty after the break-up, she was 'extremely distressed and emotional'. Maureen, who has a £400,000 London home, described Ringo as a 'sodding great Andy Capp' but adored him. Mr Doughty's firm, Withers, deny negligence. The hearing continues."

Thursday, November 5
Controversy surrounds The Beatles' music when the athletic clothing manufacturers, Nike, continue to use The Beatles' original 1968 recording of 'Revolution' in American TV commercials. This mismanagement of The Beatles' back catalogue naturally angers the former members of the group . . .

Syndicated press report, "Paul McCartney has lashed out publicly for the first time at Michael Jackson for allowing a Beatles hit to be used in a television advert. McCartney is furious that Jacko, who with EMI-Capitol Records owns publishing rights to most of The Beatles' songs, gave Nike Shoes permission to use the 1968 hit 'Revolution' in a major TV advertising campaign. Now, Paul, George, Ringo and Yoko Ono have launched a multi-million dollar law suit against EMI-Capitol and Nike . . ."

Paul "The Beatles never did any kind of advertising. We were offered money by Walt Disney, Coca-Cola and the biggest deals in Christendom and beyond. But we never took them because we thought it cheapens you to go on a commercial."

But the blame, it seems, does not stem from the athletic clothing company . . .

"With the Nike thing, it's not entirely Nike's fault," **George** announces in an interview with an American reporter. "They asked for the song. They were probably going to do a sound-alike thing, which is legitimate if they get the rights from the publisher. The publisher is no longer us, they got taken away from us and they've been sold and sold and now it's apparently owned by CBS or Michael Jackson. I get requests all the time, 'Can we use "Here Comes The Sun" for an advert for ladies knickers?' If I want, I can say, 'Yes, you can.' But they have to make up their own version of the tune, and have to licence them. With Nike, they *were* going to do this other version and apparently Yoko said, 'I want John Lennon singing it. I want The Beatles' version,' and that's what has thrown the cat amongst the pigeons, because it's conflict of interests. Apple and its directors are trying to look after and safeguard our past and our present. When we were actively The Beatles in the Sixties, we were asked to do Coca-Cola commercials and Pepsi-Cola commercials and we made a decision, the four of us, we said, 'We don't want to do that. We don't want to sell out. We want to retain some dignity,' and that's what we did. The Beatles had integrity. We tried with our songs; we tried with our recordings to make them as nicely as we could, in each period of time. We tried to make them have a good running order, with good material and good sleeves. We didn't want to take money for advertising, but now people seem to think you *can* use The Beatles for advertising. It's in The Beatles' and Apple's interest not to have our records touted about on TV commercials, otherwise all the songs we made could be advertising everything from hot dogs to bras."

Friday, November 13

Val Jones-Evans, of the UK *Today* newspaper, reports "Ex-Beatle George Harrison has done most things in his life, but he still has one ambition. He wants to fly – without his body. 'The thing I would like to accomplish is perfect peace, which is more of a spiritual sense,' he says. 'I'd like to be able consciously to leave my body at will.' "

But there's bad news for Ringo's ex-wife, Maureen when, on **Thursday, November 19**, she is stunned to learn she has lost her legal battle against the lawyer who handled her divorce. It is reported that Maureen now faces a £200,000 bill for costs and, to meet this demand, she may be forced to sell her £400,000 home. The judge, Mr Justice Bush, summed up the case, saying at the close of the hearing, "Maureen brought no money to the marriage and did nothing to contribute to Ringo's wealth. When she went to see her lawyer, Mr Doughty, he found her 'unwordly' about finances. She could spend and enjoyed it, but she could not budget. Mr Doughty secured a lump sum payment for her, which now would be worth £400,000. She was also granted £2,500 a year for each of the children, later increased to £10,000. Ringo was, and no doubt is, a generous man."

The judge clears Mr Doughty of negligence and breach of contract and orders Maureen to pay all costs. As she leaves the court, Maureen, of Maida Vale, North London, says, "I'm still smiling." But moments later, she tells a friend, "I'm feeling very shaky, I'm so surprised by the result." Asked whether Ringo would help with the legal bill, his agent, Graham Hill, says, "Unless or until she asks him, I doubt very much he'll consider it."

Thursday, January 14
The year begins with news that Ringo has sold his Ascot mansion for £4 million. The 17th century house, Tittenhurst Park, had been purchased from John back in 1973 . . .

Rick Sky, the *Sun* "Yesterday, a friend of the millionaire star said, 'It has been sold, but I don't know exactly why Ringo and Barbara are going. They have always been very happy there.' Ringo's son, Zak, who lives in a cottage in the grounds admitted to friends, 'I'm very sad to be going. I grew up here and I really love it. It holds a lot of memories for me.' It is believed that relatives of King Hussein of Jordan have bought the 26-room mansion. Ringo's friend said, 'Ringo and Barbara have not found a new home yet. There has been talk of them finding a home on the West Coast of America.' "

A workman, employed by Ringo to help remove his belongings from the house, recalls "I remember one day, Ringo came down into the garden where I was working with a bundle of items that had once belonged to John. Ringo had found them in the attic. The pile contained letters, notes, drawings, clothes and audio tapes. Ringo took the pile, threw them into a heap in the garden and promptly set fire to them. 'Why are you doing that?' I naturally asked. He replied, 'I don't want anybody else to have them. They'll only make money out of them.' Goodness knows what we lost of John that day."

Wednesday, January 20
In Los Angeles, at a star-studded event, The Beatles are admitted into the Rock And Roll Hall Of Fame. It is an event famously missed by Paul . . .

George "It didn't mean anything to me until I got there. It was just some idea that someone had and it really didn't mean that much to me. But someone said, 'It might not mean that much now, but it's history and you'll enjoy it.' So I went along and I was glad that I went. I had a great night, after everyone settled down, because it was pretty hectic and it was fantastic to see all those people. Now I've got my little statue that says, 'Beatles – Hall Of Fame'. It's an event I'm glad I didn't miss. It's a pity that Paul missed it because he would have had a good time. All the event was was to have the lads there and pat them on the back and it was a shame that Paul missed it, because he contributed so much. But it didn't spoil the night. We still had fun. He was just trying to use that situation for some personal motive, which he had. But we've gone past the squabbles now."

New York correspondent, Annette Witheridge files this report "Sulky Paul McCartney has snubbed his old pals at a prestigious awards ceremony. He refused to fly to New York to join George Harrison and Ringo Starr on stage as The Beatles were admitted into the Rock And Roll Hall Of Fame. As George and Ringo teamed up with John Lennon's widow, Yoko Ono, and son, Sean, for the ceremony, Paul sent a stroppy message to the organisers . . ."

"I was keen to go and pick up my award, but after twenty years, The Beatles still have some business differences, which I hoped would be settled by now. Unfortunately, they haven't been, so I would feel a complete hypocrite waving and smiling with them at a fake reunion."

Annette Witheridge "George and Ringo put the bad feeling behind them when they joined some of the world's greatest rock stars, including Bob Dylan, Bruce Springsteen, Elton John, Billy Joel and Mick Jagger. Les Paul, the 72-year-old inventor of the electric guitar, who was also joining the Hall Of Fame, had hoped to meet Paul. He said, 'I've got a left-hand guitar I made for him and I can't play it.' "

Tuesday, February 2

In Los Angeles, the show business correspondent, Peter MacDonald, files this report "Ringo Starr is to become a star of a different kind, in his own Hollywood comedy TV series to be produced by American heart-throb, Don Johnson. The former Beatle and the *Miami Vice* actor are expected to complete a multi-million dollar deal with a major American TV network before the end of the week. The series, tentatively titled *The Flip Side*, would feature Ringo as an ageing pop star forced to quit the concert circuit to care for his children when his former wife dies. It is the perfect role for Ringo and could be the beginning of a whole new career for him. He has long hankered after an acting career but despite critics who have described him as a gifted screen comedian, a major breakthrough has eluded him . . ."

(Note: *The Flip Side* series fails to materialise)

Wednesday, February 10

A slightly intoxicated George, accompanied by Jeff Lynne, appears on the live American radio show *Rockline*, hosted by Bob Coburn and presented by KLOS-FM in Los Angeles. During the show he takes callers questions on air . . .

On the phone line is Kenny "Hi."

George "Hi Kenny, how you doing?"

Kenny "This is a great honour to speak to you."

George (interrupting) "Me, too. So let's get on with that bit. What do you want to know?"

Kenny "Okay, my question is what was it like working with Jeff (Lynne) in the studio, producing the album?"

George (humorously) "It was terrible. He was such a rat. He's such a rat. I wouldn't have anything to do with him. Okay? What else do you want to know?"

Kenny "How did he help your sound, being that you hadn't worked with a producer in a long time?"

George "He used to have sex with me every thirty minutes just to try to keep me on my toes. No, seriously, Jeff is a great arranger, a great musician, a good singer and we had a lot in common and we had great support, not just musically but as human beings and that was the key to it all."

Host, Bob Coburn "Kenny, thanks so much for being on *Rockline* tonight and call us again sometime."

George "Piss off, Kenny . . . Just joking, Kenny, just joking. I had a *Dos Equis* earlier, that's what it is, okay, love you, Kenny, love you."

Bob Coburn "We're going to talk now with Hal, and Hal is located in Columbus, Ohio. Good evening, Hal."

Hal "Hi and hello, George."

George "Hi, how are you?"

Hal "Congratulations on *Cloud Nine* going platinum."

George "Thanks a lot. I must tell you, I do feel a bit like Dr Ruth at this moment. If you have any sexual problems, just bring them right out, okay?"

Hal "I do have an interesting question, hopefully. On the 'When We Was Fab' video, I read in this magazine *Beatlefan* that Paul McCartney had said in a London interview that he wanted to play the role of the Walrus. And I noticed, as the camera pulls back, there's Ringo, you and the Walrus with a left-hand bass in the shot, just as the guy walks across with John Lennon's *Imagine* album cover. Now, is that a reunion? Is Paul in the Walrus mask, or not?"

George "Well, here's another clue for you all, the Walrus was Paul . . . Would it make you like the video anymore if you knew it was Paul in there or could it just be BB King or Alfred Hitchcock? It doesn't really matter, you know. But it really is Paul, but he's a bit shy, lately."

Caller "Hi, is Dr Ruth there?"

George "Yeah, I'm here, yeah."

Caller "How are you doing, doc? I've got this sexual dysfunction."

George "Good, good, about time."

Caller "Listen, I'd like to know if you're planning a tour to support your latest effort."

George "Well, no. I'm not actually. I don't have a tour planned at all, actually. I'm so busy just doing this and everything else. I mean, it's so long since I made a record, you know. What else do you want? Give us a break. But I don't discount the fact that I would like to play. I would like to do some live shows but I just don't want to be stuck in some hotel in Philadelphia for the rest of my life. I've discovered things that are more important than being on the road. I don't have it planned, but don't be surprised if you see me in your home town this Saturday."

Bob Coburn "This is a caller from Jacksonville, Florida. We have Johnny on the line."

Johnny "Hi George. It's great to have you back, man."

George "I haven't been anywhere. But I know what you mean. Okay, it's great to be back but I was always there, even when you never noticed."

Johnny "My question is, are you overseeing the production of the documentary on The Beatles, *The Long And Winding Road*?"

George "Funny you should mention that, but *The Long And Winding Road* has been one of the things we've talked about lately. It's been around for years, let's face it. I mean, this road is so long and it's so winding, you'd never believe it. But eventually, it should come out. I think, at first, you're actually going to see Yoko's version of *The Long And Winding Road*. But, having said that, we are co-operating with each other, because John is also a part of our movie just as The Beatles are a part of John's life and so actually you're going to get two films eventually and one will be much sooner than the other. There may be some same footage in them, but if we're clever, we may be able to trick you into thinking different things happened."

Caller, Drew from Ontario "Hi George. I really like your new album. I think it's fab. I enjoyed hearing 'Lay His Head' on the B-side of the first single and I was considering if there is any other older, unreleased material you are planning on releasing."

George "Unreleased material? I've got more stuff than Jim Reeves ever dreamed of. It's all lying there in the attic. It's all the stuff that no one ever wanted because it wasn't commercial or it said things that no one wanted to hear. You know, maybe the chords were wrong or it wasn't produced good enough. But anyway, I've got loads of it."

Bob Coburn then throws a question at George . . .

"In the HandMade Film *Five Corners*, they were going to use 'In My Life' by The Beatles in the credits and you tried to prevent it. What was the reasoning behind that?"

George replies, "I feel we've been ripped off so much that the last thing I want to do is find that HandMade Films is ripping us off, too, if that's the way it is. But there is a situation in movies where you pay a synch licence to get the rights to a tune and you can put in on the film. The director thought it fitted the film and actually it does fit, in a way. Just like Bob Dylan singing 'The Times They Are A-Changing' . . . There's another HandMade Film, which will be out shortly. It is by a quite well known director, who is a bit of a loony. It's a film called *Track 29*, by Nicholas Roeg . . . For me, I have a bit of a problem, where the director comes to me and they say, 'Okay, we want to use John Lennon's "Mother".' And at that particular time in my life (1970), I was in one room singing 'My Sweet Lord' and John was in another room, in Abbey Road, singing 'I don't believe in Jesus, I don't believe in nothing.' He went through that situation with Primal Scream, which was really not the best thing I recommend for anything. It was the point in time where we were totally the extreme to each other and that song reminds me of that. I didn't really want it to be in the film. I tried to talk the director out of it but if you're making the movie, it's no point getting a director and then telling him he can't do what he thinks he should be doing. So I find myself in a bit of a bind, but having seen it on the film, it's such a short piece anyway. All it does is set up the scene for this situation where a boy comes back looking for his mother who left him years ago. It works in context but I also have the situation where I have to talk to Paul and Ringo and Yoko, and the last thing

I want to do is appear to be using The Beatles or my past or anything. But, at the same time, there is *Ferris Beuller's Day Off* and they've got The Beatles with 'Twist And Shout'. You have the right to get the synch licence."

Monday, February 15

Stateside, **George** offhandedly remarks to reporters, "Paul is too moody to work with nowadays. There could have been a Beatles reunion at one time, but Paul doesn't seem in such a good mood lately. But my relationship with Paul has improved. We have been having dinner together. We are friends now, the first time that we have been this close for a long time. But it doesn't mean to say that we are going to make another group or anything. I am more friendly with other musicians."

Saturday, February 27

The apparent feud between Paul and George is exposed at a pop festival in Italy . . .

Showbusiness corespondent, Mick Hamilton "The former pals were furious when they heard organisers of the star-studded event at San Remo had booked them on the same bill. Angry Paul immediately splashed out £15,000 for a private jet so he could dash in and out of the Italian resort without meeting George. And fuming George rented a yacht to hold press conferences away from McCartney. They vowed never to set eyes on each other after Paul snubbed a planned Beatles reunion in New York last month. A spokesman for Paul said, 'We'd never have accepted the San Remo booking if we'd known Harrison was to appear as well.' While an aide for George, who won the best video award for his hit 'When We Was Fab', said, 'If Paul comes near the boat, we've been told to give him his marching orders.' Friends of Harrison say he has taken the row badly. He told friends, 'I did think things were getting better, but it doesn't look like that now.' "

George "I was in San Remo the day before Paul arrived and I got a phone call from somebody at the *Daily Mail.* They said, 'Ah, is that George?' And I said, 'Er, no, sorry, George has just left.' I pretended I was somebody else. He said, 'Well, there are some people down here who are trying to get this rumour started about you and Paul.' I explained to him that the reason why we weren't together was because we didn't know that we were both going to be there. It was just one of those things where these people sit around and think, 'I know, let's have a fight between Paul and George.' "

Paul "I was hurt by reports that I had spent £15,000 hiring a private jet to leave the San Remo pop festival just because George was on the same bill. This just wasn't true. We didn't even know that we were all going to be there at the same time. But some people seem to want to exaggerate our problems."

George "But actually, I love Paul, he's my mate and it doesn't matter what I say in the papers, they're not going to get much mileage out of that one."

Wednesday, March 2

Syndicated press report "Michael Jackson is preventing the lyrics to some of Paul McCartney's most famous numbers from being included in the first-ever biography about the former Beatle, because he wants too much cash. Jacko owns the rights to The Beatles' song catalogue and author, Chet Flippo, was horrified at the American megastar's reply when he asked for permission to reprint the words to hits like 'Lady Madonna', 'Hey Jude', 'Let It Be' and 'Yesterday'. Michael said sure . . . but it would cost £600 per line! Slippo said, 'I wanted to include five songs in the book but on Jackson's terms, I'd have to pay almost £55,000 for the privilege, which I'm simply not prepared to do.' Professional needle might be at the root of the singer's demands. Flippo's book, *Yesterday*, is being published this summer by Doubleday, the same American publishers who this summer bring out Jackson's autobiography, *Moonwalk*."

Thursday, March 3

The *Daily Express* reports "Paul McCartney is putting Rupert Bear back on the big screen. Following the success of his first Rupert short animated film in 1984, Paul is recording new songs for a new story line he has written about the *Daily Express* character. The Rupert theme song, 'We All Stand Together', with its Frog Chorus, was a Top 3 hit for Paul. Paul has been a Rupert fan since he was a boy brought up on the *Express* Rupert stories . . ."

Paul "I used to like the Rupert Christmas annuals. I rediscovered Rupert in the Seventies when I started reading bedtime stories to our daughter, Heather. I am not surprised that Rupert's popularity has lasted for more than 60 years for he is an institution, like the Queen."

Friday, March 4

To a reporter from the *Daily Mail*, on the eve of George and Ringo's appearance on London Weekend Television's *Aspel & Co* programme being televised on the ITV Network, **Paul** acts quickly to play down the stories regarding his and George's apparent feud . . .

"The long feud is over," he insists. "I may even team up again with George and Ringo, possibly to write a song. We have spent the last few weeks working hard to heal the rift, which started over the group's business affairs. Things are much better between George, Ringo and me. We are seeing much more of each other now and we are going out with each other more. There are still some things to work out, but it's a definite sign. It may be that we will get together to write a song or something. But that's a long way off at the moment, although it's something we are talking about. It would be good to do something together."

Saturday, March 5

As anticipated, the ITV Network in the UK transmits George and Ringo's appearance on Michael Aspel's peak-time chat show *Aspel & Co*. . . .

Aspel "You have kept yourself to yourself in recent years and this led to stories about the Howard Hughes of Henley."

George "That's right, yeah. That's the silly newspapers. They're not all silly, of course, but some of them are very silly. Because I don't go discothequing, where people hang out with their cameras, they presumed I was Howard Hughes with my big fingernails and Kleenex tissues and bottles of urine all round the house. But I wasn't like that at all. I go out a lot of the time. I see friends, have dinner and go to parties. I'm even more normal than normal people."

Aspel "Set the record straight about today's situation. The press is keen to imply rifts, so how do you and Paul get on?"

Ringo "We get on very well."

George "We do, actually. For about ten years I didn't really know Paul. I never really saw him for much of ten years but more recently we've been hanging out, getting to know each other, going for dinner, meeting and having a laugh and it's absolutely not the way they said in the *News Of The World*."

Aspel "When I hear Lennon records, it's still, of course, impossible for us to believe he's gone. It must be a million times more for you, mustn't it?"

Ringo "Well, you've certainly brought the party down, Michael . . . I was stunned on the day."

George (interrupting) "Shocked and stunned."

Ringo "I cry easily. I still miss the man. I loved the man. I was close to them man and he went out in such a stupid way, and the guy's famous now, for God's sake."

George "I feel not so bad about it, because, unlike Ringo, when I went to Rishikesh in India, I went into meditation and I had experiences. So I believe what it says in the scriptures and in the Bhagavadgita, it says, 'It was never a time when you didn't exist and it'll never be a time when you cease to exist.' The only thing that changes is our bodily condition. The soul comes in the body, from birth to death, and death, how I look at it, is like taking a suit off. The soul is in these three bodies and one body falls off, and I feel like that. I can feel him (John) around here."

Ringo "I've seen him twice, no, I have. I felt him very strong once when I was in a hotel room in LA and I was feeling down and miserable and he was in the corner, saying, 'What are you doing?' I said, 'Being miserable,' and he said, 'Come on, get it together.' I believe, like George said, that we do continue."

George "John knew who he was. That he was a soul who happened to be in this body for this period of time. I think it's unfortunate the way he went out, but it doesn't really matter. He's okay and life flows on within you and without you."

Monday, March 28

Just over three weeks later, George makes a lightning trip to Canada and faces the Press in a hastily arranged conference . . .

Reporter "What is a typical day in the life of George Harrison?"

George "It depends really on what I'm doing. Last week, I was getting up, going for a run around my garden, eating a bowl of Scotch porridge oats and then going into the recording studios."

Reporter "Paul McCartney recently expressed an interest in working with you again. What do you feel about Paul and the possibility of a reunion?"

George "Yeah, Paul had asked and suggested maybe the chance of me and he working together and it's pretty funny, really, because I've only been there about thirty years in Paul's life and now he wants to write with me. But I think that maybe it'd be quite interesting sometime to do that. I think there's a thing with Paul where one minute he says one thing and he's really charming and then, the next minute, he's all uptight. We all go through that, good and bad, but by now, we've got to find like somewhere in the middle."

Reporter "Will you be touring with this new album?"

George "It may be time to go back out on the road again. I think it's creeping up, maybe this year or early next year. If I'm going to do anything at all, I'd better do it pretty soon otherwise I'm going to be on crutches."

Monday, August 22 (UK)
Five months later, the American author and former English professor, Albert Goldman releases *The Lives Of John Lennon*, his controversial book on the life of John Lennon . . .

60-year-old Albert Goldman "I am a workaholic but I worked harder on this book than I ever worked in my life. Every moment was necessary. Lennon was an incredibly complex man . . . Seven years ago, shortly after his death, a CBS TV crew came to interview me. I believed. I had the faith. I can now honestly say that every single thing I said in that tribute I have now debunked in the book. I was getting dismaying similarities with Elvis Presley (his previous book). They were on the same wavelength although they were products of very different worlds. They had no connection with each other, yet I was reaching into Lennon through Presley. It makes one wonder whether there is an archetypal image that is the essence of rock . . . I am like a bulldog when I lock my jaws into something. I will never give up. It just becomes a matter of the most profound urgency to get it right. I will go on and on, whatever it takes, regardless of going deeper into debt or of warnings from doctors or friends. I must find the answer. I must have the answer. There is a final revelation and, by God, I am going to get it . . . But when you pal around with John Lennon, you are playing around with a guy on his deathbed and once I peeled back the layers, I was transformed. The believer lost the faith. I was disappointed and disillusioned. People say I am always looking for sex, drugs and violence in my subjects. Frankly, I would be amazed if I found a rock star not associated with sex, drugs and violence. No, that cuts no ice with me . . . I lived, breathed and devoured Lennon with a dedicated passion and I believe that John would be the one man who would not object to the book. He left the biographer a mandate. Lennon was a man who mocked the myths and punctured them. He said outrageous things and if he had been free to do so, he might well have written some of this stuff himself."

Amongst the revelations contained in the huge publication, which Goldman claims he spent six-and-a-half years researching, are claims that the ex-Beatle "became a bag of bones because of anorexia" and he "lived like a hermit in his bedroom for nearly three years in his Dakota apartment". An excerpt reads, "Lennon believed darkness was death, so he shut himself off from the world. He could hear no sounds from the bustling streets below. Heavy wooden shutters covered by sloppily hung curtains kept out daylight . . .

The only sounds inside his huge bedroom came from the sighing noises of speakers, and the flickering of two big colour TV sets."

As expected, the publication causes outcry right around the world . . .

A spokesman for Yoko "She wants nothing to do with the book."

George "This is another symptom of a society that listens to the same drum samples. They don't realise it's the same old claptrap. People's consciousness is stuck and the Goldmans of this world can make a hell of a living, a lot of money, for slagging off someone who's dead."

Paul "Albert Goldman has written a piece of trash. It is disgusting that someone like Goldman can make up any old bunch of lies he sees fit and can be allowed to publish them without fear of repudiation. The book claims that there was a long-running affair between John and Brian Epstein but there was never even the slightest hint of this, in fact quite the opposite. John was very attracted to women. John was a great man, at times wild and wacky but always deep down a wonderful human being. I urge people to boycott this book, which in my opinion is nothing more than a piece of trash."

Beatles producer, George Martin is also particularly furious about the allegations in the book that John had a homosexual affair with Brian Epstein, The Beatles' manager. "I am furious," he blasts. "It's a load of codswallop! John did have a holiday with Brian but looking back on it, I'm sure he went to get in with Brian and make sure he was the dominant factor in the group. John was very wily like that. But, as for an affair with Brian, that's rubbish. If John was into anything at all, it was the love of women. The book has upset me deeply, as it has everyone who was close to John. Brian Epstein was a very dear friend of mine. He was unquestionably homosexual but never flaunted it. I just have very fond memories of him being a very honest person. The Beatles were his baby and he wanted to see them successful. You can't say anything more than that. The guy who supplied a lot of quotes for the book was Brian's right-hand man, Peter Brown. A few years ago, Brown did his own hatchet job, which was very nasty. He didn't actually write any lies, but he presented all the seamy bits as if there was nothing else. The irony with John was that he had gone through a lot of rubbish with Yoko and going to America and the drugs scene and so on. But the year before he died he actually had got straight again. He had come through all that and found out the value of everything, the value of his relationship with Julian, the joy of having Sean. He was coming round to becoming a happy middle-aged man. He was finding out what life was about. And then he was destroyed. I think it is iniquitous that people can libel the dead. If John were alive that book would not come out. It is largely untrue but sadly, if mud is thrown, it tends to stick. It is so cruel to the people who are still alive. It is not just John's sons and his wives; it is people such as Brian Epstein's mother, who is an ailing woman in Liverpool. She's not only lost Brian, but, earlier this year, she also lost her younger son. Think what the book is going to do to her. It's absolutely dreadful. What I've read is not the John Lennon I knew. It isn't the man my wife and I went on holiday with to St Moritz. It is significant that the people the author got his information from were not close to John. He didn't talk to me. He never actually approached me. John was a very beautiful man, very talented, very warm and very loving."

Also shocked by the homosexual reference is Denny Laine, Paul's former partner in Wings, "John's love of women was legendary. I can only think this story came about because there was a stupid rumour at one time that one of The Beatles was involved in homosexual activities. But there was never any truth in it. Where the author, Goldman, made his biggest mistake is that John was a spokesman. Why would someone that outspoken have all these secrets? The book is all about cashing in. A case of someone saying, 'How can we make money and not get sued?' "

Another celebrity joining in on the attack on Goldman and the book is the Liverpudlian singer, Cilla Black, a close friend of John's from the early Sixties. "I question the accuracy of the book," she says. "This Goldman bloke claims he interviewed over 1,000 people. Well, he never spoke to me and I knew John Lennon very, very well. How can he claim to know this person better than anyone else? That's rubbish. John was a one-off. No one has replaced him. He wasn't an angel. He was wonderfully wicked, that's why I loved him."

Cynthia Lennon is also quick to support her former husband. "John wasn't just another pop star, he was a very special person," she admits, "not just to me, but to millions of other people. I accept that people will always be interested in John and because of that, they'll always be interested in what I have to say about him. But I like to share my memories. There are so many; happy, exciting, funny and sad, just like John. And it is because of these memories that I feel so upset about recent attempts to blacken his name in the Albert Goldman book. It has made me very, very angry. There are so many lies and so much truth twisting in it. The dead can't defend themselves. It's a joke, a sick joke. I'm just trying to see it as just another grain of sand in a desert of rubbish. Before John's death, he was really getting himself together, becoming more content. He had been helped a lot by his son, Sean, and wasn't some kind of weirdo. I refused to help Goldman write his book and all the people who loved John did as well, because we know how Goldman destroyed Elvis Presley in his book on him. I hope people won't believe what's in the book. Those of us who love John will do our best to defend him . . . It was ridiculous to suggest that John was a homosexual. He was far too macho. He liked women and we didn't really know what homosexuals were then. We were so young and innocent. We did finally realise that Brian Epstein was gay, but he was a lovely man, very sweet, a gentleman and a friend. There's absolutely no way that he and John did have an affair, although John did have lots of affairs with other women."

But one supporter of the book comes in the shape of May Pang, John's one-time lover, who tells Alex Gifford and Antonella Lazzeri of *The People*, "John Lennon *was* a drug-crazed, unhappy skeleton, just as the new book says. The only thing the author got wrong was to call John a homosexual. He loved having sex with women and was a wonderful lover. Other than that, Albert Goldman's book is 99 per cent accurate. The John Lennon in the book is the John Lennon I knew . . . The last time I saw him, two years before his death, he was painfully thin and desperately unhappy. He turned up on my doorstep. I was very shocked by his appearance. He was only around nine and a half stone. I said, 'John, what the hell have you been doing?' He smiled and replied, 'I look good, don't I? It's this new macrobiotic diet I've been on.' That was the last time we made love. He was the best I ever had. But no way was John gay. He adored women and had other flings during his marriage to Yoko."

Yoko replies, "Sure, John dieted. We never hid that. He always hated how fat he thought he looked in pictures with The Beatles. He was concerned about keeping slim and looking good. He did it in the way that everyone else does. Exercise, plenty of long walks, not eating sweets, though he loved them. Not eating pork or meat in general. His diet was mostly fish and somewhere between macrobiotic and vegetarian."

After the initial shock of the book has died down, Yoko will speak further about Goldman's ill-received tome . . .

"When portions were first read to me, over the telephone," she reveals to the *Shout!* biographer, Philip Norman, "a brief thought of suicide crossed my mind. I've been undergoing character assassinations for the past twenty years, so why does it still hurt? When this whole thing started, I kept thinking of Picasso's wife and how she finally killed herself. Then I realised I could never do anything like that because I have Sean . . . There are so many allegations against John that I could never deal with them all in one interview. If I answer just a few points, people may say, 'What about all the others? Maybe those were true.' What I most detest about this book isn't so much the fact that it's all lies. It's that it robs John of all basic human dignity. The thing said about me, I hope I can prove wrong. But John isn't here to answer the things said about him. That's what chokes me up . . . He was never a recluse. Everyone in this neighbourhood saw him all the time, in restaurants, stores, in the park with Sean. He went to the theatre a lot, he read a lot, and followed everything that was happening. When reporters came to interview him about the *Double Fantasy* album in 1980, they expected to find some kind of hermit. They were amazed at how street-wise he was."

While in a separate interview, Yoko answers Goldman's allegation that "her love affair with Lennon was a cynical sham to beguile a credulous press" . . .

"There was no reason why John had to stay with me," Yoko insists. "In fact, everything was against our being together. The best thing he could have done was not to be with me, so that the world could cheer and be happy. Even as late as 1980, John was told he could sell more records if he pretended to be available and not be totally involved with one woman. Being a father and househusband wasn't commercial, but he dared to do it because that was the way we were. Neither of us was an angel. But we cherished and loved each moment we were together, and were always frightened of losing each other. I can see now how much we always acted as if time was short."

In December, Yoko will begin referring to Albert Goldman's book as "A *Monty Python* type of book – without their sense of humour."

Shortly before Albert Goldman's death, he had begun work on a book on the life of The Doors singer, Jim Morrison, which looked increasingly like another muck-raking extravaganza . . .

Ray Manzarek, The Doors "Albert had his own obsession. I talked with Albert Goldman about Morrison, the beginning in golden sands, meditation, and all Albert wanted to know about was if Jim had had sex with Jim Hendrix."

Monday, September 12

Syndicated news report "The sale of part of a Beatles bass drum was blocked at the eleventh hour by Ringo Starr today after a dispute over ownership. The former Beatle's lawyers said last night that the wrangle over the bass drum skin, used by Ringo during the Sixties, may take a long time to settle. The 1965 drum head, painted with the famous Beatles logo, had been the star item in a rock'n'roll sale at Sotheby's. It had been expected to fetch more than £30,000. The catalogue said the drum skin was originally given to George Peckham, formerly of The Fourmost, who worked in the group's Apple recording studios from 1969. A spokesman for Ringo's lawyers, Frere Cholmeley, said, 'We took out an injunction in the High Court restraining Sotheby's from selling it and restraining Mr Peckham from doing anything with it until the question was resolved. Ringo had agreed to the drum skin being in the sale on the basis that the proceeds would go to the Great Ormond Street Hospital appeal. We asked for confirmation of that but none was forthcoming. If agreement is reached, it could all be resolved very quickly but if not, then it could have to go to trial.' The injunction was obtained on Friday but Hilary Kay, the auctioneer who launched the first of Sotheby's pop music memorabilia sales in 1981, heard only moments before the sale began."

Thursday, October 6

Meanwhile, the Yoko Ono-approved, Warner Brothers film *Imagine – John Lennon* is premiered in America in Manhattan. The semi-documentary, which features narration by John, is directed by Andrew Solt and produced by David L. Wolper, a veteran of over 500 films . . .

"There's more personal footage on John Lennon than anyone who has ever lived in the Twentieth Century," Wolper announces. "I don't have a single president lying in bed with his wife, eating, sleeping, lovemaking. It's mind-boggling . . . Yoko first contacted me in 1986 while I was producing the Liberty Festivals. As chairman of Liberty Weekend, I was on the phone trying to deal with a conflict between the Secretary of the Interior and Lee Iaccoca when my secretary brought me a note that Yoko Ono was on the line. My immediate thought was, 'What was her connection to Liberty Weekend?' Yoko then assured me that the call was about something else entirely and she wanted to get together and talk. I told her that I'd be delighted to, but not until after the Statue's unveiling on the Fourth of July. I found Yoko to be articulate, charming and full of purpose. She got right to the point, telling me that she felt it was time for a definitive theatrical documentary on John's life and she wanted me to do it. Yoko asked me what I knew about John Lennon and I told her the truth. I knew nothing about him. I naturally wondered why she had picked me to work on the film and Yoko's answer impressed me. She said, 'I want someone tough. Someone I can't push around.' Her only admonition was that the movie had to be honest. She went on to say that she had some 200 hours of film and videotape, much of it unseen by the public, and all covering every aspect of John's life. We talked at length about what other elements might be involved and I thanked Yoko for her gracious offer and told her that I needed time to think about it. My main concern was simply that I wanted to be sure that we could assemble the material in such a way that we could reveal not just John's music but John Lennon, the man behind the myth. But when I began viewing the available footage, my fears were quickly put to rest. I agreed to work on the project but told Yoko that I needed total control. I also insisted that she would have no approvals of the project at any point in its editorial assemblage, nor would she have a say in the final picture. As it turned out, Yoko not only agreed unconditionally but she let me know that it was her desire *not* to have any input or approvals that would make it, in any sense, her version of John Lennon's story. Shortly after, John and Yoko's entire private film and video collection came into my possession, as well as the rights to never-before released original music written, recorded and filmed by Lennon."

Yoko "I have long considered making a film about John's life but rather than make the film myself, I turned it over to David. I did this because I was afraid to taint the film with my subjective view. I believe David Wolper has the most effective documentary production team at this time, as well as having the necessary understanding, in-depth and in-scope of the subject matter."

David Wolper "Half of the film is rare footage never seen publicly before. We built the story around the 1971 recording sessions for the *Imagine* album at John's Tittenhurst Park home in Ascot at a time when he was very much on top of the world. It was an incredibly creative time in his life and we have material that no one has seen. For instance, when John and Yoko made the *Imagine* film in 1971, they chose to show very little of John singing on camera. But in our film, we have five songs from what's considered his creative high point that were shot during the Ascot recording sessions. And then there are the times when the cameras stopped rolling, when he said he didn't want to compete, he didn't want to think about his drive to *have* to make music and to try to get a Top Ten hit. So he became a recluse of sorts, a househusband, taking care of Sean. But we have home movies from that period and, just two weeks before his death, Yoko had professional filming done in the Dakota and walking through Central Park. From the 200 hours of material we were offered, we cut it all down to an initial 20-hour version of the film. Pivotal to John's story is his Aunt Mimi, who gave Andrew Solt an extraordinary seven-hour interview. About a third of the music in the film will be Beatles tunes. We're trying to focus on the important moments that reflect who John was. For example, when he sings 'Help!' he was crying out to the world and people were dancing to it. In retrospect, that kind of moment is essential in telling his personal story. But what is critical for us is who John Lennon was, what made him tick? The material that tells the most and answers that question best comes from the period after The Beatles' break-up."

Appearing in interview sequences in the film is Cynthia Lennon, John's first wife. She recalls a meeting for the film earlier in the year at the Russian Tea Rooms in New York . . . "I went there with Jim Christie, my partner. I met Yoko there. She came with Sean. We didn't have tea; we had Bloody Marys, very strong ones. Julian was there with his girlfriend. Yoko was very nice and enthusiastic about my design work. Now I can see a time when Yoko and I will be able to sit down and talk about John. No one wants to fight."

Yoko "Paul isn't interviewed in the *Imagine* film, nor are George and Ringo. The producers tried to persuade them and failed. We're all human and it's not easy to forget the past. But I don't think we've ever been enemies. We just haven't been close friends. It's something which, in years to come, we may overcome. All four of us are doing business together in a very civilised manner as directors of the Apple Corporation. It's going very smoothly. If people really want us all to be friends, they will have to let it be, give peace a chance and give *us* a chance."

Wednesday, October 19

Back in the UK, a feature on George by Brian Case appears in the London entertainment magazine, *Time Out* . . .

"George Harrison arrived a little late for the photo session in jeans and mirror shades," Case writes. "Easy on the power pedal, he allowed himself to be coaxed out of the mirror shades. 'I'm not looking too good; I haven't had a day off since 1961.' He complied with a request for the chin-in-hand pose. 'They always want this one. It's the *Rolling Stone* shot. Unimaginative bastards.' George and Denis did a formal partner shot, George seated on a stool, Denis standing, resting a hand on his shoulder. 'Would you mind just leaning on George a bit?' asked the photographer, to the great amusement of the duo . . . 'If you go back and look at everything we've done,' says Denis, 'what has been indicative of HandMade Films is the fact that we've not stuck with the reality of the film business in the selection of film topics. In terms of the majors, our films don't get considered because they don't have a guaranteed audience. *Time Bandits* was not even close to reality, nor was *The Life Of Brian.*' "

" 'No, *Life Of Brian* was,' said **George**, perhaps at a tangent. 'It was about how people will just follow anybody. They'll miss the real guy and follow the silly guy. That's reality, to me. It depends on what you term reality . . . I am not George. I am not really George. I am this living thing that goes on, always has been, always will be, but at this time, I happen to be in this body. It depends on what's real, you know. The film industry isn't reality anyway. Once you're into that, reality flies out of the window.' "

Brian Case "HandMade and the *Monty Pythons* soon began to show cracks. Denis's idea of filming *Monty Python At The Hollywood Bowl* did not take off, despite a fortune in promotion and the Pythons moved to Universal for *The Meaning Of Life*, though both John Cleese and Michael Palin made separate deals with HandMade to produce *Privates On Parade* and *The Missionary*. George shrugged, 'Some people get disappointed we can't do their movies, but we can only do so much.' Terry Gilliam's split was less organic. He had fought with Denis over the ending of *Time Bandits* and wanted a percentage instead of a cash fee. 'I always felt we were coming from quite different directions in the brief period our paths crossed,' Denis commented. 'He went elsewhere to finance *Brazil.*' "

George "Denis and the accounts department figure out budgets because it's all a gamble. I don't get too involved in that side. My role in the film business seems to be helping people to get the money to make what they want to make. When I work with people like David Leland on *Checking Out* or Bruce Robinson on *How To Get Ahead In Advertising*, I feel pretty close to them because I admire them both and I trust them and I know I'm gonna enjoy what they're gonna make us. In most cases, I take myself away from it really, I go and see some rushes, go and see the rough assembly, but I don't go and sit around the set trying to be some heavyweight. I have much more control in music. You don't have to deal with a hundred people to make a change. I'm closer to music but I like talent."

Monday, October 24 (UK)
Meanwhile, on a new album, George's new musical venture, The Traveling Wilburys, are born . . .

UK columnist Robin Denselow "This week, a five-piece called The Traveling Wilburys released their debut LP, a refreshing and tuneful collection of songs that mostly have acoustic guitar backing, along with a good old-fashioned rock'n'roll rhythm section with no hint of fancy computerised electronics. The band doesn't give their real names. They are Lucky, Otis, Charlie T., Nelson and Lofty, but the faces lurking through the grainy cover photo were never likely to be a mystery for long. There's Bob Dylan, Jeff Lynne, Tom Petty, Roy Orbison and George Harrison himself . . . The wacky sleeves recount The Wilburys' history. 'The original Wilburys were a stationary people who realised that their civilisation could not stand still for ever, began to go for short walks . . .' They were

George and Olivia, pictured on the beach at Cannes in the South of France during the annual Midem Music Fair on January 27, 1976. *(LFI)*

Paul, playing 'Figure Of Eight', at Liverpool's King's Dock, June 28, 1990. *(LFI)*

Paul, pictured in Liverpool with his 1989/90 touring band, left to right: Chris Whitten (drums), Paul 'Wix' Wickens (keyboards), Linda, Paul, Hamish Stuart and Robbie McKintosh (guitars). *(Pictorial Press)*

Paul with Linda and Princess Diana at the French premiere of *Liverpool Oratorio* at the British Arts Festival in Lille, France, November 15, 1993. *(Rex)*

George with George Martin at the launch of the CD re-issues of The Beatles' 'Red' and 'Blue' albums, at Abbey Road Studios, September 9, 1993. *(Rex)*

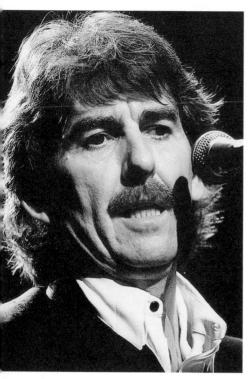

George on stage at London's Royal Albert Hall, April 6, 1992, at the concert in support of the Natural Law party. In the shot below are, left to right, Joe Walsh, George, Dhani Harrison and Gary Moore. *(Rex)*

Ringo with the third line-up of his many All Starr Bands, this one dating from 1995; back row, left to right: Mark Rivera (saxophone), Zak Starkey, Felix Cavaliere (keyboards) and Billy Preston (keyboards); front: Randy Bachman (guitar), Ringo, Mark Farner (guitar) and John Entwistle (bass). *(Henry Diltz/Corbis)*

George Martin, Jeff Lynne and Neil Aspinall at the launch of The Beatles' *Anthology* CD series in the Lancaster Rooms at the Savoy Hotel, London, November 20, 1995. Lynne produced The Beatles 'new' single 'Free As A Bird', incorporating John's vocals from a demo tape he recorded in 1977; Aspinall, who drove The Beatles' van long before they became famous, is the managing director of Apple. *(LFI)*

George in Paris on August 26, 1997, promoting his friend Ravi Shankar's album *Chance Of India*, which George produced. Asked his opinion of The Spice Girls at the press conference, George replied: "The advantage of The Spice Girls is that you can listen to them with no sound." *(Rex)*

Paul poses before a blow-up of the photograph used on the cover of Linda's *Wide Prairie* album which was released in October, 1998. *(Rex)*

George with Eric Clapton at Christie's auction rooms, London, on June 2, 1999, when Clapton sold many of his guitars to raise funds for his Crossroads Alcohol & Drug Addiction Centre in Antigua. *(Rex)*

Ringo, photographed at the turn of the millennium, in a portrait by Gillian Shaw. *(Rex)*

written by Hugh Jampton and E.F. Nortibitz, whose identity turns out to be Michael Palin, working on early ideas from Derek Taylor, once the renowned press officer for The Beatles and, of course, Harrison himself."

George humorously remarks "The name Traveling Wilburys was mostly influenced by *Dos Equis,* a brand of Mexican lager. We were going to be The Trembling Wilburys, then we sobered up . . . If you try hard to do something, then often nothing happens. At other times, you twitch your face and there's the Wilbury. I'm a great believer in destiny or some creative support that comes from a higher source, even though it's only pop music."

'Handle With Care'

George "I was in Los Angeles in April and I needed a B-side for a single I was releasing off *Cloud Nine* ('This Is Love'), so I thought, 'I'll write one tomorrow, go into a studio and do it.' As it happened, Jeff Lynne, who was in ELO and produced my last album, was having dinner with Roy Orbison and Roy said, 'If you're doing anything, I'd like to come along.' Well, the only studio I could find at that notice was this little one in Bob Dylan's garage; he's got a tiny tape machine there. I needed to pick up my guitar, which I had left at Tom Petty's, so he came along too. The next day, all five of us were assembled at Dylan's where Jeff and I sat on the lawn working out a melody. Dylan was asked to cook, he provided a barbecue, and was then asked to help. I said, 'Give us some lyrics, you famous lyricist.' He asked what the subject matter was supposed to be. I looked behind the garage door and there was a cardboard box with 'Handle With Care' on it. So I said that, and Bob said, 'That's good.' When we started the song, I thought I'd better write a lonely bit for Roy Orbison, you couldn't have him standing around and not get him on it. I thought of the first line, then everyone was writing words, with Dylan saying some hysterical things. And when it came to the middle bit, I wrote something for Tom and Bob. So we wrote that, then just sang it. The next day we added electric guitar and bass and mixed it. It was instant. But the result was too good to be stuck away on a B-side. There was no way of using the song so we decided to make a whole album . . . Nine more songs were written and recorded in just ten days, because Dylan had to go off on tour. We would assemble after breakfast, at about one in the afternoon, and just sit around with acoustic guitars. Then someone would have a title or a chord pattern and we'd let it roll . . . The drummer Jim Keltner, who joined us, used brushes. I've not heard that since Gene Vincent and 'Be-Bop-A-Lula'. He would also start drumming on a wire grill inside a fridge, to get a sound like the old Elvis records. I bet U2 will be doing it next year."

'Dirty World'

George "This started when Dylan jokingly suggested 'Let's do one like Prince,' and began to sing 'Love your sexy body,' and we just pounced on it, 'Okay.' "

George "The album has helped us rediscover the lost joys of making music. Dylan certainly seemed affected. I think this inspired him. In his recent concerts, he's been doing an acoustic set and using a little band of just guitar, bass and drums, and people close to him say that since The Wilburys, he's started writing really good songs again. For me, the experience was a welcome return to basics, because The Wilburys remind you of good old Carl Perkins tunes or Bob Dylan tunes. It's like a pastiche, a montage of all the good bits you remember . . . The album is a way of hitting back at all I hate in Eighties pop, which over the last ten years has got so computerised and so monotonous. I'm amazed that people don't realise that they've heard the same drum sample on the last 59,000 records. People have got so far from the human element with their computers. Even Michael Jackson, I can't make head or tail of it. It sounds like an IBM computer whirling around while he jerks his neck back and forward. It makes no sense to me whatsoever. I don't think hi-technology is a good thing. It's a load of crap. Give me Cab Calloway any day."

Asked whether The Traveling Wilburys will actually go on tour, **George** replies, "I hate waking up in motels in Philadelphia. I'd rather be at home, but as a fan of the other members of the band, I'd love to see them perform, so I would be inclined to do something."

OCTOBER...

Hollywood actress, Melody Stuart "It was 4am when the phone rang. Ringo Starr was on the line and he was weeping. 'I need help desperately,' he sobbed. He told me he was scared he would kill his wife, Barbara, in their next drink- and drug-fuelled fight. He told me, 'The booze and drugs have made monsters of both of us. We have got to get help.' He kept on saying, 'I'm so ashamed. I feel sick, sick, sick. I never thought we could sink so low.' I went, 'We have no choice. We have to go. We need help desperately.' Hours later, he and Barbara had checked into the Sierra Tucson drug and alcohol drying out centre in Arizona . . . It's no secret that Barbara and Ringo do cocaine now and again, but this time they had been drinking round the clock for three or four days. It was the usual pattern, drink, drugs, drink, drugs, followed by more drink. Ringo told me, 'We had one motherfucker of a fight. Barbara started screaming and throwing things around the room.' Barbara said vile things to him in drink, and Ringo shot back with some wisecrack comment. Then she went for him with an art deco lamp and cracked him across the head. He slapped her across the chops just to calm her down, but he split her lip and she started screaming the house down. Ringo told me he finished up with a bloody nose and half his hair torn out. He admitted later that he could have chopped his hands off in remorse for striking her. Apart from his kids, Barbara is the thing he treasures most in the world . . . Horrified Ringo finally realised he and Barbara were toppling into an abyss when he woke up one morning to find her lying battered and bruised beside him. When fearfully he asked how she had been hurt, she told him, 'You did it!' The real horror was that neither could remember the fighting. Both had been in a blackout induced by a deadly cocktail of drugs and booze . . ."

Ringo "It got so bad that I started getting blackouts. It got progressively worse and the blackouts got worse and I didn't know where I had been or what I had done. I knew I had the problem for years, but it plays tricks with your head. Very cunning and baffling is alcohol. God knows how it would have ended if I hadn't called it a day."

Reporters Peter Kent and Ted Hynds of *The People* newspaper "Ringo and Barbara had a typical public punch-up in front of guests at a Jamaican hotel earlier this year. They watched in amazement as the angry pair stood 20 feet apart lobbing bottles at each other then swooped and started slapping each other. One fellow guest said, 'It was like a Laurel & Hardy slapstick, only they weren't acting.' Ringo apologised afterwards to guests for their behaviour but when they returned to Los Angeles fists flew again, this time over who had started the holiday row."

Melody Stuart's husband, Bobby, who became pals with Ringo in the Sixties when he backed The Beatles on keyboards, "In The Beatles' days, you'd be lucky to see Ringo with a glass in his hand. It's so sad to see what had happened to him now."

Ringo "With The Beatles, we did the job, sometimes in a strange state of mind, but we did the gig. I drank quite a bit then. I don't think it was excessive. You had a day off and you'd party. You get caught up in thinking that's a normal thing to do . . . My battle with the bottle first began, I realise now, when I was a child in working-class Liverpool. We had parties, everyone gets drunk and passes out, that's part of my life. My mother always told me that when I was nine, I was on my knees crawling drunk. A friend of mine's dad had the booze ready for Christmas and so we decided to try it all out. I don't remember too much. That was my first blackout."

Bobby Stuart "I believe the cause of Ringo's problem is boredom. His life is empty. The burden of being the least successful Beatle preys heavily on his mind. When the voice-over part for *Thomas The Tank Engine* in the cartoon film version of the TV series fell through, it was the last straw. Ringo's just been moping around Barbara 24 hours a day."

Ringo "I had a serious drink problem. Drunks are great talkers. We'd sit around for nights on end and talk about what we were going to do and, of course, I'd get so bleeding drunk, I couldn't move. The result of being drunk was that nothing happened and, worst of all, I dragged Barbara down with me. She fell into the trap all because of me. She was an actress who used to go to bed at 10 at night and get up at eight in the morning. Till we met. Then her career went in the same way as mine. Alcohol was my drug of choice and I did not work or do anything. I wouldn't go out because that meant I would have to be in the car for 40 minutes without being able to have a single drink."

A British friend of the couple tells *The People* newspaper "He hasn't done anything creative as far as I know. There are no projects like Paul McCartney or George Harrison. It's a terrible shame."

Ringo "Every couple of months she (Barbara) would try to straighten us out but then we'd fall straight back into the trap. Certain friends thought I was getting a little over the top, too. They never actually mentioned going into a clinic or anything. They just thought it would be better if I sort of cooled it a bit. I knew I should be doing something to get help, but I just never got around to it."

Another supposedly close friend to Ringo and Barbara is also not hesitant in coming forward to tell the newspaper about the couple's private life . . . "They have both been drinking heavily every day for years. They are also cocaine users. Ringo has been snorting up to a gram of coke a day and Barbara says she has been using about half a gram."

Ringo "We did lots of booze and lots of coke. You take a bit of this and then suddenly, you're only doing that, and that's when it becomes a problem."

The close friend continues, "Barbara told me that alcohol and drugs had become the number one priority in their lives, more important than family, more important than each other, more important than anything . . . Before settling on the Tucson Center, Barbara called several other clinics but they refused to take the couple because Barbara insisted on being in the same room as Ringo at the start of the treatment. She said Ringo was so paranoid from his coke use that he refused to let her out of his sight for a minute.

Finally in desperation, she pleaded with the Sierra Tucson Center to allow her and Ringo to share a room. She told them, 'Please, if you don't help us, we're going to die.' So finally, the clinic agreed. They were even still using cocaine as they were en route to the hospital. When they arrived, they both looked like the walking dead. Ringo looked tired, old and burned out like someone who had died but had refused to lie down. He was nothing but skin and bone. So was Barbara. Her looks had gone."

Reporters Peter Kent and Ted Hynds "The clinic's doctor warned Ringo that his liver was enlarged and his heart damaged because of heavy drug abuse. Barbara's liver was also damaged. After completing the initial detoxification programme to clear all drugs and alcohol from their bodies, Ringo and Barbara were assigned separate rooms without TV or radio. The rooms have two beds and are painted in soft pastel colours. They spend their days and evenings attending lectures, group therapy sessions and meetings of groups such as Alcoholics and Cocaine Anonymous. They also clean the toilets and floors, just like any other patient at the clinic."

Ringo "I drank all the way to the clinic and got off the plane totally demented and thought I was going in to a lunatic asylum. Eight days in, I decided, 'I am here to get help because I know I'm sick.' I did whatever they asked me to. Thank God, it just pulled me through. I can never thank that clinic enough. You get so very safe in the clinic. I didn't want to leave. To begin with, I didn't know if I could handle it. They had us doing the laundry and cleaning the ashtrays. The main problem I had was the damn newspapers, who had helicopters circling above."

Monday, November 7
The lives of Ringo and Barbara reach an all-time low when it is publicly revealed that they, as planned, have admitted themselves to the Sierra Tucson Drug and Alcohol Center, the drying out clinic in Arizona, for a duration of eight weeks . . .

Columnist, Roger Tavener "Now halfway through their intensive treatment, Ringo and Barbara, cut off from the rest of the world, undergo daily therapy sessions. They are not even allowed a telephone in their room."

Maev Kennedy, the *Guardian* "Derek Taylor came back from retirement as Beatles press officer to issue the statement in an effort to stop the media hanging around the very expensive private home in the States, annoying the other inmates."

Derek Taylor "Undoubtedly, they came to the conclusion they couldn't handle their problems alone. They decided, over a time, there was something wrong and had to do something about it. That is the first step and it is a very brave one. I know he's doing OK. They are in a very convivial atmosphere. Fellow alcoholics who, by their very nature, are all very gregarious surround them. Every day for them is like being in a bar, with everyone sharing a joke and a laugh. The only difference is they don't have a drink in their hand. And that's a good thing. They all realise life can go on without alcohol. They can be just as funny, just as entertaining and just as capable. Ringo knows he wants to contain his problem and then he must take each day at a time. He will be with Barbara and I am sure they will beat it together."

Roger Tavener "The Beatles' former publicist and ex-*Daily Express* reporter, Derek Taylor, was told to inform the world, get them off the hook and allow time for them to recover in peace."

The UK tabloid reporter, Ellie Buchanan "The statement didn't spark anything like the controversy stirred when The Beatles first announced they had taken drugs, for the simple reason that despite pop's cleaner image over the past few years, the public still sees drugs as rock's main occupational hazard. 'Oh, it's only drink,' people have been heard to say, as though it was a harmless whim."

Newspaper columnist, Steve Absalom "It was the bitter secret Ringo Starr and his beautiful actress wife Barbara Bach could not finally keep. They admitted they are alcoholics. To their close showbusiness friends, the news that they had admitted themselves to a drying out clinic in America was met with virtual disbelief. Over the past few months, the couple have only been seen drinking Perrier water. And last night, rumours were spreading in the States that the problems stemmed from a different kind of bottle, drugs. There are many people in Hollywood who use non-prohibited drugs, sometimes prescribed by different advisers, to get through the tensions of life. Such use is not illegal, but in Los Angeles, indulgence is the order of the day, and many big stars have become reliant on painkillers, weight reducers and appetite suppressants as well as legal 'uppers' and 'downers' and some combine their use with alcohol. Associates of the couple are stunned at their stay in the clinic and that view is understandable . . . It emerged last night that it was Barbara who decided they needed help at the drug and alcohol detoxification clinic because she feared that Ringo was going to die. Sources close to the couple in the United States, where they moved to start a new life six months ago, said that 40-year-old Barbara was in a high state of anxiety when she made the decision. The couple's problems of chemical dependency and alcoholism had grown steadily since they married in 1981. 'Ringo never really got over John Lennon's death. On top of that, his plans to become an actor were frustrated,' said the source. 'He had tons of money but nothing really to do with his life after The Beatles.' Last night, as the shock waves of their confinement spread throughout their London celebrity circle, **Paul McCartney** refused point blank to believe it. 'It can't be true,' he said. 'He's just on holiday for a couple of weeks.'

"But confirmation came from Starr's record company. Top agent, Lawrence Myers, said he had dined privately with the couple recently in Atlanta, Georgia. 'I'm astonished by this,' he went on. 'He and Barbara appeared to be the most normal, well-adjusted couple I've ever seen. OK, he may have had a drink socially every now and then, but I never once witnessed him drink heavily, and certainly not to the extent that he or Barbara might have needed help.' "

Linda McCartney "Paul and I knew about Ringo's addiction to the bottle for years but were afraid to say anything. We were only too aware that Ringo and Barbara were wrecking their lives, but we dreaded what would happen to the friendship, we so cherished, if either tried to intervene. There was nothing we could do about it. It was up to Ringo and Barbara to sort it out. If we had said anything, they would not have stopped drinking and we would have lost our friends. Paul and I are saddened to learn that Ringo and Barbara were booked into a clinic to beat their alcoholism. While, at the same time, we are pleased that our friends had at last decided to tackle the problem. They are both winners and will beat this together. There is no way a man of such wit and humour will let this beat him. Of course, it was obvious that they were drinking too much, but that is showbusiness. It hits so many people but they can be cured. Paul and I are lucky that we have never been tempted in a way that Ringo has. I never drink. I cannot even stand the smell of the stuff never mind the taste. Barbara is a rather special friend of mine and I have spoken to her in the last few days. What she told me has given Paul and I every confidence that she and Ringo will come through this stronger than ever. Paul and I are rooting for them. What they are doing is very brave."

Thursday, December 8

The reporter, Ellie Buchanan, writes, "Former Beatle Ringo Starr caused an eyebrow or two to be raised recently when he announced that he and his wife, Barbara, were checking into the Betty Ford clinic for alcoholism therapy. After four weeks, they have emerged treated, if not cured, to face a festive season without the tipples which are supposed to make Christmas merry. Since Ringo's announcement that he has a drink problem, some of his fair-weather friends have begun to show their true colours. Sly jokes about *Thomas The Tanked-Up Engine* have found their way into conversations and some commentators have decided the reason for his drink problem is that he suddenly realised he was a useless drummer, a passenger in The Beatles with no real musical ability. Pete York, formerly drummer with The Spencer Davis Group, said recently, 'Ringo's simple, straight forward drumming style did more for pop music than all the flashy drummers put together. When kids heard Ginger Baker or Buddy Rich, they would give up trying to be drummers, but when they heard Ringo, they thought, "I can do that," and were encouraged to try.' It is so courageous for Ringo Starr, a family entertainer, to come clean about his own problem. Just as in the Sixties, his straightforward drum playing inspired ordinary punters to attempt drumming for themselves. Maybe now, ordinary alcoholics will take a look at Ringo's fight against his addiction, think, 'I can do that,' and be encouraged to try."

Ringo "I thought, 'Okay, you're sober. Now what do you do?' I couldn't regret my drinking years. I knew it was pointless to sit around regretting things. I thought I might just as well get on to the next round of my life and that's what I am doing. I only hope that work has replaced the drink but all I know is that I don't drink today . . . Not drinking is a day to day thing. I don't think about drinking all the time any more. I just get through the day and it's easier. Now, if any of my friends can't deal with me being sober, then I just don't bother with them. Because, for me, to live is more important than a friend getting uptight just because I won't have a drink. If we go out to a party now, Barbara and I usually leave around 11.30pm, when everyone else starts getting rocky. Your life is suddenly changed around. My daughter, Lee, tells me, 'It's great hanging out with you, daddy. You're not drunk or watching telly.' It makes my heart glad. Since we stopped drinking, we're having fun."

Barbara "When we stopped drinking he felt a big void and thought he'd have to go back to work. He had to fill that void."

Ringo "Since stopping, I feel 100 per cent better. I have finally left the bars. I have even got a kind of fitness regime. I take fast walks and do 50 or 60 sit-ups, nothing crazy but it just keeps you going."

Tuesday, January 3

The year begins with the news, by UK columnist Garry Jenkins, revealing that "Paul McCartney is going back on the road for the first time in 10 years with a world tour. The former Beatle, who has appeared on stage just three times since touring with Wings in 1979, desperately wants to re-launch his career. He is hoping to stage concerts in Russia but will snub one of the world's main pop nations, Japan, where he was jailed for ten days back in 1980 for possessing drugs. A spokesman said yesterday, 'Given what has happened, he won't be going there.' The tour, planned to begin in the late summer, will come at a crucial moment in his career. He has been disappointed by a series of artistic failures, which began in 1984 when his film *Give My Regards To Broad Street*, was a box-office flop. He has failed to record a hit album and his last major performance was during the *Live Aid* concert in 1985. McCartney, 44, has spent the past few months working on a new LP in the recording studios at his Sussex farm. Singer Elvis Costello has helped him, and McCartney has also formed a new group, which includes Hamish Stewart, formerly of The Average White Band."

Monday, January 9

For Ringo, meanwhile, the year starts on a happier note when, in newspaper headlines bearing the title "Ringo's Back On The Rails Again!" it is announced that he is starring in a dazzling new high-tech American TV version of *Thomas The Tank Engine*, playing an 18-inch tall train controller equipped with magic powers . . .

At the Los Angeles press conference to launch the series, *Shining Time Station*, **Ringo** announces, "I'm still the same happy-go-lucky Beatle. All I do is not drink, you know. All that is in the past. I'm the same bubbly Beatle I was 25 years ago. I'm feeling real healthy and real happy. I'm taking life one day at a time and the future is looking good. My darkest hour was too dark but everything is fine . . . now. We both feel better for quitting. I used to sink a bottle of brandy in five hefty shots, then pick up another."

Ringo's wife Barbara, who sits besides her husband at the gathering, adds, "He's back on top form. We're in good shape again."

Ringo on his role in *Shining Time Station* "Mr C, the conductor, is a magic man. I appear in gold dust and I disappear in gold dust. It's like *Star Trek*'s 'Beam me up, Scotty' all over again. I zoom in and out and the people who don't have good hearts can't see me. A trick camera process called Ultimatte turns me into a tiny tot who lives in a signal house in an enchanted station. It means that a lot of the time I am acting with props, which are 'painted' in later. I may be sitting on a couple of old boxes and on telly it looks like I'm perched on a giant hat. *Shining Time Station* is meant to be a children's series, but it's going to become a big hit with mums and dads, too. It's got that magical quality, which appeals to the kid in all of us. I've always got on with kids. Kids and mothers were my crowd. John had the intellectuals; Paul had the teenies and George the mystics. I always got the mothers and babies."

Following the conference, **Ringo** holds a private conversation with the UK reporter, Chris Anderson, "Only one thing clouds my optimism. I believe my beloved Britain turned against me when Barbara and I checked into the drying out clinic. I got terrible coverage in England. They were all supportive in America but in England, they thought I was only doing it for the publicity. They thought I had some sort of madness."

Ringo changes the conversation, announcing that the death of John still haunts him. "I've twice seen John's ghost," he says. "He came to me in a hotel room when I was feeling low. He told me to cheer up . . . The Beatles were a big part of my life and you can never get rid of that. I had a great time."

Thursday, January 26
Meanwhile, back in the UK, Paul makes a historic appearance at the BBC Radio studios in Portland Place, London . . .

Tabloid reporter, Alan Franks "The voice of Paul McCartney speaking and singing could be heard in the Soviet Union as the former Beatle took part in a phone-in radio interview broadcast from London to 18 million Soviet listeners. He chatted for more than an hour to his Russian fans, who until recently have found it impossible to buy Beatles records there. During the show, on which Sam Yossman, a Lithuanian-born presenter, was host, tracks were played from his *CHOBA B CCCP* (*Back In The USSR*) album of early rock classics. McCartney told one listener that he would love to visit Russia. 'I'm putting a band together and we are rehearsing . . . Other people go to the Soviet Union and sing "Back In The USSR" so perhaps it's about time I went out there to sing it myself.' Rudolf, a fan from Riga, wanted to know why McCartney had dedicated his newly released album to reforms in the Soviet Union. The singer said he wanted to do something to help to improve relations between the Soviet Union and Britain. 'It's important to let the people there know that there are a lot of friendly ones over here.' McCartney disclosed that there were one or two unreleased Beatles songs still in the hands of EMI. 'There is one, called "Leave My Kitten Alone", which John sings, and that's pretty good.' "

Friday, February 17
But there are bad times for **George** and HandMade Films when, following a row with his business partner, Denis O'Brien, George sensationally pulls the plug on six films currently in production and fires all his staff . . .

Michael Shanahan, the *Express* "Harrison's move has sent shock waves through the British film industry, which is currently riding high after years in the doldrums. Staff at HandMade Films was astonished when they were sent a message via a fax machine; saying that they were all fired. 'It came totally out of the blue,' said one former employee. 'Everybody was very upset. Denis O'Brien didn't even know George was going to do it.' A spokesman for the company said, 'There were nine films scheduled for this year, but now we have decided to make just three.' That means that millions of pounds that would have been injected into the movie business have now been withdrawn. One producer, to whom Harrison had offered millions of pounds in advance, said, 'Everything was fine one day and the next we were out.' A former executive at HandMade said, 'I think George got upset because he felt things were getting out of control.' Speaking in New York, Mr O'Brien said he had just returned from spending several days with Harrison in Hawaii. 'I didn't have a major difference of opinion with George Harrison,' he said. He also denied that HandMade ever intended to make nine films this year, but added, 'There has been a reduction in the amount of films in the pipeline.' "

George "To be in the film industry and still be around after eleven years, that is a miracle, but we haven't been enormously successful. We have big debts. We can't afford to make $25 million productions. We are competing with *Batman* and *Ghostbusters* and that kind of thing, which costs $45 million. It takes $30 million to buy the directors and famous five-star actors. HandMade Films will continue, but in order to get an audience, you have to make one of these big budget blockbuster movies full of crash, bang, wallop. It's a hell of a wicked business. The music industry is bad enough but the film industry is absolutely wicked."

Monday, June 5
In the UK, Paul releases his new studio album, *Flowers In The Dirt* . . .

'Motor Of Love'

Paul "In 'Motor Of Love' I talk about the heavenly father and I'm actually talking about my father, who hopefully went up top when he died in 1976. If anyone wants to put a religious meaning on the song, I'm okay with that."

Although well received by the fans, it is not acclaimed by the hard-to-please-British Press . . .

The *Sun* "Spare a tear of pity for poor Paul McCartney. His appalling new album, *Flowers In The Dirt,* has an environmentally friendly, recycled paper sleeve. Shame he couldn't have done the same for the music, though some would say he has. 'Distractions', the naffest track, and that in itself is an achievement, is a sad regurgitation of Beatles moments, illustrating brutally how times have changed. It was very important to Paul's career that this project succeeded. He desperately wants to be accepted as a creative musician. Commercially he has scored in the past, but critically he has never been that highly rated. So he pulled out all the stops for this LP. He collaborated with major talents such as the superb writer Elvis Costello."

Paul "To consider collaborating with anyone else has always been a bit difficult. I felt I wanted to write seriously with someone. Elvis's name was mentioned and I thought it would be worth having a go. If worst came to worst, it would bomb out and we would hate each other. Working with Elvis Costello was the closest experience I have had to working with John. I have not co-written with a lot of people, just Eric Stewart, of 10cc, Michael Jackson and my wife, Linda. But after writing with John, it wasn't easy. The thing with Elvis was that I kept picking up this slight feeling of John. I would sing a line and he would come up with a witty acerbic foil to it, like John used to. I said to Elvis, 'This is getting a bit like me and John. I'm being me and you're being him. How come you get all the witty lines and I get the dumb-twit ones?' But Elvis has this great sarcastic quality in his voice. I said, 'My God, that's mine and John's whole style.' I'd write some romantic line and John would write the acid put-down. It wasn't eerie; it was nice having that rapport. It is the nearest I have come to John. We sat down as equals. Writing with someone is very personal. It is like marrying someone and being able to take all their criticisms. I could easily have turned round to him and said, 'What do you know. You are younger than me, you weren't in The Beatles, so sod off.' But we sat down at my place facing each other with just two acoustic guitars, which is how I used to work with John. You mirror image each other. I can't think of anyone I would have preferred to collaborate with than John. Having come up from Liverpool together, we could read each other and he was very easy to work with. I kept saying to him, 'This sounds like The Beatles, man. We can't do this, this is dangerous.' I kept joking to him that we were going to end up sounding like one of those groups that send their cassettes into a record company saying, 'Believe me, we are the answer to The Beatles.' But his natural enthusiasm won me over. I thought, 'What the hell is wrong with it?' It is great, really. Other people imitate it. Elvis is a big Beatles fan and I suspect he's a big John fan because often, guys who wear glasses can identify with John."

The *Sun*'s negative review continues, "Paul did dozens of interviews, popping up all over the box, radio and papers, and last month was Paul McCartney month. The result? A dreadful single, 'My Brave Face', which didn't do well. A No. 1 album position, which my dealer sources say sold primarily to his hard core fans in the first fortnight and then dried up faster than cow dung. Sliding from No. 1 to No. 15 in a fortnight is not indicative of widespread popularity. His records haven't done well in the Eighties and I would not be surprised if his label was considering dropping him. A lot of money was spent pushing *Flowers In The Dirt* and the sad fact is that this could be the end of his musical career. So, say a kind word for someone who bought a lot of people plenty of happiness – in the Sixties. Thanks for the memory, Paul, but how about giving it a rest now."

Sunday, July 2

The *Sunday Mirror* reports "Ringo is going back on the road for the first time since The Beatles split nearly 20 years ago. He will sing and play drums with his new group on a six-week USA Tour, starting July 23. The group's name? The All-Starr Band, of course."

Ringo "Some guy came over to England and asked me if I would like to get a band together and take it on the road. I think he must have got me on a good day because I said yes almost right away."

Wednesday, July 12

Ringo's first concert tour since 1966 features in a syndicated news report . . .

"Ex-Beatle Ringo Starr has agreed an amazing deal to plug Diet Pepsi, in return for a newspaper advertising campaign he doesn't need! Ringo was terrified his 25-date tour of the States, which starts next month, would be a monster flop. So he signed a multi-million-dollar deal with Diet Pepsi's American bosses in a bid to obtain maximum publicity. Starr, 48, was delighted to be offered full-page advertisements in every major newspaper in America, a huge coast-to-coast poster campaign and promotional T-shirts and jackets worth more than £1 million. Ringo won't pocket a single cent from the deal and now, ironically, he doesn't need any of the publicity. Tickets for his comeback tour sold out in a matter of minutes, breaking all records. The manager of New Jersey State Arts Center says, 'I've never known anything like it. Tickets went in less than 15 minutes, faster than they did for Michael Jackson or Bruce Springsteen.' A pal of Ringo said, 'He's delighted by the response. But he's worried fans will think he is now advertising shows already sold out.' Diet Pepsi's American spokeswoman, Lisa Kolvitz, said, 'We're very pleased that Ringo's endorsing our product. Our logo is everywhere. We're also delighted that Ringo's tour is proving to be such a success. It has worked out well on both sides.' "

Sunday, July 23

American columnist, Mike Kerrigan reports, "Ringo Starr looks well. He is also busy. For two weeks he has been rehearsing flat out for a 30-city American tour opening tonight in Dallas, Texas . . . He is bright-eyed and his hair, pulled severely back off his face, is bushy-tailed. His trademark pale and puffy complexion has been replaced by a healthy looking tan . . ."

Ringo "Most of my life I have kept Count Dracula hours, sleeping all day and staying up all night. In the last year, I have been awake during daylight hours and I have acquired a tan. And what happens? The doctors come along and say it's bad for you. I wonder where they were when I needed them."

In Dallas, during a break from rehearsals, **Ringo** announces, "I feel good. It's been hard work but I really feel great about getting back to it. More important, I feel really good about myself and I know that if I had not done what I did last year, I wouldn't be able to do any of this."

Recalling his time when he booked himself into a clinic and kicked the booze, **Ringo** admits, "I was a little sick in the head and in the body as well and in the mind and the soul. I was just wasting my life. Those nights when you drank more and more than you remembered had become almost every night. So I went and got some help and I highly recommend it to anyone with addictive problems. There are a lot of folk out there who can do something for you. All you have to do is ask. The honest truth is that I would not have been able to manage the rehearsals, let alone the tour, if I was still drinking."

Joining Ringo on this 30-concerts-in-43-days tour are the musicians, Billy Preston, Dr John, Levon Helms, Nils Lofgren, Joe Walsh, Rick Danko, Clarence Clemons and Jim Keltner, who joins Ringo on drums . . .

Ringo "The great thing about these guys is that they are all stars in their own right so they don't spend all their time feeling they have to prove something. It makes for a happy group. I am really looking forward to the tour. I think we're playing towns that weren't built the last time I did this. I have also sent tour details to a couple of other guys I used to play with and they are welcome to drop by any time and sit in (an obvious reference to Paul and George) . . . Sure we keep in touch. With Paul it's a good month and then a bad month, just like a family. I see George more often because we live closer to each other."

Ringo's Tour opens in Dallas at the Park Central Amphitheater . . .

The *International Herald Tribune* "Although kids got in free on the first night of Ringo Starr's Tour For All Generations in Dallas, the audience was dominated by the over-30 crowd. The former Beatle was backed by a greying constellation of rock stars, including the former Beatles collaborator, Billy Preston, who played the organ on 'Let It Be', the singer, Dr John, the saxman, Clarence Clemons, the guitarist-keyboardist, Nils Lofgren, on loan from Bruce Springsteen's E-Street Band and the guitarist, Joe Walsh, a former

Eagle. The 49-year-old Ringo opened the first show of his 30-city tour on Sunday, singing 'It Don't Come Easy'."

Syndicated news report "It was his first solo concert, and Ringo Starr welcomed the applause with open arms. The former Beatle began a 30-city American tour in Dallas, Texas, before an audience of mainly over-40s, who were allowed to bring their children free. One woman with her two young daughters, said, 'My kids don't even know who Ringo Starr is, but they will after tonight.' Ringo, 49, who bills the concerts as A Tour For All Generations, was backed by several ageing stars . . ."

Ringo "I experienced terror facing a tour after so many years but once I had got through the first number, I was comfortable, and then I was on a roll. But just getting on the stage was the hardest bit. But really, this whole thing is a joy for me. I'm not just stuck behind the drums. I'm up there doing my thing. Many of my songs are chorus songs, like 'Yellow Submarine' and 'With A Little Help From My Friends', so we seem to have a big singalong every night. And there's also a great camaraderie now because we're all working for each other. Each of us gets the spotlight . . . Before the tour, I had done only three gigs in ten years, which is not exactly working yourself to a frazzle. But after each gig, it was really tough because I didn't know what to do with myself, because my whole body and head went into, 'Let's party!' you know, 'Let's get crazy, let's get messed up.' But there's one little seed of reality in there saying, 'But we don't do that anymore.' Thank God it won, with God's help.

"Barbara and I returned to our home in Monte Carlo straight after the tour and we were actually too excited to be physically exhausted. After the last concert, we just fell apart. It took a couple of weeks for both of us to get over it . . . It's ironic, I hadn't been on the road for years and when I finally get to do it, everybody in the world comes out with me. The Rolling Stones are still out in the States, The Who are playing again and, of course, Paul McCartney . . . It just seemed I went out and they all came out. Of course, there has been a great revival in interest in the early British bands but the secret for all our new success is that people want to hear hits. They like to hear 'With A Little Help From My Friends' or 'Yellow Submarine' over and over again."

After the final concert of Ringo's tour has taken place at the Greek Theater in Los Angeles, the UK columnist, Barry Baker reports, "Thanks to sponsorship from Pepsi, the tour grossed £5 million, which means nearly £1 million profit for him. But that pales beside the £56 million The Rolling Stones have grossed so far in their American section of a world tour, which means around £4 million for each Stone. Paul McCartney's European Tour will gross £12 million, which will make him £1 million richer . . . Ringo will tour Britain and Europe next year with a concert in Russia in April. He is writing songs again and an album is planned for May next year. 'Now I'm back in the limelight, we're getting invitations from everywhere,' Ringo announces."

Tuesday, July 25

Syndicated news report "Ringo Starr obtained a court order yesterday to stop a Memphis record company releasing an album he made in 1987. Starr's lawyers said he felt the record was not up to his standards."

The subject of the album appears in an exclusive report in the *Daily Star* newspaper (July 29) "Reformed boozer Ringo Starr has launched an amazing court battle to ban a record company from selling his old album . . . because he reckons it was ruined by drink. Ringo hit the roof when he heard that American music firm CRS Records were planning to cash in on his current tour by releasing the record. The ex-Beatle protested that the un-named LP was abandoned after Chips Moman created havoc by taking booze into the Memphis studios two years ago. Ringo demanded to re-record huge chunks of the drumming on the record, which he claims was marred by drinking bouts. But the record company insisted on releasing the album this week, just as Ringo began his 30-date comeback tour of America. Now Ringo, who gave up booze last year, wants to ban the record once and for all. At a court hearing in the Superior Court, Fulton County, Atlanta, Georgia, Ringo's lawyers claimed the producer, Chips Moman, blackmailed him by demanding £90,000 not to release the record, rejected Starr's own offer of £63,000 and ruined his performance during the recording of the album by bringing booze into the studio. Chips denies it all."

Ringo "We would send out for wine or else there would be tequila there or cognac or whatever anybody else felt like drinking. There was always plenty of alcohol on the premises. Certain nights we were all under the influence . . ."

Lawyers representing Chips Moman "Ringo came to the producer in 1987 to salvage a career bogged down by addiction to alcohol, an addiction which he had been very successful in keeping a private matter, unknown by his best friends, his agent and his attorney. He came to Moman because he has a reputation for getting careers moving again."

Chips Moman slams Ringo's claim that the album would damage the ex-Beatle's reputation "No one would notice a bad album from one who hadn't had a hit in 14 years. In my opinion, this new LP would be a £2 million hit."

(Note: the Superior Court in Georgia gives a temporary restraining order on the record's release on August 22)

Saturday, July 29
Meanwhile, back in England, in an interview with Sue Johnson published today in the *Daily Express*, it is announced that George and his wife, Olivia, have gone 'green' . . .

Sue Johnson "He is angry about pollution, Green Belt development and he is an ardent 'Friend of the Earth'. Some may feel that he is a little naive, and that it is easier for him than for others to espouse these causes, surrounded as he is by the trappings of success and international stardom, but many may agree with his desire to live in a cleaner world. At 45, age rests easily on his shoulders and he exudes an air of confidence, but there is nothing big-headed or awesome about him. He is a down-to-earth chap who goes out of his way to make you feel at ease."

George "The planet is in the hands of very greedy people," he announces. "The people in power and the people in big business, they are the people who control our fate and it's all done with so much greed."

Olivia "Things are put into food and pumped into the air and we don't have anything to say about it. You ask anyone, nobody wants it, but it's happened. What is really frightening is that information is nearly impossible to obtain about these things."

George "Such arrogance comes from the Government. They are forgetting we, the people, employ them. I'm talking now not as this famous George Harrison, I'm talking now as an ordinary member of humanity and of the British public. I'm quite a reasonable person, but the way I feel about the environment, I could just go and throttle those people. I tend to try and turn a blind eye and just do it through music, or quietly. It's not every day I talk like this, exclusively to a newspaper. You would think the Minister of the Environment would be out there looking after all the birds and the trees and the oxygen. All Nicholas Ridley ever did for the environment was concrete over it. They won't be happy until we are all squatting in the back of some fucking hatchback on the motorway, and that's the reality we are all facing. What are we going to do about all this traffic? They've got to ban it. The only vote I have ever cast is Green. By putting this present Government down, it doesn't mean to say that Neil Kinnock is going to be any better. They are all the same; they switch their policies just to suit whatever is in vogue. We can't go on and on creating more and more waste. The whole planet is operating on the waste of over-indulgence. It's just ridiculous. 'Money doesn't speak, it swears,' Dylan said that years ago."

Sue Johnson "The Harrisons avoid using chlorine bleached paper products when possible, they go to the bottle bank and have a shredder that converts newspaper and cardboard boxes to fertiliser for their vegetable garden . . . George was once a devout follower of the Hare Krishna religious body and still has an affinity for the movement . . ."

George "The things I learned from the yogis and mystics of the East are still in me. And I think in the end, no matter what happens with this planet, the only answer really lies within each one of us. Now doctors are saying Meditation should be introduced into the National Health. Why do you think we were saying this in 1967? They all said we were a bunch of lunatics, but it's proven now that we weren't that dumb after all."

Conversation then changes to The Traveling Wilburys . . .

"I hope there will be another Traveling Wilburys record," **George** announces. "It was one of the most enjoyable things I've done. I was doing it with people I admired and respected and it turned out that the public liked it too. I just have to wait for all the other Wilburys to finish being solo artists. They have all said they would like to do it again. I don't really have a desire to be a solo artist. It's much more fun being in The Wilburys. They represent the stand against this horrible computerised music. That's another thing that should be banned along with CFCs."

Friday, August 4
Meanwhile, a long-forgotten relic from the golden days of The Beatles is found when their former chauffeur has a rummage in his garden shed . . .

Tabloid reporter, John Young "A former driver employed by The Beatles expects to make up to £60,000 from the sale of a collection of tape recordings, which for more than twenty years were kept in a shed at the bottom of his garden in Cobham, Surrey. Mr Alf Bicknell, aged 60, said that he had ignored them until now because he thought they were just tapes that had been sent to the group by fans. 'I was absolutely staggered when I found they were recordings by the boys,' he said. The tapes, which are due to be auctioned by Sotheby's at a sale of rock'n'roll and film memorabilia on August 22, are not exactly a musical revelation. Among the 'highlights' is a recording made at a hotel in

Weston-Super-Mare in 1963, in which the group are joined by Gerry Marsden, of Gerry & The Pacemakers, in a rendering of hymns accompanied by hysterical laughter. John Lennon sings 'The Lord Is My Shepherd'. Mr Bicknell described it as 'more like a Goons record'. Mr Bicknell was chauffeur to the group from 1964 and accompanied them on two world tours until their last concert in San Francisco in August 1966. 'After that last concert, I told John that I would be packing it in when we got home because I was tired out,' he said. 'There were about twenty tapes in the back of the limousine and a cartoon of the famous "We're bigger than Christ" thing.' John said, "You take them and good luck." ' "

Saturday, August 5

The 'sue me sue you blues' of the modern day Beatles continues when it is announced, in a syndicated press report, that "Ringo Starr has revealed that he is refusing to drop a massive court case, which could embarrass his old pal, Paul McCartney." The report continues, "The pony-tailed Ringo, 48, claims that Macca begged him to halt the sensational legal battle over royalties from The Beatles' albums. But the drummer is determined not to give up the fight until he has picked up a small fortune in compensation . . ."

Paul "I gave Capitol six albums I had made after the group split and in return, I got increased royalties. I keep saying we've got to sort out our problems. We can't move forward while you're suing me."

Ringo "We do talk, though not lately. We have all sat down in the same room together, but then we get down to business and negotiations start to break down. The Beatles were four people and what we did was to split the records equally."

Tuesday, August 22

The *Sun* newspaper reports that "John Lennon's son, Julian, has revealed that his father left him next to nothing in his will. The ex-Beatle's estate was worth £220 million when Mark Chapman gunned him down in 1980. Julian, 26, was left £70,000 in a trust fund and says he is virtually broke. In a frank interview, Julian tells how he has been forced to sell his home because he doesn't have any cash, was ripped off by people in the business and hasn't kept a single penny from his two hit albums. He also admits that he wants to settle down but can't get a steady girlfriend . . ."

Julian tells the American *US* magazine "I got a pretty small piece of the pie considering the size of dad's estate. There was a trust fund for me and my half-brother, Sean, which is split down the middle. The will states that Yoko is the boss, so everything is up to her discretion. But I don't care. She's entitled to what she wants. I didn't show any responsibility in the past and didn't prove I was a stable son or concerned human being. Dad was very smart. If I had money I would have spent it and might have been dead by now. I thank dad for doing it. It helped me learn about life and people . . . I haven't got a cent of what I earned from my two albums. People took advantage of me because I was naive. I was totally depressed and didn't know who I could trust. Eventually I went to Switzerland to sort myself out and I've been fine ever since."

Wednesday, August 30

With three months still to go before Paul's upcoming world tour reaches the States, there is continued proof that McCartney mania is alive and well in America . . .

Syndicated news report "Ticket hungry fans sent megastar Paul McCartney screeching into the record books today when, in just 52 minutes of mayhem, they snapped up 85,000 seats for his American concert dates. Macca mania netted a thumping £2.5 million brought gasps of relief from promoters. They were unsure how a new generation of music followers would react to Paul's first live shows in America for 13 years. But the frantic scenes that blitzed ticket agents were just like the hysteria whipped up by The Beatles in the Sixties. Thousands of fans had queued up 48 hours early to get their hands on tickets for Paul's three November shows at the Los Angeles Forum. Twenty-five minutes after the goldrush began, every single ticket had gone. Then an extra two shows were announced to give fans another chance and twenty-seven minutes later they too were swallowed up. Rock experts now predict that McCartney will earn a bank-busting £20 million from his five-city American tour, including merchandise and other deals. 'He's going to make money like other people make coffee,' said one music business insider. 'It shows there's a legion of folks out there who want to see McCartney whatever the cost.' "

Thursday, September 21

The curtain-raiser to Paul's first world tour in 13 years takes place with a secret dress rehearsal show before a specially invited audience at the Elstree Film Studios in Hertfordshire . . .

Clement Burton, UK columnist and part of the packed crowd this evening, "Through BBC Radio One, Paul invited seven hundred fans, close friends and relatives to Elstree Film Studios where he performed for free a complete showcase of the show, which hits the road next Tuesday in Oslo. Plans for McCartney to present his show in front of the world's music critics at the vast Isstadion next Friday have gone awry. On discovering his first night is in Oslo, next Tuesday, the world's press is now set to descend on the Norwegian capital, which has annoyed McCartney. He wanted to have the chance to settle into the tour before facing the critics. Apart from material from his recent No. 1 album *Flowers In The Dirt*, which has now gone gold, McCartney intends to perform some of his favourite Beatles songs, including 'Let It Be', 'The Fool On The Hill' and 'The Long And Winding Road'. McCartney opens the British stage of his European tour at Birmingham's NEC on January 3. He plays ten concerts at the Wembley Arena from January 13. Paul's British fans will also then have an opportunity to see the stunning Richard Lester film show that precedes every concert on the tour . . ."

Paul "Originally I said to Dick Lester, 'Well, we're not having a support act, but we want to put something at the start of the show, which will give the kids that something extra.' I remember when I had to pay for tickets, from a hard-earned wage, and it makes a big dent in your wage to pay for a ticket. So we decided we wanted to give something of great value. We did the free programme and I said to Dick, 'Let's put a film there.' So he went away and did what he wanted. He included all those film clips, including those shots of Michael Jackson, from archive footage we had. The 'Say Say Say' footage was on file at our office and he said, 'Do you mind if we use it?' I said, 'No, I don't mind what you do. It's a great movie.' It was Dick's personal opinion to include that. I didn't say, 'Hey, we'd better not have that.' It was funny, the reaction to the inclusion from Beatles fans who are annoyed at the commercialisation. I think they're annoyed because The Beatles never commercialised songs like 'All You Need Is Love' and 'Revolution'. They have a meaning to people. On some parts of the world tour, fans booed that particular piece of footage."

Sunday, September 24
As a further promotional push for his world tour, Paul announces that he is only going back on the road again thanks to Princess Diana . . .

Paul "I had never considered going back on tour until I got the royals rocking at the Prince's Trust concert three years ago. I joined Tina Turner on stage for a duet on 'Get Back' and the packed crowd went crazy and I noticed that Princess Diana had jumped on to her feet to bop along. I had missed playing live shows but I didn't realise how much until I did the Prince's Trust gig. When I saw Diana up in the stands dancing it was then that I started to plan this tour. That concert left me feeling so good that I thought it wouldn't be unthinkable to get back on the road again. But I will be petrified when I step out on stage for the first time on Tuesday. I am still haunted by the memories of *Live Aid* when I sang 'Let It Be' into a dead microphone."

Tuesday, September 26
Just months after Ringo has undertaken his first major tour in two decades, Paul, Linda and his band begin their massive tour in Norway in Oslo. But the run-up to the shows at the Drannenhallen Stadium is not free from problems when the demand for first show tickets causes Norway's post office computer to crash . . .

Norwegian press release "Tickets for the opening date of Paul's first world tour in 13 years went in a few hours. An organiser of the 5,700-ticket concert in Oslo said the plan was to sell tickets from three hundred post offices all over Norway. But the computer collapsed minutes after the sale started. Parents and youngsters had queued all night outside the offices ready for when they opened at 8am on Monday. But the computer broke down and by the time it had been fixed at noon, the central offices in Oslo had sold all 6,000 tickets. McCartney's Norwegian agent, Gunner Eide, said he had received countless calls from disappointed fans, many of which were weeping. He announced that he had asked McCartney to give an extra concert but was told it was impossible."

It is Paul's first series of concerts in a decade . . .

Present at McCartney's great concert comeback is American music critic, Clark Gamble, "In an average-sized sports hall in Scandinavia, a living legend of pop put his reputation on the line. For the first time in 13 years, Paul McCartney embarked on a world tour and chose to include a repertoire of fifteen Beatles songs. The start, it has to be said, was not too auspicious. A black stage lit by stark white lights picked out Paul, wife Linda and their brand new band as they played 'Figure Of Eight', a track from his latest album. But by the end of the evening, after a medley of classics such as 'The Fool On The Hill', 'Sgt. Pepper', 'Eleanor Rigby', 'Back In The USSR', 'Hey Jude' and 'Yesterday', there was no doubting that the McCartney reputation was more than intact. Drawing from music he made famous throughout his career, McCartney rolled back the years from the early days of The Beatles, through Wings, and up to his more recent solo work. At a press conference earlier in the day, he had stressed that this band was about musicianship, not image and he was right. While he could have fallen into the trap of surrounding himself with talented but dry session musicians, the assembled line-up of Hamish Stuart, Robbie McIntosh, Wix and Chris Whitten were anything but. There was no question that they were treading dangerous ground to dabble with the triumphs of the Fab Four like 'Can't Buy Me Love', but it worked. At times McCartney's voice sounded hoarser than normal, but he put as much gusto into his performance as he did thirty years ago. The atmosphere was similar to a good wedding party as they played all the old favourites that had everyone singing, clapping, tapping their feet and had parents dancing with their children. Hydraulic lifts, laser beams, light shows and explosions, added to the spectacular, but it was the songs and McCartney who stole the show."

Daily Mail "In Oslo, the £23 tickets were changing hands for up to twenty times the price. Many of those who did have tickets weren't even born when The Beatles split up twenty years ago. Katrina Hague, 18, said, 'I wasn't born when The Beatles played and I was too young to see his next band, Wings, perform.' McCartney's tour will take in 15 countries, including Britain, Scandinavia, Brazil and America. Paul's astonishing climax to the show includes three numbers from the *Abbey Road* album, which neither he nor The Beatles ever played live. The millionaire will use his concerts to publicise the work of Friends Of The Earth."

Paul "Friends Of The Earth are our sponsors and they're getting it for nothing. I am not doing this because it is hip to be Green or as a gimmick for the tour. I'm doing it because I am a parent and I am worried about my kids. I fear for what shape the planet will be in by the time my children are my age. Linda and I do every little bit we can to help the environment. We use the right washing powder and liquids. It doesn't seem much, but if we all do it, every little bit will help."

This long and winding road of performances will continue until next June . . .

Linda "When Paul started planning this world tour, I couldn't bear the thought of leaving our zoo of cats, dogs, chickens, horses, geese and sheep. The idea of getting in and out of aeroplanes for months didn't excite me. But the thought of playing with Paul did. And what was special about it was that at least we could be together. That's the whole point about me being in the band, so we can be together. That's why you marry someone, so you can be with him. Once the tour started, I really enjoyed it. Best of all, I could go round the world talking about not slaughtering animals."

Paul "We had formed the band gradually. Chris Whitten had jammed with me at sessions in London and then sat in to drum on *CHOBA B CCCP*, my Russian album. I had long admired Hamish Stuart, the linchpin of The Average White Band, and called him in to play on *Flowers In The Dirt*. Hamish recommended Robbie McIntosh, Chrissie Hynde's sidekick in The Pretenders . . ."

Robbie McIntosh "In the beginning, I didn't want to tour and so I turned down the offer of joining Paul's band. I didn't want to be away from my family. But I had grown up listening to all of these songs of Paul's, playing them at home as a kid and the chance to perform them, with him, on stage was pretty amazing. I wouldn't have toured with any other bands, and I'd had offers, but this was different."

Paul "Robbie, in turn, recommended Wix, his old pal from Chris Thompson & The Islands. So the band all sort of fell together through friends putting up each other for the jobs. So, once I had a band, the next logical step was to get out on the road again . . .

They'd all toured before but nothing like this. At the start of it all, I had warned them that we had to be a little cautious and we had to work hard as a band."

Music reporter, Kevin Connal "McCartney assembled a crack line-up for the tour, wife Linda on keyboards, Robbie McIntosh of Pretenders fame on guitar, Hamish Stewart, formerly of The Average White Band on guitar, keyboardist Paul 'Wix' Wickens and drummer, Chris Whitten . . ."

Paul "Even from the early days of the band, the fun of that friendship between all of us was very much a distinctive aspect of the group. And in putting a band together, that brought on the idea of going on tour. People had asked me why I hadn't toured for so long before this, the simple reason was that I didn't have a band. But once I did have a band, the next logical step was to get out on the road again. It's one thing to tour around the world playing with a bunch of very fine musicians, but it's even better when you can all have a good laugh together. These are the sort of people you'd want to go around the world with and these guys and my lovely wife are making my songs fun again."

Kevin Connal "Anyone who caught one of McCartney's shows admits that it was nearly impossible to take your eyes off the charismatic ex-Beatle once he trotted onstage, spinning like a windmill gone awry. He'd play 'Figure Of Eight', 'Put It There' and other tracks from *Flowers In The Dirt*. He'd do several old Wings hits, such as 'Jet' and 'Band On The Run' . . . But from city to city, the high points were The Beatles numbers. McCartney would strap on his vintage Hofner bass and remind us that 'I Saw Her Standing There' was *not* a Tiffany original . . . He'd jog memories with touching updates of 'Hey Jude' and 'Yesterday'. He'd rile up the crowd with fiery, guitar-riffling versions of 'Sgt. Pepper' and 'Golden Slumbers/Carry That Weight/The End'. Then he'd come floating to centre stage on a rotating baby grand piano and recite an extended version of 'The Fool On The Hill', following a brief dedication to 'My mates, George, John and Ringo!' The crowds go crazy. After each show, the ubiquitous media people follow McCartney, waiting for a chance to talk with the amicable bassist . . ."

Linda "After a short while, I realised that this tour was going to be fun, and a lot of that had to do with the way the fans reacted. It all became very intimate for us. Even when we were playing in the huge stadiums, there was an intimacy with the crowd. You could feel the warmth of the people and I think that's down to Paul's talent; he's a great showman. He warms them up to the point where they feel they are in a living room with Paul McCartney. They were in the same space with a great talent who is also a real person, he loves entertaining but he also loves and that had a lot to do with the fun the fans had."

Keyboard player, Wix "I had my work cut out on that stage, recreating on the keyboards a lot of orchestral parts to get the sound as authentic as you could to the records. And that's quite a challenge, playing everything from straight rock and roll piano and organ through to being a string quartet on 'Eleanor Rigby' and half an orchestra on 'Live And Let Die'. It was a pretty varied job. There were nights when the lump would swell up in your throat during 'Hey Jude' or 'The Long And Winding Road'. It wasn't just the crowd that got affected."

Throughout the tour, Paul is asked about the choice of songs in his repertoire . . .

"It took months and months of list-making," **Paul** says. "I took out a piece of paper and thought, ' "Maybe I'm Amazed", pretty good, "Let It Be", good, "Hey Jude", not bad, "The Long And Winding Road", yeah.' I carried on until the list numbered thirty-five. I didn't want to do John's Beatles stuff. That's for Julian or Yoko to put together. That's for his side of things. I figured out that there was enough stuff of mine, like 'The Fool On The Hill' and 'Yesterday', which was mine. There's a lot of stuff, which is definitely mine, like 'Eleanor Rigby'. These are ones, which were basically recognised to be mine; the ones I knew were mine. So I thought, 'That's fine, what I'm doing is going out as a performer and showing you what I writ.' When I took my band the list of songs I had written down, and we whittled the songs down, certain things in rehearsal weren't as fun as they were on the records. It wasn't fun to play them and that was a pretty big criterion. If it's not fun to play it, I'm not taking it out on tour. It had better be fun now, because it's going to get boring later. But the best thing about it was that there were certain old songs that I had never done before. I kept thinking to myself, 'Why does this seem so fresh, doing "Sgt. Pepper"?' And then I suddenly realised that I had only sang it once, at Abbey Road, the night we recorded it. That was the vocal take and I never had any cause to do it after that. Nobody ever asked me. What's nice about 'Sgt, Pepper' is the way John and I conceived it. It's all directed to an audience. The whole idea of *Sgt. Pepper* is a show, a circus. So this song works great live. And then 'Hey Jude'. I realised that I had never done that either. 'God,' I thought. 'This is great. I've got an audience participation number, which I've always wanted.' The *Abbey Road* medley, which closed the album, was suggested for this tour by our keyboards player and when we were rehearsing it, one of my old mates, who manages my studio, had to excuse himself. He started crying because it brought back so many memories. He was there when we recorded it, twenty years ago.

"Originally we were going to open with 'I Saw Her Standing There' but I got really upset by the idea. I was going home one night and I thought, 'That's really betraying our new material, sending it right down the line.' It's the obvious thing, boom, bang, Beatles, Beatles. Then you say, 'Now we'd like to do some new material.' Boo! Hiss! I've seen The Rolling Stones try and do it and it doesn't go down that great. Even with The Beatles, our new material didn't always go down that well. It was the older tunes that the crowds preferred. 'Baby's In Black' never went down nearly as well as 'I Feel Fine' or 'She Loves You'. That's just the nature of the beast. So when I was compiling a list of songs for these shows, I'd get in a certain mood and scratch songs that evoked a lot of pain. But ultimately I tried to unselfishly amass a set of songs that my fans would want to hear. For the first time in years, I played some Beatles tunes. I shied away from them at the time of The Beatles' break-up and decided to do just Wings stuff. But now I've decided that enough water has gone under the bridge. I like those songs still and there is a mass of great stuff to choose from. Once all the songs had fallen into place, we thought, 'Are we going to have an army of backing singers?' But we decided to keep it to just the six of us. 'Got To Get You Into My Life' would have sounded cool with a horn section, but we made a decision to keep it as just the six."

'The Fool On The Hill'

Paul "That song sums up how it (The Beatles) ended, in my mind. We had it all and sometimes I think we never even realised it. It happened so quickly that four sets of egos practically grew overnight, and I think there's a piece of each of us recognisable as that fool on the hill. I believe that if we had stayed honest with each other and committed to one another, like we were when we started, that things might have turned out differently . . . When I wrote 'The Fool On The Hill', the idea for me was always just someone who's got the right answer, but people tend to ridicule him. Whether he's a little guy in a cave at the top of the hill, whether he's an activist and so I was looking for a speech from someone like that. And I think that probably the greatest recorded speech in that vein is the Martin Luther King speech. It is so moving and so dramatic and we found that it fitted exactly the piece of music. So it's great. It's a stirring thing to put in."

'PS Love Me Do'

Paul "We did a version of that in Japan and we dropped it. I didn't like it that much. It was okay, but we weren't that wild on it and we put 'Birthday' in instead and we liked that better."

Reporter on tour, "You never played several Beatles classics, like 'Hey Jude' and 'Sgt. Pepper', prior to this tour. In fact, in the past, you hinted that you would never play these songs again."

Paul "Well, those things and things like 'I Want To Hold Your Hand' are really fresh to me again, probably because I've never played them out live."

Ringo jokingly announces to a UK reporter, "I would have no problems now about seeing a Paul McCartney concert. Paul always puts on a good show and, after all, I taught him everything he knows."

Paul "I never really meant to be political. My main thing is just to be a musician but when we started this tour, this big hole appeared over the Antarctic, this big 50-mile hole and it worries people. Obviously, most people you meet are worried about it . . . I also feel very optimistic about it and I feel that we are going to turn it around."

Sunday, October 1

There's tabloid scandal afoot when the reporter Alan Shadrake writes, "Ringo Starr has secretly paid out nearly £250,000 in 'hush money' to his former lover to stop her revealing the truth about his excessive boozing and drug taking. The deal, thought to be Hollywood's biggest ever palimony payout, was agreed when girlfriend of seven years, Nancy Leigh Andrews, threatened to sue him. The money was paid in annual instalments over an eight-year period after an initial payment of £90,000. The final cheque for £18,000 was handed over earlier this year. Former actress, Nancy, was furious at being abruptly dropped by the ex-Beatle for her friend, 'James Bond' star, Barbara Bach . . . Nancy admitted she was alarmed at Ringo's drug and drink problems when they lived together. 'I feared for his health. The body can take only so much and I was afraid it was going to kill him,' she announces. 'I suggested he go into a clinic or just get away from everything and go camping in the desert.' "

Tuesday, October 3
Macca's world tour rolls on . . .

Syndicated press release "Green loving Paul McCartney has been hit by a walkout of four of his tour team, after he tried to ban them from eating meat. The Texans quit his American Friends Of The Earth Tour because they can't stomach a daily diet of veggie burgers and greens. The £100 a day riggers were hired to set up his stage equipment in American cities next month. A spokesman said of the deserters, 'Texans ought to be a little more adventurous rather than just eating hamburgers. Paul's not worried. There's no shortage of people wanting to join this tour. If the Texans had tried the food, they'd have discovered that the caterers can make excellent sausage rolls, burgers and chilli *non carne*, without meat.' "

Friday, October 20
The continued mis-use of The Beatles' back catalogue forces Paul to blast at Michael Jackson . . .

Syndicated press release "Superstar Paul McCartney is fuming after he failed to stop Michael Jackson selling permission for a Beatles' classic to be used in an advert. Paul has been quietly battling for six months to stop the 1967 hit 'All You Need Is Love' being featured in a 60-second advert for Panasonic cameras. Paul wrote a strongly worded letter to his one-time pal begging him not to devalue the music of the Fab Four. But Jacko, 31, who now owns the best Beatles songs, decided to pocket the staggering £150,000 fee from admen Saatchi & Saatchi. He has made just one concession by ordering Panasonic to use the music for a mere 45-seconds. Macca stormed, 'It's disgusting. The Beatles never allowed their songs to be used in adverts because we believed our music would be cheapened.' "

Sunday, October 22

UK reporter, Annette Witheridge "Potty pop moguls aim to bask in the sweet smell of success, by flogging Paul McCartney's perspiration. They collect the drops that fall from the ex-Beatle's brow during a concert, can them and sell them at £8 a time. The nifty notion was floated last week when sixty girls fainted during a wild concert by McCartney. The mass collapse was triggered by Paul flicking sweat from his face and hair into the crowd clustered in front of the stage in Paris last week. Suddenly a Marseilles businessman in the audience had a grand idea. And at the end of the show, he and a group of associates approached McCartney's aides to ask about merchandising rights. An organiser of Paul's current world tour said afterwards, 'They want to can his sweat and reckon they'll make a bomb. God knows how they'll collect it. They'll probably have to stand at the front holding up buckets.' It is not the first time that McCartney's natural functions have been exploited for cash. Twenty-five years ago, American entrepreneurs sold canned Beatles breath . . ."

Thursday, November 2
Paul and his band reach Spain . . .

Paul "There are a lot of words to remember in a two-hour show and I must admit, some of them elude me, occasionally. I was in Europe, in Spain and I had two funny incidents, where I got it right and they, the audience, got it right and they know it better than me. They really know these records, where maybe I haven't heard them for the past twenty years, and there was this girl in the audience and I was doing 'I Saw Her Standing There' and I saw her sing 'I'll never dance with a number.' So I thought, 'Right, I've got this one, that's one up for me.' I was doing that one right."

Wednesday, November 8
There's some good news on The Beatles front when Paul, George and Ringo call a halt to their long-running legal wrangle over record royalties . . .

David Wigg, the *Daily Express* "The music world eagerly awaited a new Beatles era last night after the three surviving stars called an end to their argument over royalties. They settled a rift, which began nine years ago, when it was revealed that Paul McCartney had signed an individual deal with Capitol Records, which guaranteed him extra cash from the Fab Four recordings. George Harrison, Ringo Starr, McCartney and John Lennon's widow, Yoko Ono, yesterday decided to give peace a chance when they reached a secret deal and abandoned all lawsuits between them and their companies. As the decision was announced, speculation began in music circles that the three superstars might re-form for special concerts . . ."

Paul "There are a lot of exciting possibilities with George and Ringo. We might even write some new music. George and I have never written together, which is a staggering fact. We could even finally do *The Long And Winding Road,* our documentary movie on The Beatles' story and set the record straight."

On the secret agreement reached between all concerned parties, EMI's spokesman, Bhaskar Menon, announces, "The parties have agreed as a term of the settlement, that no one would be permitted to make any comment on the deal. The Beatles' recordings are a unique legacy in the history of popular music, which EMI has been privileged to represent since 1962. We are most delighted to have resolved all the differences that arose between us in recent years, and looking forward to the continuation of our long-standing and close relationship with the artists and Apple."

Friday, November 10

The *Daily Express* "In the same week in which he resolved his nine-year legal differences with George Harrison, and Ringo Starr, Paul McCartney has a new fight on his hands, to stop the illegal distribution of bootleg tapes of Beatles songs he sang in Italy recently. As in the rest of Europe, it is illegal to record rock concerts in Italy. However, Italy's muddled laws make it perfectly legal to mass-produce and sell any tape recorded in this way, provided the song is more than twenty years old. Italian bootleggers couldn't believe their luck when McCartney sang a batch of Beatles hits, including 'The Fool On The Hill', for the first time since the Fab Four broke up in 1970. Our man in Rome said, 'The bootleggers had a field day. Backstreet tape-copying plants are churning out copies as fast as they can. Beatles fans are snapping them up at £3 a time and it's legal.' Ironically, McCartney will get a share of the loot as the Italian Performing Rights Society looks after its artists and collects a percentage from each of the bootleg tape sales. But the Italian division of the international record labels doesn't like it one bit because they get nothing. There is little hope of McCartney's fans in Britain getting hold of copies of the tapes, despite the continuing move towards the free exchange of goods between European Community countries, unless, of course, you hop on a plane to Rome. 'Once these tapes entered Britain, their sale would be governed by Britain's copyright laws and they'd be illegal,' says a spokesman for the ever-alert, British Phonographic Industry's anti-piracy unit. 'You could only bring a copy back for personal use.' "

Paul's second leg of American concerts begins in Los Angeles at the Los Angeles Coliseum on **Thursday, November 23**, where a host of top celebrities are in attendance. Their verdict on Paul's performance?

Actor, Jack Nicholson "It was one hell of a concert. I've never seen anything like it. McCartney is the ultimate performer. When I heard 'Jet' and 'Live And Let Die' in the same hour, I wanted to die."

Singer, Stevie Wonder, who took to the stage for a duet with Paul on 'Ebony And Ivory', remarks, "McCartney is and always will be the best in the business. The old songs like 'Let It Be' and 'Sgt. Pepper' brought back some great memories."

Actor, Tom Hanks "I was a Beatles fan but I never saw them live so this was a show I couldn't miss. 'Back In The USSR' was the best number for me."

Singer and Paul's former friend and collaborator, Michael Jackson, "Wow! I had a good, good time. Paul is a great friend and his show proved that he is one of the world's best performers."

Actress, Raquel Welch "Paul may be 47 but he is still one of the sexiest men in rock. I loved every minute of the show. 'Hey Jude' was out of this world."

An unusual string of incidents resulting from Paul's decision to include classic Beatles tunes in his repertoire is that passionate pop followers are caught making love in the aisles while Paul is on stage belting out his classic songs. One of Paul's security guards remarks, "We spotted the randy couples after bouncers pounced on cameramen who were making pirate videos of the concerts. When we replayed their tapes, we found couples who were really going at it during the show. There's always been a bit of snogging and petting at shows but recently, in Florida, fans started getting very, very intimate. We're amazed. It seems that all those Beatles songs from the Summer Of Love have a strange effect. The fans seem to get overcome by the music and then, the next thing you know, they're making love in the aisles."

Monday, November 27

In New York, the VISA credit card corporation announces that it has signed a multi-million dollar contract with Paul, meaning that they will sponsor his 1990 American Tour. Besides paying him an undisclosed seven-figure sum, the company will spend $8.5 (£5.4) million on television advertising promoting Paul's concerts . . .

The Times newspaper writes, "Ten years ago, the notion of a Sixties icon allowing himself to be used in credit card commercials would have been deemed a sell-out. But McCartney is a fairly late arrival in the business of celebrity sponsorship. He was beaten to the act by Mr Ronald Reagan, who has just completed a promotional tour of Japan for the Fujisankei Corporation for a fee of $2 million. And, for the past three weeks, Mrs Nancy Reagan has been touring the country to promote her book. But under his contract, McCartney, who has never appeared in an advertisement, will not have to endorse the credit card directly and he will not have to sing about it. The commercials will make clear, however, that Visa is the only card that ticket-sellers will accept."

Paul "Someone said to me, 'But The Beatles were anti-materialistic.' Well, that's just a huge myth. John and I used to sit down and say, 'Now, let's write a swimming pool.' We said it out of innocence. Out of our normal, working-class glee, we were able to write a swimming pool. For the first time in our lives, we could actually do something and earn money. Anyway, I don't believe any person, whether he's a businessman or not, would turn down millions of dollars just to be associated with a name. I'm actually very flattered that VISA thinks so much of Paul McCartney and his band's tour that they would back us. If VISA want to film us, show the tour, show me getting in and out of limos and then talk about their card without me ever turning round to the viewer and saying, 'Yes, this card,' then I'm happy. The money that VISA puts into the tour allows us keep ticket prices at a reasonable rate. If people aren't perceptive enough to understand that, I guess I don't care."

New Year's Eve, **Sunday, December 31**

George recalls the evening on the dawn of a new decade . . . "I was watching the moon," he recalls. "It was actually a Blue Moon on New Year's Eve and I was in the Pacific on an island and I saw the moon come up out of the ocean and I just watched that. I had the flu at the time so I didn't have a big party this year."

1990

JANUARY...

Paul "The Nineties are going to be the time when people finally realise that we've got to clean this world up. The Nineties are going to be the time when we do it in order to have a clean 21st century. That's my wish, anyway."

Tuesday, January 2
Paul's world tour reaches the UK with a string of sold-out concerts beginning at the NEC in Birmingham. Covering the opening show is *The Times'* rock columnist, Steve Turner...

"The Paul McCartney who returned to the British stage was the Paul McCartney many have longed for years to see," Turner writes. "In a 29-song set, lasting two-and-a-half-hours, he took the audience through hits that had inspired him as a teenager, Beatles songs that inspired a generation and the best of his own recent work. With a crack, five-piece band recruited for *Flowers In The Dirt*, a stunning light show and the most elaborate staging he has ever used, McCartney managed to turn the 12,000-seat auditorium into a huge party. 'It's good to be back in Britain,' he said after singing 'Band On The Run'. 'It's dead good. Hope you all let your hair down, have some fun and get groovy.' And groovy they got. They got out of their seats for Beatles stompers like 'I Saw Her Standing There' and 'Can't Buy Me Love', swayed their arms to 'Let It Be' and sang along to 'Hey Jude'. The fact that a few coachloads of McCartney's relatives were down from Liverpool added to the feeling of celebration. Every now and then he would spot a familiar face and up would go the thumbs. 'Live And Let Die' was dedicated to his cousin, 'A wonderful old lady who is 57 today.' During the concert there were fifteen Beatles songs, over half of which The Beatles never played in concert. 'We are going to go back to a land they call the Sixties,' he said as he sat down at a psychedelically painted piano to play 'The Long And Winding Road'. 'The Fool On The Hill' was dedicated to 'My mates, George, Ringo and John, without whom I would not have been here.' Paul McCartney must have one of the best-loved back catalogues of any living musician and to hear him play through it can only be a privilege. A splendid time was had by all."

Another most favourable review of the NEC's opening show is written by the UK music reporter, Jack Jasper, "Beatlemania is back, whipped up by Paul McCartney. His 29-number set, a triumphant trip down memory lane proved that, at 47, he is even better now than he was in his Beatles days. There is no doubt that McCartney's voice is stronger, deeper and more soulful than it was first time around. The sell-out 12,000 crowd at Birmingham's NEC Arena, split between Paul's middle-aged contemporaries and teenagers, obviously agreed with me that Macca is magic. This will be remembered as one of the great shows of the Nineties, I promise you. Mums old enough to remember the Fab Four's heyday linked arms and screamed along with their daughters, some young enough to call McCartney granddad. The mums borrowed mini-skirts from their daughters to bring back their fab memories of The Beatles years. And dads, who haven't worn their winkle-pickers for 25 years, donned their flares, paisley shirts and caftans again and rocked in the isles like teenagers. Age didn't matter as McCartney rock'n'rolled his way through a scintillating two-hour set of his classic hits. He announced 'Got To Get You Into My Life' as 'something we made up in the cab down here, which we thought we would try out on you.' He was loving every minute of it and so were we. I don't mind admitting that McCartney's rendering of 'Let It Be' tore into my tear ducts. He followed with 'Hey Jude', 'Yesterday' and ended a memorable night with a brilliant Abbey Road medley. As he left the stage to tumultuous cheers, McCartney turned and punched the air. It had been a magical evening. Forget a Beatles reunion. This was it."

Sunday, January 7

Meanwhile, back in the States, there is news of Ringo's Atlanta court hearing against the record producer, Chips Moman . . .

The *Sunday Mirror* newspaper reports "Ringo Starr was yesterday counting the £46,000 cost of keeping his own record out of the shops. The ex-Beatle took legal action to block the release of an LP recorded before he swore off alcohol. He said the songs were substandard because of his boozing. Now, a judge in Atlanta, Georgia, has ordered Ringo to pay record producer Chips Moman the cost of the recording sessions plus seven per cent interest. The album included new songs and several oldies, including 'I Can Help' and 'Ain't That A Shame'. Moman told the judge that Bob Dylan made a guest appearance on one song. But Ringo blocked the LP's release after listening to the tapes. He later admitted that he and his actress wife, Barbara Bach, were being treated for drink problems. Though Ringo claimed he owed nothing for the recording, his lawyer said he was happy with the court's £46,000 ruling. Moman, who had demanded more than £90,000 from the ex-Beatle, may now appeal."

Paul, Linda and his band's string of British concerts continue at the Empire Pool in Wembley on **Thursday, January 11**. Following the opening night's concert, a review of the show appears in the respected *Financial Times*, where Antony Thorncroft writes . . .

"The easiest way to judge the impact of a concert is not to watch the audience, they are usually hopelessly uncritical fanatics, but the attendants and bouncers manning the barricades. For the first of Paul McCartney's ten nights at the Wembley Arena they were having a whale of a time, singing their hearts out to 'I Saw Her Standing There' and 'Get Back'. They gave their insiders thumbs up, Paulie's show was just about the most professional seen at the place in years . . ."

Monday, January 29

On the strength of Paul's successful concert tours, a syndicated news report appears, revealing that "Pop superstar Paul McCartney was fuming over a bizarre bid to revive his Sixties supergroup, The Beatles. This scheme is Cynthia Lennon's brainchild and she wants her son, Julian, to stand in for John. Now Cynthia, 47, has put together a band to play a one-off concert to nudge the surviving Beatles closer to a get-together. She is so keen to see son Julian, 26, perform with Paul, George and Ringo that she has already booked her new line-up to play for thousands at Berlin's Brandenburg Gate in April. Apparently she has approached Pink Floyd to act as support and even requested official United Nations letters to present to the remaining Beatles, demanding that they reform in the interest of world peace. A UN spokesman said, 'We have heard of this scheme but we're sceptical about The Beatles' contribution to world peace.' "

Paul, halfway through his successful world tour, is quick to defuse the latest reunion rumours, "I am furious about this. Julian is a nice boy but not in the same league as John. John is irreplaceable and without him, there can never be a Beatles again."

Yoko is also quick to join in on the story, announcing through her spokesman, "This is in the worst possible taste."

But Cynthia is unrepentant, "I don't feel I'm exploiting the Lennon name," she says. "Once Mrs Lennon, always Mrs Lennon. My heart is in rock'n'roll and always will be."

Thursday, February 1
The next leg of Paul's American Tour kicks off with shows at The Palace of Auburn Hills, near Detroit in Michigan . . .

Paul "Even when the European shows had gone great, I'd be saying, 'We can't let up, guys. America's a whole different game. We can't relax yet.' But then we cracked America together, and I was proud, because, in the end, there was only ever just the six of us on that stage. We didn't have any troupe of dancers or a massive brass section. It was just us six. Six of the best."

Monday, February 5
While Paul's World Tour is playing to packed-out crowds, John and Ringo's former home in Ascot, Berkshire, Tittenhurst Park, again figures in the news, predominantly revealing who the mystery buyer was . . .

Syndicated news report "While Ringo Starr vowed never to reveal to whom he sold his Berkshire mansion nearly two years ago, the buyer has failed to keep the secret. The man now spending £40 million as he turns John Lennon's original home, the seventeen-bedroom Tittenhurst Park, in Sunninghill, into a palace is Sheikh Zayed bin Sultan, the ruler of Abu Dhabi and President of the United Arab Emirates. However, the Sheikh has incurred the wrath of neighbours as builders work day and night to create his 'Arabian Nights romanticism'. Once completed, the property will have an underground pleasure-dome and a pool with bulletproof walls. That will not be as soon as Zayed had hoped. Noisy weekend work has been banned. As one of the neighbour's sniffs, 'Ringo never made a whisper.' "

Wednesday, February 21
There's further glory for Paul this evening at the Shrine Auditorium in Los Angeles . . .

Mike Hartley, *LA News* correspondent, "Paul McCartney stole the show at the annual Grammy awards ceremony in Los Angeles tonight. All those hard days' nights paid off for the ex-Beatle when he was given a Lifetime Achievement Award for 25 years of hits. Film star, Meryl Streep, who presented the trophy to Paul, confessed during the ceremony that she had carried a sign, which said, 'I love you forever, Paul' when she went to a Beatles concert in 1965. 'But,' joked the star, 'I don't think he noticed it.' Paul replied, 'I remember you well, Meryl, in row 116. You looked great, even then.' Accepting his award,

Paul made an emotional speech to the celebrity filled audience. 'I've got to take this opportunity to thank John, George and Ringo for being beautiful people,' he said. The speech sparked fresh rumours that the remaining Beatles may still get back together again . . ."

Friday, April 20
Paul's World Tour reaches Rio in Brazil, where they play sell-out concerts at the Maracanã Stadium in front of the highest ever recorded attendance, beating Frank Sinatra's previous figure . . .

Hamish Stuart "It was the biggest crowd that any of us had ever played to. In fact it was the biggest crowd that anybody had ever played to. After that, I think the whole band hit another level of performing. We got the same sort of buzz off the crowd in Liverpool . . ."

Robbie McIntosh "The most emotional night was in Rio. I think I was close to tears that night. Usually I feel quite happy when I come off stage but that night was a different sort of happy. I think it got to me because nobody really goes to play there. It's only in the last few years that name bands have started going to Brazil and when we played, you could really feel a lot of gratification. Those people thought the world of us for going and playing there, a place where living conditions are appalling. That whole feeling of them giving this big thank you was very emotional."

But there's trouble afoot in Brazil when Paul nearly drowns when a force nine gale batters his tiny sailing boat whilst sailing in the waters off the coast of Rio de Janeiro . . .

Paul "I was sailing alone off Copacabana Beach in my tiny little boat when a huge gale whipped up a large wave and capsized my hired Laser craft. My boat actually went over. My two minders in a nearby powerboat watched helplessly as their own craft was repeatedly smashed by waves. I still managed to control my boat and struggled back to shore."

Paul's loyal assistant, John Hammel "Paul often goes sailing alone whenever the band visits a city near a coast. He's an absolute fanatic. Linda hardly ever goes out with him and nor do the band, unless he's got hold of a bigger boat. Paul's a very good sailor. He's into all that Boy's Own stuff. When we were in Indiana, he went out on a huge lake alone. I'm sure he was winding up everyone on the shore because he capsized four times, righting the boat four times. But this time, it was for real. He might not think it was dangerous but we all knew full well how bad it was."

Saturday, May 5
A special day-long memorial cum charity music concert takes place in Liverpool at the Pier Head, honouring what would have been John's 50th birthday. Both Paul and Ringo contribute, via video clips, separate musical offerings but, as expected, **George** is conspicuous by his absence . . .

"I don't think John would want it," he explains, "and I don't want to keep dabbling in the past. Personally, I've made a pact with myself not to get involved in anything to do with ex-Beatles. The Beatles ceased to exist in 1969. They meant whatever they did to various people across the world and it was fun at the time, but it has affected the rest of our lives.

The very nature of our success got in the way of me being a musician. I suffered for years as a guitarist. Let sleeping dogs lie."

Thursday, June 28

Paul's World Tour reaches the UK with performances in Glasgow, subtitled *Get Back To Glasgow* and Liverpool, in a show called *Let It Be Liverpool*, which takes place at the King's Dock . . .

Just weeks before the Liverpool show, **Paul** says, "I'm convinced I'll start crying once I'm up there. It'll be a struggle to keep from weeping. Going back to Liverpool is going to be a very emotional experience for me because the people there matter so much. Times like this really choke me up. It's not just the fans who get affected by some of those songs. They move me too. 'Hey Jude' is a bit of a choker at times because it always reminds me of John and singing it in Liverpool is going to remind me of John a whole lot more. 'Put It There' can be a bit of a tear-jerker, too, because it's about my father and I'll be thinking of him too in Liverpool."

Ray Johnston of Cavern City Tours, the Liverpool-based Beatles tourist organisation who are helping to promote Paul's concert, "I had been promoting the gig for the past three weeks and I had recruited a team of girls and took them all over the north of England. I dropped them off with posters and flyers and basically I went back at the end of the day and picked them up again. We spent three weeks doing that in a hired car paid for by MPL. We went round the major department stores in Liverpool, Manchester, Wigan etc., persuading radio and TV departments to play this looped video MPL had made. Another part of my job was to contact the local charities we thought were of a worthy cause and try and distribute a number of tickets for Paul's show. I used the car all the time and I accidentally wrote it off a week before the show. On the day of the concert, that was, in fact, the first time I had got to meet Paul. We were told that when he arrives, we were to keep out of the way and not to approach him in any way. But it was by pure accident that I got to meet him. When Paul arrived at the King's Dock for the show, and was getting out of his car to walk towards his dressing room, I was actually walking out of his dressing room at the same time. I was helping put the room together on behalf of Ray Edwards of Marshall Arts, the promoter, and as I walked out, I thought, 'Oh shit, here's Paul,' and all I said to him was, 'Welcome back. Macca. Nice to see ya.' He looked at me and said, 'A Scouse voice at last.' I said, 'What do you mean?' And he said, 'My God, I've been all over the world for the last eighteen months, touring with an American crew, and I come back home and the first person to speak to me is a Scouser!' So I said, 'Well, nice.' We got chatting and then I got really cheeky, saying, 'Well, Paul, I'm a Beatles guy, I drive the *Magical Mystery Tour* bus and it's actually the first time that I've got to meet a real-life Beatle, is there any chance of a photograph?' And he said, 'Why not?' So luckily I had a camera with me and Paul put his arm around my shoulder. We were about to have a photo taken when Paul said, 'Hold on a minute,' and shouted, 'Linda, come and get in this one.' So Linda came over and he introduced me to her and she was so charming. I fell in love with her there and then. She was just so friendly. We took the photograph and I asked Paul to sign the back of my access pass, which he did. I said, 'Thanks, have a good gig,' and he said, 'Thanks, see you later.' "

Two hours before the show, Paul faces another press conference . . .

Reporter, William Leith, "These days, a Paul McCartney press conference is a simple matter. Paul appears, everybody claps, Paul bows, feigning embarrassment, and sits down . . ." During the get-together with Press, Paul tells of his project for a talent school in Liverpool . . . " 'I don't wanna be some J. Paul Getty character and just wave a magic wand,' Paul says. 'I just want to see if we can get it up and running.' A reporter asks, 'Will you be teaching at the school?' To which, Paul replies, 'Well, not exactly teaching. I'll probably just come along with me guitar and say sort of, me hand goes about there and I kind of hold it like that. You see, I can't read a note of music.' "

Paul's concert at the King's Dock is a great success . . .

Paul "We were playing at the Docks, by the banks of the River Mersey where we had played around as kids."

UK columnists Gill Pringle and David Hancock "The rainy, miserable day had given way to perfect sunshine. Clouds scudded across a pale blue sky . . . and Paul McCartney was back in Liverpool. To Scousers, he is more than just a pop star who made it to the top. He's the one who took the whole city along with him. Now Liverpool's most famous son was home again for the first time in eleven years. And, as if on cue, the words almost leapt from the lyrics of The Beatles hit, 'A Hard Day's Night', 'When I'm home, everything seems to be right.'

" 'People of Liverpool, welcome to the banks of the Mersey,' Paul roared as he took the stage for what was to be an evening of nostalgia for 40,000 fans packed into the King's Dock. And, as if desperate to make up for the clumsy John Lennon tribute staged by Yoko Ono last month, the Scousers welcomed him in real style. Huge banners outside city pubs screamed 'Welcome Home, Paul'. Juke boxes played Beatles tunes non-stop. Local radio blasted tributes all day. Paul already holds the key to the city and this homecoming seemed to unlock the people's hearts. They all knew that Liverpool was going to be an occasion but even he must have been startled by the mountain of goodwill he received."

" 'People of Liverpool, welcome,' and he was off, the city's most famous son," writes Spencer Bright of the *Daily Mail*. "It has been a long time since Paul McCartney has played in his home town. He says he pays regular visits but he hasn't performed in Liverpool since 1979 with his group, Wings. Now, as the sun set in a clear blue sky, McCartney looked as though he had truly come home. He had a big grin on his face. He looked satisfied, youthful and somehow even taller. The concert, proceeds of which are going towards the setting up of a Liverpool Fame school and several other charities, was held in a specially constructed arena at the King's Dock. It kicked off with a film that spanned The Beatles years up to the present. Paul and his band appeared in matching clean-cut khaki jackets and launched into 'Figure Of Eight' from the current *Flowers In The Dirt* album. But, inevitably, the star numbers were The Beatles' hits. He played 'The Fool On The Hill' sitting at a psychedelically decorated piano that raised him ten feet in the air. Then came 'Sgt. Pepper'. He stormed through it . . .' "

Gill Pringle and David Hancock " 'I'd like to dedicate this next song to three mates of mine, John, George and Ringo,' he said with typical understatement. 'The Fool On The Hill' saw his piano rise ten foot in the air as it spun round, splashing coloured lights over the heads of his audience. 'Back In The USSR' raised the tempo and 'Sgt Pepper' raised the roof as a spectacular fireworks sky burst over the Mersey."

Ray Johnston "I couldn't have wished for a better view of the Liverpool gig. I stood right at the side of the stage. We had no idea that he was going to do the Lennon tribute. Even in the soundcheck that afternoon, I don't recall him playing any of the songs he played that night. He was messing around with tracks like 'Hit The Road, Jack' and stuff like that. It was a surprisingly short soundcheck. The night before the concert, Paul was checking the PA, so most of the work had been done then. Incidentally, during the soundcheck on the day of Paul's show, one of my jobs was to keep Paul and Linda's son, James, occupied. So I was told to go and buy him a remote-controlled boat. And when I brought it back to the King's Dock, the motor of the remote control was interfering with the security guys' walkie-talkies, so he was told to stop using it for a while."

Spencer Bright "Was this concert history? It will probably be talked about as one of the great moments in his career. During the show Paul paid tribute to his former colleague, John . . ."

Paul "We wanted to do something by way of a nod to John, you know, because he was my best mate. We knew the people of Liverpool would relate to it. Originally I was going to get up there with an acoustic, all on my own, but I thought, 'Maybe that's a little too precious,' so I wanted to include the band because they all wanted to be in on the tribute. So we just did a little medley of three songs that meant a lot to us, and which said John to us. We did it and it went down great. We enjoyed doing it so much that we kept it in our act. In Liverpool, the people wouldn't stop singing. We finished with 'Give Peace A Chance' and I thought this was really brilliant, you know. It was ten years after John's death and people were putting their fingers up, singing 'Give Peace A Chance'. I think that's really important."

Gill Pringle and David Hancock "Try as he might, Paul just couldn't stop the audience chanting 'Give Peace A Chance', the words as poignant today as they were when Lennon wrote them. In the end, he had to give in to the crowds who wanted to sing. And they did, until they were hoarse. Fighting back tears, McCartney moved into a different era then, the Seventies, belting out his *James Bond* theme, 'Live And Let Die' accompanied by a spectacular laser and fireworks show. Time has been kind to Paul. At 48, he has a few grey hairs and his face is a little chubby, but Scouse wit has stopped him taking himself too seriously."

Spencer Bright "McCartney did not attend Yoko Ono's tribute in Liverpool last month. He only appeared there in video form. That had been a limp, artistically uneven affair. But this concert really felt as though the spirit of The Beatles was present. Liverpool is unlikely to see anything like it again . . ."

JULY

Robert Sandall of the *Sunday Times* asks George about Paul's recent suggestion that he and George should get together to write songs. It produces a frosty response . . . "He's left it a bit late, is all I can say," **George** replies. "I'm enriched with Bob Dylan, Tom Petty and Jeff Lynne, The Traveling Wilburys, and I don't see any reason to go back to an old situation."

Wednesday, July 4
Paul's band performs a Fourth of July concert in Washington DC . . .

Hamish Stuart "That was incredible! We'd learnt up 'Birthday' for that show and I remember all those cheers as Paul intro-ed, saying, 'Hey America, they say it's your birthday.'"

At a press conference in Washington, **Paul** takes the opportunity to reply to George's recent anti-Beatles reunion blast . . .

"I heard that George said that there won't be a Beatles reunion. But I mean, as far as we're concerned, there *can't* be a Beatles reunion because John died and that was The Beatles. I don't think any of us would be interested in substituting someone for John, even Julian, which has been suggested. It wouldn't be The Beatles. It wouldn't be a Beatles reunion. So I think that is what George was talking about. But there is a film that we might get round to in a couple of years, which we have been meaning to do and there might be some involvement there, where we might play together, me, George and Ringo. But we wouldn't call it The Beatles, but *you* probably would."

Tuesday, July 24
Paul's World Tour is almost at an end. Backstage at the Sullivan Stadium in Foxboro in Massachusetts, the music reporter Kevin Connal interviews Paul following another successful show . . .

Connal "How have the crowds changed in thirteen years?"

Paul "It's not that different, really. There is still that state of pandemonium in the arenas and stadiums. The one difference is that now I'm seeing kids, moms, dads and grandfolk. In the early Beatles years, it often seemed like we were the mums' and dads' worst headaches!"

Connal "How bad did things get between you and John Lennon when The Beatles broke up?"

Paul "Wouldn't you rather talk about the new record now? One more time I'll say it. We were a team, and teams sometimes fight amongst themselves. And then other times, teams are broken up. I was living there in London in the mid-Sixtiess during the artsy period when the Indica Gallery and that whole community was thriving. I was into it to a point but didn't think it was the whole world's business. Then John got into it and as usual his excessiveness took over – thus the love-in thing with Yoko and all the media overkill that attracted."

Connal "Will you ever reunite with George Harrison and Ringo Starr?"

Paul "What's it matter what I think about that? George has taken the liberty of answering that question with shocking regularity for you media guys. He's had a field day getting publicity from his negative responses. So, obviously, it's never going to happen, no matter what I think."

Connal "What are your thoughts on Michael Jackson's purchase of much of your publishing catalogue?"

Paul "Obviously I was not very thrilled. But that's all I care to say on the record about that sore subject."

Connal "As the tour progresses, you've become more and more persistent in mentioning, during shows, the disintegrating world environment. Has anything in particular prompted this, or is it a combination of factors that you see going on around you?"

Paul "I guess the Exxon oil spill in Alaska stimulated my involvement more than anything. I've got four children and I want to help save this planet for them, and for many generations beyond them. I think it was a total joke the way that Exxon 'cleaned up'. It's still a mess up there. They've got crude oil seeped two feet below the rocks on the beaches. So I've become involved with an organisation called Friends Of The Earth. They are out to clean up the planet, eliminate toxic wastes, and stop acid rain, issues like that. By mentioning it from the stage every night, I'm trying to create an awareness to get as many people as possible involved."

Pundits continue describing Paul as "the self-appointed torch-bearer of The Beatles' legacy". Passing through Massachusetts at this time is George, prompting a question to him as to whether he could be persuaded to see his former colleague in performance . . . **George** swipes back, "I saw The Beatles. Why would I want to go and see a man pretending to be The Beatles? I suppose somebody's got to do it. I'm just glad it's not me."

On **Sunday, July 29**, Paul's World Tour concludes at Soldier Field in Chicago . . . "We had a few options of where to finish the tour," Paul announces, "and this was the most exiting. I always liked Chicago. It's one of my cities."

. . . And faces the mandatory press conference . . .

Reporter "What's next for you?"

Paul "I don't know that you follow it up. But I do know that you keep trying to go forward. I'd like to make another album before too long. I actually enjoyed making *Flowers In The Dirt* and I think it showed. It was my best record in recent memory. For the immediate future, I've been working on a classical project with the British conductor, Carl Davis, that I'm very excited about. It's due to be performed by the Liverpool Philharmonic Orchestra in the Liverpool Cathedral at their 150th anniversary celebration in 1991."

Reporter "Are you going to tour again?"

Paul "Yeah, quite possibly. Being that this is a big tour on the heels of The Stones, people tend to think, 'Oh, this is bound to be his last tour, you know.' And my great venerable age would suggest this kind of thing but I've had a great time on this tour. The band has got better and better, we're putting a live album out from this tour, we've got a film, and then we'll make a new studio album. And I'd like to think that, after that, we'll come back on tour."

Reporter "What is the latest on The Beatles' film *The Long And Winding Road*?"

Paul "Well, *The Long And Winding Road* is a film that we, The Beatles, have been trying to make for a long time, because everybody else makes films about us and people write books about us and they are, basically, not correct. They get a bunch of facts and then screw them all up and make a sensational book, which probably sells quite well. So, *The Long And Winding Road* is going to be an attempt to put the story straight, you know. The story of The Beatles, that we could, maybe, narrate over it."

Reporter "What about the BBC tapes and any other unreleased Beatles tapes?"

Paul "The BBC tapes will be getting released at some point. These will be the radio shows we used to do in England called *Pop Go The Beatles*. We did a deal recently so that will be released at some point and there are a couple of other tracks, but there isn't an awful lot lying around, because we were very tidy. I'm not too keen on them because they were tapes we rejected, you know, and it's like pulling out old articles you did that the editor turned down and releasing them. It doesn't make any sense to me. But, maybe there is some good stuff, you know."

Linda, Hamish and **Paul** reflect on the World Tour . . .

"Looking back, I'm heartened at just how much this tour achieved," she announces. "Not just with Paul taking his music to so many people, but there were other successes too. For instance, Paul and I are vegetarians and this was rock and roll's first ever fully vegetarian tour. We went all around the world without eating flesh, spreading the message of kindness to animals and I think it paid off. People actually listened. The press made a big thing of this huge veggie tour coming to town and that made some people think better about animals. I think this tour did a lot to raise the image of being veggie. We showed it's not cranky to be vegetarian. In fact, it's very rock and roll to be vegetarian now. The other big achievement was how the tour made a stand on behalf of the planet. We wanted to do something, do some good, so we linked up with Friends Of The Earth to spread the message that we need to Save The Planet. Every night on stage, Paul would make this little speech about saving the planet and the great thing was that, whatever country we were playing in, the messages hit home. The roars from the crowd told you that."

Hamish Stuart "I think people came away from the shows wrapped up in a good feeling. That was what the shows were all about. It is like what Paul said about having a party."

Paul "We started off the tour thinking it would be a good idea to support people like Friends Of The Earth and we're supporting them basically through the whole tour. All we've been doing is bringing publicity to the issues. I'm not an expert and Friends Of The Earth have got a lot of new members. The kinds of things I've noticed are when I see a kid who says, 'I just did a class lecture to all my school friends and I used your programme to get all the facts.' It's having some effect . . . In Rio we saw more than Lambadaring going on. It's very interesting but they're a very hot-blooded race over there. During 'Let It Be' we've seen couples necking. It depends on what the effect is on them. I've seen grown men crying. It's the nostalgia thing that gets them. The concerts we played in stadiums, it seemed to be very young kids coming to see us so we saw an interesting perspective from the stage."

Paul and Linda's world tour is over, so Linda finds time to give an interview to *Woman's Own* magazine, which is published in the UK on **Monday, September 3** . . .

"I'm a musician, a photographer, a mother and most of all, an animal activist," she announces. "I would do almost anything to stop people eating meat. I don't mean I would harm people but I'd gently convert them. All my kids are vegetarians and so are most of their friends. I am planning to bring out a range of instant microwave meals and the proceeds will be ploughed back into my crusade. Paul has been a vegetarian for as long as I have. At first he missed the smell of bacon and so he started eating it again. Then we got lots of meat substitutes. I would never marry a man who ate meat. If I was not with Paul, and with someone else, I would play on his heartstrings to stop him eating it and if he started arguing with me, it would repulse me and I would kick him out."

The reasons why she and Paul have remained married for twenty-one years? "A major factor is that we are friends," Linda reveals. "We like each other and we get on. But because we are people living together, especially as we are of the opposite sex, it's a constant battle. Paul thinks it's healthy to have a row, as long as you make up afterwards."

And as for other women running after her husband, Linda replies, "I would probably kick her in the face, especially if she wasn't a veggie. Seriously, Paul and I are a little bit beyond that. We are both grown up. I have risen above a lot in life. I float above a lot of things and don't even notice them. But I take each day as it comes. I won't change when my kids leave home. I don't have any special plans. You are a singular person in life anyway. Paul and I are going to get go-karts when we are 90. That's our plan."

Friday, September 14 . . . the squabbles continue.

Paul "I Loved John . . ." Yoko "No You Didn't!"

UK columnist, Andrew Young, "Sparks are flying again between Paul McCartney and the widow of murdered Beatle, John Lennon. They clashed after multi-millionaire McCartney spoke for the first time of his reconciliation with Lennon shortly before his death. He said, 'One of the great joys for me was that we had made up. It really would have been pretty difficult for me to cope with his death if we hadn't made up.' But Yoko Ono, interviewed for the same radio show, claimed McCartney only revealed his feelings because Lennon was loved all over the world. She said, 'If John died and nobody cared, if John died as a person whose last album was number twenty in the charts or something like that, Paul wouldn't have said that. After John's death, there was a reverence all over the world and therefore it is important to know that the person who is revered did actually love you.' McCartney also added, 'No matter what happened, even though John's dead, I don't feel like we are ever going to be apart. I think we're a part of each other's lives, we're a part of each other's karma, man. There's something deeper than all the business troubles we went through.' "

Tuesday, October 9
Celebrations take place around the world on what would have been John's 50th birthday, including a worldwide simultaneous broadcast of his 1971 recording, 'Imagine' . . .

Syndicated news report "The haunting voice of John Lennon was heard by a record radio audience of a billion around the world today, the 50th anniversary of his birth. His peace anthem 'Imagine' was broadcast simultaneously by more than 1,000 stations, thirty of them in Britain, after a ceremony at the United Nations headquarters in New York. The former Beatle's widow, Yoko Ono, made a tearful plea for global harmony and said, 'When this was discussed we had no knowledge of what would happen in Iraq and Kuwait. But now it seems very appropriate that this be sung all over the world. The timing is incredible.' Soldiers in the Saudi desert tuned in to the broadcast, also beamed at Iraq and Iran. Lennon's words urged people to think of children, adding, 'The choice we have . . . is war or peace.' His music and interviews about him were heard in Moscow where The Beatles were once dubbed decadent . . .'"

The *Guardian* "At 8pm, more than 1,000 radio stations in 120 countries played his peace anthem 'Imagine'. Even the Soviet Union marked the occasion with a Red Army band performing 'Yellow Submarine' in a Moscow park . . .'"

It seems that the entire world is united in recognising John's 50th birthday, that is all except the BBC, who decide to snub the landmark event . . .

The *Guardian* "The BBC said Radio One was doing enough already with its current series *In My Life: Lennon Remembers*, and added that the anniversary was noted in its birthday file. The Corporation was accused of 'churlishness' by Harry Rimmer, leader of the city council in Lennon's birthplace, Liverpool. Rimmer, 62, said from the city, ' "Imagine" was John's way of trying to push the idea of universal peace and you cannot underestimate its importance.' "

Reuters news report "Hundreds of fans flocked to Liverpool today to mark what would have been the 50th birthday of rock idol, John Lennon. They crowded into the Cavern Walks precinct and heard a service for the murdered Beatle. A tearful vigil also took place in New York at the Dakota apartment block, where Lennon was shot, and in Central Park. . . ."

George "The clamour surrounding John Lennon's 50th birthday is, at best, irrelevant. I just had a bloke from Swedish Television harping on forever about John. It's nice that we remember people that we have loved but you can do that any day of the week. It doesn't have to be an anniversary. But I suppose some people need to do it, like putting wreaths on soldiers' graves each year. I don't personally need it."

Paul, who rejects Yoko's invitation to appear in a memorial concert for John in Tokyo in December, says, "If John was alive now he would have been the first to laugh at all this. He'd say, 'How many tributes can you have in one year?' "

Monday, October 29 (UK)
The Traveling Wilburys release their second album, perversely titled *Volume Three* . . .

George "With the first album, we were all a bit nervous of each other, but this time no one even thought about it. We rented a house in LA and I was just hanging around the first morning and all of a sudden I heard acoustic guitars start up. I went down and Jeff and Tom were there and I picked up a guitar. Bob walked in and said, 'Hello mate, how are yer?' Within an hour we'd got the first song, 'Inside Out'. We did two that day. We just banged 'em out like that, Monday to Friday and we had ten songs by the end of it. Lyrics were added later, some of them plain daft like the dance step instructions on 'Wilbury Twist' and others with a more serious angle . . ."

'The Devil's Been Busy'

George "This came to me when I recalled a story about golf courses. In order to keep them nice and smooth and free of weeds, they put so much toxic chemicals on them that in certain places it's seeping through into the water supply. In England, there was a golfer who died and now they have a sign on the golf course, 'Do Not Lick Your Balls', because that's how he died."

George is asked how the untimely death of an original Traveling Wilbury, Roy Orbison, who died of a heart attack in December 1988, affected the new album . . .

"If he had died while we were actually making the record, it might have been a bit different. But it has been two years and Roy was full of fun, whatever his image might have been. He wouldn't have wanted anyone mourning too much."

The UK columnist David Sinclair, during a promotional interview for The Traveling Wilburys new album, notes that "For Harrison it is clearly a great relief to have found such a partnership of (relative) equals to which he can repair . . . Despite making a spectacular comeback with *Cloud Nine* in 1987, he remains an ensemble player at heart."

George replies, "My ideal situation would be to play in a proper driving big band like the old Cab Calloway Band. I'd love to play somewhere that people can go along, maybe dance a bit of whatever, but where the emphasis is on enjoying the music rather than being in awe of some superstar mob on stage. I'd like to play the Holiday Inn in some out of the way place. Somewhere where your myth and your past are not attached to what you're doing now. Like we did before we were famous. I'd tour again if it weren't such a big deal. But nowadays it's like the third world war every time you go on the road."

David Sinclair writes, "Between us on the desk is a copy of a new biography on Harrison called *The Quiet One*, by Alan Clayson. It is wrapped in a plain white cover. Harrison has not read it. 'This Italian guy called Red Ronnie just gave it to me,' he says picking it up gingerly. 'I don't know who this writer is. All he knows about me is what he's read in the papers or heard in interviews. He doesn't know me. There was another one last year. God knows why these people bother, to make some money I suppose, because it's not important to history to have a stranger's version of what my life is supposed to be. There have been far too many Beatles books and it's depressing when you read a load of nasty things and even if you read about good things, it doesn't serve any purpose. I expect that I'll just leave it lying around the house and then my wife can read all the extra-marital affairs I'm supposed to have had and all the drugs I'm supposed to have taken.' "

Friday, November 9
An interview with **George**, conducted by DJ, Simon Bates on his BBC Radio One show, appears in the *Daily Mail*, in which he attacks the current record charts . . .

"The rap and dance music dominating the pop charts is rubbish," he announces. "I listen to *Top Of The Pops* and after three tunes, it makes me want to kill somebody. It's just so nauseating. And all this rap rubbish. It's just computerised rot. Everybody's got the same keyboard sound. Anybody who can use those pathetic drum machines to the extent they do and haven't even noticed how rubbish they sound, well, they sound real rubbish."

When asked about rap and dance music, **Paul** defends it, saying, "It's a vibrant form of music, which is attempting to push back the barriers like The Beatles did. It's wrong to say it's tuneless or just noise because it means a great deal to a lot of kids."

But the long-running British DJ, Tony Blackburn, is quick to agree with George "A lot of rap is rubbish," he announces. "You can't hear the words and it's boring and monotonous."

. . . The debate continues.

Tuesday, November 13

Twelve years after The Beatles had briefly toyed with the idea of returning to the Cavern Club in Liverpool for a unique, one-off gig, **Paul** announces to the UK reporter, Alec Low, "I have secret plans to return to the Cavern Club, the birthplace of The Beatles. I plan to play there this Christmas or early in the New Year. The Beatles never played enough live shows. We were a great band but instead we became this huge edifice, which stopped us performing. I'm going back to play the Cavern again and why not? I want to return there because the people of Liverpool are the best in the world. And we understand each other."

Paul's spokesman, Geoff Baker "Paul played in front of 2.8 million fans during his recent world tour. He did 102 dates in twelve countries but performing in Liverpool means all the world to him. The Cavern holds just over one hundred people and tickets will go on sale on the night. I wouldn't be surprised if they fetched £2,000 each. There will be a riot."

Liverpool-based Billy Heckle, the Cavern Club's future co-proprietor, "As a Beatles fan on the ground, nothing ever escapes me via the variety of sources I used and I was astonished when I heard about this years later. If I had have known anything about this in November 1990, I would have been banging down the doors of MPL."

Monday, November 26 (UK)
Paul again courts controversy when critics including the pop pundit Jonathan King, say his new single 'All My Trials' is nothing more than a "cheap publicity stunt for a ghastly record" . . .

" 'All My Trials' was an attack on eleven years of cruel Tory rule," **Paul** explains in an exclusive letter to the *Daily Mirror*. "I was bowled over by the public's support to the song and I shall be giving the profits from the single to hospitals and the homeless. And in answer to those people who say I shouldn't have made this record, I suppose you could have looked at Live Aid and the Amnesty and Mandela concerts and say that they were cheap publicity stunts, too. But I don't subscribe to that. I feel that too little attention is given to the groups who are seen in the video for the single, the homeless, the jobless and the cash-starved NHS. I will continue to speak out until something is done about these groups. It is ridiculous to try to shut me up on this. It is only a record but it seems to have touched a few nerves. Perhaps it is guilt they are feeling, not anger. Perhaps Jonathan King would like to persuade the thousands of homeless people in Britain that it is better to say nothing and produce completely meaningless, twitty records like his latest release, 'I Can't Let Maggie Go', a single in praise of Margaret Thatcher. This man King is well known as a bit of an idiot. Millions detest his views on events like *Live Aid*. Why doesn't he instead ridicule the people in Government who are failing to address the problems instead of those of us who care to stand up and be counted? If I were doing this record and this video just for me, I wouldn't need to have any footage of the homeless. Of course, the argument against me is, 'Well, he's got a lot of dough, why doesn't he do something?' And the answer to that is, 'Well, I do.' We've indicated already that I shall not be making any money out of this record and any money that is made from the record will be going towards solving the problems we're addressing. But that is not the answer. The real answer is to get to the root of these problems. Of course, it shouldn't be like that. But you can't stay quiet in the face of such wrongs. I will continue to speak out until something is done about these things. It is ridiculous to try to shut me up on this. This song, 'All My Trials', has been a tool throughout the generations and this is not the first time that it has been used to protest a wrong. It started innocently because I like the words and the chord changes and I got a good take when I was singing it with passion. I saw it as an offbeat Christmas song that would be an antidote to the sugary messages that abound this time of the year. But it has become something bigger now. It is fitting for all the modern trials that are bringing misery to millions like joblessness, homelessness and the collapse of the NHS. My mother was a nurse and was always very proud of the health care in this country. When I first went abroad with The Beatles and saw how they handle the sick in America, I was proud, too. I am a great believer in the health service. The closing down of so many hospitals is absolute madness. It makes me really sad now to see the NHS in such a bad way."

Paul's spokesman, **Geoff Baker** "None of the words of 'All My Trials' have been changed, because they still ring true today. There may not be slavery in Britain anymore but there is still rich and poor. It is a song about despair and the hope that the trials will soon be over."

Paul "And as for Jonathan King's outburst, it strikes me that he's doing exactly what he's accusing me of, which is jumping on the bandwagon and he's far more guilty of that than I am. One of the trials in Britain today is that we've got people like Jonathan King around. Just think about a world that didn't protest these things. Think about Jonathan King's world, a world of not doing *Live Aid*, of not protesting against Vietnam, of letting them take down the rain forests. Go on, fuck the rain forests, fuck the poor. Perhaps it's an opinion, but you'll never get me voting for it in a million years."

Almost four months after recording an appearance for MTV's *Unplugged* series, Paul takes the idea one step further by turning his back on big stadium gigs and appearing in tiny nightclubs and venues on a low-key UK and European tour. Critics describe the series of concerts as a "re-run of gigs of thirty years ago before The Beatles made it. The spellbinding tour will go down in pop history as one of the most amazing ever undertaken by McCartney and his red-hot five-piece band . . ." On **Friday, May 10**, Paul's second gig on this tour takes place at the Mean Fiddler Club in Harlesden, South West London . . .

UK columnist, Linda Duff "While Macca could fill the nearby 72,000-seater Wembley Stadium for a month, he opted to play in front of just 400 wide-eyed fans. Some had paid £100 to ticket touts outside. Only last year, Paul played to 183,000 people at the Rio Festival but the weekend gig was a repeat of the time twenty years ago when he set out on a university tour with his new band Wings. And now McCartney is determined to give something back to the fans who have loved him since the Sixties . . ."

Paul "I just wanted to go out and play some real gigs to real people. I like to see what the people at the back look like. I just wanted to see what it felt like to play small places where we all sweat and have a good time. I just wanted to have a go at seeing what it would be like if we tried to recapture some of the spirit of the old days."

Linda Duff "McCartney stunned the crowd by ambling on stage, picking up a six-string, acoustic guitar, and playing a selection of his best songs spanning thirty years. In the tiny Western saloon-style nightclub, open-mouthed fans watched Paul, in a casual white and peach T-shirt and black jeans, in awe. He thrilled them with a selection of his best-loved numbers, from Beatles classics like 'We Can Work It Out' and 'Get Back' to later hits like 'Band On The Run' and 'Ebony And Ivory'. Perched on the low stage, and with a new longer haircut, similar to his look in the early Wings days, a tanned and fit-looking McCartney greeted the audience with a chirpy, 'Good evening, y'all.' Then he burst into a blistering version of the blues standard 'Mean Woman Blues'. Shaking his head moptop style as scenes of Beatlemania erupted throughout the baying crowd, he tore through the rock'n'roll classic 'Be-Bop-A-Lula', before overwhelming the tiny audience with songs like 'Here, There And Everywhere', 'And I Love Her' and 'I've Just Seen A Face'. The fans almost wept when Macca belted out a scorching version of The Beatles' smash 'She's A Woman'. McCartney also charmed the crowd with a mixture of jokes and the surprises kept on coming. Macca told fans, 'Here's something that's never been done before on a British stage,' before sitting down to play the drums on the soul classic 'Ain't No Sunshine', and there were loud cheers when he plugged in his famous Sixties Hofner violin bass. . . ."

One month after his gig at the Mean Fiddler, Paul and his band continue with their string of low-key whistle-stop concerts by appearing in Cornwall at the cliff-top Coliseum. The 2,000 tickets for the show were snapped up within just minutes of going on sale . . .

Syndicated news report "Paul McCartney has a message for those desperate to see him in concert tonight: 'Tell the touts to take a hike. The £16 tickets for the gig could be up for grabs for as much as £70. It is too much to pay and my staff will do everything they can to stop the touts from exploiting my fans.' Paul's spokesman, Geoff Baker, said, 'Paul's security men are planning tough measures to deter the touts. We are asking fans who don't have a ticket for the show, not to attempt buying one on the street. The agents are very evil people who prey on the desperation of genuine fans who can't get into the gig. We know who they are and they are coming down from London and they will be at the Coliseum. We will be looking for them. The Coliseum is a small venue and it was Paul's request to come here.' "

Friday, June 28
The *Liverpool Oratorio*, Paul's first venture into classical music, receives its world premiere in Liverpool at the Anglican Cathedral in front of a capacity 2,500 audience. His collaborator on the project is Carl Davis . . .

Paul "For years I have been flirting with classical music. On 'Yesterday' I had a string quartet and on 'Eleanor Rigby' we had used string players so I always enjoyed the experience. And, in the back of my mind, there was always this thought that if I ever get a great offer to do something big in the classical world, I'd leap at it. So, the Liverpool people rang up (in 1989) and asked me to do this for their 150th anniversary. So it was my hometown orchestra, it was to be performed in the Cathedral, which is right next-door to the school where I did all my schooling and it was in an area of a million great memories for me. I always had the idea that I might do this one day so I just leapt at the offer and said, 'Okay, in two years time we'll deliver. Carl Davis and myself will deliver something that you can celebrate your 150th anniversary with.' "

Saturday, July 13
Cynthia Lennon meanwhile, surprises many by revealing that she is to sell her collection of John Lennon memorabilia at an auction in London at Christie's on August 29 . . . Back in 1986, talking to a *Mail On Sunday* reporter, she had blasted The Beatles memorabilia trade as 'indecent' . . .

"This whole industry has grown on the back of someone who has died," Cynthia angrily said at the time. "It is sick, it is like taking the pennies off the eyes of a dead man." Five years on, Michael Robotham, a reporter for the *Mail On Sunday*, visits her bungalow in the Isle of Man to ask her about her sale. But instead he is greeted at the door by a man who says his name is 'Harry' and tells Michael that Cynthia has already sold her story to *Hello* magazine but will still give him one quote. He hands the reporter a scrap piece of paper upon which she had scrawled, "Yes, I am selling my memorabilia. But I will retain the memories. It's about time other people had the opportunity to enjoy what I have enjoyed for the last twenty-five years."

Among the priceless artefacts put up for sale by Cynthia is a hand-written letter by John dating from 1965, which is expected to fetch up to £5,000. In it, John provides an interesting and unique view of his feelings about fatherhood . . . *"I spend hours in the dressing rooms,"* **John** wrote, *"thinking about the times I've wasted not being with him (Julian) . . . I really want him to know I love him and miss me like I seem to be missing both of you so much . . . it's only sort of three o'clock in the afternoon and it seems the wrong time of day to feel so emotion. I really feel like crying."*

On **Friday, July 19**, the *Standard* newspaper reports "Former Beatle George Harrison was at the centre of a security alert after a prowler was seen jumping over a wall into his multi-million pound estate. Police with sniffer dogs who were called to Friar Park mansion at Henley-on-Thames failed to find any trace of the intruder but the incident is bound to increase Mr Harrison's fears of attack. Since the shooting of John Lennon, he has lived in fear of becoming a target himself and has gone to extreme measures to protect his 20-acre estate. A 10-foot-high wall equipped with lights runs round the perimeter and guards regularly patrol the estate. The estate's alarm is also directly linked to the local police station, which is only 400 yards away, and Mr Harrison has installed electronically controlled gates at the entrance and has a keep out sign in seven languages posted nearby. The security scare happened at around 8.45am on Tuesday when Mr Harrison, his wife Olivia and children (*sic*) were at home. A Henley police spokesman said that six officers with dogs searched the grounds for an hour but were unable to find any trace of the intruder."

Wednesday, July 24

A sample of how crazy collecting 'original' Beatles memorabilia has become is demonstrated in a syndicated news report today . . . "A corner of toast is up for auction at a Beatles souvenir auction, labelled 'A piece of George Harrison's breakfast – 2/8/63.' A jelly baby given to George in Manchester and a sock are also on offer. Merseyside teenager, Susan Houghton, George's number one fan, hopes to get £2,000 for her collection at Christie's."

When told of the sale of a piece of his breakfast, **George** slyly remarks, "I didn't have toast that day."

Wednesday, September 18

Paul's documentary *Get Back*, a documentary-concert film of Paul's band on the road, taken during their 1989/1990 World Tour, receives its world premiere in Hamburg, Germany at the Passage Kino Cinema. The movie is directed by Richard Lester, famed, amongst other things, for his work on The Beatles' films *A Hard Day's Night* and *Help!* . . .

Paul "The film was Richard's idea. He wanted to climax his 25-year relationship with me by filming my return to the road. Richard had been involved in the World Tour from the start. It was he who made the striking 11-minute movie that began each concert, played on a giant screen behind the stage."

Richard Lester "What I most wanted to put on film was the genuine connection between Paul McCartney and his audience, who obviously had such a highly emotional response to him. There was such a wonderful sense of exuberance, such good spirit between each member of the band and between the band and the audience, that my primary aim became to convey that. I used to say that this was a kind of love affair, a love story. Paul's audience brings a lot of romantic and nostalgic baggage with it. And with the use of 25 years of music, including classic Beatles songs and the extraordinary newsreel footage that we were able to obtain, we tried to recreate that feeling of romantic nostalgia that hopefully makes the film work well on an emotional, as well as a musical, level."

Paul had chosen Hamburg for the premiere because it was there that the Fab Four had famously played at the start of the Sixties. But during a press conference for the film's launch, **Paul** interestingly announces that the "three surviving Beatles are closer than ever to a concert reunion," adding, "We are good friends again. We have dinner and we talk and the idea is always in the air somewhere. But the question is how, where and when. I do think it's possible but the trouble is that there's so much pressure in a thing like that. What would we do that would stand up to that legend? George and I have privately discussed writing songs that could form the basis of a reunion. But it has to be handled delicately. Any relationship is delicate but writing together as ex-Beatles is very delicate. We've just spent twenty years arguing with each other through lawyers. But at least there's more of a glimmer of The Beatles getting back together than ever in the past."

Paul also uses the get-together with the Press to launch a tirade about some of today's so-called pop superstars – in particular, the Australian singer, Kylie Minogue . . .

"It's all just conveyor belt stuff and I don't think that sort of music improves the scene. I don't see too many performers like Kylie Minogue being able to handle the big tours and the big concerts the way that The Stones and even the remaining Beatles can. I think it's something to do with humour, enjoying experience and experience." Jokingly, McCartney adds, "I also put it down to drugs. It's nothing new that in the Sixties I experimented with drugs. From *Rubber Soul* in 1965 on, every Beatles album was produced under the influence of drugs, especially marijuana and LSD. Everything in the Sixties was drug-inspired; music, literature, cinema and Vietnam was carried out under drugs."

On **Friday, November 15**, in Lille, France, Paul courts controversy by keeping Princess Diana waiting in the wings . . .

Royal correspondent, Martin Phillips "Di, in a sleek red velvet evening dress, was ready to meet McCartney backstage after a performance of his classic work, the *Liverpool Oratorio*, in France. But she was left clicking her heels as Paul and co-composer, Carl Davis, soaked up a standing ovation from an ecstatic audience. Di passed the time by chatting to Macca's wife Linda until Paul joined them for a photo session. She smiled as she told Linda she did not mind the delay and had enjoyed the concert. The audience at the Palais de la Musique loudly applauded Di as she arrived as guest of honour, but even that welcome was put in the shade when they went for McCartney. He returned their cheers by blowing kisses before the Royal Liverpool Philharmonic Society's rendition of the *Oratorio*. After the concert, Di left to catch a royal flight back to England while Paul, Linda and their children, were mobbed in their stretch limousine. Macca wound down the window to sign autographs and shake hands with fans who had blocked Lille's streets. Paul said the concert was 'lovely' and 'brilliant'."

Monday, November 18

Three days later, Paul's *Liverpool Oratorio* receives its North American premiere at New York's Carnegie Hall. Sitting among the excited crowd is the American reporter, Andrew Porter . . . "The place was packed, security was tight and at the close, the ushers tried in vain to enforce the house rule against unauthorised photography, and the hall was glittering with flashes as if under a Fourth of July fireworks display. The *Oratorio* has had a rough ride from music critics but in New York I found its honest, easy communicativeness more enjoyable and more moving than most of the new music that the month has brought. McCartney, does it need saying, can write good tunes, and he sets words well and Carl Davis, in his easy eclectic way, is a very skilful composer and orchestrator . . ."

Sunday, December 1

George surprises many by beginning a 12-date concert tour of Japan, beginning at the Yokohama Arena. It is his first string of concert appearances since his ill-fated *Dark Horse* North American tour seventeen years ago. Joining him throughout the series of shows is Eric Clapton . . .

George "When we decided we would do this tour, Eric said, 'Where do we want to go? Where should we go to have fun and have a good time?' And the reason we came to Japan was because Eric and his manager like Japan. Eric suggested to me that it would have to be this time of the year if I wanted to do a concert tour because he was not working and his band was available to become my band. I'm not into touring so much. I toured in the Seventies, and just did little bits of concerts, just a song here and a concert there but nothing much, because I was always doing other things, and plenty of travelling around. It always seemed like hard work to me. But now I'm ready to try it again and see, because I'm convinced I can master the art of touring. But I hate the idea of being the front man of a band. In The Beatles we had two other people who had enormous desire to be in the front and for me, it was a nice position. I could be in The Beatles but at the same time I didn't have to be the front of The Beatles . . . This tour will be very special for me because it will be the tour that will decide whether I want to do any more touring or not. This could be my first and last tour or it could just be something that begins a new period for me."

Eric Clapton "I've always thought that George is a great songwriter, a great musician, a very unique man and he gave up smoking, and I have to respect that. He's very brave to come here to Japan. He hasn't worked on stage for a long time. It can be a very frightening experience. I've always thought of George as being the older brother I never had. I respect his judgement and his values and I think he's a wonderful man, and I like the way he bends the strings. He's a great slide player, too."

George "Eric's more perfect in as much as he's got a great band. I know a lot of people in the band, I've known him for so long, and he's played on so many of my records, going right back to the Sixties, going right through to the Nineties. We have this on-going relationship that was this magical mystical, relationship, which is interesting . . . Eric convinced me to do the tour and to do it in Japan because the audience would be so receptive to me. For him to be a back-up musician, which is what he is, he just stands there in the background with the rest of the band and he's quite happy to do that, which is good, because his ego is such that he can do that, and he can handle that. A lot of our relationship has been romanticised and mystified by writers who have written stuff. They have made it into such a big thing, I suppose because of the fact that I divorced Patti and he married her and then he divorced her. They've made it as if it is some funny stuff, but to me, it is just life. Doesn't everybody do that?"

Reporters in Japan ask **George** how he felt about making a return to concert performances . . .

"I didn't really know how my physical body would stand up to touring. I'm not an athletic kind of person, some people are always out there playing tennis or jogging. For a tour, Mick Jagger jogs backwards for twenty miles every day, but I'm not like that at all. Over the last few years it has taken all my strength just to sit on the couch and watch TV. I'm not the most physical person, so I needed to get myself together. I didn't want to collapse on stage halfway through. That wouldn't look good. I had stopped smoking and I used the tour as an excuse to get rid of this horrible curse of nicotine. Eric was so generous and I thought, 'Well, if I'm going to do this, the least I can do is try to do it as good as I can and maybe make him proud to have been a part of it.' I didn't want to flunk out so I stopped smoking and tried to get some breathing exercises so I could sing and have a bit more power to my voice."

Shortly after arriving in Japan, George and Eric face their one and only press conference on the tour in the Red Pearl Room at the Capitol Tower Hotel in front of 500 reporters. The first question, as one would expect, concerns his former group . . .

George "The Beatles as a group, to me, seems like something that happened in a previous lifetime. It's so long ago. We were only together, really, for about six years and we were finished by 1969. I've been much longer as me than I have been a Beatle, but The Beatles were such a phenomenon, nobody could forget it. It's very interesting to have been in The Beatles, to have experienced it, but I'm glad it's over. The Beatles' producer, George Martin, said recently how he always felt sorry because he always concentrated on them and should have paid more attention to me. He said to me personally, 'I hope you'll forgive me.' But I'm quite happy with my role in The Beatles, you know. It split up because of all those problems, because there were too many songs and because we had got too close to each other. But I'm quite happy with the way things went, but I feel that whatever I am, I have always been that. Maybe different things have taken longer to reach the surface or whatever, you know, but I am what I am. I'm not really that much different to how I was then, maybe I'm more able to express it now. Many people are more interested now in what I had to say because, in the Sixties, and early Seventies, they thought I was a loony because I went to India."

While another reporter asks George about The Beatles' continuing influence on the world . . .

George "You can't turn on the telly without there being something to do with The Beatles. All the kids pick up on The Beatles because of *Yellow Submarine*. I made a point about not saying anything about them, but by the time my son Dhani was five, he wanted to know how the piano part on 'Hey Bulldog' went, which completely threw me. I didn't understand where he had heard a song like that. I hadn't heard that one much myself and then I realised it was in *Yellow Submarine*."

Recalling The Beatles' humour?

George "I miss that side at press conferences. We used to have fun at press conferences. They used to be really funny. There would always be someone with a wisecrack. I miss that side of The Fab Four. Now, people seem to give me respect, which is quite nice."

His favourite music?

George "My favourite music at the moment is the Bulgarian Choir. It is called *The Mysterious Voices Of Bulgaria* and it is the most brilliant vocals. It is quite beautiful. I feel there are some good things I genuinely like, whereas, a couple of years ago, I couldn't find anything there that was interesting. Now, in the top twenty, there tends to be the same stuff in every country. But I think it's getting better. I think as soon as we can have programme planners and disc jockeys that don't have to bow down to the sponsors, because that's the problem. Ten years ago, when I was more actively involved in it, you'd get a playlist that the DJs were allowed to play, maybe three new records a week. Now, one record company may put out twenty or thirty and then you've got like fifty record companies. So what they'd do is, any record over three minutes 30, they don't even listen to and then usually it's the programme planners, for his own personal motives, like back handers, or how you'd go and bow and scrape, those records would get played. And so, I'm not really into that anymore. We (The Beatles) genuinely got popular by people playing them because they liked them. And the business is going to get more and more money and more and more greed and selfish and, on that basis, people have tin ears as far as I'm concerned. I hear some stuff that's happening now and it's people who are just tone deaf with 15-million-selling albums. It takes all sorts."

His religious views today?

George "I keep it to myself unless someone asks me about it. But I still feel the same as I felt back in the Sixties. I lost touch with the Krishnas when the Swami died, maybe eight years ago. I know one or two of them but I don't really hang out with them. I used to go and see the old master, you know, AC Bhakevividandta, quite a lot. He was real good. I'm still involved but it is more like a thing you do inside yourself. You don't actually do it in the road. It's a way of just trying to get in touch with yourself. I still write songs with a bit of it in there, you know, bits and pieces. Sometimes I feel that it is a shame that it's musicians who seem to go round saving, you know, the world. I think that some of the politicians should get their fingers out occasionally."

The questions from the Japanese Press continue . . .

Reporter, referring to the fact that this tour corresponds with John's death eleven years ago, "Will you be doing anything as a tribute to John Lennon?"

George "No, we won't be doing anything other than singing songs. We won't be doing anything special."

Reporter "Does the anniversary have any special meaning to you?"

George "No, the day doesn't have any special meaning to me."

Eric Clapton, breaking into the conversation, "I think the fact that George will be playing is tribute enough, really."

George "The day John Lennon got killed or anything, I'm not into days. I don't remember my own birthday. I don't remember anniversaries. I'm just not into remembering days or anniversaries."

Reporter "How have things changed in the 25 years since you last played in Japan?"

George "Everything, everything has changed over 25 years. First of all, I'm much younger now than I used to be then. I think I can sing better, I can play better (laughter fills hall), I can be a happier person, everything has changed."

Reporter, turning to Eric, "Will you be playing 'Layla'?"

Eric "I don't think so, unless there is some kind of a riot, or public outcry, where we *have* to play it. I've played it at nearly every show for the last twenty years, so it doesn't bother me not to play it now and again. George has only given me a very limited space so I'll try and do a couple of new songs. But it's all negotiable, don't worry."

George "I don't mind if he does it."

Eric "We'll see, we'll see."

At the conclusion of the highly successful tour, **George** discusses the concert's repertoire . . .

"I wanted to do those songs in the spirit of the original records," he admits. "But that can be an elusive thing. A lot of the things on my records have been difficult because you need to know what you're playing. There are a lot of chords and they've got a lot of little bits and bits that are important to the structure of the song. So a song like 'All Those Years Ago', when you listen to the record, you take it for granted, it's just a simple tune with a simple melody. But when you dissect it in a situation like a rehearsal, you say, 'Okay, who's playing what? Who's going to do this bit? Who's going to do that bit?' But I want people to see the songs as they remember it. I want them to be in that spirit so people can say, 'Oh yeah, I remember that.' On 'What Is Life?' there was a slight problem. Every time, at the end of the verse, and it stops and goes into another verse, it has this funny little bit. And if it's not going into the verse, or if it goes turning around and keeping going, it goes something different. So trying to get it so that everyone hits the same one is very hard. It's funny, because on the version that's on the record (*Live In Japan*), Eric looked at me and said, 'It looks like it's going wrong,' and as he said that, he misses his cue to come back in and then he fell about playing. But on the mix, to cover up that big mess that occurred, I decided to cut a couple of the people off and in the end, the only person who got it right now sounds like he got it wrong, the drummer, Steve. He really got it right."

Monday, April 6

Just over three months after his tour of Japan, and with General Election fever gripping the UK, George performs at the Royal Albert Hall in London as part of a gala show in aid of the Maharishi's National Law Party, Britain's newest political party . . .

Ringo jokingly remarks, "They're not standing for seats, they're the ones pinging all over the place. They'll have to take the benches out of the House of Commons."

Jeff Postlewaite, the *Standard* "Starr, in London to launch his first album in nine years and promote his first-ever tour with son Zak Starkey, said he knew little about politics and even less about the NLP (National Law Party). Asked if he would play tonight with George, he replied, 'I will not appear on stage tonight at the Albert Hall. It's the other fellow that's playing the Albert Hall. I'm here to do this and he's there to do that. I will be going along to support him, but just as a member of the audience. The NLP is new to me. I just heard about it on the plane coming over. I don't really know what they stand for. I saw George this morning in an interview and he wasn't sure what it stood for either, but didn't like what the others stood for.' Nevertheless, some star performers are expected to join the bill for tonight's concert, for which tickets have been selling for up to £200. The Beach Boys flew into London today pledging support for the NLP, but still did not know whether they would play tonight. Bruce Johnston said, 'If you ask us why we're supporting the National Law Party, you have to ask, "Is the other stuff working?" Like George Harrison, we believe it is time for a complete change.' Colleague Mike Love added, 'The Beach Party has come to join the National Law Party.' "

Aside from the brief 1987 Prince's Trust cameo, the show becomes George's first concert appearance in his homeland since 1966 and his first as a solo artist . . .

George "The last time I played in England was with The Beatles in 1966 (May 1 – the *NME* Poll Winners Concert at the Empire Pool, Wembley). But I did do two tunes at the Prince's Trust and I did the Carl Perkins TV special, but I had never performed at a concert as a solo artist in England. Not many people know this, but not many people care. They (the audience at the Royal Albert Hall) loved it. That was the best thing for me. For a number of years, the British press has been pretty nasty, not necessarily to me, but to everybody, particularly to people who are British. They don't seem to like their own people or they build you up and then knock you down, and for years the British press always seemed bitchy to me and nasty and I had built up this impression that the British don't like me and my music. So I thought, 'Well, that's all right by me. I can live here quietly.' But when I stepped on the stage of the Albert Hall, it was unbelievable. The audience was so happy. It was the most incredible buzz; it was like a 'love-in'. It was one of those things where I could have just stood on my head and done anything and they would have just loved it. So perhaps absence *does* make the heart grow fonder."

Sunday Times (April 12) "It may have been a dull campaign but this election will be remembered as the one which nearly sparked a reunion of The Beatles. In the event, only two of the three surviving Fabs turned out for last Monday's surprise concert at the Royal Albert Hall in support of the National Law Party. But it was a nostalgic treat all the same to hear George Harrison and Ringo Starr whacking their way through the encores, 'Roll Over Beethoven' and 'While My Guitar Gently Weeps'. For the rest of the 90-minute show, Harrison was supported by The Hijack Band, so called because he had borrowed six of them from his friend Eric Clapton, and by the residual appeal of songs he wrote at least 20 years ago. If The Beatles hadn't stopped touring in 1966, a set-list headed by tunes such as 'Taxman', 'Something' and 'Here Comes The Sun' might have sounded like middle-aged revivalism. Given the lack of more recent material, it might also have raised the awkward question of exactly what Harrison has been up to since he wrote about 'My Sweet Lord' in 1971. As it was, though, most of these numbers had never been performed in public before and despite some slightly shaky vocals on 'Piggies' and 'Old Brown Shoe', George seemed well up to the task of premiering them. But any Natural Lawyer hoping for inspirational words from the Fab One went away disappointed. A brief dismissal of 'those stiffs in parliament' was Harrison's only direct contribution to the political debate."

Thursday, June 18
Paul reaches fifty years of age and marks the occasion by speaking about his love and admiration for his wife, Linda . . .

"We've been married for over 23 years now, so it must be love," **Paul** announces. "I am very proud of Linda. It's not like she's got one job, she's got many. First and foremost she is a mother of four children. Then she's a photographer and now she's got this whole new career writing her cookery books and bringing out her own range of foods. Then on top of all that, she sings and plays in my band. That's because I want and ask her to."

Linda "Kindness is the thing I find most attractive in a man. I think being kind is the most macho thing a guy can be. That's what I still find attractive about Paul. Even after all these years, he still stops off after meetings to bring me flowers home."

Thursday, July 2
Ringo begins the European leg of his latest All-Starr Band tour in Sweden, reaching the Hammersmith Odeon in London on Tuesday, July 7 . . .

David Cheal, the *Telegraph* "At the Hammersmith Odeon on Tuesday, a motley collection of some of rock music's most talented, eccentric personalities performed songs from their repertoires. Together they played some terrific music and occasionally, though, a man with dark glasses, a big nose, a beard and an amazing Technicolor drapecoat would saunter on, sing a song or two, play drums a bit and saunter off. The gentleman in question was Ringo Starr, ex-Beatle and the purpose of this event was to promote Ringo's latest solo album (*Time Takes Time*). In the event, Ringo probably spent no more than half an hour on stage, and much of that was taken up with renditions of Beatles songs and vintage numbers from his solo career. His album received pretty short shrift. Indeed, as the show progressed, it became clear that Ringo was here in little more than name, and that most of the hard work was being done by the other troubadours . . . As the show approached its climax, Ringo wandered back on to sing the lachrymose 'Photograph', surely his finest moment as a solo artist. 'With A Little Help From My Friends', The Beatles song with which he is most closely associated, ended the show. 'Thanks for coming,' he said in his best *Thomas The Tank Engine* voice. It had been our pleasure."

Max Bell also reports on the concert for the *Evening Standard* "Mr Starr was celebrating his 52nd birthday with the help of some once-famous friends. Ringo's All-Starr Band includes Nils Lofgren, Joe Walsh, Todd Rundgren, Tim Schmidt, Burton Cummings, Dave Edmunds, a hairy sax player and son Zak, on drums of course. They should really be called Eight Men And A Baby. The All-Starr format wasn't so bad if you were prepared to put critical faculty, taste and embarrassment on ice, though a fairly strong stomach was necessary to endure the sight of so many old codgers forcing the jollity buttons for His Ringoness. True, most of the show was conducted at the level where tongues are kept firmly in cheek and an element of send-up is expected. Even so, I often felt like the kid on the Happy Eater logo who seems to have two fingers heading straight for his throat . . . Ringo chose not to hang about much but managed to con his way though 'You're Sixteen', 'Photograph', 'Act Naturally', 'Boys', a vile singalong version of the appalling 'Yellow Submarine' and an equally tiresome 'With A Little Help From My Friends'. Nostalgia, sadly, ain't what it used to be."

But the day before, on **July 6**, Ringo's tour reached his hometown of Liverpool, where he plays an historic show at the Empire Theatre, a venue he played with The Beatles . . . "I wanted to go back to Liverpool and play where I started out," he says. "I also want to give my dad and my auntie a day out."

Sunday, January 10

The *News Of The World* reports "Ex-Beatle Paul McCartney has been banned by radio and telly chiefs over a four-letter rant on his new record. The do-gooder star blurts out 'fuck' six times on 'Big Boys Bickering', a protest song about world leaders. The track is one of four on his new EP 'Hope Of Deliverance', which was named record of the week by Simon Mayo's *Breakfast Show*. But Radio One chiefs have banned 'Big Boys Bickering'. A spokesman for the station said, 'We don't play records with the f-word in them.' And *ITV Chart Show* boss, Keith Macmillan said, 'I agree with the song, but I can't play it for youngsters.' The song includes the line, 'Big boys bickering, fucking it up for everyone.' "

Paul "I sympathise with people who are not into swearing and I admit I don't like to hear people swearing in front of the kids. But in this case, I believe it's essential to the song. I felt I had to use the word, otherwise it would have been a cop-out. I could have sung 'mucking it up' but I thought, 'What do I feel about the hole in the ozone layer?' Basically I think, 'That fucking hole,' so the words stay. It's the first time I've used this word in a song but this whole thing about Governments got me annoyed. They all went down to the Earth Summit in Rio but didn't sign an agreement."

Tuesday, February 2 (UK)

Paul releases *Off The Ground*, his first new studio album since *Flowers In The Dirt* in 1989 and his first new music release since the *Liverpool Oratorio* in 1991. Critics describe the album as "His best work since his days with The Beatles . . ."

Paul "I had a definite idea about the kind of album I wanted to do. I knew that I wanted it to be different from my last music album, *Flowers In The Dirt*, and the good thing about this band is that we can make a pretty good sound, just the six of us. I didn't worry if the album sounded 'Beatley' or anything, because if anyone has the right to do Beatles-type music, it's me or George or Ringo. So I didn't worry about that. REM have been doing very Beatles-type things and a lot of what is in the charts now are very suggestive of Sixties-type stuff . . . I said to my co-producer on the album, Julian Mendelson, 'My most pleasant, easiest memories of recordings were with The Beatles.' In those days, we would record from ten-thirty to one-thirty, in one session, and then we'd go for lunch. Then, from two-thirty to five and this was the next session. And that was practically all we did. We'd do a couple of songs in each of those three-hour sessions and you'd do three or four songs a day. The songs didn't suffer; you just had to be more prepared. You had to do your homework. You really had to know your songs. So I said to Julian, 'How do you fancy me recording that way?' And he was quite up for the whole idea. So we went for feel instead of perfection. Some of the songs on this album were first takes, like 'Biker Like An Icon'. That didn't take us long to record."

'Off The Ground'

Paul "I happened to be speaking to my daughter, who was working in London, and she said, 'What did you do today, dad?' And I said, 'Well, we did this song,' explaining how I did it. And she said, 'What's it called?' And I said, ' "Off The Ground".' She said, 'Oh, that's a great album title.' Then I thought, 'Yeah, I never thought of that.' She saw it immediately as an album title, whereas I hadn't even considered it. So when the question of an album title came up, I said, 'I've got one.' We thought of a couple of others but they weren't so good. I had an image to go with the *Off The Ground* title, which was a picture where people accidentally cut heads off whenever they try and take a picture. So I thought, 'Perhaps we should try and cut the whole thing off and just have feet disappearing off the top of the CD.' It would just be the band's feet. That was the image I kept seeing. You can explain it, 'Well, we didn't quite get a picture of the band but here is their feet.' I then thought that if everyone were barefoot, it would be quite good because our drummer is black and it would be quite a funny image to see five pairs of white feet and one pair of black feet. But when we came to shoot it, you can't actually tell which pair of feet belongs to our black drummer. His feet and legs are very tanned. We all looked the same, which I liked even better."

The first single off the album is 'Hope Of Deliverance' . . .

Paul "With 'Hope Of Deliverance' you'd think I was inspired by something terrible on the news. But, in actual fact, I went up into the attic of the house, just to get away from everyone and I took a 12-string guitar with me and the sound of that inspired me. The tune came very simply. I don't know where it came from. The jingly-jangly sound just inspired me. I released this as the first single because it's catchy, bright and memorable. It's good to have a song that is spiritually uplifting. The message of it is that it is going to be all right. Like Bob Marley said, 'Everything's gonna be alright.' It has that message."

'C'mon People'

Paul "The song is very 'C'mon, let's get it together,' and it was only later that I realised that the theme of the album was quite positive and I was quite glad to find that theme. I didn't realise I was putting so much of that theme into the album. I would rather have that instead of doom and gloom."

'Mistress And Maid'

Paul "It is very difficult to compare the partnership I had with John with the partnership I have going with Elvis Costello. In reality, the Lennon & McCartney partnership has to be seen as a very special one, and it's very unfair to Elvis to make him live up to John's thing. Obviously, the best collaboration I had was with John. It's no doubt in my mind. But when Elvis came round, I found it easier to work with him than many others I had worked with. Elvis is good with words, which John was. He wears glasses, like John did. So there are funny little similarities. The song 'Mistress And Maid' turned out to have a very womanly point of view, which is kind of strange because the two of us are fellows and we shouldn't really understand how the woman is thinking. I had the title and it's actually the title of a painting that I admire very much. The mistress is a lady in medieval days and the maid is her maid and the painting shows something about a love letter. It's one of those old story paintings. It really is an incredible painting. I loved the title 'Mistress And Maid' and I kept it at the back of my mind and in my mind, it was going to be a little bit sexy. I thought, 'Oh, a little bit sexy, all this kinky gear, French maid.' I was seeing it that way, you know, how Madonna might interpret it. When we started writing it, I still had that image in my mind. But the minute the song started to unfold and she said, 'Come in my dear,' to this fellow, and he walked in to the song, sat down and didn't take a lot of notice of her, it didn't suddenly go into a sex scene. He started to ignore her. We thought it was a much better way to go. And at the end of the song, she leaves him saying, 'I'm not your mistress and maid, I'm not your skivvy.' "

'Biker Like An Icon'

Paul " 'Biker Like An Icon' is a straight song about a runaway, about a girl who likes a biker and the only thing you never find out from the song is whether it works out okay or not. The idea of the song came from Linda."

On **Thursday, February 18**, at The Forum, near Milan in Italy, Paul begins his latest world tour, entitled World Tour Two . . .

Paul "I had this idea of going out on the road at fifty. That's because few of us guys from the Sixties have got old enough yet to play on over that threshold. Back when I was in my twenties, around the time I had written 'Yesterday', I thought that there was no way I would still be rocking at 30! But I'm well beyond that now and I'm still raring to go. And why not? The jazz stars of the 20s went on as they got older. The blues guys that I grew up listening to have done it. It's just that, as a musical form, rock's not old enough yet to have thrown up the older stars who can't still go out there and cut it. But I'm up for that . . . The set list for this tour includes 'Drive My Car', 'All My Loving', 'Can't Buy Me Love', 'Yesterday', 'Sgt. Pepper', 'Hey Jude' and many, many more. A lot of The Beatles' stuff seems fresh because they were recorded after The Beatles stopped touring in 1966, so they've not been done live before. You've got to be aware of what the people want. If I went to see The Rolling Stones in concert, I would want them to do 'Satisfaction'. So I do stuff like 'Can't Buy Me Love' and 'Sgt. Pepper' because I know people are going to want to hear those songs . . .

"The thought of planning the tour is fun but there is always the aspect of, 'Now I'm really planning my next year, or so.' I like to leave a bit of space in case something comes along, which I want to do. I'm a great believer in being flexible, but, of course, you can't do that if you're on tour. You've got to commit . . . Something like a tour also stops the rumours. The critics can't say, 'Is he alive? Is he dead?' because you're there. They can't say, 'Is he dead?' when you're up there on the stage. There's obviously going to be some nutter saying, 'That's not him, that's his double.' On tour you also get a chance to meet people, meet the media and chat more than I normally do. Touring also lays to rest some ghosts, like, 'Can he sing?' Well, if I'm going to be out there on stage for two-and-a-half hours, every night, you've got to be able to sing. 'Can he still play the bass?' Well, I'm going to be playing bass up there and after a couple of months' touring, these questions go away, because you've proved it. And if you sell out, you prove that you've still got pulling power. It's good for your confidence and it's also good for the band's confidence."

Thursday, March 4
Paul's latest world tour reaches Australia . . .

Syndicated press release "Paul McCartney is being hounded by a busty fan who wants to jump up on stage with him and strip. Linda Chamberlain, from Chicago, has written to the superstar threatening to do it during his Australian tour. McCartney has doubled security for the tour, which kicks off in Perth tomorrow . . ." Geoff Baker, Paul's spokesman, "We've dubbed her the Mad Stripper but Paul is a bit concerned. Judging by the photos she sent, she is a well-endowed lady and may cause older fans some distress."

Friday, March 5

In a press conference in Perth at the Subiaco Oval, start of his latest tour down under, **Paul** lashes out at Princess Di and Fergie, the young members of the Royal Family . . . "Princess Di and Fergie goof around and act like kids," he blasts. "When I was young, the Royal Family deserved respect and were treated accordingly. When I grew up, the Queen was Your Majesty, touch your forelock sort of stuff. I probably still think that way. But the young generation of Fergie and Di have been goofing around and acting like kids. When you're a Royal you're not supposed to act like that."

Thursday, July 15

Paul's American leg of his world tour runs into trouble when he sensationally fires his manager, Richard Ogden . . .

Syndicated press release "Pop legend Paul McCartney has split with his long-time manager after a furious bust-up on a US tour. Macca, who plays a string of UK dates in September, parted company with manager Richard Ogden after rowing about the cost of Paul's spectacular new stage show. Ogden has worked with the ex-Beatle for more than six years and was in charge of overseeing his massive pop empire. McCartney, the richest rock star in the world, paid Ogden a salary of £200,000 a year for co-ordinating his record releases, tour schedules and juggling his complex £200 million investments. A source close to Paul says, 'Paul relied on his level-headed approach.' But the pair fell out over the spiralling cost of Macca's sold-out American tour. Reveals the source, 'Paul insisted on using the best and most spectacular stage effects available. The crunch came when Paul was told he would have to play another thirty concerts if he wanted to break even. He was furious because no one tells Paul McCartney what to do.' Now scores of managers have contacted Macca offering to oversee his career."

Friday, July 16

One day after firing his manager, Paul finds himself back in the papers, but this time for quite another reason . . .

New York correspondent, Tim Miles "The world's largest car company has halted animal experiments after protests from Paul McCartney. He refused to accept adverts from General Motors in his world tour programme. The former Beatle objected to the company using live animals in crash testing, which included hanging upside down in harnesses and hurling steering wheels at them to simulate accident injuries. American animal rights campaigner, Mary Beth Sweetland, said, 'We called General Motors and told them that Paul McCartney is getting involved. And I asked them whether or not they really want to take on Paul McCartney? They issued a statement a few days later confirming the accident trauma tests on animals would be halted.' Paul, animal lover and vegetarian, gave the advert space that General Motors wanted to the organisation Ethical Treatment of Animals (PETA). A newsletter from PETA claimed that General Motors pounded dog's hearts with a pneumatic device and used rats and mice in exhaust poison tests . . ."

Paul "This is absolutely barbaric and inhumane. They're conducting systematic torture in the name of science. It makes me sick. We all have an obligation to fight this kind of thing."

An associate said, 'Paul was livid when he heard General Motors was conducting crash tests with helpless animals. He was determined to stop them by leading the crusade. He threatened to make TV and radio spots exposing the tests. In the end, the idea of McCartney's vocal opposition was just too much for General Motors, so they dropped the testing programme.' "

A spokesman for General Motors, "We no longer have any animal trauma research activity and do not plan to do any trauma testing in the future."

Friday, August 13
Even though work has been going on full-time in London since the start of 1992, Apple Corps release to the Press today the first details, albeit brief, of the long-mooted official Beatles documentary series. Once titled *The Long And Winding Road*, work has been continuing on the programme under the new title of *The Beatles Anthology*, a change fitting in with the requests of George Harrison . . .

Sam Scott, the *Guardian* "First it was fab, then it was chaos and then it all became too dramatic to talk about. Now, though, the three surviving Beatles have finally joined egos to make and pay for a television documentary series on their world-famous pop group. Produced by their own Apple Productions, the series is currently being edited and is expected to be shown late next year. It will be the first time that George Harrison, Ringo Starr and Paul McCartney have joined forces to tell the tale. John Lennon's widow, Yoko Ono, will also recount his side of the story and tell of his assassination. But Philip Norman, author of The Beatles' biography, *Shout!*, believes that arriving at an agreed version could be an uphill task . . ."

Philip Norman "For years they just wouldn't talk about it all. More recently they have talked about the band individually but not together. Ringo doesn't have a lot to say and George has done a lot since. McCartney has always talked most freely but he always paints himself as the central character. But the problem is, the most interesting one is dead."

Paul, speaking on September 5, "It's not a Beatles reunion. You can fantasise that if we get together on one instrumental, which would be enough for me, then maybe I might have a song and George might have a song. I suspect that if we get into it, then we *will* get into it. But I don't think we'll ever tour but getting together for this TV thing, it might be fun to see what noise we can make."

Anthony Harrington, the *Telegraph* "Will 1994 be the year that The Beatles reform? Probably not, but next year, apart from marking Paul and Linda McCartney's silver wedding anniversary, will see the three surviving Beatles working at closer quarters than they have for more than two decades. And it seems possible that they will even be making a little sweet music together. The occasion is a massive television documentary on the rise and fall of the Fab Four. Entitled *The Beatles Anthology*, the ascent of the Mop Top civilisation will be told in ten one-hour parts and is being made with the full co-operation of Paul, George,

Ringo and Yoko. It seems certain that the surviving Beatles will compose some additional music for the documentary. A Harrison-McCartney instrumental as a requiem for John Lennon has been mentioned. Could this collaboration lead to greater things? The Beatles certainly don't need the money. Their bank balances will swell to bursting point later this month (September) when EMI releases the two classic 1973 compilations, *The Beatles 1962–1966* (known as the Red album) and *The Beatles 1967–1970* (known as the Blue). Though the Red album features just over one hour's worth of music, both records will be double CDs retailing at full price, somewhere in the region of £20 to £25. EMI, it is said, argued that the Red album should be put out as a single CD because it is only 62 minutes in total but Apple demurred. According to *Q* magazine, 'Apple refused any variation of the original format and, in EMI's view, then ensured that they would have to sell the very short double-CD at full price by insisting on top whack royalties.' "

Sunday, September 5

The UK columnist, Virginia Hill writes, "Paul McCartney is rocking his way round the world with the biggest tour of his career. The long and winding road has already taken in Australia, New Zealand, Canada and eighteen states of America. Now Macca and his band are conquering Europe with three sell-out performances in Earl's Court, London, as the centrepiece. And wherever he goes, the response is the same – rave reviews. After thirty years in the business, Macca's relaxed formula has made him the richest pop star in the world, outselling even Michael Jackson. But behind that cool exterior is a lot of hard work. He has spent seven months of this year travelling abroad and can't imagine a time when he won't be writing lyrics and singing songs . . ."

Paul "Nobody used to ask me why I worked so hard when I was in The Beatles. But because I'm getting older, others suddenly see doing what I have always done as hard work. But I still enjoy it. If you're quite good at something and you believe it's magic, then it's not hard work. If you could stand in front of an audience in somewhere like Paris, and you hear the cheers and applause for you, it is very easy to understand why I still do it. I also enjoy being tagged as an ageing sex symbol. Put it this way, most guys would like to go into the room where all the girls are saying, 'Wow, he's my favourite.' It's a good feeling. But, really, there's only one girl for me, and that's Linda. She's rarely from my side and I like it. I tried all the wilder stuff, the all-night clubbing and stuff, when I was a single guy. But the point is that you are very, very lucky to find someone like Linda. I feel sorry for those people who never find the right someone. I used to feel sorry for myself until I met Linda and then a whole different thing happened and I can't explain it. It wasn't just wild, romantic love. It was more than that."

Saturday, September 12
As planned, Paul's New World Tour Two rolls into London with three performances at London's Earl's Court. Watching from the crowd on the opening night is the UK music correspondent, Mark Whineburg . . .

"The moment the lights went down on Paul McCartney's New World Tour show, Earl's Court was engulfed in a tidal wave of nostalgia," Whineburg writes. "The first fifteen minutes plundered history with a film projection of quirky Beatles moments accompanied by such tracks as 'Help!' and 'Maybe I'm Amazed'. Women in the audience near to me were screaming at Paul's film images. McCartney could have come on stage and belched and they would have begged for more. Those girls caught crying and screaming three decades ago are still there and still at it. But now they're married, have had kids and are now nudging into early grand-motherhood. Yet, they're still in love with him. And for them, the image of their baby-faced Paul has never altered. But for those of us watching in the Nineties, the key to the night's success was the dominance of Paul's thoroughbred band. It has been together some four years now and they have clearly spent the majority of that time in rehearsal, fine-tuning the things that matter. They even pulled off an embarrassing 'Whooooh,' during 'I Saw Her Standing There'. Of course, the fifteen Lennon & McCartney songs on offer this evening were all McCartney songs. Who would want to bear witness to Paul taking a stab at John's 'I Am The Walrus'? These classics comprised approximately fifty per cent of the evening's material. Mostly they are played straight and when they are not, the results are mixed. For instance, Robbie McIntosh's mean-picking string work set the soulful 'We Can Work It Out' ablaze, yet the Santana-like interlude during 'Sgt Pepper's Lonely Hearts Club Band' should stand trial for heinous crimes against pop. Between tracks, McCartney kept the needle flickering on the nostalgimetre. 'This is a song from the Sixties,' and 'This is a song from the Seventies,' and these were all numbers that needed no introduction. But new material, from the *Off The Ground* album, required a more formal introduction. Naturally, albums have to be shifted, but it might have made more business sense for Paul not to have dipped quite so heavily (six tracks) into his last disc, with their pat lyrics and nursery-rhyme tunes. But, heck, you could excuse a sentimental old Beatle a few duffers on a night that was, after all, a searing blitz through the McCartney classics. Reminding us again and again of the songwriting talent, succinct melodies and commercial awareness that gave us 'Hey Jude', 'Yesterday' and 'Let It Be'. You could bet your pension or pocket money that no one in Saturday's audience will be rushing out to buy Nirvana's new album, certainly not the 60-year-old rocking in the aisle with his grandson . . ."

David Cheal, *Daily Telegraph* "At Earl's Court, a rapturous crowd, clutching their free programmes, sang and clapped along while the bloke-ish McCartney raised those beseeching eyebrows and wagged his head to such songs as 'Drive My Car', 'Michelle', 'Back In The USSR', 'Magical Mystery Tour', 'Penny Lane', 'Let It Be', 'Lady Madonna', 'Paperback Writer' and 'Sgt. Pepper's Lonely Hearts Club Band'. All of which were performed with admirable authenticity and attention to detail. There was too the inevitable smattering of songs from McCartney's most recent album, *Off The Ground*, but these served little purpose other than to pad the evening out and to provide further proof that, while McCartney may have once been one of the world's finest popular song writers, in the year's since The Beatles' demise, his powers have slowly been deserting him. The juxtaposition of new songs such as 'Peace In The Neighbourhood' and 'Hope Of Deliverance' with old tunes like ''We Can Work It Out' and 'Here, There And Everywhere', was quite simply cruel. The former are little more than musical doodles with gratingly anodyne lyrics, while the latter are masterful examples of the songwriter's art, melodic, fluid, simply worded and expertly structured. Perhaps one of his gifts will come flooding back but in the meantime, Paul McCartney, judging by his triumphant response to the crowd's adulation, seems content to bathe in the reflected glory of his illustrious past. And his fans, in turn, judging by their emotional arm-waving reaction to 'Hey Jude', which closed the show, are delighted that at last they can hear these songs being sung by the man who wrote them."

Wednesday, January 19

In New York, at the Waldorf-Astoria, Paul inducts John into the Rock And Roll Hall Of Fame, during which he confirms that there will a musical reunion of the three surviving Beatles . . .

" 'For old times' sake, we're going to give it a whirl,' " **Paul** announces, forcing a report in the *Independent* . . . "And the most celebrated feud in rock history came to an end as McCartney and Yoko Ono embraced after he handed her the award at the induction dinner in New York, also attended by Sean, son of Lennon and Ono. Lennon's widow had long been blamed for breaking up The Beatles, who were inducted into the *Hall Of Fame* in 1988. The hug between Paul and Yoko brought tears to the eyes of many. McCartney later contemplated a possible Lennon reaction to the honour. 'John would have been the guy in the crowd heckling,' he said. 'And kicked out, maybe,' Ono added. The musical reunion with George Harrison and Ringo Starr will be part of a television documentary on the Fab Four, who split up in 1970. 'We said we'd try and do a little incidental music for it,' McCartney said, adding, 'Unfortunately, the world's press has kind of blown it up like we're trying to better The Beatles, which we're certainly not trying to do.' "

Paul "I knew Yoko had bits and pieces of tapes of John's so I just happened to ring her up on New Year's Day. I said, 'Happy New Year.' She was a bit surprised. I had been up North, had a great New Year and I had come back full of bonhomie thinking, 'Everyone's great and humanity is okay this year,' so I rang her. I thought it would be a great move and we started to chat. We were ringing each other a lot over the next couple of weeks and we got real friendly. And it suddenly occurred to me that it would be terrific to have John on this record. That solved all of the problems. I rang the other guys, George and Ringo, and said, 'Look, if we could get hold of a cassette of something of John's, would we be up for that?' And it seemed that we were. I flew to the States with Linda and Yoko had promised to play me the Lennon tapes when we went over. I sighed when I heard John's vocal on this tape for the first time. She played us three songs, 'Free As A Bird', 'Real Love' and 'Grow Old With Me'. I liked 'Free As A Bird' immediately. I thought, 'I would have loved to have worked with John on that.' I liked the melody, it's got strong chords and it really appealed to me. If John had played those three tunes to me, I would have said, 'Let's work on "Free As A Bird" first.' I took the tapes back to England, got copies made for the guys, they like it and so we decided to do it. In fact, I warned Ringo to have his hanky ready when he listened to the tapes."

But news of the remaining Beatles reunion causes immense scepticism in the newspapers and magazines around the world . . .

The *Sunday Times* (January 23) "Amid the banner headlines about a reunion of The Beatles, of the Fab Three, as they must now be known, the most appropriate response was probably a sceptical, 'Yeah, Yeah, Yeah'. We may still love them madly, in advance of the aural evidence we have made them the bookmakers' favourite for next Christmas's No. 1 single, but the sad truth is that the strokes of individual genius and miracles of group chemistry that once touched these fiftysomethings with greatness went missing long ago. Not even the guiding presence of their silver-haired tonmeister George Martin seems likely to restore three elderly Beatles to their youthful glories. Paul McCartney's well publicised embrace of Yoko Ono in New York last Thursday, at a ceremony to induct the late John Lennon into the Rock And Roll Hall Of Fame, was a clear sign that he would like bygones to be bygones. The fact that neither of the other surviving Beatles bothered to turn up to witness McCartney's 'John and me' speech, was an equally clear indication that a lingering spirit of disunity blights the legacy of the world's most popular pop group. Their individual CVs are now starting to look decidedly dog-eared. George Harrison and Ringo Starr have been, for the past decade, only part-time musicians. Harrison has been running a film company, HandMade Films, launched to acclaim with Monty Python's *Life Of Brian*, but now struggling . . . Harrison was last sighted in concert here at the Albert Hall during the 1992 general election campaign, supporting the cranky Natural Law Party. For most of the Eighties, Starr was an alcoholic without a recording contract, best known for his unseen role as the Scouse voice of the children's television series *Thomas The Tank Engine And Friends.* The eternally cheery, thumbs aloft, figure of Paul 'Macca' McCartney is still never far from the media spotlight, despite the fact that he has gradually lost his golden touch as a songwriter . . . His mimicking of the cover of the *Abbey Road* album on the sleeve of his latest release, *Paul Is Live,* was hardly a smart diplomatic move. There are reasons to doubt whether relations will remain cordial enough for the three of them to feel comfortable inhabiting the same studio. The news that they intend to reconvene next month to record 'incidental music' for a documentary video series about themselves was not strictly news at all. *The Long And Winding Road,* 10 one-hour films made by their own company, Apple, to tell the story of The Beatles, has been two years in the making and is expected to be broadcast worldwide next year. A plan to conclude it with new recorded material had already been agreed and aired in public several times before the *New Yorker* magazine belatedly decided to splash a reunion story. McCartney, who has been urging Harrison and Starr to join him in the studio for years, announced it at a press conference during his last solo tour. Harrison talked about it, though markedly less enthusiastically, on an interview with MTV last September. 'We'll try it, and if it doesn't work, then we'll just put out a song that says, "We Can't Work It Out",' he deadpanned. The nature of Starr's involvement in this project is best illustrated by his recent unavailability for a recording session, pencilled in for January 11. After deciding to extend his skiing holiday, Ringo phoned to say he would be unable to attend . . . As a consistently close friend of Lennon's, Harrison has been giving especially short shrift to the talk of a Beatles reunion. 'John is dead. Whatever we do it won't be The Beatles,' he told MTV. Speaking off the record to a journalist in America, he stated his position more bluntly. 'Listen love, I've spent twenty years backing Paul McCartney's fucking ego.' . . . Unlike groups such as The Rolling Stones, The Who and The Kinks, The Beatles split while they were still in their twenties and were preserved in the aspic of nostalgia, which has surrounded the Sixties ever since. They were never seen to get old in public, before now."

Shout! author Philip Norman "I tend to agree with The Rolling Stones' ex-manager, Andrew Loog Oldham, who, on American television recently, was asked, 'How would you get The Beatles back together?' 'Three more bullets,' Oldham replied."

Friday, February 11

At Paul's Mill Studios in Sussex, after years of resisting the offers to reunite under The Beatles' banner, Paul, George and Ringo commence work on the first new Beatles song since 1970, utilising some of John's home-made demos. One of the tracks secretly recorded is 'Free As A Bird', a track of John's from 1977. The producer on the sessions is Jeff Lynne . . .

Paul "Yoko gave us the cassette with John's voice on it and even then I gave her a veto on the project, saying that if she didn't like what we did on the song, we wouldn't put it out. When we did *Sgt. Pepper* we pretended we were other people. It sometimes helps to get a little bit of a scenario going in your mind. So we pretended that John had just rang us up and said, 'I'm going on holiday to Spain and there's this one little song that I like. Finish it up for me, I trust you.' Those were the crucial words, 'I trust you.'

"I think we were all emotional before we started work, wondering how it would be. Before the session started, we were talking about it, and I was trying to help set it because we never even knew if we could be in a room together, never mind make music together after all these years. But we know each other so well, we just put on the headphones and got on with it. There was some tension between George and I when it came to the time to write a few new lines for the song. We were vying for the best lyric. I think we've done it well. Yoko sent over a sheet of lyrics and we tried them, but they didn't fit. When Ringo heard 'Free As A Bird' in the control room, he couldn't contain himself. He shouted, 'It sounds like the bloody Beatles!' It actually takes off because there are a lot of harmonies that come in and stuff. I thought, 'Wasn't it strange playing along with John Lennon's cassette?' It was very strange and very magic. It was very spooky and very wonderful. We pulled it off and that's the thing. I don't care what anyone says . . . To do this song, we took a cassette of John's, not multi-tracked . . . it was him and piano, interlocked. You couldn't pull the fader down and get rid of the piano. We did a lot of technical stuff on the tape to make it work. And, not being boastful with Jeff Lynne, we did a really good job. We recorded it, George, Ringo and me, and Jeff Lynne was very good."

Jeff Lynne "The mood in the studio was mostly upbeat. It's the only session I've ever done where the talk in between the takes was so good that I didn't even want to start recording. They were all doing all the old anecdotes and one of them would laugh and say, 'What about you, you old bugger!' "

Paul "We had Geoff Emerick, our old Beatles engineer, and he's solid, really great. He knows how Ringo's snare should sound. George Martin wasn't involved. He doesn't want to produce much anymore because his hearing's not as good as it used to be. He's a very sensible guy, and he says, 'Look, Paul, I like to do a proper job,' and if he doesn't feel he's up to it, he won't do it. It's very noble of him, actually, more people would take the money and run."

George Martin "The historic recording by the three remaining Beatles took place in secret in London. They got together and did it entirely on their own in private. They are going to play it to me very soon and I'm looking forward to that."

But the secrecy of the recordings are not kept secret for long . . .

David Wigg, Show business editor, *Daily Express* "The three surviving Beatles have secretly recorded again for the first time since they split in 1970. Paul, George and Ringo teamed up to record their new material. To complete the revival, their old producer, George Martin, will add the finishing studio touches to the tracks. The reunion will spark the most cut-throat race for recording rights in pop music history . . ."

A spokesman for EMI Records, "We hope we will be able to release the new recordings as we have all The Beatles' material. But it is entirely up to Paul, George and Ringo whether or not they do it with us or another company."

But the grand reunion of the surviving members of the Fab Four does not excite everyone, including Ray Coleman who writes in the *Daily Mail* under a title of "The Reunion I Hoped Would Never Take Place" . . .

"Are we about to witness the return of The Beatles? News that Paul, George and Ringo are making music at Harrison's mansion in Henley-on-Thames will inevitably refuel speculation that they will go back on the road. The latest manifestation of Beatlemania began when Paul McCartney hugged Yoko Ono at a function in New York and laid to rest one of the most famous feuds in show business history. For 25 years, fans had blamed Yoko for breaking up The Beatles. At last, Paul's rift with the widow of his old friend and partner seemed to have healed. Inducting Lennon posthumously as a solo artist into the Rock And Roll Hall of Fame, McCartney spoke tearfully about his early days with John in Liverpool. Afterwards, away from the cameras, in a suite at the Waldorf-Astoria Hotel, years of acrimony within The Beatles camp ended in embraces, Paul and Linda with Yoko and her 19-year-old son, Sean. The Beatles grapevine is the hottest gossip circuit in the world and as word of this new affection filtered out, it was heady stuff indeed for Beatles fans awaiting a symbolic reunion of any substance. In America, where each year 25,000 fans make pilgrimages to three Beatles conventions, feverish predictions followed the sighting of Paul and Yoko as friends. Now that the heads of the family were at peace, this meant, surely, that the long-awaited reunion of The Beatles could finally happen. For weeks, radio stations in America played Beatles songs non-stop. They even ran contests asking listeners to suggest names for the new 'Beatles'. Disc jockeys who were not even born in the Sixties were speechless at the prospect of Paul, George and Ringo recreating on stage the greatest group in history. But one such craving was totally flawed because John Lennon was murdered in 1980. But for the three ex-Beatles now to attempt to recreate the old magic, ignoring the march of time by reuniting on stage, would be as sad as it would be impossible. Cherishing their past is one thing, trying to rekindle it in 1994 is another. With Lennon dead, it would have little artistic merit and a vital cog would be missing. And, in fact, it is doubtful whether they will actually heed the clarion calls for a reunion that follows every sighting of them together. They all have better things to do than try to recapture a glorious memory."

Sunday, February 13
Two days into the comeback session, the three remaining Beatles, through Paul, declare that, although they have recorded together again, they will, however, never perform on stage together again . . .

Paul, speaking at his farmhouse in Peasmarsh, East Sussex, "We are furious about these reports, which say that we are about to link up on stage in New York. It's rubbish! There's as much chance of a Beatles reunion as re-heating a soufflé. When John was alive, there was a possibility but without John, it will never happen."

Geoff Baker, Paul's spokesman, "Look, everyone's talking about a live Beatles reunion but it will not happen! It demeans the memory of John Lennon. Apart from that, the only other motive might be money, but what you have to grasp are the full financial implications of this Beatles *Anthology* programme. Once it is sold to TV networks around the world at a premium, then it may well be made into a video, as a collector's item. It is dynamite and will make them a fortune in sales and deals."

While **George** repeats his previous statement, "There will never be a Beatles reunion as long as John Lennon remains dead."

A month later, during a break from a family vacation in Los Angeles, Linda holds a press conference to launch her latest range of vegetarian foods, but the subject of The Beatles and their imminent official *Anthology* documentary series rears its head into the proceedings . . .

"We have a documentary series, which is coming out in a year or two and we said we might do one piece of music for that, just for old times' sake, really," **Paul** announces to the gathered Press. "In fact, we got back together about a month ago in England and we have recorded a track and it's great, really. When you think about a new Beatles track, it's impossible because John's not around, you know. But we've managed to get a track of John's that's unreleased and we just pretended that he had gone on holiday and he said, 'Look, just finish it up. I trust you, just do it.' So that gave us a nice free feeling that we didn't worry what he would think about it and we got on with it and we just treated it like any old track The Beatles might have done. I'm quite proud of it. I think it really worked out great. It's kind of spooky because John's on it and it's actually a Beatles record. But it worked out great!"

Reporter "You didn't think more specifically about what the song is about?"

Paul (firmly) "No!"

(Roars of laughter around the hall)

Press conference's compere "Any food questions, please?"

(Further laughter)

Reporter "I heard the other day that Ringo has become a vegetarian, as well."

Linda "It's very true. He's really into health and his nutritionist said, 'Oh, you've got to go veggie if you want to get healthy.' He jogs and he eats veggie food and he's a very happy person."

Paul "A little while ago, he wasn't that healthy. It was one of these cases where he went to the doctor and he was told what to do and it pointed to him going veggie. Ringo went back to the doctor and the doctor said, 'You've got the body of a 45-year-old man now.'"

Friday, May 19
George and Denis O'Brien's company, HandMade Films, which almost single-handedly kept alive the British film industry in the late Seventies and Eighties, reaches the end of the line when George sells the company for $8.5 million (£5.6 million) in cash to the Toronto based Paragon Entertainment, one of Canada's fastest-growing independent film-makers . . .

Stephen Kahn, the *Daily Express* "It was unclear last night whether Harrison would have a continuing interest in the new concern. Paragon's chairman, Jon Sian, said the purchase gives it a strategic foothold in the international feature film market. Among HandMade's biggest hits was the Monty Python film, *The Life Of Brian*, which grossed $21 million (£14 million) at North American box offices. Other names in the 23-title library include *The Long Good Friday, Mona Lisa, Withnail And I* and *Nuns On The Run*. After a succession of hit films, HandMade's sure touch failed for a time at the beginning of the decade. In 1991, Harrison was reported to have lost half his fortune, once estimated at £14 million, in a succession of flops. HandMade's biggest flop was Madonna's *Shanghai Surprise*, which cost £8 million."

Thursday, September 15

Daily Telegraph "The distinctive voice of John Lennon filled an auction room at Sotheby's today when his earliest known recording with a teenage group in the late 1950s sold for £78,500. A few bars of Lennon singing Lonnie Donegan's skiffle hit 'Putting On The Style', top of the charts that week, was played to applause from a packed sales room. It was part of Lennon's performance at St Peter's church hall, Walton, Liverpool, on July 6, 1957. The date also marked the first meeting between Lennon, then 16, and Paul McCartney, which began the best known partnership in pop music. The tape, Lot 804, and recorded by Bob Molyneux, a retired Liverpool policeman, was bought by EMI, the recording company of The Beatles. Mr David Hughes, the executive who acquired the three-inch tape together with a bulky portable Grundig recorder, admitted the firm had paid slightly more than it had expected to."

David Hughes, EMI "We paid slightly more than we expected to, but this is a unique piece of Beatles history and as the group's record company, we felt it right for us to own it. It will go into our archives and we will be discussing what to do with it in the coming weeks and months."

Bob Molyneux "Despite it missing the estimate of £100,000 to £150,000, I am delighted with the price. I am delighted that it is going to such a good home. It was exactly the right place for it."

Thursday, November 17
George's unusual appearance at last weekend's Adelaide Grand Prix reaches the UK tabloids . . .

The *Sun* "George Harrison has been driving racing hero Damon Hill round the bend with his strange behaviour. Damon clashed with the former Beatle when Harrison gatecrashed a press conference and bombarded him with questions immediately after last weekend's Adelaide Grand Prix. Armed with a camcorder, Harrison repeatedly referred to the Schumacher shunting incident and shouted out, 'Why don't you say what really happened?' Stunned Damon then put his hands over his ears and replied, 'I'm not listening to you, Mr Harrison. I'm not listening to you.' An onlooker remarked, 'George was like a man possessed. He was furious that Damon had been knocked out of the race and seemed intent on getting him to blame Schumacher. But Damon was having none of it. It was a bizarre scene, with George behaving like an over-keen groupie.'
Haggard-looking Harrison is a keen motor racing fan and often turns up for Grand Prix events . . ."

Monday, November 21
Live At The BBC, the first 'new' Beatles album to be released since 1977, is unveiled in a press launch in London . . .

Jane Thynne, UK media correspondent, "The first Beatles LP for 24 years is to be released after being unearthed from the BBC archives. Songs recorded for 39 shows in the Sixties but never commercially recorded are included in *Live At The BBC*, to be released for Christmas with a single in the New Year. Mr Kevin Howlett, a Radio One producer researching a documentary, found them in 1981. He compared his discovery to finding Tutankhamun's tomb."

Kevin Howlett "It took thirteen years for The Beatles to give their consent to the album. They chose George Martin to represent their interests and he acted as quality controller."

Jane Thynne "The three remaining Beatles could not be present at the launch, nor could the album. Given the hopes for its success, the secrecy surrounding *Live At The BBC* would be more suited to the latest royal book or an exposé of next week's National Lottery numbers. Guests at the launch were played a 'sample' of the songs, with instructions not to review them before November 30, the official launch date of the album. Publicity material was available only to those prepared to sign an agreement not to lend it to their friends. 'We're not letting everyone have the album yet. This was an awareness exercise,' a spokesman at EMI explained mysteriously. Fortunately awareness of The Beatles remains high enough for the 56 songs to be regarded as a goldmine. They were included on 39 shows made in 1963 including the Light Programme's *Saturday Club, Easy Beat, From Us To You* and *Pop Go The Beatles*. The songs, most of them rock'n'roll classics, including 'Sweet Little Sixteen', 'Johnny B. Goode' and a rare Lennon & McCartney song, 'I'll Be On My Way', were digitally re-mastered and transformed into a 130-minute double CD by George Martin, The Beatles' former producer . . ."

George Martin, speaking at the launch, "I am amazed because the album sounds so impressive. Some of the stuff they did was not that good and I am the keeper of the flame. These recordings show how good they were live, before we started doing the production tricks."

In the early hours of **Thursday, December 1**, the first copies of The Beatles' new album are sold at Tower Records in Piccadilly Circus, London . . .

Daily Express "At a minute past midnight, the doors opened and fans dressed in Sixties gear made a frenzied rush to get their hands on the double-album entitled The Beatles *Live At The BBC*. It features 56 songs never heard before, recently discovered in the BBC archives. At the head of the late night queue was Steve Bennett, 33, from Surrey. He jumped for joy as he collected the album. 'This is better than winning the lottery,' he cried. By 2am, more than 250 copies of the £19.99 double-album had been snapped up. Big queues built up at stores throughout the country as the record went on general sale later today . . ."

Tony Parsons writes in the *Daily Telegraph* "Here we are in Tutankhamun's tomb and the early Beatles sessions have been unearthed in the BBC archives. And just when you are starting to think that perhaps you have encountered 'Dizzy Miss Lizzy', 'Lucille' and 'Long Tall Sally' one time too many, you find yourself yet again mugged by the overwhelming charm of four boys who shook the world. *Live At The BBC* features The Beatles at the crossroads. No longer the group that honed their skills in Hamburg, but not yet the prodigies who pushed back pop music's final frontiers. This is the flop-haired Fabs poised between being merely a great band and true greatness. The music on *Live At The BBC* is more exciting than you could reasonably expect but the banter in between the tracks is touched with genius."

Ringo "I get excited listening to the tracks because it was a band I was in, and you tend to forget that we were a working band. Everyone thinks of *Sgt. Pepper* but before that we did every club in the planet. All the groups in Liverpool were doing the same numbers. We were very lucky coming from Liverpool because it was a port and it seemed that half of Liverpool was in the Merchant Navy and all these records were coming from America, so you could find out about Arthur Alexander and people like that . . .

"Hearing them again knocked me out. It has been a while since I had heard them. It shows that we were a pretty good band, even in the olden days. Some of the tracks we would rehearse in the morning, then do them live on the radio that afternoon. I really like 'I'll Be On My Way', 'A Shot Of Rhythm And Blues', which is an all-time classic, 'Sure To Fall', which has always been one of my favourites and 'You've Really Got A Hold On Me' is still a Beatles classic. It was a lot of fun and a lot of work. But that was what we wanted to do . . ."

Tuesday, December 6

Marianne MacDonald of the *Independent* reports, "Record company executives have been taken aback by sales of the new Beatles album, which has had middle-aged and elderly buyers reaching for it with the enthusiasm of Hollywood matrons for HRT. *Live At The BBC* was released by EMI last Wednesday and was No. 1 in the charts on Sunday. Although EMI does not give out sales figures, a spokeswoman described the response as 'overwhelming. We expected it to do well obviously, but sales have gone beyond our wildest dreams.' Such has been the interest in the release that the Oxford Street branch of WH Smith in London reversed a four-year-old policy of not selling vinyl to accommodate diehard Beatles fans . . ."

But the *Live At The BBC* album is regarded as more of a missed opportunity to some of the more hardened Beatles connoisseurs, like Allan Kozinn, who writes in *The New York Times* on **December 7** . . .

"Anyone who knows these recordings, either from their abundant representation on bootlegs or from the BBC radio specials that have been broadcast annually since 1982, will find this collection more flawed than satisfying. What's wrong? To begin with, the set offers only 56 of the 88 songs and only 30 of the 36 non-EMI items. Among the missing rarities are a rocked-up version of 'Beautiful Dreamer' and a goofy but topical 'Lend Me Your Comb'. Also glaringly absent are radio renderings of several hits and favourites, including 'Please Please Me', 'She Loves You' and 'Twist And Shout'. EMI apparently believes that only fanatics could want it all. Still, a third disc, hardly unheard of for this kind of release, would have allowed the inclusion of one version of every song the band played to the BBC . . . Not that the set is a total washout. EMI has refurbished these recordings, many of which come from bootlegs or off-the-air tapes, and although a few tracks have the slightly hollow sound that digital noise-reduction processes sometimes yield, most sound far better than anything previously bootlegged or broadcast . . . In a rare example of BBC fudging, the solo from the EMI version of 'A Hard Day's Night', Harrison on 12-string with the group's producer, George Martin, doubling on piano, was edited into the BBC performance. Collectors have long assumed that Harrison was unable to play it properly that day, although he later performed it in concert. But the *Live At The BBC* album cannot compare to the nine-CD bootleg box set *The Complete BBC Sessions*, which was recently released in Italy. The lavishly annotated Great Dane box set includes 239 performances and a few outtakes that were not broadcast but some of the tracks, 'I'll Be On My Way' and 'Johnny B. Goode' sound better than on *Live At The BBC*."

While frenzied scenes of modern day Beatlemania surround the *Live At The BBC* album, attention returns to The Beatles' long-mooted documentary film, *The Beatles Anthology*, with reports appearing in the press regarding the UK TV bidding war for the programme . . .

UK columnist, Samuel Roberts (December 9) "Bosses at the BBC and ITV are at each other's throats in a £20 million battle to win the rights to screen a historic series about The Beatles. The 12-part documentary, which chronicles the history of The Fab Four, has been made with the co-operation of the three remaining Beatles and John Lennon's widow, Yoko Ono. The series will hit our screens next autumn and will feature a wealth of never-before-seen and home movies of the band. The programme will also feature The Beatles performing the only song that they have recorded since their bust-up in 1969. The song, 'Free As A Bird', was written by John Lennon and Paul, George and Ringo have used the wonders of modern technology to marry their recording to that of John Lennon's demo tape. The single will be released to coincide with the series . . ."

While the *Daily Express* columnist, Louise Gannon (also on December 9), is quick to reiterate this, "It has been believed that the BBC has already secured the rights to the series but last night it was revealed that ITV look most likely to win the battle. A source at ITV said, 'The BBC have been tacitly implying that *The Long And Winding Road* is their biggest gig for next year. But this isn't true! Offers of around £10 million were put in some time ago but that is about half the actual value. ITV have put up the stakes by double but the BBC just don't want to lose out on something which is of such sociological importance. It will be the jewel in the crown of any TV scheduling. There are some fraught executives racing around at the moment.' "

A source close to the *Anthology* series is heard to remark, "It will be the hottest thing to hit our television screens next year. Many people thought that the programmes were going to be shown by the BBC, but ITV is desperate to broadcast them, too. Whoever gets the series will have the biggest jewel in all their programming."

Six days later, on **Thursday, December 15**, The Beatles' *Live At The BBC* album again reaches the newspapers but for quite another reason . . .

Daily Mirror "The Beatles' new album slipped from the No. 1 slot because shops ran out of copies. EMI originally pressed up 200,000 copies of the album but it sold so fast that record company chiefs had to order a new batch. Sources at the record company say that shops were only able to satisfy half the demand for the record from fans desperate to buy a copy. Record shops up and down the country admit that they have lost thousands of pounds because of the mix-up over the double-album, which was released last Monday."

1995

Sunday, January 22

The new year begins with further bad news for **George** . . .

Stuart White, the *News Of The World* "Millionaire Beatle George Harrison was staring bankruptcy in the face last night after accusing a close friend of conning him out of £16 million. The 51-year-old pop legend has filed a lawsuit against business partner, Denis O'Brien, claiming the accountant milked him of a fortune over twenty years. In court papers, filed in Los Angeles, the star accuses O'Brien of setting up a tangled web of investments so complex Harrison was unable to keep track of his money; allowing the value of those investments to nose-dive through poor management and bad judgement; secretly siphoning off millions of pounds to fund a jet set lifestyle, which featured yachts and villas in various parts of the world; and conning Harrison into believing O'Brien shared liability for their company's bad debts when, in truth, the star was on his own. Yesterday Harrison left his stately home in Henley-on-Thames, Oxfordshire, and drove for three hours to stay with friends in a bid to escape the media spotlight. The *News Of The World* was the only paper to track the star down. Last night, he told us exclusively, 'It's kind of crazy. This is one of these things that happen in life. I think the court papers tell the whole story, it's a long one and everything is contained in there. The action is proceeding and I'm letting my lawyers handle it. I'm not saying it's not been a strain. It's just something you cope with. I'll just get on with it. I'm really tired by the whole thing.' It is not clear whether the star's lavish lifestyle is under threat. But he may be advised to go voluntarily bankrupt in America to protect him from losing his £16 million fortune . . ."

The story also features in a report by Andrew Alderson in the *Sunday Times* "George Harrison, the former Beatle, has filed a $25 million (£16 million) lawsuit against his former business partner and financial manager for allegedly mishandling his investments and defrauding him for twenty years. Harrison, who moved into the film business after The Beatles disbanded, has claimed that Denis O'Brien, once a close friend, misused 'his client's assets and credit' to finance secret profit and a lavish lifestyle fore himself. O'Brien, who was unavailable for comment yesterday, is expected to contest the allegations . . . According to a lawsuit, filed at the Los Angeles Superior Court, O'Brien used a 'Byzantine structure of investments to ensure Harrison could not keep track of his money and the management of HandMade Films'. HandMade Films was sold last year to a Canadian company. Initially, the company made successful films, including *The Life Of Brian*, starring the Monty Pythons and *Mona Lisa*, starring Bob Hoskins. More recent films, including *Shanghai Surprise*, starring Madonna, have been costly flops."

Sunday, March 26

Rebecca Fowler, the Arts Correspondent for the *Sunday Times* reveals that "Yoko Ono and Paul McCartney have come together after nearly three decades of hostilities to make a secret musical recording with their families in a gesture of peace. Insiders saw the private reconciliation, which took place at McCartney's studio in East Sussex, as the final conclusion to the bitter recriminations that followed the break-up of The Beatles. The recording took place when Ono and her son, Sean, spent a weekend with the McCartney family at their country home in Rye. To mark the end of one of rock's most enduring feuds, the two clans played a work by Yoko entitled 'Hiroshima Sky Is Always Blue'. It was written as a memorial for the 50th anniversary of the dropping of the atom bomb on Japan. Ono and Sean performed alongside McCartney, while his wife, Linda, accompanied them on the organ. McCartney's three daughters, Mary, Stella and Heather, played percussion and son James was on the guitar. The lyrics of the song, described as being in the style of The Plastic Ono Band, consisted of the title words being repeated in different ways. Afterwards, McCartney gave Ono the master tape to use as she likes. It is also understood Ono has agreed to give him some of Lennon's unfinished songs, reportedly with permission to turn them into new Beatles numbers . . ."

Sean Lennon "The recordings were not planned. It was more the result of our reconciliation after twenty years of bitterness and feuding bullshit. It was incredible working with Paul. Here were these people who had never played together actually making music."

On **Monday, June 12**, Paul and Linda's fashion student daughter, Stella, steps out of the shadows and grabs the limelight for her catwalk show, which surprisingly features appearances by the supermodels Kate Moss, Yasmin LeBon and Naomi Campbell . . .

Fashion correspondent, Sarah King "Rival designers at the Central St Martins college show even suggested that Paul had paid for the notoriously expensive models. One of Stella's peers said, 'It just proves what money and fame can do.' Kate Moss flew in especially for the show. Sitting in the middle of the front row, Paul, Linda and their family seemed to be riveted by the catwalk displays. McCartney said later, 'I am the proudest dad in the world. I thought that it was brilliant. Stella has come a long way since she first started out.' "

Monday, July 31
The repercussions of **George**'s lawsuit against Denis O'Brien are revealed in an exclusive report, syndicated by the famed UK journalist, David Wigg . . .

"George Harrison may have to sell his much-loved mansion," the report reads. "The former Beatle has had meetings with a top London estate agent who handles property for the rich and famous. Magnificent Friar Park, near Henley-on-Thames, is worth around £10 million. Harrison is currently embroiled in a £16 million legal fight with his former manager and film company partner, Denis O'Brien. He has filed papers through the Los Angeles Superior Court accusing O'Brien of mismanaging his money. Harrison complains, 'O'Brien made secret decisions, concealed and misrepresented the facts and took actions contrary to Harrison's wishes and directions. And through his improper and inept management, caused the film organisation to lose huge sums of money.' According to court papers, the disaster left Harrison liable for £16 million in loans and guarantees. His Los Angeles lawyer, Brian Edwards, explained, 'This is a very serious and heated dispute, but it's very early days yet.' The case is set to be heard in Los Angeles this month. Harrison's attorneys are trying to hurry things up, but so far O'Brien has not filed a defence. All Harrison will say is, 'I'm letting my lawyers handle it.' If he loses the case, the musician could be down to his last £10 million and that could spell a move from the 120-room mansion. If Friar Park goes, all the rock star trappings will go with it. The house has a 120-track recording studio, part of £1.5 million worth of renovations completed a few years ago . . ."

Saturday, October 21

As the build-up to The Beatles *Anthology* continues, sound recordist Paul Le Marre announces that he is intending to sell a fifteen-minute tape, which comprises music and chatter made by The Beatles and recorded on the eve of their last public performance, which took place on the roof of the Apple building on January 30, 1969 . . .

"I made the tape during the *Let It Be* film sessions because I feared that Apple was going broke and I might not get paid, " Paul reveals. "The recording is of the group talking about how they were going to record the track 'I Want You'. John Lennon was being an absolute pain in the neck. He wasn't a happy man and made things very difficult. The others all turned up at seven in the morning but John didn't arrive until much later. Ringo was the wit. He was as sharp as a razor and quite cutting in some of his remarks to Lennon. Paul was the nice guy. He was always sunny natured and encouraging the others. George can also be heard but he doesn't say much."

Sunday, October 22

The following day, **Paul** hits out at the British establishment for failing to make him a Sir . . .

"All The Beatles are MBEs except John, who sent his back," Paul blasts. "It's the lowest honour you can have from Britain. Jimmy Savile, Andrew Lloyd-Webber and Cliff Richard all have knighthoods. All these people are Sirs. Even George Martin, The Beatles' producer, has a higher honour than we have. But I'm not bitter. You can't sit around saying, 'God, I wish they'd make me a Sir.' Funnily enough, in his early days, John was very much wondering how he would be remembered. I said, 'You're crazy, man. What are you talking about? You'll be remembered as something fantastic and you'll be out in the cosmos somewhere. And I have a feeling that other things will be of more consequence at that point.' "

Sunday, November 19

With immense anticipation, The Beatles *Anthology* television special receives its world premiere on the ABC TV Network in America . . .

Paul "We wanted to set the record straight. There's all these books written about The Beatles and me, and most are by people I've never met. We did a lot of interviews for the *Anthology* film, with the intention of setting a few myths straight, although it doesn't always work. The funniest thing is that we don't always agree on the memories, because it was thirty years ago. It can be hilarious . . . There's one bit where Ringo's telling a story, and he says, 'At that point, George had a sore throat,' and the camera pans to George and he says, 'I thought it was Paul' and the camera pans to me and I say, 'Well, I know it was John.' I've worked it out since. If Ringo thought it was George, it wasn't Ringo. If George thought it was me, it wasn't George and if I thought it was John, it wasn't me. It must have been John, he's the only one left. But this is funny, for the definitive bloody thing on The Beatles; you've got to laugh. It's fucking human, and so real. We forgot, who cares? We did some great stuff, but exact analysis was never our bag."

Ringo "It did become fun and it just started evolving and we became more and more involved. I've seen every frame of the show. We've been totally involved. It shows what we feel about The Beatles rather than what people feel we feel. We've spent hours hanging out together and we've got rid of the dog dirt that we were involved in with each other. That's all gone out of the window."

George "We all have different memories and one concerns Elvis when we all went to his house in Bel Air in, I think, 1965. We were talking about Priscilla and one of us said, 'Oh yeah, Priscilla came in wearing a green dress and she had a green bow in her hair.' Then somebody said, 'I remember that she had a blue dress and a diamond tiara.' So what we've got is actually four different stories. Paul remembers so many stories and just to get together with him was interesting. We'd be talking about stuff and he would mention something we hadn't thought of for years and years."

Paul "The scary thing for me is how young we were because you'll see us on things like *The Ed Sullivan Show* and *The Royal Command Performance*. I was only about 22 and you see the footage and think, 'God, we were just kids, and younger than what most of my kids are now.' Over the years, insiders and hangers-on have told their own story of The Beatles and I have enjoyed being able to tell my side of the story. If things weren't true, we've tried to put the record straight but we've concentrated on just laying out the story as it happened. In these hours, my life just flashes by in front of me."

Chips Chipperfield, executive producer for the *Anthology* series, "It's the first time they have ever done anything like this and I can't think of a bigger series in terms of international broadcasting. It will go out to more or less every country. It is marvellous to have a musical contribution from them."

The UK TV premiere takes place across the ITV Network a week later during the evening of **Sunday, November 26**. But the reviews are mixed . . .

Pete Clark, *Evening Standard* "To call the first film dull would be to do dull a disservice. Beyond a couple of scenes of John, Paul and George in the earliest days, manfully attempting to fuse the newly learned skills of guitar-playing and cigarette smoking, there was nothing to tingle the spine. The film failed to provide any sense of the manic excitement, which must have been felt as the young Beatles learned the language of American rock'n'roll and then, without missing a beat, translated the whole lot into English. Worse than that, the film succeeded in fatally downplaying those incidents in the group's career, which have become cornerstones of The Beatles' myth. The Beatles *Anthology* promised so much but delivered so little. All traces of strife, skulduggery, bad behaviour and lunacy, all vital elements in the making of a rock'n'roll band, had been scrubbed from the tale. For this we have to thank Apple and the surviving Beatles, who retained editorial control. *Anthology* director, Geoff Wonfor, vehemently denied any attempt had been made to sanitise the story . . ."

Geoff Wonfor "My only problem is that I don't have enough time. There are so many anecdotes that just had to go. I was certainly not told to gloss over anything."

Pete Clark "The Beatles *Anthology* is the perfect example of alchemy in reverse, gold transmuted into base metal. And all to make us fork out for a new record containing inferior versions of songs we already own. Roll over Beethoven and let John Lennon spin in his grave."

Six days previously, on **Monday, November 20**, the extraordinary countdown to the worldwide launch of the *Anthology 1* double-album and the premiere airing of the first Beatles song in 25 years, is also worthy of saturation newspaper coverage . . .

UK reporter, Giles Coren "At 4 o'clock in the morning, the B-Day landings began. Thanks to a worldwide embargo for US Television (ABC), it was in the grim cold hours before dawn that the first new Beatles song for a quarter of a century took off into the air from radio stations all over Britain to launch the biggest campaign Beatlemania has known since the 1960s . . ."

UK reporter, Tim Crystal "Under the sort of secrecy more appropriate to D-Day, the first new Beatles song for a quarter of a century made its way in the early hours from Abbey Road to BBC Broadcasting House in London . . ."

Radio One DJ, Clive Warren, live on air shortly after 4am, "Here it is, the first new song in 25 years from The Beatles . . ."

It marks the media release of 'Free As A Bird' and immediately the judgements are passed . . .

Giles Coren " 'Free As A Bird' is more than unreleased. It was not even recorded. It is a product of virtual pop. John Lennon's voice taken from a demo tape and rearranged with accompaniment by the three musicians who grew old as he did not."

The Beatles producer, George Martin " 'Free As A Bird' is a super song. I like the way the harmonies move. I like the lyrics. I don't think it's as good as 'Strawberry Fields', which didn't actually get to No. 1, but I think 'Free As A Bird' is much better than other No. 1s we've had. Having heard it now, I wish I'd produced it. This will certainly be No. 1 all over the world."

But the UK disc jockey, Jonathan King, never worried about upsetting The Beatles fraternity, is quick to blast, "It is total rubbish! It sounds like a very bad demo made by elderly session musicians struggling to earn a crust. It reeks of money, not of enthusiasm or musical inventiveness. John Lennon would have been ashamed to think it would ever see the light of day. You can almost hear him at the end of the record saying, 'What a load of rubbish. Thank God no one will ever hear it.' McCartney has provided the most plodding bass line I've ever heard and George sounds like he's got arthritis. If it was by a new band, it would be rejected immediately."

UK disc jockey, Tony Blackburn " 'Free As A Bird' will be an enormous hit because it's The Beatles but had it been by anybody else, I don't think that it would get the air time. It is not a good record but people will certainly buy it."

The big thumbs-down for The Beatles' new disc continues when the highly respected writer and commentator, Germaine Greer remarks, "They're flogging a dead horse. I think the record is leaden and awful. If it is No. 1 this Christmas then it is going to be a grim Christmas."

But The Beatles' official biographer, Hunter Davies, is quick to say, "It doesn't worry me what it's like. Beatles fans will lap it up even if it is rubbish. Wordsworth fans read his crap poems just because they're Wordsworth. Even if they keep digging out scrag-ends, and unfinished stuff, and there must be more, we'll still buy it."

And what of the thoughts of the three surviving Beatles?

Ringo "It's great and I'm not just saying it because I'm on it. It really is an amazing Beatles track. I had taken myself away from it for so long that it was like listening as an outsider and it really sounds like them. It's just brilliant!"

George "It's a very happy occasion for me to hear that it actually works and to hear John's voice in a song again. That was very nice. Maybe I'm peculiar but I don't think of him as dead."

Paul "George (Harrison) is a very forthright character and he just says what he thinks. In fact, he wasn't really keen on 'Free As A Bird'. He was saying to me, 'I sort of felt that John was going off a little bit towards the end of his writing.' I personally found that a bit presumptuous but I don't think we should get into that because this is going to sound sour. I always felt that John was a great songwriter. Anyway, I don't think that this whole *Anthology* thing would have happened if John was still alive. It could have been very difficult. This is conjecture, but I think it would have been okay with John and me. And I think it would have been okay with Ringo. I had managed to make my peace with John before he was killed but George hadn't. I'm not sure whether they were talking or what it was. George did his big book, his life story, and he's (John) barely mentioned in it and John was naturally upset."

Later on the morning of November 20, at the Savoy Hotel in London, June Southworth, reports on the official launch for the *Anthology 1* album for the *Daily Mail* "Only one of The Beatles turned up for the biggest record launch in the history of hype yesterday. As 800 journalists stared at the empty stand where the drum kit bearing the band's name was as familiar as an exit sign, John Lennon's presence was everywhere. You could almost hear that flat, laconic voice asking what the hell was going on. And his cynical laughter as the five-man backing group, which the surviving Beatles had sent along in their place, sat uneasily dodging questions. There was their former roadie, Neil Aspinall, who is still working for Apple Corps, the eternally laid-back Derek Taylor, still their PR; George Martin, who produced the 'new' *Anthology* albums just as he produced them the first time around; Jeff Lynne, producer of 'Free As A Bird', the single that resurrects John Lennon, the man who thought The Beatles were more famous than Jesus; and a record company supremo nobody had heard of. What the world's press wanted to know, and never found out, was why Paul McCartney, George Harrison and Ringo Starr had stayed away themselves. More to the point perhaps, how a load of outtakes, the rejected tracks that didn't make the original Beatles records, were now considered fit to issue . . ."

Reporter "Where are The Beatles today?"

Derek Taylor "At home, but they send their love. They are everywhere, but here."

Reporter "Why is The Beatles *Anthology* being released when Parlophone staff had always maintained that there was nothing left worth releasing?"

George Martin "People are ready for it now and they probably weren't in 1970 and 1980."

Reporter "Why does 'Free As A Bird' sound like something by The Traveling Wilburys?"

Jeff Lynne "It doesn't sound anything like The Traveling Wilburys. I put a lot more work into this one. The Wilburys take ten minutes and this took fifteen!"

The *Anthology 1* album is released simultaneously around the world the following day . . .

Derek Taylor, Apple Corps "*Anthology 1* is the musical equivalent of the Churchill Papers."

Paul "What was so lovely was having an excuse to see the guys a lot, sitting with Ringo, George and George Martin in Studio Two at Abbey Road again. People questioned us as to whether or not we should have recorded 'Free As A Bird' but don't they think I checked under every little stone? John and I used to discuss this situation when we were young boys sitting in his Auntie's living room in Liverpool. After Buddy Holly died, some records were released with a backing group dubbed on to his voice, and credited to Buddy Holly & The Fireballs. And we said, 'No way, it should be still credited to Buddy Holly & The Crickets.' This new record isn't John & The Fireballs, it's John & The Beatles and that's the difference. I worried what Yoko might think but she was the one who gave us the cassette with John's voice on it, so she must have been happy."

George "The Beatles exist apart from myself. I am not really 'Beatle George'. Beatle George is like a suit or shirt that I once wore on an occasion, and until the end of my life, people may see that shirt and mistake it for me. I want someone like U2 to watch the *Anthology* series and then they'd see a band that was *really* famous."

Paul "Promoters have begged me, George and Ringo to get back up on stage. We have had a major offer from America to do just ten dates across the States and the money is ridiculous, about $100 million! It's scandalous. From the money point of view, most people would do it but to me, at this moment, the three of us isn't as exciting as the four of us. You couldn't fill that hole on stage. The Beatles was always the four of us. People will say we could get someone else in, but it's still not the same. The Beatles was The Beatles."

On **Friday, December 1**, the New York media correspondent, Mark Tran writes, "The new double-album, The Beatles *Anthology*, has sold so well in the US that it could have set the biggest first-week total in recording history. *Anthology* sold an estimated 1.2 million copies in the week ended last Sunday. The success is a financial windfall for EMI-Capitol. 'This is the equivalent of a movie opening,' said Charles Koppelman, chairman and chief executive of EMI-Capitol, adding that the new Beatles album has boosted sales of earlier Beatles albums to more than 200,000 copies last week . . ."

Sunday, December 10

Two of The Beatles feature in a news report with a difference. The piece, written by David Brown, is entitled "Let It Pee! Soaking For Macca Rose" and reads, "Beatle George Harrison has a dog that pees on Paul McCartney every day. Whenever Winston, the Yorkshire terrier, goes for walkies in George's garden, he cocks his leg and showers a rose bush named after fellow Beatles and Wings star Macca. Former head gardener, Derek Mann, said George, currently top of the charts with 'Free As A Bird', The Beatles' first track in 25 years, 'always takes Winston for walks past the two foot shrub. George said, "It is great baying Winston around because he can piss on Paul McCartney once a day. It was just a joke in the family. He didn't mean it maliciously."' Winston has answered the call of nature on the bush so often it now has dieback, a disease that attracts the stem. Derek added, 'I don't think it is going to get much bigger. It has done all the growing it is going to do.' He also revealed that Harrison has a keepsake of another band member at his Friar Park estate in Henley, Oxon. There is a mosaic of a space monster crafted by John Lennon, who was shot dead in 1980 . . ."

Monday, December 11

Far removed from the excitement surrounding the *Anthology*, the year ends on a bad note when it is announced that Linda McCartney has had an operation to remove a lump from her breast. The lump was discovered when she went to hospital for a routine breast scan. She underwent surgery at the Princess Grace Hospital in London . . .

Paul "We were totally scared. She'd had a lump under her arm, which she'd gone and seen our local doctor about, and he'd given her some antibiotics and told her, 'Don't worry about it, it's nothing.' But she talked to a couple of women friends and they said she should get it checked out. So she did and I was out of the house one day, and she rang me. She said, 'I've got the results of the tests back,' and she said, 'I've got breast cancer.' Naturally, our lives just turned round at that second. She said, 'You had better come home.' I said, 'Don't worry, I'm on my way.' So I just ran home. We immediately got into the car and drove up to London to try and get some facts, because we were two hours away from any sort of medical help. And from then on, we just embarked on a two-and-a-half year programme of trying everything we possibly could to turn it round. As anyone who knows anything about breast cancer, if you're unlucky it will travel from the breast and go to your nodes, which are like your safety valves under your arm. Depending on how many nodes are infected that's generally the seriousness of your illness. Linda had met some friends who were good supporters and who had had it and they'd sort of say, 'It had gone into three of my nodes,' and stuff. We sort of knew it was a little more than that, but to tell you the truth, we'd try to block it out, trying to keep positive. We knew we had a battle on and so we tried everything. The biggest difficulty is miracle cures coming out of the woodwork. Everyone's got a miracle cure and some of them say what you really don't want to do is to go the traditional medical route. I hate to say this, but I still don't know the answer. For instance, when Stella was born we had to go the traditional medical route, as there were complications at the birth. If we hadn't, both Linda and the baby would have died. So we'd learned that there were times when you needed traditional modern medical science and we opted for that route. We found really good people, who were the best, who knew the most about her condition and who knew the very best treatments. And the truth of the matter is, she tried them all. She had her first bout of treatment, and she tried that and the sad thing is, she coped with it so well because she was such an up person. She hardly ever lost her appetite, and you're really

453

supposed to lose your appetite on these things. But Linda was such a sort of lusty person. She never went like an ill person. People around her would be dropping and she'd be saying, 'No, don't worry, we're going to lick this thing.' She really stayed so positive."

Further bad news is heaped on the couple when it is announced that their St John's Wood home in London had been ransacked on the day that Linda was undergoing surgery . . .

Paul "This house has been broken into many times during the past thirty years as this part of London is a favourite area for burglars. We are improving security and obviously an incident like this doesn't help at a time like this."

Thursday, March 7

There's bad news for The Beatles' second comeback single, 'Real Love', when BBC Radio One announces that they will not be adding it to their playlist on the grounds that it is "not of sufficient merit" . . .

Paul "The Beatles don't need our new single to be a hit. It's not as if our careers depended on it. We've done all right over the years and if Radio One feels that we should be banned now, it's not exactly going to ruin us overnight. Is Radio One as important as it once was? As Ringo said to me, 'Who needs Radio One when you've got all these independent stations?' "

The *Independent* newspaper "The single 'Real Love', only the Fab Four's second single since their split in 1970, has entered the midweek charts at No. 4 but the BBC station has decided that the track will not interest its listeners and have left it off their playlist of 60 records. Instead, Radio One has selected less established chart names for their playlist, such as Gap Decor, 99th Floor Elevators, Benz and Goldie. Oasis, the band who have admitted to basing their sound around The Beatles, have two tracks on the playlist . . ."

Geoff Baker, The Beatles' spokesman blasts, "We are obviously very furious with Radio One. Over the years, The Beatles have made a fortune for the BBC. There is obviously a public demand for and interest in the record because it is No. 4. We conducted research, which showed that 41 per cent of the buyers of the last single were teenagers. They were the largest single group of buyers in the survey."

Rock critic, Tony Parsons "Anybody that has got any curiosity about contemporary music would want to hear a Beatles song. The jumped-up little men at Radio One are getting a little bit above themselves with this one. They're being self-consciously cool. But really, there is nothing so square as people trying to be trendy."

But a spokesman for the BBC answers back, "We haven't banned the record, 'Real Love'. We are a contemporary music station and each week there are 250 new releases. Each record is chosen for its own merits. It's not an ageist decision. Sting is on our playlist, and so is David Bowie."

The *Independent* concludes, "However, there was better news for The Beatles last night when it was announced that the more sedate Radio Two has decided to put 'Real Love' on its playlist. But Radio One's stance contrasts with its views on The Beatles last autumn when it was desperate to be the first station in Britain to play 'Free As A Bird'. The station played it at 4am."

Monday, March 18

The Beatles release the album *Anthology 2* simultaneously around the world . . .

Paul " 'Revolution 9' is probably John's most experimental song with The Beatles, but the year before (1967), I wrote a piece called 'Carnival Of Light', which was very avant-garde. It didn't get on The Beatles *Anthology* because some of the people involved thought it was too far out. But it's a 15-minute piece, which has so far been unheard. I like it, but you've got to think John Cage was important to appreciate it, which I do. John (Lennon) could only do 'Revolution 9' because I put a couple of tape recorders together and showed him how to do it. That's how he came to do *Two Virgins*. John could never have done it otherwise. He was hopelessly untechnical."

Wednesday, October 23

Five days before the issue of *Anthology 3*, the *Daily Express* reports "George Harrison, the ageing Beatle who so enlivened the last election with his sponsorship of the absurd Natural Law Party, has had his karma shattered by Bob Dole. The Republican presidential candidate has been playing Harrison's 1966 Beatles hit 'Taxman' as a rousing anthem for his electioneering rallies. No one told George and the first he knew of it was when he overheard a Dole speech televised from Chicago. 'What cheek,' snaps Harrison's spokesman, Derek Taylor. 'He wrote the song as an apolitical statement. He believes no one should pay taxes. George thinks all politicians are equally deplorable whether they are Indonesian, Belgian or American.' Sadly there is not a lot that Harrison can do about it. The rights to this tune and almost all The Beatles' other songs are owned by Michael Jackson."

Monday, October 28

The third and final album in the *Anthology* trilogy appears simultaneously around the world, and again receives mixed reviews. For instance, Roger Catlow of the *Hartford Courant* newspaper speaks for many columnists when he writes . . .

"And now it ends, a year of unprecedented success for a band that has been gone for more than a quarter-century. A flood of unreleased tracks, more than 150, released on six-discs during 11 months and reels and reels of video-ography, ten-hours over eight volumes of home video, sold in a boxed set for $150. It's obvious now that The Beatles have made more money with the 1995–1996 *Anthology* series than they did even when they were at the apex of the planet's rock scene 30 years ago. But nowhere has it been as clear as it is on the final instalment how pale most of the outtakes were compared with the real songs. *Anthology 3* will complete the series of double-disc outtakes when it is released. The Beatles were the world's most important rock group not only because of the genius in writing and performing, but also in choosing to release the correct takes on the finished albums. By the time we reach the chronological period covered by *Anthology 3*, the band had long since stopped touring, so there are no live performances or TV appearances to leaven the studio work. It's obvious the work became a grind to them, because it does so to the listener as well. Unlike the other two sets in the *Anthology* series, there is no unreleased track here that deserved to have been issued previously, such as 'Leave My Kitten Alone' from the first set. Most noticeable of all is that there is no third 'new' Beatles track, with the surviving Beatles reuniting around the work tapes of John Lennon. After the shameful radio response to 'Real Love', the new Beatles track on *Anthology 2* earlier this year, the group decided not to push the novelty of these posthumous jams. Yet the absence of such an event robs 3 of much of its surprise.

"So the *Anthology* series, like The Beatles themselves, end with a sneer, shrug and a whimper instead of a shake, rattle and roll, which they cover in a middling Fifties rock medley on the new set. Aside from a totally incongruous symphonic opening by George Martin, *Anthology 3* begins with a sparkling series of previously unheard home demo tracks for the *White Album*, songs that probably alone are worth the price. Back from their spiritual sojourn in India, Lennon and Paul McCartney lay down tracks for songs they could include in their next album. They gather at the estate of George Harrison, who by then had become an accomplished songwriter near the stature of his band mates. In a format that today sounds like the perfect, unfettered *Unplugged* performance, Lennon delivers two-thirds of what would soon become 'Happiness Is A Warm Gun' in a version that's made more compelling by the crispness of his vocal and guitar work. He also brings out 'Mean Mr. Mustard' and 'Polythene Pam', songs that wouldn't appear until *Abbey Road*, and an amusing double-tracked version of 'Glass Onion'. McCartney, for his part, throws in the lyrical 'Junk' and 'Honey Pie'. Harrison includes 'Piggies'. Other songs of this calibre include stripped-down studio recordings of Lennon's 'Cry Baby Cry' and 'Sexy Sadie' and especially Harrison's acoustic take of 'While My Guitar Gently Weeps'. Yet many unplugged versions of solo acoustic songs on *Anthology 3* are merely redundant. There just isn't enough difference in the run-throughs of Lennon's 'Julia' or McCartney's 'Blackbird', 'Mother Nature's Son' and 'I Will'. Perhaps the earlier *Anthology* gems have spoiled us. But there seem to be too many tracks that are only slightly different than released versions, all of them inferior to the actual recordings. For instance, a cluttered 'Ob-La-Di, Ob-La-Da', a plodding, pre-fiddle 'Don't Pass Me By', versions of 'Octopus's Garden' and 'Maxwell's Silver Hammer' with obvious flubs. Beatles fans tend to put a fixed wall between group projects and later solo efforts, but *Anthology 3* breaks that down as McCartney tries out a couple of songs that would appear on his first solo album, 'Junk' and 'Teddy Boy'. The version here has Lennon playfully singing along and mocking in the background. More notably, Harrison presents a dreamy version of his 'All Things Must Pass' accompanied only by a vibrato-rich electric guitar. It's one of three songs he recorded as a demo along with 'Old Brown Shoe' and 'Something' that appear on *3* that were all recorded on the same day, February 25, 1969, his 26th birthday.

"Fans who've followed the *Anthology* series will want this, if only to complete the series. There are certainly far more double-albums out there that are worse. But it's troubling that this series has actually outsold the original Beatles albums, and for some young people actually represents The Fab Four. Some of the best of The Beatles' output, for instance 'In My Life' and 'Revolution', are not reflected in a series never meant to be a greatest-hits package or comprehensive career overview. My advice: round out your collection of original Beatles albums first."

On **Wednesday, November 27**, the normally quiet **George Harrison** comes public to announce his distaste towards one of the current pop scene's big stars . . .

Daily Mail "George Harrison says, 'Oasis would be better off without controversial singer, Liam Gallagher.' In a startling attack, the former Beatle calls Liam 'The silly one' and says his rock'n'roll antics are outdated. 'His older brother, Noel, is the real talent behind the band,' says Harrison. The criticism is certain to hurt Liam, who has said The Beatles were the biggest single influence on the brothers. Liam, 24, even once said they meant 'everything' to him. Referring to Liam's alleged heavy use of drink and drugs, Harrison said, 'He's a bit out of date. What's the point? It's silly and I feel a bit sorry for him really because he's missed the bus.' "

George says in a radio interview, "The Beatles showed far more variety in their songs than Oasis. I don't think they have as much flexibility in their songs. It's not a criticism. It's an observation. We had songs, which went through a bigger spectrum. They've written some good songs, which I've enjoyed and I like their *Unplugged* show on MTV but that was mainly because the silly one wasn't there. They don't actually need him. Noel is really good, he writes the tunes and he sings better than Liam as far as I'm concerned. They are a tidy band. I think it is proven when you see the band without him singing. They are more in tune. He's just excess baggage I think and all he does is make people think what a bunch of prannies they are.'

A source close to Noel Gallagher remarks, "Liam was furious when he heard what George said."

While Noel Gallagher adds, "George doesn't even know Liam. I've met George once and he's a nice guy."

Tuesday, March 11

This morning, Paul is knighted in an investiture at Buckingham Palace in London . . .

Paul "When you become a Sir, you're supposed to leave all that working-class stuff behind you and get a bit elevated and everyone's supposed to call you, 'Sir Paul'. But, because of the way I am, being called Sir embarrasses me. I say to people, 'Look, if you want to call me Sir Paul, fine, you go ahead.' It tends to be people on aeroplanes. They say, 'Can I get you a coffee, Sir Paul?' But with people I know, I say, 'Look, don't do that stuff. I'm still the same guy.' "

Syndicated news report "More than 1,000 screaming teenagers, many of whom weren't even born when The Beatles were fab back in the Sixties, were waiting in front of Buckingham Palace when Paul was knighted. Some had been there as early as 6am."

After the ceremony, **Sir Paul** speaks to the waiting reporters . . .

"This is the best day of my life," he reveals. "To come from a terraced house in Liverpool to this house is quite a journey and I am immensely proud. I would never have dreamed of this day. If we had had that thought when we started off in Liverpool it would have been laughed at as a complete joke. Today is fantastic, there is a blue sky and it's springtime. My mum and dad would have been extremely proud today – and perhaps they are. George Harrison and Ringo Starr keep ringing me up, calling me 'Your Holiness'."

A reporter asks Paul about Linda . . .

"Linda is fine," he replies. "I would have loved the whole family to have been here but we only had three guest tickets so we had to draw straws. Linda and Heather decided to stay out of the limelight today . . . I'm still heavily involved in music and I have a new album, called *Flaming Pie*, coming out in May. It's mainly a solo album but Ringo plays on it. And I'm also writing a full-length orchestral piece for the London Symphony Orchestra. It is due to be performed at the Albert Hall on October 14."

Syndicated news report "When Paul finally left Buckingham Palace after two-and-a-half-hours, he smiled to the fans and gave them his familiar thumbs-up sign. The crowd sang 'A Hard Day's Night' and 'Hey Jude' when Paul passed through the gates. They even honoured him by changing 'Yesterday' to 'Yes Sir Day'."

A possible instigator for Paul's award is the long-time Beatles fan, Laurence Moore "I remember thinking that Paul McCartney has contributed so much to this world, what with his music, animal rights, promoting vegetarian food and peace in the world. So I wondered why has he only got the title MBE after his name when he collected it with the other Beatles in 1965? I guess that's how it all started and so I wrote a letter to the Queen at Buckingham Palace and to John Major, the Prime Minister at the time in 1997.

However, I wrote the letters in the last few months of 1996 and got a reply from both Buckingham Palace and Downing Street in December, which was so exciting. Although Buckingham Palace said it had been forwarded onto the nominations department at Downing Street, I got a reply from them as well saying something like 'Thanks for nominating Paul McCartney MBE for a knighthood, it will now be forwarded to the Prime Minister.' It was funny because when I heard that Paul had been awarded that honour, I was watching a repeat of *The Beatles Anthology* on TV. And then I saw the news report, 'A Hard Day's Knight For Paul McCartney' and I was so overjoyed and excited that perhaps I played a small part in him being awarded this honour. Then, in March 1997, I travelled down to London on a coach to Buckingham Palace to see Paul's special day. I arrived just after Paul McCartney had just driven into the Palace. It was pretty exciting seeing so many people there. There were so many photographers, reporters and different camera crew outside filming the event. I then bumped into Paul's spokesman, Geoff Baker, who was with some other reporters chatting outside the Palace, and I said it was wonderful that Paul was getting knighted. Then I showed him the letters I received from Buckingham Palace and Downing Street and the other reporters got hold of it and wanted to do a story with me. Geoff then said to me, 'It's just like Beatlemania all over again.'

"I then joined the crowd outside the gates and was standing looking up at the Palace when a lady approached me. She heard about my story for nominating Paul and said she was a reporter for Sky News, and would I like to do a live interview for their main lunchtime story? So I asked would there be many people watching, she smiled and said, 'Well, it's only broadcast around the world 24 hours a day with millions of people watching!' So I said okay and I was told later that they would only interview two people for this story. One of them was me and the other was Paul McCartney. To this day I'm not sure how she knew I had nominated Paul, although I have always believed that Geoff Baker had something to do with it, I guess that he had told her about me. My interview would take place after Paul had received his knighthood inside the Palace and so I just waited around until he drove out. When he left in his car he opened his window and waved, then drove off giving the thumbs-up sign as the car went past the Palace. Walking back to give the interview, I then met Jane Foley of Sky News who had just interviewed Paul inside the Palace and she gave me her Royal Rota Press TV Pass to enter the Palace on that day. She said only six were given out on that day, including Sky News, BBC1, ITV, C4 and an American television station. Then just before the interview, Geoff Baker emerged from the Palace and gave me a piece of paper, which I noticed had been signed by Paul McCartney. It read, 'To Laurence, Paul McCartney.' I was so excited as I just did not expect that at all, although I thought that it was unusual that earlier on Geoff had asked me how I spelt my name! I guess that was the reason why. So I was now ready to give the live interview for Sky, who filmed me holding the autograph. After that, several reporters came to interview me from the national newspapers. One in particular, the *Mirror*, did a whole story and brought one of their photographers from the city to take a few photos of me outside the Palace with me holding the autograph. The article appeared on page 3 the next day. I've always wanted to appear on 'PAGE 3'. After that a film crew came up to me and said they just watched Sky News and would like to do a similar interview for their station, it was for Australian News, this time it was recorded. I think that was just a perfect end to an amazing day. A few days later I also appeared on the front page of my local newspaper and I did a couple of radio interviews for Radio Norfolk and Beach Radio. By the way, it was rumoured that Sky News were trying to arrange with Paul that after he was given the knighthood, perhaps he could walk out of the Palace and stand with me on top of the Queen Victoria statue for a double interview! Wow, that would have been awesome, although not on this occasion."

Monday, May 5 (UK)

As announced at the Palace, Paul releases his new album *Flaming Pie*, his first studio album since *Off The Ground* almost five years ago . . .

Paul "I wanted to have some fun and not sweat it. That's been the spirit of making this record. You've got to have a laugh, because it's just an album. So I called up a bunch of friends and family and we just got on and did it. We had fun making it. Hopefully you'll hear that in the songs."

'The Song We Were Singing'

Paul "I was remembering the Sixties, sitting round late at night, dossing, smoking, drinking wine, hanging out. We were taking a sip, seeing the world through a glass, talking about the cosmic solution. It's that time in your life when you get a chance for all that. This was a song that we kept very faithful to the original demo, because you can lose that feel, that atmosphere and all the inspiration if you're not careful. It was a bit like 'Real Love' or 'Free As A Bird' in that way."

'The World Tonight'

Paul "It's got a bit of a tougher guitar riff on it. There's a bit more of my heavier guitar on this album. When Linda and I first met, she'd say, 'I didn't know you played heavy guitar like that, I love that.' But I've always done quite a bit of that for myself. So when it came to this album, Linda said, 'Really play guitar. Don't just get someone in to play it.' It's a little naive my guitar style; it's not amazingly technical. It's a bit like Neil Young. In fact, I still haven't done the guitar as much as she wanted."

'If You Wanna'

Paul "I describe this as a very stereotyped American road song. I wrote this when we were in Minneapolis on tour. We were in a skyscraper with its head in the clouds. We had a day off between shows and I was inspired because it is Prince's hometown and I like his stuff. It has simple chords and most of the stuff on this album is simple. I just wanted to write something that was rocking, the kind of thing you could hear when you're driving across the desert on that big road with the flat horizon. I love all that."

'Somedays'

Paul "I wrote this when I drove Linda to a photo session in Kent. I knew that Linda would be about two hours doing the shoot so I set myself a deadline to write a song in that time. And that was it. I wanted to finish it so that when Linda had finished and would say, 'What did you do? Did you get bored?' I could say, 'Oh, I wrote this song. Wanna hear it?' It's just a little game that John and I used to play and I don't think it ever took us more than three or so hours to write a song."

'Young Boy'

Paul "I wrote on Long Island in the time that it took Linda to cook lunch. It also gave me the chance to renew my friendship with Steve Miller, which we had struck up one night at Olympic Studios in London in the Sixties, when we had recorded 'My Dark Hour' together. I rang Steve up, said I had this song, how about it? He's got this studio in Sun Valley, Idaho, and we went out there. Working with him was like falling back into an old habit. We worked on 'Young Boy' over three days at his place and it was fun. It's very straightforward, just a song straight from the shoulder."

'Calico Skies'

Paul "I wanted to write something acoustic, in the vein of 'Blackbird', something simple that would stand on its own. So if anyone said, 'Give us a song,' you could just do it . . . I spent a lot of time on my acoustic guitar, making up little bits and pieces. 'Calico Skies' was one of them."

'Heaven On A Sunday'

Paul "I wrote this on holiday and when I'm on holiday, I like to sail, not a big boat, just a little sunfish. It's a great relaxation for me, away from the high-profile stuff, that's often when I come up with that kind of song, relaxed, peaceful. I wrote it and was playing it at home and Linda was singing along with the chorus and it was getting nice. My son James is credited on the song. I thought it would be a nice idea to play with him as he's getting really good on guitar. When you've been in a band with someone for twenty years, you read them and they read you. I thought, 'Well, I haven't been in a band with James for all those years, but I've known him for all those years. I've heard him play and he's heard me play. We've got so much in common that I bet we could do it.' "

'Used To Be Bad'

Paul "Steve (Miller) came to England saying, 'I want to get you singing Texas blues.' That sounded like a good offer and he turned up with millions of little blues riffs. It was just a jam, really with Steve whacking out these riffs. I got on the drums and we went for it, a little duet, sung on one mike, from a jam, and we did it in one take."

'Souvenirs'

Paul "I like some songs because they can get covered by a black singer. 'The Long And Winding Road' was written with Ray Charles in mind. This one was like Wilson Pickett. I could imagine someone really getting to grips with that one. I cut a demo of the track when I was on holiday in Jamaica and I was anxious that I stayed close to the feel of the original take when I started work on the track in England with Jeff Lynne. I said to Jeff, 'Let's take this demo but instead of what we normally do, take all the information off and renew it, and wreck it. Let's make sure that everything that's going on is at least as good and has the flavour of the demo.' That song's a little favourite of mine. I'm looking forward, I hope, to an R&B singer doing it. I would have loved it as a single but I knew that no one on earth would ever have chosen it as a single."

'Little Willow'

Paul "The morning I heard the news of the death of Ringo's ex-wife, Maureen, I couldn't think of anything else, so I wrote this to convey how much I thought of her. It's certainly heartfelt and I hope it'll help the kids. Instead of writing a letter, I wrote a song."

'Really Love You'
(Featuring Ringo Starr)

Paul "When I played it back to Ringo, he said, 'It's relentless, it's relentless.' He's a one with words."

'Beautiful Night'
(The second track on *Flaming Pie* to feature Ringo)

Paul "I had written it a few years ago and I had always liked the song. I had done a version in New York but I didn't feel we had quite pulled it off. So I got this song out for when Ringo was coming, changed a few of the lyrics and it was like the old days. I realised we hadn't done this for so long, but it was really comfortable and it was still there. So we did 'Beautiful Night' and we tagged on a fast bit on the end, which wasn't there before."

'Great Day'

Paul "I wanted a short, simple song to close the album and I remembered this one, which goes back twenty years or so to when the kids were young. Linda and I used to sing it around the kitchen. It's just a little upbeat song of hope, to the point of and in the sprit of this whole album."

To coincide with the release of *Flaming Pie*, an interview with Paul, carried out by Vic Garbarini, is published in the magazine *Guitar World* . . .

Garbarini "Were you aware, when you were recording *Flaming Pie*, that it was a definite improvement on your other recent efforts?"

Paul "You do get a feeling that something is working, though you can always be wrong. I've thought I was working on something good and then it turned out that people thought it was average. I don't know if I was right or they were right. Time will tell."

Garbarini "What did you do differently this time?"

Paul "I was checking the songs in my own mind against some of the early Beatles stuff, because I had just been doing the *Anthology* and it surprised me how simple, and yet complete, some of the early Beatles work was. I didn't see any reason why my new stuff shouldn't be just as simple and complete. So whereas I might have been a little bit lazy in the past, and just thought, 'Ah, near enough,' which is very tempting to do, I made it a point to go in and sharpen the chisel and get it a bit tighter."

Garbarini "Not including greatest hits and live sets, you've released 20 albums since The Beatles broke up."

Paul "Yeah, too large an output is probably a major reason for a slip in quality. I did a bloody record every bloody year for a long time. But I think there may be some revisionism to come on those sloppy lyrics. Take *Back To The Egg* (1979). Linda and I were so disappointed, thinking, 'God, this is a terrible bloody record.' But my son pulled it out recently and it's really not as bad as I thought it was. It's not easy to do your tightest, most succinct work all the time, and I think if my work does slip, it probably is in the lyrics. And I hate to tell you, but I put a lot of it down to laziness, where I just thought, 'Yeah, that'll do.' And in mitigation, I think that sometimes I probably was right."

Garbarini "Do you get bored with answering questions about The Beatles?"

Paul "Sometimes you don't wanna go through that fucking stuff again. You hear yourself for the 50th time go into your routine. But it's an occupational hazard, like being a doctor at a party, everyone's going to ask you about their heath problems."

Garbarini "What's next for Paul McCartney?"

Paul "I don't know. Something will happen. I've told this story before, but once in the early days of The Beatles, we broke down on the motorway going back to Liverpool. One of us said, 'What are we going to do now?' And another said, 'Well, something will happen.' Immediately, a lorry came up and said, 'Wanna lift, lads?' We all piled in. I'm a great believer in 'Something will happen.' You can look at it in two ways, like the 'enjoy' thing with the Maharishi . . . He had given us a book that he had written and he wrote a message in it. It was one word, 'Enjoy'. I was totally freaked out because this guruish guy's best advice was 'Enjoy'. But I think it's seriously good advice. If, at the end of the day, we have enjoyed it, it's better than having a shitty day. That sounds horribly simplistic, but I'm a great believer in that . . . It's either true or you're totally naive. We always used to say 'Something will happen.' That's like the village idiots, but something always did happen. There's a lot of magic about; you know what I mean? You've got to believe that shit. If you've come from where I've come, and what's happened to me has happened, then you've gotta believe that."

Meanwhile, in America, George joins Ravi Shankar in promotions for the *Chants Of India* album. On **Thursday, June 12**, the duo appear on the *CBS This Morning* programme . . .

Interviewer "You said as a Beatle you had met captains of industry, politicians and royalty, yet no one impressed you until you met Ravi Shankar."

George "That's true, yeah."

Interviewer "Why?"

George "During that time, you know, we met just about everybody and I just thought, 'Well, I'm looking for something really, really beyond just the ordinary, the mundane, and that's when I wanted somebody to impress me.' And you know, I didn't expect it to be this little Indian man but you know good things come in small packages."

Interviewer "Now it's your turn Ravi. You've called him many things. Three words that stand out, friend, disciple, son."

Ravi "Presently, chum, because he makes me laugh more than anyone else."

Interviewer "What is it like having him in the studio with you?"

Ravi "This was a great experience. He helped me so much in real producing. It's taking being there in the recording booth from the very beginning, balancing, to editing, mixing, and everything."

Interviewer "Ravi, in this country when we hear chants, we tend to think of Gregorian chants. We think of religious chants. This album is not like that. This is more mainstream."

Ravi "I chose the chants which are not so much into religion. No matter who listens to it feels that special spiritual feeling."

George "Something like this is totally new. It's like, and now for something completely different, and you know, I think it's worthy. It's something that I believe in, and I think it's a benefit if people during the day, you know everybody gets stressed out, and this music is particularly inclined to calm you down. It's an antidote to stress."

Interviewer "You brought your mates Paul and John to India in the Sixties, to hear his music and to taste the culture. They left, you stayed. I'm speaking more, your soul stayed, as it were. Why do you think that is?"

George "Well, from my point of view, it's the only place to be really. For every human is a quest to find the answer to, why are we here? Who am I? Where did I come from? Where am I going? That to me became the only important thing in my life. Everything else is secondary. So for me there is no alternative."

And then, six weeks later, on **Thursday, July 24**, George joins Ravi for an appearance on the pre-taped VH-1 special, *George Harrison & Ravi Shankar: Yin & Yang . . .* John Fugelsang, a self-confessed Beatles fanatic, asks the questions . . .

John "It's been a great year for music fans. Last year saw the release of Ravi Shankar's four-CD boxed set *In Celebration*, and this year has brought us the release of the new album *Chants Of India* produced by George Harrison. And it's a great thrill for me to be here today with two of the greatest living artists in music, from the east and from the west, Ravi Shankar and George Harrison. Thank you both for joining us."

George and Ravi "Thank you."

John "I'd like to start off talking about the *Chants Of India* album, because it's a real beautiful CD, record, whatever we call them these days. Do you think that an American audience is gonna be able to relate to the music on the album?"

George "I think so. It's like, first of all it's not really like sitar music. I know Ravi's sitting here with his sitar, everybody knows him from sitar music, but it isn't really sitar music. I mean it's basically spiritual music, spiritual songs, ancient mantras, and passages from the Vedas, which are the most ancient texts on earth. And so it's these ancient songs, which are all spiritual music, but trying to put it in a context where it doesn't change it from

465

what it basically is but at the same time the instrumentation to make it palatable to not only westerners but to everybody."

Ravi "Well I always had in my mind not to make it so difficult for hearing for people who are not used to our music for instance. But apart from the words which are very old and they all mean almost the same thing, you know, peace, love, for equality, for trees, for nature, for human beings, body, soul, everything. About 30, 40 years ago these were absolutely not heard. You were not permitted. You had to give it only to your disciples and also listen privately in the ear, not loudly. But now books are all printed. Everything is out even in network. So as far as the words are concerned they are open now, but the tune, that I had to give, or added slight orchestration in the background, was with this very thought, that it should match this old sentiment of whole spiritual context that it has. At the same time not be too much, or sound too ritualistic, or fundamentalist, or anything like that. That's the main thing that I tried."

John "George, how did you first come to meet Ravi and discover the music?"

George "During the days when there was the mania, the Beatlemania, well I got involved with the records, you know. I bought some of Ravi's records, and I listened to it, and although my intellect didn't really know what was happening, or didn't know much about the music, just the pure sound of it and what it was playing, it just appealed to me so much. It hit a spot in me very deep, and it was, you know, I just recognised it somehow. And along with that I just had a feeling that I was going to meet him. It was just one of those things and at the same time when I played the sitar, very badly, on a Beatle record, then Ravi was coming to London. A lot of the press was trying to set it up that we'd meet, but I just avoided that. You know, I didn't want it to, you know, be on the front page of a newspaper as a gimmick, because it meant more to me than that. So I thought, well I'll wait and meet him in my own time. And that arrived on an occasion, there was a society called Asian Music Circle, and the fellow who ran that, who I'd got to know, he said Ravi's gonna come, he was in London, he was going to come for lunch, and we met like that way. Then he came to my house and got me to learn how to hold the sitar and put me through the basic lessons of sitar."

John "Ravi, I've always wanted to ask you, how did you feel the first time you heard 'Norwegian Wood'? What did you honestly think of George's sitar playing?"

Ravi "When my niece and nephews, they made me hear this, and that was after I met George, I hadn't heard anything before that, and I wasn't much impressed by it you know. But I saw the effect on the young people; I couldn't believe it, even in India. It was not only in the west, it seemed they were just lapping it up as you say. They loved it so much."

John "How did the other guys in The Beatles react when you started bringing this instrument into the studio?"

George "Well in those days, you know we were growing very quickly, and there was a lot of influences that we were into. I mean that was the best thing about our band. We were very open-minded to everything and we were listening to all kinds of music you know. Like avant-garde music, which later became known as avant-garde a clue, and various things like that. So you know, they just thought well that's good, they liked the sound of it, and on 'Norwegian Wood' it was just one of those songs that just needed that little extra. And the sitar I'd bought, a very cheap one in a shop called India Craft in London, even though it sounded bad it still fitted onto the song and it gave it that little extra thing. So they were quite happy about it. I went to India to be with Ravi, to see India, to learn some music, and just to experience India, but I also wanted to know about the Himalayas . . . I mean it sounds like a lofty thing to say on VH-1 but basically, you know, what are we doing on this planet? And I think throughout the Beatle experience that we'd had, we'd grown so many years within a short period of time. I'd experienced so many things and met so many people but I realised there was nothing actually that was giving me a buzz anymore. I wanted something better, I remember thinking, 'I'd love to meet somebody who will really impress me,' and that's when I met Ravi. Which is funny, 'cause he's this little fella with this obscure instrument, from our point of view, and yet it led me into such depths. And I think that's the most important thing, it still is for me. You know I get confused when I look around at the world and I see everybody's running around. And you know, as Bob Dylan said, 'He not busy being born, he's busy dying,' and yet nobody's trying to figure out what's the cause of death and what happens when you die. I mean that to me is the only thing really that's of any importance, the rest is all secondary. I believe in the thing I read years ago, which I think was in the bible, it said, 'Knock and the door will be opened,' and it's true. If you want to know anything in this life you just have to knock on the door. Whether that be physically on somebody else's door and ask them a question or, which I was lucky to find, it's meditation, you know it's all within. And that's really why for me this record's important, because it's another little key to open up the within. For each individual to be able to sit and turn off, 'Turn off your mind, relax and float downstream,' and listen to something that has its root in a transcendental, because really even all the words of these songs, they carry with it a very subtle spiritual vibration. And it goes beyond intellect really. So if you let yourself be free to let that have an effect on you, it can have an effect, a positive effect."

John "Ravi, how was it for you when you first met George? What was your take on Beatlemania?"

Ravi "I'm ashamed to say that I knew almost nothing about them when I first, you know, met them excepting that they're very popular. And meeting them in the parties I was so impressed by George at that time, who looked so much younger and was so inquisitive. Asking about so many different things. Mostly music, sitar and of course along with that certain spiritual . . . and the only thing . . . I felt that his enthusiasm was so real, you see, and I wanted to give as much as I could through my sitar, of course, because that is the only thing that I know of. The rest I cannot express. He [George] talks so beautifully. He is used to words. He writes poems. He writes songs. I do sometimes foolishly but I'm not that much . . . I express myself through notes, musical notes, so it's a different way of . . . but anyway. As you said when I met him and we started off immediately after a few days, as he said earlier, to sit properly, how to hold the sitar and you know, how to handle the finger position and all that, the basic things. And he was so interested and he was so quick in learning and then we fixed immediately for him to come to India and he came. We fixed it for six weeks but unfortunately it didn't happen because people recognised him after a week or so and there was such a commotion in Bombay that we had to run away to Kashmir and live in a houseboat and all that. But unfortunately he had to leave. Then I thought, 'My God.' I couldn't believe that any four people could create such a storm all over the world."

George "The Spice Boys."

Ravi "And it was not that I was unknown or anything you know. I was playing concerts in Carnegie Hall and different places, but as a classical Indian musician, but the moment it was known that he has become my disciple, it was like wildfire. I became so popular with the young people all of a sudden, and I was rediscovered as they say and then I took that role of a superstar for a number of years because of him. 'Cause you know the whole thing was going a bit not to my liking because of the association of drugs and things like that. So I really had a very difficult time for the next few years putting my music in the right register or right place but because I did that is why I am here today also. Sitting with you. Otherwise I wouldn't have been here. People have really come to understand the depth and the seriousness of our music along with all the, you know, enjoying part of it, the entertainment part, that is there, but the true root and that's what is also projected in this particular record."

John "I want to talk about the early 1970s, *The Concert for Bangladesh*. Now how did this all come about? Was it Ravi who set it in motion?"

Ravi "Yeah, it was that period when Eastern Pakistan and the Pakistan government had problems and they wanted to get separate, and they wanted to name it Bangladesh. It was mainly the language issue. It started with that and then became a big political issue. They come as refugees, a lot of children. So all that was very painful to me. And I was at that time planning to give a benefit show and maybe raise $20,000, $25,000, $30,000 and send it, you know and George happened to be in Los Angeles at that time and he saw how unhappy I was, and I told him. He said, 'That's nothing, let's do something big,' and immediately he, like magic, phoned up, fixed Madison Square Garden and all his friends, Eric Clapton, Bob Dylan, and it was magic really. And he wrote that song also, 'Bangla Desh'. So overnight that name became known all over the world, you know."

George "America was actually shipping armaments to Pakistan who were, you know, just massacring everybody, and the more I read about it and understood what was going on I thought, well, we've got to do something and it had to be quick. And what we did really was only to point it out. That's what I felt."

John "It was a very controversial thing in Bangladesh. John Lennon used to get in trouble all the time for his activism. Did anyone tell you, you know it's a little bit hot, don't go there? Were you discouraged at all by people for pursuing it?"

George "No, not really. I think that was one of the things that I developed, just by being in The Beatles, was being bold. And I think John had a lot to do with that, you know, because John Lennon, you know, if he felt something strongly he just did it. And you know I picked up a lot of that by being a friend of John's. Just that attitude of, well we'll just go for it, just do it."

Ravi "This was something unique. The whole spirit was so beautiful, the Bangladesh concert."

George "It was just pure adrenalin, and it was very lucky that it came off because all musicians weren't there for rehearsal. We rehearsed bits and pieces with different people but we didn't have everybody all on at one time until the show itself. And we were just very lucky really that it all came together."

Monday, September 29

Back in the UK, Paul releases a 75-minute symphonic work called *Standing Stone – A Symphonic Poem*, his most ambitious album yet . . .

Paul "When Lennon & McCartney wrote a song, separately or together, it took three hours. John and I just knew the form, a couple of verses, a chorus, middle eight, a new verse, a chorus. Now instead of the short story, this is the novel. I think it's good coming to it now, having written a lot of short stories. It's a question of scale, to keep an interest for 75 minutes, compared with seven minutes on 'Hey Jude', one of the longest Beatles songs . . . I'm taking a huge risk although Elvis Costello and one or two others have done classical pieces. You see in the end, we know and love music and I just don't see the dividing lines. I'm listening a lot to Monteverdi and I can hear what he's trying to do, musically. He didn't know many chords, like early Beatles. I love Chopin. There is so much more. I've no idea what's in store for me musically, but I know it's going to be interesting, a fascinating voyage. It's like someone said to me the other day, I would really like Messiaen. Well, I don't know Messiaen, as a mate of mine used to say, from a bar of soap!"

To assist with the orchestration on *Standing Stone*, Paul is helped by the trained musicians Richard Rodney Bennett, John Harle and David Mathews . . .

"There were one or two difficult moments," **Paul** recalls. "I would often fax sections of music from my computer to Richard Rodney Bennett. I sent him one, thinking it was pretty good. A few minutes later, I got a fax back with the words 'Feeble' scribbled across it. I phoned him straight back and said, 'Richard, that's what my teacher wrote on my essays. You're a sensitive artist, if you don't like something, could you please write, 'That's a little below par.'"

Thursday, October 2

Paul releases *Many Years From Now*, his official biography, written by his long-time friend, Barry Miles . . .

Paul in an interview for the *New Statesman* newspaper "Since giving the interviews a couple of years ago for the biography, I have thought about whether or not I should have done it. I don't want to carry on trying to justify myself. But I don't regret co-operating with the book . . . I got this reputation of being the balladeer, the one who's into love. I was called 'The cute one'. Well, I can tell you that when I went home I wasn't cute at all. So, without wanting to put John down, or to look as if I was justifying myself, I did want to put the record straight. Don't just put me down as an idiot who didn't know any of it and John taught me it all. So there you go. If anyone historically wants to delve into that period they will know that I wasn't just twiddling my thumbs while John was informing me of all this stuff."

Paul reflects on some turbulent times . . .

"We, Linda and I, were in New York, having tests and they took a routine mammogram of Linda's other breast and something was discovered there. So, holy cow, we had it all over again to deal with and then she had to lose her hair, which was the kind of thing she hated. I think women are particularly vulnerable when that kind of thing happens, because you can't ignore it. Many men go bald and so it's maybe a little less scary. But for a woman, and a beautiful woman, with the most beautiful hair, strawberry blonde and natural too, it was a terrible tragedy for her to lose that. But she was really so courageous. She said, 'Right, let's cut it off,' and she had a Marine crew cut. It looked great actually, because she had a beautiful bone structure and a beautiful neck. She looked gorgeous and eventually, when she realised that even her little crew cut was going to go, she shaved it all off. She looked like a Buddhist monk and then unfortunately this year, the worst news, the worst possible scenario, just when we thought we'd got it licked, actually. We'd come back off holiday and her hair was growing back and each time they said it'll grow back dark and curly, and I must say she didn't really fancy that, having been straight and blonde, but it grew back beautifully, it was slightly darker but still blonde. But she was so brave with all of that. And so it was almost going okay.

"But then, we got back off holiday and she didn't feel too well. We went to see a doctor and he said, 'You've got an enlarged liver and unfortunately with your history it's most likely to be cancer.' We were just dumbstruck. But again, we said, 'Is there anything we can do? Do people ever come back from this? Yes, sure,' we thought. There's statistics, which show that people have licked this, which is true, so we always went with that side of it. Linda never once said, 'Oh, I'm going to be a bad statistic.' I think that's what sustained us. She'd say to all of us, 'You're the best support group a girl could ever have,' and we'd say, 'We couldn't do it without you, babe.' She had such courage. We could be strong because she was. I don't even think that until the last week she even knew. I think the last week, you know, things were going so badly, but we were riding horses. I said to her, 'Tell you what, babe, I'll get the horses ready, you don't have to even do anything. I'll get them all ready, get a little bale of hay and you can hop off of it.' That was always one of our horrors, of being eighty and you can't ride. We'd joke that we'd design a special crane and have you lifted up, because that was the horror of her life that she couldn't ride. Thank God that she was able to, two days before she died and, as I said, the crowning moment was this big rattler stretched across the track. We just looked at it and felt awed. Like it was some sort of magic sign. I bet it is in Indian folklore."

But on **Friday, April 17**, Paul's wife, Linda, as expected, loses her brave battle against breast cancer . . .

Paul "Thank the Lord, she went into a coma as the doctors had predicted, which wasn't the worst of all scenarios, as it happened. She just felt tired, and I said, 'Would you like to sit by the pool?' She said, 'No. I don't really fancy it today.' I thought I'd try her in about an hour's time. I tried her in about an hour's time and she still felt tired. I joked, 'Well, do you just fancy a lie-in?' She said, 'Yeah,' and the next day she died. She was just in a coma for one day. It was as if she was so smart that something in her said, 'We can't lick this one. Let's get the hell out of here, quick,' and she didn't hang about. She'd spent that day in bed and I went to bed that night with her figuring, 'God, things are getting desperate but we'll just keep hoping.' I went to bed and she got restless in the middle of the night, as they'd warned me they might. So I called the nurse about three in the morning and at five o'clock she died. She didn't hang about. In her last sort of moments she got very peaceful. As she died, something told me to just say something to her and I said what I'd say when she'd be going into anaesthetic when she'd had a couple of operations in previous years. I'd used this sort of trick of saying, 'You're up on your beautiful horse,' just to give her a beautiful peaceful moment and she'd drift off into the anaesthetic beautifully and peacefully. In fact the doctors used to say, 'We've never had such a quiet patient.' One of the doctors said that after her first operation she woke up, looked around at us and said, 'Hello.' He said, 'Boy, we've never had that before.' So it suddenly came to me at the moment when she was just about to die. I really have no idea why, but I just thought, 'I've just got to say this.' It was as if I was guided and I said, 'You're up on your beautiful Appaloosa stallion; it's a fine spring day, we're riding through the woods. The bluebells are all out, and the sky is clear blue.' And she just drifted off. It's a terrible tragedy. But I don't think it could have happened in a much better way in a better place. I talked to the doctor after Linda died and he was saying that the amount of cancerous nodes involved was scary. He said that it wasn't just three, it was in tens. Luckily though, the medical evidence wasn't totally conclusive and you could read it two ways, so we always took the most optimistic reading. The word you were always scared to hear was 'aggressive', that it was an aggressive cancer. But thank God we never heard that. I only heard that after she died. I was always waiting to hear that, as she was. But we thought, 'Well, we haven't heard that word yet, so we're still okay.'

"After Linda's death, I don't know what I would have done without my kids. We are such a close family and it hit us pretty much equally. They lost their mum as well as their best friend. It hit us all really hard, but they have been very strong and very helpful. We cried a lot together. None of us has held that back. We pretty much still cry because Linda was so important, so much the centre of everything in our lives. So it was mainly the kids. But I did get a counsellor, realising that I would need some sort of help. And although it's not much of a British tradition to do that, I was married to an American so I know quite a lot of people who have no problem with psychiatrists and counsellors. Funnily enough, Linda used to know psychiatrists when she was young. She'd say, 'I used to sort out all their problems for them.' And you know that's true. So I knew a particular one, who I talked to. He was a good help. It was mainly to get rid of some of my guilt. When anyone you love this much dies, one of the first things is that you wish you could have been perfect for every minute of every day. But nobody is like that. I would say to Linda if we were arguing, 'Look, I'm not Jesus Christ, you know. I'm not a saint. I'm just some normal man. I'll try to do something about it but that's who I am, that's who you're married to.' So I had quite a bit of guilt and probably still have. You remember arguments and when you're married you don't remember them quite so much. You just get on with the next day and as long as you don't have too many arguments and they're not too bad, you figure that it evens itself out. But when someone dies, you remember only the arguments in the first couple of weeks and the moments when I wasn't as nice as I would have wanted to be. So I needed counselling with that and I found it really helpful.

"I must say that our friends have been very supportive. We've got a lot of lovely sincere friends who, because of the nature of Linda and I, unless they're sincere, they're not our friends anyway, and they've been very helpful. And funnily enough, and something that I didn't expect, the public at large have been a huge help. I thought that if you didn't know Linda, you might not get it. But I was so wrong. So many of the thousands of letters that I got said, 'Although we never met Linda, you could tell that she was a great woman.' For some of them, it was because of her wonderful attitude to animals. A lot of others said it was because of the way that she brought up our kids. Yet they wouldn't even know that we had kids, you hardly ever saw their pictures in the paper, we guarded their privacy in case when they grew up they wanted it. We figured you couldn't rob them of that. The public sent very uplifting quotes and prayers. A lot of them had been through a similar grief. They'd write and say how they'd lost their wife and this little poem they'd enclose had sustained them. A lot of people sent me a lot of good stuff that helped me. But it was mainly the kids. Now, when I get sad, as I do pretty often, like if I go for a ride, she's not with me and I find myself going down. I let myself go down for a moment, just because I have to and then I try to counterbalance it and think that Linda's life was very upbeat. She wasn't a downbeat kind of person, so she wouldn't like it now if I went downbeat. She was always the one for the joke. If you spat inadvertently while you were talking to her, she'd say, 'Do you serve towels with your showers?' She just had a line for everything. If you looked a little inattentive while she's talking, she'd say, 'What, am I boring you?' She was a really funny lady and very, very witty. She had a delicious sense of humour. She was happy. So I use that now. I balance every sad moment with a happy moment. That kind of helps day to day. It helps me get through. I was really worried after Linda died that I would not be able to sleep at all. I have had the feeling ever since that she's seen to it that I'm sleeping. That's my theory. I don't know how correct it is but somehow I manage to sleep okay and it's really a blessing because I need to. The rest of the day can be pretty traumatic with the memorials and all the stuff you have to do, and just missing her. It's great, I feel like she's blessed me with the ability to get some sleep. It's a blessing."

Tuesday, June 16 (USA)
In these most unfortunate times, there is a brief pause for joy when Ringo releases *Vertical Man*, his first studio album since *Time Takes Time* back in 1992 . . .

Ringo "During these last few years, I mainly devoted myself to the golf and well, I'd had enough of it! As with any young person into music, I dreamt of becoming better and this passion did not leave me. I am a musician, and to play is good for my heart. But recently I had written, painted, went to the restaurant and I did all that that everyone else likes to do. I visited my friends, I cooked or, quite simply, I looked at the television like everyone else. I carried out a life that is more normal. But more than all, I still liked the music. My mother always said to me that nothing made so me happy than to play in a band and she was right. And more than all, I like to play with good musicians. Paul was in the studio with me. George could not move for the recording but he sent a tape to me. It is a tradition between us to play on the solo albums of the others. Steven (Tyler) telephoned me at the studio. He really wanted to come. Apparently, this guy never takes holidays. But me, I like to have loads of time free. He played the harmonica on 'Love Me Do'. After, I suggested to him playing with the band on 'Drift Away'. Few people know it better. When I played in Boston with my All-Starr Band, he came on and played with my band. But in the studio, at the beginning, he did not want to play with the band. He said, 'I haven't practised for a long time.' And I said to him, 'I assure you, play with us and you will never forget it.' So he played on *Vertical Man* and it was good. I was very satisfied. But then we got a message from his record company saying that we had to take Steven off. At the time, they did it late because we had mixed and mastered the album. So then I called a fabulous guy, Tom Petty, and he agreed to appear without even knowing what he had to do. He said, 'Don't worry, I'll do it.' "

Vertical Man was recorded in the Santa Monica Boulevard offices belonging to the musician and lyricist Mark Hudson. Hudson's office shares the building with a Thai restaurant, a ticket agent, an optometrist, a graphic artist and some other small offices . . .

CNN Report "With a little help from his friends, Ringo Starr feels he can do anything. For instance, when Starr decided to put together another album, he called friends old and new to help. The result is *Vertical Man,* which was created with the aid of fellow former Beatles Paul McCartney and George Harrison, as well as Joe Walsh and Steve Tyler. Ringo says the album thrived with the help of an open-door policy at the studio where it was recorded."

Ringo "We were in this little studio, and we had this open-door policy: if you came in the door, you were on the record. That's a lot of fun. It's not strictly true, but the likes of Alanis Morissette came to visit, and we were doing a track that was, in my opinion, perfect to have her on. And we just said, 'Would you like to be on the record?' It came spontaneously from us just saying hello and as I was going to record the voices, I invited her to join us. She answered, 'Of course,' and she is a marvellous woman. One gets along well with her."

Dean Grakal, the lyricist who co-wrote most of the album's 13 songs, "In the cramped quarters of the Los Angeles studio chosen by Ringo Starr for the making of *Vertical Man* there was a magical atmosphere that oozes through to the listener. Ringo is one of those special people who makes you feel good about yourself. You could see it on everyone's faces as they were drawn into the excitement of making the album. The room had such great vibes. I know everyone talks about good vibes this and good vibes that, but something magical happened there that you cannot put your finger on. It was such a great feeling to be a part of it. When Alanis (Morissette) came into the room, she said she had never felt such happiness in a place before. There were so many funny things that happened during the recording of the album. For instance, the footsteps heard at the end of the track 'Mindfield' come from the Thai restaurant owner coming up the stairs to ask for quiet during the dinner hour. She had a restaurant full of people who were trying to eat, and we could be heard through the floor. She was not pleased."

Ringo "The album's called *Vertical Man* because when I was sitting at my home in Monaco, I was just paging through this huge book of quotes that my stepdaughter, Francesca, had won ten years ago at school. It's a huge thing with a million quotes in it. I was flipping through it and I saw this quote that said, 'Let's hear it for the vertical man, because so much praise is given for the horizontal one,' and I thought, 'What a cool thing.' It's true, when you've gone, they're all saying, 'What a good guy he was,' and I thought, 'Well, let's hear it now. And let's hear it for everyone still standing.' It relates to musicians. We've lost quite a few over the years and I feel blessed that I'm still here. It's also for everyone else out there who's vertical. So for all those reasons, I thought I'd call the album *Vertical Man* and we didn't have a song for it, at all, until the last week. The song came from us just sitting around, humming."

'One'

Ringo "That was the first song we wrote. We just sat there and said, 'What should we write about, boys?' That's how we started. It's really a love song. That's what it is. It's one of the few love songs on the album and there's a great line at the end, as we fade out, where the chorus goes 'Two.' Because all through the song, it's 'One' girl, and it takes the edge off."

'The King Of Broken Hearts'

Ringo "It's a beautiful song. The song is one hundred per cent but then George and his guitar made it a two hundred per cent song. It was funny with George, when we were in England, I went to see him and I played him some of the tracks to try and get him to play on some. I really wanted him to play on 'The King Of Broken Hearts' so I played him the track and said, 'Come on, I really want you to play,' and he said, 'Well, it seems like I'm on it already.' He wasn't that excited then but two weeks later, I called him and he had changed his mind. I found him in a better mood and he said, 'Sure, send the tape over.' He is the killer with slide. There is so much emotion. He gets into every note. He never fails to move me. He should play more. He should get out there and get a band together."

'La De Da'

Ringo "When things get tough, you've got to let go sometimes. It's no use getting angry. I co-wrote this."

The album includes a re-recording of The Beatles' 'Love Me Do'

Ringo "Well, after almost thirty years, I simply thought, 'That devil, what good is it?' And then, I did not even exploit the first recording. I approached this song in a serious way, well, perhaps not as much as that. It is quite simply a song, which I always wanted to play and sing for the pleasure. My version will not change the world, that's for sure.

Ringo "It is the best album that I have recorded in these last fifteen years. Why? It's simple, because it is one in which I took the most pleasure! I enjoyed myself during the recording, the playing of my band was good and my singing out front is better, quite simply because I stopped smoking, I eat better and I drink a lot of water. I even play drums better . . . I can't hide the enthusiasm I feel over the direction of my own life. I feel just good. I feel like I have a purpose. I am a player. I'm playing. I just made a really good record in my opinion, and I hope in everyone else's opinion out there. In our business sometimes it gets a little down, but when you're doing an album with love, and lots of friends around, you realise why you stay in the business. And do you know why I stay? Because this is what I do. I'm a drummer. This is my dream from the age of thirteen. I wanted to be a drummer . . . The success of this album depends on the next one. I stand by this album. It's a dynamite album."

One day later, in New York, on **Wednesday, June 17**, Ringo makes a live appearance to promote his new album on the controversial *Howard Stern's* 92.3 WXRK FM radio show. It is quite possibly the most different kind of interview Ringo has ever had to encounter . . .

Howard "Can I say something? You've aged better than all of the other Beatles. You've actually become the handsome Beatle. You're the cutest Beatle, now."

Ringo and Barbara, pictured at a charity function in North London on December 1, 1998. *(PA Photos)*

Paul with his 'rock'n'roll' band at the Liverpool Cavern, December 14, 1999, left to right: Mick Green (guitar), Pete Wingfield (keyboards), David Gilmour (guitar), Ian Paice (drums) and Chris Hall (accordian), with Paul in the foreground. *(LFI)*

Paul, with Julia Baird, John Lennon's half sister (left) and Billy Heckle, the Cavern Club's co-manager (right), at the party after the Cavern show. *(Cavern City Tours)*

The Cavern Club's replica of Paul's famous Hofner violin bass guitar, as inscribed by Paul on the night after the Cavern show. *(Cavern City Tours)*

An aerial view of Friar Park, Henley, George's home since March, 1970. Built in the eighteenth century by the noted British eccentric Sir Francis Crisp, it has benefited during George's occupation by vast sums being spent on renovation. "I'm just the caretaker," says George. *(Rex)*

George and Olivia at Goodwood racetrack for the Festival Of Speed, June, 2000. *(Rex)*

Paul with *Sgt Pepper* fan Clara Tait, for whom he signed his book of paintings at Watersons bookshop in Piccadilly, London, December 13, 2000. *(LFI)*

aul with Heather Mills, shopping in New York's Madison Avenue, June 13, 2000. *(Rex)*

Paul attending the Chloe fashion show in Paris, October 11, 2000. On his right is former model Twiggy with actor Leigh Lawson, and on his left is his daughter Mary. *(LFI)*

Paul with Keith Richards at the VH1 2000 Fashion Awards in New York, October 20, 2000. *(LFI)*

Yoko showing a picture of John to children at Dovedal School in Liverpool, his primary school, July 2, 2001. Yoko was visiting the city to attend the ceremony at which Liverpool Airport was renamed Liverpool John Lennon Airport. *(PA Photos)*

Paul at a poetry reading at the Everyman Theatre, Liverpool, March 21, 20001, left to right: Adrian Mitchell, Willy Russell, Paul and Tom Pickard. Paul attendance was unannounced, and he read extracts from his *Blackbird Singing* poetry book. *(PA Photos)*

George and Olivia on holiday in Turin, Italy, on May 3, 2001. George flew to Italy on actor Jim Carey's private plane to rest after cancer surgery in America. *(PA Photos)*

Paul promotes his *Wingspan Hits & History* retrospective album at the Cannes Film Festival, May 9, 2001. Follwing his appearance in Cannes, Paul visited George and Olivia in Italy. *(PA Photos)*

Paul with Heather Mills at the Adopt A Minefield event at the Regent Beverly Wilshire, Los Angeles, June 14, 2001. With them is the recipient of the Adopt-A-Minefield Humanitarian Award, Radosav 'Zika' Zivkovic, a land-mine survivor. *(Reuters)*

Ringo "I am."

Howard "Did you have a nose job?"

Ringo "Are you kidding? But I do feel good. I'm working out and I'm eating good."

Howard "Obviously, you're here because of your new CD, *Vertical Man*, but there's so much to ask you about. First of all, all the women you've banged. I mean, that could take up a two-hour show."

Ringo "Two minutes."

Howard "Do you laugh at that guy, Pete Best?"

Ringo "No, I don't laugh. Pete was doing the gig and then I got the gig. They asked him to leave and me to join."

Howard "All the time I used to go and see The Beatles' movies, I remember I used to sit in the theatres and the girls were screaming and I used to think how great it was. But then I thought, 'The movie I'd really like to see is *The Pete Best Story*.' Like, where is he right now? I'd like to make it. Am I the only one interested in that? I can star in that. I'm a great actor."

Ringo (changing subject) "Barbara thinks you're so charming."

Howard "Is that right? I think your wife is so hot! So, what is the most amount of women you've had at one time?"

Ringo "Two. We (The Beatles) did a show in Florida (*The Ed Sullivan Show* – February 16, 1964). They (the two girls) took me out in a Lincoln Convertible and took me to my first drive-in but I didn't see much of the movie."

Howard "You hooked up with two girls? You go to this drive-in, you go out in this limo and they have sex with you, just because you are with The Beatles?"

Ringo "Right there and then, Howard."

Howard "Wow, young beautiful girls. They banged their heads together trying to please you. Were you thinking, 'I've died and gone to heaven'?"

Ringo "Yeah."

Howard "How old were you when you first got laid?"

Ringo "Sixteen, in the park."

Howard "No kidding . . . I bet Barbara looks great naked! Does she work out all the time? I wished you had brought her in, no offence."

Ringo "Then you wouldn't have talked to me."

Howard "I would have ignored you and she's great in bed, I imagine? Let me ask you a question. The Beatles in the early years . . ."

Ringo (slightly agitated, interrupting) "Oh, The Beatles, come on . . ."

Howard "No, this is an important question. We're not moving on until we're ready. It's my show. Listen to me . . . You've seen all The Beatles naked together?"

Ringo "I have no big vision of us all being naked."

Howard "Well, who was the largest Beatle?"

Ringo "Me!"

Howard "You were?"

Ringo "I am! I'm the big one. I'm the biggie! You know, I haven't really inspected the others."

Howard "I've seen John (*Two Virgins* sleeve). I believe he was a little bit aroused in that picture. If I was going to go naked, I would be a little bit aroused. So seriously, you are the biggest one?"

Ringo "I don't know. I'm just bullshitting you. We never said, 'We've got nothing to do, so let's measure ourselves.' "

Howard "It's funny, George told me he was the largest."

Monday, June 22

Five days later, Linda's memorial service is held in New York at the Riverside Church. It surprises many people that Yoko Ono and Sean are not among those in attendance . . .

Paul, in conversation with Chrissie Hynde, of The Pretenders for *USA Today*, "The thing we decided on the memorial services was instead of inviting people who we maybe ought to have invited out of duty, that we would stay true to Linda's spirit and only invite her nearest and dearest friends. Seeing as Yoko wasn't one of those, we didn't invite her. We had helicopter pilots who'd helped us in New York when Linda was travelling a lot for treatments. They became good friends and I said to one of them that I'd like them to come to the memorial, and he was shocked. He said, 'Oh, I don't want to get in the way of all the various dignitaries,' and I said, 'Don't worry, there won't be any, this isn't that kind of thing. This is for people who Linda genuinely loved and for those who genuinely loved Linda.' Those were the only people invited. I'm really glad that we did do it like that because everyone who went remarked that there were so many friends there and it was such a warm atmosphere and everyone who spoke, spoke from the heart, genuinely. Linda would have hated anything else. There were some very nice people. For instance, Senator Ted Kennedy sent a really nice condolence letter to me. It was very thoughtful of him. But I knew that she wasn't a friend of his so he didn't get invited, either."

Four months later, on **Monday, October 26**, simultaneously around the world, EMI releases Linda's posthumous album *Wide Prairie . . .*

Paul "A couple of years ago, Linda got a letter from a girl who said she had really liked hearing one of Linda's songs, 'Seaside Woman' and she asked if she had any other songs. Well through the years, since the early Seventies, Linda had been writing and recording her own songs. But because of being in the shadow of The Beatles or of me and being so much in the public eye, she always felt very nervous and because it wasn't her main career she was reluctant. It was like she was on a hiding to nothing and people would be bound to criticise her. So she was shy to release it all. But this letter from this fan made her think that maybe she should put an album together. So in the last couple of years of her life, we spent time finding all the old tapes and looking at songs that didn't have lyrics. Then, during one of many trips to London where Linda was having treatment, we'd get a cassette of one of the melodies she'd written and we'd come up with the words. On one such journey we wrote the words to 'Appaloosa', 'I Got Up' and 'The Light Comes From Within', three of the sixteen tracks on this album. And that was good, writing like that. We would have a good laugh and forget that she was going up for treatment. It kept us both positive.

"Before we went out to Arizona, about a month before she died, we were putting the finishing touches to the album, making a couple of tracks and doing the backing vocals. We put the finishing touches to the vocals and there was nothing left to be done. We were going to come back from Arizona and I was going to mix the album. We were going to work on promotion now, this time of the year, and she was going to be doing the promotional interviews and we were going to release the album at Christmas. So when she died, I thought, 'I've just got to fulfil that plan.' I thought that some people might think that it's a tribute album that we'd rushed out. But I wanted to make it clear that it is something we were planning anyway. Releasing this album was something that very much Linda wanted. She was very proud of it. We decided the title would be *Wide Prairie.* Anyway, a couple of months after she died, I managed to get into the studio and we called those studio sessions *Tears & Laughter* because the engineer, my old friend Geoff Emerick, who I've known since The Beatles days, he lost his wife to cancer, too. So the pair of us were just crying on the console. But then we'd listen to Linda's spirit and we'd laugh and remember her. So it was *The Tears & Laughter* sessions. It was very moving to do it, but it was very uplifting to do it and when we finally got the whole album together we thought she'd be damn proud of this. And she should be too, because her personality comes over. You see that she's a very strong singer, a strong writer and she got a lot of flack over the years. Critics would say, 'Oh, she only plays keyboard with one finger,' or 'She can't sing.' People would even isolate microphones very cruelly, which devastated her; she hated that stuff as anyone would. I used to say, 'If I ever catch up with those DJs, I'll give them a word.' And believe me, that is really difficult.

"Many people were cruel to Linda. But you know, after a time you forgive. She didn't hold grudges. She'd just say, 'No, let it go. Don't dwell on it.' So we finished up the album and I am really proud of it. There are some really cool songs. She said, 'If we do an album there are three videos already,' which was like animated pieces that she'd done to three other tracks, which is good. So that means that that's all there. And a friend of ours was always going to make a trilogy of the third animation piece, so he's currently making 'The Light Comes From Within' where Linda rather shockingly swears on it.

"It's quite funny because some people view Linda as the sort of dutiful wife. But she really wasn't. I mean she was plenty dutiful but she was something else besides. But there were these words, and it was basically this song, 'The Light Comes From Within', which is basically her getting back at her critics and the people who had been cruel to her. And even though she didn't hold a grudge, she figured it's a pretty good subject for a song where she could vent her emotions, you know get it out and let it go. So I looked at the second verse and there's swearing, and I said, 'Well, I don't know about this,' and she said, 'What's wrong with it?' And I said, 'Well, it's pretty forthright. You're singing this?' And she said, 'Watch me.' She grabbed on the microphone and bang. She did it in one take. She sang it beautifully. You know, she just had guts, nerves. She just had the nerve to carry that kind of thing off completely. So she did it. It's a beautiful vocal take, very strong. She got all of the work done, got the whole thing done, and then she said, 'Now I've put the whole thing together, with some sleeve notes giving my recollections of each song. We're releasing it at the end of October.' I think it will surprise a lot of people. I think it's a really good album to have. That was her concern: that if you went into a record shop 20 years from now and said could you have a Linda McCartney record they'd have to guide you to one of my records, or a Wings record. We thought that it would be a bit sad that there wouldn't be a Linda McCartney record but now there is. I'm very proud of it and I know she would have been. I think it shows that there's a lot more to this lady than a lot of people knew."

Thursday, February 11
On the eve of Ringo's tenth anniversary All-Starr Band tour, the former Beatle and Todd Rundgren hold an online AOL live webchat . . .

AOLiveMC3 "Welcome to AOL Live, Ringo Starr and Todd Rundgren."

Ringo "Hi."

AOLiveMC3 "Are you ready to start answering questions? Here we go."

Question "Ringo, what is your all-time favourite Beatles song?"

Ringo "That's an interesting question. I have so many. I really don't break it down to one, but if you are forcing me to pick one, let me pick 'Rain'."

Question "Ringo, do you miss the times of the Sixties at all? Or do you just go with the flow?"

Ringo "I have great memories of the Sixties, but I am a man of the Nineties."

Question "Thanks to you, Paul and George for reuniting for 'Free As A Bird'. What was the atmosphere like on the sessions?"

Ringo "It was really lovely. It was interesting because we hadn't played together in such a long time."

Question "We wanted to know how Ringo liked his visit on *The Howard Stern Show*. Was he nervous about it?"

Ringo "My visit with Howard was great. He's a very charming human being. He was fine."

Question "Ringo, what do you feel was your most important accomplishment in your life?"

Ringo "Being born!"

Question "Hello, Ringo. I'm Lisa. I love you and your music. Your album *Vertical Man* is exceptional. My question to you is, would you ever consider doing movies again?"

Ringo "I consider doing movies many times, but I'm afraid the people who make them don't consider me."

Question "What have you found most gratifying about the success of The Beatles' music with a whole new generation of fans, many of whom were not born when the band recorded?"

Ringo "That they listen to it. I think it's fabulous that generation after generation get into the music. That's the thing I am proud of."

Question "Hi Ringo, my question is about Ludwig drums. I heard they are giving out Ringo Starr replica maple Ludwig sets on *The Price Is Right* (TV show) now. Did you know about that?"

Ringo "No, I'm afraid I won't be giving up my replica drum set for *The Price Is Right*. This is news to me. But it would be interesting to see what the price would be for them."

Question "Ringo, I loved your work on 'Beautiful Night'. Will you and Paul co-write any other songs?"

Ringo "We have no plans to at the moment."

Question "Ringo, I was wondering what your thoughts are on the music scene today, in particular, bands like Metallica."

Ringo "I like a lot of the music that's out today, it's just that Metallica passed me by."

Question "What are the factors that you feel led to The Beatles' break-up?"

Ringo "Read any newspaper or magazine from 1970 and you'll find the answers there."

Question "What drummer had the biggest influence on you?"

Ringo "Gene Krupa. I saw him in two movies."

Question "Hi, Ringo, I want to wish you the best of luck with the All-Starr Tour. My question is how come you have not been wearing all of your rings lately? Love you always, Linda from New York."

Ringo "Good question! Let me tell you, Linda, I'm playing so much lately, I'm playing more and more and more and if I wear the rings, I get blisters on my fingers, and so I take them off now."

Question "Do you think you will ever retire and if so, why?"

Ringo "I feel I'm always going to retire, halfway through all of my tours. Then when it's over and I have a couple of months' holiday, I want to play again. But Barbara, my wife, and my children laugh at me now whenever I mention retirement, as they've heard it so often."

Question "Hello, Ringo. How has your daughter been doing since her surgery in Boston?"

Ringo "Great, thank you! Thanks for asking. She is just fabulous."

Question "When John died, how did it affect your lifestyle, partying, relationships, etc.?"

Ringo "It affected my lifestyle in the way that he wasn't there."

Question "Will there be any special box set or book or anything to celebrate ten years of All-Starr Bands?"

Ringo "Yes there will be a compilation box set of all the All-Starr Bands. It should be out around May or June. If you come to the show, you'll be able to buy your ten-year hat and T-shirt and key ring. Also to find out any information about the 10th All-Starr Tour, log onto the ringotour.com website to see if I'm playing in your town, with Jack Bruce, Todd Rundgren and Gary Brooker and Simon Kirke."

Question "Ringo, what keeps you motivated at this stage of your career?"

Ringo "Blood transfusions!"

Question "Is there any way that fans can get your autograph?"

Ringo "With difficulty! Oh, that's enough fun."

AOLiveMC3 "Wow, where has the time gone? We have time for one more question."

Question "How does it make you feel knowing that you are still a role model to kids and adults everywhere still to this day?"

Ringo "I don't really think of myself as a role model, but if I am, thinking peace and love every moment of the day like I do, then it's good. I'd like to thank everybody for sending their questions to me and I hope they had as much fun as I did. Lots of love from Ringo and Todd."

AOLiveMC3 "Thank you for being our guests tonight, Ringo Starr and Todd Rundgren. Thank you, audience, for sending such great questions. Good night."

Tuesday, June 8

"Go Veggie with Paul McCartney and *Viva!*" Paul gives his second interview since Linda's death to Juliet Gellatley, Founder & Director of *Viva!*

Press Release "Sir Paul McCartney has put his weight behind a *Viva!* campaign to turn Britain veggie. A joint colourful, upbeat leaflet has been produced to coincide with 1999's National Vegetarian Week (taking place between June 14–20) encouraging people all over Britain to 'Go Veggie With Paul McCartney And *Viva!*' Hundreds of thousands of copies will be distributed in the coming months, from one end of the UK to the other."

Paul "Going veggie saves animals and people, protects the environment and is one of the healthiest things you can do. Linda became the spokesperson on vegetarianism largely because she had the time available. I'd be off making music somewhere but in fact she was speaking for both of us and for all our family. I really worry that good people around the world might think that we've lost a powerful voice. Well, we have but my voice is there now and I'm trying to use it. I've helped raise a family of four kids and they couldn't be healthier. My son James is a big surfer, fit and healthy, and he's a vegan. There's now a whole heap of science to show that vegetarians and vegans are healthier and live longer."

Viva! Press Release "In a passionate appeal for a better, saner world, **Paul** is clear about what motivates him . . ."

"It's always been and will always be compassion for animals. That's it! It's respect for our fellow species. We're just another animal yet we think we're so clever, know so much, but what have we done? We're headed towards disaster and won't even acknowledge it. From the biggest to the smallest we have beaten all the other animals into submission. Couldn't we be magnanimous in victory? Isn't it time to see if there's anything they can teach us before we obliterate the whole lot of them and ourselves as well."

Paul then talks about factory farming. "We can't go on cramming creatures into battery cages, broiler sheds, pig pens and so on," he insists. "Where's the compassion in that? For the sake of the animals, support *Viva!*"

Speaking of their joint campaign, Ms Gellatley said, "People greatly respect Paul McCartney and will listen to his plea for change. *Viva!* has all the practical experience to offer support and information necessary to anyone wanting to change their diet. It's a great combination."

Monday, September 13 (UK)
The Beatles' 1968 film *Yellow Submarine* undergoes a major overhaul and is re-released on DVD, home video and as a new songtrack album, featuring newly re-mixed tracks . . .

George "Everything has a different mix on it now because when they set up to do this new, wraparound five-speaker mix for the film, they were working away doing that for months and months at Abbey Road. You see, a lot of the time The Beatles were only working on 4-track tape, so we'd get to the fourth track and then what we'd do is mix the four tracks onto one track of another 4-track machine, and then we'd do another three tracks. So what they've gone and done in these new mixes was connect all the four tracks together and have the first four tracks all separated. So for the first time you've actually got a much bigger, cleaner mix, because you've got the original bass and drum and guitar tracks unmixed-together, you know. And also, with all the old equipment and all the compressors and the stuff that we used in those days, you'd spend ages trying to improve the final 4-track mix you figured you were stuck with. This engineer, a fellow named Peter Mew, did a lot of the work with a guy called Allan Rouse, who's kind of in charge of all The Beatles' catalogue. So we went in and listened to all these new, fully remixed tracks, and they really are good, with the sound coming all around you."

Monday, October 4 (UK)
Paul meanwhile, releases *Run Devil Run*, an album comprising covers of rock'n'roll classics and a few new McCartney originals . . .

Paul "I got together about 25 songs that I just remembered fondly from the early days. We hadn't done them with The Beatles, but I just liked them. My fondness for the tracks was the important thing about picking them. A lot of the songs were obscure B-sides from way back. In preparing for this album, I just sat at home with a bunch of cassettes, played them, and wrote down the words to the songs that I wanted to do on this album. Doing that was great. I sat at home exactly as I had done when I was a teenager, listening to a 45 I wanted to learn . . . There were a couple of songs that I wanted to stay faithful to the originals because my memory of them was so clear and I loved them so much. 'Blue Jean Bop' was off a Gene Vincent album we had in Liverpool and it wasn't as big a hit as 'Be-Bop-A-Lula', but it was one we loved. There were two songs I turned Mick Jagger onto that The Stones have done. One was 'She Said Yeah', which was by Larry Williams and the other was 'Ain't Too Proud To Beg' by The Temptations. Mick will deny it, 'What? No mate, never saw him, never met him,' but I distinctly remember having him up into a little music room and playing them to him in the Sixties. He loved them and he went and covered them. I thought, 'I can't cover "She Said Yeah" because he's covered it', but then I thought, 'Na, I will, because I love it so much.' We've messed around with the track a bit but it is sort of like my memory of the original. We left it until the end of the week because it's hard to sing when you're playing bass as well. It was the last song we recorded in that first week.

"I really made *Run Devil Run* because Linda had urged me to do it. I like to play a lot of loud rock'n'roll guitar around the house. Linda loved me to play real loud, real dirty rock'n'roll guitar and that's what I like to do too . . . I realise that *Run Devil Run* is going to get compared to John's *Rock 'N' Roll* (1975) and because of that, I deliberately didn't look up John's album again before I did mine. I wanted to go on my gut instinct and go for the spontaneity in recording this one. That's why we cut it all in less than a week. When I was thinking about who to use on the album, I first thought of the guitars and I thought of Dave Gilmour of Pink Floyd. He had played on my track 'No More Lonely Nights'. Then, when I had chosen my other musicians, Ian Paice, Pete Wingfield, Mick Green, we booked Abbey Road for just five days. I arrived at 10am on the first morning and I hadn't even met two of the musicians. So we worked from Monday to Friday and by the end of that time, we had recorded 19 songs, 15 of which are on this album. We raced through them just like we did in the early days with The Beatles. We'd arrive at the studio, set up our gear, and we'd record two songs before lunch, have a break for lunch, and then record two more songs in the afternoon. I deliberately planned it like that. I remembered the early recording sessions at Abbey Road with The Beatles, which happened in a very specific way. We'd arrive at the studio for 10am, get your guitar in tune and your bass set up, everything to go by 10.30, when the producer and the engineer would arrive and ask what you'd be doing. In the next three hours, until 1.30pm, you'd record two songs, have lunch until 2.30 and then do another two songs before 5.30. That was the way we worked for quite a while with The Beatles, on albums like *Rubber Soul* and *Revolver*. I remembered loving it because it was so fast. As far as what I think about John these days, he's always with me. I think about him a lot. I always was and always will be a John Lennon fan. I say we both loved our rock'n'roll. We wrote all those songs together with The Beatles and you can't do all that stuff together if you differ. I'm still very proud of the fact that John only ever had one songwriting partner and that was me."

'All Shook Up'

Paul "I have the loveliest memory of 'All Shook Up'. We were mad Elvis fans before he went into the army. We all thought the army made him a little too grown-up, but he was fantastic. Back in Liverpool, my best mate, Ian James, who I still know, and me we used to go around in these draped flecked jackets. We thought they were really cool, that you could not have a cooler item of clothing, and we would wander around the fairgrounds in

Liverpool trying to pick up girls. We thought the girls would come flooding to us, us being in these jackets. But of course they never took any notice of us. We could not get arrested. That got us down, that got us depressed, so much so that it gave us a headache. So we went back to his granny's house in the Dingle, round by where Ringo lived, and we put 'All Shook Up' on the record player. And I swear that hearing that song got rid of the blues. My headaches went and we were lifted out of that depression."

'Run Devil Run'
(A McCartney original)

Paul "I was in Atlanta with my son and he wanted to visit the funky side of town. So we went down there and were just wandering around the block and we came across this sort of voodoo shop selling cures for everything. I was looking in the shop window and I saw this bottle of bath salts called Run Devil Run and I thought that was a good title for a song. So when I was on holiday after that, I started thinking of words for it and it came out quite easily. I was actually out sailing when I did the verses. It's nothing about sailing; it's about a swamp in Alabama, but imagination roams. Some people have said that the harmonies on the song had a Linda feel to them and I thought that too. She didn't record on it. It was done more recently, but it is like she is singing on it. I wrote this with Chuck Berry in mind. When we were recording it, I remember someone saying, 'Who did that originally? Who was that by?' And I thought, 'Yeah, I've got 'em.' I had great pleasure in telling them, 'It's by me!' The producer, Chris Thomas, said, 'Well, have you got any others?' "

'No Other Baby'

Paul "It's a strange track because I didn't have a record of it. I did not know who had recorded it or who had written it. But I knew that I had loved the song from the late Fifties. And luckily, I just remembered the words. Thank goodness for memory. That was the one I pulled out of my envelope and when I asked if anybody knew it, nobody did. We used to do it at the soundchecks when we were last on tour, so the tour guys probably know it. I found out recently that an English skiffle group called The Vipers recorded it. Funnily enough, I was talking to George Martin about this song, and I suddenly remembered that he recorded The Vipers. Talk about things coming full circle."

'Lonesome Town'

Paul "When I first heard it, it was just a nice ballad about lonesome people that Ricky Nelson did. With that one, I got into the studio fully intending to do it like Ricky Nelson, just a complete remake because I thought I won't be able to better it. Then I thought I'd take it higher and sing it in my middle voice. So we did that and it was going great until we got to the middle and because I was taking it higher, I was having to sing so high in the middle it got ridiculous. It was like Mickey Mouse. So I tried to take it down but that didn't work. It was going to spoil the mood. Then, in two seconds flat, I thought, 'Dave (Gilmour), you sing the melody and I will sing the harmony above it.' That was good and that was exactly how we would work with The Beatles. Someone would come up with a good idea and you didn't take two weeks to go through the bureaucracy of whether it was a good idea or not."

'Movie Magg'

Paul "It's a Carl Perkins song and The Beatles were really major fans of Carl. We did a lot of his songs and 'Movie Magg' was a crazy little song that I always liked. This one is about Carl trying to take his girlfriend, Maggie, to the movies on a horse called Becky, which turned out to be a mule. This is a real story. He actually had a mule called Becky, he had a girlfriend called Maggie and they rode on Becky's back to the movies. I thought that was just so wild. I wanted to do it because it was kind of a homage to Carl."

'I Got Stung'

Paul "After Elvis got out of the army, he did 'I Got Stung'. I remembered us not being too keen on it at the time, but recently I remembered the intro and I just loved it. I thought I just had to do it because of that intro. We do more of a shouty version than Elvis's version and I'm pleased with the way it turned out."

'Honey Hush'

Paul "That song has very, very early memories for me. I remember that John Lennon and Stuart Sutcliffe had an art school flat at a place called Gambier Terrace, which looks out onto Liverpool Cathedral. It was an amazing place, just a bare flat, a mattress, a record player, a little ashtray and that was it. George and I stayed there on one of the first times I'd stayed out all night. It was a great experience for us kids to stay over at someone's flat and not sleep at home. I remember waking up in the morning after having virtually no sleep and it felt so cool. The record player was next to the mattress and the first thing we did in the morning was put on this Johnny Burnette record, 'Honey Hush'. When we were making this record, I came in one morning a little tired and confused and did this one just to blow all the cobwebs away. It was one of those songs that I hadn't been able to get all the lines down when I was writing out the lyrics at home. I just couldn't figure out the lyric on one line. So I thought I'd just write it down phonetically and find a lyric sheet later, when we went to record it. But I never did get the lyric sheet. I never did find out the real words. So when we were recording it, I thought I'd just sing it phonetically. The real lyrics are nothing like I sing but it was in the spirit of the album, not to even care what the lyric was. It just sings great. It's a great song to sing."

'Shake A Hand'

Paul "When we were working in Hamburg with The Beatles, there was this one jukebox in a pool hall we used to go to. This jukebox had records on it that the other jukeboxes didn't. So that was where we went to get down and learn the words to the songs, because we couldn't buy the records. My favourite was 'Shake A Hand' by Little Richard. I never got the record; I just listened to it on the jukebox. To this day, I still haven't got the record."

'Party'

Paul " 'Let's Have A Party' was one that Elvis did in *Loving You*. It's such a great song and again it's one of those that as kids we could never get the words right and there was no authority that we could consult on them. We thought it said, 'I've never kissed a bear, I've never kissed a goo.' We kept on putting the record back and then we found out he said, 'I've never kissed a goon.' But that didn't help much. We said, 'What? Is he talking about Spike Milligan?' But it was great to do a tribute to Elvis."

Monday, November 1

Paul records a *Run Devil Run* promotional interview with Gary Crowley of the London radio station GLR at his MPL headquarters in Soho Square. For Gary, it is a dream come true . . .

"I've been an enormous Beatles fan for years," Gary admits. "I discovered them when I was about thirteen or fourteen. I wanted to find out more about them so I went down to the record shop, like many other people, and bought the *Red* and the *Blue* albums and these were my initial introductions to the group. Prior to that, I had been into all that normal glam rock stuff, you know, Slade, Gary Glitter, and that sort of thing. I got into The Beatles a couple of years before punk and prior to punk, The Beatles became almost my whole life, really. I started off by buying their records, and at that time, it was a bit like a secret society of Beatles fans in my school and I found a couple of others who were really big Beatles fans. We started swapping Beatles records and a friendship grew out of that. And because I was such a big fan, what I used to do, in every English or Social Studies project, I would always try and pull it around so that I would always write about The Beatles or Sixties culture in general. One of my Beatles projects was shown in the reception of the school. My love for the group has just snowballed from there, really. It's been never ending. It's funny, a lot of my best friends, like Terry, Simon and Michael, are all massive Beatles fans and after a while, you invariably end up talking about them. Talking about The Beatles is almost like an introduction to meeting people. Later, I remember watching Tony Palmer's documentary on The Beatles in the *All You Need Is Love* series (ITV network, May 14, 1977). I watched that on a Saturday night and recall being completely bowled over. The clip that really got me excited was 'Some Other Guy' at the Cavern Club. I hadn't seen that before and I was totally fascinated by it and excited by it as well. The show set me off on another journey, really.

"But, before my meeting with Paul in November 1999, I had never met any of The Beatles. But I remember, when I was a kid, in 1979, when I first started working for Clive Banks, Pete Townshend of The Who paid for me to go to New York to see The Who. It was a payment for my work I did in getting some kids together for his 'Rough Boys' video and I remember we went to the Dakota buildings and stood around there for about an hour. I remember Carly Simon came out because she was living there at the time. In 1994, I came close to interviewing Paul when I was presenting *The Beat* (ITV). There was talk because I know Paul gets on well with the executive producer of the programme and a date was set for an interview and I got very, very excited about that but that got pulled at the last minute for some reason. It just seemed to go away, it just never happened. So that was the closest I had got until my mate Kevin, at Parlophone, made that fateful call.

"I remember it vividly, it was on the Friday, and Kevin McCabe, who is the head of radio promotion at Parlophone, he called and said, 'What are you doing on Monday?' and I said, 'Well, nothing really. Why is that?' He said, 'Well, there's a good chance that you might be interviewing McCartney.' Of course, I keeled over, hit my head on the sofa and knocked myself out. He said, 'It looks as though it could happen. I'll call first thing on Monday morning just to confirm.' So, over that weekend, I was, without wishing to put too fine a point on it, absolutely shitting myself! I wasn't sleeping that much and I was constantly going back and forwards to my computer, working on the questions. I kept asking myself, 'Oh, is that one right?' And saying, 'Oh no, I can't really ask him that.'

Then, on Monday morning, the phone rang at about ten o'clock, and it was Kevin saying that the interview with Paul was definitely on. So I met my producer, Jim, he came over to my flat and picked me up. Then we drove down to Oxford Street, parked the car in a car park and walked round to MPL. There was me, Kevin, Jim and also a man called Tony Howels, who was the man who got me involved at Capitol Radio many years ago. He was recording the interview. So we got there, hung around in MPL's reception for about ten minutes and then we were taken upstairs to the first floor into an office, which overlooks Soho Square and I had a dry mouth. I consumed gallons of water and I must have literally used the MPL toilet a half a dozen times. I'm sure the girls sitting outside must have thought, 'What's he up to?' Then I came back in, sat down and then, all of a sudden, Paul walked in with Geoff (Baker) and the great thing about it was that he has done this millions and millions of times. He knows what to say with regards to relaxing you, so when he saw me, he said, 'Aye, it's the man off the telly.' Which I thought was a bit funny, because I haven't been on the telly for a couple of years. But he was great. He kept picking the phone up, even though it wasn't ringing, and said, 'No, he's not here.' It just kind of relaxed everybody. I know he certainly relaxed me.

"I had literally just finished that book about Robert Frazer, called *Groovy Bob,* so we spoke a little about that, which was a kind of warm-up question. Paul was quoted a lot in that book and Robert was a good friend to him and Linda and then we were away. Originally we were only going to have about forty minutes or something but we did about an hour and a half. I had so many great bits in my interview with Paul that it's hard to say which was my favourite part. I think we really got him on a good day. But one bit I did like was the bit where Paul was talking about the time they, The Beatles, spent at the flat in Gambier Terrace in Liverpool, which was brilliant. It had me in hysterics . . ."

Paul "John and Stuart, the first bass player in The Beatles, they went to art school. Stuart was a really good painter and they used to have a flat with some other people, like you do, and there was one room they had. We were invited to that, me and George one night, and this was truly living, staying out all night, that was really cool. We just chatted all night, we had hyper chats, speeding away, 'I love him, he's great.' 'What about Scotty Moore?' 'What about that solo?' ' "Don't Be Cruel"? Are you kidding?' 'I'm not kidding you?' It was like that all night and then tiredness would kick in and then you'd flake. I woke up with the burning eyes syndrome, thinking, 'Oh no. I usually get sleep when I'm at home. I lie in when I'm at home.' But then we'd say, 'Ah yes, but we're having fun, aren't we? This is great. We're staying out all night.' I just remember John turning over, lighting a 'ciggie' and putting this Johnny Burnette album on, and I think the opening track was 'Honey Hush'. I've always loved it since then. I know John would have liked to record it, so that was an added bonus. There are songs you're always going to get around to so I finally got round to this one. It's the greatest song to sing. You like singing it. It's got a chilling lyric to the last verse. You couldn't get that one past the censor now. It's very un PC. I don't listen to the lyrics. It feels great to sing. I'll advise anyone, if you're feeling bad, to sing that song. It takes care of anything."

"Paul also told some lovely stories about Gene Vincent and Little Richard in Hamburg," Gary recalls.

"He also told the Elvis story and the other thing for me that was interesting was when he told me that he had met all of his rock'n'roll heroes, like Fats Domino, you know, all the people that inspired them to form a band. They actually met them all. Spending the day with Paul was euphoric. Up until that point, passing my driving test was my most incredible feeling. I didn't pass until the third time but the meeting with Paul surpassed it by miles. It's funny really, after I had done the interview, I asked him to record a little trail which could be played on the station, which he was only too happy to do. I got him to sign a picture for my girlfriend, because she's a massive fan as well, and also I had my picture taken with him. He just couldn't be any more accommodating, really. He couldn't have been any nicer. I didn't walk out of MPL; I floated out of there. I then walked down Oxford Street and drifted into the afternoon."

Thursday, December 2

After a twenty-six year wait, Paul finally agrees to an appearance on *Parkinson*, the top-rated BBC1 talk show hosted by Michael Parkinson . . .

Parkinson "Back in 1973, when Paul made the hit album *Band On The Run*, he asked me if I would pose alongside him and Linda and a bunch of other celebrities in prison garb on the sleeve. I agreed to do the photo shoot, requesting in return that he would be a guest on my chat show. I said to him, 'Look, I've never interviewed you. You're top of my hit list, so can we do a deal that I'll do your album cover and you'll do an interview?' He said, 'Done!' So the little bugger owes me."

Shortly before appearing with Michael Parkinson on his show, Paul gives an interview with Keith Little of the *TVTimes* magazine . . .

Keith "How are you coping without your late wife, Linda?"

Paul "If you are lucky enough, like I was, to have a soulmate for 30 years who you just love, it's a terrible tragedy when you lose her. But then you can look at it and just think, 'God, that's luckier than most people.' That doesn't happen to everyone, a really beautiful romance like that. So it took me at least a year to just grieve and let the whole thing out. And if I had to cry, I cried. I didn't hold anything back. But after a while, I started to think, 'Well, Linda herself was such an upbeat lady, she wouldn't want me to cry too long.' So that started to kick in. And then the rays of sunshine start coming back, your kids start making you laugh and so I'm feeling really good now."

Keith "Do you think that the remaining Beatles will ever get back together?"

Paul "The thing is that it's really hard to do that because we haven't got John and without John, it's not the four of us. The Beatles were all four of us, all for one and one for all. Nobody is closing any doors on the idea. When we're 90, we may well fall on stage out of our wheelchairs."

Keith "Do you think you'll go out on tour again?"

Paul "I put a band together for the rock'n'roll album and we really haven't known each other for that long. We cut the album and then we went over to Los Angeles and did a charity gig (PETA). Doing that gig was great and it certainly got the juices flowing again . . . After that LA show, we were all having a drink together and the band was really eager to do more. When your band is keen to gig, that's when it gets really exciting. So now I'm thinking that, maybe, I'll get out there again next year. Once Christmas is over, I'll probably be setting up to record a new album and then, maybe, play live again."

Keith "How do you see your future?"

Paul "I've never seen my future and I don't intend to start now. I've no idea. The Beatles used to have an expression, 'Something will happen,' and that's about as far as I get in philosophy. There's no point in mapping out next year. It's going to happen anyway. I believe in fate and I'm ready to accept the future rather than try to tell it what to do."

During the taping of *Parkinson,* which was recorded at the BBC TV Centre in London on **Thursday, December 2**, Paul reminisces about the people of Liverpool . . .

"The people there are headcases," **Paul** affectionately jokes. "They've got a strange brilliance, I think. I love 'em. They're such lovely people. I've met Prime Ministers and high falutin' people around the world, but I've never met people as good as these people, or as wise or as funny as these people. I had this Uncle Harry, Auntie Gin's husband, Harry Harris, his name was. He was a bit of a boozer, he wouldn't mind me saying, and once, my cousin Betty had decorated her flat. She was newly married and she and her husband, Mike, had decorated her flat a kind of nice pale mushroom colour. And Harry came round and he was having a little drink and stuff and she happened to say, 'What do you think of the colour, the mushroom colour? Do you like it, Harry?' Because his opinion was valuable and he said, 'Ah, yeah,' looking at it. 'Ah, yeah, it's all right, Fan. It looks like boiled shite!' Shite's bad enough but there's this image of him with this little pan of water, 'That's the colour.' "

At the conclusion of the BBC1 show, transmitted the following day, Paul unexpectedly reveals that he will playing Liverpool's famous Cavern Club on **Tuesday, December 14** . . .

Parkinson "You're actually going to take this band on the road, aren't you?"

Paul "Well, we're actually going to do a gig, before the end of the year, at the Cavern in Liverpool."

(Squeals of delight come from the packed studio audience)

Parkinson "But it only takes about 150 people."

Paul "It takes about 300, we'll get you all in. It'll be rocking out the century, I reckon."

Obviously this announcement is not unexpected for those who had been involved with the organisation of the concert . . .

Billy Heckle of Cavern City Tours, the Liverpool-based Beatles tourist organisation who owns the Cavern Club, "Jean Catharell, of *Liverpool Beatlescene*, went to the taping of *Parkinson* on the Thursday. And as she left, she rang us up, shouting, 'He's announced it, he's announced it.' And when Paul did that, we knew that there was no going back, because up until then, it had only been phone calls from Geoff Baker, Alan Crowder and a few executives from MPL. But when Paul announced it, it was like, 'Fucking hell!' It was like all your Christmases coming at once. On the Friday morning, we woke up to the papers who had a snippet about the concert. We came into our office at 8am and from the second I came in, Paul's gig at the Cavern became a 24 hours a day concern. It was incessant. The phones never stopped ringing. We had five lines in our office and if it had been 55 lines, it would not have been any different. As soon as you put the phone down, it would ring again. We were manning the phones every night until 10 o'clock. That went on for eleven straight days. We even worked on Sundays. It was not only us, but it involved everyone who had something to do with Paul or The Beatles. Everyone got inundated with calls. We only had five lines so when people couldn't get through to us, they were ringing up EMI, Apple, MPL, The Beatles Shop, and The Beatles Story. They all got hammered. Anything remotely to do with Paul or The Beatles had a nightmare time with people looking for tickets . . .

"Definitely, the whole thing about Paul at the Cavern came about as a result of the reissue of the *Yellow Submarine* film. We at Cavern City Tours had gone for years without any formal recognition from Apple, The Beatles' company. But we did get a phone call from Derek Taylor, God rest his merry soul, in 1987 and he was very entertaining on the phone and very friendly. He basically said that they would never ever come out and authorise anything we ever did. It was a bit of a Mexican standoff. He said, 'Don't be worried if other conventions get closed down and don't be worried if other bands, who are using The Beatles' image without permission, are stopped from performing elsewhere. In Liverpool, it would be all right for the simple fact that it was in Liverpool.' After the problems of Heysel, Toxteth and Hillsborough, there was a great deal of sympathy and empathy from Apple about the role that The Beatles could play and were playing in the regeneration of the city, with tourism and jobs. Derek basically said to us, 'We've checked you out, we've found out you're honest, you're not taking the piss and, at the end of the day, you're making your money in Liverpool by providing jobs and improving the image of the city.' He concluded by saying, 'As long as that continues, you'll never hear from us. But if you ever cross that white line, we'll come down on you like a fucking ton of bricks. Enjoy your conventions, enjoy your tours and if you don't bother us, we won't bother you. The walls have eyes and ears, especially in Liverpool.'

"That phone call in 1987 was a complete surprise. It wasn't a discussion; it was a listening phone call. But he was very entertaining and very sweet. After that, the only other person we had a relationship with was Geoff Baker at MPL. He included us in lots of fans' stuff and gatherings. We helped promote Paul's Kings Dock concert in 1990 and when Paul played at Westcliffe in St Austell in 1991, we were invited to the gig. We started to get recognition and he started to look after us. We talked to Geoff three or four times a year. We'd give him information if he wanted it. It was all very casual. But then, in January 1999, we got a phone call from Geoff saying, 'You are never going to believe this but I think you're going to get a phone call in the next couple of days from Neil (Aspinall, head of Apple Corps).' So I said, laughing, 'Well, what have we done?' He said, 'Well, basically, they are going to re-launch *Yellow Submarine* in September and I've been to a meeting in Hollywood, at the Capitol Records Tower, and we were discussing how we are going to re-launch it.' Geoff told me that one of the American executives suggested that they re-launch *Yellow Submarine* in Liverpool because he had heard that The Beatles' convention in Liverpool was really big with the street festival, which has hundreds of thousands of people. But Neil's apparent reaction to that was very, very negative and Geoff got involved because he did know, from talking to us, exactly how many attended the convention and the Mathew Street Festival, and he was aware of the international appeal. So when Neil was being very reticent and very negative, Geoff jumped in with a number of positives. But at the end of the day, Neil, who had the overriding say anyway, was convinced enough to say, 'Well, let's speak to them.' Geoff won that battle for us with the knowledge that he had. So, sure enough, I got that phone call from Neil and I was asked to go down to see them in London with a number of ideas of how we could re-launch *Yellow Submarine* in Liverpool.

"As I walked through the doors at Apple I remember I felt very intimidated. I had not been intimidated by anything in my life. I remember thinking to myself, 'Fuck, shit! This is Apple! This is Neil Aspinall!' His reputation has been very well documented but I found him to be most charming and he treated me very gently. We talked for about an hour-and-a-half and what was really gratifying after talking with Neil, Geoff and a couple of other Apple executives, was that Neil really took on board everything that was initially suggested. One of which was an idea that the tower, which is now Radio City, we could turn on from dusk onwards and, using special lights, we could turn the sky yellow. We came up with the idea that when the people were going into the *Yellow Submarine* premiere, they could see that the whole of the city centre was yellow. Apple liked that one as well as a few other ones like the renaming of the Mathew Street Festival as the *Yellow Submarine* Festival. I also proposed to them the idea of the *Yellow Submarine* stage, which Colin Jones, our electrician, constructed. Anyway, in terms of budgets, Apple ended up putting about £40,000 into the project, which was nice. They said they preferred not having a sponsor. I ended up attending another two meetings at Apple. We refined everything and put everything into play. So for the *Yellow Submarine* premiere in August, Neil came down, George Martin came down, and Neil was noticeably impressed and amazed by the number of people there in the city centre. We had 300,000 there that day and the police had to tell the locals not to go into town. Everything about that day was phenomenal! I even persuaded Neil to allow a band, Lenny Payne, to perform after the *Yellow Submarine* film was shown. I was surprised when Neil said, 'Okay then.' The whole day went like a dream and Apple was very impressed and we ended up establishing a very nice working relationship. And what was also very nice was that Apple endorsed the premiere. It was an official Apple day. EMI endorsed it and so it became an official Apple, Beatles day. So even though Derek Taylor had said back in 1987 that they would never endorse us, they eventually did. It was a unique one-off event. We had a debriefing meeting at Apple in October and Neil was very complimentary, very nice, and everything was hunky-dory.

"Going back slightly, on the Sunday before the *Yellow Submarine*/Mathew Street Festival, we were in full swing at the convention. And I had a phone call from Geoff Baker saying that the American Post Master General, who was at the convention to launch the *Yellow Submarine* stamps outside the USA, had arrived with an entourage of about four or five and she had expressed a desire to walk around the Town Hall, where the stamp was being unveiled and also to see the Cavern Club. Geoff asked me to show her the Cavern so I said I would meet them there in about half-an-hour. I got there and Mathew Street was really busy for a Sunday. I met her, took her down into the Cavern and showed her round the backroom where the band who was on were playing Beatles music. It was packed, sweaty and in all its glory. I was doing the PR bit. I got my T-shirt and stuff, thanked her for coming and told her what an honour it was for Liverpool. We spent about fifteen minutes doing this and all the time I was aware that Geoff Baker wasn't around. But then I suddenly kept seeing him, whizzing around like a dog on heat. Anyway, the Cavern was hot and stinking of smoke so I suggested that we go upstairs to get some air and, as I said my farewells to the lady, Geoff came up to me and said, 'You bastard!' I said, 'Why, what have I done?' He said, 'You know what you've done.' I had an inkling of what he was talking about so I said, 'It was pretty good down there, wasn't it?' He said, 'It was amazing! I've only met you down there when it was empty. And although the place still had a certain degree of atmosphere, with that band on, it was simply awesome!' Pausing for breath, Geoff then said, 'I'll tell you, before I die, we'll have McCartney here to play. I don't know how we're going to do it but Paul is going to come here and play.' So after the Apple debriefing meeting in October we heard no more and then *Run Devil Run* came out. We were invited to the launch at The Equinox in London. Six of us were invited into the VIP area. It was another pat on the back, which we appreciated.

"Then, about three weeks after, Geoff rang me up and said, 'Bill, you don't how to get in touch with the guy at 3 Gambier Terrace do you?' And I said, 'Yeah, I'll go round for you.' Geoff said, 'Would you knock on his door and find out who the gaffer is.' So I asked, 'Are you shooting a video?' and Geoff said, 'You smart arse bastard. Don't tell anybody but, yeah, that's what we're looking to do with the new single.' ('Honey Hush') Geoff asked if I would go round to see the fellow at Gambier Terrace but was told not to tell the man in any way that it was anything to do with McCartney. So I went round with Dave Jones, of Cavern City Tours, and we knocked on the guy's door. But he wasn't in. So we just left a message saying, 'Please contact Cavern City Tours, urgently. It is in your interest.' I rang Geoff back saying we had still not heard from the bloke at Gambier Terrace. So, 24 hours later, we went back, knocked again on his door and he still wasn't in. We were told that he was away for the weekend. But within an hour, the guy came back. He rang us up and asked us what the message was about. We told him that an American film crew might be interested in using his place for location work. Geoff came up and looked at it, thanked the bloke and that was it. We never heard for a week and then, the next thing I know, we get a phone call from Geoff and he says, 'How does the Cavern sound?' I said, 'Fuck off!' He said, 'No, honestly. It's on the agenda. We've been talking about it for a couple of hours. The idea of putting the Cavern together with *Run Devil Run* for promotion makes sense. Paul would have played a lot of these tracks at the Cavern; it's on old retro album, so it just makes sense. Don't say anything to anybody, but we're actually talking about it.' We were sworn to secrecy. Then we started to have daily phone calls from Geoff and then he said, 'We think we are going to go with the Cavern idea. It's not one hundred per cent but it looks like we're going ahead with the idea. Now, you're going to get a phone call from Alan Crowder, of MPL. You'll most probably get that in the next couple of days.' But within an hour, our secretary takes a phone call and says, 'It's Alan Crowder on line one for you,' and everybody in the office went deathly silent. Everybody was very excited. I got on the phone and he said, 'Hi Bill, I think you probably know why I'm phoning.' I said, 'Yes, I've spoken to Geoff.' So he said, 'There are only two days we can do it and both of them are in December.' The first date he gave me we were already booked for and we couldn't get out of it. The other date he gave me was for the 14th. I told him we could do December 14th. Now, that date was only two weeks and a day away. But then, a phone call comes back from Geoff an hour later and he says, 'You won't fucking believe this, but it's not working. The dates aren't working. Paul's schedule is so tight that they are now talking about Paul doing the gig at the Hammersmith fucking Odeon in London. I've been trying to tell them that it's far more interesting to see Paul at the Cavern than Paul just doing a gig at the Hammersmith Odeon. Well, hang fire, they're in the office discussing it now.' An hour becomes two hours and then five o'clock came. I stayed in the office while they continued talking in London and then, at seven o'clock, the phone rings and it was Geoff, and he told me, 'Yeah, it's on. The 14th. I'll be up in the next couple of days. You'll get loads of phone calls tomorrow. You've dealt with Barry Marshall (the promoter) before and the team will start moving in very quickly.' And that was it. It was just two weeks to go. Geoff also told me, 'If you tell anybody, it's off. You must keep it under wraps.' So the only person I told, apart from my wife and staff, was Dave Jones."

Ray Johnston, Cavern City Tours employee, "When Billy Heckle announced to key members of staff that he *might* be playing at the Cavern, we were all sworn to secrecy. In all honesty, our jobs depended on this. We couldn't say a thing. We were soon told that Paul *would* be playing at the Cavern as soon as his staff thought that the club would be suitable. It then became our jobs to make sure it was suitable. Anything that had to be done to get that gig on, we were prepared to do. All of us were prepared to work seven days a week, 24 hours a day if we had to because we knew it was going to be the ultimate accolade."

Billy Heckle "The event just took over everything for the next two weeks. The first person who visited us was the man who put the lines in, which we needed for the Internet. This guy arrived largely unannounced and, after I showed him round the area, he put it together in basically six hours. When he arrived and introduced himself, I discovered that he was the Senior Executive for Microsoft. He had flown from San Francisco to Manchester on the first available plane and then from Manchester he had taken a limo to bring him to our humble offices. We were just expecting a BT engineer. When the guy arrived, that was when we realised that we were playing with the big boys. What was gratifying was when Mark Hammill, the head of security, came down, 99 per cent of all our original security plans were the plans that they went with. Then for the next two weeks, it was someone every day. Barry Marshall, Geoff Wonfor, the director, came down, to have a look round and we were literally on call for 24 hours from different people."

Colin Jones, Cavern City Tours employee, "MPL came down to the Cavern and videoed it. They were checking the club out. They went through the club with a video camera so that they could go back to Paul and show him how the Cavern Club looked. They liked it."

Ray Johnston "When we were told that the gig *was* happening, it was a sense of disbelief at first."

Dave Jones of Cavern City Tours, "We knew that it was going to be announced on *Parkinson* and we knew that once that announcement was made, all hell was going to be let loose. We knew that, on the Monday when we came into work, it was going to be hell. We were going to deal with all sorts of serious enquiries from the Press and dealing with a whole range of requests and pleas for tickets from all and sundry, including your mates and people from Greenland. Many of which, you are never likely to see."

Paul's announcement that his gig at the Cavern would be taking place naturally opens the floodgates to mass hysteria, unseen on Merseyside since the days of The Beatles and produces a deluge of requests for Cavern Club tickets to the Cavern City Tours workers . . .

Dave Jones "We had requests from people who were marginally close to you. They were coming up with all sorts of excuses like, 'I've got a terminally ill sister, it's her last wish,' and that put us under a lot of pressure. Many people were quite blatant, saying 'I'll do anything for a ticket,' and people *would* have done anything for a ticket. Many women were definitely prepared to offer their bodies for a ticket to the show, without any shadow of a doubt. But we treated them light-heartedly and the press picked up on it. We were also offered all sorts of strange things, like free holidays and I think we showed our mettle by remaining incorruptible or inscrutable. But we did have genuine requests from people who, quite rightly, wanted to buy a ticket. But I had to try and explain to them that it was all by invitation and the tickets were free. It was quite difficult. It was an unusual concept, really. So that was the first hurdle. Also, there was the competition scheme, which MPL introduced, and we were answering those enquiries as well. But as far as my mates were concerned, the vast majority of friends showed their quality by not even asking me for a ticket, which took the pressure off you, because we really were under a lot of pressure."

Billy Heckle "I went into the Cavern Club and some girl came up to me and said, 'You're Bill, aren't you?' I said, 'Yeah.' She said, 'Can you get me a ticket for this McCartney gig?' So I said, 'Don't be silly. I can't even get my brother one.' So she said, 'I'll make it worth your while.' I asked, knowingly, 'What do you mean?' She said, 'Well, what do you want?' I said, 'I suppose a shag's out of the question?' She started laughing but said, 'No, you'll get a shag if you get me a ticket.' So I said, 'Fuck off.' I told this story the next day to Geoff Baker on the phone and he thought it was hilarious. The next thing you know, it's in the papers, 'Bill Heckle gets offered sex for Cavern tickets'. He rang me up and said, 'Have you seen the papers?' The story had gone right around the world. It was Baker at his best."

Dave Jones "This was such a special gig for us that we had to appear untouchable. We had to maintain such a strict stance on things. We only had a short time to organise and prepare for the event and we were working 16 to 18 hours a day from the moment it was announced on *Parkinson*. We took calls from the whole world. No country stood out more than another."

Monday, December 6
People begin queuing outside the HMV store in Liverpool to obtain an application form for a chance of winning tickets to Paul's Cavern Club gig. Many of them had been sleeping there since the early hours of the morning. Ten thousand forms are made available at HMV stores across the country and had to be returned to Paul's record company by 5pm on Thursday. Over 8,500 forms were returned, with only 1,500 boasting the correct answers to the questions. The draw for the tickets takes place on **Friday, December 10** when seventy-five pairs of tickets for Paul's concert are chosen randomly in a draw held at the EMI offices in London. First out of the drum is Kevin Reavey, 55, of Aigburth, Liverpool . . .

"I was actually on a ladder in the bathroom painting when I heard the phone go," Kevin recalls. "It normally switches over to the answering machine after four rings so I tried to catch it before that. I stayed in knowing that there was a chance I could have won but I was very doubtful. The odds were against it with so few tickets. I've been a fan of The Beatles since the beginning. I used to go to the Cavern but I never saw them there. It's going to be a fantastic night at the Cavern. Paul will never do anything like this again. It will revive a lot of memories for the people present."

Geoff Baker "Around twenty per cent of the winners came from the Merseyside area."

Another Liverpool-based fan who succeeds in his attempt for tickets is the 18-year-old fan, John Lennon, a name changed by deed poll. Amongst the foreign winners are Tomohiro Konyashi from Tokyo and Raphael Vandenbergh from Belgium. Fans will also arrive from Birmingham, Blackburn, Derby, Essex, Glasgow, Swindon and Wales.

Billy Heckle "Although the Cavern could hold 350, we decided that we would do just 300, to accommodate the cameras and such like, so it wasn't uncomfortable for people. MPL and EMI were doing 150 tickets for fans at HMV and I told Geoff, 'We'll need the other 150,' and he said, 'Yeah, no problem. But hold off from inviting anybody yet.' So we provisionally invited just 80 or 90 people, and that included people from The Beatles

Story and people that you really wanted to invite, as well as the Lord Mayor, dignitaries and then our close friends and families. The next thing that happened, with just four days to go, Geoff rang me up and said, 'Bill, you can't have that 150 tickets. But how many do you need?' I said, 'Fucking hell, Geoff. I've invited up to 80 already.' He then went through our list, saying, 'No, fuck them, fuck them,' and he got our list down to about 55. He said, 'No, sorry, it's the biggest little gig in the world. Sorry, but you're just going to have to be hard. I've said no to loads of people. Even Madonna wanted tickets but I've said no. It doesn't matter how big you are, but we've only got 350 tickets and that's the end of it. 150 have gone already. They've gone to Paul's family, who need to be there and MPL people, who need to be there. If you want 80, you're not going to get 80. Work on 50.' Well, I was nearly crying when I thought of the number of people I was going to let down."

Dave Jones, Cavern City Tours, "We got fifty tickets for the gig. Remembering that there are three directors of the company, with partners and we've all got children, so there were ten tickets gone straight away. That left us with forty tickets. But we employ 130 people so it was hard to decide where the other 40 tickets should go and we did it with great difficulty. So we went to our closest friends, but then again, it was only our closest friends who were Beatles fans. We said, 'If you're not a Beatles fan, then we're sorry.' I have a friend in Holland who has been a close friend of mine for twenty years and I phoned him up and he came over for the event. But his wife didn't get a ticket. Another problem for us was, 'How many friends are we going to lose?' But when you look at it, in reality, they wouldn't be real friends anyway if they fell out with you because they couldn't get a McCartney concert ticket. So what we were able to do was to utilise De Coubertins, our sports bar and all the screens there are monitors. We agreed with MPL to broadcast the concert live into there and this enabled us to televise it to another 350 specially invited guests and what was the icing on the cake for those people was that Paul came in there after the gig. So they all got to see him anyway. He stayed the night with his family and we had a really good time."

Billy Heckle "I also came up with another, really good idea to solve the problem with our friends and tickets for the concert. I have fifteen people who are really good friends, people who are really close to us and have been with us for years and years. And they also work for us. Then I looked at our Cavern Club bar staff, people that have been with us for five minutes. So I thought, 'I'll make our friends barmaids and barmen.' But I'll keep my security on because of their knowledge. So, on the night of Paul's gig, we ended up having the worst trained bar staff you'll ever see in your life. I saw one fellow order a pint of lager and the froth was three quarters of the glass and I just pissed myself laughing. The fellow was complaining and the barman was pleading, 'Sorry mate, but it's the best I can do.' It was just friends and family behind the bar on the night of Paul's gig."

Colin Jones, Cavern City Tours' 'Mr. Fix It' and electrician, "The build-up to the gig really started, for us, just under two weeks before. I always remember my eldest daughter, who worked for the NAAFI, down in London, for the horse guards, she said, 'The Royal Family always thinks that everywhere is specially painted, because wherever they go, the whole place is specially painted out for them.' So we painted out the whole Cavern Club. We also altered the stage and we built a dressing room at the back that wasn't there before. We put mirrors up and even my wife came in, for three days, to help paint the place out. But she unfortunately didn't get a ticket for the concert. We also took a wall out so that the mixing desk could fit in alongside the stage."

Ray Johnston "We had started to liaise with Paul's people, the TV people and the sound engineers a couple of days before the concert. We had to dismantle parts of the club, taking walls down and build a dressing room and get it as good as we could. We were screwing scaffolding bars into the roof so that they could hang lights and cameras onto these bars. We had the stage carpeted. We did everything we had to do to get the gig ready."

Friday, December 10

Billy Heckle "About four days before the concert, on the train coming into work, I decided that I wanted to buy Paul and the band something. I thought that it had to be something to do with Liverpool and, with my connections with David Moores of Liverpool Football Club, I suggested to Dave Jones, that we get five shirts signed by all the players. We would then get them framed, with a little plaque, with the date, and a thank you. Dave said, 'Yeah, okay, it's a good idea.' So I rang Bob Young, a good friend of ours who is best mate with David Moores and we went straight down to Anfield, Liverpool's ground. I think they were on their way to play Newcastle and their coach was already running. It was six o'clock at night. We bought the shirts at the club shop and Gerard Houllier, Liverpool's manager, was there to meet me at the ground. He took me in to see David Moores. Half of Liverpool's players were already on the coach, ready to leave so David said, 'Look, we can't get them off the coach so why don't you take the shirts onto the coach.' So we went onto the coach and we told the players whom the shirts would be signed for. Now, footballer's signatures are notoriously just a squiggly line, but this time, every Liverpool player's signature was so neat. They were all taking the piss out of each other, saying, 'Fucking hell that's the neatest I've ever seen you write.' The players were putting the shirts out on straight surfaces and they were all really taking their time. They were even arguing about the position where they'd put their signatures. It took us about twenty minutes to get the five shirts signed. Naturally, the players were all clamouring for tickets and the one who was really desperate was Gerard Houllier. He begged me for tickets. He gave me his mobile number and said, 'Please, please try and get me a ticket.' One other Liverpool player most keen to see Paul's Cavern gig was Diddier Hamman, who had played for Hamburg FC, and one of the reasons why he had gone there was because he was a big Beatles fan. And one of the reasons why he came to Liverpool was because of The Beatles. He's a massive fan and he desperately wanted a Cavern ticket. But I explained to them that there wasn't any. Soon after, Bob Young told me that he had a Cavern Club ticket and an 'access all areas' pass and he said, 'Look, I don't need both of these. I can give up my ticket.' So, at six o'clock on the night of Paul's gig, I rang up Gerard Houllier on his mobile to tell him that we had got him his ticket but he was on his way to a Bolton reserve match to watch a player. He told me that he was nearly at Bolton at that point and said, 'If you had phoned me a couple of hours ago, I would have gone.' He was really pissed off.

"Anyway, four days before Paul's gig, I got the signed shirts and dropped them off at our framers, and because it was for Paul, they dropped all their work. We had jumped the queue. Two days before the gig, I had the engravers working on the inscription and then Dave Jones came into our office and said, 'I've just had this horrible thought about those Liverpool shirts.' I said, 'Like what?' And Dave said, 'Well, McCartney is an Evertonian!' I said, 'Oh, fucking hell, you're kidding me? I've forgotten about that.' At that point, we've got on the back of the Liverpool shirts 'Cavern 99'. So I asked my framer, 'Have you started framing McCartney's yet?' And he said, 'No, we're doing the other four first.' So I told him to hold off until tomorrow because McCartney was an Evertonian. The framer told me that he had a contact at Everton Football Club and said he'll try and get an Everton shirt and double-mount it. He also said that he'd put on the back of the new shirt 'Macca 19' so, once framed alongside the Liverpool shirt, it would read, 'Macca Cavern 1999'. The Everton goalkeeper, Thomas Meyrer, rented my house when I moved to the Wirral and he had a guy, Bill Ellaby, who looked after all the foreign players at Everton and I got to know him very well. So at 9am, on the day before Paul's gig, I rang Bill up, told him the story and he said, 'We've got a shirt up here. If you can get the numbers done by the end of today's training, I'll get the lads to sign it.' So we went up to Everton's ground, got the shirt, took it to the sports shop, had '19' and 'Macca' printed on it, rushed round to Bellfield, where Everton's players were training, got them to sign it, whizzed it up to the framers and they rang me up at five o'clock that night saying that both shirts had been framed and I could pick all the frames up first thing the following morning, the morning of Paul's gig. The first time that I actually saw all the frames was at one o'clock the next day, when they were presented to the band, and they looked beautiful. Peter Wingfield was knocked out because he is a football fan and Ian Paice was nearly crying because he is a Liverpudlian. We left McCartney's frame in his dressing room. The dressing room was so small that we had to find somewhere that it would fit. We never even presented it to him. Apparently, he was most touched. He put it straight into his car to take it back home. I've been told that it is in The Mill recording studio at his home in Sussex."

Later Friday, December 10

Billy Heckle "It was Friday night, I had been rushing around all day, it was just days before the gig and we had been on the phones all week. Exhaustedly, I looked up at the clock and said, 'I don't care. I'm not working past ten o'clock. I'm going straight for a pint.' Then, at five to ten, with the telephone's constantly ringing, I picked up my phone and a guy said, 'All right, lads. I'm ringing up about McCartney on Tuesday,' by which time the whole world knew about McCartney. The guy said, 'This gig on Tuesday?' and I said, 'Yeah, how can I help you?' Then he said, in all seriousness, 'Is it all right if I pay on the door?' I just pissed myself laughing and this scally said, 'What's funny about that?' I said, 'Well, it's just funny, isn't it?' And he said, 'Well, what is funny about that? I only wanted to know if I could buy a ticket on the door?' I said, 'Look, there's been a million people who have enquired for tickets in the last few days.' And he said, 'Well, you don't have to laugh at me, mate. You usually pay at the door of Cavern gigs.' So I just respectfully got off the phone and thought, 'How detached from reality can you be?' "

Saturday, December 11

Richard Felton reports in the *Liverpool Echo* "A massive security operation is underway to beat ticket touts for Sir Paul McCartney's historic Cavern concert. Organisers are issuing the audience with secret identity codes, rather than risk sending out tickets for the gig and giving counterfeiters the chance to cash in. Already more than £10,000 has been offered by one desperate fan in a bid to be there. Meanwhile, around 15,000 Macca fans are expected to gather on Chavasse Park to watch their hero's performance live on a giant screen. The telecast of the event was confirmed late last night after a deal was clinched between Cavern directors, Liverpool City Council and regeneration group, Liverpool Vision. It will be free for people to go and watch and is expected to improve safety by keeping crowds away from the Cavern in Mathew Street . . ."

Paul's spokesman Geoff Baker "Paul is absolutely ecstatic about the giant screen. He really wanted it to happen. There were a lot of disappointed people who wanted to be in the Cavern, but Chavasse Park will be great as well."

Cavern City Tours director, Billy Heckle remarks to the *Liverpool Echo* "Paul McCartney was pushing and pushing from his end for this to be done because he just wants as many people in Liverpool as possible to see the concert. We have taken thousands of calls from people asking for tickets and by sorting this out, it will take a lot of the pressure off us. We just hope people will go along to Chavasse Park and enjoy what should be a fantastic concert and a fantastic night."

Liverpool Vision's chief executive, Layth Bunni "We have known that this gig was taking place for about a week and the unfortunate thing is the size of the Cavern and the enormous number of people wanting to go. We decided the best way to try to solve the problem was to get a screen and relay the gig live to a wide open area like Chavasse Park, so we have been working to secure funds to do that. It is something that the people of Liverpool and the country at large will be able to be a part of and we are delighted to be able to offer it to them."

Richard Felton "Planning is so tight and so secretive that even those lucky enough to have won a ticket will not be issued with it until Tuesday, a few hours before the concert. Paul's spokesman, Geoff Baker, said today, 'There are quite complex and tight security arrangements in place for the gig, which will ensure we don't get forgeries. This is the tightest security I have seen for any of Paul's gigs around the world. If we sent these tickets in the post, there would be about 3,000 forgeries on the streets tomorrow. If people get offered tickets, they will definitely be forged. If anyone buys one of these tickets, they would need their head tested.' Fans from as far afield as Argentina and Australia were among the thousands to apply for the limited number of tickets."

Dave Jones, Cavern City Tours "We had to come up with suggestions on how all the ticketing arrangements would be made. How people would get their tickets, how the tickets would be taken off them, so we came up with a ticketing issuing system in the car park next to the club and a whole range of systems had to be put into place. It was also our suggestion that the concert be broadcast live outdoors in Chavasse Park, in terms of giving the people of Liverpool this free show because we knew so many people would want to see it but couldn't get in the club."

Monday, December 13
The eve of Paul's concert . . .

Colin Jones "We wanted Paul's dressing room to look smart. We had got big bunches of fruit and two massive flowerpots. We even had soft drinks in there for Paul and his guests, everything, water, Cokes, beers, in fact we had everything for them."

Billy Heckle "We all mucked in to get Paul's dressing room looking smart. We were all chipping in. I had a full-length mirror, which my daughter had in her bedroom and this went in Paul's dressing room. This was nice because, as it had been used all day, we thought, 'Right, that mirror can go into our *Run Devil Run* room at our hotel when it opens.' We'll put a plaque on it saying, 'This mirror was used by Paul at the Cavern Club gig in December 1999'."

Ray Johnston "My job was to get Paul's dressing room ready and to get everything that he would need. We decided we needed furniture in his dressing room. I thought, 'He's got to have something nice to sit on, hasn't he?' So we went round all these shops, trying to find something suitable but we couldn't get anything. So we rang up the Lord Mayor and said, 'Excuse me, Mr Lord Mayor, Sir, but have you got any furniture we can borrow for Paul McCartney to sit on?' The Lord Mayor's secretary said, 'Oh, yeah. We've heard this one before.' We said, 'No, honestly, it's true. We only want to borrow it for a day. It's to go in Paul McCartney's dressing room.' The Lord Mayor said, 'Well, I suppose if we can help, we will. Do you want to come over to the municipal offices and pick some furniture?' So I went over with one of McCartney's crew. We drove over in this bloody big lorry and I picked, what looked to be, the newest three-seater sofa, and it was a bloody heavy thing. We eventually got it in the truck and we drove it over to the Cavern. We managed to squeeze it into the lift, finally managed to get it into McCartney's dressing room and then we realised that the sofa was leather!"

Colin Jones "We carried this settee down into the Cavern and it wasn't light. It was bloody heavy and then someone said, 'Oh look. It's leather.' I think it was Ray who spotted it. So we had to get another one."

Billy Heckle "Mark Hamilton, the head of security, came in and said, 'Is that leather?' And we said, 'Yeah, it's nice, isn't it?' He said, 'There's no way that Paul's going to have that in his dressing room.' Of course, we never even thought of it. We had trouble getting it in and trouble getting it out."

Ray Johnston "I said, 'Oh, shit!' So we had to get it out as quick as we possibly could. We got it out and we managed to borrow a cloth chair from a shop around the corner."

Billy Heckle "We went round to the furniture shop and they wouldn't believe it was for Paul McCartney. They said, 'Do you think we're stupid? No way.' The only way that they would loan us a chair was if we paid them £700 and if we brought it back the next day, he'd pay us our money back, which we were about to do until Steven Griskin came off the phone and said, 'It's okay, sorted it. We can get a chair from the chief executive's office.' He had a small non-hide sofa in his office and it was brought over by two council workers. They carried it over into the Cavern dressing room."

Ray Johnston "The leather chair was our biggest boob but it created a lot of humour around the crew. Even Barry Marshall was laughing at that one. He knew it was a mistake and we meant well."

Tuesday, December 14

The day of Paul's historic Cavern concert dawns . . .

Dave Jones, Cavern City Tours "It was just mad! It was just so horrendously mad! There was so much going on that I didn't really have much time to think about the gig because we were constantly trying to make sure that everything was going right, going to schedule and going to plan. Our offices were completely taken over by Barry Marshall, the promoter, and all the concert security people. We had a lot to do in trying to facilitate all the people for two days as well as trying to facilitate the mob who turned up on the Tuesday. The whole thing went very, very well. I didn't, at any stage, ever see anybody losing their tempers and our staff was exemplary, considering we had never done anything of this magnitude before. We earned praise from Barry Marshall and praise from MPL."

Billy Heckle "We were in around 6am and one fellow I missed on the day was Geoff Emerick, who was doing the live mixing of the show. I would love to have met him. The place was just swarming with world-class technicians. I think there were 119 there on the day of Paul's show."

Colin Jones, Cavern City Tours "I was in the Cavern Club at 5am and we got everything ready. But then somebody came in and said, 'We want to alter the stage.' They needed another four-foot on the stage. So I had to go up to the timber yard and put another four-foot on the stage in front. So, for the concert, Paul could stand right on the very edge of the stage."

Ray Johnston "Colin went out and got the wood and it was done. He painted it black and told McCartney's crew, 'Give it ten minutes for the paint to dry and you can use it.' Colin was absolutely brilliant on the day."

At 2pm, Paul arrives . . .

Dave Jones, Cavern City Tours "Paul arrived in Harrington Street, at the back of the club, and drove straight down into the car park. It was very convenient for him. It meant that he was basically driven to the back fire exits, got out of the car, walked ten yards and he was on the Cavern stage."

Ray Johnston "I remember Paul arriving in the underground car park. He got out of his car and walked into the Cavern Club with John Hammel. I was standing in the doorway, but I didn't say anything at first, because everyone was saying, 'Hi, Paul.' So I thought, 'I'm going to be professional here. I'm going to keep out of this.' So I just kept on doing my job. He walked into his dressing room and was talking to a few people and I just walked past and said, 'Hi Paul. Nice to see you back,' and he went, 'Not you again. How you doing? Nice to see you.' He remembered me. I thought to myself, 'Well, if only he could remember my name, it would be the icing on the cake.' I then just let him go about his business."

Billy Heckle "I welcomed him as he came in. I said, 'Welcome to the Cavern.' I didn't say I owned it or anything. I said, 'If there's anything you need, just ask. We'll sort it out.' Every one of our staff had been threatened with the sack if anyone approached him. It was a complete no-no to ask him for an autograph."

Dave Jones "Almost immediately, Paul went straight on stage, picked up his guitar and soundchecked for a couple of hours."

Billy Heckle "When Paul came in, he went on the stage, stood in front of the band, who had already been in the club for an hour, and said, 'We all know what we're in for here. We're totally unrehearsed. We last recorded back in May, we all know the songs but I'd like us to be as tight as possible. So now we'll run through the songs very loosely until we're all happy.' With this, Paul walked on stage, slapped on his Hofner and said, 'Right, I think we'll start with . . .' and they immediately started playing. About two-thirds of the way through a song, he'd stop everybody and say, 'No, no, that wasn't quite right,' and he'd talk to the band musically. On the sound desk, they had a CD player and the technicians would play the *Run Devil Run* album over the system. So you had all the band on stage not playing, just miming and listening and Paul would go, 'Okay, listen to how this bit goes. That's what I want.' Then the band would play again and they'd get it right first time. Then Paul would say, 'Okay, right, that's it. Let's put that one to bed.' This went on for three fucking hours. Paul never came off the stage. He came in at 2pm and never came off until 5pm. I watched it all. It was like your own private gig. It was surreal."

Ray Johnston "In all honesty, when Paul arrived and walked onto the stage to start soundchecking, I looked at Bill Heckle and Bill Heckle looked at me and we were both standing there with tears in our eyes. We both thought, 'This is not happening.' It was very emotional because we thought, 'He's here, he's going to do it.' But, in all honesty, I was more pleased for Dave Jones and Billy because it was a reward for all their years of hard work."

Dave Jones "I saw bits of the soundcheck. I always find soundchecks more intriguing than the gig really. When he did his soundcheck, Geoff Wonfor's people were chucking people out of the club. Everyone who was thrown out knew the professional angle and the situation that existed. So we just stayed in the background, listening, talking and clapping. Other than the production staff, there were only about a half dozen or so of us watching. There was Billy, myself and a couple of others, guys who had worked for Bryan Adams who know Barry Marshall. One of the people watching was David Moores, the chairman of Liverpool Football Club and he's a big Beatles fan. He booked the group back in 1963 (April 4) at Stowe School in Bucks. So Dave came down for the soundcheck and he was there for the gig as well."

Billy Heckle "There were eight people in the room during the soundcheck. We rang David Moores up and asked if he'd like to come down. He had important Liverpool FC business that day but just dropped it. Dave Gilmour was also a big hero to him, as well, so David came down for the soundcheck. Neil Aspinall was stood next to David just watching. Neil didn't know David and after one of the songs, I introduced them to each other, these two powerful men. Neil is a Liverpool fan and David is a Beatles fan, so they instantly had a rapport. At the soundcheck, Geoff Wonfor, the director, told me that Paul had said to him, 'I've played the Cavern nearly 300 times and there's only a couple of minutes of footage of me here. I'm going back to do this one gig and so, from the second I arrive, to the second I go, I want cameras recording every moment.' So Paul had everything filmed, his arrival, the soundcheck, everything."

Ray Johnston "I think Paul was maybe struggling a little bit with his voice during the run-through but he still sounded as sweet as a nut. All the guys who were working with him were optimistic that there wouldn't be a problem."

Colin Jones "They did an awful lot of filming at the soundcheck. After which, Paul went round to the front of the club where he did his press conference."

Billy Heckle "At 5pm, Paul said, 'Okay, thanks lads. I'll see you back here at half seven, quarter to eight,' and then he walked out of the club, through the car park. He re-entered the club through the side door, put his thumbs up to the press and immediately walked to the back of The Beatles stage and kissed it. Then, with his hands in his pockets, he went to the microphone and spoke for maybe three minutes . . ."

Paul "I just want to say that it's fantastic to be back at the Cavern. What better place to rock out the century? This is where it all began and for me, the century is going to end with playing rock'n'roll. You'll remember that before The Beatles were The Beatles, they were a fabulous little rock'n'roll band, which is what held us together for so long and made us so good. I think. And I'm back here because I love Liverpool and I'm playing the music I love best in the city I love most. There is no more fantastic place to rock out the century."

Billy Heckle "After Paul had spoken, the band joined him on stage for photographs and then the press were asked to leave."

Ray Johnston "Immediately after the conference, Geoff Baker came up to me and said, 'Paul wants to meet Bob Wooler (the original Cavern Club DJ). Have you any idea how to find him?' So I said, 'I'll put the feelers out. I'll track him down.' I had been told that he was in Mathew Street. So I said to Geoff, 'Tell you what. I'll nip out and try and find him.' So I went out into Mathew Street and somebody told me that Bob was with Allan Williams in a little French bar around the corner. I went in and found him. He was sitting around with a few mates and I said, 'Bob, Paul would like to meet you,' and Bob, in his typical manner, said, 'Raymond, if Paul wants to come and speak to me, he can come here.' So I said, 'Oh, come on, Bob. He can't do that. Look, I've been asked to come round and take you down into the Cavern. Paul would love to say hello to you.' So Bob said, 'Raymond, I'm having a drink with my friends.' Even Allan Williams said, 'Oh, come on, Bob. You old fart. He's waiting to meet you. Just go!' It took me half an hour to get him out of the bar. He said, 'I'll only go if my friend can come with me.' His friend was Jerry Devine, a well-known singer in Liverpool. So I took them round to the Cavern and I said to Jerry, 'When we get to the lifts, you may have to wait outside because with my pass I can only get Bob in. So I'm going to take him down into the lifts and take him into the back to meet Paul.' Jerry was fine about this but Bob said, 'Raymond, I'm not going in without my friend!' So I said, 'Okay, we'll try it.' When we got to the bottom of the stairs, and got out of the lift, the security guy stopped us and I said, 'I've been told to get this guy, it's Bob Wooler,' as I pointed to Bob. 'Paul wants to meet him.' Then the security guy said, 'He can't come in without a pass.' So I said, 'Okay. Bob, you just wait here. I'll go and arrange your passes.' Luckily, at that point, Mark Hamilton was walking past and I explained the situation to him. So Mark grabbed Bob and Jerry's arms and brought them into the club. When Paul met Bob it was a great moment."

Billy Heckle "Paul gave Bob a big, big hug and made a big fuss of him. Paul said, 'Bob, I haven't seen you for a while. How are you?' They chatted and I took a back step while they reminisced. Then Bob said, 'Paul, I'm going to go now,' and Paul said, 'Well, aren't you going to come here tonight?' Bob replied, 'Well, I don't know, Paul. I'm unsteady on my legs.' After they discussed making provisions for Bob, Paul was insistent. 'I want you to come, Bob,' Paul said, 'and if you do come, you've got to do me a favour.' So Bob said, 'What can I do? I'll do anything. What do you want me to do?' And Paul said, 'Could you bring me on stage one more time?' Bob's eyes welled up and he was speechless. Bob composed himself before saying, 'I really, really don't know if I can.' Paul said, 'I'd like you to, so just come back at half past seven and it doesn't have to be anything other than, "Ladies and gentlemen, Paul McCartney." I want you to do it like you used to. It's up to you what you want to do.' So Bob said, 'Thank you, I'll think about it and hopefully I'll see you at 7.30pm.'"

Ray Johnston "Bob was kind of very much himself. He hadn't seen Paul for many, many years and he still remembered the Paul he knew from the Sixties. They chatted for ten minutes and then Paul said to Bob, 'Before you go, there's something that I've always wanted to ask you. Give us your autograph.' Bob said, 'Oh, Paul, you don't mean that.' Paul said, 'No, please give me your autograph. I never got your autograph.' So he signed something for Paul. That was a nice thing for Paul and a very nice thing for Bob."

Billy Heckle "Bob went off and when Paul came back to the Cavern at about half seven, he got a message saying that Bob was just not up to it and he felt that he could not do it justice. And if he couldn't do it justice, he wouldn't do it."

Ray Johnston "Later in the afternoon, after Paul and the band had gone off to meet their families and friends, I was helping out by keeping an eye on the back door while the security guy went to do something. He said, 'Do me a favour. Can you help the security girl here a minute?' He insisted, 'Remember, nobody comes through this door without a pass. Nobody!' He told me that he would be back in ten minutes and I said, 'Yeah, fine.' The next thing, a car pulls up and a young guy gets out. He goes to walk in the club but I stop him. I said, 'Excuse me, mate. Have you got your pass?' And he said, 'Well, no, not yet.' So I said, 'Well, you'll have to hang on here a moment until you get passed up.' So he said, 'I'm looking for me dad.' I said, 'I'm sorry. I can't let you in until you've got a pass. Who's your dad?' And he said, 'Paul McCartney!' As he was saying this, Geoff Baker went by and said, 'Oh, hi James. Come in.' I thought, 'Oh, fuckin' hell.' I just wanted the ground to open up and swallow me. I just couldn't believe it! Anyway, James walks in and goes into the dressing room. Geoff Baker comes out and I said, 'I'm awfully sorry I wouldn't let him in,' and he said, 'What have you got to be sorry about? You were just doing your job. There's no problem whatsoever.' I thought, 'Thank God for that.' Ten minutes later, I plucked up the courage and went into the dressing room and there was James just sitting there, drinking a soft drink, and I said, 'Sorry about that, James. I didn't recognise you,' and he went, 'No problems, mate.' I said, 'You don't remember me, do you?' And he said, 'Why is that?' I said, 'Do you remember when your dad played the Kings Dock in 1990?' and he said, 'Yeah.' I said, 'Well, do you remember some guy getting sent out that day and coming back with a huge remote-controlled boat that they wouldn't let you use because it was interfering with the walkie-talkies?' He said, 'Yeah.' I said, 'Well, I'm the guy who went out and bought that huge boat.' James said, 'My God, what a memory you've got.' I said, 'You were only a young boy then. You've grown up quite a bit since then. It's been nearly ten years.' I said goodbye and I went back to my business."

Colin Jones "When the band returned from their break, after seeing their families, they came back to the Cavern without wearing their passes and these two security guards wouldn't let them in. They honestly wouldn't let them in. That was Dave Gilmour, Ian Paice, all of them. They came back, went down the ramp and just as they were about to re-enter the Cavern, the two security guards told them they were not coming through the door until they put their passes on. Dave Gilmour said, 'Do you know who I am?' And one of the security girls said, 'I don't care who you are. You're not coming through this door until you put your pass on.' I remember when Paul came back, he joked with one of the girls, 'Even I could get pass you,' and she replied, jokingly, 'Well, go on, if you want to come and try.' The girls really knew their job. She knew he was mucking around."

Billy Heckle "An hour before we were due to open the gates, Geoff Wonfor, the director, and Mark Hamilton, the head of security, went round going berserk. A lot of the production people, whose jobs were earlier in the day, probably about eighty of them, were just hanging around the club and Geoff and Mark got rid of them like you have never seen. They told them, 'You're not here to watch, you've been working, you're not working through the concert, so fuck off now!' They threw them all out onto the streets because room in the Cavern was too tight."

Shortly before the concert, the specially invited audience began arriving . . .

Dave Jones "We were nervous because we had the problem of getting everyone in and making sure that everything was right and actually getting them into the auditorium. But we had to keep space for all the McCartney family who were in the De Coubertins (sports bar) prior to the gig. They came into the Cavern through the back way, down the car ramp and into the Cavern. The same route as Paul took. They all congregated at the front of the stage. To make it fair for the other people, as they arrived they were given a ticket with a number on it and then we called the numbers of the people. For instance, if you arrived at 7pm, and your ticket number was 15, you were in the first group of people that we called into the auditorium, and you were able to get the space you wanted. If you arrived early, you got a good spot. I came up with that idea and it worked."

At 8pm, the show begins . . . "And now, with his band, Paul McCartney . . ."

Debbie Johnson, *Liverpool Echo* "The Cavern was packed to the rafters and the atmosphere was electric . . . Striding on to the stage under the purple and green neon lights, McCartney and his all-star band were given a rapturous reception. They played a 50-minute set of rock'n'roll classics, plus The Beatles' 'I Saw Her Standing There'. One song, 'Twenty Flight Rock', was dedicated to the day Macca met John Lennon. He said, 'When I met John, I knew all the words to this song and I think that's why I got to join the band.' Paul seemed as overwhelmed as his fans at appearing on the tiny club stage once more. He said, 'Hey, we're playing the Cavern. It just came to me. Wow!' Later he joked, 'It's good up here. Isn't it?' And the Cavern is up there somewhere, in the rubble. Another brilliant city council decision, 'Let's demolish the Cavern.' "

Peter Grant, *Liverpool Echo* "The minute he opened up with 'Honey Hush', it was as if he had turned back the clock. He rocked and rolled and tilted his head and 'Oohed' like we are used to seeing these days only on the archive film. Outside the Cavern, hundreds braved the rain just to catch a glimpse of him, screaming as if it were the Sixties. They, and particularly us, the lucky ones inside, were part of something unique. And that was probably clearest when he sang 'Brown Eyed Handsome Man', his own tribute to Buddy Holly. Cavern City Tours, the organisers, have longed to see one of the Fab Four return on stage. So as they stood at the back of the arched walls, watching the show, they were awe-struck, just the way Brian Epstein was once besotted three decades ago."

Billy Heckle "When the concert started, I noticed that there was a big space by the bar at the back. I thought that we could get another twenty-odd people in easily. So, as soon as I saw this space, and knowing that we were twenty-five under our fire safety number of 375, I legged it up to De Coubertins where everyone was watching the gig on the TVs, and I found Lillian, of MPL. I shouted to her, 'Listen, we can get a good twenty-five more in down there,' so she got twenty-five more of McCartney's family, like the aunties, uncles, the kids and they all came down and we got them all ushered in by the end of the second song. They were all so happy. When I had them ushered in, I realised that the only thing I hadn't seen was the video screen in Chavasse Park. I hadn't seen it at all, all day, because I had been so busy. So I legged it out of the Cavern, up the ramp into Harrington Street and ran up into the park, and saw the screen. I believe it was the biggest one in England. The images on the screen were pristine. I stayed there for about a minute, saw how many people were there in the park and then legged it back to the Cavern and got back as Paul finished the third song."

Dave Jones "The gig was tremendous! But it was the shortest forty minutes of my bloody life. You wanted more. You didn't want it to stop. The group of us, my family and friends stood by the bar. We must have been the last ones in there. We had all sorts in there that night, politicians, professional musicians and ordinary members of the public. Everybody was just knocked out. You had to pinch yourself to believe that it was happening and you were there watching it."

Colin Jones "Dave said it was short but we'd had it all day, so it was a long gig. For most of the concert, I was stuck by the mixing desk, which was stage left. There were so few of us at the concert, it was almost like a private showing. Not many people have seen Paul McCartney playing privately for them, have they? The concert itself went so quickly. The concert just flew by. I couldn't believe it when they went off stage and that was the end. For the people going to listen to it, it must have been really quick. I remember the radio DJ, Billy Butler, was there in the crowd. Because I was 'access all areas', I could go out different doorways and come in different places to watch the concert. I am a big Beatles fan, so the concert was a dream."

Billy Heckle "It was a great event. I was just numb, seeing Paul McCartney up there on stage, I was in a state of shock."

Dave Jones "There were 350 ticket holders in the Cavern that night. 150 were given away in an EMI raffle, 50 were given to us, Cavern City Tours and the remainder went to Paul McCartney's family, Apple, but even Neil Aspinall was short on tickets. There was Neil Aspinall asking for tickets to see Paul McCartney. How bizarre! But true."

Billy Heckle "I had to get Neil Aspinall a ticket and there were no tickets left. He was waiting outside the Cavern about half-an-hour before the gig started, because Geoff Baker had told him, 'You'll have to get your ticket off Bill, because all of our tickets have gone.' Neil had arrived at the Cavern at 4pm but I was really busy and they couldn't find me. Neil got his ticket because I made someone else I knew a barman."

Dave Jones "In the club on the night of the concert, we had about forty people working and some of those forty had definitely never seen or worked behind a bar before. We had some very strange-looking bar staff that night. They were our mates and a lot of our Cavern City Tours staff who had really wanted to go to the concert. But our poor security guys had to stay on the door."

Billy Heckle "Paul's gig was broadcast on the Internet and Madonna picked up the idea with her Brixton Academy concert. She broke Paul's record three times with her gig but the bandwidth between those two shows, which was about twelve months, had increased ten-fold. We didn't really have the knowledge of broadcasting a gig on the Internet in December 1999 like we had a year later. But Paul's groundbreaking Cavern Club gig on the Internet did get recognised in the *Guinness Book Of Records*."

After the show, Billy Heckle drew Paul's attention to their Hofner violin bass, which had been kept securely in the Cavern Pub across the road, "I asked Paul to sign it and he wrote, 'Cool Cavern! Cheers! Paul McCartney' and dated it. It took him 35 seconds. Because of that autograph, it is now worth about £45,000! We have drawn up an agreement though, that if it is ever sold for any reason, the money will go to charity. We put in the contract stipulations saying that if it was ever offered for sale, we would default on ownership. We made that contract so that Paul didn't think he was putting his signature on our Hofner just for us to make £40,000. But, to be honest, I think it will stay in the Cavern pub for the next 200 years at least. Paul thanked us for thinking like that. He said, 'I would have done it anyway, but I appreciate you thought like that.' We also got Dave Gilmour to sign a guitar as well."

Ray Johnston "Paul agreed to sign for us our Hofner bass. Billy Heckle got a message through to me saying, 'We need someone to go across the road to the Cavern Pub and get the Hofner bass out of the case and bring it over to the dressing room because Paul is going to sign it.' So I thought, 'Right, I'll take that one on.' So I got one of our security guys and he came over with me to the Cavern Pub. To get the bass out of the cabinet, we had to unscrew all the casing and turn off the alarm and obviously the pub was very busy. If was full of people who didn't have tickets so the pub was doing a roaring trade. Anyway, we went in, managed to get the guitar out and I said to this guy who was with me, 'Just follow me over to the Cavern.' There was this barrier outside the Cavern Club where the people were queuing and I said to the guy, 'All I want you to do is cross the street with me until you see me disappear down into the Cavern. And once I'm in the Cavern, I'm all right.' As we came out of the Cavern Pub to cross the street to go to the Cavern Club, at least 300 people turned to see me walking across the street clutching this Hofner violin bass. They obviously thought it was McCartney's. The crowd was shouting, 'Look! What's he doing with Macca's guitar?' and I froze! I went, 'Oh oh, I've made a mistake here.' Little did they know that it was a replica and it was going down to be signed. Luckily, the security outside the Cavern Club was good. They saw me rushing across the street and they moved the barriers so I could get in quick. Thankfully, it was unscathed."

Billy Heckle "After Paul signed the bass, he said to me, 'Well, what was it like for you, Bill? Was it all right?' And I said, 'Paul, it was amazing! Just amazing! But you want to see who we've got on next week.' He pissed himself laughing."

Colin Jones "After the gig, I was backstage with Julia (Lennon) most of the time and she was quite upset. I don't know for certain why, but I think it was to do with a mix-up with security. The two girls who did the main security at the dressing room and Mark Hamilton didn't know who she was. Naturally, quite a lot of people wanted to go in and the girls didn't know who she was and Julia was trying to get in to see Paul. They wouldn't let her go through. Those two security girls were bloody good."

Billy Heckle "After the gig, Geoff Baker got hold of me and said, 'Look, we're going to clear this place out and if you're not in the backstage part, you're not going to get in.' I said, 'But I'm with Julia and my wife, Diane.' So Geoff said, 'Well, bring them.' So we went backstage and the area was so fucking small. The dressing room must have had about seventy people in there! Every one of which, you knew. There was Paul's brother, Mike, Paul's daughters, Stella and Mary, John Eastman and Neil Aspinall. If there was such a thing as a Beatles Mafia, that was it. We were all literally standing shoulder to shoulder. You couldn't swing a cat. But every one was buzzing. Neil came up to me and said, 'Where do you get a drink round here?' So I said something like, 'Wasn't the gig fantastic? It was a bit of history. What did you think?' And Neil shrugged his shoulders, smiled at me and said, 'Yeah, it was good. But I've seen it all. I've seen this night replicated a thousand times. It was just another great night. There's no bigger and no better.' He wasn't being a smart arse, but he's seen all the big nights, like the Hollywood Bowl and Shea Stadium. You name it, he was at everything. Backstage, Will Schillinger presented Paul with an original 1961 Reslo microphone, which was still in its original packaging. Paul was naturally intrigued by how he had come across it. Will, who owns Pilot Studios in New York City, and had flown in especially for the gig, told Paul how two hundred mikes had been impounded by customs men forty years ago and Will had acquired them, along with the customs documentation, from a pawn shop. Will also told Paul that Yoko had purchased six of the microphones off him. Paul also spent time talking backstage to Julia."

Dave Jones "The relief when the gig was finished was like, 'Oh, thank God!' Everything had gone well. There had not been a problem and then everybody just got drunk. Everyone was just so joyous. I didn't even meet Paul after the gig was finished. I just stayed in the Cavern to make sure everything was all right in there."

Ray Johnston "At the end of the night, I found a plectrum on the stage but I didn't know from whom it came. It could have been Mick Green's, it could have been Dave Gilmour's or it could have been Paul's. I thought, 'I'm going to keep this as a keepsake,' and when I showed it to the bass player in my band, he said, 'That's a bass player's plectrum.' So I said, 'Hold on, it might have been Macca's!' So that plectrum has gone into my box of souvenirs as a 'maybe'."

Dave Jones "After I had done my checking of the Cavern Club, I came out of the front door of the club and went over to the Cavern Pub to make sure everything was all right over there. Then I wandered round to De Coubertins with my accompaniment of people. I got into the sports bar and stood at the bar, having a drink, not realising that Paul was in there. Then, the next minute, everyone was jumping round and Paul was leaving, going out of the side door. I didn't even know he was in there."

Billy Heckle "Paul had a great time in our sports bar after the gig. There was a policeman at the door stopping people trying to get in. He had a yellow raincoat on and a truncheon and Paul noticed him. He stood up and said, 'Oi, come here. Give me that here,' grabbing his hat and truncheon. With the policeman's hat on his head, Paul started singing still clutching the truncheon. Paul and all his family were having a ball. They were all laughing and joking. It was one hell of a party atmosphere. The place was electric. Then, at 11.45pm, it was announced that Paul was leaving. But one thing that Geoff Baker had said to me, all through the day, was, 'We'll get Paul on his own and you can have a photograph taken of just the two of you. I'll sort that out with our official photographer.' But the day just went so fast and I never spoke to Paul again after he arrived until he was in the sports bar with his family. Then it was announced that he was going and I said to Geoff, 'I haven't had my photograph taken.' So he said, 'Do you know anyone with a camera?' We had our official photographer so I whizzed out to get him, whizzed back and Paul was fighting his way out because he was shaking hands with everyone and posing for photographs. Geoff said to me, 'Get in, it's your place. He won't mind.' So I said, 'Paul, it's me again. It's been a great day. Thank you very much. Could I just have a quick photograph before you go? Geoff promised me.' Paul said, 'Yeah, no problem.' So I had a ten-second photograph."

Dave Jones "It was a great night. It all went like a dream. The planning that went into it all paid off. It was like a military operation and it was a great, great night. My biggest memory of the night was knowing that I co-owned the club. I thought, 'This is my gaff.' Obviously Billy and George own it as well, but it was partly my gaff. I thought, 'I own this place and Paul McCartney is playing in it and it is being seen by the world.' It was pride, really. For me, it was the culmination of twenty years in business doing this and fifty years as a fan. I'm not the greatest Beatles fan in the world but I was enough of a fan to go and see them three times in 1963. Paul's Cavern gig was a memorable occasion and a piece of rock'n'roll history. Normally you don't know that you're in an environment where rock'n'roll history is happening, you only find out years later. But Paul's Cavern gig was planned rock'n'roll history in the making and it was organised to be history, which is quite unusual, really. Historical events cannot be manufactured usually. But this one was. It wasn't phoney. This was Paul McCartney's last gig of the 20th century and it happened in our Cavern Club. Following Paul's show, it once again cemented, to me and everyone else, the association with Liverpool and The Beatles. It made me realise that it's never going to go away. If Paul's gig had taken place in say, Birmingham, in some small venue, it wouldn't have had a tenth of the impact that the Cavern gig had. Even if it had happened in London, it wouldn't have had the impact. The impact of Paul McCartney appearing again at the Cavern Club in Liverpool is the ultimate. It is irresistible."

Billy Heckle "It was weird, just weird. Paul was in from two o'clock and stayed until half past five. He was back at 7.45 to go on stage at eight and he was there in the Cavern for the hour he played and the hour afterwards until 10pm and he was in the sports bar from just after ten until 11.45pm. So he had been with us for ten hours, apart from the time he went and met his family and got changed. So he was with us for seven and a half hours, on our patch, in places we owned and I'm very proud of this."

Ray Johnston "We all said, 'How can you top that?' The only way we could top that was if we got all three of The Beatles back, but that's not going to happen, is it? But, having said that, years ago we all said, 'You'll never get McCartney back,' but it happened. So we're never going to give up on anything now."

Wednesday, December 15
Merseyside basks in the aftermath of a highly successful event . . .

Debbie Johnson reports in the *Liverpool Echo* "Liverpool was basking in worldwide glory today after Sir Paul McCartney's return to the Cavern. Tourist chiefs reckon the concert earned the city £25m worth of publicity and put us at the centre of world attention. The former Beatle's appeal meant the live Internet broadcast of the concert broke world records for a music event, with three million people watching globally at any time. The lines were jammed. Despite the cold weather, 12,000 fans watched a video relay of the event in Chavasse Park. Mathew Street was packed with fans, some of which were offering thousands for a ticket. One even offered a £10,000 holiday to California. Sir Paul, and Liverpool, are today on the front pages of newspapers all over the world."

Colin Jones "I came into work the next morning and everyone was still in the pub and Billy said to me, 'I've got a present for you. Go over to the dressing room. There's a present for you.' There I found the Hofner bass guitar that is in our Cavern Pub cabinet and it was signed by Paul. Quite a few newspapers had photos of me holding it, including the *Liverpool Echo*."

Billy Heckle "I've been up all night and just started to get copies of the papers in. I've just read one from Venezuela, a front-page headline about 'El Cavern Club'. The publicity for the city has been estimated at being worth about £25m."

Dave Jones "The media were asking us, 'Well, how much were you paid?' And we said, 'We weren't paid anything.' And they said, 'You mean they didn't pay you?' We said, 'They asked us if wanted paying but we didn't want anything.' We didn't want paying for the club. It was as simple as that. What can you say to Paul McCartney? 'Well, normally we charge £100 if you want to hire the gaff and if you spend more than £1,000 at the bar, you get your £100 back.' How much would you have to pay to get Paul McCartney at the Cavern? There's no money involved. It was a unique occasion. It was special for him and was special for us, special for the venue and special for everyone in there. Money didn't matter. We guessed that between 10 and 15,000 people came into Liverpool last night."

Billy Heckle "Everyone at Cavern City Tours worked their hearts out on the Cavern gig, and so did Geoff Baker. He had also worked flat out on promoting *Run Devil Run*. I last saw him on December 15, the day after the gig, and we spoke about how the gig was a part of Beatles history. The papers were all going mad about the concert and we guessed that this was going to be the last major Beatles-related event of the century. I said to him, 'Have a good Christmas. What are you going to do?' He said, 'I'm going to fucking bed. I'm going to have a break, see my kids and have a nice, relaxing Christmas.' Then, two weeks later, when the story with George broke, it was Geoff Baker who was called up again, because George hasn't got his own publicist."

Thursday, December 30

E! On Line reporter, Emily Farache reports "George Harrison, called the Quiet Beatle for his reclusive ways, was stabbed several times in the chest by a knife-wielding intruder during a pre-dawn attack today inside the legendary rocker's British estate. The guitarist, who penned such classics as 'Here Comes The Sun', 'Something' and 'While My Guitar Gently Weeps', suffered a collapsed lung and is recovering in a London hospital. The attack comes nearly 19 years after John Lennon was gunned down outside his New York apartment building by a crazed fan. Harrison's spokesman said the 56-year-old Rock And Roll Hall of Fame was in a stable condition after fighting off the assailant at the musician's sprawling estate in Henley-on-Thames, west of London. The couple was able to put up a fight, and detained the attacker until police, who were phoned by a member of the Harrisons' staff, arrived at 3.30am GMT, according to a police spokesperson. He's expected to be released in a few days. His wife, Olivia, slightly wounded in the attack, did not require hospitalisation and is at her husband's bedside. 'Since he's been in a hospital bed, he's been getting much better and is comfortable,' a hospital spokesperson said. 'Generally, they are very happy and concerned to let the world know they are recovering well.' Harrison, stabbed four times, did not require surgery for his collapsed right lung, but had been fitted with a chest drain to remove fluid build-up. Doctors say Harrison was lucky to survive the attack. The knife just missed a major chest artery. The 33-year-old attacker, who hails from The Beatles' hometown of Liverpool, was arrested on suspicion of attempted murder at the 100-room, heavily guarded mansion where the Harrisons have lived for 20 years. There is no immediate word on how the intruder got by the security and into the house. He has been identified in British media reports as Michael Abram, and his mother is quoted in a Liverpool newspaper as saying he 'has been running in pubs shouting about The Beatles . . . he hates them and even believes they are witches.'

Lynda Abram says her son has had a history of mental-health problems, and she says he recently became obsessed with The Beatles. Apple, The Fab Four's record label, said the surviving members of the band, Paul McCartney and Ringo Starr, as well as Lennon's widow, Yoko Ono, had all been informed of the attack and were being updated on Harrison's condition. 'Thank God that both George and Olivia are all right,' McCartney said in a statement. 'I send them all my love.' Added Ringo, 'Both [wife] Barbara and I are deeply shocked that this incident has occurred. We send George and Olivia all our love and wish George a speedy recovery.' "

Sunday, May 7
Five months into the new century, Ringo promotes his forthcoming All-Starr Band American tour by conducting an hour, online webchat with Century 21 – highlights of which follow . . .

Century21 "Welcome to the Live Chat with Ringo Starr. Century21.com is proud to present our special guest, Ringo Starr, as he travels across the United States on his Ringo Starr and his All-Starr Band Connections Tour 2000! Welcome, Ringo Starr."

Ringo "Hey, everybody! Welcome to our web site! What's the *big* question?"

Guest-Barb "Mr Starkey, have you given any thought to having Badfinger's Joey Molland in one of your All-Starr bands?"

Ringo "The short answer is no."

Dream girl "What goes through your mind right before a concert? Has it changed since you started performing?"

Ringo "The moments just before I go on stage, most of me wants to go home. There's five seconds of madness there and I have to run on stage. The thoughts are, 'Do I remember the songs? Are they good?' There are a million thoughts that go through your head in five seconds."

Guest "Ringo, any plans for recording an album of new material? I really liked *Time Takes Time* and *Vertical Man.*"

Ringo "Thank you. There are no big plans, at this moment, to make a new CD. Maybe next year."

Becky6582 "Growing up and getting in music, who was your biggest influence?"

Ringo "Many influences from Hank Williams to Elvis Presley."

Ludwig-guest "Will you use any sets on tour that were used with The Beatles?"

Ringo "No. I'm sure you're asking about drums, and no."

Guest Billy "Hi, Ringo. Any chance of hearing some of your other songs on this tour, like 'Don't Pass Me By' or 'What Goes On?' PS – Many thanks for the continuous magic over all of the years."

Ringo "No, not on this tour."

Guest Me Myself and I "How many songs are you playing on this tour? I saw you and the band one year and you were great! And is there a new CD on the way?"

Ringo "We're doing 22–24 songs and as I've said before, there is no new CD on the way."

Guest Me Myself and I "Will there be any signed copies of The Beatles *Anthology* book available on the net? I'd love to get one. I'm getting the book anyway, but a signed copy would be excellent!"

Ringo "There will be signed copies of The Beatles *Anthology*. I believe it's three-and-a-half thousand, but very expensive! You might get lucky."

Guest Raspbernie "During rehearsals, what songs have you and the All-Starr Band jammed on to loosen up that are not on the official set list?"

Ringo "Very little jamming, very heavy schedules, and very heavy rehearsals."

Texasroselinda "Hello. I would like to know what you think of the music of today in comparison to the Sixties and Seventies."

Ringo "I think all the music is great, but I relate more to the music of the Sixties and Seventies. There are musicians out there today. But I'm not really involved in that much."

Mystery Girl "Ringo, how did you get involved with Century 21?"

Ringo "I was asked to do the commercial for Connections 2000 and they loved me soooo much that they decided to sponsor the tour. And we made a very nice connection."

Guest Jamie Starkey "What was your favourite Beatles album?"

Ringo "That's very hard to nail down. The *White Album, Rubber Soul, Abbey Road*; it's very hard."

Donna905 "My son wants to know how did it feel to be the star of the movie *Help!*?"

Ringo "Great! If anyone has the ring, I'd like it back."

Guest Pat "Ringo, is there any chance in the future that you may possibly release a box set of rarities and unreleased songs from the course of your solo career?"

Ringo "We have released already two CDs of the *Best Of Ringo* and in June or July, we'll be releasing the All-Starr Band Anthologies."

Bostonbird "Tell us about your new All-Starr Band. Some of the members have toured with you before and some to be exact, have not?"

Ringo "Yes, Dave Edmunds was in the All-Starrs in 1992. Jack Bruce and Simon Kirke have been in the last three All-Starrs; this is their fourth. Mark Rivera has been in all four, and this is the first year for Eric Carmen. Those are all the members."

Guest Raspbernie "Eric Carmen's voice, capable of handling soulful ballads as well as rip-roaring rockers, has often been compared to Paul McCartney's. How's the All-Starr Band faring with its newest member's solo songs?"

Ringo "Great! Eric is a really fine singer and he has great songs. This is probably from Eric, isn't it?"

Guest Busy Brat "On your new CD, *VH 1 Storytellers*, does the All-Starr band perform songs with you or is this a solo effort?"

Guest Pat "Ringo, is there any chance that any of your solo albums will be digitally re-mastered or re-mixed?"

Ringo "I do believe they're all on CD, now."

Guest Beatlefool "How do you feel about your upcoming 60th birthday?"

Ringo "Don't mention it."

Symmy "If you could work with anyone you haven't worked with yet, who would it be, and why?"

Ringo "There's no answer to that. There are so many people I have worked with and yet to work with. I am just letting time take its course."

Sasi "Your career has been going strong for many, many years. Do you ever plan to retire? If so, how will you spend your time?"

Ringo "I retire after every tour. Guess what! Here I am again!"

Sarahsong "It looked like you were having fun doing your commercials. Is it fun, and will we be seeing you on any more soon?

Ringo "It is fun, and it's a short day. Pays well, and the next one you see me in will be the Century 21 Connections 2000 commercial that premieres on May 15th on the *Today Show*. I know you'll all be watching!"

Andy "What is the most important thing you'd like the world to remember about Ringo Starr, 100 years from now?"

Ringo "He was a damn fine drummer!"

Honey "If you were having dinner with the three people in history most important to you, who are they and why?"

Ringo "Can I have 5 people, Barbara, Zak, Jason, Lee, Francesca, Jianni and Titia, and Louie?"

Tiger-five "There was a time when you guest-starred on *The Simpsons*. Did you enjoy it?"

Ringo "It was so nice meeting Homer in real life."

Guest MeSue "Will you ever wear your hair long again?"

Ringo "No, I love it short."

Guest Sentimental "What do you remember about recording *Two Sides Of The Moon*? You and Keith (Moon) sound to be having so much fun together. It's something I can always listen to, to make me smile. Love Sentimentalist."

Ringo "You're absolutely right! I had a lot of fun making that record."

Guest Jamie Starkey "I was told that you are a vegetarian? Is this true?"

Ringo "Yes."

Guest Brianna "Hi Ringo, Near the end of the song, 'Free As A Bird' there is the ukulele with a voice-over by John. I was wondering if it is true that this is actually a backward playback of John talking that just happens to sound like 'made by John Lennon'. Either way, who thought to add that part to the song?"

Ringo "We all did. And it is a ukulele."

Guest Barb " 'Yellow Submarine' and 'Octopus's Garden' would go well together in a concert. Would you reconsider doing both?"

Ringo "No, I feel one underwater song is plenty."

Guest "What was the first song you ever wrote?"

Ringo " 'Don't Pass Me By'."

Guest "Are you planning on doing any more acting or directing in the future?"

Ringo "No."

Guest Sally G "How many times over are you a grandfather now?"

Ringo "Twice."

MS-Cassie "What things do you do to stay in good health, as you seem to be. Do you take herbs at all?"

Ringo "Yes, I work out, and I take vitamins and herbs and I drink lots of water."

Gbarioni "Hi, Ringo. Thanks for all the great music through the years. I have heard that The Beatles' song 'Rain' was one of your favourites to drum to. Is this true?"

Ringo "It's one of my all-time favourite tracks, as far as a Beatle album or anybody else's. I particularly enjoy my drumming."

Guest Fan in Florida "If the All-Starr Band had booked an opening act for the tour, who would it be? Are you a fan of any bands on the scene these days?"

Ringo "Elvis!"

MS-Cassie "What are some of the biggest lessons you have learnt about life, and would you do anything different?"

Ringo "You can't do anything different. You have to live with the life you have."

Auburnprincess1 "I was one of those screaming fans when you first toured America. Do you find your fans calmer today, or the same?"

Ringo "I find the fans a lot calmer today. If you were in the audience then, and you're in the audience now, I bet you've quietened down a lot."

EZGuest419 "When you're not working, do you listen to a lot of music at home? If so, who was the last artist's work you listened to?"

Ringo "I was listening at home to Moby and Nick Lowe's 'Dig My Mood', everybody should have that CD. As a rule, I play lots of blues and lots of rock."

Thursday, September 28
Paul McCartney releases his latest book, *Paul McCartney Paintings* . . .

"I don't think there is any great heroic act in going in slavishly every day and saying, 'I must do this,'" says **Paul**. "So what I find is that I do it when I am inspired, and that's how I can combine it with music. Some days the inspiration is a musical one and other days it has just got to be painting."

While on **Thursday, October 19** at 5.00pm UK time (noon EST/9am PST), following Ringo's online chat in May, Paul chats live about his paintings and new book . . .

(Highlights of the webchat . . .)

Yahoo Lisa "Paul is here! Welcome!"

Paul "Hello all you cyberspace people."

Lisa "Dominic Mohan (the *Sun*) asks, 'You said that your first interest in art came by drawing naked ladies when you were at school in Liverpool. When will you exhibit in Liverpool and would any such exhibition include the naked ladies from your schooldays?'"

Paul "Well, Dominic, I did start off drawing naked ladies, but my mum caught me and reported me to my dad and that put an end to that. As a matter of fact, the Walker Art Gallery in Liverpool, where John and I used to spend many a pleasant afternoon, has offered me an exhibition of my paintings. So I am really excited about that. It's from October 2001 till January 2002."

Lisa "Do your paintings and music express the same things?"

Paul "The paintings come from the mood I am in at that particular time, but there are one or two like C Minor and the Key of F, which illustrate how I think those particular musical sounds might look, otherwise music and painting are separate."

Sergei from Moscow, "You've said that you are wary of being seen as a celebrity who paints because art critics appear to be prejudiced against them. But what is the difference between a celebrity who paints and a painter who achieves celebrity?"

Paul "Dear Sergei, hi. Give my regards to Moscow. I'm a bit worried about being a musician who suddenly decides to paint because I think a lot of people tend to dismiss your work, assuming it won't be worthwhile. But if you're a painter who achieves great celebrity then I think it's different because people will give your work a chance before criticising or judging it for that reason. I didn't tell anybody I painted for about 15 years, but now I'm out of the closet it doesn't mean to say I'm a bad person."

Eleanor Hawkins "G'day Paul! Do you know it's 2am in the bloody morning here in Aussie land! Jeez, the things I do for you! Any road, do you think we'll see an exhibition down under, because we miss you? PS Yeah, my dad named me after your song, not that he's a fanatic or anything."

Paul "Dear Eleanor, have you ever considered changing your surname? It's not my fault you're still up at 2am in the bloody morning but thanks for being there. There are no plans at the moment for an Aussie visit but I do love the place and look forward to getting back there in the not too distant future. By the way, fantastic Olympics and Para Olympics! You guys know how to put on a show, congratulations."

Goodolhonestboy 2001 "Paul, I'm sure I'm just one of millions of people who've been inspired to take up music and songwriting as a direct result of inspiration from your music. Do you think your paintings will have a similar impact, in terms of getting scores of people to take up painting?"

Paul "Dear good ol' honest boy. I'm really chuffed that people have been inspired to take up music because of my buddies and me. It'd be great to think that people who are interested in taking up painting might now dare to do it because of something I've said."

Arlene Leal Maia "Hi, Paul, you know you have tons of fans here in Brazil. Just remember the gig at the Maracanã Stadium. So, when will you bring your paintings down here? Love to you and your family."

Paul "Dear Arlene, hi to you and all those lovely Brazilian folks. At the moment the only two exhibitions planned is one in New York at the Matthew Marks Gallery in early November and the one I mentioned before at the Walker Art Gallery in Liverpool in October 2001. Maybe someone in Brazil will make an offer I can't refuse . . . I'm here with my friend Brian Clarke and he just said that someone already has made an offer, so who knows?"

Hudson Valley Sunshine "Paul, what was your inspiration for *Big Mountain Face*?"

Paul "The inspiration for *Big Mountain Face* was the painted self and the colour of the desert sand. While I was playing about trying to get the earth colour, a face appeared and I followed that inspiration that came through in the paint."

Egyptionisis "I was wondering if Linda had influence on your painting. She was such a magnificent photographer."

Paul "Hey Egypt, Linda's influence on my painting came mainly from the fact that she loved it and encouraged me to do more and more of it. Her fantastic photographs were not often a basis for anything I did in painting, but the general art vibe she gave off was infectious to say the least. She said, 'You paint like a real painter,' and that was good enough for me."

Chris Berg "Why haven't we seen your art on the album covers?"

Paul "Hey Chris, the only time I can remember doing any artwork of my own for an album cover was The Beatles fan club records that we used to put out and more recently the *Liverpool Sound Collage* CD, which used my collage from the exhibition."

Maurizio62_99 "Hello Paul, Italy here, I was just wondering what you thought of John's lithographs, back in the Sixties."

Paul "Dear Maurice of Italy, hi to your beautiful country. I loved John's drawings from his books in the Sixties and feel that, had he have lived, he might by now have been getting round to some serious painting."

Morten Nielsen, Copenhagen, Denmark "Paul, do you listen to music while painting? In that case what kinds?"

Paul "Dear Morten, you're not the guy out of A-Ha, are you? No, as it happens, even though many people I know listen to music whilst painting, I rarely do but *Pictures At An Exhibition* is one I've had a go with and the *Liverpool Sound Collage* more recently, it works quite well. Normally it's just the sound of the brush."

Linda from Minneapolis "Looking at some of your paintings, I picked up on a bit of the Ancient Celtic spirit. Am I correct?"

Paul "Hey Linda, great name. When I was asked to do this exhibition I'd been looking at some Celtic stuff and realised that it would link Germany and Britain as the two places both were home to Celts. Also being of Irish origin, I figured I am one myself so I did a series of pictures based on that good old ancient Celtic spirit. They were not ashamed to call a Dick a Dick, so I suppose that was part of the attraction."

Macca luvaz "Mr McCartney, you inspired us both to become vegetarians. We've been veggie for over a year. Thank you!"

Paul "Well done on being veggies. It's a great step to take and the animals of the world join with me in applauding your action."

Eileen562000 "Paul, didn't you draw the cake on *Flaming Pie*?"

Paul "C'mon, Eileen, yeah, I happened to do a drawing with a chinagraph on the mixing desk and it ended up as the *Flaming Pie* logo."

Mrhosehead "My apartment needs painting, are you available?"

Paul "Hey, Mr hose head, I am available for apartment painting but I must warn you, my rates are extremely steep. But I'm not sure I want to go there."

Johnlennonandyoko "What do you think of Andy Warhol, Paul?"

Paul "Hey folks, I met Andy in the Sixties and he seemed to me to be a really cool guy, perhaps a little shy but extremely sure of what he was doing and that worked. His work has stood the test of time and I suspect will do so for many years to come."

Think magnetically "Have you ever eaten peanut butter and tomato sandwiches?"

Paul "Dear Mr Magnet. I must say I have not had the pleasure of a peanut butter and tomato sarnie but my dad used to make a fine pea sandwich, unfortunately my mates would only eat them in extremely dire circumstances."

Andreaitem "Paul, when you start a painting, do you know exactly how it will look once completed? Is it the same with your music?"

Paul "Dear Andrea, most of the time I haven't got a clue how a painting is going to end up when I start and it's the same with music. I look for something inspiring and follow its lead. It may be a chord in music or a brush stroke in painting. The picture *Andy In The Garden* came from two accidental white brush strokes."

Caller "Have you ever considered computer art?"

Paul "The only thing I really do on a computer is play with my music programme and compose on it otherwise I'm afraid I'm a complete idiot and computer illegitimate or should that be illiterate boo boom!"

Degready "Do you speak French?"

Paul " 'Oui un petite peu je vous emprisi.' I used to joke that I spoke French, 'Un petite pois', but nobody got it and my dad kept making them into sandwiches."

Anna maria42 "Is the Apple logo inspired by a Magritte painting?"

Paul "Dear Anna, cool name, we know a song about that don't we children. Yeah, the Apple logo was inspired by one of Rene Magritte's paintings. It's an apple with au revoir written across it. My friend Robert Fraser arrived at my house one summer's day and left the painting propped up on a table and left without saying anything. It was possibly his coolest ever conceptual act."

As1serge "Do you plan to exhibit in Hermitage Museum, in Russia?"

Paul "Dear Serge, it's one of those places I've been longing to get to for many years but I've never got around to it I keep promising myself that I'll get to Russia one of these days and if I do that a visit there would be a must."

Ford Prefect01 "Do you have any unfulfilled ambitions?"

Paul "Dear Ford practice makes prefects yeah, I've got too many unfulfilled ambitions but I'm working at fulfilling them. Hey, by the way, anyone listening or looking, this is really cool, chatting to you all."

Oobujoobu2 "Paul, do you enjoy going on line and chatting with people from all around the world?"

Paul "Dear Oobujoobu, I sure do. We were just saying that it's cool to imagine people around the globe clueing in to this little session but there is one Aussie woman who should go to bed or pay for it in the morning."

Ryan from SF "How long does it usually take you to finish a painting?"

Paul "Hey, Ryan, it varies, but I'm quite a quick painter, sometimes it can be three or four hours. Other times it can take longer. My friend told me about a school of painters called the alla primists who liked to paint all at one go so I sometimes refer to myself as Britain's foremost alla primist, which of course is bullshit."

Bonjovibabe 2000 "Do you have any tips for struggling student artists of our time? Love you always, Kat from Liverpool!"

Paul "Dear Kat, regards to the 'pool. When I started painting I asked a lot of good people for advice and they just said, 'Paint more at the time,' and I thought that they were fobbing me off with crummy advice but now I think it's about the best advice anyone could give."

Chicken54601 "Will you create an art book for children?"

Paul "Hey chicken. When my kids were growing up I often made up stories and drew pictures for them but never thought of making a children's book, but who knows, maybe one of these years I'll get round to it. Hey guys, all you cyber people out there, I've run out of time and I've got to get my cute little ass in gear and get ready for my next thang. So thanks for looking in, it's been a pleasure for me so let's do it again some time, lots of love, Paul."

Monday, November 20

Jam! Music reports, "Beatles *1* hits No. 1 in Britain. Even though The Beatles reached the end of their long and winding road, their music and mystique still maintains a strong allure for British record buyers. *Reuters* reports that Beatles *1*, the new collection of the group's No. 1 hit songs, is officially Britain's fastest-selling album of the year. According to British retail sales data, Beatles *1* sold 319,000 copies in Britain during its debut week and entered the charts at No. 1. By comparison, Robbie Williams, one of the UK's hottest musical acts, sold just 313,000 copies of his new album during his first week, Reuters said. Geoff Baker, The Beatles' spokesman, remarked, 'The Beatles are extremely pleased.' The album arrived in Canadian record stores last Tuesday, and SoundScan, the company that monitors record sales, won't release sales results for North America until Wednesday. Observers in Britain were keenly following the Fab Four's sales, given that they were up against new albums from U2 and Spice Girls, as well as a live album from the heavily Beatles-influenced Oasis."

On **Wednesday, November 22**, The Beatles' *1* album debuts at the No. 1 spot in Canada . . . Paul Cantin, American show business correspondent, "The Beatles enjoyed first-week sales of their new collection Beatles *1* that can only be described as . . . fab! Beatles *1* entered the Canadian retail album chart at No. 1, selling 54,668 copies in one week, according to sales data compiled by SoundScan Canada. The album, which collects 27 of the group's chart-toppers, has benefited from a massive marketing campaign and a release timed to coincide with the Christmas gift-giving season. The group's achievement is even more impressive when you consider that the week's album chart includes seven debuts in the Canadian top 15, including four new entries landing in the first four chart positions . . . While in the US, The Fab Four's results were almost identically impressive. Beatles *1* entered the US charts in top spot, selling 594,666. Given the usual one-tenth sales comparison for Canada's smaller population, US and Canadian sales were proportionately similar."

DECEMBER

The following month, George returns, undertaking *All Things Must Pass* reissue promotional interviews by phone from New York . . .

The Spanish magazine, *Musician* "Since arriving in New York, Harrison has agreed to promote the reissue of his album (published by EMI), but only by telephone. The attack by Michael Abram in his house near London in 1999, a paranoid schizophrenic who stabbed him and his wife, Olivia Arias has served to make him keep his distance. A little after the anger expressed through his 22-year-old son Dhani, he acknowledged that Abram was also a victim, of the British insane system because he had not received any treatment for his illness. When at last he calls to speak of music, the rage has been dissipated and the surprise is his desire to talk about everything (except the attack) and the amount added to his life by the Hindu mysticism learned during one of the more crazy periods of his life."

Musician "Your son Dhani has collaborated in the recording. Does he seem to have a talent for music?"

George "When he returned from university he began to play the guitar with us. He has a pretty good voice and doesn't do badly, but for the time being at 22 years old he is at university. It is always painful to see how children of famous parents, Julian Lennon included, are obliged to prove they are better than anyone else because of who their parents are. This industry is despicable and it seems that Dhani understands that very well."

Musician "The cover of the disc is not ready yet but it seems that has been modernised too?"

George "On the original box I appeared sitting down in the garden with some gnomes. We have added a motorway flyover over my head and some industrial chimneys spitting out smoke, and some high-rise buildings as found in cities. It is a statement I want to make about the chaos in which we live."

Musician "Your album *Cloud Nine* in the Eighties was awarded a platinum disc for sales numbering in the millions. You were also No. 1 in the United States with 'Got My Mind

Set On You', not to mention the legendary 'Concert for Bangla Desh'. Despite this you were not considered a good composer for years?"

George "When I was in The Beatles it turned out to be very difficult. Paul McCartney and John Lennon had serious talent and they formed a good partnership, but they also had huge egos and that left little space for others. When you write a tune alone and it is flawed or could be improved, nobody helps you. I composed for myself and they saw me as competition, although I am peaceful and I was not like them. It is like throwing a stone in a lake: when the wave arrives the fish are set apart. But yes I felt ignored and undervalued for years but I have exceeded that in all ways."

Musician "How do the songs of The Beatles seem to you today? Would you subscribe to them all?"

George "You have to look at it in perspective. You must recognise that not all the songs from those days were good, far from it. Since the break-up, I have written some songs that are just as good and more that are even better than The Beatles."

Musician "What is your relationship to Paul and Ringo Starr at the moment?"

George "They form part of my life. We knew each other as adolescents and it is fun to go to a birthday celebration at Ringo's home and see how we have matured. Paul and I are more distant. It was through writing that we would find ourselves."

Musician "You were a movie producer with HandMade Films; do you still have an interest in it?"

George "I sold it because of serious differences with my manager who was also my associate. We made some very popular films like Monty Python's *Life of Brian*, but my interest in the film business has gone now."

Musician "He concludes by wishing us Happy Christmas with the best of telephone smiles."

Wednesday, December 13

Paul causes commotion by holding a *Paintings* book signing session at the Waterstone's bookstore in Piccadilly, Central London, an event that naturally attracts hundreds of excited McCartney fans. One of which is Jean Herbaut, who travels down to the capital from her home in Hertfordshire . . .

"I set out from home in Stevenage on Tuesday with my sleeping bag, pillow, several dustbin liners and a very large umbrella," Jean recalls. "I drove to Hendon, parked the car, and made my way by tube to Piccadilly and arrived at Waterstone's at around 11pm, having agreed this time with a couple of other fans, Nina and her little sister Helen, and Eleanor, who would be arriving from Nottingham and Cheshire respectively. They had arrived just minutes before me so we were separated in the line by a fellow who had brought along his guitar to entertain us throughout the long cold night. There were already some 50 people in the queue in front of us. The first in line being a fan from Poland who had arrived at 9am that day. We recognised quite a few people, as you do at these events, Shuji from the Japanese fan club amongst them. People who were in the queue before the shop had closed for the evening had already been given numbers, to secure their position in the queue. So we had to wait until the morning. Several late revellers passed the queue on their way home, and every one of them wanted to know why we were camped out on the pavement. It became a game to see who could think up the most ridiculous answer. I think Nina won with 'This is the end of the Harrods sale. You should see the front of the queue!' We spent the night playing silly games like I-spy, and singing along to tapes.

"When morning broke, and the streets once more became very busy, the staff from Waterstone's asked us if we would keep all the other shop doorways clear, and came along the line, taking our names, and giving us a number. I was number 56. Now we could relax a little, knowing that we almost certainly would get in to meet the great man himself. By now the queue was really growing, with people not having a hope in hell of getting into the shop, but still joining the queue. One of the most amusing things was a number of people getting on their mobile phones, to phone their employers to say they would not be in today as they were 'feeling sick, and didn't get much sleep last night.' This, of course, was not a lie. Nobody got any sleep, and we were certainly feeling sick, sick with excitement. I have to say at this point that I was well and truly going down with the flu. I had a temperature, and I was feeling quite poorly, but so determined was I to make this trip, having planned it for about a week before, nothing was going to stop me. As more and more people arrived, girls started to put make-up on and the shops along the route opened for business, we duly left the front doorways clear. Some people saw this as an opportunity to try to push into the queue, they obviously got very short shrift from all of us, but there were some who were quite determined to stand their ground. Waterstone's staff came to the rescue and they soon moved people on, explaining that we had spent the night outside etc. I have to say the staff from Waterstone's was extremely friendly, helpful and efficient, in fact they were brilliant. Soon the press and camera crews arrived, asking for the usual interviews. Eleanor did a brilliant interview for Reuters news. They had singled her out because she was covered in badges, and really looked 'the part'. Then the great moment came – Paul arrived, the customary 10 minutes late, and all hell broke loose, crowds were pushing, police were doing their best to control the crowds. I did manage to get a photo of his arrival, but it was from a distance, as I was not prepared to give up my place in the queue. At last the long 14-hour wait was over. Well almost, we were now on the final stretch.

"When we eventually got into the shop, our bags and baggage were taken from us and placed over the other side of the shop. There were piles of Paul's book lining the way to the desk where he sat, in front of a semi-circle backdrop of posters, and in front of the world's press. There were so many press! You took a book from the pile, walked up to Paul, a distance of about 10 feet away, and said just what you wanted to say to him. This had a marked effect on a lot of people. Some couldn't say anything at all. There was no rush to move you on, and he seemed genuinely interested in what you had to say. He asked your name, so that he could dedicate the signature. Nina, Eleanor and Helen went before me. It was Nina's birthday, so he wrote 'Happy Birthday, Nina. Love Paul McCartney' in her book. When he asked Eleanor her name, he made reference to 'Eleanor Rigby,' and Helen was just lost for words and couldn't speak at all, you know, being just the tender age of 16, and meeting her idol. The girls had bought Paul Christmas presents, a book on Magritte, *Goon Show* scripts, photo frame, and a wind chime and were anxious that he should get them, as we had to leave all our belongings with the staff. Eleanor told Paul of this. So Paul shouted across to John Hammel, his assistant and driver, 'These lovely ladies have bought me a Christmas present, what's the deal?' John turned around and said, 'It's okay! All taken care of.' Eleanor breathed a sigh of relief, and as Paul turned back to face her, he saw the numerous badges she was wearing, pointed and said, 'Wow, great.' Then came my turn. This was such an emotional moment for me, and everybody said the same, that I felt myself welling up with tears, but was determined not to show myself up, at least not until it was all over. I remember my conversation, 'I'd like to say thanks for all the pleasure and music you've given to everybody over the years. And Paul, I know you've been working on a new album, if and when you take to the road to promote it, could you please think about a performance in Liverpool, to coincide with the annual Beatles convention, during August bank holiday.'

"He thought for a moment and replied, 'Hmm, good idea, but can't promise mind.' The moment was over far too quickly, I picked up my book, thanked him, and turned to walk away, and began to sob uncontrollably. I met up with everybody else at the bag collection point and I noticed that all of us were doing the same thing. We were all crying! Even grown men were reduced to tears. The fellow who had entertained us all night with his guitar, was crying and had collapsed on the floor, and had to be helped away by Waterstone's staff. Nobody wanted to leave the area, nobody wanted this very special moment to end. Eventually we composed ourselves enough to make our way to the till to pay for the books. Just recalling this moment still has a very emotional effect on me, and probably will forever. I don't know why. It's not that I've never been close to him before. After all, I'd been fairly close to him at the HMV Oxford Street signing, even though I didn't quite make the front, and I'd managed to get a ticket for the *Run Devil Run* launch party in Leicester Square. I was only two feet away from him there, and I managed to get a ticket for *Parkinson*, and was in the second row of that. I even managed to get a photo through the Beeb's window of Paul with Mary Parkinson, but that's another story. But to actually speak to him, and have him answer you personally, well, that was just the icing on the cake. You can't top that! It certainly was a day in the life!"

2001

Monday, January 22
After a two-month delay, George reissues his classic 1970 album *All Things Must Pass* in the UK, which includes amongst the bonus tracks a reworking of his memorable song 'My Sweet Lord' . . .

George in the Spanish *Musician* magazine, "What we have added now is new guitars to compensate for the echo of the Seventies. We have also united the original choruses with the voice of vocalist Sam Brown, as a backing for me on the song. The result is relative. It sounds similar but the arrangements are different. The same thing happens with 'Isn't It A Pity'. That has two versions, both are on the compact disc."

A favourable review of *All Things Must Pass* (issued in the States the following day) by Luke Smith of the newspaper, *Michigan Daily* "Never mind that George Harrison was the second worst Beatle. Never mind that the only Beatle he could say he was better than was, well, Ringo. Forget that Harrison settled a lawsuit against the validity of 'My Sweet Lord'. And no matter what, forget that Harrison video for 'Got My Mind Set On You', where the patron saint of dull sat in a chair and wouldn't move, so the director had to move everything around him (thank you VH1's *Pop-Up Video*). Harrison is by no means a disposable member of the Fab Four. He is not to be confused with that Starr fellow. Remember though, this is the album that outsold both Lennon and McCartney's first solo releases, but the whole lawsuit thing kinda rained on that parade. What a bitch! Nonetheless, despite all these things, Capitol Records went back, re-mastered and repackaged this Harrison vehicle, and made it a bit more road-worthy than the original. *All Things Must Pass* is a lucidity layered record, thick with texture and filled with heavy rhythm tracks. Harrison's album features Eric Clapton (unable to receive credit for the record till now), and Genesis post-Gabriel maestro Phil Collins (*Invisible Touch* anyone?). Complacent and lengthy (running 7:08), 'Isn't It A Pity' is a tunefully rueful love song winding behind a tambourine, piano and drums. The track is propelled by a series of lengthy guitar solos, and in my Nineties-bred pop mind that translated to, 'Hey, he ripped off "Champagne Supernova".' An infectiously written riff-age launches 'What Is Life'. Harrison combines so much on this track like gang vocals, 'Hello Goodbye'-esque horn sections and a fabulous hook. Songs like this, 'Band on the Run' and 'Oh Yoko' show absolutely no drop-off in quality from when the moptops were still together. Harrison effectively moves back and forth between Beatles-y pop and his own ornately fashioned songsmithery. 'Behind That Locked Door' even teeters on the edge of being a country song, it does have that Bryan White twang to it à la 1996's *Between Now And Forever*. These Harrison hooks and arrangements do seem to find a niche somewhere in the back of my head. Exchanging confused glances with other Beatles' fans and then plucking the CD off of the shelf is more than a good idea, for a lot of you out there, it will be necessity. You will read this review and go, 'Luke Smith, this dude, he knows his shit. And since he said that Beatles' fans should own this record and I certainly am a Beatles fan,' you will march your ass down to the record store and you'll shell out something like $25 bucks for this Harrison joint. You'll marvel at the packaging, which is a sexy black box with both CDs stored in freefall small cardboard slippers because he says it's 'environmentally friendly' or something. Grade? What the hell do you mean 'Grade'? It's George Harrison."

Thursday, February 15
George continues with his *All Things Must Pass* promotional interviews by giving his first ever on-line chat, hosted by Yahoo Chat . . .

Yahoo "We're here with George Harrison. Please welcome EMI recording artist George Harrison. Hi."

George "Hello. It's nice to be here. It's my first time on a computer. I'm pretty illiterate."

Yahoo "What made you decide to reissue *All Things Must Pass* now?"

George "It's the 30th anniversary and I'm in the process of re-mastering my entire catalogue, which I want to get back into the stores. So we started with that one and hopefully during the year we'll be able to come with the next batch and so on, so that everything I have ever done will be available."

Yahoo "Are you planning a new studio album?"

George "Yeah. After I'm through with all that stuff I hope to put out a new studio album, possibly November, and I have at the moment many songs in various states of completion, possibly 35 songs that I have been working on over the years."

Yahoo "Do you surf the Internet much? What types of things do you do online?"

George "No, I never surf. I don't know the password."

Question from willowy blonde, "Hi, my boyfriend wants to know what is your favourite electric guitar and do you still have Rocky, your 161 Fender stratocaster?"

George "Hello, willowy blonde. I still have Rocky and he can be seen at Cyril's rare guitar shop on www.allthingsmustpass.com."

Question "Will you be releasing *Living In The Material World* in a re-mastered extra tracks version?"

George "Well, as I said before, that would be the next one to be re-mastered. I have to get into my tape library to find out if there are any alternate versions of anything."

Question "What did you think of Bob Dylan getting nominated for an Oscar?"

George "I think he should win it. I think he should win all the Oscars, all the Tonys, all the Grammies."

Question "How has The Rutles influenced your career?"

George "I got all my ideas from The Rutles. Particularly the 12-string Rickenbackers and slide guitar styles I got from Stig O'Hara. I met him once and he is a super chap."

Question "Hi, George. I'm Natalie, an 18-year-old girl from Australia and I'm a huge fan. Any hints for a budding guitarist?"

George "Yes. Buy a ukulele."

Question "George, do you ever see a reunion tour with you, Paul and Ringo?"

George "Not really. But stranger things have happened."

Question "George, which version of 'My Sweet Lord' do you like best. The original or the new version?"

George "I like the new version better because it's new. And I like Sam Brown singing it."

Yahoo "Why did you revisit it?"

George "At the time, the song was so popular and also so controversial that the most important thing about it for me was that it, in its small way, conjured up a touch of spirituality, something we are very short of."

Question "Hi George, Christopher here. Thank you for being such an inspiration. What was it like working with Phil Spector? Although I can hear his influence, your influence and leadership in the production is clear. God Bless You, George."

George "Phil Spector was probably the greatest producer from the Sixties and it was good to work with him because I needed some assistance in the control box. Phil was very funny, loveable, and sometimes annoying. But we love him."

Question "I have several teenage friends who have just discovered *All Things Must Pass*. They were wondering about radio airplay. I explained that this was a re-mastered etc. album, a re-release essentially. They, however, as I do, feel the music is just as cool as it was when you first released the work. Wouldn't it be great if a single was selected and the whole cycle could start again?"

George "It's nice to know that teenagers find *All Things Must Pass* cool. As far as a single goes, I suppose that's really up to Capitol Records. I have no objection."

Question "Hi, Mr Harrison. How do you feel about The Beatles' *1* album being top of the charts?"

George "It's very nice. It helps pay the bills. It's also nice that young children seem to be hearing it for the first time. And I think that as an alternative form of music for today it has its place alongside all this other stuff."

Question "Out of curiosity, why the garden gnomes on *All Things Must Pass*?"

George "Originally when we took the photo, I had these old Bavarian gnomes, which I thought I would put there, like kinda John, Paul, George and Ringo. Gnomes are very popular in Europe, and these gnomes were made in about 1860. So while building the website, the gnomes just seemed to get into it and we just couldn't stop them."

Question "Is Indian music still a big influence on your music?"

George "Yes!"

Question "Following the incident at your house in December 1999, has your outlook on life changed at all?"

George "Yes and no. Adi Shankara, an Indian historical spiritual groovy type person once said, 'Life is fragile, like a raindrop on a lotus leaf,' and you'd better believe it."

Question "I'm curious about your website and the way the cover photo is altered by adding roads and urban development to the picture. Does that symbolise anything?"

George "Yes. It symbolises that our world is being concreted over. Haven't you noticed?"

Question "Mr Harrison, what is the opening chord you use for 'A Hard Day's Night'?"

George "It is F with a G on top, on the 12 string. But you'll have to ask Paul about the bass note to get the proper story."

Question "What do you think of Eminem's Grammy nomination?"

George "What is Eminem? Aren't they chocolates or something?"

Question "What did you record with Bill Wyman last month?"

George "An old Ketty Lester song called 'Love Letters'."

Question "Why was 'I Live For You' left out of the original mix? I think it's lovely. Thanks for putting it out at last."

George "I didn't think that we had got a good enough take on it, except for Pete Drake, the pedal steel guitar player. At that time I had so many other tracks as well, so we just left it off. It did need patching up in the drum department."

Question "George, what do you miss most about John Lennon?"

George "John Lennon."

Question "George, in the *Anthology* book you talk about the unwound G-string. What is that? I play guitar and I'm not sure what you're talking about."

George "It's one of those little things that goes up your butt so people can't see your panty lines. No, it's actually a 3rd string that doesn't have a winding around it."

Question "Does Paul still piss you off? Tell us the truth."

George "Scan not a friend with a microscopic glass. You know his faults, then let his foibles pass. It is an old Victorian proverb. I'm sure there is enough about me that pisses him off, but I think we have now grown old enough to realise that we're both pretty damn cute."

Question "Mr Harrison, I was wondering if you might tell us a bit about your ideas on love, romantic love that is. I recall you having written some of The Beatles' most beautiful love songs. It will be interesting to hear how your religious attitudes have impacted on your beliefs concerning romanticism."

George "Well, the lover that we miss is actually God. The beauty that you see within each other is actually God. So Krishna was the greatest romanticist. He had girlfriends on every corner. I can't separate the two. A beautiful girl is the Divine Mother. A beautiful man is the manifestation of potential."

Question "You're joking in a most *Pythoni*stic manner tonight, George. It's great to hear you online."

George "Piss off! You nosy bastard."

Question "Given the drug experimentation of the Sixties, how do you feel about the legalisation of pot?"

George "Well, I saw someone on TV last night pulling out huge loads of pot out of various fields in California. My feeling is as long as you can go into a store and buy whiskey, bourbon, vodka, gin and all the rest of it, then a little grass is nothing. The authorities are just causing the price to be high. Excuse the pun."

Question "Have you any tips to budding songwriters? Do you, as John apparently advised you, stick at it until you have finished it?"

George "Try and write some melodies and some words that mean something. It is true that if you are on a roll then it's best to finish it in one go. That's what Johnny said."

Question "Hey George, will you ever be back on Yahoo?"

George "Possibly. It's pretty painless for me."

Saturday, March 10
... An Interview with a Poet

Daily Telegraph "From his Los Angeles recording studio, Sir Paul buoyantly reports that the recording of his new album is going well. Last Saturday evening, Sir Paul took time between tracks to discuss his newly released book of poetry, *Blackbird Singing: Poems and Lyrics 1965–1999*, with fellow Liverpudlian poet and London *Daily Telegraph* reporter, Roger McGough ..."

Roger "What is the difference between writing poetry and song lyrics? Does the melody ever get in the way?"

Paul "I think so. There is a little bit of a crutch with the music. I do think of them separately, although Adrian Mitchell (who edited and introduced the book) doesn't. He's into 'Sweet Little Sixteen' and rock'n'roll lyrics and he sees the poetry in them. Originally I only wanted poems in the book, but he talked me into, or rather, persuaded me into including the song lyrics. I used to hang out a bit with Allen Ginsberg in the Sixties, and later on during the last couple of years of his life we became good friends. And he said to me, 'That Eleanor Rigby is a fucking good poem, man.' So I thought, 'Well, he's no slouch,' and so, with Adrian pushing me, I looked at them again, and thought, 'Yes, some of them could be read.' "

Roger "Is having a book published different from having an album released?"

Paul "Yes, there's a big difference. I'm used to doing albums, but this is a bit special. My neck is on the line."

Roger "Were you interested in poetry as a student?"

Paul "I did A-level English at the Inny [Liverpool Institute], which is my scholastic claim to fame, and we had Alan 'Dusty' Durband, a lovely man, who showed us the dirty bits of Chaucer. You know, *The Miller's Tale*, and *The Nun's Tale*, which were dirtier than anything we were telling each other. He had studied under FR Leavis at Oxford, and he brought a rich pool of information to us guys, and when we would listen, which was occasionally, it was great. He introduced us to Louis MacNeice and Auden, both of whom I liked. It was a good period of my life and I enjoyed it."

Roger "In the early Sixties, poetry wasn't really regarded as a macho thing to do."

Paul "I agree. It was all very well to be artistic, but poetry was just that bit too far. I used to hang around book shops like Phillip, Son and Nephew and surreptitiously read the stuff and be turned on by it. I would go and see plays at the Playhouse and the Royal Court and get excited by what I experienced, but I was never going to do anything with it."

Roger "Do you use a computer?"

Paul "Pencil and paper. I'm not a typist. Funnily enough, John became a red-hot typist towards the end of his life. He had always had this Arts Correspondent in Kowloon kind of dream. But for me it's pencil and paper by the bed . . . those moments between falling asleep and just before waking are good. I've got this little book that Stelly [his daughter, Stella] gave me and it's full of scribbles and drawings."

Roger "Will there be another poetry book?"

Paul "It depends how many I write. I think a lot of the poems in this book were written out of grief. The one for my friend Ivan, for John and the ones for Linda are like private notes, confidential letters that seemed to me more powerful than writing songs. I really felt that it was Linda who was moving the wind chimes and only a poem could express that feeling. I remember Peter Ustinov saying, 'I like being interviewed, it allows me to know what I'm thinking.' It's a little bit true of poems. It's like therapy; you write something down and then you can remember what you were thinking. In my case the depths, in your case the poems are more humorous, but with an underlying sadness that you're probably just covering up."

Wednesday, March 21
Paul returns to Liverpool and holds another book signing session, this time for *Blackbird Singing* at the WH Smith's store in Church Street . . .

Emma Gunby, *Liverpool Echo* "More than 1,000 people turned up to see one of the city's favourite sons return home to sign copies of his new book. It was more like a pop concert with screaming fans pushed against crash barriers and The Beatles' music blaring out of loudspeakers into a very chilly city centre. For some, meeting Sir Paul was just a little bit too much. Seven-year-old, Charley McKeon, from Waterloo, burst into tears when he realised he was going to meet his idol. His mum, Stephanie said, 'Charley was crying and one of Paul McCartney's people saw him. He took Charley over and said he could be one of the first people to meet Paul. He said hello and signed his book. It was absolutely wonderful, although I do feel a bit guilty because Charley should have been in school.' Tearful Tomohiro Kobayashi, who travelled from Tokyo to meet Sir Paul, was overwhelmed after meeting his favourite Beatle. The 21-year-old, who had queued since 10am on Tuesday, said, 'I can't talk. I'm just so happy.' Stephen Bailey, manager of The Beatles Shop in Mathew Street, had a very special present for Sir Paul, a record sleeve from the Phillips recording studio where The Beatles first recorded when they were known as The Quarry Men. 'If I was going to give this to anybody, it had to be Paul McCartney,' said Stephen."

While in another report in the *Liverpool Echo*, "Some fans were not so happy and vowed not to buy the book in protest after failing to meet their idol. Elena Perez had flown all the way from Spain and queued from 3am yesterday morning in the snow. She was furious that she was left out in the cold. She said, 'I am very disappointed with Paul and am going to return my book to the shop. He could have stayed for just a little while longer and made sure that he met his fans who had queued up all night and day. I am absolutely devastated.' A spokesman for WH Smith's said that stewards had gone along the queue informing people that they might not get in. She said, 'We were aware that people had queued for a long time and come from far away so we sent stewards along the crowd to tell them to move to the front of the store where they would have the best chance of taking photos.' But Ania Rakowski, 25, from Crosby, and her sister Stella, who joined the queue at 5am, said that nobody had approached them. Ania said, 'We had no idea that we might not meet him. When he came out and began signing books for people at the front barriers who had only been there for about half-an-hour, I could not believe it.'"

After the book signing session, Paul makes a surprise appearance in the city at the Everyman Theatre where he makes his poetry reading debut alongside established poets Adrian Mitchell, Tom Pickard and Willy Russell . . .

Paul Kennedy, *Liverpool Echo* "To make his poetry debut, Paul has had offers from all over the world. The Shakespeare Library in Washington DC, *LA Times Book Review* and London's Royal Theatre have all wanted him at their prestigious events. But he turned them all down to come back home to read to a small audience at Liverpool's Everyman Theatre, exactly 40 years after a young Macca made his night-time debut with The Beatles on stage at the Cavern . . ."

Joe Riley, *Liverpool Echo* "Britain's artistic everyman, singer, composer, painter and now bard, was at the 500-seater Everyman for a socially levelling experience. The near billionaire ex-Beatle wore battered trainers that would have been the envy of the *Big Issue* sellers on the door. The still princely looking king of pop was suddenly on stage, relaxed, humorous and nostalgic about his Liverpool childhood. Strangely, as McCartney's new tome includes a lot of very famous lyrics, 'Penny Lane', 'Yellow Submarine', 'Yesterday', etc., he only chose to recite one lesser known opus from the days of Fabdom, 'Maxwell's

Silver Hammer'. It would have been fun (surely?) to hear some familiar anthems spoken by the chap who penned the libretto. But instead, there were ditties inspired by love, loss, nature, and even Mark Chapman, John Lennon's killer . . ."

Paul "I was naked. I'm used to sticking a guitar in front of me. I picked Liverpool to make my poetry debut because it is a lovely place. It just seemed like the right place. Liverpool means everything to me. I grew up here. I love coming back, just driving around the old haunts, looking at the buses . . ."

Blackbird Singing . . .

Paul "Many of the pages are devoted to Linda. I just wanted to get my feelings out on to the page. It's like a kind of therapy, I think. They just came, they arrived and it's the way I felt. So I thought I would write them down and it helps you get through it."

A month later, on **Thursday, April 19**, Paul McCartney and his girlfriend, Heather Mills, meet with the U.S. Secretary of State, Colin Powell, in Washington to discuss their efforts to clear minefields around the globe.

Powell remarks, "There are a number of areas where the U.S. government can co-operate with them even though the United States opposes an international convention that would ban the use of landmines."

Following the meeting, Heather Mills announces that issues they discussed with Powell included the *Adopt-A-Minefield* campaign to remove mines and the use of 'smart mines' that can be identified after minefields have been abandoned. While **Paul** is heard to remark, "We basically expressed our point of view and Powell expressed support for many of the programmes to get rid of landmines."

Syndicated press report "The *Adopt-A-Minefield* campaign is sponsored by the UN Association of the USA and the Better World Fund. It raises money for the clearing of minefields worldwide. The former Beatle, Paul McCartney became interested in the landmine issue after becoming acquainted with Mills, who has aided efforts to provide artificial limbs to landmine victims. Mills, a former model, lost her left leg below the knee in a traffic accident in 1993."

While in another report, the issue is reiterated by Associated Press "Once upon a time, the US government wanted to kick former Beatle John Lennon out of the country. But today, the Secretary of State met with a former Beatle to talk about minefields. Colin Powell and Paul McCartney, along with Macca's girlfriend Heather Mills, discussed the singer's *Adopt-A-Minefield* campaign, which raises money to help clear minefields around the world. Despite America's well-documented reservations about landmine clearance, McCartney says the meeting was productive."

Paul "We basically explained to him our point of view, a lot of which he agreed with. He expressed his support for *Adopt-A-Minefield*, which is hoping to clear all the mines in the world and allow people to go back to their fields and to their towns. Basically, we are hoping to clear these landmines through *Adopt-A-Minefield*, and we are looking forward to a landmine-free future."

After the meeting, Secretary Powell talks about US efforts to help with the programme and his time with the pop legend . . .

"We had a good meeting," says Powell, "and I'm very proud of US efforts to support the *Adopt-A-Minefield* campaign. And also, we contributed something like 500 million dollars over the last seven years to remove minefields."

Thursday, May 3
It is revealed that George has had another operation for cancer . . .

Daily Mail (May 4) "George Harrison has undergone a lung operation after being diagnosed with cancer for a second time. Recuperating with his wife, Olivia, in Tuscany, Italy, he posed for photographs with her to prove he is well on the road to recovery. 'God bless and not to worry,' he said. Harrison, who had surgery for throat cancer three years ago, joked that he had 'no plans' to die. Harrison's new problem was diagnosed when a regular check-up at the Mayo Clinic in Rochester, Minnesota, revealed that the disease had returned. Following the operation, he flew to Milan in a private jet belonging to actor Jim Carrey to begin his recuperation in the sun."

George's lawyer, Nick Valner, reads a statement revealing details of the operation . . .

"George recently underwent an operation on one of his lungs at the Mayo Clinic in the USA," Nick said. "Because of his previous health problems, he is checked regularly to ensure that if there are any problems they can be discovered immediately. Thankfully after one of these checks they discovered the very small tumour. A tiny part of his lung was removed along with a very small cancerous tumour. They also checked his throat to see if the cancer had returned there but thankfully it hadn't. The operation was a complete success and he is now recuperating with his wife. He has made a very good recovery and is fit and well, all things considering. He is now enjoying a holiday in Tuscany, Italy. Although All Things Must Pass Away, George has no plans right now and is still Living In The Material World, and wishes everyone all the very best, God Bless and not to worry."

Professor Ray Donnelly, founder of Liverpool's Roy Castle Lung Foundation, tells the *Liverpool Echo* he would be contacting Harrison and his family to offer his personal support and urged George to use his high profile to raise awareness of the disease . . .

"It takes between 25 and 30 years for lung cancer to develop and so it is highly likely that George Harrison developed it while he was playing with The Beatles in Liverpool," Donnelly said. "Lung cancer is extremely common in Liverpool. In the city alone, approximately 500 people every year get lung cancer. . . . Of course, his risk of contracting the disease is high because he was a very heavy smoker. As such, it is really important that he urges the government and other agencies to give increased funding for research."

Monday, May 7
Paul releases, simultaneously around the world, *Wingspan: Hits And History*, a two-CD compilation of Wings' most recognised hit singles and choice album tracks . . .

Paul "The great thing about this story is it's got a lot of human drama because it was a struggle trying to put it together after The Beatles. I mean, The Beatles' career itself was a struggle, and then having reached those heights, to try and do it over and at the same time bring up a young family was quite an interesting human interest story. And that comes over, I think. It's quite dramatic and pretty moving. And then, I think, you realise that Wings was a pretty good band. This album comes so close after the release of The Beatles' *1* but we didn't plan that timing, because *Wingspan* started being made about three years ago. My son-in-law, Alistair Donald, directed *Wingspan*. But what's been happening is like when I was out in Los Angeles, six weeks ago, and a lot of people were saying, 'Gosh, my 6-year-old, my 8-year-old, my 10-year-olds are really into you guys from the *1* album.' I was being asked to sign by all these kids, a lot of stuff, which was really interesting to me. And then people say to me, 'You know what they want to know now? What happened next?' And I say, 'You know what? The timing's right, because what happened next for me was the Wings band.' "

Thursday, June 14

The *Times Of India* reports, "Former Beatle Paul McCartney and his girlfriend Heather Mills appealed to a celebrity-studded audience to open their wallets and adopt-a-minefield so their dream of a world without the killer weapons can become a reality. The British pop star asked the two hundred guests to imagine living in a country where there had been a terrible war. And after it ended being unable to walk on the beach or in the countryside for fear of stepping on a mine and being killed or severely injured. 'My take on the whole thing is that it's not a brave weapon,' Paul said. 'That's why I want to see the world rid of these weapons.' He urged those who back a mine-free world to support the *Adopt-A-Minefield* campaign, which seeks sponsors to adopt minefields identified by the united nations as being in urgent need of clearance. The cost ranges from thousands to millions of dollars, depending on the complexity."

Bill Leurs, President of the United Nations Association of the USA, which implements the campaign, says today, "There are still between seventy and one hundred million landmines planted around the world. The campaign has so far raised 2.9 million dollars and I hope to top three million dollars with further contributions on Friday night."

On the evening of **Thursday, June 14**, Paul performs at the *Adopt-A-Minefield* benefit gala in Los Angeles at the Regent Beverly Wiltshire Hotel. Amongst the crowd is the American reporter, diner guest and long-time Beatles fan, Greg Nowak . . .

"At 5.30pm, there was a photo call for the press," Greg recalls. "Paul and Heather posed with the recipient of the *Adopt-A-Minefield Humanitarian Award*, Radosav 'Zika' Zivkovic, a landmine survivor. He had unfortunately lost a part of a leg in Bosnia and Herzegovina when he stepped on a mine in April 1994. An hour later, at 6.30, we had a cocktail hour. I took a few pictures as Paul walked with Heather down the steps, which led to the ballroom. A guy shouted at him and Paul graciously shook his hand. It was amazing to see him again because I have been such a big Beatles fan for so many years. When we took our seats, Paul sat three tables away from us at number twenty-four. We were shown two films about landmines. One of them Heather narrated, while the other featured both Heather and Paul's voices. After the movies and award, which Paul presented, we had the main course. Later, after Paul Simon had finished his set, Paul took to the stage and *Tonight Show* host, Jay Leno, the MC, introduced him. Jay cracked jokes while Paul's band set up. Leno asked John Hammel, Paul's roadie, 'Is the lad from Liverpool ready yet?' It took a while for Paul to get ready. Jay finally introduced Paul and he said, 'It's a great pleasure for me to do this. I remember when I was eight years old watching these guys on *The Ed Sullivan Show* and my father shouting at me to 'Shut the damn music off!' Well, we've all come a long way since then.'

"Paul came on by himself and John Hammel handed him his acoustic guitar and Paul played 'Yesterday'. The band came out next and they played 'The Long and Winding Road' with Paul playing his Hofner bass, remaining on the instrument for the other songs he performed this evening. After finishing that song, he said, 'As you may know, I've been in Los Angeles recording a new album,' said to a rousing cheer from the celebrity packed crowd, 'and here's a song from the new album that nobody's ever heard before.' Paul did not announce the title but it's a good rocker, reminiscent of his 1993 track 'Get Out Of My Way'. I think it may be called 'Drive In The Rain'. After which, he said, 'Now I'm gonna do something I've never done before. You may know that I've got this book out,' said while he held up a copy of *Blackbird Singing*, and said, 'It's a book of my poems.' He then read *Jerk Of All Jerks*. When he read the last line, he tossed the book into the air and performed 'Let It Be'. Then he said, 'Goodnight,' and left to a standing ovation. A short time later, he came back out with Paul Simon and they played The Beatles' classic, 'I've Just Seen A Face'. Paul was playing along on bass. At its conclusion, they both took a bow and left the stage. It was a great, albeit brief, performance on a most memorable night."

Sunday, July 22

In an interview with the UK newspaper, the *Mail On Sunday*, Sir George Martin is erroneously quoted as saying that George Harrison says he's losing his battle with cancer. Sir George, "He is taking it easy and still hoping that the thing will go away. He has an indomitable spirit but he knows that he is going to die soon and he is accepting that. However, George has maintained a positive attitude. George is very philosophical. He does realise that everybody has got to die sometime . . . He has been near death many times and he's been rescued many times as well. But he knows he is going to die soon and he's accepting it perfectly happily."

Monday, July 23

One day after George Martin's shock admission, a **George Harrison** spokesman issues a press release denying the reports that he is near to death's door. "We are disappointed and disgusted by the report. It was unsubstantiated, untrue and totally uncalled for, when in fact Mr. Harrison is active and feeling very well. It has caused untold distress amongst our family and friends. The original 'story' was conjured up by the *National Enquirer*, the *Globe* and the *Daily Mail*."

Adam Sharp, George Martin's agent, tells CBS News, "George Harrison is fine and working on his new album. George Martin emphatically denies speaking to anyone from the *Mail*."

Ringo tells the American television programme *Access Hollywood*, on **Wednesday, July 25**, "George is fine. I saw him three weeks ago. I did not believe the reports. If he had been bad he would have told me. I didn't panic because I will wait until it becomes a reality. The news is real when either George tells me or Paul tells me. We do that to each other. We say, 'Watch out, something's happened and they will be calling you.' The thing is people still think we're one body with three heads."

And in a web chat with Yahoo, **Ringo** remarks, "The problem with George Harrison's situation is that the press went crazy over the weekend, and printed a whole deal supposedly said by George Martin, and we had to wait till Monday for George Martin to deny he said it. As we all know, George has had an operation, I saw him three weeks ago, he was in great spirits, but of course he is recovering. End of story . . . As you know, it's been retracted in England now . . . George Martin came out and said he didn't actually say it. That's the problem sometimes with the media, they take some craziness. It's not their fault and they blow it up."

One day earlier, on **Tuesday, July 24**, at the Casino Rama, in Ontario, **Ringo** holds a press conference to launch the latest tour by his All-Starr Band. He is backed by another host of top rock legends, which include this time Marc Rivera (Foreigner), Sheila E (Prince), Howard Jones, Emerson, Lake & Palmer's Greg Lake, Mott The Hoople's Ian Hunter, Supertramp's Roger Hodgson and Ringo's son, Zak, on drums . . .

At the conference, **Ringo** discussed the lack of radio play his recent albums have received. "I've crossed the threshold into golden-oldiedom," he remarks in the *New York Daily News.* "You have to be heard on the radio. If you aren't promoted, people don't know your record exists and we just couldn't get programmers to play it. It doesn't matter how many lunches you have with the buggers. You're beating your head against a wall. So, after a while, you just say, 'Okay, I worked hard on this record and, musically, it stands up. I'm proud of it and that's as far as I can go.' If radio had the attitude in 1964 that it has today, no one would have ever heard The Beatles." Ringo also addresses the question of whether this would be the last All-Starr Band. "Every one is the last one," he jokes. "It's gotten to the point where my family just laughs at me. I come home at the end and say, 'That's it,' and they say, 'Sure, Dad. Sure it is.'"

At the get-together, Ringo again faces the country's press . . .

Reporter "This is the seventh tour for your group. Is that more than you expected when you started?"

Ringo "Yes it is. I thought I'd do a tour one year, then have a year off, then tour the next year. But this is like the fourth in a row. I suppose I'm just on a roll, really, so I might as well take advantage of it. And I do enjoy it. It gives me a chance to play, so that's why we're here."

Reporter "You have an all new batch of All-Starrs, compared to the last few when you had some carry-overs."

Ringo "After last year's tour, I went back to the initial idea of having the All-Starrs change personnel every year. I didn't really do that the first two years. I had Joe Walsh with me those first two and I've done the last three years with Jack Bruce and Simon Kirke. I thought, 'No, I'm getting a little too comfortable.' Jack is an incredible bass player and Simon is a brilliant drummer. But we were becoming more like an act. So I said, 'Well, if I'm going out this year, I'm going to change everybody.'"

Reporter "How did you go about making the changes?"

Ringo "It's always the same process. We get calls from managers who are putting their artists forward, and we get calls from the artists saying they'd like to do it. But in the end, win or lose, I have to sit down and say, 'Well, I'll have him as the bass player and him as the guitar player, and OK, let's have him on keyboards.' It's just from the top of my head, really. The night before rehearsals you just pray that it's going to work, and then I think, 'Hey, it has so far. What are you worried about?' "

Reporter "You have Sheila E on percussion, the first female you've had in the band."

Ringo "She's something. She's talented and has a beautiful soul."

Reporter "What about the other members?"

Ringo "We have Roger Hodgson. He did 'Logical Song'. He's great and he's the lead guitarist. So it's a mixed bag. We go from him to Ian Hunter, from the old rock'n'roll school and Howard Jones on the piano and Greg Lake on bass. It's actually a very varied band, this one. But we all have hits and we're all pulling together. I support them. They support me. We do our best for each other and I'm just a band member, too. I like being in bands."

Reporter "Did you hear about the *Abbey Road* tour this summer with Todd Rundgren, Alan Parsons, Ann Wilson, and John Entwistle?"

Ringo "Yes, I did. And they had two former All-Starrs [Rundgren and Entwistle]. But it's fine. People have to work. It's just playing music. The Beatles wrote some great songs, so why not?"

Reporter "Due to the success last year of The Beatles *1* album, are there any other Beatles projects in the pipeline?"

Ringo "Yes, there will be a new Beatles product next year, but I can't say what it is because I will get into trouble with the Beatle police."

The first show of this latest All-Starr tour takes place on **Thursday, July 26 . . .**

Concert review: "When Ringo Starr chose the line-up for his latest All-Starr Band he wanted to reflect music from the Sixties, Seventies and Eighties. Thus the former Beatles drummer, who turned 61 years old just three weeks ago, was joined at Casino Rama by Ian Hunter of Mott The Hoople and Roger Hodgson of Supertramp, both alternating on guitar and piano, bassist Greg Lake of Emerson, Lake & Palmer and King Crimson, percussionist Sheila E, the first female to grace the stage with the All-Starr Band, keyboardist Howard Jones and multi-instrumentalist Mark Rivera. The North American launch of his latest All-Starr tour, his seventh in 12 years, saw the impressive group easily navigate Starr's solo hits, four Beatles songs, 'Boys', 'Yellow Submarine', 'I Wanna Be Your Man' and 'With A Little Help From My Friends' and classics from the other members. In other words, it was hard to go wrong with a 26-song, hit-heavy set list although after two hours and 10 minutes, it wouldn't have been so bad to leave the audience of 5,000 wanting more. Starr and his All-Starrs arrived in this Central Ontario town just under two weeks ago to begin 10-hour-a-day rehearsals for their pending tour. And the drummer certainly acknowledged his rural setting early on by asking, 'Are there any cowboys in the audience?' Starr seemed eager to share the spotlight, which meant no one performer had to carry the entertaining load for very long. Instead, they all seemed pleased to pass the baton, as it were, opening the evening with Starr's own solo hits

'Photograph' and 'Act Naturally' (sic), before moving easily into King Crimson's 'Court Of The Crimson King', then Supertramp's 'Logical Song' followed by Jones' 'No One Is To Blame', Hunter's Drew Carey show theme, 'Cleveland Rocks' and Sheila E's 'A Love Bizarre'. And so it went for the rest of the night. Starr made no mention last night of the other two surviving Beatles, despite this being a big news week for both of them. As Starr himself said at the beginning of the concert, 'Good music and fun, that's what it's all about.' "

Thursday, July 26, at 4.32pm, it is announced that Paul has become engaged to Heather Mills . . .

Beth Gardiner, Associated Press Writer, "Sir Paul McCartney, the former Beatle who lost his first wife to cancer three years ago, is engaged to be married to Heather Mills, an activist for the disabled. McCartney, 59, proposed on Monday during a trip to Britain's Lake District, his spokesman said Thursday. The two plan to marry some time next year. The 33-year-old Mills is a former swim wear model whose left leg was amputated below the knee after she was run down by a police motorcyclist in 1993. The spokesman said McCartney bought the sapphire and diamond engagement ring in India earlier this year . . .

"Paul and Heather said today they would like to thank their relatives and friends for all the great support they have shown them since they met two years ago," said a statement from McCartney's office.

"McCartney spoke briefly with journalists Thursday evening outside his home in St John's Wood, north London. Asked how he proposed to his fiancée, the former Beatle said, 'That's private, that's just for me.' He then went back inside for a quiet dinner with his future wife."

Paul had met Heather Mills at a charity function in May 1999 when she appealed for help for her own foundation, The Heather Mills Trust, which provides limbs for victims of war.

Paul "I was smitten instantly. So I found out her telephone number, like you do and rang her up and said we should talk about some charity stuff. I did fancy her from the start but I was playing it cool. She came to the office to talk about the charity and I realised that I fancied her."

Heather "I fancied the pants off him. But I'm not flirtatious at all and for months I had no idea that he fancied me. I just thought he was a lovely man who wanted to help my charity, so when it sank in it was a shock. But his fame is irrelevant. He's just Paul, my boyfriend who happens to have a great voice."

Tim Castle, Reuters, "McCartney, 59, got down on one knee to propose to Mills, a 33-year-old model and charity worker, during a short holiday in Britain's Lake District on Monday, his publicist said. The singer and songwriter gave Mills an Indian sapphire and diamond ring he bought in Jaipur during a holiday in January. The pair thanked their friends and relatives for all their great support since they met two years ago. McCartney has spoken of how his relationship with Mills helped him overcome the pain of losing his wife Linda, who died in April 1998 as a result of breast cancer after a happy marriage of more than 30 years. 'Obviously, I'd been going through a hard time,' he was cited as saying last year. 'Now I've got romance back in my life. I love her, and I get a lot of pleasure from that.' "

Friday, July 27 . . . 11.54am

Sir Paul McCartney steps out of his house today in St John's Wood, London, hand in hand with his fiancée Heather Mills and says, "We are really happy."

Paul "I was a bit nervous about proposing to Heather but I managed. We've had a good reception from relatives and friends and from the media."

Heather "I am still in shock and over the moon."

But when the gathered photographers ask for the couple to kiss, Heather responds by saying, "We don't kiss on demand. It's spontaneous. I won't be using the title Lady, I'm not into all that pretence."

Syndicated news report, "It was his first public announcement since news broke of his engagement to the former model and anti-landmines campaigner. Sir Paul has seen plenty of large crowds gathered outside his house during his long and winding career. Today a pack of 100 cameramen, photographers and reporters jostled for space with fans to hear him declare his love for his new fiancée. As he stepped out of the five-bedroom St John's Wood house with Miss Mills, she proudly showed off her large sapphire and diamond engagement ring. Photographers jostled for space and two children presented them with two large bouquets."

Paul "Good morning everybody, hope you're all well. There's not much to say. We're engaged and that's it. It's a very personal thing, the wedding, and we're not giving any details out, whatsoever . . . That's it, we have to go, we're only posing for photographers, we've got to get to work. But first we're off to the boozer. Thanks for all your support."

Syndicated press report "Sir Paul then drove off in his Mercedes estate with Miss Mills in the passenger seat and his driver in the back. The crowds had started gathering for a glimpse of the happy couple from around 6am outside the 6ft high steel gates of the five-bedroom mansion Sir Paul has occupied since the Sixties. Rumours abounded that the singer and composer would make a brief appearance with his new fiancée, a former model turned anti-landmines campaigner. The former Beatle is thought to have popped the question on Monday, while the couple was taking a short break in Ullswater in the Lake District. For the nostalgic among us today's events were a faint reminder of the excitement that surrounded the singer's engagement and subsequent marriage to Linda, in nearby Marylebone Register Office in March 1969, when Miss Mills was just a year old. Then, the couple married with a modest £12 wedding ring, there was a furious reaction from hysterical female fans."

To be continued . . .